Fodor's 94
Scandinavia

Fodor's Travel Publications, Inc.
New York • Toronto • London • Sydney • Auckland

Fodor's Scandinavia

Editor: Nancy van Itallie
Contributors: Katrine Osa Aaby, Hannah Borgeson, Margaret Hunter, Hilary Jacobs, Caroline Liou, Brian Owens, Karina Porcelli, Marcy Pritchard, Enrique Tessieri, Anna Yates
Creative Director: Fabrizio La Rocca
Cartographer: David Lindroth
Illustrator: Karl Tanner
Cover Photograph: Robert Maas

Design: Vignelli Associates

Contents

Foreword *vi*

Highlights '94 *viii*

Fodor's Choice *x*

Introduction *xviii*

Money-Saving Tips *xxiii*

1 Essential Information *1*

Before You Go *2*

Government Information Offices *2*
Tour and Packages *2*
When to Go *4*
What to Pack *5*
Taking Money Abroad *7*
Getting Money from Home *7*
Scandinavian Currency *8*
What It Will Cost *9*
Passports and Visas *9*
Customs and Duties *10*
Traveling with Cameras, Camcorders, and Laptops *11*
Language *13*
Staying Healthy *13*
Insurance *14*
Car Rentals *16*
Rail Passes *17*
Student and Youth Travel *18*
Traveling with Children *19*
Hints for Travelers with Disabilities *21*
Hints for Older Travelers *22*
Further Reading *23*

Arriving and Departing *23*

From North America by Plane *23*
From the United Kingdom by Plane *26*
By Ship *27*

Staying in Scandinavia *27*

Getting Around *27*
Shopping *29*
Sports *30*
Beaches *30*
Dining *31*
Lodging *31*
Credit Cards *33*

Great Itineraries *33*

Sand, Surf, and Ships, Scandinavia-style *33*
Scandinavian Mountains *34*
Tracing the Vikings *35*
Architecture and Handicrafts *36*

Scandinavia at a Glance: A Chronology *38*

2 Denmark 44

Before You Go *48*
Arriving and Departing *52*
Staying in Denmark *54*
Copenhagen *60*
Sjælland and Its Islands *91*
Fyn and the Central Islands *104*
Jylland *116*
Bornholm *129*
Greenland *139*
The Faroe Islands *148*

3 Finland 156

Before You Go *157*
Arriving and Departing *163*
Staying in Finland *163*
Helsinki *170*
South Coast and Ålands *199*
Lapland *207*
The Lakelands *215*

4 Iceland 226

Before You Go *229*
Arriving and Departing *234*
Staying in Iceland *236*
Reykjavík *244*
Golden Circle Excursion *260*
The West and the Western Fjords *264*
The North *268*
The East *274*
The South *277*

5 Norway 282

Before You Go *286*
Arriving and Departing *291*
Staying in Norway *292*
Oslo *302*
Excursions from Oslo *332*
Sørlandet *335*
Bergen *348*
Mountains and Valleys of the Interior *361*
Central Fjord Country *377*
Trondheim and the North *387*

6 Sweden 407

Before You Go *411*
Arriving and Departing *416*

Staying in Sweden *417*
Stockholm *422*
Excursions from Stockholm *449*
Göteborg *453*
Excursions from Göteborg *463*
The South and the Kingdom of Crystal *472*
Dalarna: The Folklore District *485*
Norrland *492*

Conversion Tables *501*

Vocabulary *503*

Index *515*

Maps

Scandinavia *xiv–xv*
World Time Zones *xvi–xvii*
Denmark *46*
Copenhagen *66–67*
Copenhagen Dining and Lodging *82–83*
Sjælland and Its Islands *94*
Fyn and the Central Islands *107*
Jylland *119*
Bornholm *132*
Greenland *143*
The Faroe Islands *151*
Finland *158*
Helsinki *176–177*
Helsinki Dining and Lodging *190–191*
The South Coast and Ålands *201*
Lapland *211*
The Lakelands *218*
Iceland *228*
Reykjavík *249*
Norway *284*
Oslo *308–309*
Oslo Excursions *316*
Oslo Dining and Lodging *322–323*
Sørlandet *339*
Bergen *353*
Mountains and Valleys of the Interior *363*
Central Fjord Country *380*
Trondheim and the North *390*
Sweden *409*
Stockholm *428–429*
Excursions from Stockholm *434*
Stockholm Dining and Lodging *438–439*
Göteborg *456*
Excursions from Göteborg *465*
The South and the Kingdom of Crystal *475*
Dalarna *488*
Norrland *495*

Foreword

We would like to express our gratitude to Lillian Hess of the Danish Tourist Board, Ritva Muller and Eeva-Liisa Nyberg of the Finnish Tourist Board, Harald Hansen of the Norwegian Tourist Board, Einar Gustafsson of the Icelandic Tourist Board, and Viveca Nordström of the Swedish Tourist Board in New York City for their valuable assistance during the preparation of this new edition of Fodor's *Scandinavia*.

While every care has been taken to ensure the accuracy of the information in this guide, the passage of time will always bring change, and consequently the publisher cannot accept responsibility for errors that may occur.

All prices and opening times quoted here are based on information supplied to us at press time. Hours and admission fees may change, however, and the prudent traveler will avoid inconvenience by calling ahead.

Fodor's wants to hear about your travel experiences, both pleasant and unpleasant. When a hotel or restaurant fails to live up to its billing, let us know and we will investigate the complaint and revise our entries where the facts warrant it. Send your letters to the editors of Fodor's Travel Publications, 201 E. 50th Street, New York, NY 10022.

Highlights'94 and Fodor's Choice

Highlights '94

The 1993 recovery of the dollar in relation to Scandinavian currencies means less expensive travel here for Americans. The dramatic **changes in Eastern Europe,** the **Baltic,** and the **Commonwealth of Independent States** have also brought shifts in prices, new opportunities to combine visits to the two regions, and a greater need to reserve ahead, as travel to and from these countries has become easy and rapid.

In 1994 **Finland** commemorates the 90th anniversary of the assassination of the notorious Nicholas Bobrikov, the Russian Governor-General of the Grand Duchy of Finland, on June 16, 1904, by nationalist hero-martyr **Eugen Schauman.** Finland will also be celebrating the 150th anniversary of the birth of one of its foremost playwrights, **Minna Cant.** Her plays about the plight of Finnish women during the last century helped to lay the foundations of Finland's strong sense of equality between the sexes.

The most important political event in Finland in 1994 is the presidential election in the spring. President Mauno Koivisto, who took over from the late President Urho Kekkonen (who ruled Finland for 25 years) in 1982, will step down after two terms. This year also marks the 75th anniversary of Finland's first president in 1919.

If everything goes as planned, Finland will welcome 1995 as a new member of the European Community (EC). Apart from the European Economic Area (EEA), Finland's EC membership will strengthen the country's economic and political ties with Western Europe. Greater economic reciprocity with Western Europe is expected to make Finland even more competitive and accessible to tourists.

On June 17, 1994, **Iceland** celebrates the 50th anniversary of the foundation of the modern republic, when the Icelanders formally cut their age-old ties to Denmark in 1944. The event is marked by celebrations at Þingvellir, the seat of the ancient Alþing. The anniversary also coincides with the biannual Reykjavík Arts Festival, which offers, as usual, a feast of visual and musical arts.

Currently **Norway** remains undecided on whether to join the EC. The issue is creating divisions among the various elements of society, and the road to full membership seems remote for the moment, even though most Norwegians feel very much a part of western Europe. The pressures of the influx of eastern European and other refugees, however, may spur Norwegians to join other Europeans in coping with them.

Oslo will soon have a new airport, at Gardermoen, 40 kilometers (25 miles) outside the city. It is scheduled for completion by 1998 at a projected cost of NKr 11.7 billion.

The **XVII Olympic Winter Games** in Lillehammer, February 12–26 this year, have been planned with a view to the future. Great care was taken in the construction of the facilities to preserve the local ecology, and the installations are all intended for public use after the games are over.

Sweden, anticipating increased trade with and travel to and from the continent in the wake of its application for EC membership, started construction in 1993 on an 18-kilometer (13-mile) rail and road bridge across the Öresund, linking the country with Denmark. Good news for travelers in 1992 was the reduction of the value-added tax on hotels and transportation from 25% to 12% and on restaurants from 25% to 21%. Most restaurants and hotels have responded by keeping their prices down in order to attract budget-minded visitors.

Fodor's Choice

No two people will agree on what makes a perfect vacation, but it can be fun and helpful to know what others think. We hope you'll have a chance to experience some of Fodor's Choices yourself while visiting Scandinavia. For detailed information on individual entries, see the relevant sections of this guidebook.

Dining

Denmark Kommandanten, Copenhagen (*Very Expensive*)

Skt. Gertrudes Kloster, Copenhagen (*Very Expensive*)

Ida Davidsen, Copenhagen (*Moderate*)

Finland Alexander Nevski, Helsinki (*Very Expensive*)

Kosmos, Helsinki (*Expensive*)

Garlic Restaurant Kynsilaukka, Helsinki (*Moderate*)

Iceland Perlan, Reykjavík (*Very Expensive*)

Fiðlarinn, Akureyri (*Expensive*)

Við Tjörnina, Reykjavík (*Expensive*)

Norway Refnes Gods, Moss (*Expensive*)

Spisestuen (Alexandra Molde Hotel), Molde (*Expensive*)

Bryggestuen & Bryggeloftet, Bergen (*Moderate*)

Sweden Den Gyldene Freden, Stockholm (*Expensive*)

Kokska Krogen, Malmö (*Expensive*)

Nils Emil, Stockholm (*Moderate*)

Jukkasjärvis Wärdshus och Hembyggdsgård, Jukkasjärvi (*Inexpensive*)

Lodging

Denmark D'Angleterre, Copenhagen (*Very Expensive*)

Falsled Kro, Faborg, Fyn (*Very Expensive*)

Cab-Inn, Copenhagen (*Inexpensive*)

Vandrehjem (Family and Youth Hostels), anywhere in Denmark (*Inexpensive*)

Finland Kalastajatorppa, Helsinki (*Very Expensive*)

Lord, Helsinki (*Expensive*)

Anna, Helsinki (*Moderate*)

Iceland Hotel Holt, Reykjavík (*Expensive*)

Valhöll, Þingvellir (*Expensive*)

Norway Oslo Plaza, Oslo (*Very Expensive*)

Karasjok SAS Hotell, Karasjok (*Expensive*)

Kvikne's Hotel, Balestrand (*Moderate*)

Sweden Grand Hotel, Stockholm (*Very Expensive*)

Clas på Hörnet, Stockholm (*Expensive*)

Mäster Johan Hotel, Malmö (*Expensive*)

Castles and Churches

Denmark Hammershus, Bornholm

Kronborg, Helsingør, Sjælland

Valdemars Slot, Troense, Fyn

Finland Olavinlinna, Savonlinna

Temppeliaukion Kirkko, Helsinki

Turun Linna (Turku Castle), Turku

Iceland Árbæjarsafn Church, Reykjavík

Skáholt Church, Skáholt

Norway Akershus Slott, Oslo

Heddal Stave Church, Heddal

Tromsø Cathedral, Tromsø

Sweden Drottningholm Palace, Stockholm

Glimmingehus, Skåne

Läckö Slott, Läckö

Royal Palace, Stockholm

Towns and Villages

Denmark Gudhjem, Bornholm

Møn, Sjælland

Ribe, Jylland

Skagen, Jylland

Finland Eckerö

Porvoo

Rauma

Iceland Akureyri

Bakkagerði

Norway Lom

Lyngør

Røros

Sweden Rättvik

Sigtuna

Simrishamn

Visby

Parks and Gardens

Denmark Dollerup Bakker, Jylland

Frederiksberg Have, Copenhagen

Kongens Have, Copenhagen

Finland Kultaranta rose gardens, Luonnonmaasaari

Urho Kekkonen National Park, Saariselkä

Iceland Grasagarðurinn (Botanical Gardens), Reykjavík

Skaftafell National Park

Norway Frogner Park, Oslo

Hardangervidda, Geilo

Jostedalsbreen (glacier), Loen

Mountains above Tromsø

Sweden Djurgården, Stockholm

Muddus National Park, Norrland

Trädgårdsföreningen, Göteborg

Museums

Denmark Carlsberg Glyptoteket, Copenhagen

Louisiana Modern Art Museum, Copenhagen

Finland Suomen Kansallismuseo, Helsinki

Iceland Árni Magnússon Institute, repository of the Saga manuscripts, Reykjavík

Skógar Folk Museum

Norway Norwegian Folk Museum, Bygdøy, Oslo

Munch Museum, Oslo

Sami Collections, Karasjok

Sweden Millesgården, Stockholm

Vasa Museum, Stockholm

Zorn Museum, Mora

Lakes, Fjords, and Islands

Denmark Aerø, off Fyn

Bornholm

Strømfjord, Greenland

Finland Sruomenlinna Fortress Island, Helsinki

Iceland Flatey, Breiðafjörður

Lake Mývatn

Norway Geirangerfjord

Lofoten Islands

Svalbard

Sweden Siljan and Sollerön

Mälaren and Björkö

Special Moments

Denmark Eating an old-fashioned ice-cream cone on a Bornholm beach

Walking through Tivoli at dusk

Watching a bonfire on Skt. Hansaften (the longest day of the year)

Finland Cloudberry-picking in Lapland in August

Crayfish-eating in August

Sailboat regatta in Hanko

Iceland Bobbing among glacial ice floes in Jökulsárlón lagoon

Watching the northern lights in December from Þingvellir

Norway Eating reindeer meat in a Sami tent, with your reindeer parked outside

Midsummer or a blizzard at the North Cape

The train journey from Flåm to Myrdal

Sweden Dogsledding in Norrland

Eating a Shrove Tuesday bun during Lent

Sailing in the Stockholm archipelago

Scandinavia

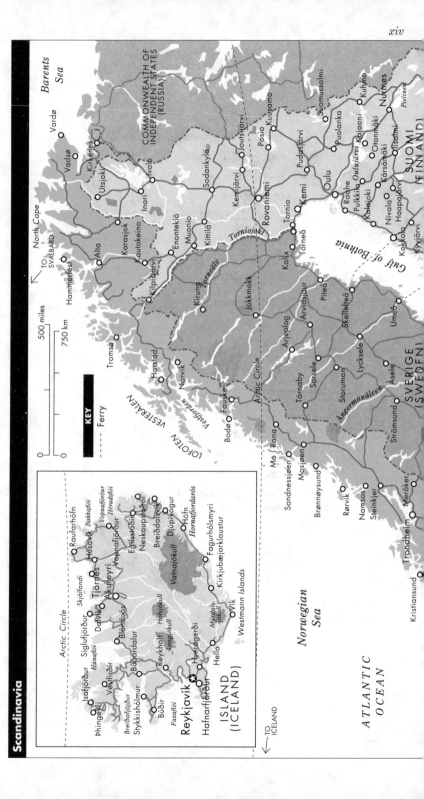

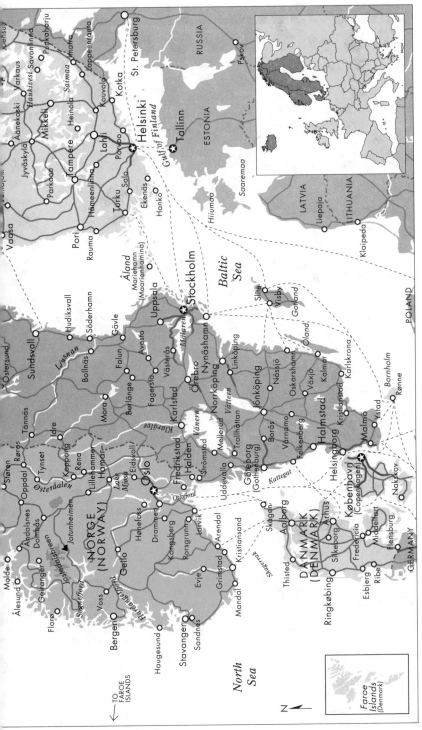

World Time Zones

Numbers below vertical bands relate each zone to Greenwich Mean Time (0 hrs.).
Local times frequently differ from these general indications,
as indicated by light-face numbers on map.

Algiers, **29**
Anchorage, **3**
Athens, **41**
Auckland, **1**
Baghdad, **46**
Bangkok, **50**
Beijing, **54**

Berlin, **34**
Bogotá, **19**
Budapest, **37**
Buenos Aires, **24**
Caracas, **22**
Chicago, **9**
Copenhagen, **33**
Dallas, **10**

Delhi, **48**
Denver, **8**
Djakarta, **53**
Dublin, **26**
Edmonton, **7**
Hong Kong, **56**
Honolulu, **2**

Istanbul, **40**
Jerusalem, **42**
Johannesburg, **44**
Lima, **20**
Lisbon, **28**
London (Greenwich), **27**
Los Angeles, **6**
Madrid, **38**
Manila, **57**

Mecca, **47**

Mexico City, **12**

Miami, **18**

Montréal, **15**

Moscow, **45**

Nairobi, **43**

New Orleans, **11**

New York City, **16**

Ottawa, **14**

Paris, **30**

Perth, **58**

Reykjavík, **25**

Rio de Janeiro, **23**

Rome, **39**

Saigon (Ho Chi Minh City), **51**

San Francisco, **5**

Santiago, **21**

Seoul, **59**

Shanghai, **55**

Singapore, **52**

Stockholm, **32**

Sydney, **61**

Tokyo, **60**

Toronto, **13**

Vancouver, **4**

Vienna, **35**

Warsaw, **36**

Washington, D.C., **17**

Yangon, **49**

Zürich, **31**

Introduction

By Eric Sjogren

Eric Sjogren, a Swedish travel writer based in Brussels, is a frequent contributor to The New York Times *and other publications. He has also served as area editor for* Fodor's Belgium and Luxembourg.

The islands of Stockholm mirrored in the water, the ships and Little Mermaid of Copenhagen, Oslo and its majestic fjord, the bay and peninsulas of Helsinki, Reykjavík with its busy deep-blue harbor: the capitals of Scandinavia are unthinkable without the water that surrounds and sustains them.

What is true for the capitals is equally true for the countries. Denmark consists of one peninsula and 400 islands, half of them inhabited. Finland and Sweden used to dispute which country was really "the land of a thousand lakes." Finland settled it, after counting almost 190,000. An island summer in the archipelago is part of every Stockholmer's childhood memory. The mail packets of Norway's Hurtigruten sail north from Bergen along the fjord-indented coast and turn around at Kirkenes on the Russian border, 1,250 miles later. Iceland is so dependent on the surrounding sea that it has been known to take on the British navy to protect its fishing limits.

Water has never separated the Scandinavian nations. In the early days it was far easier to cross a stretch of water than it was to penetrate dense and trackless forests. It was their mastery of shipbuilding that enabled the Vikings to rule the waves 1,000 years ago. Their ocean-going ships could be beached, and this gave them the advantage of surprise.

Viking exploration and conquests ranged from North America to the Black Sea and from Greenland to Mallorca. These voyagers developed the angular Runic alphabet, ideal for carving in stone. In Sweden alone, over 2,000 rune stones still stand, in memory of Vikings who fell in far-away battles. The Vikings also devised a complex mythology and created literature of such realism and immediacy that even today the Icelandic sagas can be read with admiration and enjoyment.

You might think that, with so much in common, the Scandinavians would keep peace among themselves, but this was not to be. By the 11th century the passion that had inflamed the Vikings was spent, and Christianity defeated the old beliefs. The Swedes departed on a dubious crusade to conquer the Finns and annex their land. The Norwegians, having colonized Iceland, squabbled among themselves and disappeared as a nation for 500 years. By the 16th century, Scandinavia was divided between Denmark and Sweden, bound together by mutual antagonism. The two countries were at war with one another for a total of 134 years, and the conflict was perpetuated by history books written from nationalistic points of view.

What happened in the distant past acquires the status of myth and influences in many ways the image that a people has of itself. What has happened more recently sometimes leaves more obvious marks. Allegiances and dependencies were reshuffled early in the 19th century, as a consequence of the Napoleonic Wars, which transformed the European landscape. Sweden lost Finland, which spent the next 100 years as a czarist province. Norway declared its independence from Denmark but was thrust into a union with Sweden.

Finland learned more about her cultural identity while a Russian province than she did during centuries of Swedish rule. Akseli Gallen Kallela painted the scenes of a mythological past that Jean Sibelius fashioned into tone poems. Norway, too, was to experience a cultural renaissance, led by artists such as Edvard Grieg, Henrik Ibsen, and Edvard Munch. From Denmark came philosopher Soren Kierkegaard, writer Hans Christian Andersen, and the composer Carl Nielsen. Sweden produced the painters Anders Zorn and Carl Larsson and dramatist August Strindberg.

Large-scale emigration to the United States (including a million Swedes) peaked during the latter half of the century, only decades before new industries transformed the old farming economy.

In the early years of this century the Norwegians finally became masters in their own house. This could not have happened without strong nationalist sentiment, and it is to the credit of both Norway and Sweden that the divorce was amicable. The Russian revolution brought civil war to Finland, followed by independence, for the first time in that nation's history. Finland was attacked again in 1939, by Stalin's forces, and was eventually defeated but never occupied. Denmark and Norway, attacked by Germany in 1940, were not spared that fate. After the war had ended, Iceland declared its independence from Denmark.

Denmark, Norway, and Iceland are members of NATO. Denmark is also a paid-up member of the European Community; and Sweden has applied for membership, with Norway and Finland bringing up the rear.

Scandinavians, like the British, often talk of Europe as though they were not part of it. They see themselves as different. They dream of the *joie de vivre* that they believe all southerners enjoy but maintain that the moral fiber and know-how of the Scandinavians are superior to anything you find south of the border.

Nevertheless, it is sometimes said that sick-leave levels are now so high in Sweden that there are more sick people in a factory than in a hospital. As people often do with the good things in life, Scandinavians in all five countries have become used to high levels of social services. The political coloration of the government seems to matter less, as long as the services are delivered. This requirement is not easily squared with the vociferous demand for lower taxes.

More than the rest of Europe, Scandinavia has been influenced by the American lifestyle and its ethos of professionalism. This coexists, sometimes precariously, with the "socialism with a human face" that has influenced these societies for the past 50 years or more. Among the measures introduced recently is Sweden's 12-month maternity/paternity leave. Husband and wife can split it between them as they see fit: An idea that was decried as madness has done wonders for marriage and fatherhood.

Scandinavian women know how to assume power with ease and grace. Denmark's Queen Margarethe was pushed into her position as reigning monarch but has acquitted herself so well that royalism in Denmark is at an all-time high. President Vigdis of Iceland first achieved narrow victory on a platform that emphasized cultural values; she has subsequently seen her majority grow by leaps and bounds. When Gro Harlem Bruntland became prime minister of Norway, she appointed a cabinet consisting of 40% women. Her popularity may have influenced the main opposition party to elect another woman as their leader. Sweden's Antonia Axelsson Johnson runs one of the country's largest business empires. And, with more than 250 policemen reporting to her, Margareta Linderoth is district police commissioner of one of Stockholm's most difficult precincts. "I have had nothing but support from my male colleagues," she says. Officially 101 languages are spoken in her district. This can be read as an indication of the richness of new ethnic contributions to Scandinavian culture, although it is not necessarily seen that way by the host country.

There is still much truth in the myth of the taciturn Scandinavian. A story tells of the two Danes, two Norwegians, and two Swedes who were marooned on a desert island. When a rescue party arrived six months later, they found that the two Danes had started a cooperative, and the two Norwegians had founded a local chapter of the patriotic society Sons of Norway. The two Swedes were waiting to be introduced.

Stereotypes about national characteristics abound among Scandinavians. Danes believe the saving grace of humor will take the sting out of most of life's vicissitudes. The Finns attribute their survival to their *sisu*, or true grit. Icelanders are known as a nation of hard workers, singers, and drinkers, who think there is always a way for things to get fixed. The Norwegians find virtue in being, like Ibsen's Peer Gynt, *sig selv nok*, which means self-reliant in all things. The Swedes, the most introspective of the lot, take pride in their reliability and admit to "Royal Swedish envy" as their principal vice.

There's no denying that there is a definite strain of melancholy in the Scandinavian character, more pronounced the farther you penetrate into the lonely north. In Finland, the most popular dance—one in which dance halls specialize to the exclusion of all others—is the tango, precisely because it is so sad. But there's no need to look only to Argentine imports: Virtually all Scandinavian folk music, even when rhythms are rapid and gay, is in a minor key.

The Scandinavians are not bound by a native language. Iceland was colonized from Norway, but present-day Icelandic is incomprehensible to other Scandinavians. Finnish, like Hungarian, is one of the enigmatic Finno-Ugrian languages. Danish, a language rich in glottal stops, is not understood by many Swedes, and Danish TV programs have to be subtitled. Norwegian, in pronunciation and vocabulary halfway between the two, sometimes serves as an intra-Scandinavian mode of communication. But get a group of Scandinavians together, and what are they most likely to speak? English.

Those who think a sauna is nothing but a steam bath are greatly mistaken. To the Finns, who invented it, a sauna has a spiritual dimension, with the cleansing of the body accompanied by the enjoyment of nature, because a beautiful location is a vital part of a true Finnish sauna. Most of the major decisions made in the country are reached during a sauna.

Denmark is in many ways a garden of delight. The Denmark of beech woods, dappled paths, half-timber farmhouses, and rolling fields still exists. Only Skåne, the southernmost Swedish province, which was part of Denmark until the 17th century, resembles agricultural Denmark.

Farther north the woods close in, pine and spruce mingling with white-trunked birches, with here and there a clearing or a field. As you continue north, the hegemony of the forest becomes complete, challenged only by the lakes. On a clear night, from an aircraft, the moonlight is reflected in so many lakes that it seems to cut a shining path to the horizon.

The forest is not as silent and lonely as you might think. Walk along a Scandinavian country road on an evening in early summer, and you will hear roe deer barking at your approach and the forlorn hooting of loons from the lakes. You will see stately moose coming out of the woods to graze in the fields. Juniper bushes cast long, eerie shadows, and on a hilltop skeletal pines are silhouetted against a still clear sky. No wonder that in ages past popular imagination peopled these forests with sprites and trolls and giants.

Having a summer home is not a great luxury in Scandinavia. On Friday afternoon there are traffic jams in Oslo, as the Norwegians escape to their cabins in the mountainous interior. In Stockholm the waterways are clogged with motorboats heading for summer cottages in the archipelago. The Finns and Icelanders, less urbanized than their neighbors, almost always have a village or isolated farmstead they consider their real home.

Modern Scandinavia is largely a secular society, but woods and lakes hold a special mystique. A midnight boat ride on an island-studded lake, with the moon suspended just above the treetops, is very close to a religious experience for the people of the North, as their souls fill with a tremendous wistfulness and a sense of simultaneous sadness and joy.

Money-Saving Tips

Denmark

Shopping For original and inexpensive gifts, peruse the hundreds of "*Antik*" shops in Copenhagen and throughout Denmark. Even if you have to dig through dusty boxes and cajole crotchety shopkeepers, the finds are unusual, and often a fraction of the cost of what you'll find in department stores. Look for crystal, including Orrefors and Holmegaard bowls and glasses, Royal Copenhagen, including the ubiquitous blue-fluted porcelain, and silver. Twin towers on the back of a piece signify silver plate and triple towers signify sterling. The central antiques shops in Copenhagen, around Strøget, tend to be the most expensive. Venture farther afield into Frederiksberg, Nørrebro, and Valby, as well as provincial towns outside the Copenhagen area. Also check flea market (*loppemarket*) listings in local city guides. While frantic bargaining is not a Danish custom, quiet negotiation is perfectly acceptable.

Books are expensive in Denmark, and an unusual value-added tax (MOMs) of 25% makes them even pricier. Bring your own, then sell them at used bookstores, most of which are eager to pay for English-language tomes.

Finally, appreciate Danish design, and know that even if you pay an exorbitant price, you're getting what you paid for. These items are known the world over, and, even though they cost a small fortune in Denmark, they cost a bigger fortune abroad.

Dining In Copenhagen, sample the ethnic restaurants in and around Vesterbro and Nørrebro. Scores of Indian, Pakistani, Greek, and Asian restaurants provide inexpensive (and sometimes all-you-can-eat) fare.

For inexpensive Danish food, try a *smørrebrød* shop for open-faced sandwiches, or an all-you-can-eat breakfast buffet, offered in most large hotels. Remember too, that while artistry makes a smørrebrød pretty, you can buy all the ingredients (black bread, liver pâté, cheese, and cucumbers) from a grocer, sit on a park bench or beach, and enjoy.

If you want to eat out three square meals a day, an Entertainment book, at DKr400, is a good investment. Most of the coupons are two-for-one main courses, but there is also a back section, which gives a 50% discount on hotels around the world, including some in Scandinavia, plus an outing section, with discounts for car rentals and museum and attraction admissions. In Copenhagen, call 33/15–35–11. However, the book is in Danish, and geared for residents.

Buy it only if you want to take advantage of the restaurant section. For discounts to museums, sights, and transportation, a Copenhagen or other regional card or pass (particularly the Jutland Pass, which is loaded with restaurant deals), available from all tourist information offices (and sometimes distributed free in hotels and on ferries), offers better deals.

Accommodations Before you leave the U.S., purchase a Scandinavia Bonus Pass, which costs $23, through your travel agent. The pass is valid mid-May through August for a 50% family discount at all Danway Hotels. Travel agents can make first- and last-night reservations.

In some cities, including Copenhagen, you can cash in on a 50% hotel discount by booking your hotel room at the last minute. Prebooking in private homes and hotels must be made two months in advance, but last-minute (same-day) hotel rooms can also be found. Ask at the local tourist information office. If you are venturing out of the city, you can also check into a small traditional inn or farm holiday (*see* Staying in Denmark, *below*), which is usually cheaper than a hotel.

During the summer months, when Danish businesses traditionally close for the entire month of July, hotels offer weekend and other specials to fill up empty rooms. Ask!

Iceland

Iceland is a very expensive country to visit, and even money-saving aptitude cannot make it cheap.

Transportation Do not assume you need to hire a car. Not only is it very costly, but you should also consider whether you will be happy driving on rough gravel roads and along precipitous coasts. Many of Iceland's more hair-raising routes require 100% of the driver's attention, which means that the driver tends to miss all the marvelous views. Bus services run regularly to every corner of the country, with a daily bus on most routes, while airlines serve many towns and villages in the regions. Both airlines and bus companies offer a variety of discount tickets, valid either for a specific combination of routes or for a specified period of time. You can even combine air and bus travel with an Air/Bus Rover. Some of the discount air tickets are only available when you book your Icelandair flight, so ask your Icelandair agent for details.

Dining Eating out in Iceland is a very expensive proposition. Even if you only want a burger, the price may shock you, while a good three-course meal at a pleasant restaurant can easily cost IKr5,000 or more. A hot dog from a hot-dog stand, however, remains a bargain at around IKr100. There is a lot to be said for planning a self-catering holiday of some kind, perhaps through the Farm Holiday Service or youth hostels, and eating at restaurants only occasionally. On the bright side, many restaurants in the regions, and some in Reykjavík, are participants in a Tourist Menu scheme, with set menus at IKr1,000 to 1,200 for lunch, and IKr1,300 to 2,000 for dinner, with discounts for children. These restaurants display a Tourist Menu sign in the window, and a list of them is available from the Icelandic Hotel and Restaurant Association. In addition, some of Reykjavík's finest restaurants offer bargain-price lunches. At Hotel Holt, for instance, you can eat a wonderful three-course lunch, with first-class service, and pay a fraction of the price the same fare would cost in the evening. So consider eating out at midday, then dining more frugally in the evening.

Drinks Prices of alcoholic drinks in Iceland's bars and pubs are brain-numbing to outsiders, so be forewarned. Half a liter of beer will cost IKr500, a mixed drink more. If you like to have a little drink in the evening, seize the opportunity to buy your low-price duty-free allowance at the airport, and mix your own drinks. If you are visiting friends in Iceland, a duty-free bottle is often a welcome gift.

Accommodations Hotel accommodation is expensive and can be hard to find at the peak of the season. Many hotels, however, especially, the Edda summer hotels, which operate in schools during the long summer vacation, offer cheap sleeping-bag accommodation in rooms or dormitories. Farmhouse accommodation, available through the Farm Holiday Service, is usually cheaper than a hotel, as well as friendlier. Both Edda hotels and the Farm Holiday Service often offer voucher schemes, with a discount for several nights.

Norway

Norway can be an expensive vacation option, but there are ways to stretch out your travel funds.

Admission Discounts Students and senior citizens should bring their ID's to take advantage of many discounts at movies, museums, trains, and so on. Ask about family-price tickets at museums and other attractions and go for the citycards in Oslo, Bergen, Stavanger, and Kristiansand, which offer discounts to various attractions.

Transportation Buses and trams (*trikks*) offer tickets that include transfers, usually valid for one hour after purchase. In Oslo, children with an adult travel free by tram on Sunday. Trains and airlines often offer good bargains for midday or off-season travel, respectively. Another money-saving option is a rail pass, with discounts on train travel and often rebates at hotels or ferries.

For the true Norwegian experience, take a hike, or at least a walk. On Sundays, especially, you'll meet hordes of Norwegians out stretching their legs on city streets or country roads.

Shopping Try the **H&M** department stores, secondhand stores, and home furnishings stores in Oslo and other major towns. It's hard to find a souvenir more "authentic" than one that was actually used in a Norwegian household, and the quality and prices are first-rate. **Majorstuhallen, Brukt & Antik** (Middeltuns Gate 19, tel. 22/60–97–40), in Oslo, is the largest secondhand market in Norway. Here you'll find kitchen utensils, tables, paintings, silver picture frames, old records, and used clothes. Oslo's **Tonico Secondhand Boutique** (Sorgenfrigt. 1, tel. 22/60–22–06) is a good place to find fashionable outfits that have been worn by celebrities. **Sportsboden** (Jacob allé gt. 11, tel. 22/60–19–41), in Oslo, carries secondhand sports articles. In summer there are bicycles and accessories, while in winter, skiing and skating equipment is for sale.

Dining To save money on meals, pack your own lunch or take advantage of midday and early-dinner specials at restaurants. Be sure to ask about the *dagens meny* (special of the day).

Ask for water, which is clean and very good instead of soft drinks and beer, which are pricey. At small establishments, the second cup of coffee is usually free, or at least cheaper.

There are many money-saving dining options in Oslo. The **Kafe Nordraak** (St. Olavsgt. 2, tel. 22/42–10–59) at the Art Academy is a good place to stop for a bite; it's informal and cheap, with prices around NKr50 and up. **Olsens Cafe** (Bogstadvn. 8, tel. 22/46–39–65) is also popular and cheap, with prices ranging from NKr24 to NKr68 for a hot meal. The NKr49 lunch buffet at the **Sebastian Rock Cafe** (Karl Johans gt. 35, tel. 22/42–97–10) is a good bargain. For a cheap beer (about NKr23), head to **Sub Pub** (St. Olavs gt. 23, tel. 22/11–02–49).

Accommodations Before registering in hotels, check with the local tourist information office for special hotel rates, which sometimes the hotels themselves cannot offer. Many hotels honor discounts with special passes, such as Fjord Pass (discounts at more than 300 hotels), Scandinavian Bonus Pass (Inter Nor Hotels) and Nordturist.

Hostels are a way to keep accommodation costs down. There are more than 90 in the country, including family hostels that come equipped with a kitchenette. Other popular options are farms, mountain cabins, *rorbuer* (rustic fishermen's cabins), and the more than 1,400 authorized campsites.

Sweden

As one of Europe's most expensive and highly taxed countries (Sweden has a 25% value-added tax on consumer products), Sweden does not offer the same bargains and money-saving opportunities that are more typically available in other countries. Nevertheless, with patience, foresight, and a little research, they can be found.

Sweden's three major cities—Stockholm, Gotheburg, and Malmö—offer a "key to the city" card that provides not only discounted or unlimited travel on city subways, buses, and rail services, but also free admission to museums, sightseeing trips, and discounted prices at restaurants and shops. For example, the Stockholmskort (Key to Stockholm) costs SKr150 for 24 hours, SKr300 for two days, and SKr450 for three days and entitles you to free transportation and museum entrance. Contact the tourist office in the city you are visiting to find out how to purchase this card.

Transportation The VAT on transportation has been reduced to 12%. Statens Järnvägar (SJ, the Swedish state railway company) offers the Reslutskort (Desire-to-travel card) which costs SKr150 and entitles the holder to 50% discounts on "red" day fares (less frequently traveled days) and 25% discount on regular fares (Tues.–Thurs. and Sat., tel. 020/757575). SJ has introduced the Nordturistkort, a pass that gives the holder unlimited travel by train throughout Denmark, Finland, Norway, and Sweden for 21 days. It costs SKr1,980 for adults over 25, SKr1,480 for young people ages 12 to 25, and SKr1,000 for children ages 4 to 11. Children under 4 travel free.

Communications Purchase a Telefonkort (telephone card) from any Telebutik, pressbyrå, or hospital for SKr45 or SKr80, depending on the number of calls you wish to make. The cost per call is much cheaper if you make numerous domestic calls.

Shopping More than 13,000 shops are part of a tax-free shopping service for visitors. When you buy goods, you are given a voucher for the value-added tax paid on them for which you can obtain a 14%–18% refund when you leave the country. Look for the blue and yellow TAX FREE sign. Cotton-made children's clothes at Hennes & Mauritz, a Swedish department store chain, are priced at a level that is at least on a par with the most expensive U.S. stores, where 100% cotton clothes can be difficult to find.

Dining The restaurant VAT is 21%, but even the fanciest restaurants have what is called *dagens rätt* (today's special) for lunch, which typically costs SKr60–80 and includes a main dish, a salad, a drink, and a cup of coffee. One of the most common eateries is the Konditori, a cross between a bakery and a café that offers coffee, soft drinks, and sandwiches at reasonable prices. They exist on practically every other street in the cities, towns, and villages of Sweden. *Korv* (sausage), which tastes better than its U.S. counterpart, costs SKr10 at the ubiquitous city hot-dog stands. Ice cream is also a good deal in Sweden, costing as little as SKr10 for a standard yogurt ice-cream cone if you buy it from a kiosk.

Accommodations The VAT on hotel accommodations has been reduced to 12%. All hotels in Sweden offer as much as 50% off the regular rate on weekends and during the summer. In addition, most of the major hotels provide some kind of discount program. Ask for Reso's Piccolo Card, which costs SKr150 and entitles the holder to a 20% discount on summer rates (June 1–Aug. 31), which are already reduced by 50%. The Scandic Hotel summer check plan enables you to pay for your accommodations in advance, with a weekend check costing SKr550 and a supplement of SKr150 for inner-city hotels. Sweden Hotels offers the Scandinavian Bonus Pass which costs SKr160 and gives discounts of between 15% and 50% during May 15–Oct. 1. Biltur-Logi (Go-as-you-please) is a hotel pass that offers discount rates to some 200 hotels and bed-and-breakfasts through Sweden. With an SKr65 pass, you have a choice of rooms ranging from SKr158 per person for a modest room to SKr198 per person for a room with a bathroom and shower. Contact Biltur-Logi, S-793 Tällberg, Sweden, tel. 0247/509 25, fax 0247/509 25.

Whatever program you ultimately choose, be sure to find out exactly what is included: taxes, tips, transfers, meals, baggage handling, ground transportation, entertainment, excursions, sports or recreation (and rental equipment if necessary). Ask about the level of hotel used, its location, the size of its rooms, the kind of beds, and its amenities, such as pool, room service, or programs for children, if they're important to you. Find out the operator's cancellation penalties. Nearly everyone charges them, and the only way to avoid them is to buy trip-cancellation insurance (*see* Trip Insurance, *below*). Also ask about the single supplement, a surcharge assessed to solo travelers. Some operators do not make you pay it if you agree to be matched up with a roommate of the same sex, even if one is not found by departure time. Remember that a program that has features you won't use, whether for rental sporting equipment or discounted museum admissions, may not be the most cost-wise choice for you.

Fully Escorted Tours

Escorted tours are usually sold in three categories: deluxe, first-class, and tourist or budget class. The most important differences are the price, of course, and the level of accommodations. Some operators specialize in one category, while others offer a range.

Contact **Maupintour** (Box 807, Lawrence, KS 66044, tel. 800/255–4266 or 913/843–1211), **Tauck Tours** (11 Wilton Rd., Westport, CT 06881, tel. 203/226–6911), and **Abercrombie & Kent** (1520 Kensington Rd., Oak Brook, IL 60521, tel. 800/325–7308 or 708/954–2944) in the deluxe category; **American Airlines Fly AAway Vacations** (tel. 800/321–2121), **Bennett Tours** (270 Madison Ave., New York, NY 10016, tel. 800/221–2420 or 212/532–5060), **British Airways** (tel. 800/247–9297), **Caravan Tours** (401 N. Michigan Ave., Chicago, IL 60611, tel. 800/227–2826 or 312/321–9800), **Continental Airlines' Grand Destinations** (tel. 800/634–5555), **Delta Dream Vacations** (tel. 800/872–7786), **Gadabout Tours** (700 E. Tahquitz Way, Palm Springs, CA 92262, tel. 800/952–5068 or 619/325–5556), **Globus-Gateway** (95–25 Queens Blvd., Rego Park, NY 11374, tel. 800/221–0090 or 718/268–7000), **SAS** (tel. 800/221–2350, press "3" for tour desk), and **Trafalgar Tours** (21 E. 26th St., New York, NY 10010, tel. 800/854–0103 or 212/689–8977) in the first-class category; and **Cosmos,** a sister company of Globus-Gateway (*see above*), in the budget category.

Most itineraries are jam-packed with sightseeing, so you see a lot in a short amount of time (usually one place per day). To judge just how fast-paced the tour is, review the itinerary carefully. If you are in a different hotel each night, you will be getting up early each day to head out, travel to your next destination, do some sightseeing, have dinner, and go to bed; then you'll start all over again. If you want some free time, make sure it's mentioned in the tour brochure; if you want to be escorted to every meal, confirm that any tour you consider does that. Also, when comparing programs, be sure to find out if the motorcoach is air-conditioned and has a restroom on board. Make your selection based on price and stops on the itinerary.

Independent Packages

Independent packages, which travel agents call FITs (for foreign independent travel), are offered by airlines, tour operators who may also do escorted programs, and any number of other companies from large, established firms to small, new entrepreneurs.

All the airlines listed above (**American, Delta, Continental, British Airways,** and **SAS**) and **KLM Royal Dutch Airlines** (tel. 800/777–1668) offer independent packages. Other operators include **Bennett Tours** (*see above*), **DER Tours** (11933 Wilshire Blvd., Los Angeles, CA 90025, tel. 800/937–1234 or 213/479–4140), **Gadabout Tours** (*see above*), **Jet Vacations** (1775 Broadway, New York, NY 10019, tel. 800/538–0999 or 212/247–0999), and **Travel Bound** (599 Broadway, Penthouse, New York, NY 10012, tel. 800/456–8656 or 212/334–1350).

Their programs come in a wide range of prices based on levels of luxury and options—in addition to hotel and airfare, sightseeing, car rental, transfers, admission to local attractions, and other extras. Note that when pricing different packages, it sometimes pays to purchase the same arrangements separately, as when a rock-bottom promotional airfare is being offered, for example. Again, base your choice on what's available at your budget for the destinations you want to visit.

Special-Interest Travel Special-interest programs may be fully escorted or independent. Some require a certain amount of expertise, but most are for the average traveler with an interest and are usually hosted by experts in the subject matter. When the program is escorted, it enjoys the advantages and disadvantages of all escorted programs; because your fellow travelers are apt to be passionate or knowledgeable about the subject, they can prove as enjoyable a part of your travel experience as the destination itself. The price range is wide, but the cost is usually higher—sometimes a lot higher—than for ordinary escorted tours and packages, because of the expert guiding and special activities.

Biking **Backroads** (1516 5th St., Suite Q333, Berkeley, CA 94710, tel. 800/245–3874 or 510/527–1555) offers a seven-day inn trip through Norway, in July and August.

Educational **Arrangements Abroad** (50 Broadway, New York, NY 10004, tel. 212/514-8921) specializes in educational programs in Scandinavia for alumni groups and museum members.

When to Go

Tourist season is in June, July, and August, when daytime temperatures are often in the 70s (21°C to 26°C) and sometimes rise into the 80s (27°C to 32°C). Detailed temperature charts are included in individual country chapters. In general, the weather is not overly warm, and a brisk breeze and brief rainstorms are possible anytime. Nights can be chilly, even in summer.

Truly delightful are the incredibly long days, particularly in June, when the sun rises in Copenhagen at 4 AM and sets at 11 PM, making long evenings of sightseeing possible. Days are even longer farther north. Many attractions extend their hours during the summer, and some shut down altogether in winter. Fall, spring, and even winter are pleasant, despite the area's reputation for gloom. The days become shorter quickly, but the sun casts a golden light one does not see farther south. On dark days, fires and candlelight will warm you indoors.

The Gulf Stream warms Denmark, the western coast of Norway, and Iceland, making winters in these areas similar to those in London. Even the harbor of Narvik, far to the north in Norway, remains ice-free year-round. Away from the protection of the

Gulf Stream, however, northern Norway, Sweden, and Finland experience very cold, clear weather that attracts skiers.

Climate
Information
Sources
For current weather conditions for cities in the United States and abroad, plus the local time and helpful travel tips, call the **Weather Channel Connection** (tel. 900/932–8437; 95¢ per minute) from a touch-tone phone.

What to Pack

Pack light, then take half of what you thought you needed and leave it at home as well. A light suitcase with wheels is a real joy, as porters are usually difficult to find and baggage restrictions are tight on international flights. Be sure to check your airline's policy before you pack. Make sure, too, to leave room for the bulky sweaters, furs, and crystal that you may bring home from Scandinavian shops.

Clothing
Don't forget to bring a bathing suit even in winter, as many hotels have pools and in Iceland, the volcanic springs are particularly delightful then. Also bring a warm sweater, socks, and slacks during summer, wherever you travel in Scandinavia. Fresh summer days become cool evenings, and the wind is often brisk, particularly on the water, if you plan to travel by boat.

Take a folding umbrella, but be prepared for gusty winds that can destroy even the sturdiest. Take a lightweight raincoat too as it can double as a windbreaker. You will probably find yourself taking them with you every day, everywhere you go, as it is common for the sky to be clear at 9 AM, rainy at 11 AM, and clear again in time for lunch. Don't forget that your feet get wet, as well: an extra pair of walking shoes that dry quickly will come in handy. Except in summer, you'll be glad to have waterproof boots to keep you cozy.

Perhaps because of the climate, Scandinavians tend to be practical and resilient, and fashion follows suit. It is safe to generalize that, with the possible exception of the Swedes, most Scandinavians—from bicyclists in Copenhagen, to businesspeople in Oslo, to shopkeepers in Reykjavík and Helsinki—dress more casually than their Continental brethren in Germany and Italy. Slacks and comfortable shoes are almost always acceptable attire. That said, don't forget to bring one nice outfit for your visit to a fancy Stockholm restaurant.

Miscellaneous
If you can't sleep when it is light and you are traveling during summer, bring a comfortable eye-mask, so you won't wake up automatically at the 4 AM sunrise.

Bug repellent is a good idea if you plan to venture away from the capital cities. Large mosquitoes can be a real nuisance on summer evenings in Denmark, as well as in the far northern reaches of Norway and Sweden.

Because of the far northern latitude, the sun slants at angles unseen elsewhere on the globe, and a pair of dark sunglasses can prevent eyestrain if, for example, you're unlucky enough to drive westward at sundown. Sunscreen is less a requirement here than in most places but can nonetheless be a good idea during summer and for winter skiing.

Bring an extra pair of eyeglasses or contact lenses. If you have a health problem that may require you to purchase a prescription

drug, pack enough to last the duration of the trip, or have your doctor write a prescription using the drug's generic name, since brand names vary from country to country. And don't forget to pack a list of the addresses of offices that supply refunds for lost or stolen traveler's checks.

Electricity   The electrical current in Scandinavia is 220 volts, 50 cycles alternating current (AC); the United States runs on 110-volt, 60-cycle AC current. Unlike wall outlets in the United States, which accept plugs with two flat prongs, outlets in Scandinavia take plugs with two round prongs.

Adapters,   To plug in U.S.-made appliances abroad, you'll need an adapter
Converters,   plug. To reduce the voltage entering the appliance from 220 to
Transformers   110 volts, you'll also need a converter, unless it is a dual-voltage appliance, made for travel. There are converters for high-wattage appliances (such as hair dryers), low-wattage items (such as electric toothbrushes and razors), and combination models. Hotels sometimes have outlets marked "For Shavers Only" near the sink; these are 110-volt outlets for low-wattage appliances; don't use them for a high-wattage appliance. If you're traveling with a laptop computer, especially an older one, you may need a transformer—a type of converter used with electronic-circuitry products. Newer laptop computers are autosensing, operating equally well on 110 and 220 volts (so you need only the appropriate adapter plug). When in doubt, consult your appliance's owner's manual or the manufacturer. Or get a copy of the free brochure "Foreign Electricity is No Deep Dark Secret," published by adapter-converter manufacturer Franzus (Murtha Industrial Park, Box 142, Beacon Falls, CT 06403, tel. 203/723–6664; send a stamped, self-addressed envelope when ordering).

Luggage   Free baggage allowances on an airline depend on the airline,
Regulations   the route, and the class of your ticket. In general, on domestic flights and on international flights to or from the United States, you are entitled to check two bags—neither exceeding 62 inches, or 158 centimeters (length + width + height), or weighing more than 70 pounds (32 kilograms). A third piece may be brought aboard as a carryon; its total dimensions are generally limited to less than 45 inches (114 centimeters), so it will fit easily under the seat in front of you or in the overhead compartment. There are variations, so ask in advance. The single rule, a Federal Aviation Administration safety regulation that pertains to carry-on baggage on U.S. airlines, requires that carryons be properly stowed and allows the airline to limit allowances and tailor them to different aircraft and operational conditions. Charges for excess, oversize, or overweight pieces vary, so inquire before you pack.

If you are flying between two foreign destinations, note that baggage allowances may be determined not by piece but by weight, which generally allows 88 pounds (40 kilograms) of luggage in first class, 66 pounds (30 kilograms) in business class, and 44 pounds (20 kilograms) in economy. If your flight between two cities abroad *connects* with your transatlantic or transpacific flight, the piece method still applies.

Safeguarding Your   Before leaving home, itemize your bags' contents and their
Luggage   worth; this list will help you estimate the extent of your loss if your bags go astray. To minimize that risk, tag them inside and out with your name, address, and phone number. (If you use

your home address, cover it so that potential thieves can't see it.) At check-in, make sure that the tag attached by baggage handlers bears the correct three-letter code for your destination. If your bags do not arrive with you, or if you detect damage, do not leave the airport until you've filed a written report with the airline.

Taking Money Abroad

Traveler's Checks Although you will want plenty of cash when visiting small cities or rural areas, traveler's checks are usually preferable. The most widely recognized are **American Express, Barclay's, Thomas Cook,** and those issued by major commercial banks such as **Citibank** and **Bank of America.** American Express also issues *Traveler's Cheques for Two*, which can be countersigned and used by you or your traveling companion. Some checks are free; usually the issuing company or the bank at which you make your purchase charges 1% of the checks' face value as a fee. Be sure to buy a few checks in small denominations to cash toward the end of your trip, when you don't want to be left with more foreign currency than you can spend. Always record the numbers of checks as you spend them, and keep this list separate from the checks.

Currency Exchange Banks and bank-operated exchange booths at airports and railroad stations are usually the best places to change money. Hotels, stores, and privately run exchange firms typically offer less favorable rates.

Before your trip, pay attention to how the dollar is doing vis-à-vis Scandinavian currencies. If the dollar is losing strength, try to pay as many travel bills as possible in advance, especially the big ones. If it is getting stronger, pay for costly items overseas, and use your credit card whenever possible—you'll come out ahead, whether the exchange rate at which your purchase is calculated is the one in effect the day the vendor's bank abroad processes the charge, or the one prevailing on the day the charge company's service center processes it at home.

To avoid lines at airport currency-exchange booths, arrive in a foreign country with a small amount of the local currency already in your pocket—a so-called tip pack. **Thomas Cook Currency Services** (630 5th Ave., New York, NY 10111, tel. 212/757–6915) supplies foreign currency by mail.

Getting Money from Home

Cash Machines Automated-teller machines (ATMs) are proliferating; many are tied to international networks such as **Cirrus** and **Plus.** You can use your bank card at ATMs away from home to withdraw money from an account and get cash advances on a credit-card account (providing your card has been programmed with a personal identification number, or PIN). Check in advance on limits on withdrawals and cash advances within specified periods. Ask whether your bank-card or credit-card PIN number will need to be reprogrammed for use in the area you'll be visiting—a possibility if the number has more than four digits. Remember that on cash advances you are charged interest from the day you get the money from ATMs as well as from tellers. And note that, although transaction fees for ATM withdrawals

abroad will probably be higher than fees for withdrawals at home, Cirrus and Plus exchange rates tend to be good.

Be sure to plan ahead: Obtain ATM locations and the names of affiliated cash-machine networks before departure. For specific foreign Cirrus locations, call 800/424–7787; for foreign Plus locations, consult the Plus directory at your local bank.

American Express Cardholder Services

The company's **Express Cash** system lets you withdraw cash and/or traveler's checks from a worldwide network of 57,000 American Express dispensers and participating bank ATMs. You must *enroll first* (call 800/227–4669 for a form and allow two weeks for processing). Withdrawals are charged not to your card but to a designated bank account. You can withdraw up to $1,000 per seven-day period on the basic card, more if your card is gold or platinum. There is a 2% fee (minimum $2.50, maximum $10) for each cash transaction, and a 1% fee for traveler's checks (except for the platinum card), which are available only from American Express dispensers.

At AmEx offices, cardholders can also cash personal checks for up to $1,000 in any seven-day period (21 days abroad); of this $200 can be in cash, more if available, with the balance paid in traveler's checks, for which all but platinum cardholders pay a 1% fee. Higher limits apply to the gold and platinum cards.

Wiring Money

You don't have to be a cardholder to send or receive an **American Express MoneyGram** for up to $10,000. To send one, go to an American Express MoneyGram agent, pay up to $1,000 with a credit card and anything over that in cash, and phone a transaction reference number to your intended recipient, who needs only present identification and the reference number to the nearest MoneyGram agent to pick up the cash. There are MoneyGram agents in more than 60 countries (call 800/543–4080 for locations). Fees range from 5% to 10%, depending on the amount and how you pay. You can't use American Express, which is really a convenience card—only Discover, MasterCard, and Visa credit cards.

You can also use **Western Union.** To wire money, take either cash or a check to the nearest office. (Or you can call and use a credit card.) Fees are roughly 5%–10%. Money sent from the United States or Canada will be available for pick up at agent locations in Scandinavia within minutes. (Note that once the money is in the system it can be picked up at *any* location. You don't have to miss your train waiting for it to arrive in City A, because if there's an agent in City B, where you're headed, you can pick it up there, too.) There are approximately 20,000 agents worldwide (call 800/325–6000 for locations).

Scandinavian Currency

Currency values fluctuate, of course. The strengthening of the dollar in 1993 made travel to Scandanavia more appealing to Americans. In this book currencies are abbreviated DKr (Danish kroner), FM (Finnish mark), IKr (Icelandic kroner), NKr (Norwegian kroner), and SKr (Swedish kronor). In individual countries you may see prices indicated with Kr only, and you may see exchange rates in banks quoted for DKK, FIM, ISK, NOK, and SEK, respectively. The currency exchange rates quoted in the following chapters fluctuate daily, so check them at the time of your departure.

What It Will Cost

Costs are high in Denmark, Norway, and Sweden, higher still in Finland, and highest in Iceland, where so many things must be imported. Throughout the region, be aware that sales taxes can be very high, but foreigners can get some refunds by shopping at tax-free stores. *See* Shopping, *below*, for details. City cards can save you transportation and entrance fees in many of the larger cities.

You can reduce the cost of food by planning. Breakfast is often included in your hotel bill; if not, you may wish to buy fruit, sweet rolls, and a beverage for a picnic breakfast. Electrical devices for hot coffee or tea should be bought abroad, though, to conform to the local current. Restaurant lunches are often significantly less expensive than the same or a comparable dinner. Drink water instead of beer or wine, which can cost four times the price of the same brand in a store—but do specify tap water, as the term "water" can refer to soft drinks and bottled water, which are also expensive. The tip is included in the cost of your meal. After a filling hot lunch, dinner could be lighter—a picnic of delicious open-face sandwiches from a delicatessen, for instance—or eaten at a snack bar or cafeteria.

Passports and Visas

If your passport is lost or stolen abroad, report it immediately to the nearest embassy or consulate and to the local police. If you can provide the consular officer with the information contained in the passport, he or she will usually be able to issue you a new passport. For this reason, it is a good idea to keep a copy of the data page of your passport in a separate place, or to leave the passport number, date, and place of issuance with a relative or friend at home.

U.S. Citizens All U.S. citizens, even infants, need a valid passport to enter any Scandinavian country for stays of up to three months. Note that this three-month period is calculated from the time you enter *any* Scandinavian country. You can pick up new and renewal application forms at any of the 13 U.S. Passport Agency offices and at some post offices and courthouses. Although passports are usually mailed within two weeks of your application's receipt, it's best to allow three weeks for delivery in low season, five weeks or more from April through summer. Call the Department of State Office of Passport Services' information line (1425 K St. NW, Washington, DC 20522, tel. 202/647–0518) for fees, documentation requirements, and other details.

Canadian Citizens Canadian citizens need a valid passport to enter any Scandinavian country for stays of up to three months. Note that this three-month period is calculated from the time you enter *any* Scandinavian country. Application forms are available at 23 regional passport offices as well as post offices and travel agencies. Whether applying for a first or subsequent passport, you must apply in person. Children under 16 may be included on a parent's passport but must have their own passport to travel alone. Passports are valid for five years and are usually mailed within two weeks of an application's receipt. For fees, documentation requirements, and other information in English or French, call the passport office (tel. 514/283–2152).

U.K. Citizens Citizens of the United Kingdom need a valid passport to enter any Scandinavian country for stays of up to three months. Applications for new and renewal passports are available from main post offices as well as at the six passport offices, located in Belfast, Glasgow, Liverpool, London, Newport, and Peterborough. You may apply in person at all passport offices, or by mail to all except the London office. Children under 16 may travel on a parent's passport when accompanying them. All passports are valid for 10 years. Allow a month for processing.

A British Visitor's Passport is valid for holidays and some business trips of up to three months to Scandinavia. It can include both partners of a married couple. Valid for one year, it will be issued on the same day that you apply. You must apply in person at a main post office.

Customs and Duties

On Arrival Limits on what you can bring in duty-free vary from country to country. *See* individual chapters for limits on alcohol, cigarettes, and other items. Also be careful to check before bringing food of any kind into Iceland.

Returning Home Provided you've been out of the country for at least 48 hours
U.S. Customs and haven't already used the exemption, or any part of it, in the past 30 days, you may bring home $400 worth of foreign goods duty-free. So can each member of your family, regardless of age; and your exemptions may be pooled, so one of you can bring in more if another brings in less. A flat 10% duty applies to the next $1,000 worth of goods; above $1,400, the rate varies with the merchandise. (If the 48-hour or 30-day limits apply, your duty-free allowance drops to $25, which may not be pooled.)

Travelers 21 or older may bring back 1 liter of alcohol duty-free, provided the beverage laws of the state through which they reenter the United States allow it. In addition, 100 non-Cuban cigars and 200 cigarettes are allowed, regardless of your age. Antiques and works of art more than 100 years old are duty-free.

Gifts valued at less than $50 may be mailed duty-free to stateside friends and relatives, with a limit of one package per day per addressee (do not send alcohol or tobacco products, nor perfume valued at more than $5). These gifts do not count as part of your exemption, unless you bring them home with you. Mark the package "Unsolicited Gift" and include the nature of the gift and its retail value.

For a copy of "Know Before You Go," a free brochure detailing what you may and may not bring back to the United States, rates of duty, and other pointers, contact the **U.S. Customs Service** (Box 7407, Washington, DC 20044, tel. 202/927–6724).

Canadian Customs Once per calendar year, when you've been out of Canada for at least seven days, you may bring in $300 worth of goods duty-free. If you've been away less than seven days but more than 48 hours, the duty-free exemption drops to $100 but can be claimed any number of times (as can a $20 duty-free exemption for absences of 24 hours or more). You cannot combine the yearly and 48-hour exemptions, use the $300 exemption only partially (to save the balance for a later trip), or pool exemptions with family members. Goods claimed under the $300 exemption

may follow you by mail; those claimed under the lesser exemptions must accompany you on your return.

Alcohol and tobacco products may be included in the yearly and 48-hour exemptions but not in the 24-hour exemption. If you meet the age requirements of the province through which you reenter Canada, you may bring in, duty-free, 1.14 liters (40 imperial ounces) of wine or liquor *or* two dozen 12-ounce cans or bottles of beer or ale. If you are 16 or older, you may bring in, duty-free, 200 cigarettes, 50 cigars or cigarillos, and 400 tobacco sticks or 400 grams of manufactured tobacco. Alcohol and tobacco must accompany you on your return.

Gifts may be mailed to friends in Canada duty-free. These do not count as part of your exemption. Each gift may be worth up to $60—label the package "Unsolicited Gift—Value under $60." There are no limits on the number of gifts that may be sent per day or per addressee, but you can't mail alcohol or tobacco.

For more information, including details of duties on items that exceed your duty-free limit, ask the Revenue Canada Customs and Excise Department (Connaught Bldg., MacKenzie Ave., Ottawa, Ont., K1A OL5, tel. 613/957–0275) for a copy of the free brochure "I Declare/Je Déclare."

U.K. Customs   If your journey was wholly within EC countries, you no longer need to pass through customs when you return to the United Kingdom. According to EC guidelines, you may bring in 800 cigarettes, 400 cigarillos, 200 cigars, and 1 kilogram of smoking tobacco, plus 10 liters of spirits, 20 liters of fortified wine, 90 liters of wine, and 110 liters of beer. If you exceed these limits, you may be required to prove that the goods are for your personal use or are gifts.

From countries outside the EC, you may import duty-free 200 cigarettes, 100 cigarillos, 50 cigars or 250 grams of tobacco; 1 liter of spirits or 2 liters of fortified or sparkling wine; 2 liters of still table wine; 60 millileters of perfume; 250 millileters of toilet water; plus £36 worth of other goods, including gifts and souvenirs.

For further information or a copy of "A Guide for Travellers," which details standard customs procedures as well as what you may bring into the United Kingdom from abroad, contact HM Customs and Excise (New King's Beam House, 22 Upper Ground, London SE1 9PJ, tel. 071/620–1313).

Traveling with Cameras, Camcorders, and Laptops

About Film and   If your camera is new or if you haven't used it for a while, shoot
Cameras   and develop a few rolls of film before leaving home. Pack some lens tissue and an extra battery for your built-in light meter, and invest in an inexpensive skylight filter, to both protect your lens and provide some definition in hazy shots. Store film in a cool, dry place—never in the car's glove compartment or on the shelf under the rear window.

Films above ISO 400 are more sensitive to damage from airport security X-rays than others; very high speed films, ISO 1,000 and above, are exceedingly vulnerable. To protect your film, don't put it in checked luggage; carry it with you in a plastic bag and ask for a hand inspection. Such requests are honored at

American airports, up to the inspector abroad. Don't depend on a lead-lined bag to protect film in checked luggage—the airline may very well turn up the dosage of radiation to see what you've got in there. Airport metal detectors do not harm film, although you'll set off the alarm if you walk through one with a roll in your pocket. Call the Kodak Information Center (tel. 800/242–2424) for details.

About Camcorders Before your trip, put new or long-unused camcorders through their paces, and practice panning and zooming. Invest in a skylight filter to protect the lens, and check the lithium battery that lights up the LCD (liquid crystal display) modes. As for the rechargeable nickel-cadmium batteries that are the camera's power source, take along an extra pair, so while you're using your camcorder you'll have one battery ready and another recharging. Most newer camcorders are equipped with the battery (which generally slides or clicks onto the camera body) and, to recharge it, with what's known as a universal or worldwide AC adapter charger (or multivoltage converter) that can be used whether the voltage is 110 or 220. All that's needed is the appropriate plug.

About Videotape Unlike still-camera film, videotape is not damaged by X-rays. However, it may well be harmed by the magnetic field of a walk-through metal detector. Airport security personnel may want you to turn the camcorder on to prove that that's what it is, so make sure the battery is charged when you get to the airport. Note that although the United States, Canada, Japan, Korea, Taiwan, and other countries operate on the National Television System Committee video standard (NTSC), Scandinavia uses PAL technology. So you will not be able to view your tapes through the local TV set or view movies bought there in your home VCR. Blank tapes bought in Scandinavia can be used for NTSC camcorder taping, however—although you'll probably find they cost more abroad and wish you'd brought an adequate supply along.

About Laptops Security X-rays do not harm hard-disk or floppy-disk storage. Most airlines allow you to use your laptop aloft but request that you turn it off during takeoff and landing so as not to interfere with navigation equipment. Make sure the battery is charged when you arrive at the airport, because you may be asked to turn on the computer at security checkpoints to prove that it is what it appears to be. If you're a heavy computer user, consider traveling with a backup battery. For international travel, register your laptop with U.S. Customs as you leave the country, providing it's manufactured abroad (U.S.-origin items cannot be registered at U.S. Customs); when you do so, you'll get a certificate, good for as long as you own the item, containing your name and address, a description of the laptop, and its serial number, that will quash any questions that may arise on your return. If your laptop is U.S.-made, call the consulate of the country you'll be visiting to find out whether it should be registered with customs in that country upon arrival. Some travelers do this as a matter of course and ask customs officers to sign a document that specifies the total configuration of the system, computer and peripherals, and its value. In addition, before leaving home, find out about repair facilities at your destination, and don't forget any transformer or adapter plug you may need (*see* Electricity, *above*).

Language

Despite the fact that four of the five Scandinavian tongues are in the Germanic family of languages, it is a myth that someone who speaks German can understand Danish, Swedish, and Norwegian. Fortunately, English is widely spoken in Scandinavia. German is the most common third language. Outside major cities, English becomes rarer, and it's a good idea to take along a dictionary or phrase book. Even here, however, anyone under the age of 50 is likely to have studied English in school.

Danish, Norwegian, and Swedish are similar, and fluent speakers can generally understand each other. A foreigner will most often be struck by the lilting rhythm of spoken Swedish, which takes a bit of getting used to for Danes and Norwegians, who often choose to speak English with Swedes.

Characters special to these three languages are the Danish "ø" and the Swedish "ö," pronounced somewhat like the "oo" in "goop," but with a bit more r-sound to it; "æ" or "ä," which sounds like the "a" in "ape" but with a glottal stop, or the "a" in "cat," depending on the country; and the "å" (also written "aa"), which sounds like the "o" in "ghost." The important thing about these characters isn't that you pronounce them correctly—foreigners usually can't—but that you know to find them in the phone book at the very end. Mr. Søren Åstrup, for example, will be found after "Z." Æ or Ä and Ø or Ö follow.

Icelandic, because of its island isolation, is the language closest to what the Vikings spoke 1,000 years ago. Although Norwegian, Danish, and Swedish have clearly evolved away from the roots common to all four languages, Icelandic retains a surprising amount of its ancient heritage, and Icelanders want to keep it that way: a governmental committee in Iceland has the express task of coming up with Icelandic versions of new words such as "computer." Two characters are unique to Icelandic and Faroese: the "Þ" or "þ," which is pronounced like the "th" in "thing"; and "Ð" or "ð," which is pronounced like the "th" in "the."

Finnish is a non-Germanic language more closely related to Hungarian than to the other Scandinavian languages. A visitor isn't likely to recognize anything on the average newspaper's front page. A linguistic cousin to Finnish is still spoken by the Sami (Lapps), who wander in the northernmost parts of Norway, Sweden, Finland, and Russia.

Staying Healthy

If necessary, many clinics in Scandinavia will write a prescription for you free of charge, which you can pick up at a nearby *apotek* (drug store), often at subsidized prices.

Finding a Doctor The **International Association for Medical Assistance to Travellers** (IAMAT, 417 Center St., Lewiston, NY 14092, tel. 716/754–4883; 40 Regal Rd., Guelph, Ontario N1K 1B5; 57 Voirets, 1212 Grand-Lancy, Geneva, Switzerland) publishes a worldwide directory of English-speaking physicians whose qualifications meet IAMAT standards and who have agreed to treat members for a set fee. Membership is free.

Assistance Companies Pretrip medical referrals, emergency evacuation or repatriation, 24-hour telephone hot lines for medical consultation, dis-

patch of medical personnel, relay of medical records, up-front cash for emergencies, and other personal and legal assistance are among the services provided by several membership organizations specializing in medical assistance to travelers. Among them are **International SOS Assistance** (Box 11568, Philadelphia, PA 19116, tel. 215/244–1500 or 800/523–8930; Box 466, Pl. Bonaventure, Montréal, Qué. H5A 1C1, tel. 514/874–7674 or 800/363–0263), **Near Services** (450 Prairie Ave., Suite 101, Calumet City, IL 60409, tel. 708/868–6700 or 800/654–6700), and **Travel Assistance International** (1133 15th St. NW, Suite 400, Washington, DC 20005, tel. 202/331–1609 or 800/821–2828), part of Europ Assistance Worldwide Services, Inc. Because these companies will also sell you death-and-dismemberment, trip-cancellation, and other insurance coverage, there is some overlap with the travel-insurance policies discussed below, which may include the services of an assistance company among the insurance options or reimburse travelers for such services without providing them.

Insurance

For U.S. Residents Most tour operators, travel agents, and insurance agents sell specialized health-and-accident, flight, trip-cancellation, and luggage insurance as well as comprehensive policies with some or all of these features. But before you make any purchase, review your existing health and homeowner policies to find out whether they cover expenses incurred while travelling.

Health-and-Accident Insurance Supplemental health-and-accident insurance for travelers is usually a part of comprehensive policies. Specific policy provisions vary, but they tend to address three general areas, beginning with reimbursement for medical expenses caused by illness or an accident during a trip. Such policies may reimburse anywhere from $1,000 to $150,000 worth of medical expenses; dental benefits may also be included. A second common feature is the personal-accident, or death-and-dismemberment, provision, which pays a lump sum to your beneficiaries if your die or to you if you lose one or both limbs or your eyesight. This is similar to the flight insurance described below, although it is not necessarily limited to accidents involving airplanes or even other "common carriers" (buses, trains, and ships) and can be in effect 24 hours a day. The lump sum awarded can range from $15,000 to $500,000. A third area generally addressed by these policies is medical assistance (referrals, evacuation, or repatriation and other services). Some policies reimburse travelers for the cost of such services; others may automatically enroll you as a member of a particular medical-assistance company.

Flight Insurance This insurance, often bought as a last-minute impulse at the airport, pays a lump sum to a beneficiary when a plane crashes and the insured dies (and sometimes to a surviving passenger who loses eyesight or a limb); thus it supplements the airlines' own coverage as described in the limits-of-liability paragraphs on your ticket (up to $75,000 on international flights, $20,000 on domestic ones—and that is generally subject to litigation). Charging an airline ticket to a major credit card often automatically signs you up for flight insurance; in this case, the coverage may also embrace travel by bus, train, and ship.

Baggage Insurance   In the event of loss, damage, or theft on international flights, airlines limit their liability to $20 per kilogram for checked baggage (roughly about $640 per 70-pound bag) and $400 per passenger for unchecked baggage. On domestic flights, the ceiling is $1,250 per passenger. Excess-valuation insurance can be bought directly from the airline at check-in but leaves your bags vulnerable on the ground.

Trip Insurance   There are two sides to this coin. **Trip-cancellation-and-interruption insurance** protects you in the event you are unable to undertake or finish your trip. **Default** or **bankruptcy insurance** protects you against a supplier's failure to deliver. Consider the former if your airline ticket, cruise, or package tour does not allow changes or cancellations. The amount of coverage to buy should equal the cost of your trip should you, a traveling companion, or a family member get sick, forcing you to stay home, plus the nondiscounted one-way airline ticket you would need to buy if you had to return home early. Read the fine print carefully; pay attention to sections defining "family member" and "preexisting medical conditions." A characteristic quirk of default policies is that they often do not cover default by travel agencies or default by a tour operator, airline, or cruise line if you bought your tour and the coverage directly from the firm in question. To reduce your need for default insurance, give preference to tours packaged by members of the United States Tour Operators Association (USTOA), which maintains a fund to reimburse clients in the event of member defaults. Even better, pay for travel arrangements with a major credit card, so that you can refuse to pay the bill if services have not been rendered—and let the card company fight your battles.

Comprehensive Policies   Companies supplying comprehensive policies with some or all of the above features include **Access America, Inc.,** underwritten by BCS Insurance Company (Box 11188, Richmond, VA 23230, tel. 800/284–8300); **Carefree Travel Insurance,** underwritten by The Hartford (Box 310, 120 Mineola Blvd., Mineola, NY 11501, tel. 516/294–0220 or 800/323–3149); **Tele-Trip** (Mutual of Omaha Plaza, Box 31762, Omaha, NE 68131, tel. 800/228–9792), a subsidiary of Mutual of Omaha; **The Travelers Companies** (1 Tower Sq., Hartford, CT 06183, tel. 203/277–0111 or 800/243–3174); **Travel Guard International,** underwritten by Transamerica Occidental Life Companies (1145 Clark St., Stevens Point, WI 54481, tel. 715/345–0505 or 800/782–5151); and **Wallach and Company, Inc.** (107 W. Federal St., Box 480, Middleburg, VA 22117, tel. 703/687–3166 or 800/237–6615), underwritten by Lloyds, London. These companies may also offer the above types of insurance separately.

For U.K. Residents   Most tour operators, travel agents, and insurance agents sell specialized policies covering accident, medical expenses, personal liability, trip cancellation, and loss or theft of personal property. Some policies include coverage for delayed departure and legal expenses, winter-sports, motoring abroad, or their accidents. You can also purchase an annual travel-insurance policy valid for every trip you make during the year in which it's purchased (usually only trips of less than 90 days). Before you leave, make sure you will be covered if you have a preexisting medical condition or are pregnant; your insurers may not pay for routine or continuing treatment, or may require a note from your doctor certifying your fitness to travel.

For advice by phone or a free booklet, "Holiday Insurance," that sets out what to expect from a holiday-insurance policy and gives price guidelines, contact the **Association of British Insurers** (51 Gresham St., London EC2V 7HQ, tel. 071/600–3333; 30 Gordon St., Glasgow G1 3PU, tel. 041/226–3905; Scottish Provincial Bldg., Donegall Sq. W, Belfast BT1 6JE, tel. 0232/249176; call for other locations).

Car Rentals

Driving through Scandinavia is delightful. You'll notice that drivers keep their headlights on even during the day—it is required by law in most of Scandinavia. Take a good pair of sunglasses—the slanting sunlight creates a lot of glare. Drivers' licenses from Britain, Canada, and the United States are valid in Scandinavia. Several countries require drivers to be over 20 years old, but some car-rental companies require that drivers be at least 25, so it is wise to ask.

Most major car-rental companies are represented in Scandinavia, including **Avis** (tel. 800/331–1084, 800/879–2847 in Canada); **Budget** (tel. 800/527–0700); **Dollar** (tel. 800/800–6000); **Hertz** (tel. 800/654–3001, 800/263-0600 in Canada); **National** (tel. 800/227–3876), known internationally as InterRent and Europcar. In cities, unlimited-mileage rates range from about $55–$75 per day for an economy car and $70–$103 for a large car; weekly unlimited-mileage rates range from $235–$315 to $330–$425. Prices vary according to country as well as exchange rates; these prices do not include VAT tax, which in Scandinavia ranges from 22%–25%.

Requirements Your own U.S., Canadian, or U.K. driver's license is acceptable. An International Driver's Permit, available from the American or Canadian Automobile Association, is a good idea.

Extra Charges Picking up the car in one city or country and leaving it in another may entail drop-off charges or one-way service fees, which can be substantial. The cost of a collision or loss-damage waiver (*see below*) can be high, also. Automatic transmissions and air-conditioning are not universally available abroad; ask for them when you book if you want them, and check the cost before you commit yourself to the rental.

Cutting Costs If you know you will want a car for more than a day or two, you can save by planning ahead. Major international companies have programs that discount their standard rates by 15%–30% if you make the reservation before departure (anywhere from two to 14 days), rent for a minimum number of days (typically three or four), and prepay the rental. Ask about these advance-purchase schemes when you call for information. More economical rentals are those that come as part of fly/drive or other packages, even those as bare-bones as the rental plus an airline ticket (*see* Tours and Packages, *above*).

Other sources of savings are the several companies that operate as wholesalers—companies that do not own their own fleets but rent in bulk from those that do and offer advantageous rates to their customers. Rentals through such companies must be arranged and paid for before you leave the United States. Among them are **Auto Europe** (Box 1097, Camden, ME 04843, tel. 207/236–8235 or 800/223–5555, 800/458–9503 in Canada), **Europe by Car** (mailing address, 1 Rockefeller Plaza, New

York, NY 10020; walk-in address, 14 W. 49th St, New York, NY 10020, tel. 212/581–3040 or 212/245–1713; 9000 Sunset Blvd., Los Angeles, CA 90069, tel. 213/252–9401 or 800/223–1516 in CA), and **Kemwel** (106 Calvert St., Harrison, NY 10528, tel. 914/835–5555 or 800/678–0678). You won't see these wholesalers' deals advertised; they're even better in summer, when business travel is down. Always ask whether the prices are guaranteed in U.S. dollars or foreign currency and if unlimited mileage is available. Find out about any required deposits, cancellation penalties, and drop-off charges, and confirm the cost of the CDW.

One last tip: Remember to fill the tank when you turn in the vehicle, to avoid being charged for refueling at what you'll swear is the most expensive pump in town.

Insurance and Collision Damage Waiver The standard rental contract includes liability coverage (for damage to public property, injury to pedestrians, etc.) and coverage for the car against fire, theft (not included in certain countries), and collision damage with a deductible—most commonly $2,000–$3,000, occasionally more. In the case of an accident, you are responsible for the deductible amount unless you've purchased the collision damage waiver (CDW), which costs an average $12 a day, although this varies depending on what you've rented, where, and from whom.

Because this adds up quickly, you may be inclined to say "no thanks"—and that's certainly your option, although the rental agent may not tell you so. Note before you decline that deductibles are occasionally high enough that totaling a car would make you responsible for its full value. Planning ahead will help you make the right decision. By all means, find out if your own insurance covers damage to a rental car while traveling (not simply a car to drive when yours is in for repairs). And check whether charging car rentals to any of your credit cards will get you a CDW at no charge.

Personal accident insurance covers medical injuries. One expense not generally covered by rental-car personal accident insurance policies is emergency transportation home (*see* Insurance, *above*).

Rail Passes

The **EurailPass,** valid for unlimited first-class train travel through 17 countries, including Denmark, Finland, Norway, and Sweden, is an excellent value if you plan to travel around the Continent.

The ticket is available for periods of 15 days ($460), 21 days ($598), one month ($728), two months ($998), and three months ($1,260). For two or more people traveling together, a 15-day rail pass costs $390 each. Between April 1 and September 30, you need a minimum of three in your group to get this discount. For those younger than 26, there is the **Eurail Youthpass,** for one or two months of unlimited second-class train travel at $508 and $698.

If you like to spread out your train journey, you can use the **Eurail Flexipass.** With a Flexipass you can choose between 5, 10, or 15 days unlimited first-class train travel within a period of two months. You pay $298, $496, and $676 for the **Eurail Flexipass,** sold for first-class travel; and $220, $348, $474 for the

Eurail Youth Flexipass, available to those under 26 on their first travel day, sold for second-class travel.

Ask also about the **EurailDrive** Pass, which lets you combine four days of train travel with three days of car rental (through Hertz or Avis) at any time within a two-month period. Charges vary according to size of car, but two people traveling together can get the basic package for $289 per person.

The **EurailPass** is available only if you live outside Europe and North Africa. You can apply through an authorized travel agent or through **Rail Europe** (226–230 Westchester Ave., White Plains, NY 10604, tel. 914/682–5172 or 800/848–7245 from the East and 800/438-7245 from the West).

The **Scanrail Pass** is valid for unlimited rail travel in Scandinavia, and offers free and discounted crossings on several ferry lines. A second-class pass costs $155 for four travel days within a period of 15 days, $265 for nine days travel within 21 days, and $369 for 14 travel days within one month. The first-class rates are $189, $325, and $475, respectively. If you want the flexibility of a car combined with the speed and comfort of the train, try **Scanrail 'n Drive** (from $289 per person, based on two adults sharing an economy car). This pass gives you a four- or nine-day Scanrail pass, plus three days of car rental to use within a 14- or 21-day period. Both of these passes can be purchased from Rail Europe (*see above*) or from the **NSB** (Norweigian State Railways) travel agency in London (tel. 071/930–6666).

Don't make the mistake of assuming that your rail pass guarantees you seats on the trains you want to ride. Seat reservations are required on some trains, particularly high-speed trains, and are a good idea on trains that may be crowded. You will also need reservations for overnight sleeping accommodations. Rail Europe can help you determine if you need reservations and can make them for you (about $10 each, less if you purchase them in Europe at the time of travel). (*See also* Staying in Scandinavia: Getting Around by Train, *below*).

Student and Youth Travel

Most major cities in Scandinavia (including Helsinki, Oslo, Stockholm, Reykjavík, and Copenhagen) offer special **City Cards,** which entitle the holder to unlimited, reduced-rate travel on public transportation as well as free or discounted admission to museums, theaters, and other attractions. The cards can be purchased at tourist offices and major rail stations. (For more information, *see* individual destination chapters.) Additional information is available from the **Scandinavian Tourist Board.**

Travel Agencies The foremost U.S. student travel agency is **Council Travel,** a subsidiary of the nonprofit Council on International Educational Exchange. It specializes in low-cost travel arrangements, is the exclusive U.S. agent for several discount cards, and, with its sister CIEE subsidiary, **Council Charter,** is a source of airfare bargains. The Council Charter brochure and CIEE's twice-yearly *Student Travels* magazine, which details its programs, are available at the Council Travel office at CIEE headquarters (205 E. 42nd Street, New York, NY 10017, tel. 212/661–1450) and at 37 branches in college towns nationwide (free

in person, $1 by mail). The **Educational Travel Center** (ETC, 438 N. Francis St., Madison, WI 53703, tel. 608/256–5551) also offers low-cost rail passes, domestic and international airline tickets (mostly for flights departing from Chicago), and other budgetwise travel arrangements. Other travel agencies catering to students include **Travel Management International** (TMI, 18 Prescott St., Suite 4, Cambridge, MA 02138, tel. 617/661–8187) and **Travel Cuts** (187 College St., Toronto, Ont. M5T 1P7, tel. 416/979–2406).

Discount Cards Most major cities in Scandinavia (including Helsinki, Oslo, Stockholm, Reykjavik, and Copenhagen) offer special **City Cards,** which entitle the holder to unlimited, reduced-rate travel on public transportation as well as free or discounted admission to museums, theaters, and other attractions. The cards can be purchased at tourist offices and major rail stations. (For more information, *see* individual destination chapters.)

For discounts on transportation and on museum and attractions admissions, buy the **International Student Identity Card** (ISIC) if you're a bona fide student, or the **International Youth Card** (IYC) if you're under 26. In the United States the ISIC and IYC cards cost $15 each and include basic travel accident and sickness coverage. Apply to **CIEE** (*see* address *above*, tel. 212/661–1414; the application is in *Student Travels*). In Canada the cards are available for $15 each from **Travel Cuts** (*see above*). In the United Kingdom they cost £5 and £4 respectively at student unions and student travel companies, including Council Travel's London office (28A Poland St., London W1V 3DB, tel. 071/437–7767).

Hosteling An **International Youth Hostel Federation** (IYHF) membership card is the key to more than 5,300 hostel locations in 59 countries; the sex-segregated, dormitory-style sleeping quarters, including some for families, go for $7–$20 a night per person. Membership is available in the United States through **American Youth Hostels** (733 15th St. NW, Washington, DC 20005, tel. 202/783–6161), the American link in the worldwide chain, and costs $25 for adults 18–54, $10 for those under 18, $15 for those 55 and over, and $35 for families. Volume 1 of the two-volume *Guide to Budget Accommodation* lists hostels in Europe and the Mediterranean ($13.95, including postage). IYHF membership is available in Canada through the **Canadian Hostelling Association** (1600 James Naismith Dr., Suite 608, Gloucester, Ont. K1B 5N4, tel. 613/748–5638) for $26.75, and in the United Kingdom through the **Youth Hostel Association of England and Wales** (8 St. Stephen's Hill, St. Albans, Herts. AL1 2DY, tel. 0727/55215) for £9.

Traveling with Children

In Scandinavia children are to be seen AND heard and are genuinely welcome in most public places. Even so, on some occasions hiring a babysitter may be warranted. Rates in Denmark, for instance, range from DKr30 to DKr50 per hour; try bonded services in the capital cities and through your hotel in the countryside.

Publications *Family Travel Times,* published 10 times a year by Travel With
Newsletter Your Children (TWYCH, 45 W. 18th St., 7th Floor Tower, New York, NY 10011, tel. 212/206–0688; annual subscription $55), covers destinations, types of vacations, and modes of travel.

Books   *Great Vacations with Your Kids*, by Dorothy Jordon and Marjorie Cohen ($13; Penguin USA, 120 Woodbine St., Bergenfield, NJ 07621, tel. 800/253–6476) and *Traveling with Children—And Enjoying It*, by Arlene K. Butler ($11.95 plus $3 shipping per book; Globe Pequot Press, Box 833, Old Saybrook, CT 06475, tel. 800/243–0495, or 800/962–0973 in CT) help plan your trip with children, from toddlers to teens. *Innocents Abroad: Traveling with Kids in Europe*, by Valerie Wolf Deutsch and Laura Sutherland ($15.95 or $4.95 paperback, Penguin USA, *see above*), covers child- and teen-friendly activities, food, and transportation.

Tour Operators   **GrandTravel** (6900 Wisconsin Ave., Suite 706, Chevy Chase, MD 20815, tel. 301/986–0790 or 800/247–7651) offers international and domestic tours for grandparents traveling with their grandchildren. The catalogue, as charmingly written and illustrated as a children's book, positively invites armchair traveling with lap-sitters aboard. **Families Welcome!** (21 W. Colony Pl., Suite 140, Durham, NC 27705, tel. 919/489–2555 or 800/326–0724) packages and sells family tours to Europe. **Rascals in Paradise** (650 5th St., Suite 505, San Francisco, CA 94107, tel. 415/978–9800, or 800/872–7225) specializes in programs for families.

Getting There   On international flights, the fare for infants under 2 not occupy-
Air Fares   ing a seat is generally 10% of the accompanying adult's fare; children ages 2–11 usually pay half to two-thirds of the adult fare. On domestic flights, children under 2 not occupying a seat travel free, and older children currently travel on the "lowest applicable" adult fare.

Baggage   In general, infants paying 10% of the adult fare are allowed one carry-on bag, not to exceed 70 pounds or 45 inches (length + width + height). The adult baggage allowance applies for children paying half or more of the adult fare. Check with the airline for particulars, especially regarding flights between two foreign destinations, where allowances for infants may be less generous than those above.

Safety Seats   The FAA recommends the use of safety seats aloft and details approved models in the free leaflet "**Child/Infant Safety Seats Recommended for Use in Aircraft**" (available from the Federal Aviation Administration, APA–200, 800 Independence Ave. SW, Washington, DC 20591, tel. 202/267–3479). Airline policy varies. U.S. carriers must allow FAA-approved models, but because these seats are strapped into a regular passenger seat, they may require that parents buy a ticket even for an infant under 2 who would otherwise ride free. Foreign carriers may not allow infant seats, may charge the child's rather than the infant's fare for their use, or may require you to hold your baby during takeoff and landing, thus defeating the seat's purpose.

Facilities Aloft   Airlines do provide other facilities and services for children, such as children's meals and freestanding bassinets (to those sitting in seats on the bulkhead, where there's enough legroom to accommodate them). Make your request when reserving. The annual February/March issue of *Family Travel Times* gives details of the children's services of dozens of airlines ($10; *see above*). "Kids and Teens in Flight" (free from the U.S. Department of Transportation, tel. 202/366–2220) offers tips for children flying alone.

Getting Around Children are entitled to discount tickets (often as much as 50% off) on buses, trains, and ferries throughout Scandinavia, as well as reductions on special City Cards. During summer months children under 12 pay half price and children under two fly free or pay maximum 10% on SAS and Linjeflyg round-trips. The only restriction on this discount is that the family travel together and return to the originating city in Scandinavia at least two days later. With the Nordturist Pass—good for rail journeys throughout Scandinavia for 21 days—children under four travel free and children four to 11 pay half-fare.

Lodging In most Scandinavian hotels children stay free or at reduced rates when sharing their parents' rooms; there is a nominal charge for an extra bed.

Many youth hostels offer special facilities (including multiple-bed rooms and separate kitchens) for families with children. Family hostels also provide an excellent opportunity for children to meet youngsters from other countries. Contact the **AYH** (*see* Student and Youth Travel, *above*) for information.

Baby-Sitting Services For information on local baby-sitting agencies, contact the tourist office in the city or region you are visiting.

Hints for Travelers with Disabilities

Facilities for the disabled in Scandinavia are generally good, and most of the major tourist offices offer special booklets and brochures on travel and accommodations for disabled visitors.

Organizations Several organizations provide travel information for people with disabilities, usually for a membership fee, and some publish newsletters and bulletins. Among them are the **Information Center for Individuals with Disabilities** (Fort Point Pl., 27–43 Wormwood St., Boston, MA 02210, tel. 617/727–5540 or 800/462–5015 in MA between 11 and 4, or leave message; TDD/TTY tel. 617/345–9743); **Mobility International USA** (Box 3551, Eugene, OR 97403, voice and TDD tel. 503/343–1284), the U.S. branch of an international organization based in Britain (*see below*) and present in 30 countries; **MossRehab Hospital Travel Information Service** (1200 W. Tabor Rd., Philadelphia, PA 19141, tel. 215/456–9603, TDD tel. 215/456–9602); the **Society for the Advancement of Travel for the Handicapped** (SATH, 347 5th Ave., Suite 610, New York, NY 10016, tel. 212/447–7284, fax 212/725–8253); the **Travel Industry and Disabled Exchange** (TIDE, 5435 Donna Ave., Tarzana, CA 91356, tel. 818/368–5648); and **Travelin' Talk** (Box 3534, Clarksville, TN 37043, tel. 615/552–6670).

In the United Kingdom Main information sources include the **Royal Association for Disability and Rehabilitation** (RADAR, 25 Mortimer St., London W1N 8AB, tel. 071/637–5400), which publishes travel information for the disabled in Britain, and **Mobility International** (228 Borough High St., London SE1 1JX, tel. 071/403–5688), the headquarters of an international membership organization that serves as a clearinghouse of travel information for people with disabilities.

Travel Agencies and Tour Operators **Directions Unlimited** (720 N. Bedford Rd., Bedford Hills, NY 10507, tel. 914/241–1700), a travel agency, has expertise in tours and cruises for the disabled. **Evergreen Travel Service** (4114 198th St. SW, Suite 13, Lynnwood, WA 98036, tel. 206/776–1184 or 800/435–2288) operates Wings on Wheels Tours for

those in wheelchairs, White Cane Tours for the blind, and tours for the deaf and makes group and independent arrangements for travelers with any disability. **Flying Wheels Travel** (143 W. Bridge St., Box 382, Owatonna, MN 55060, tel. 800/535–6790 or 800/722–9351 in MN), a tour operator and travel agency, arranges international tours, cruises, and independent travel itineraries for people with mobility disabilities. **Nautilus,** at the same address as TIDE (*see above*), packages tours for the disabled internationally.

Publications In addition to the fact sheets, newsletters, and books mentioned above are several free publications available from the Consumer Information Center (Pueblo, CO 81009): "New Horizons for the Air Traveler with a Disability," a U.S. Department of Transportation booklet describing changes resulting from the 1986 Air Carrier Access Act and those still to come from the 1990 Americans with Disabilities Act (include Department 608Y in the address), and the Airport Operators Council's *Access Travel: Airports* (Dept. 5804), which describes facilities and services for the disabled at more than 500 airports worldwide.

Twin Peaks Press (Box 129, Vancouver, WA 98666, tel. 206/694–2462 or 800/637–2256) publishes the *Directory of Travel Agencies for the Disabled* ($19.95), listing more than 370 agencies worldwide; *Travel for the Disabled* ($19.95), listing some 500 access guides and accessible places worldwide; the *Directory of Accessible Van Rentals* ($9.95) for campers and RV travelers worldwide; and *Wheelchair Vagabond* ($14.95), a collection of personal travel tips. Add $2 per book for shipping.

Lodging Some hotels are suitable for unaccompanied travelers, but, in many others, individuals will require the assistance of an able-bodied companion. Contact the organizations listed above for further information.

The **Best Western** chain (tel. 800/528–1234) offers properties with wheelchair-accessible rooms in Helsinki, Oslo, and Stockholm and just outside Copenhagen. If wheelchair rooms are not available, ground-floor rooms are provided.

Hints for Older Travelers

A **Senior Rail Card** can be bought for about $25 in Scandinavia that gives a year's worth of 30% to 50% discounts on train travel in 19 European countries for travelers over 60.

Organizations The **American Association of Retired Persons** (AARP, 601 E St. NW, Washington, DC 20049, tel. 202/434–2277) provides independent travelers the Purchase Privilege Program, which offers discounts on hotels, car rentals, and sightseeing, and arranges group tours, cruises, and apartment living through AARP Travel Experience from American Express (400 Pinnacle Way, Suite 450, Norcross, GA 30071, tel. 800/927–0111); these can be booked through travel agents, except for the cruises, which must be booked directly (tel. 800/745–4567). AARP membership is open to those 50 and over; annual dues are $8 per person or couple.

Two other membership organizations offer discounts on lodgings, car rentals, and other travel products, along with such nontravel perks as magazines and newsletters. The **National Council of Senior Citizens** (1331 F St. NW, Washington, DC

20004, tel. 202/347–8800) is a nonprofit advocacy group with some 5,000 local clubs across the United States; membership costs $12 per person or couple annually. **Mature Outlook** (6001 N. Clark St., Chicago, IL 60660, tel. 800/336–6330), a Sears Roebuck & Co. subsidiary with 800,000 members, charges $9.95 for an annual membership.

Note: When using any senior-citizen identification card for reduced hotel rates, mention it when booking, not when checking out. At restaurants, show your card before you're seated; discounts may be limited to certain menus, days, or hours. If you are renting a car, ask about promotional rates that might improve on your senior-citizen discount.

Educational Travel **Elderhostel** (75 Federal St., 3rd floor, Boston, MA 02110, tel. 617/426–7788) is a nonprofit organization that has offered inexpensive study programs for people 60 and older since 1975. Programs take place at more than 1,800 educational institutions in the United States, Canada, and 45 other countries; courses cover everything from marine science to Greek myths and cowboy poetry. Participants generally attend lectures in the morning and spend the afternoon sightseeing or on field trips; they live in dorms on the host campuses. Fees for two- to three-week international trips—including room, board, and transportation from the United States—range from $1,800 to $4,500.

Interhostel (University of New Hampshire, 6 Garrison Ave., Durham, NH 03824, tel. 800/733–9753), a slightly younger enterprise than Elderhostel, caters to a slightly younger clientele—that is, 50 and over—and runs programs in some 25 countries. But the idea is similar: Lectures and field trips mix with sightseeing, and participants stay in dormitories at cooperating educational institutions or in modest hotels. Programs are usually two weeks in length and cost $1,500–$2,100, not including airfare from the United States.

Tour Operators **Saga International Holidays** (222 Berkeley St., Boston, MA 02116, tel. 800/343–0273), which specializes in group travel for people over 60, offers a selection of variously priced tours and cruises covering five continents. If you want to take your grandchildren, look into **GrandTravel** (*see* Traveling with Children, *above*).

Further Reading

A History of the Vikings (Oxford University Press, 1984) recounts the story of the aggressive warriors and explorers who during the middle ages influenced a large portion of the world, extending from Constantinople to America. Gwyn Jones's lively account makes learning the history enjoyable.

Arriving and Departing

From North America by Plane

Flights are either nonstop, direct, or connecting. A **nonstop** flight requires no change of plane and makes no stops. A **direct** flight stops at least once and can involve a change of plane, although the flight number remains the same; if the first leg is late, the second waits. This is not the case with a **connecting**

flight, which involves a different plane and a different flight number.

Airlines The following is a list of the major airlines that fly nonstop or direct from the United States or Canada to Scandinavia. Additional airlines offer connecting flights to Scandinavia.

Scandinavian Airlines (SAS) (tel. 800/221–2350) offers nonstop flights to Scandinavia, with flights from Copenhagen to New York, Seattle, Los Angeles, London, and Reykjavík, as well as direct service from New York to Oslo. **Delta Airlines** (tel. 800/ 221–1212) flies from New York to Copenhagen, Oslo, and Stockholm. **Finnair** (tel. 800/950–5000) operates nonstop flights between Helsinki and Copenhagen, Göteborg, London, Los Angeles, Malmö, New York, Oslo, Stockholm, and Toronto. **Icelandair** (in the U.S., tel. 800/223–5500; in Oslo, 02/42–39– 75; in Copenhagen, 33–12–33–88) offers nonstop flights linking Reykjavík to New York, Copenhagen, London, Orlando, Oslo, Stockholm, Amsterdam, Baltimore, and Glasgow. Overnight stopovers in Reykjavík are available; during winter months, stopovers for business class and EuroClass passengers are free and include hotel.

Cutting Flight The Sunday travel section of most newspapers is a good source
Costs of deals. When booking, particularly through an unfamiliar company, call the Better Business Bureau to find out whether any complaints have been registered against the company, pay with a credit card if you can, and consider trip-cancellation and default insurance (*see* Insurance, *above*).

Promotional All the less expensive fares, called promotional or discount
Airfares fares, are round-trip and involve restrictions. The exact nature of the restrictions depends on the airline, the route, and the season and on whether travel is domestic or international, but you must usually buy the ticket—commonly called an APEX (advance purchase excursion) when it's for international travel—in advance (seven, 14, or 21 days are usual). You must also respect certain minimum- and maximum-stay requirements (for instance, over a Saturday night or at least seven and no more than 30, 45, or 90 days), and you must be willing to pay penalties for changes. Airlines generally allow some changes for a fee. But the cheaper the fare, the more likely the ticket is to be nonrefundable; it would take a death in the family for the airline to give you any of your money back if you had to cancel. The lowest fares are also subject to availability; because only a certain percentage of the plane's total seats will be sold at that price, they may go quickly.

Consolidators Consolidators or bulk-fare operators—also known as bucket shops—buy blocks of seats on scheduled flights that airlines anticipate they won't be able to sell. They pay wholesale prices, add a markup, and resell the seats to travel agents or directly to the public at prices that still undercut the airline's promotional or discount fares. You pay more than on a charter but ordinarily less than for an APEX ticket, and, even when there is not much of a price difference, the ticket usually comes without the advance-purchase restriction. Moreover, although tickets are marked nonrefundable so you can't turn them in to the airline for a full-fare refund, some consolidators sometimes give you your money back. Carefully read the fine print detailing penalties for changes and cancellations. If you doubt the reliability of a company, call the airline once you've made your book-

ing and confirm that you do, indeed, have a reservation on the flight.

The biggest U.S. consolidator, C.L. Thomson Express, sells only to travel agents. Well-established consolidators selling to the public include **UniTravel** (Box 12485, St. Louis, MO 63132, tel. 314/569–0900 or 800/325–2222); **Council Charter** (205 E. 42nd St., New York, NY 10017, tel. 212/661–0311 or 800/800–8222), a division of the Council on International Educational Exchange and a longtime charter operator now functioning more as a consolidator; and **Travac** (989 6th Ave., New York, NY 10018, tel. 212/563–3303 or 800/872–8800), also a former charterer.

Charter Flights Charters usually have the lowest fares and the most restrictions. Departures are limited and seldom on time, and you can lose all or most of your money if you cancel. (Generally, the closer to departure you cancel, the more you lose, although sometimes you will be charged only a small fee if you supply a substitute passenger.) The charterer, on the other hand, may legally cancel the flight for any reason up to 10 days before departure; within 10 days of departure, the flight may be canceled only if it becomes physically impossible to operate it. The charterer may also revise the itinerary or increase the price after you have bought the ticket, but if the new arrangement constitutes a "major change," you have the right to a refund. Before buying a charter ticket, read the fine print for the company's refund policy and details on major changes. Money for charter flights is usually paid into a bank escrow account, the name of which should be on the contract. If you don't pay by credit card, make your check payable to the escrow account (unless you're dealing with a travel agent, in which case, his or her check should be payable to the escrow account). The Department of Transportation's Consumer Affairs Office (I–25, Washington, DC 20590, tel. 202/366–2220) can answer questions on charters and send you its "Plane Talk: Public Charter Flights" information sheet.

Charter operators may offer flights alone or with ground arrangements that constitute a charter package. Well-established charter operators include **Council Charter** (205 E. 42nd St., New York, NY 10017, tel. 212/661–0311 or 800/800–8222), now largely a consolidator, despite its name, and **Travel Charter** (1120 E. Long Lake Rd., Troy, MI 48098, tel. 313/528–3500 or 800/521–5267), with Midwestern departures. **DER Tours** (Box 1606, Des Plains, IL 60017, tel. 800/782–2424), a charterer and consolidator, sells through travel agents.

Discount Travel Travel clubs offer their members unsold space on airplanes,
Clubs cruise ships, and package tours at nearly the last minute and at well below the original cost. Suppliers thus receive some revenue for their "leftovers," and members get a bargain. Membership generally includes a regular bulletin or access to a toll-free telephone hot line giving details of available trips departing anywhere from three or four days to several months in the future. Packages tend to be more common than flights alone, so if airfares are your only interest, read the literature before joining. Reductions on hotels are also available. Clubs include **Discount Travel International** (114 Forrest Ave., Suite 203, Narberth, PA 19072, tel. 215/668–7184; $45 annually, single or family), **Moment's Notice** (425 Madison Ave., New York, NY

10017, tel. 212/486–0503; $45 annually, single or family), **Travelers Advantage** (CUC Travel Service, 49 Music Sq. W, Nashville, TN 37203, tel. 800/548–1116; $49 annually, single or family), and **Worldwide Discount Travel Club** (1674 Meridian Ave., Miami Beach, FL 33139, tel. 305/534–2082; $50 annually for family, $40 single).

Enjoying the Flight Almost all flights to Scandinavia are night flights, unless you prefer to take a morning flight to London or Reykjavík and stay overnight before continuing on. Because the air aloft is dry, drink plenty of beverages while on board; remember that drinking alcohol contributes to jet lag, as do heavy meals. Sleepers usually prefer window seats to curl up against; restless passengers ask to be on the aisle. Bulkhead seats, in the front row of each cabin, have more legroom, but since there's no seat ahead, trays attach awkwardly to the arms of your seat, and you must stow all possessions overhead. Bulkhead seats are usually reserved for the disabled, the elderly, and people traveling with babies.

Smoking Since February 1990, smoking has been banned on all domestic flights of less than six hours' duration; the ban also applies to domestic segments of international flights aboard U.S. and foreign carriers. On U.S. carriers flying to Scandinavia and other destinations abroad, a seat in a no-smoking section must be provided for every passenger who requests one, and the section must be enlarged to accommodate such passengers if necessary as long as they have complied with the airline's deadline for check-in and seat assignment. If smoking bothers you, request a seat far from the smoking section.

Foreign airlines are exempt from these rules but do provide no-smoking sections, and some nations, including Canada as of July 1, 1993, have gone as far as to ban smoking on all domestic flights; other countries may ban smoking on flights of less than a specified duration. The International Civil Aviation Organization has set July 1, 1996, as the date to ban smoking aboard airlines worldwide, but the body has no power to enforce its decisions.

From the United Kingdom by Plane Many of the airlines listed above make stops in London en route to Scandinavia. The list below includes other major carriers from Great Britain.

SAS (in London, tel. 071/734–6777; fax 071/465–0125) offers nonstop flights connecting London to Århus, Bergen, Copenhagen, Göteborg, Malmö, Oslo, Stavanger, and Stockholm. **British Airways** (tel. 081/897–4000) flies from Heathrow to Bergen, Copenhagen, Gothenburg, Helsinki, Oslo, Stavanger, and Stockholm. **Maersk Air** (tel. 071/638–7920) flies between London and Copenhagen. **Air Europe** (tel. 0345/444737), **Aer Lingus** (in London, tel. 081/569–555; in Dublin, 0001/377–777), **Cimber Air** (tel. 0652/688491), and **Icelandair** (tel. 071/388–5599) all have flights between Great Britain or Ireland and major Scandinavian cities.

Flying Time The following are typical in-air times between major airports in North America, London, and Scandinavia. Add extra time for stopovers and connections.

From New York: to Reykjavík, 5 hours 30 minutes; to Copenhagen, 7 hours 40 minutes; to Stockholm, 8 hours; to Oslo, 7 hours 30 minutes; to Helsinki, 8 hours.

From Los Angeles: to Copenhagen, 9 hours 50 minutes; to Helsinki, 11 hours 15 minutes.

From London: to Copenhagen, 2 hours; to Stockholm, 2 hours 25 minutes; to Reykjavík, 3 hours 10 minutes; to Helsinki, 3 hours.

From Reykjavík: to Copenhagen, 3 hours 30 minutes.

From Helsinki: to Stockholm, 55 minutes; to Copenhagen, 1 hour 45 minutes; to Oslo, 1 hour 45 minutes.

From Copenhagen: to Oslo, 1 hour 5 minutes; to Stockholm, 1 hour 10 minutes; to Reykjavík, 3 hours 20 minutes; to Helsinki, 2 hours 35 minutes.

By Ship

Only one firm now offers trans-Atlantic crossings: **Cunard** (tel. 800/221–4770; in the United Kingdom, through British Airways, tel. 081/897–4000), sailing the famed *Queen Elizabeth 2* between New York and Southampton. The trip takes five days. Those arriving at Southampton wishing to sail on to Scandinavia should be aware that the Scandinavian ferries leave from Harwich, on the other side of London from Southampton. (For information on ferries between Scandinavian ports and England, Germany, and Holland, *see* Getting Around by Ship in Staying in Scandinavia, *below. See also* Arriving and Departing in each country chapter, *below.*)

Staying in Scandinavia

Getting Around

Particularly between Sweden, Norway, and Denmark, travel is practical by car, bus, train, boat, and plane. The choice depends on personal preference.

The Norwegian Tourist Office publishes an unglamorous brochure called "Tourist Timetables" that is particularly useful. It includes information about ships, trains, planes, buses, and ferries traveling to and around Norway, but much of the information is pertinent to all of Scandinavia.

By Plane Scandinavia is larger than it looks on a map, and many native travelers choose to fly between the capital cities, using trains and buses for domestic travel.

If you are traveling from south to north in Norway, Sweden, or Finland, flying is a necessity: Stavanger in southern Norway is as close to Rome, Italy, as it is to the northern tip of Norway.

For international travelers, one or two stopovers can often be purchased more cheaply along with an international ticket. With SAS, the least expensive tickets are round-trip, must include a Saturday night, and can be bought only within Scandinavia from 7 to 14 days ahead. Ask about low rates for hotels and car rental in connection with SAS Jackpot tickets. Slightly more expensive are APEX tickets, which require purchase seven days in advance, and SAS miniprice tickets, which require no advance purchase. SAS also gives couples traveling together a discount off some tickets and significant discounts on SAS hotels booked through SAS.

By Car   Driving is a marvelous way to explore Scandinavia. The roads are generally excellent and well marked, but it is expensive; the price of gasoline runs about $1.25 per liter of lead-free gas, or roughly four times the typical American price. Ferry costs are steep, and reservations are vital. Tolls on some major roads add to the expense.

Also be aware that there are relatively low legal blood-alcohol limits and tough penalties for driving while intoxicated in Scandinavia. Penalties include suspension of the driver's license and fines or imprisonment, and are enforced by random police roadblocks in urban areas on weekends. In addition, an accident involving a driver with an illegal blood-alcohol level usually voids all insurance agreements, so the driver becomes responsible for his own medical bills and damage to the cars.

In a few remote areas, especially in Iceland and northern Norway, Sweden, and Finland, road conditions can be unpredictable, and careful planning is required for safety's sake. It is wise to use a four-wheel-drive vehicle and to travel with at least one other car in these areas.

By Train   Trains are clean, comfortable, on schedule, and deliver passengers directly downtown. They also offer special smoking and quiet sections, plus bunk beds for overnight trips. The prices are reasonable, and the network is extensive, allowing passengers to go wherever they wish, either by train or by links to local bus networks, which are coordinated with train schedules. Trains are often cheaper than flying, you see more of the country, and an overnight train costs less than many Scandinavian hotels; they do take longer, however.

If you are over 65 or traveling with children, ask about discounts whenever you buy single-trip train tickets, as special prices are available in many places on many routes. Reservations are sometimes necessary.

Available from train stations and travel bureaus in Denmark, Finland, Norway, and Sweden, the **Nordturist Card** gives 21 days of unlimited rail travel in Denmark, Sweden, Norway, and Finland and is valid on many ferries. It costs roughly $305 for adults, $230 for young people from 12 to 25, and $150 for children from 4 to 11. Rebates of up to 50% are granted on other ferries and buses and by some hotels. Travelers over 60 may find the **SeniorRail Card** more advantageous. It can be bought in Denmark for about $25 and gives 30–50% discounts on train travel in 19 European countries for a whole year. For details on other rail passes, *see* Rail Passes in Before You Go, *above.*

By Bus   Buses are ideal for local trips. Detailed information on bus routes is available through local tourist offices (*see* Essential Information in destination chapters).

By Ship   Taking a ferry isn't only fun, it's often necessary in Scandinavia. Many of the operators below arrange package trips, some offering a rental car and hotel as part of the deal.

Cruises often last overnight. The trip between Copenhagen and Oslo, for example, lasts approximately 16 hours, most lines leaving at about 5 PM and arriving about 9 the next morning. The cruise between Stockholm and Helsinki takes 12 hours, usually leaving at about 6 PM and arriving the next morning at 9. The shortest ferry route runs between Helsingør, Denmark, and Helsingborg, Sweden, and takes only 20 minutes.

The main shipping operators running within Scandinavian waters are: **Larvik Line** (Hoffsvn. 15, 0212 Oslo, Norway, tel. 47/02–52–55–00), **Color Line** (Box 30, DK–9850 Hirtshals, Denmark, tel. 45/99–56–19–66, fax 45/98–94–50–92; c/o Bergen Line, Inc., 505 Fifth Ave., N.Y., N.Y. 10017, tel. 800/323–7436, fax 212/983–1275; Tyne Commission Quay, North Shields NE29 6EA, Newcastle, England, tel. 091/296–1313, fax 091/296–1540), and **ScandLines** (Jernbaneveg 1b, DK–3000 Helsingør, Denmark, tel. 45/49–26–26–83, fax 45/49–26–11–24).

The chief operator between England and many points within Scandinavia is **DFDS/Scandinavian Seaways** (Vesterbrogade 4A, 1620 Copenhagen V, Denmark, tel. 45/33–15–63–41; DFDS Travel Centre, 15 Hanover St., London WIR 9HG, tel. 071/493–6696, fax 071–493–4668; DFDS Seaways USA Inc., 6555 NW 9th Ave., Suite 207, Fort Lauderdale, FL 33309, tel. 800/533–3756, fax 305/491–7958) with ships connecting Harwich and Newcastle to Esbjerg, Göteborg, and ports farther up the Norwegian coastline. Another cruise connects Travemünde, Stockholm, Helsinki, and Leningrad.

Connections from Holland and Germany to Norway are available through DFDS and the **Stena Line** (Stenaterminalen DK–9900 Frederikshavn, Denmark, tel. 45/96–20–02–00.

Connections to the Faroe Islands from Norway are available through the **Smyril Line** (DFDS—*see above*—or J. Bronksgøøta 37, Box 370, FR–110 Tórshavn, Faroe Islands, tel. 298/15–900, fax 298/15–707).

Connections to Finland from Sundsvall or Umeñ, Sweden, are available through **Wasa Line** (Box 213, SF–65101 Vaasa, Finland, tel. 358/61–326–0600).

Travel by car often necessitates travel by ferry. Some well-known vehicle and passenger ferries run between Dragør, Denmark, just south of Copenhagen, and Limhamn, Sweden, just south of Malmö; between Helsingør, Denmark, and Helsingborg, Sweden; and between Copenhagen and Göteborg, Sweden.

On the Dragør/Limhamn ferry (ScandLines), taking a car one way costs DKr330 (about $54 or £35). An easy trip runs between Copenhagen and Göteborg on **Stena Line** (in Sweden, tel. 031/75–00–00). The Helsingør/Helsingborg ferry (ScandLines also) takes only 20 minutes; taking a car along one way costs DKr 280 (about $45 or £30).

Shopping

Prices in Scandinavia are never low, but quality is high, and specialties are sometimes less expensive here than elsewhere. Swedish crystal, Icelandic sweaters, Danish Lego blocks and furniture, Norwegian furs, and Finnish fabrics—these are just a few of the items to look for. Keep an eye out for sales, called *udsalg* in Danish and *rea* in Swedish.

One way to beat the prices is to take advantage of tax-free shopping. In all of Scandinavia, you can make major purchases free of tax if you have a foreign passport. Ask about tax-free shopping when you make a purchase for $50 (about £32) or more. When your purchases exceed a specified limit (which var-

ies from country to country), you receive a special export receipt. Keep the parcels intact and take them out of the country within 30 days of purchase. When you leave, you can obtain a refund of the tax in cash from a special office at the airport, or, upon arriving home, you can send your receipts to an office in the country of purchase to receive your refund by mail. Be aware that limits for EC tourists are higher than for those coming from outside the EC. In Sweden, for non-EC tourists, the refund is about 14%; in Finland, 11% to 15% for purchases over FM200; in Norway, 16.67% of purchases over NKr300; in Denmark, 18% of purchases over DKr600; in Iceland, 15% of purchases over IKr5,000.

Sports

Biking is pleasurable throughout Scandinavia, but if you don't like hills, stick to Denmark and southern Sweden. Bikers' clubs in most countries (*see* chapters, *below*) publish maps with information in English about local biking routes and camping places.

Sailing is a sport dear to many Scandinavian hearts. Five excellent routes include: The sail south from Stockholm along the Swedish coast to Copenhagen; among the islands of Stocholm's archipelago; from Copenhagen to the Danish island of Bornholm and back; south from the Danish island of Fyn, where the sea is studded with many small uninhabited islands; and up the western coast of Denmark and Norway. Be aware that the weather can change suddenly and dangerously, the water is cold enough that swimmers numb quickly, and you must be able to navigate from sea charts to avoid going aground or getting lost; these waters are not for beginners. Boats can be chartered in major cities and harbors.

Skiing—downhill, cross-country, and trekking—is excellent much of the year; snow in northern Sweden and Norway lasts often as late as May, and in some areas is present year-round. Disadvantages in winter include short days and bitter cold, as low as −35°C (any temperature below −10°C makes the danger of frostbite great enough to prohibit skiing, advises one experienced Scandinavian skier). It is a good idea to ski here in fall or spring, when the days are longer and warmer—November and March are preferable.

Other popular sports in Scandinavia include **wind-surfing** (in wetsuits, year-round), **hiking, fishing,** and **mountain climbing.** *See* the individual country chapters for details.

Beaches

Although Scandinavia is better known for its craggy coastlines, the region does have some lovely beaches. After the last great Ice Age, the retreating glaciers left the southern parts of Norway, Sweden, and all of Denmark with a flattened landscape and rich soil, which is why these regions are today known for their farmland—and for their beaches. This fact is not lost on landlocked Germans, who drive northward in such numbers every summer that many shopkeepers advertise their wares in English and German as well as Danish. All national tourist offices (*see* Tourist Information in Before You Go, *above*) have in-

formation on beaches in their areas; additional resources are listed in individual country chapters below.

Truly hot summer days are rare in Scandinavia, and frequently a cool sea breeze can chill wet skin. So take plenty of towels, a light jacket or sweater, and perhaps a beach umbrella as a wind break. Look for sand dunes when you arrive: Sleeping behind a warm sand dune in the Scandinavian sun is a cozy, but not sweaty, experience.

Dining

Eating is fun in Scandinavia, and consists of a lot more than the well-known *smörgåsbord*, which can be found throughout the region. Because it's inevitable you'll encounter one of these lavish buffets, here's how the locals tackle them: Begin with strong-tasting herring, served in a myriad of cream- and vinegar-based marinades, eaten with whole-grain brown bread or a hot boiled potato with a spoonful of fermented cream and chives. Follow with marinated or smoked salmon with dill sauce. Then the main course: cold meats, salads, fish, "Swedish" meatballs, and occasionally reindeer meat or the Swedish Jansson's temptation, made with potatoes, onions, and anchovies. Desserts include well-ripened cheeses, cakes, and terrific amounts of chocolate and whipped cream.

Local liquor laws arouse almost obsessional interest among Scandinavians. In most of Scandinavia, liquor and strong beer (over 3% alcohol) can be purchased only in state-owned shops, at very high prices, during weekday business hours, usually 9:30 to 6. A 70 or 75 centiliter bottle of whiskey in Sweden, for example, can easily cost SKr230 to SKr260, or about $40. Denmark takes a less restrictive approach, with liquor and beer available in the smallest of grocery stores, open weekdays and Saturday morning. Danish prices, too, are high. (When you visit relatives in Scandinavia, a bottle of liquor or fine wine bought duty-free on the trip over is often a much-appreciated gift.)

Lodging

In the larger cities, lodging ranges from first-class business hotels run by SAS, Sheraton, and Scandic, to good-quality tourist-class hotels, such as SARA, RESO, Best Western, and Scandic Budget, to a wide variety of single-entrepreneur hotels. In the countryside, look for independently run inns and motels. In Denmark they're called *kro;* in Norway, *fjellstue* or *pensjonat;* in Finland, *kienvari;* and elsewhere, guest houses. Check with your travel bureau for information on the many hotel discounts available, including summer hotel checks for Best Western, Scandic, and Inter Nor hotels, a summer Fjord pass in Norway, and enormous year-round rebates at SAS hotels for travelers over 65. All EuroClass passengers can get discounts of at least 10% at SAS hotels when they book through SAS and can have a double room for the price of a single.

Two things about hotels usually surprise North Americans: the relatively limited dimensions of Scandinavian beds and the generous size of Scandinavian breakfasts. Scandinavian double beds are often around 60″ wide or slightly less, close in size to

the U.S. queen size. King-size beds (72″ wide) are difficult to find and, if available, require special reservations.

Older hotels may have some rooms described as "double," which in fact have one double bed plus one fold-out sofa big enough for two people. This arrangement is occasionally called a "combi-room" but is being phased out.

Many older hotels, particularly the country inns and independently run smaller hotels in the cities, do not have private bathrooms. Ask ahead if this is important to you.

Scandinavian breakfasts resemble what many people would call lunch, usually including breads, cheeses, marmalade, hams, lunch meats, eggs, juice, cereal, milk, and coffee. In contrast, the typical Continental breakfast served in other parts of Europe is just a roll and coffee. A general rule is that the farther north you go, the larger the breakfasts become. Breakfast is often included in the price of the hotel, except in Finland and in deluxe establishments elsewhere.

All five Scandinavian countries offer **Inn Checks,** or prepaid hotel vouchers, for accommodations ranging from first-class hotels to country cottages. These vouchers, which must be purchased from travel agents or from the Scandinavian Tourist Board (*see* Tourist Information, *above*) before departure, are sold individually and in packets for as many nights as needed and offer savings of up to 50%. Most countries also offer summer bargains for foreign tourists. For further information about Scandinavian hotel vouchers, contact the Scandinavian Tourist Board.

Reservations The need for reservations depends on where you want to stay and when. In general, reservations are a good idea. It is virtually impossible to get a room on a weekday in Stockholm in the late spring because large conventions soak up all available space. Countryside inns usually have space, but not always: Norwegians and Danes call vacationing Germans *vandhunde* (water-dogs) because waterside areas attract them in large numbers. With eastern Germans suddenly more mobile, some coast-side inns have recently been filling their summer vacancies by January.

Be aware that different countries define their tourist seasons differently: Sweden's official season is much shorter than Norway's, for example. Some hotels lower prices during tourist season, others raise them during the same period. It's best to ask when making reservations.

Home Exchange This is obviously an inexpensive solution to the lodging problem, because house-swapping means living rent-free. You find a house, apartment, or other vacation property to exchange for your own by becoming a member of a home-exchange organization, which then sends you its annual directories listing available exchanges and includes your own listing in at least one of them. Arrangements for the actual exchange are made by the two parties to it, not by the organization. Principal clearinghouses include **Intervac U.S./International Home Exchange** (Box 590504, San Francisco, CA 94159, tel. 415/435–3497), the oldest, with thousands of foreign and domestic homes for exchange in its three annual directories; membership is $62, or $72 if you want to receive the directories but remain unlisted. The **Vacation Exchange Club** (Box 650, Key

West, FL 33041, tel. 800/638–3841), also affiliated with HomeLink International, has thousands of foreign and domestic listings and publishes four annual directories plus updates; the $50 membership includes your listing in one book. **Loan-a-Home** (2 Park La., Apt. 6E, Mount Vernon, NY 10552, tel. 914/664–7640) specializes in long-term exchanges; there is no charge to list your home, but the directories cost $35 or $45 depending on the number you receive.

Apartment and Villa Rentals If you want a home base that's roomy enough for a family and comes with cooking facilities, a furnished rental may be the solution. It's generally cost-wise, too, although not always—some rentals are luxury properties (economical only when your party is large). Home-exchange directories do list rentals—often second homes owned by prospective house swappers— and there are services that can not only look for a house or apartment for you (even a castle if that's your fancy) but also handle the paperwork. Some send an illustrated catalogue and others send photographs of specific properties, sometimes at a charge; up-front registration fees may apply.

Among the companies is **Rent a Home International** (7200 34th Ave. NW, Seattle, WA 98117, tel. 206/789–9377 or 800/488–7368), with properties in Denmark, Finland, and Sweden. **Hideaways International** (767 Islington St., Box 4433, Portsmouth, NH 03802, tel. 603/430–4433 or 800/843–4433) functions as a travel club. Membership ($79 yearly per person or family at the same address) includes two annual guides plus quarterly newsletters; rentals are arranged directly between members, not by the club staff.

Ratings Each of the national tourist offices distributes lists of hotels with nformation about opening times, pricing, accommodations for disabled travelers, and discounts for children and senior citizens.

Credit Cards

The following credit card abbreviations are used in this book: AE, American Express; D, Discover; DC, Diners Club; MC, MasterCard; V, Visa. It's a good idea to call ahead to check current credit card policies.

Great Itineraries

The itineraries that follow suggest ways in which Scandinavian destinations can be combined and give an idea of reasonable (minimum) amounts of time needed in various destinations. Elements from different itineraries can be combined to create an itinerary that suits your interests.

Sand, Surf, and Ships, Scandinavia–Style

Scandinavia is defined by water. Glaciers, rivers, and sea tides shape the geography; oceans inform the history and culture. Tiny Denmark, for example, would probably not exist today, except that it sticks up like a cork in the bottleneck entrance to the Baltic Sea, making it strategically important for great shipping and trading countries such as England, which has both attacked and defended the country over trading issues

during the last 400 years. What better way, then, to see the land of the Vikings than by water?

Length of Trip Two weeks

The Main Route **Three nights: Denmark.** Fly to Copenhagen. Explore the city and its waterways: Nyhavn's tall ships and myriad restaurants; Christianshavn with its encircling moat and canals reflecting colorful old buildings, including the beautiful Royal Naval Museum; and the canal-ringed palace of Christiansborg, where you can visit the Danish Parliament and the royal reception rooms. Enjoy the twinkling lights and happy atmosphere of Tivoli, from May to September. Take a harbor cruise, passing the Little Mermaid perched on her rock. Sun on the beaches north of town or sail the Oresund—maybe even all the way around Sjælland. You'll love the museum Castle of Frederiksborg, set in its lake an hour north of Copenhagen. Continue by air to Stockholm.

Six nights: Sweden. Beautiful Stockholm comprises 14 islands surrounded by sparkling water, clean enough for fishing and swimming even in the center. You can take ferries all around town and out into the enchantingly lovely archipelago with its 24,000 islands. Don't miss the picturesque Old Town, the new museum for the salvaged 17th-century warship Vasa, or Skansen, the world's oldest open-air museum.

From Stockholm, take the canal route across Sweden to Göteborg, where you explore the West Coast beaches warmed by the Gulf Stream. Try sea fishing or windsurfing, and visit the 17th-century fortress of Elfsborg, guarding the harbor entrance. Take a ferry to Oslo.

Five nights: Norway. In Oslo, visit the Viking Ship and Kon-Tiki museums. You'll also enjoy the Frogner sculpture park. The Bergen Railway will carry you across the roof of Norway in 6½ dramatic hours. If you can spare an extra day, stop in Myrdal for a side trip on the Flåm Railway and a short cruise on the beautiful Aurland Fjord before continuing to Bergen. Here you'll enjoy Bryggen, a collection of reconstructed houses dating from the Hansa period in the 14th century, the famous fish market, and the funicular. Marvel at the magnificent, everchanging Norwegian coastline aboard a steamship to Trondheim, from which you can fly to Oslo or Copenhagen, then home.

Information *See* Chapters 2, 4, 5, and 6.

Scandinavian Mountains

For those who like snow-clad mountains, Scandinavia has plenty to offer: glacier climbing, reindeer and dog sledding, cross-country skiing, and just plain old hiking in gorgeous surroundings.

Length of Trip Two weeks

The Main Route **Five nights: Norway.** Fly to Oslo then on to Bodø or another destination in northern Norway. Some of the country's most striking ranges are the Lofoton and Vesterålen mountains, near Bodø, along with the Lyngen peninsula in Troms. Begin with a four-day hiking tour or a glacier walk guided by **Den Norske Turistforening (DNT, Norwegian Mountain Touring Association)** (Postboks 1963 Vika, N–0125 Oslo 1, tel. 02/832550 or 02/

838040). From Bodø, fly to Narvik then take the train to Kiruna, Sweden, the largest town in Swedish Lapland.

Five nights: Sweden. Welcome to the Arctic Circle, the land of the midnight sun, where the sun is above the horizon 24 hours during summer solstice. In Kiruna, join a three-day white-water-canoeing trip. Take a rest, rent a car, and visit the beaver colonies at Ramsele and the fine collection of Lapp art in Jokkmokk. Drive to Gällivare, where the Lapps celebrate their annual church festivals, and go monster-spotting on Storsjön (Great Lake) near Æstersund. Drive or take the train to Rovaniemi, Finland, about 323 kilometers (200 miles) from Kiruna, a five- or six-hour drive. Watch out for deer and other animals on the road.

Four nights: Finland. Rovaniemi is the beginning point for The Road of the Four Winds, or, simply, the Arctic Road, which runs 1,000 kilometers (620 miles) north to the Arctic Circle. In summer, look for the salmon-fishing competition, reindeer herding, gold panning, logging, and the Russian Orthodox Skolt Lappish festivals that are held throughout the region. Fly from Rovaniemi to Helsinki and then home.

Information *See* Chapters 3, 5, and 6.

Tracing the Vikings

Traces can still be found of the seafaring warriors who, from the eighth through 11th centuries, traded with, settled in, or raided what today is the Soviet Union, western Europe, Iceland, Greenland, Labrador, and Newfoundland. The Vikings' 1,000-year-old remains are scattered throughout Scandinavia and provide a fascinating record of their culture.

Length of Trip 10 days

The Main Route **Three nights: Denmark.** Begin in Copenhagen with a visit to the Danish National Museum, which has many Viking exhibits labeled in English; one discusses how the Vikings could navigate their ships across vast oceans at a time when most people believed the world was flat. Take the train to the Viking Ship Hall in Roskilde (less than an hour west of Copenhagen), where five ships, found in the Roskilde Fjord and dating from around AD 1000, have been restored. In nearby Lejre, you can see how the Vikings lived. On the way back, visit Trelleborg in western Sjælland, where you'll find the remains of a staging area for troops led by Knud (Canute), who in 1016 became king of England, Denmark, Norway, and part of Sweden. In May, you can enjoy a colorful viking pageant in the lovely park at Frederikssund.

Rent a car or take a train and stay overnight in Vejle, on the large peninsula of Jylland, then head for Jelling, where two Viking kings—Gorm the Old and his son, Harald Bluetooth, Knud's great-grandfather—reigned. They left two large burial mounds and two runic stones, dating from around AD 950. In June, attend a performance of the Viking play *The Stoneship* on Fårup Sø.

If you have time, you can visit many other Viking sites in Denmark: Ribe, Denmark's oldest town; Hedeby; Høje, where graves are marked by four-foot-tall stones placed in the pattern of a ship; Moesgård museum near Århus; Fyrkat, a

10th-century ring fortress near Hobro; Lindholm; Mammen; Aggersborg; and Viborg. Return to Copenhagen and fly to Oslo, Norway.

Three nights: Norway. Go straight to the Oslo Viking Ship Hall, where you'll see the finest single collection of excavated and preserved Viking ships, once used as burial sepulchers for nobles. The next day, in Oslo's Historical Museum, you'll find beautiful jewelry from the 9th century: gold necklaces, silver ornaments, and "gripping beasts," whimsical monsters fashioned from amber and other materials. Fly to Stockholm.

Four nights: Sweden. In the State Historical Museum, you'll find swords and amulets in the shape of a hammer, the symbol of Thor, the thunder god. At Gamla Uppsala (old Uppsala), an easy drive north of Stockholm, there are burial grounds for three sixth-century Viking monarchs. In summer take the ferry to the island of Gotland in time for the Folk Sports Olympiad to see games played the way they were in the distant past. One contest, known as *varpa*, is won by tossing a stone nearest a stake. Another, *stångstörtning*, involves the tossing of 16-foot poles. In the Gotland Historical Museum, you'll find valuables that were buried with the Vikings, including Arabic, Byzantine, German, Bohemian, Hungarian, and Anglo-Saxon coins that reflect the warriors' wanderings. Return to Stockholm and then home.

Architecture and Handicrafts

Scandinavian furniture, architecture, and handicrafts are world renowned.

Length of Trip 11 days

The Main Route **Three nights: Denmark.** Strolling through Copenhagen, you'll find a treasure trove of beautiful buildings, punctuated by green copper spires and tinkling fountains. Don't miss the 15th-century Church of the Holy Ghost and the Baroque Church of Our Saviour. Brick Renaissance buildings from the reign of King Christian IV include the Stock Exchange surmounted by a spire of twisting dragontails; the exquisite Rosenborg Castle, housing the crown jewels and set in a flowery park; and the Round Tower, Copenhagen's first observatory, from which you'll see the old town spread out like a map. Enjoy charming Gråbrødrestorv and the colorful old buildings reflected in the canals of Nyhavn and Christianshavn. Monumental are Christiansborg Palace, housing the Parliament and Royal Reception Rooms, and Amalienborg Palace, home of the royal family. Examples of modern monumentality are the exciting new planetarium and the golden brick mass of Gruntvig's Church. An hour north of Copenhagen, visit the museum castles of Frederiksborg in Hillerød and Kronborg (Hamlet's castle) in Helsingør.

Danish applied art is famed for fine design and high quality. To see contemporary furniture, in Copenhagen visit Illum's Bolighus, a mecca for all kinds of home furnishings. Enjoy the porcelain showrooms of Royal Copenhagen and Bing & Grøndahl. Watch exquisite glass being blown at the Holmegård Glass factory about an hour south of town. Visit the Georg Jensen Museum and the Kunstindustrimuseet, with its Rococo

buildings and fine exhibits of European and Oriental handicrafts. Historical walking tours in English are held each day and are the best introduction to the city's architecture. They are often led by Helge Jacobsen, a local historian. Take the overnight train or fly to Stockholm.

Two nights: Sweden. Stroll around Stockholm's old town (Gamla Stan) for views of the magnificent 700-year-old cathedral and the 608-room Royal Palace. From the tower of the beautiful modern Town Hall, with its golden mosaics, gaze over Stockholm's 14 islands and glittering, clean waters. Visit the Skansen Open Air Museum with 150 buildings full of handicrafts, ending with dinner, a concert, or outdoor entertainment. The Nordic museum documents daily life for 500 years, and the Vasa Museum is noteworthy for its new building as well as the fabulous warship, recently raised from where it sank on its maiden voyage in 1628. Take a ferry or drive to Gripsholm Castle or Drottningholm, the royal residence in its lovely park. Slightly outside the city, visit the Ulriksdal Castle and park and the Carl Milles Sculpture Garden in Lidingö. If you can spend an extra day, drive to Insjöen to visit Säterglänten, a center for courses in traditional handicrafts. From Stockholm, take the overnight ferry to Helsinki.

Five nights: Finland. The Museum of Finnish Architecture and the Museum of Applied Arts will give you an overview of the development of Finnish architecture and design, and the Helsinki Information Center offers exhibitions, films, and slide shows. See the fine Neoclassical Senate Square and the Art Nouveau buildings at Eira and Katajanokka, as well as Eliel Saarinen's Helsinki railway station from 1914. Don't miss Finlandiatalo, the concert hall designed by Finland's greatest architect, Alvar Aalto; the Temppeliaukio Church, hollowed out from rock with only its dome showing; or the magnificent sculpture commemorating the composer Jean Sibelius. The Gallen-Kallela Museum is a studio-castle in the National Romantic Style built on a rocky peninsula. It was designed by the artist Gallen-Kallela and houses his paintings, drawings, sculpture, textiles, and furniture. Check with the University of Industrial Arts in Helsinki, the largest of its kind in Scandinavia, on its current exhibits, often held in collaboration with Design Forum Finland. Fine china and pottery are displayed at the Arabia Museum and traditional folk handicraft at the Virkki Museum of Handicrafts. Visit the Artek factory, which features furniture by Alvar Aalto, and the Marimekko and Vuokko textile factories. Rent a car to visit the Finnish Glass Museum, 50 kilometers (31 miles) north of Helsinki in Riihimäki, with permanent exhibits on glassmaking and exhibitions of old Finnish glassware and crystal as well as works by contemporary designers. Stop by the Hvitträsk, a turn-of-the-century studio designed by and for three Finnish architects as a laboratory for their aesthetic principles.

Take a ferry to Suomenlinna Island fortress, partly built by Russians, where you will find the Nordic Art Center. Also stop in the garden city of Käpylä, a residential area built in the 1920s in a unique neoclassical style reminiscent of traditional Finnish wood architecture. If you have time, drive or take a bus along the King's Road, west to Lovisa or east to Turku. This historic

road affords spectacular coastal views and is studded with buildings and monuments of interest.

Information *See* Chapters 2, 3, and 6.

Scandinavia at a Glance: A Chronology

c 12,000 BC The first migrations into Sweden.

c 10,000 BC Stone Age culture develops in Denmark.

c 8,000 BC The earliest human settlers reach the coast of Norway.

c 7,000 BC First nomadic settlers come to Finland.

2,000 BC Tribes from Southern Europe, mostly Germanic peoples, migrate toward Denmark.

c 500 BC Migration of Celts across central Europe impinges on Denmark's trade routes with the Mediterranean world. Trade becomes less economically crucial because of the growing use of abundant iron.

c AD 100 Ancestors of present-day Finns move to Finland.

c 770 The Viking Age begins. For the next 250 years, Scandinavians set sail on frequent expeditions stretching from the Baltic to the Irish seas and even to the Mediterranean as far as Sicily, employing superior ships and weapons and efficient military organization.

c 800–c 1000 Swedes control river trade routes between the Baltic and Black seas; establish Novgorod, Kiev, and other cities.

830 Frankish monk Ansgar makes one of the first attempts to Christianize Sweden and builds the first church in Slesvig, Denmark. Sweden is not successfully Christianized until the end of the 11th century, when the temple at Uppsala, a center for pagan resistance, is destroyed.

c 870 The first permanent settlers arrive in Iceland from western Norway.

911 Scandinavian, Rollo, rules Normandy by treaty with French king.

930 Iceland's parliament, the Althing, is founded.

995 King Olaf I Tryggvadlson introduces Christianity into Norway.

1000 Leif Eriksson visits America. Olaf I sends a mission to Christianize Iceland.

1016–1035 Canute (Knud) the Great is king of England, Denmark (1018), and Norway (1028).

1070 Adam of Bremen composes *History of the Archbishops of Hamburg-Bremen*, the first important contemporary source for Danish history.

1169 King Valdemar, who was acknowledged as the single king of Denmark in 1157 and who undertook repeated crusades against the Germans, captures Rugen and places it under Danish rule, signifying the beginning of the Danish medieval empire. It culminates in 1219 when Valdemar marches to Estonia

and builds a fortress at Ravel. In 1225, Valdemar, after being kidnapped by a German vassal, is forced to give up all his conquests, except for Rugen and Estonia, in exchange for freedom.

1217 Haakon IV becomes king of Norway, beginning its "Golden Age." His many reforms modernize the Norwegian administration; under him, the Norwegian empire reaches its greatest extent when Greenland and Iceland form unions with Norway in 1261.

1248 In Sweden, Erik Eriksson appoints Birger as Jarl, in charge of military affairs and expeditions abroad. Birger improves women's rights, makes laws establishing peace in the home and church, and begins building Stockholm.

1250 Stockholm, Sweden, is officially founded.

1282 At a meeting of the Hof, or Danish parliament, Danish king Erik Glipping signs a coronation charter that becomes the first written constitution of Denmark.

1319 Sweden and Norway form a union that lasts until 1335.

1349 The Black Death strikes Norway and kills two-thirds of the population.

1370 The Treaty of Stralsund gives the north German trading centers of the Hanseatic League free passage through Danish waters and full control of Danish herring fisheries for 15 years. German power increases throughout Scandinavia.

1397 The Kalmar union is formed as a result of the dynastic ties between Sweden, Denmark, and Norway, the geographical position of the Scandinavian states, and the growing influence of Germans in the Baltic. Erik of Pomerania is crowned king of the Kalmar Union.

1477 University of Uppsala, Sweden's oldest university, is founded.

1479 University of Copenhagen is founded.

1520 Christian II, ruler of the Kalmar Union, executes 82 people who oppose the Scandinavian union, an event known as the "Stockholm blood bath." Sweden secedes from the Union three years later. Norway remains tied to Denmark and becomes a Danish province in 1536.

1523 Gustav Ericsson founds Swedish Vasa dynasty as King Gustav I Vasa.

1534 Count Christoffer of Oldenburg and his army demand the restoration of Christian II as king of Denmark, initiating civil war between supporters of Christian II and supporters of Prince Christian (later King Christian III).

1611–16 The Kalmar War: Denmark wages war against Sweden in hope of restoring the Kalmar Union.

1611–1660 Gustav II Adolphus reigns in Sweden. Under his rule, Sweden defeats Denmark in the Thirty Years War and becomes the greatest power in Scandinavia as well as Northern and Central Europe.

1660 Peace of Copenhagen establishes modern boundaries of Denmark, Sweden, and Norway.

1668 Bank of Sweden, the world's oldest central bank, is founded.

1700–1721 Sweden, led by Karl XII, first broadens then loses its position to Russia as Northern Europe's greatest power in the Great Northern War.

1754 Royal Danish Academy of Fine Arts is established.

1762 Duke of Gottorp becomes tsar of Russia and declares war on Denmark. Catherine, the tsar's wife, overrules her husband's war declaration and makes a peaceful settlement.

1763 The first Norwegian newspaper is founded.

c 1780 A volcanic eruption causes a famine in Iceland that kills one-fifth of the population.

1801–1814 The Napoleonic wars are catastrophic for Denmark economically and politically: The policy of armed neutrality fails, the English destroy the Danish fleet in 1801, Copenhagen is devastated at the bombardment of 1807, and Sweden, after Napoleon's defeat at the Battle of Leipzig, attacks Denmark and forces the Danish surrender of Norway. The Treaty of Kiel, in 1814, calls for a union between Norway and Sweden despite Norway's desire for independence. The Danish monarchy is left with three parts: the Kingdom of Denmark and the duchies of Schleswig and Holstein.

1807 During the Napoleonic wars, Swedish king Gustav III joins the coalition against France and reluctantly accepts war with France and Russia.

1809 Sweden surrenders the Åland Islands and Finland to Russia, Finland becomes a Grand Duchy of the Russian Empire, and the Instrument of Government, Sweden's constitution, is adopted.

1811 University of Oslo is established.

1818 Sweden takes a Frenchman as king: Karl XIV Johann establishes the Bernadotte dynasty.

1818 National Library of Iceland is founded.

1849 Denmark's absolute monarchy is abolished and replaced by the liberal June constitution, which establishes freedom of the press, freedom of religion, the right to hold meetings and form associations, and rule by parliament with two elected chambers as well as the king and his ministers.

c 1850 The building of railroads begins in Scandinavia.

1863 National Museum of Iceland is established.

1864 Denmark goes to war against Prussia and Austria; the hostilities end with the Treaty of Vienna, which forces Denmark to surrender the duchies of Schleswig and Holstein to Prussia and Austria.

1874 Iceland adopts a constitution.

1884 A parliamentary system is established in Norway.

1885 The Art Gallery of Iceland is founded.

1887 The Norwegian Labor Party is founded.

1889 The Swedish Social Democratic Party is founded.

1901 Alfred Nobel, the Swedish millionaire chemist and industrialist, initiates the Nobel prizes.

1904   Iceland is granted home rule. The first Icelandic minister takes office. Rule by parliamentary majority is introduced.

1905   Norway's union with Sweden is dissolved.

1914   At the outbreak of World War I, Germany forces Denmark to lay mines in an area of international waters known as the Great Belt. Because the British fleet makes no serious attempts to break through, Denmark is able to maintain neutrality. Norway and Sweden also declare neutrality but are effectively blockaded.

1916   Iceland establishes a national organization of trade unions.

1917   Finland declares independence from Russia. Danish writer Henrik Pontoppidan is awarded the Nobel prize for Literature.

1918   Iceland becomes a separate state under the Danish crown; only foreign affairs remains under Danish control. Sweden, Denmark, and Norway grant women the right to vote.

1919   A republican constitution is adopted by Finland. Kaarlo Juho Stahlberg is elected president.

1920   Scandinavian countries join the League of Nations.

1929–1937   The first social democratic governments take office in Denmark, Sweden, and Finland. During this period, Norway is ruled by a labor government.

c 1930   The Great Depression causes unemployment, affecting 40% of the organized industrial workers in Denmark.

1939   Denmark and the other Nordic countries declare neutrality in World War II. Finnish novelist Frans Eemil Sillanpaa wins the Nobel prize for literature.

1939–1940   Russia defeats Finland in the Winter War. Russia invades Finland primarily for its larger strategic interests in the area and not because Finland poses a threat.

1940   Germany occupies Norway and Denmark. British forces occupy Iceland until 1941 when U.S. forces replace them.

1941–1944   The Continuation War begins when Finland joins Nazi Germany in attacking the Soviet Union. After Russia defeats Finland, an agreement is signed calling for Finnish troops to withdraw to the 1940 boundary lines of Finland and for German troops on Finnish soil to disarm.

1944   The Icelandic Republic, with British and U.S. support, is founded on June 17. Sveinn Bjørnsson is Iceland's first president.

1945   Norway joins the United Nations.

1948   Treaty of Friendship, Cooperation, and Mutual Assistance between Finland and the Soviet Union obligates Finland to defend the U.S.S.R. in the event of an attack through Finnish territory.

1949   Denmark, Norway, and Iceland become members of NATO. Sweden and Finland decline membership.

1952   The Nordic Council, which promotes cooperation among the Nordic parliaments, is founded.

1955 Finland joins the United Nations and the Nordic Council. Halldor Laxness of Iceland receives the Nobel prize for literature.

1970 Finland hosts the Strategic Arms Limitation Talks (SALT).

1972 Sweden, on the basis of its neutral foreign policy, and Norway decline membership in the EC; Denmark becomes a member in 1973.

1975 Sweden's Instrument of Government of 1809 is revised and replaced with a new Instrument of Government. This constitution reduces the voting age to eighteen and removes many of the king's powers and responsibilities.

1976 The "cod wars," between Britain and Iceland over the extent of Iceland's fishing waters, end.

1980 Fifty-eight percent of Sweden's voters advocate minimizing the use of nuclear reactors at Sweden's four power plants. Iceland elects as president Vigdis Finnbogadottir, the world's first popularly elected female head of state.

1981 Gro Harlem Brundtland, a member of the Labor party, becomes Norway's first female prime minister.

1982 Poul Schluter becomes Denmark's first Conservative prime minister since 1894.

1983 In Finland, the Greens gain parliamentary representation, making them the first elected environmentalists in the Nordic region.

1985 The Alþing, Iceland's parliament, unanimously approves a resolution banning the entry of nuclear weapons into the country.

1986 U.S. president Ronald Reagan and Soviet premier Mikhail Gorbachev discuss nuclear disarmament at a summit meeting in Reykjavík, Iceland. Sweden's prime minister, Olof Palme, is assassinated for unknown reasons. Ingvar Carlsson succeeds him.

1988 Due to U.S. pressure, Iceland consents to reducing its quota of whales caught for "scientific purposes." The United States argues that Iceland is acting against a moratorium imposed by the International Whaling Commission.

1989 Tycho Brahe Planetarium opens in Copenhagen; and Denmark becomes the first NATO country to allow women to join frontline military units.

Denmark becomes the first country in the world to recognize marriages between citizens of the same sex.

1990 Finland becomes the fourth major route for Jewish emigration from the Soviet Union. Helsinki, Finland, hosts the summit meeting between George Bush and Mikhail Gorbachev.

1991 The Karen Blixen Museum, in Rungstedlund, Denmark, is founded.

Norway's King Olav V dies. King Harald V ascends the throne. His wife, Queen Sonja, becomes the first queen since the death of Maud in 1938.

Sweden's Social Democrats voted out of office and the new government launches a privatization policy.

1992 Denmark declines to support the Maastricht Treaty setting up a framework for European economic union. Denmark wins the European Soccer Championships.

Sweden's Riksbank (National Bank) raises overnight interest rates to a world record of 500% in an effort to defend the Swedish krona against speculation.

1993 Denmark is the president of the EC for the first half of 1993. In a second referendum, the country votes to support the Maastricht Treaty, as well as its own modified involvement in it. Tivoli celebrates its 150th year, Legoland celebrates its 25th birthday, and the Little Mermaid turns 80. Denmark also commemorates the 50th anniversary of the World War II rescue of Danish Jews, in which they were smuggled into Sweden.

Norway applies for EC membership.

Norway's minister of foreign affairs, Thorvald Stoltenberg, is appointed peace negotiator to war-torn Bosnia-Herzegovina.

In secret meetings near Oslo, Norwegian negotiators help bring about a historic rapprochement between Israel and the Palestine Liberation Organization.

1994 The XVII Olympic Winter Games are held in Lillehammer, Norway, from February 12 to February 27.

2 **Denmark**

By Karina Porcelli

Karina Porcelli is a freelance travel writer who divides her time between Copenhagen, Denmark, and Washington, D.C.

The kingdom of Denmark dapples the Baltic Sea in an archipelago of some 450 islands and the arc of one peninsula. Measuring 43,069 square kilometers (17,028 square miles), with a population of 5 million, it is the geographical link between Scandinavia and Europe. Half-timbered villages and well-groomed agriculture cozy up to provincial towns and a handful of cities, where footsteps, not traffic, mark the tempo. Mothers safely park baby carriages outside bakeries, while outdoor cafés fill with cappuccino-sippers, and lanky Danes pedal to work in lanes thick with bicycle traffic. Clearly this is a land where the process of life is the greatest reward.

Many visitors pinch themselves in disbelief and make long lists of resolutions to emulate the Danes. The lifestyle is certainly enviable. Many of the qualities that have pressure-cooked life in other Western countries have barely touched this land. Long one of the world's most liberal countries, Denmark has a highly developed social-welfare system. The hefty taxes are the subject of grumbles and jokes, but Danes remain proud of their state-funded medical and educational systems and their high standard of living. They enjoy life with month-long vacations, 7.6-hour workdays, and overall security.

Educated, patriotic, and keenly aware of their tiny international stance, most Danes travel extensively and have a balanced perspective of their nation's benefits and shortfalls. As in many provincial states, egalitarianism is often a constraint for the ambitious. In Denmark, this "Don't think you're anything special" notion is the *Jante* law, an insidious cultural barrier to talent and aspiration. On the other hand, free education and state support give refugees, immigrants, and the underprivileged an opportunity to begin new, often prosperous lives.

The history of the tiny country stretches back 250,000 years, when Jylland (Jutland) was inhabited by nomadic hunters, but it wasn't until AD 500 that a tribe from Sweden, called the Danes, migrated south and christened the land Denmark.

The Viking expansion that followed, based on the country's strategic position in the north, saw struggles for control of the North Sea with England and Western Europe, for the Skagerrak (the strait between Denmark and Norway) with Norway and Sweden, and for the Baltic with Germany, Poland, and Russia. With high-speed ships and fine-tuned warriors, intrepid navies navigated to Europe and Canada, invading and often pillaging, until, under King Knud (Canute) the Great (995–1035), they captured England.

After the British conquest, Viking supremacy declined as feudal Europe learned to defend itself. Internally, the pagan way of life was threatened by the expansion of Christianity, which was introduced under Harold Bluetooth, who in AD 980 "baptized" the country, essentially to avoid war with Germany. For the next several hundred years, the country tried to maintain its Baltic power under the influence of the German Hanseatic League. Under the leadership of Valdemar IV (1340–1375), Sweden, Norway, Iceland, Greenland, and the Faroe Islands became a part of Denmark. Sweden broke away by the mid-15th century and battled Denmark for much of the next several hundred years, while Norway remained under Danish rule until 1814, and Iceland until 1943. Greenland and the Faroe Islands are still self-governing Danish provinces.

Denmark

North Sea

Skagerrak

Skagen

SWEDEN

TO GREENLAND

TO FAROE ISLANDS

Hirtshals

Hjørring

Frederikshavn

Sæby

Brønderslev

Hanstholm

Limfjord

Aalborg

Læsø

11

Thisted

Lim-fjord

Aalborg Bugt

Kattegat

Nykøbing

Hadsund

13

Lemvig

Skive

Anholt

Struer

Viborg

Holstebro

Jylland

Randers

16

16

Grenå

Ringkøbing

Herning

Silkeborg

15

Århus

Ebeltoft

Skanderborg

Tisvildeleje

Hornbaek

11

Grindsted

Horsens

Samsø

Nykøbing

Helsingør

Hillerød

Skjern

Billund

Vejle

E45

Frederikssund

Esbjerg

E20

Holsted

Fredericia

Samsøbælt

Kalundborg

Holbæk

Copenhagen

Fanø

Kolding

Middelfart

Store-bælt

Jyderup

Roskilde

21

E47

Ribe

Vojens

E45

Odense

Kerteminde

Slagelse

Sjælland

Amager

Køge Bugt

Rømø

Haderslev

Assens

Fyn

Nyborg

E20

Ringsted

Køge

Skærbæk

Åbenrå

Lillebælt

Fåborg

Korsør

St. Heddinge

Tønder

8

Als

Svendborg

Næstved

Karrebæksminde

Sønderborg

Troense

Langeland

Tranekær

Vordingborg

Ærøskøbing

Rudkøbing

Stege

Møn

Ærø

Marstal

Nakskov

Nykøbing

TO BORNHOLM

E47

Maribo

Falster

Rødby

Lolland

Nysted

Ostsee

GERMANY

N

SWEDEN

Baltic Sea

Bornholm

Rønne

0   50 miles

0   75 km

Denmark prospered again in the 16th century, thanks to the Sound Dues, a levy charged to ships crossing the Øresund, the slender waterway between Denmark and Sweden. Under King Christian IV, a construction boom crowned the land with what remain architectural gems, but his fantasy spires and castles, compounded with the Thirty Years' War in the 17th century, led to state bankruptcy.

By the 18th century, absolute monarchy gave way to representative democracy, and culture flourished. Then, in a fatal mistake, Denmark sided with France and refused to surrender its navy to the English during the Napoleonic Wars. In a less than valiant episode of British history, Lord Nelson turned his famous blind eye to the destruction and bombed Copenhagen to bits. The defeated King Frederik VI handed Norway to Sweden. Denmark's days of glory were unequivocally over.

Though Denmark was unaligned during World War II, the Nazis invaded in 1940. Against them, the Danes used the only weapons they had: a cold shoulder and massive underground resistance. After the war, Denmark focused inward, refining its welfare system and concentrating on its main industries of agriculture, shipping, and financial and technical services. In spring 1993 it was still the sole Scandinavian member of the European Community (EC).

Though expensive, Denmark is in many ways less pricey than the rest of Scandinavia. At the height of summer, when businesses shut down (usually for all of July), conference hotels often lower prices and offer weekend specials. Denmark is also the only Nordic country with relaxed drinking laws and moderate beer and wine prices, an attraction that induces other Scandinavians to hop over for splurge weekends.

Copenhagen fidgets with its modern identity, trying to integrate its role as a Scandinavian-European link and cozy capital. The center of Danish politics, culture, and finance, it copes through balance and an absurd sense of humor. Stroll the streets and you'll pass classical architecture painted in candy colors, businessmen clad in jeans and T-shirts, and on sunny days, ebullient Danes stripping down on beaches and in parks.

Copenhagen is the attention-getter, but it would be a shame to miss the surrounding countryside of Sjælland (Zealand). Less than an hour away, the land is checkered with fields and half-timbered cottages. Roskilde, to the east, has an impressive 12th-century cathedral, while in the north, Helsingør is crowned with the Kronborg castle of *Hamlet* fame. Beaches, some chic, some deserted, are powdered by fine white sand that drives Danes to bliss.

Fyn (Funen) has rightly earned its storybook reputation by making cute a local passion. The city of Odense, Hans Christian Andersen's birthplace, is cobbled with crooked old streets and lilliputian cottages. Jylland's landscape is the most severe, with Ice Age–chiseled fjords and hills (which the Danes sheepishly call mountains). Nonetheless, its provincial towns have timbered neighborhoods, while the cities of Århus and Aalborg offer museums and nightlife rivaling Copenhagen's.

The best way to discover Denmark is to strike up a conversation with a Dane. Affable and hospitable, they'll probably approach you before you get the chance to ask the time. They have

a wonderful word, *hyggelig*, which defies definition but comes close to meaning a cozy and charming hospitality. A summertime beach picnic can be as hyggelig as tea on a cold winter's night. The only requirement is the company of a Dane.

Before You Go

Government Tourist Offices

In the United States — **Danish Tourist Board,** 655 3rd Ave., New York, NY 10017, tel. 212/949–2333

In Canada — **Danish Contact Center,** Box 115 Station N, Toronto, Ontario, M8V 3S4, tel. 416/823–9620

In the United Kingdom — **Danish Tourist Board,** Sceptre House, 169–173 Regent St., JB London W1R 8PY, tel. 071/734–2637

When to Go

Most travelers visit Denmark in the warmest months, July and August, but there are advantages to coming in May, June, or September when sights are less crowded and many establishments offer off-season discounts. However, few places in Denmark are ever unpleasantly crowded, and when the Danes make their annual exodus to the beaches, the cities have more breathing space. In winter months the days are short and dark, and important attractions such as Tivoli are closed.

Climate — The climate is greatly tempered by the Gulf Stream, which makes for warm summers and soggy, gray winters, with little snow. The following are average daily maximum and minimum temperatures for Copenhagen.

Jan.	36F	2C	May	61F	16C	Sept.	64F	18C
	28	– 2		46	8		52	11
Feb.	36F	2C	June	66F	19C	Oct.	54F	12C
	27	– 3		52	11		45	7
Mar.	41F	5C	July	72F	22C	Nov.	45F	7C
	30	– 1		57	14		37	3
Apr.	52F	11C	Aug.	70F	21C	Dec.	39F	4C
	37	3		57	14		34	1

Festivals and Seasonal Events

April 16: The Queen's Birthday is celebrated with the royal guard in full ceremonial dress, as the royal family appears before the public on the balcony of Amalienborg Castle.
May: The Copenhagen Carnival includes boat parades in Nyhavn and costumed revelers in the streets.
May–August: The **Tivoli Gardens** in Copenhagen open with rides, concerts, and entertainment. Special activities and concerts are planned for the 145th anniversary of the Tivoli Guard.
May–September: Legoland, a park constructed of 35 million Lego blocks, opens in Billund, Jylland.
June: The Around Fyn Regatta starts in Kerteminde.
June: The Round Zealand Regatta, one of the largest yachting events in the world, starts and ends in Helsingør.

Mid-June: The Aalborg Jazz Festival fills the city with four days of indoor and outdoor concerts, many free.

June: The Viking Festival in Frederikssund includes open-air performances of a Viking play.

June: On Midsummer's Night, Danes celebrate the longest day of the year with bonfires and picnics.

June–July: The Roskilde Festival, the largest rock concert in northern Europe, attracts dozens of bands and 75,000 fans.

July: The Copenhagen Jazz Festival gathers international and Scandinavian jazz greats for a week of concerts, many free.

July 4: The Fourth of July celebration in Rebild Park, near Aalborg, sets off the only American Independence Day festivities outside the United States.

Mid-July: The Århus Jazz Festival gathers European and world-renowned names, with indoor and outdoor concerts.

July–August: The Hans Christian Andersen Festival brings the author's fairy tales to life in street theater and free events for children and adults.

September: The Århus Festival, Denmark's most comprehensive fete, fills the city with concerts, sports, and theater.

Danish Currency

The monetary unit in Denmark is the krone (DKr), which is divided into 100 øre. At press time (summer 1993), the krone stood at 6.1 to the dollar, 9.48 to the pound sterling, and 4.8 to the Canadian dollar. Most major credit cards are accepted in Denmark, American Express less frequently than others, and Carte Blanche rarely. Traveler's checks can be exchanged in banks and at many hotels, restaurants, and shops.

What It Will Cost

Denmark's economy is stable, and inflation remains reasonably low. While considerably lower than Norway and Sweden's, the Danish cost of living is nonetheless high, especially for such luxuries as cigarettes and alcohol. Prices are highest in Copenhagen, lower elsewhere in the country.

Taxes All hotel, restaurant, and departure taxes and VAT (what the Danes call MOMS) are automatically included in prices. VAT is 25%; non-EC citizens can obtain a 20% refund. The more than 1,500 shops that participate in the tax-free scheme have a white TAX FREE sticker on their windows. Purchases must be at least DKr600 per store and must be sealed and unused in Denmark. At the shop, you'll be asked to fill out a form and show your passport. The form can then be turned in at any airport or ferry customs desk, where you can choose a check or charge-card credit. Keep all your receipts and tags; occasionally, customs authorities do ask to see purchases, so pack them where they will be accessible.

Sample Costs Cup of coffee, DKr12–16; bottle of beer, DKr15–25; soda, DKr12–15; ham sandwich, DKr35; 1-mile taxi ride, DKr25.

Passports and Visas

U.S., Canadian, and British citizens must have a valid passport to enter Denmark for a stay of up to three months. Visas and health certificates are not required. If you lose your passport, go to the police immediately and report it. Bring the report, with positive ID and a photocopy of the photo page (do this be-

fore you leave home, and keep it separate from your passport) to the embassy in Copenhagen, (*see* Copenhagen, *below,* for embassy addresses).

U.S. Citizens   For more information, contact the **Royal Danish Embassy** (3200 Whitehaven St. NW, Washington, DC 20008, tel. 202/234–4300).

Canadian Citizens   **Royal Danish Embassy,** 85 Range Rd., Apt. 702, Ottawa, Ontario, K1N 8J6, tel. 613/234–0704.

U.K. Citizens   **Royal Danish Embassy,** 55 Sloane St., London SW1x 9SR, tel. 071/333–0200.

Customs and Duties

On Arrival   If you purchase goods in a shop within an EC country, and have paid that country's taxes, you may bring in 1.5 liters of alcohol; 300 cigarettes, 75 cigars or 400 grams of tobacco. There are no longer restrictions on any other purchases of less than DKr80,000 in value made for private use within an EC country.

If you purchase goods in a non-EC country or tax-free, for example, in an airport, on a ferryboat or in another airport untaxed in the EC, you will pay Danish taxes on any amounts greater than: 1 liter liquor or 2 liters strong wine; 2 liters wine; 200 cigarettes, 50 cigars or 250 grams tobacco and 50 grams of perfume. Other articles include DKr350 worth of goods.

On Departure   *See* Customs and Duties in Chapter 1.

Language

Students of Danish are taught that if they can't pronounce a word, they should say it faster and swallow most of it. It's a difficult language for foreigners, except Norwegians and Swedes, to learn to understand, let alone speak. Most Danes, except those in rural areas, speak English well, but it's a good idea to ask before launching into a conversation. Bring a phrase book if you plan to visit the countryside or the small islands.

Car Rentals

Major international car rentals are available throughout Denmark. Smaller companies include: **Europcar** (Kastrup Airport, tel. 32/50–30–90) and **Pitzner Auto** (Kastrup Airport, tel. 32/50–90–65). In Copenhagen, most car-rental agencies are located near the Vesterport Station.

Rail Passes

The **Copenhagen Card** provides unlimited transportation on trains and buses in the metropolitan area, as well as admission to a number of attractions in Copenhagen and surroundings, and discount passage to Sweden. The card costs approximately DKr130 (one day), DKr210 (two days), or DKr260 (three days); half price for children; and is available at tourist offices and hotels and through travel agents.

The **Danish State Railways (DSB)** also offers discount tickets for senior citizens, children, and groups of three or more traveling together. Inquire at any train station for **Gruppe Rabat (group rebate), Gruppe Billetter (group tickets),** or off-peak

fare, which offers considerable reductions on certain days of the week.

Student and Youth Travel

Copenhagen's main railway station features a useful **Inter Rail Center,** open June 14 to September 14, where young travelers can meet, exchange notes, and even partake of a free shower. Students can obtain information on inexpensive accommodations in Copenhagen at **Use It,** the **Youth Information Center** (Raadhusstraede 13, DK–1466 Copenhagen K; tel. 33/15–65–18). It is open June 15 to September 14, daily 9 AM to 7 PM; and September 15 to June 14, Monday to Friday 10 AM to 3 PM.

Hints for Travelers with Disabilities

In Denmark, wheelchair users will find short-distance rail travel difficult, because **Danish State Railways (DSB)** has few special carriages or toilets for disabled passengers. Travelers are advised to bring a companion to help them on and off trains; however, for longer trips, especially to Jylland, assistance both on and off the trains is provided as long as it is specifically requested at least two days in advance (call 33/14–17–01). On the Copenhagen–Esbjerg and Copenhagen–Aalborg routes, as well as other direct IC–3 routes to Jylland, trains offer special facilities for the disabled, including hydraulic wheelchair lifts and accessible toilets. Advance reservations are required. A number of major stations provide wheelchairs for customers' use. A brochure with information about train facilities is available from the state railroad, in train stations, and from the state railroad's travel agency, **DSB Rejsebureau** (Terminus Vesterbrogade 5, DK–1620 Copenhagen V, Denmark).

In Denmark, most buses and coaches are not equipped to carry wheelchair users, though all long-distance routes now have a minimum of one daily departure each way using buses with lifts and extra space for wheelchairs. Advance reservations are required. Some Danish taxi firms also have large, London-size cabs for passengers in wheelchairs. For information on travel and accommodations in Denmark, ask the Danish Tourist Board for its 100-page booklet "Access in Denmark—A Travel Guide for the Disabled," or contact the **Dansk Handicap Forbund** (The Danish Handicapped Association, Kollektivhuset, Hans Knudsens Plads, 1A, 1, DK–2100, Copenhagen Ø, tel. 39/29–35–55, fax 39/29–39–48).

Many hotels, particularly among the larger chains, have facilities for the disabled. You may also wish to contact the **Committee for Housing, Transportation and Technical Aids: Bolig-, Motor- or Hjælpemiddeludvalget** (Landskronagade 66, 4 salle, DK–2100 Copenhagen Ø, tel. 31/18–26–66).

Hints for Older Travelers

One of the only travel agencies that offer tailor-made senior-citizen tours is **Robinson Scandinavia** (Carit Etlarsvej 3, 1814 Frederiksberg, Copenhagen, tel. 31/31–71–77). Packages and special arrangements inside Scandinavia include bus tours, accommodations, and sightseeing tours at rates substantially cheaper than those for independent travel.

Further Reading

Excellent reading on Denmark includes: those works of Karen Blixen (Isak Dinesen) set in Denmark; *Pelle the Conqueror* (volumes I and II) by Martin Andersen Nexø (a novel about a young Swedish boy and his father who work on a stone farm in Bornholm under hateful Danish landowners); *Laterna Magica* by William Heinesen (a novel of the Faroe Islands by perhaps Denmark's greatest writer since Karen Blixen); and the satirical trilogy by Hans Scherfig—*Stolen Spring, The Missing Bureaucrat,* and *Idealists.* Wallace Stegner's novel *The Spectator Bird* follows a man's exploration of his Danish heritage. Finally, **Fjord Press** (Box 16349, Seattle, WA 98116, tel. 206/935–7376, fax 206/938–1991) has one of the most comprehensive selections of Danish titles of any bookseller in the United States.

Arriving and Departing

From North America by Plane

Airports and Airlines Copenhagen's **Kastrup Airport,** the hub of Scandinavian air travel, is 10 kilometers (6 miles) from the capital's center. **Scandinavian Airlines System (SAS)** (tel. 800/221–2350), the main carrier, makes nonstop flights from Los Angeles, Newark, and Seattle. **British Airways** (tel. 800/247–9297) makes connecting flights via London from Atlanta, Boston, Chicago, Dallas, Detroit, Los Angeles, Miami, New York, Orlando, Philadelphia, Pittsburgh, San Francisco, Seattle, and Washington, D.C. **Icelandair** (tel. 800/223–5500) makes connecting flights via Reykjavík from Baltimore and New York. **Delta** (tel. 800/221–1212) is planning to start direct service from New York.

Flying Time From New York, flights to Copenhagen take 7 hours, 40 minutes. From Chicago they take 8 hours, 15 minutes. From Los Angeles the flight time is 10 hours, 55 minutes.

Discount Flights Airfare to Denmark is expensive, but it is possible to save money on regular coach tickets. Start with a flexible schedule and make your reservations as early as possible. Discounted, advance-purchase tickets sell out quickly. Generally, the airfare is much more economical if you travel with a tour operator.

From the United Kingdom by Plane, Car, Ferry, Train, and Bus

By Plane The major airlines flying to Copenhagen from the United King-
Airlines dom include **British Airways** (156 Regent St., London W1, tel. 081/897–4000), which flies nonstop from Heathrow, Gatwick, Birmingham, and Manchester; **SAS Scandinavian Airlines** (SAS House, 52–53 Conduit St., W1R 0AY, London, tel. 071/734–6777), which flies nonstop from Heathrow, Manchester, and Glasgow; **Brymon European Airways** (Plymouth City Airport, Croenhill, Plymouth, PL6 8BW, tel. 021/782–0711), which flies nonstop from Birmingham; and **Aer Lingus** (67 Deans Gate, Manchester, tel. 061/832–5771), which flies direct from Manchester. SAS also flies round-trip from London to Århus, while **Maersk Air** (Liverpool Station, London EC2, tel. 071/623–3813) flies nonstop from Gatwick to Billund and Copenhagen.

Flying Time   From London to Copenhagen the flight takes 1 hour, 55 minutes.

Discount Flights   Though intra-European flights into Scandinavia are often as expensive as flying directly from the United States, it's worth scanning the newspapers and London's local *Time Out* magazine for fares. The major airlines also offer APEX tickets that must be bought at least two weeks in advance, require a Saturday night stay, and have other restrictions, including severe penalties for flight cancellations.

By Car and Ferry   **Scandinavian Seaways Ferries (DFDS)** (Scandinavian Seaways, DFDS Ltd., Scandinavia House, Parkeston Quay, Harwich, Essex, CO12 4QG, England, tel. 0255/24–02–40; in Denmark, tel. 33/11–22–55) sail from Harwich to Esbjerg (20 hours) on Jylland's west coast and from Newcastle to Esbjerg (21 hours). Schedules in both summer and winter are very irregular. There are many discounts, including 20% for senior citizens and the disabled and 50% for children between the ages of 4 and 16.

The only part of Denmark connected to the European continent is Jylland on the E–45 highway from Germany. The E–20 highway then leads to Middelfart on Fyn and east to Knudshoved. From there a ferry crosses to Korsør on Sjælland and E–20 east leads to Copenhagen. Another option is to take the three-hour car ferry from Århus directly to Kalundborg in western Sjælland. From there, Route 23 leads to Copenhagen. Make reservations for the ferry in advance through the **Danish State Railway (DSB)** (tel. 33/14–88–80). (*Note:* During the busy summer months, passengers without reservations for their vehicles can wait hours.) The completion of the Storebælt Bridge, connecting Fyn and Sjælland, should speed up rail connections by 1996 and auto traffic by 1997.

By Train   Trains within Europe are well connected to Denmark, with Copenhagen serving as the main hub; however, it's often little cheaper than flying, especially if you make your arrangements from the United States. **Eurorail-** and **Eurail Saverpass** passes, which can only be purchased in the United States, are accepted by the **Danish State Railway** and on some ferries operated by DSB. From London, the crossing (23 hours including ferry) can be arranged through the **British Rail European Travel Center** (Victoria Station, London, tel. 071/834–2345), **Eurotrain** (52 Grosvenor Gardens, London SW1, tel. 071/730–3402) and **Wasteels** (121 Wilton Rd., London SW1, tel. 071/834–7066).

By Bus   Not particularly comfortable or fast, bus travel is inexpensive. The **JCP Sally Express** (23 Bourne End Rd., Northwood, Middlesex, tel. 0923/835–696; Copenhagen office, tel. 33/14–27–99) departs from the Great Eastern Hotel (Liverpool St., London) at 2:45 Saturday between June and late August and makes stops in Copenhagen (26 hours), as well as Århus (24 hours), Odense (24 hours), and Frederikshavn (22 hours). **Eurolines** (23 Crawley, Luton, Bedfordshire, LU1 1HX, tel. 058/240–4511; Copenhagen office, tel. 33/25–95–11) travels from London's Victoria Station Saturday at 9:30 PM and arrives in Copenhagen 24 hours later.

Staying in Denmark

Getting Around

By Plane Copenhagen's **Kastrup Airport** is the hub of all domestic routes. Most other airports are located in areas that serve several cities. Flight times within the country are all less than one hour. Probably the best bet for tourists for intra-Scandinavian travel, which is usually expensive, is the SAS Scandinavia Pass. One coupon costs about $70; six about $420, for unlimited air travel in Scandinavia; it is sold only in the United States. Coupons can be be used year-round for a maximum of three months and must be purchased in conjunction with transatlantic flights.

The major carriers in Denmark are **SAS** (tel. 33/13–62–66), **Danair** (tel. 31/51–50–55), **Maersk Air** (tel. 32/45–35–35), and **Cimber Air** (tel. 74/42–22–77).

By Train and Bus Traveling by bus or train is easy because DSB and a few private companies cover the country with a dense network of services, supplemented by buses in remote areas. Hourly intercity trains connect the main towns in Jylland and Fyn with Copenhagen and Sjælland, using high-speed diesels, called Lyntog (lightning trains), on the most important stretches. All these trains make one-hour ferry crossings of the Great Belt, the waterway separating Fyn and Sjælland. You can reserve seats on intercity trains and Lyntog, and you *must* have a reservation if you plan to cross the Great Belt. Buy tickets at stations for trains, buses, and connecting ferry crossings. Bus tickets are usually sold on the bus itself. Children under 5 travel free, and those between 5 and 12 travel for half price. Ask about discounts for senior citizens and groups of three or more. The **Scanrail Pass,** for travel anywhere within Scandinavia (Denmark, Sweden, Norway, and Finland), **Interail** and **Eurail** are also valid on all DSB trains, as well as some ferry passages. Call the DSB Travel Office (tel. 42/52–92–22) for additional information.

By Car Roads here are good and largely traffic-free (except the manageable traffic around Copenhagen); you can reach the many islands by toll bridges.

Rules of the Road Drivers need a valid driver's license, and if you're using your own car it must have a certificate of registration and national plates. A triangular hazard-warning sign is compulsory in every car and is provided with a rental car. No matter where you sit in a car, you must wear a seat belt, and cars must have low beams on at all times. Motorcyclists must wear helmets and use low-beam lights as well.

Drive on the right and give way to traffic—*especially to cyclists*—on the right. A red-and-white YIELD sign or a line of white triangles across the road means you must yield to traffic on the road you are entering. Do not turn right on red unless there is a green arrow indicating that this is allowed. Speed limits are 50 kilometers per hour (30 miles per hour) in built-up areas; 100 kph (60 mph) on highways; and 80 kph (50 mph) on other roads. If you are towing a trailer, you must not exceed 70 kph (40 mph). Speeding and, especially, drinking and driving are treated severely,

even if no damage is caused. Americans and foreign tourists must pay fines on the spot.

Parking You can usually park on the right-hand side of the road, though not on main roads and highways.

PARKERING/STANDSNING FORBUNDT means no parking or stopping, though you are allowed a three-minute grace period for loading and unloading. In town, parking discs are used where there are no automatic ticket-vending machines. Get discs from gas stations, post offices, police stations, or tourist offices, and set them to show your time of arrival. For most downtown parking, you must buy a ticket from an automatic vending machine and display it on the dash. Parking costs about DKr9 or more per hour in town, DKr7 elsewhere.

Gasoline Gasoline costs about DKr6.15 per liter.

Breakdowns Before leaving home, consult your insurance company. Members of organizations affiliated with **Alliance International de Tourisme (AIT)** can get technical and legal advice from the **Danish Motoring Organization (FDM)** (Firskovvej 32, 2800 Lyngby, tel. 45/93–08–00, open 10–4 weekdays). All highways have emergency phones, and you can call the rental company for help. If you cannot drive your car to a garage for repairs, the rescue corps, **Falck** (tel. 33/14–22–22), can help anywhere, anytime. In most cases, they do charge for assistance.

Telephones

Telephone exchanges throughout Denmark, especially those in Sjælland and Bornholm, were changed recently. If you hear a recorded message or three loud beeps, chances are the number you are trying to reach has been changed. KTAS information (tel. 118) can always find current numbers.

Local Calls Phones accept 1-, 5-, 10-, and 20-kroner coins. Pick up the receiver, dial the number, always including the area code, and wait until the party answers, then deposit the coins. You have roughly a minute per krone, so you can make another call on the same payment if your time has not run out. When it does, you will hear a beep and your call will be disconnected unless you deposit another coin. Dial the eight-digit number for calls anywhere within the country. For calls to the Faroe Islands (298) and Greenland (299), dial 009, then the three-digit code, then the five-digit number.

International Calls Dial 009, then the country code (1 for the United States and Canada, 44 for Great Britain), the area code, and the number. It's very expensive to telephone or fax from hotels, and the regional phone companies offer no discount times, so it's best to make calls from either main rail stations or post offices, many of which have telephone offices.

Operators and Information Most operators speak English. For national directory assistance, dial 118; for an international operator, dial 113; for a directory-assisted international call, dial 115. To reach an AT&T direct operator in the United States, for collect, person-to-person, or credit-card calls, dial 80–01–0010.

Mail

Postal Rates Airmail letters to the United States cost DKr5 for 20 grams and postcards. Letters and postcards to the United Kingdom and EC countries cost DKr3.75. You can buy stamps at post offices or from shops selling postcards.

Receiving Mail You can arrange to have your mail sent general delivery (called *Poste Restante* in Denmark) to any post office, hotel, or inn. If you do not have an address, **American Express** (Amagertorv 18, 1461 KBH K, tel. 33/12–23–01) will also receive and hold card holders' mail.

Tipping

The egalitarian Danes do not expect to be tipped. Service is included in bills for hotels, bars, and restaurants. Taxi drivers round up the fare to the next krone but expect no tip. The exception is hotel porters, who receive about DKr5 per bag.

Opening and Closing Times

Banks Most banks are open weekdays 9:30 to 4, Thursday until 6, but check in smaller towns, where times vary.

Museums As a rule, museums are open 10 to 3 or 11 to 4 and are closed on Monday. In winter, opening hours are shorter, and some museums close for the season. Check the local papers or ask at tourism offices for current times.

Shops Shops are generally open weekdays 10 to 5:30; most stay open until 7 on Friday and close at 1 or 2 on Saturday. Everything except bakeries and kiosks is closed on Sunday, and most bakeries take Monday off. The first Saturday of the month is a Long Saturday, when shops, especially in large cities, stay open until 4 or 5.

Shopping

Danish design has earned an international reputation for form and function, and any visitor will have a hard time resisting the boutiques and crafts shops. The summer season is as good as any for shopping, though the most drastic sales are after Christmas until February. Skip clothing and stick to the best buys, which are to be found in glassware, stainless steel, pottery, ceramics, and fur, though Danish antiques and silver are also much cheaper than in the United States. The best selection of shops and department stores is in Copenhagen, though crafts shops are also located in the pedestrian streets of most smaller towns.

Sports and Outdoor Activities

Bicycling Without a doubt, Denmark is one of the world's best places for cycling. Three-quarters of the population have bicycles, and more than half make use of them, on roads that effectively coordinate public transportation and cycle traffic. Many towns, particularly Copenhagen, have good cycling lanes alongside auto traffic, but the cyclist should be aware of cars at all times and pedal with caution, especially at intersections. The countrysides are also lined with paths, especially Jylland and

the island of Bornholm. Bicycles can be sent as baggage between most train stations and can also be carried onto most trains and ferries. Contact **DSB** (tel. 33/14–17–01) for more information. All cabs must be able to take bikes and are equipped with racks. Most towns have rentals, but check with local tourism offices for referrals. For more information, contact the **Danish Cyclist Federation** (Rømersgade 7, DK–1362 KBH K, tel. 33/32–31–21). The Danish Tourist Board also publishes bicycle maps and brochures.

Boating and Sailing
Well-marked channels and nearby anchorages make sailing and boating easy and popular throughout the 7,300-kilometer (4,500-mile) coastline. Waters range from the open seas of the Kattegat and the Baltic to Smålandshavet (between Sjælland and Lolland Falster) and the calm Limsfjord in Jylland. Boat rentals are available in most areas. Canoe and kayak rentals are also available for exploring the country's calm streams. For details, contact the Danish Tourist Board.

Camping
See Camping, in Lodging, *below.*

Golf
Because of its low greens fees and the more than 60 well-maintained courses, golfers throughout Europe and Japan are heading to Denmark. Visitors are welcome to all courses, but you do need a valid membership card from your own club. For general information about golfing in Denmark, contact the **Danske Golf Union** (Golfsvinget 12, DK–2625 Vallensbæk, tel. 42/64–06–66).

Hiking
Because Denmark is basically flat, the most interesting hikes are day walks between towns. Local tourism offices have maps of paths and can help plan specific routes.

Horseback Riding
Riding schools throughout the country rent horses for day or package holidays. You can also rent a covered wagon for an inexpensive and unusual accommodation and transport (*see* Off the Beaten Track in Fyn, *below*). For details, contact the Danish Tourist Board.

Tennis
Tennis, as well as badminton, handball, and other court-and-ball games, is extremely popular in Denmark, which boasts some of the world's best players and teams. Courts are at a premium, but most cities and towns have public gyms where you might get a court. Ask at your hotel or the local tourist board.

Water Sports
Surfing and scuba diving take second place to windsurfing, which is quite popular, especially in southern and northern Sjælland and off the shores north of Copenhagen and southern Fyn. A wet suit is advisable year-round. The Danish Tourist Board has more information.

Beaches

Denmark's best beaches are located on the northwest coast of Jylland and just north of Copenhagen on the northeast coast of the island of Sjælland. Topless sunbathers are common on Danish beaches and in public parks. In addition to information from the national tourist office, an up-to-date map of Danish beaches can be purchased for DKr58 from the **Dansk Miljø Styrelsen (Danish Environmental Department)** (Strandgade 29, 1401 Copenhagen K, Denmark, tel. 32/66–01–00).

Dining

Danes take their food seriously, and Danish food, however simple, is excellent, with an emphasis on fresh ingredients and careful presentation. Fish and meat are both of top quality in this farming and fishing country, and both are staple ingredients of the famous *smørrebrød* (open-face sandwich). Some smørrebrød are huge meals in themselves: Innocent snackers find themselves faced with dauntingly large (but delicious) mounds of meat or fish, slathered with pickle relish, all atop *rugbrød* (black bread) and *franskbrød* (white bread). Among the other specialties are *frikadeller* (butter-fried pork meatballs), *flæskesteg* (pork roast baked with crisp rind), *æggekage* (fluffy bacon, tomato, and cucumber omelets), *biksemad* (cubed potatoes, bacon, and beef panfried and served with an egg), and the original Danish pastries, called *wienerbrød*, which shame all imitations.

All Scandinavian countries have versions of the cold table, but the Danes claim that theirs, *det store kolde bord*, is the original and the best. It's a celebration meal: The setting of the long table is a work of art, and the food itself is a minor miracle of design and decoration.

In hotels and restaurants, the cold table is served at lunch only, though you'll find more limited versions at hotel breakfasts—a good bet for budget travelers because you can eat as much as you like. The price-conscious should also be on the lookout for establishments with fixed-price menus (look for *tilbud*, which means "special") and cafés, where an overstuffed sandwich and a steaming cup of cappuccino rarely cost more than DKr45. Even less expensive are the *pølservogn* (sausage wagons), where you can pick up a lip-smacking Danish sausage or hot dog and a separate roll for less than DKr18. Vegetarians sometimes feel slighted in this meat-and-potatoes land, but there are vegetarian restaurants in large cities, and fresh fruit and vegetable stands are almost everywhere. Fresh fish, including plaice, cod, eel, and the ubiquitous herring, are also excellent.

Liquid refreshment is top-notch. Denmark boasts more than 50 beers; the best-known are Carlsberg and Tuborg. Those who like harder stuff should try the *snaps*, the famous akvavit traditionally drunk with cold food.

Ratings Meal prices vary little between town and country. Though approximate ratings are given below, remember that careful ordering can get you a Moderate meal at a Very Expensive restaurant. Prices are per person and include a first course, entrée and dessert, plus taxes and tip, but not wine. Best bets are indicated by a star. At press time (summer 1993), there were DKr6.1 to the dollar.

Category	Copenhagen	Other Areas*
Very Expensive	over DKr400	over DKr350
Expensive	DKr250–DKr400	DKr200–DKr350
Moderate	DKr150–DKr250	DKr100–DKr200
Inexpensive	under DKr150	under DKr100

Lodging

Accommodations in Denmark range from spare to resplendent. Even inexpensive hotels offer simple designs in good materials, and good, firm beds. Many Danes prefer a shower to a bath, so if you particularly want a bath, ask for it, but be prepared to pay more. Farmhouses and *kro* (old stagecoach inns) accommodations offer a terrific alternative to more traditional hotels. Except in the case of rentals, breakfast and taxes are usually included in prices, but check when making a reservation.

The very friendly staff at the **Hotel Booking desk** (tel. 33/12–28–30) in the main tourist office (Bernstorffsgade 1, DK–1577 Copenhagen V) can help find rooms in hotels, hostels and private homes, or even at campsites. Prices range from budget upward. Prebooking in private homes and hotels must be done two months in advance, but last-minute (as in same-day) hotel rooms can also be found and will save you 50% off the normal price. When Tivoli is open, hours are 9–midnight; mid-Sept.–Oct. 9 AM–10 PM; Oct.–Apr., Mon.–Sat. 9–5.

For bed-and-breakfast accommodations, contact **Dansk Bed & Breakfast** (Box 53, Hesselvang 20, DK–2900 Hellerup, tel. 31/61–04–05) before you leave home. For either pre- or last-minute booking, contact **SLM** (Scandinavian Lodging and Breakfast, Store Kongensgade 94, DK–1264 Copenhagen, tel. 33/91–91–15, fax 33/91–91–85). A standard double room with either agency runs between DKr275 and DKr350.

Hotels Luxury hotels in the city or countryside offer rooms of a high standard, and in a manor-house hotel you may find yourself sleeping in a four-poster bed. Less expensive accommodations, however, are uniformly clean and comfortable. Make your reservations well in advance, especially in resort areas near the coasts, to avoid having to overnight in costly, last-minute hotels. Many places offer summer reductions to compensate for the slowdown in business travelers and conferences.

Inns A cheaper and charming alternative to hotels are the kro (old stagecoach inns) scattered throughout Denmark. You can save money by investing in **Inn Checks,** valid at 79 inns. Each check costs DKr375 per person or DKr535 per couple. Prices include one overnight stay in a room with bath, breakfast included. Contact **Dansk Kroferie** (Vejlevej 16, DK–8700 Horsens, tel. 75/62–35–44, fax 75/64–87–20).

Farm Vacations These are perhaps the best way to see how the Danes live and work. You stay on a farm and share meals with the family and can even get out and help with the chores. There's a minimum stay of three nights; half-board accommodation runs around DKr230, while lunch and dinner can often be purchased directly from the family for DKr25 to 35. Contact the **Horsens Tourist Information Office** (Søndergade 26, DK–8700 Horsens, Jylland, tel. 75/62–38–22).

Youth and Family Hostels The country's 100 youth hostels are excellent, with kitchen and family rooms available to all, regardless of age. If you have an International Youth Hostels Association card (obtainable before you leave home), the average cost is DKr60 to DKr84 per person. Without the card, there's a surcharge of DKr22. The hostels fill up quickly in summer, so make your reservations early. Most hostels are particularly sympathetic to students and will usually find them at least a place on the floor. Bring

your own linens or sheet sleeping bags, though these can usually be rented at the hostel. Sleeping bags are not allowed. Contact **Landsforeningen Danmarks Vandrehjem** (Vesterbrogade 39, DK–1620, Copenhagen V, tel. 31/31–36–12). It charges for information, but you can get a free brochure, "Camping/Youth and Family Hostels," from the Danish Tourist Board.

Rentals Many Danes rent out their summer homes, and a stay in one is another good way to see the countryside on your own. A simple house with room for four will cost from DKr2,500 per week upward. Contact **DanCenter** (Falkoner Allé 7, DK–2000 Frederiksberg, tel. 31/19–09–00).

Camping Denmark has over 500 approved campsites, with a rating system of one, two, or three stars. You need an International Camping Carnet or Danish Camping Pass (available at any campsite and valid for one year). For more details on camping and discounts for groups and families, contact **Campingrådet** (Hesseløgade 16, DK–2100 Copenhagen Ø, tel. 39/27–88–44).

Ratings Prices are for two people in a double room and include service and taxes, and usually breakfast. Best bets are indicated by a star. At press time (summer 1993), there were DKr6.1 to the dollar.

Category	Copenhagen	Other Areas*
Very Expensive	over DKr1,100	over DKr850
Expensive	DKr800–DKr1,100	DKr650–DKr850
Moderate	DKr670–DKr800	DKr450–DKr650
Inexpensive	under DKr670	under DKr450

Copenhagen

Copenhagen (København in Danish) has no glittering skylines, few killer views, and only a handful of meager skyscrapers. Traffic is manageable, events are organized, and the pace is utterly human. Even at the height of the busy summer, there is always a quiet café or a lakeside bench available to ponder this European capital with a provincial soul.

In the streets, bicycles spin alongside smooth auto traffic. In the early morning in the pedestrian streets of the city's core, Strøget, the air is redolent of freshly baked bread and soap-scrubbed store fronts. If there's such a thing as a cozy city, this is it.

Extremely livable and relatively calm, Copenhagen is not a microcosm of Denmark; indeed, it speeds past the rest of the mostly rural country. The headquarters of Denmark's political, cultural, and financial operations, it is inhabited by 1.5 million Danes, a fifth of the population, as well as a growing immigrant community. Filled with museums, restaurants, cafés, and lively nightlife, it has its greatest resource in its spirited inhabitants. Imaginative and unconventional, the affable Copenhageners exude an egalitarian philosophy that embraces and respects nearly all lifestyles and leanings.

The town was a fishing colony until 1157, when Valdemar the Great gave it to Bishop Absalon, who built a castle on what is now Christianborg. It grew as a center on the Baltic trade route and became known as *købmændenes havn* (merchants' harbor), and eventually København. In the 15th century it became the royal residence and the capital of Norway and Sweden. A hundred years later, Christian IV, a Renaissance king obsessed with fine architecture, began a building boom that crowned the city with towers and castles, many of which still exist. They are almost all that remain of the city's 800-year history; much of the city was destroyed during two major fires in the 18th century and Lord Nelson's bombings during the Napoleonic Wars.

Despite a tumultuous history, Copenhagen survives as the liveliest Scandinavian capital. With the backdrop of copper towers and crooked rooftops, the venerable city is humored by playful street musicians and performers, soothed by one of the highest standards of living in the world, and spangled by the thousand lights and gardens of Tivoli.

Important Addresses and Numbers

Tourist Information
The main tourist information office is **Danmarks Turistråd** (Danish Tourist Board, Bernstorffsgade 1, tel. 33/11–13–25). It is open in May, weekdays 9–5, Saturday 9–2 and Sunday 9–1; June through mid-September, daily 9–6; and mid-September through April, weekdays 9–5 and Saturday 9–noon. Packed with brochures and maps covering Copenhagen and the rest of the country, it's run by a pleasant and knowledgeable staff. Youth information in Copenhagen is available at **Use-It** (Huset, Rådhusstræde 13, tel. 33/15–65–18), which also has a café, a video gallery, and three music clubs.

Embassies
U.S. Embassy, Dag Hammarskjölds Allé 24, tel. 31/42–31–44. **Canadian Embassy,** Kristen Bernikows Gade 1, tel. 33/12–22–99. **U.K. Embassy,** Kastesvej 36–40, tel. 35/26–46–00.

Emergencies
For **police, fire,** and **ambulance,** dial 112. If you cannot drive your car to a garage for repairs, the rescue corps, **Falck** (tel. 31/14–22–22), can help.

Hospital Emergency Rooms
Rigshospitalet (Blegdamsvej 9, tel. 35/45–35–45) is located north of the city, next to the large Fælled Park. **Frederiksberg Hospital** (Nordre Fasanvej 57, tel. 38/34–77–11) is two blocks north of the zoo.

Doctors
After normal business hours, **emergency doctors** make house calls in the central city. In Osterbro and Norrebro, call 33/12–00–41; in Frederiksberg, 31/10–00–41; and in Vesterbro, Valby, and Sydhaven, 31/22–00–41. Fees are payable in cash only; night fees are approximately DKr300–400.

Dentists
Emergency dentists (14 Oslo Plads, no tel.) near Østerport Station, are available daily 8 PM–9:30 PM and Saturday, Sunday, and holidays 10 AM–noon. Only cash is accepted as payment.

Late-Night Pharmacies
Steno Apotek (Vesterbrogade 6C, tel. 33/14–82–66) and **Sønderbro Apotek** (Amangerbrogade 158, tel. 31/58–01–40) are open 24 hours a day.

Where to Change Money
Almost all banks (including Den Danske Bank at the airport) exchange money. Most hotels cash traveler's checks and major foreign currency, but they charge a substantial fee and give a

lower rate. After normal banking hours, an exchange is open at the **main railway station** October to mid-April, daily 7 AM–9 PM, and mid-April to September 6:45 AM–10 PM. **American Express** (Amagertorv 18, tel. 33/12–23–01) is open weekdays 9–5 and Saturday 9–noon. In the same area, the three locations of **Danish Change** (Købmagergade 19 and on Strøget, Østergade 61 and Frederiksberggade 5, tel. 33/93–04–18) are open April to October, daily 10–8; November to March, daily 10–6. **Tivoli** (Vesterbrogade 3, tel. 33/15–10–01) also exchanges money; it is open May to September, daily noon–11 PM.

English-Language Bookstores **Steve's Books and Records** (Ved Stranden 10, tel. 33/11–94–60) has new and used English books. **Boghallen** (Rådhuspladsen 37, tel. 33/11–85–11, ext. 309) and **Arnold Busck** (Kobmagergade 49, tel. 33/12–24–53) are Danish bookstores with excellent English-language sections.

Travel Agencies **American Express** (Amagertorv 18, tel. 33/12–23–01), **Thomas Cook,** c/o **Wagons-Lits** (Vesterport 6, tel. 33/14–27–47), and **Skibby Rejser** (Vandkunsten 10, tel. 33/32–85–00) are among the leading agencies. For student and budget travel, try **Kilroy Travels Denmark** (Skindergade 28, tel. 33/11–00–44). **Spies** (Nyropsgade 41, tel. 33/11–84–84) handles charter packages.

Arriving and Departing by Plane

Airport and Airlines Copenhagen's **Kastrup Airport,** 10 kilometers (6 miles) southeast of downtown, is the gateway to Scandinavia. In addition to international flights, domestic flights are served by **SAS** (tel. 33/13–72–77). Among the many airlines that serve Kastrup are **British Airways** (tel. 33/14–60–00), **Icelandair** (tel. 33/12–33–88), and **Delta** (tel. 32/52–02–15).

Between the Airport and Downtown Traffic in Copenhagen, even during rush hour, is manageable; you will find that travel between the airport and downtown is both quick and easy.

By Bus **SAS coach buses** leave the international arrivals terminal every 15 minutes, from 5:42 AM to 9:45 PM, cost DKr28, and take 25 minutes to reach Copenhagen's main train station on Vesterbrogade. Another SAS coach from Christianborg, on Slotsholmsgade, to the airport runs every 15 minutes between 8:30 AM and noon, and every half hour from noon to 6 PM. The **HT** city buses depart from the international arrivals terminal every 15 minutes, from 4:30 AM (Sunday 5:30) to 11:52 PM, but take a longer, more circuitous route. Take Bus 32 or 32H for the Town Hall Square (Rådhuspladsen), Bus 9 for Kongens Nytorv and Østerport, and Bus 78E for Valby Station. Tickets cost DKr14.25.

By Taxi The 20-minute ride downtown costs from DKr75 to DKr120. Lines form at the international arrivals terminal. In the unlikely event there is no taxi available, call 31/35–35–35.

Arriving and Departing by Car, Train, and Ship

By Car The E–66 highway, via bridges and ferry routes, connects Fredericia (on Jylland) with Middelfart (on Fyn) and Copenhagen. Farther north, from Århus (in Jylland), there is direct ferry service to Kalundborg (on Sjælland). From there, Route 23 leads to Roskilde. Take Route 21 east and follow the signs to Copenhagen. Make reservations for the ferry in advance through **DSB** (tel. 33/14–88–80).

Once in Copenhagen, leave your car in the garage and walk. The charm of the pedestrian malls comes at the cost of a complicated system of one-way streets and difficult (and expensive) parking. Attractions are relatively close together, and public transportation is excellent.

By Train Copenhagen's **Hovedbanegården** (central station) is the hub of the DSB network. Intercity trains leave every hour, usually on the hour, from 6 AM to 10 PM for principal towns in Fyn and Jylland. Find out more from **DSB Information** (tel. 33/14–17–01). You can make reservations at the central station, at most other stations, and through travel agents.

By Ship If you are coming from Sweden, there are frequent ferry connections, including several daily ships from Malmö, Limhamn, Landskrona, and Helsingborg, that arrive in Copenhagen. There is also a high-speed craft from Malmö.

Getting Around

Copenhagen is small, with most sights within its square-mile center. Wear comfortable shoes and explore it on foot. Or follow the example of the Danes and rent a bike. For the footsore, an efficient transit system is available.

By Train and Bus The **Copenhagen Card** affords unlimited travel on buses and suburban trains, admission to more than 40 museums and sights around Sjælland, and a reduction on the ferry crossing to Sweden. You can buy the card, which costs DKr130 (one day), DKr220 (two days), or DKr260 (three days)—half-price for children—at tourist offices and hotels and from travel agents.

Trains and buses operate from 5 AM (Sunday 6 AM) to midnight. After that, night buses run every half hour from 1 AM to 4:30 AM from the main bus station at the Town Hall Square to most areas of the city and surroundings. Trains and buses operate on the same ticket system and divide Copenhagen and surrounding areas into three zones. Tickets are validated on a time basis: On the basic ticket, which costs DKr9.50 per hour, you can travel anywhere in the zone in which you started. A discount *klip kort*, good for 10 rides, costs DKr70 and must be stamped in the automatic ticket machines on buses or at stations. Get zone details from the 24-hour information service (tel. 36/45–45–45 for buses, 33/14–17–01 for S trains).

By Taxi The shiny computer-metered Mercedes and Volvo cabs are not cheap. The base charge is DKr15, plus DKr8–DKr10 per kilometer. A cab is available when it displays the sign FRI (free); it can be hailed or picked up in front of the main train station or at taxi stands, or by calling 31/35–35–35.

By Bicycle Bikes are delightfully well suited to Copenhagen's flat terrain and are popular among Danes, as well as among visitors. Bike rental costs DKr25–DKr60 a day, with a deposit of DKr100–DKr200. Contact **Københavns Cyclebørs** (Track 12, Copenhagen main train station, tel. 33/14–07–17), **Danwheel-Rent-a-Bike** (Colbjørnsensgade 3, tel. 31/21–22–27), or **Urania Cykler** (Gammel Kongevej 1, tel. 31/21–80–88).

Opening and Closing Times

Banks and businesses follow the same hours as the rest of the country, but grocery stores stay open later, until 7 most

nights. Shops stay open until 5:30 Monday through Thursday and until 6 or 7 on Friday. On the first Saturday of the month some shops stay open until 4 or 5.

Guided Tours

The Copenhagen Tourist Board monitors all tours and has brochures and information. Most tours run through the summer until September. Only the Grand Tour of Copenhagen is year-round.

Orientation All tours begin at Lurblæserne (Lur Blower Column) at the Town Hall Square, and reservations are not necessary. **The Royal Tour of Copenhagen** (2¾ hours) covers the exhibitions at Christiansborg and Rosenborg, and visits Amalienborg Square. **The Grand Tour of Copenhagen** (2½ hours) includes Tivoli, the Carlsberg Glyptotek, Christiansborg Palace, Børsen, the Royal Theater, Nyhavn, Amalienborg Palace, the Gefion Fountain, the Grundtvig Church, and Rosenborg Castle. The **City Tour** (1½ hours) is more general, passing the Carlsberg Glyptotek, Christiansborg Palace, Thorvaldsen's Museum, the National Museum, Børsen, the Royal Theater, Rosenborg, the National Art Gallery, the Botanical Gardens, Amalienborg, the Gefion Fountain, and stopping at the Little Mermaid. For more information on all tours, call **Copenhagen Excursions** (tel. 31/54–06–06).

Special-Interest Tours of the **Carlsberg Brewery** meet at the Elephant Gate (Ny Carlsbergvej 140, tel. 31/21–12–21, ext. 1312), weekdays at 11 and 2. **Tuborg Breweries** also offers tours (Strandvejen 54, Hellerup, tel. 31/29–33–11, ext. 2212). **The Royal Porcelain Factory** (Smallegade 45, tel. 31/86–48–48) has tours, which end at its shop, on weekdays at 9, 10, and 11 from mid-September until April and weekdays at 9, 10, 11, 1, and 2 from May through mid-September.

Boat Tours The **Harbor and Canal Tour** (1 hour) leaves from Gammel Strand and the east side of Kongens Nytorv from May to mid-September. Contact **Canal Tours** (tel. 33/13–31–05) or the Tourist Board. The **City and Harbor Tour** (2½ hours) includes a short bus trip through town and sails from the Fish Market on Holmens Canal through several more waterways, ending near Strøget. Call Copenhagen Excursions (*see* Orientation, *above*).

Walking Tours **Guided strolls** (2 hours) with English-speaking guides start at 4:30 Sunday and 5:30 Wednesday, May through September, at the town hall and include the double square of Gammel and Nytorv, Vor Frue Kirke, the university, and the Round Tower. Other walks are also planned. Call 31/51–25–90 or 42/73–00–66, or look for the latest schedule in the tourist magazine *Copenhagen This Week*.

Highlights for First-Time Visitors

Amalienborg Castle (*see* Tour 2)
Christiansborg Palace (*see* Tour 1)
Langelinie and **the Little Mermaid** (*see* Tour 2)
Ny Carlsberg Glyptotek (*see* Tour 3)
Nyhavn (*see* Tour 2)
Rosenborg Castle (*see* Tour 3)
Rundetårn and **Trinitas Church** (*see* Tour 3)
Strøget (*see* Tour 3)

Tivoli (*see* Tour 3)
Vor Frelsers Kirke (*see* Tour 1)

Exploring Copenhagen

Numbers in the margin correspond to points of interest on the Copenhagen map.

The city core consists of the five consecutive pedestrian strands known as Strøget and the surrounding tangle of roads and courtyards. Less than a mile square, it is best explored on foot. North of Kongens Nytorv, the city becomes a fidgety grid of wider boulevards and parks that point toward the upscale Østerbro area. To the south are the working-class and immigrant neighborhoods of Vesterbro, where you'll find a good selection of inexpensive ethnic restaurants and shops. Across the main harbor is the smaller, historic haven of Christianshavn.

The city is surrounded by water, be it sea or canal; it is built on two islands—Sjælland and Amager—and connected by bridges and drawbridges. The maritime atmosphere is indelible, especially around Nyhavn and Christianshavn. Leave enough time in your tours to linger, to enjoy the views of life from the sidewalk cafés in the shady squares.

Tour 1: Town Hall Square to the Citadel

The best place to begin a stroll is **Rådhus Pladsen** (City Hall Square), the hub of Copenhagen's commercial district. The mock-Renaissance building dominating it is **Københavns Rådhus** (Copenhagen's City Hall), completed in 1905. A statue of Copenhagen's 12th-century founder, Bishop Absalon, sits atop the main entrance. Inside you can see the first World Clock, a multidialed, superaccurate astronomical timepiece that took inventor Jens Olsen 27 years to complete before it was put into action in 1955. It contains a 570,000-year calendar. If you're feeling energetic, take a guided tour up the 106-meter (350-foot) bell tower for the panoramic, but not particularly inspiring, view. *Rådhus Pladsen, tel. 33/66–25–82 or 33/66–25–83. Admission free. Open weekdays 10–3. Tower tours in English: admission, DKr10, Oct.–May, Mon.–Sat. noon; June–Sept., weekdays 10, noon, and 2 and Sat. noon. Guided tours in English: admission, DKr20, weekdays at 3, Sat. at 3. World Clock: admission DKr10 adults, DKr5 children, Mon.–Fri. 10–4, Sat. 10–1. Combination admission tickets DKr30.*

Diagonally across the square, atop a corner office building, you can check the local weather forecast. Look above the neon thermometer to the gilded barometer: On sunny days a golden sculpture of a girl on a bicycle appears; on rainy days there's a girl with an umbrella. The bronze sculpture was created by the Danish artist E. Utzon Frank in 1936.

On the right of Rådhus Pladsen is **Lurblæserne** (the Lur Blower's Column), topped by two Vikings blowing an ancient trumpet called a *lur*. The 1914 sculptor took a great deal of artistic license—the lur dates from the Bronze Age, 1500 BC, while the Vikings lived a mere 1,000 years ago.

If you continue to the square's northeastern corner and turn right, you will be in **Frederiksberggade**, the first of the five pedestrian streets that make up **Strøget**, Copenhagen's shopping

Amalienborg, **15**
Amalienhaven, **16**
Børsen, **10**
Botanisk Have, **29**
Christiansborg Slot, **5**
Den Hirschsprungske Samling, **31**
Den Lille Havfrue, **22**
Det Kongelige Bibliotek, **7**
Frihedsmuseet, **20**
Gefion Springvandet, **23**
Helligånds Kirken, **12**
Kastellet, **21**
Københavns Bymuseum, **35**
Københavns Rådhus, **1**
Københavns Synagoge, **26**
Københavns Universitet, **25**
Kongelige Teater, **14**
Kunstindustrimuseet, **19**
Lurblæserne, **2**
Marmorkirken, **17**
National Museet, **4**
Nikolaj Kirke, **13**
Ny Carlsberg Glyptotek, **33**
Rosenborg Slot, **28**
Rundetårn, **27**
Russiske Ortodoks Kirke, **18**
Statens Museum for Kunst, **30**
Strøget, **3**
Teaterhistorisk Museet, **8**
Thorvaldsens Museum, **6**
Tivoli, **32**
Tøjhusmuseet, **9**
Tycho Brahe Planetarium, **34**
Vor Frelsers Kirke, **11**
Vor Frue Kirke, **24**

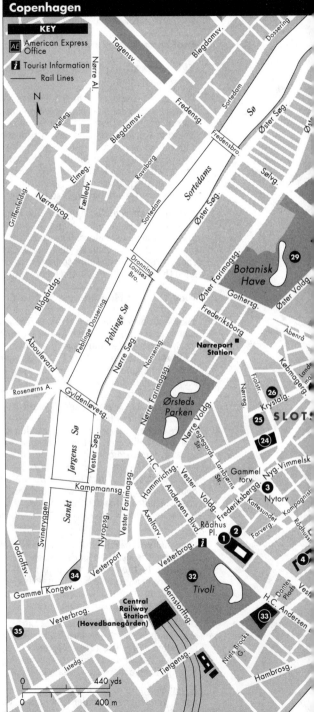

Copenhagen

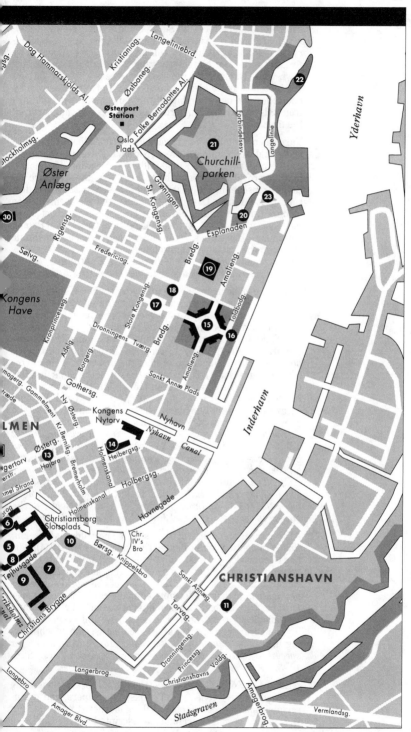

district. Walk past the cafés and trendy boutiques to the double
square of **Gammeltorv** (Old Square) and **Nytorv** (New Square),
which are lined with street vendors selling inexpensive jewelry. In 1728 and again in 1795, this area was heavily damaged by
fire, with the later blaze destroying the original 15th-century
town hall. During the renovation process the city fathers
straightened and widened the streets. Between the swanky
boutiques and newer architecture, you can still see buildings
from this reconstruction period, as well as a few that survived
the fires.

❹ Turn down Rådhusstræde toward Frederiksholms Kanal. Here
you'll find the **National Museet** (National Museum), which recently underwent a DKr450-million renovation. Originally
built as a royal residence in the 18th century, the structure became a museum in the 1930s and now houses extensive collections that chronicle Danish cultural history from prehistoric to
modern times, including one of the largest collections of Stone
Age tools in the world, as well as Egyptian, Greek, and Roman
antiquities. If you are a Viking enthusiast, check out the Runic
stones in the Danish cultural-history section. *Frederiksholms
Kanal 12, tel. 33/13-44-11. Admission: DKr30 adults, DKr20
senior citizens; children under 16 free. Open Tues.-Sun. 10-5.*

❺ Cross Frederiksholms Kanal to Christiansborg Slotsplads, a
small atoll divided by the canal and dominated by the massive
granite **Christiansborg Slot** (Christiansborg Castle), where the
queen officially receives guests. The complex, which contains
the **Folketinget** (Parliament House), **De Kongelige Repræ-
santationlokaler** (the Royal Reception Chambers; where you'll
be asked to don slippers to protect the floors), and **Højesteret**
(the Supreme Court), is located on the site of the city's first fortress, built by Bishop Absalon in 1167. While the castle was being built at the turn of the century, the National Museum
excavated the **ruins** lying beneath the site. From 1441 until the
fire of 1795 Christiansborg was used as the royal residence.
*Christiansborg, tel. 33/92-64-92. Ruins: admission DKr12
adults, DKr5 children; open daily 9:30-3:30; closed Mon. and
Sat., Oct.-May. Reception chambers: admission DKr27
adults, DKr10 children; open to guided tours only: June-
Aug., Tues.-Sun., English tour at 11 and 3; Sept.-May,
Tues.-Thurs. and Sun., English tour at 11 and 3. Folketinget:
tel. 33/37-55-00; admission free, tours June-Sept., daily,
hourly 10-4; Oct.-Nov. and Jan.-May, Sun. hourly 10-4.*

❻ Also on the island, north of the castle, is **Thorvaldsens Museum.**
The 19th-century artist Bertel Thorvaldsen (1770-1844), perhaps Denmark's greatest sculptor, is buried at the center of the
museum. Greatly influenced by the statues and reliefs of classical antiquity, he is recognized as one of the world's greatest
neoclassical artists and completed many commissions all over
Europe. In addition to his own interpretations of classical and
mythological figures, there is an extensive collection of paintings and drawings by other artists that he assembled while living in Italy. *Porthusgade 2, tel. 33/32-15-32. Admission for
special exhibitions: DKr20; otherwise free. Open Tues.-Sun.
10-5.*

❼ Nearby **Det Kongelige Bibliotek** (the Royal Library) houses the
country's largest collection of books, newspapers, and manuscripts. Look for records of the Viking journeys to America and
Greenland, as well as original manuscripts by Hans Christian

Andersen and Karen Blixen (Isak Dinesen). Afterward, leave time to ramble around the statue of philosopher Søren Kierkegaard (1813–1855), the formal gardens, and the tree-lined avenues that surround the scholarly building. *Christians Brygge 8, tel. 33/93–01–11. Admission free. Open weekdays 9–7, Sat. 10–7.*

8 Close to the library is **Teaterhistorisk Museet** (the Theater History Museum), in the Royal Court Theater of 1766. You can see extensive exhibits in theater and ballet history and then wander around the boxes, the stage, and the dressing rooms. *Christiansborg Ridebane 18, tel. 33/11–51–76. Admission: DKr20 adults, DKr10 senior citizens and students, DKr5 children. Open Wed. 2–4, Sun. noon–4.*

Also at this address are **De Kongelige Stald** (the Royal Stables), which display vehicles used by the Danish monarchy from 1776 to the present. *Tel. 33/40–26–67. Admission: DKr5 adults, DKr2 children. Open Nov.–Apr., weekends 2–4; May–Oct., Fri.–Sun. 2–4.*

9 Across the street that bears its name is **Tøjhusmuseet** (the Royal Danish Arsenal Museum), housed in one of the oldest buildings in central Copenhagen. The Renaissance structure, built by King Christian IV, a scholar and a warrior as well as the architect of much of the city, contains impressive displays of uniforms, weapons, and armor in an arched hall 200 yards long. *Tøjhusgade 3, tel. 33/11–60–37. Admission: DKr20 adults, DKr5 children. Open Tues.–Sun. 10–4.*

10 A few steps from Tøjhuset is **Børsen,** believed to be the oldest stock exchange still in use, though now only on special occasions. It was built between 1619 and 1640 by Christian IV. The king is said to have helped to twist the tails of the four dragons that form the structure's whimsical green copper spire. With its steep roofs, tiny windows, and gables, the building is one of Copenhagen's treasures. *Not open to the public.*

To the left (near Højbro Plads) is a delightful row of houses bordering the northern edge of Slotsholmen. The quays in front of them were long used for Copenhagen's fish market, though today a lone early morning fisherwoman hawking fresh fish, marinated herring, and slithering eel is the only person who carries on the tradition.

Across from Børsen is **Holmens Kirke** (the Islet's Church), where two of the country's most revered naval heroes—Niels Juel, who crushed the Swedish fleet at Køge in 1677, and Peder Tordenskjold, who defeated Charles XII of Sweden during the Great Northern War in the early 18th century—are buried. *Holmens Kanal, tel. 33/13–61–78. Admission free. Open May 15–Sept. 15, Mon.–Fri. 9–2, Sat. 9–noon; Sept. 16–May 14, Mon.–Sat. 9–noon.*

From Børsen, look east across the drawbridge (Knippelsbro) that connects Slotsholmen with **Christianshavn,** one of the oldest parts of Copenhagen. Three hundred years ago it was designed for trade, commerce, housing for the shipbuilding workers, and as a defense area against sea attacks. Now gentrified, its old tangles of cobbled avenues, antique street lamps, and Left Bank atmosphere have been preserved, as has the old system of earthworks—the best preserved of Copenhagen's original fortification walls. Restaurants, cafés,

and boutiques have moved in, and the ramparts are now edged with green areas and walking paths—a popular neighborhood for afternoon and evening promenades.

⑪ Dominating the scene is the green-and-gold spire of **Vor Frelsers Kirke** (Our Savior's Church). The Gothic structure was built in 1696. Local legend has it that the staircase encircling it was built curling the wrong way around, so that when its architect reached the top and realized what he'd done, he jumped. The tower itself is closed until 1998 for repairs. *Skt. Annægade, tel. 31/57–27–98. Admission free. Open Mar. 15–May, Mon.– Sat. 9–3:30, Sun. noon–3:30; June–Aug., Mon.–Sat. 9–4:30, Sun. noon–4:30; Sept.–Oct., Mon.–Sat. 9–3:30, Sun. noon– 3:30; Nov.–Mar. 14, Mon.–Sat. 10–1:30, Sun. noon–1:30.*

Cross the Knippels Torvegade Bridge and walk straight down the street about a mile (or take Bus 2 or 8 to the canal and walk about two blocks north) to the Amagertorv section of Strøget.
⑫ On your left is the 18th-century **Helligånds Kirken** (Church of the Holy Ghost), one of the city's oldest. The choir contains a font by the sculptor Thorvaldsen. *Niels Hemmingsengade 5, tel. 33/12–95–55. Admission free. Open Mon.–Fri. noon–4.*

In Østergade, the easternmost of the streets that make up
⑬ Strøget, you'll see the green spire of **Nikolaj Kirke** (Nicholas Church). The current building was finished in 1914; the previous structure, which dated from the 13th century, was destroyed by the 1728 fire. Today the church is an art gallery and an exhibition center. *Nikolaiplads, tel. 33/93–16–26. Admission free. Open daily noon–5.*

Time Out   **Café Nikolaj,** inside Nikolaj Kirke, is a reliable, inexpensive café where you can enjoy a good Danish pastry or a light meal.

Although Strøget is a famous shopping area, and elegant stores and trendy boutiques abound, it's also where Copenhagen comes to stroll. Outside the posh displays of the fur and porcelain shops, the bustling cafés and restaurants, the sidewalks have the festive air of a street fair.

Tour 2: Around the Royal Palace

Kongens Nytorv (the King's New Square) marks the end of Strøget. In its center is a mounted statue of Christian V. Every year, at the end of June, graduating high-school students wearing white caps arrive in horse-drawn carriages and dance
⑭ around the austere statue. The stoic, pillared **Kongelige Teater** (Danish Royal Theater), flanked by statues of Danish authors Adam Oehlenschläger and Ludvig Holberg, sits on the south side. Its two stages and sumptuous red-velvet interiors are the home of Danish opera and ballet, as well as theater. The Danish Royal Ballet remains one of the world's great companies, with a repertoire ranging from classical to modern works (*see* The Arts and Nightlife, *below*). *Tordenskjoldsgade 3, tel. 33/14–10– 02. Not open for tours.*

Located just behind the theater is **Charlottenborg,** which 300 years ago was planned as a residential palace with a large garden. Since 1754, however, the main section of the palace (which was built in 1670) has housed the faculty and students of the Danish Academy of Fine Art. On the western side of the

square, you'll see the stately white New Georgian facade of the 200-year-old **D'Angleterre** (*see* Lodging, *below*), the grande dame of Copenhagen hotels.

The street leading southeast from Kongens Nytorv is **Nyhavn** (New Harbor). The harbor is actually a canal that was dug 300 years ago to draw traffic and commerce to the center of the city. The plan worked, attracting merchants and warehouses to the area, many of which have been well preserved and give Nyhavn its authentic 18th-century maritime atmosphere. Until 1970, this area was the favorite haunt of sailors. Now gentrified, the restaurants, boutiques, and antiques stores outnumber the tattoo parlors, but the area still retains a genuine charm, with a fleet of old-time sailing ships that you can view from the quay. Hans Christian Andersen lived in the houses at numbers 18, 20, and 67 at various times.

Time Out Dozens of restaurants and cafés line Nyhavn. Among the best is **Cap Horn** (Nyhavn 21, tel. 33/12–85–04), for moderately priced hearty and light Danish specialties served in a ship's-galley atmosphere.

Beside the main harbor are old shipping warehouses, including two—Nyhavn 71 and the Admiral—that have been converted into comfortable hotels (*see* Lodging, *below*). The end of Nyhavn is the departure point for the high-speed craft to Malmö, while on the other side, on Kvævthusbroen (at the end of Skt. Annæ Plads) is the quay for boats to Oslo and Bornholm.

Turn left at the end of Nyhavn to see the harbor front and then take an immediate left onto Skt. Annæ Plads and the second right onto Amaliegade. Walk through the imposing wooden colonnade and you'll be in the cobbled square of **Amalienborg,** the four identical Rococo buildings that have been the royal residence since 1784. Every day at noon, the Royal Guard and band march from Rosenborg Slot through the city for the changing of the guard. On Queen Margrethe's birthday, April 16, at noon, hundreds of Danes gather to cheer their monarch, who stands and waves from her balcony. Plans are under way to open the Christian VIII palace across from the Queen's residence. Interiors will chronicle royal lifestyles between 1863 and 1947. As of press time (summer 1993), details had not yet been finalized. Call Amalienborg (tel. 33/12–21–86) for information. In the center of the square is a magnificent statue of King Frederik V by the French sculptor Jacques François Joseph Saly. One of the finest equestrian statues in the world, it reputedly cost as much as all the buildings combined.

On the palace's harbor side are the trees, gardens, and fountains of **Amalienhaven** (Amalia's Gardens). Across the square, it's a step to Bredgade and the ponderous Frederikskirke, commonly called **Marmorkirken** (the Marble Church), a Baroque church begun in 1749 in high-priced Norwegian marble that lay unfinished (because of budget restraints) from 1770 to 1874 before it was finally completed and consecrated in 1894. Perched around the exterior are 16 statues of various religious leaders from Moses to Luther, and below them stand sculptures of outstanding Danish ministers and bishops. *Bredgade, tel. 33/15–37–63. Admission free. Open daily 11–2*.

On Bredgade as well, you can see the exotic gilded onion domes of the **Russiske Ortodoks Kirke** (Russian Orthodox Church).

⑲ Farther on is the fine Rococo building of the **Kunstindustri-museet** (Museum of Decorative Art), which was formerly a royal hospital. Inside there's a large selection of European and Oriental handicrafts, as well as ceramics, silverware, and tapestry. Leave enough time to stop for a cup of coffee in the little café. *Bredgade 68, tel. 33/14–94–52. Admission: DKr30; DKr20 students and senior citizens. Permanent collection: open Tues.–Sun. 1–4; changing exhibits, Tues.–Sat. 10–4, Sun. 1–4.*

Parallel to Bredgade, you can walk down Store Kongensgade to the neat mustard-colored enclave of **Nyboder,** a perfectly laid-out compound of flat, long, former sailors' homes built by Christian IV. Like Nyhavn, this salty sailors' area was seedy and boisterous at the beginning of the 1970s, but today it has become one of Copenhagen's more fashionable neighborhoods.

Back on Store Kongensgade, turn right onto Esplanaden, and
⑳ you'll arrive at **Frihedsmuseet** (the Liberty Museum), situated in Churchill Park. Flanked by a homemade tank the Danes used to spread the news of the Nazi surrender after World War II, the museum gives an evocative picture of the heroic Danish resistance movement, which managed to save 7,000 Jews from the Nazis by hiding them then smuggling them to Sweden. *Churchillparken, tel. 33/13–77–14. Admission free. Open Sept. 16–Apr., Tues.–Sat. 11–3, Sun. 11–4; May–Sept. 15, Tues.–Sat. 10–4, Sun. 10–5.*

At the park's entrance stands the English church, St. Albans,
㉑ and, in the center, **Kastellet** (the Citadel), with two rings of moats. This was the city's main fortress in the 18th century, but in a grim reversal during World War II, the Germans used it as the focal point of their occupation. *Admission free. Open 6 AM–sunset.*

Continue to Langelinie, which on Sundays is thronged with
㉒ promenading Danes, and at last to **Den Lille Havfrue** (the Little Mermaid), the somewhat overrated 1913 statue commemorating Hans Christian Andersen's lovelorn creation, and the subject of hundreds of travel posters. Donated to the city by Carl Jacobsen, the son of the founder of Carlsberg Breweries, the innocent waif has also been the subject of some cruel practical jokes, including decapitation and the loss of an arm, but she is
㉓ currently in one piece. Back toward Esplanaden, the **Gefion Springvandet** (Gefion Fountain) illustrates another dramatic myth, that of the goddess Gefion, who was promised as much of Sweden as she could carve in a night. The story goes that she changed her sons to oxen and carved out the island of Sjælland.

Time Out The **Langelinie Pavillonen** (Langelinie, tel. 33/12–12–14) serves a steady flow of tourists, but other than that, the nearest cafés are either back on Østerbrogade or toward the center of the city.

Tour 3: Around Strøget and down Vesterbrogade

From Langelinie, take the train from Østerport Station to
㉔ Nørreport Station and walk down Fiolstræde to **Vor Frue Kirke** (Church of Our Lady), Copenhagen's cathedral since 1924. The site itself has been a place of worship since the 13th century, when Bishop Absalon built a chapel here, but was recon-

structed in neoclassical style after it was destroyed during the
Napoleonic Wars. Inside you can see Thorvaldsen's marble
sculptures of Christ and the Apostles, and Moses and David in
bronze. *Nørregade, Frue Plads, tel. 33/15–10–78. Open Mon.–
Sat. 9–5, Sun. 12–5. Closed during mass.*

㉕ Head north again on Fiolstræde to the main building of
Københavns Universitet (Copenhagen University), constructed
in the 19th century on the site of the medieval bishops' palace.
Past the university, turn right on Krystalgade. On the left is
㉖ the arklike **Københavns Synagoge** (Copenhagen Synagogue),
designed by the noted contemporary architect Gustav
Friederich Hetsch.

㉗ Just across Købmagergade is **Rundetårn** (the round tower),
built as an observatory in 1642 by Christian IV and still maintained as the oldest such structure in Europe. It is said that
Peter the Great of Russia rode a horse alongside his wife, Catherine, who took a carriage up the 600 feet of its smooth, spiral-
ing ramp. You'll have to walk, but the view of the twisted
streets and crooked roofs of old Copenhagen is worth it.
*Købmagergade, tel. 33/93–66–60. Admission: DKr12 adults,
DKr5 children. Open Dec.–Mar., daily 10–5; Apr.–Oct., daily
10–8.*

㉘ Straight down from Rundetårn on Landemærket is Gothersgade and **Kongens Haven** (the King's Garden), with expansive
lawns, park benches, and shady walking paths. Carefully
tended gardens surround **Rosenborg Slot,** the Dutch Renaissance castle built by Christian IV. Intending it first as a summer residence, the king loved the castle so much that he ended
up living, and dying, there. It remained the royal residence until the early 19th century, when it became a museum. It still
contains the crown jewels, as well as a collection of costumes
and royal memorabilia—Christian IV's pearl-studded saddle
and bejeweled tables are showstoppers. In 1849, when the absolute monarchy was abolished, the royal castles became state
property, except for Rosenborg, which is still inherited from
monarch to monarch. *Øster Voldgade 4A, tel. 33/15–32–86. Admission: DKr35 adults, DKr5 children. Open May, daily 11–3;
June–Aug., daily 10–4; Sept.–Oct., daily 11–3; Nov.–Apr.,
Tues., Fri., and Sun. 11–2.*

㉙ Across Øster Voldgade from the palace is **Botanisk Have** (the
Botanical Garden), 25 acres of trees, flowers, ponds, sculptures, and a rather spectacular *Palmehuset* (Palm House) containing tropical and subtropical plants. There's also an
observatory and a geological museum. *Gothersgade 128, tel. 33/
12–74–60. Admission free. Gardens open May–Aug., daily
8:30–6; Sept.–Apr., daily 8:30–4. Palm House open daily
10–3.*

㉚ Leave the gardens through the north exit to get to the **Statens
Museum for Kunst** (National Art Gallery), which is flanked by a
sculpture garden filled with classical, modern, and whimsical
works. The collections range from Danish art to works by Rubens, Dürer, the Impressionists, and Matisse. *Sølvgade 48–50,
tel. 33/91–21–26. Admission: DKr30 adults, children free.
Open Tues.–Sun. 10–4:30.*

㉛ An adjacent building houses **Den Hirschsprungske Samling** (the
Hirschsprung Collection) of 19th-century Danish art. The
modest museum features works from the country's Golden

Age, in particular a group of late-19th-century painters known as the Skagen School, whose illuminated images capture the play of light and water that is so characteristic of the Danish countryside. *Stockholmsgade 20, tel. 31/42–03–36. Admission: DKr20 adults, DKr10 children under 12. Open Wed.–Sat. 1–4, Sun. 11–4.*

Walk back to Nørreport station and take a train to Copenhagen's Main Station. When you exit on Vesterbrogade, make a right and you'll see the city's best-known attraction, **Tivoli.** In the 1840s, Danish architect George Carstensen persuaded a worried King Christian VIII to let him build an amusement park on the edge of the city's fortifications, rationalizing that "when people amuse themselves, they forget politics." In the comparatively short season, from May to September, more than 4 million people come through the gates. Tivoli is more sophisticated than a mere funfair: It boasts a pantomime theater, an open-air stage, elegant restaurants (24 in all), and frequent classical, jazz, and rock concerts. There are also fantastic flower displays both in the lush gardens and floating on the swan-filled ponds. On weekends elaborate fireworks displays are presented, as well as maneuvers by the Tivoli Guard, a youth version of the Queen's Royal Guard. Try to see Tivoli at least once by night, when 100,000 colored lanterns illuminate the Chinese Pagoda and the main fountain. *Vesterbrogade 3, tel. 33/15–10–01. Admission, not including rides: DKr35 adults, DKr18 children. Open end-Apr.–mid-Sept., daily 10 AM–midnight.*

At the southern end of the gardens, on Hans Christian Andersen Boulevard, is the neoclassical **Ny Carlsberg Glyptotek** (New Carlsberg Museum), one of Copenhagen's most imposing museums. Its nucleus is a lush indoor garden—a green sanctuary where you can write a few postcards and relax. From there, start to explore the nooks and chambers that house a vast collection of works by Gauguin and Degas and other Impressionists, as well as an extensive assemblage of Egyptian, Greek, Roman, and French sculpture—and what is considered the best collection of Etruscan art outside Italy and Europe's finest collection of Roman portraits. The museum was a gift to the city from Carl Jacobsen, the son of the founder of the Carlsberg Breweries, and is maintained by the Carlsberg Foundation, one of the largest cultural and scientific benefactors in Denmark. *Dantes Plads 7, tel. 33/91–10–65. Admission: DKr15 adults (free Wed. and Sun.), children free. Open Sept.–Apr., Tues.–Sat. noon–3, Sun. 10–4; May–Aug., Tues.–Sun. 10–4.*

Tucked between St. Jørgens Lake and the main arteries of Vestersøgade and Gammel Kongevej is the **Tycho Brahe Planetarium.** The modern, cylindrical building (which appears to be sliced at an angle) is filled with astronomy exhibits and an Omnimax Theater that takes visitors on a visual journey up through space and down under the seas. *Gammel Kongevej 10, tel. 33/12–12–24. Admission: DKr60. Show times vary. As the answering machine at the planetarium leaves only a Danish message, it is less frustrating to stop by in person.*

Continue down Vesterbrogade into Copenhagen's equivalent of New York's Lower East Side. Populated by many of the city's immigrants, students, and union workers, it's full of ethnic groceries, discount shops, and inexpensive international restaurants. Parallel to it is **Istedgade,** Copenhagen's half-hearted

red-light district, where mom-and-pop kiosks stand side by side with seedy porn shops. Though it's relatively safe, with several fine hotels, avoid it for a late-night stroll.

35 Farther down Vesterbrogade is **Københavns Bymuseum** (Copenhagen City Museum), a 17th-century building flanked by a meticulously maintained model of medieval Copenhagen. Inside there are exhibits chronicling the city's history and a memorial room for philosopher Søren Kierkegaard, the father of existentialism. *Vesterbrogade 59, tel. 31/21–07–72. Admission free. Open May–Sept., Tues.–Sun. 10–4; Oct.–Apr., Tues.–Sun. 1–4.*

Short Excursions from Copenhagen

Eksperimentarium Eight kilometers (6 miles) north of Copenhagen is the beachside town of Hellerup, where the newest attraction is the user-friendly **Eksperimentarium** (Experimentarium). More than 200 exhibitions are clustered in 15 Discovery Islands, each exploring a different facet of science, technology, and natural phenomena with a dozen hands- and body-on exhibits. Visitors can take skeleton-revealing bike rides, measure their lung capacity, stir up magnetic goop, play ball on a jet stream, and gyrate to gyroscopes. Take bus No. 6 from Rådhus Plads or the S-train to Hellerup. *Tuborg Havnevej, tel. 39/27–33–33. Admission: DKr50 adults, DKr35 children under 15. Discounts for combined adult/child admission. Open Mon., Wed., and Fri. 9–6; Tues. and Thurs. 9–9; weekends 11–6.*

Louisiana A world-class collection of modern art is housed in the **Louisiana,** a museum on the "Danish Riviera," the north Sjælland coast. Even if you can't tell a Rauschenberg from a Rembrandt, you should make the 35-kilometer (22-mile) trip to see this elegant rambling structure surrounded by a large park. In the permanent collection, Warhols vie for space with Giacomettis and Picassos. There are contemporary exhibits, as well as concerts and films. In the summer, Danes bring their children and picnic in the sculpture garden and on the banks of the sound. The museum is a half-hour train ride from Copenhagen and a 10-minute walk from the station. It's also accessible by the E4 highway and the more scenic coastal road, Strandvejen. *Gammel Strandvej 13, Humlebæk, tel. 42/19–07–19. Admission: DKr42 adults, children under 16 free. Open Mon., Tues., and Thurs. 10–5; Wed. 10–10, weekends 10–6.*

Dragør On the island of Amager, less than an hour from Copenhagen, is the quaint fishing town of **Dragør** (pronounced Drah-wer). The town's history is separated from the rest of Copenhagen's because it was settled by Dutch farmers in the 16th century. The community was ordered by King Christian II to provide fresh produce and flowers for the royal court. Still meticulously maintained, it has neat rows of white, terra-cotta-tiled houses trimmed with wandering ivy, roses, and the occasional waddling goose. The Dragør Museum, located in one of the oldest houses in town, contains a collection of furniture, costumes, drawings, and model ships. According to local legend, its chimney was built with a twist so that town meetings couldn't be overheard. Take Bus 30 or 33 from Råhuspladsen. *Strandlinien 4, tel. 32/53–41–06. Admission: DKr25. Open Tues.–Fri. 2–5, weekends noon–6.*

Frilandsmuseet Just north of Copenhagen is Lyngby, and the **Frilandsmuseet,** an open-air building museum. About 50 farmhouses representing different periods of Danish history have been painstakingly dismantled, moved, reconstructed, and filled with period furniture and tools. In addition to its historical appeal, the museum is located in a verdant setting of trees and gardens. Bring a lunch and plan to spend the day. Take the S-train to Lyngby Station and then Bus 84 or the train to Sorgenfri Station. When you exit from the stairs, walk right and follow the signs. *Frilandsmuseet. 100 Kongevejen, Lyngby, tel. 42/85-02-92. Admission: DKr20 adults, children free. Open mid-Apr.–Sept., Tues.–Sun. 10–5; Oct.–Nov. 14, Tues.–Sun. 10–3.*

Copenhagen for Free

Many museums in Copenhagen skip admission fees or offer free entrance on certain evenings or days. These museums include the Royal Library (admission free), Frihedsmuseet (admission free), the Ny Carlsberg Glyptotek (admission free Wed. and Sun.), and the Bymuseum (admission free). The **Davids Samling** (Kronprinsessegade 30, tel. 33/13–55–64), which has an unusual exhibition of Islamic art, European handicrafts, and porcelain; the **Royal Copenhagen Museum** (Amagertorv on Strøget 6, tel. 33/13–71–81); and the **Zoological Museum** (Universitetsparken 15, tel. 35/32–10–00), with models and exhibits of animal life, are also free. Of course, the green parks and gardens, which include the Botanical and Kings gardens are free, too, and on a sunny day, priceless.

What to See and Do with Children

Few cities are as accommodating to children and families. Most museums have free or half-price admission for kids, in addition to providing strollers and changing facilities for the smallest travelers. **Tivoli** shouldn't be missed, but as it costs between DKr10 and DKr20 per ride, the most zealous thrill-seekers should buy a **Tur-Pas,** which affords admission and tickets for all rides for about DKr150. Keep your eyes open for the whereabouts of the **Benneweis Circus,** an old-fashioned family-run circus with acrobats, seals, horses, and an army of clowns. Also in town is the **Sømods Bolcher** (Nørregade 36, tel. 33/12–60–46, open Mon.–Fri. 10–5:30 and Sat. 10–1), where hard candy is made the traditional way by pulling and cutting it by hand. Up north, near the Klampenborg train station, Copenhagen's other amusement park, **Bakken** (tel. 31/63–73–00; admission free; open Apr.–Sept., daily noon–midnight) has more old-time fun. Once you arrive at the train station, walk through the lush Dyrehaven (Deer Park) or take a horse-drawn carriage. The park-bound **Zoological Gardens** (Roskildevej 32; tel. 36/30–25–55; admission DKr50 adults, DKr25 children 3–11; open weekdays 9–5, weekends 9–6) boasts more than 2,000 animals and a small petting zoo. There's also the fantasy world of the **Toy Museum** (Valkendorfsgade 13; tel. 33/14–10–09; admission DKr22 adults, DKr12 children; open Sat.–Thurs. 10–4) and **Danmarks Akvarium** (Charlottenlund; tel. 31/62–32–83; admission DKr35 adults, DKr18 children; open daily 10–6).

Off the Beaten Track

If you are nostalgic for the '60s counterculture, head to **Christiania** (at the corner of Prinsessegade and Badsmandsstræde, on Christianshavn), an anarchists' commune founded in 1971 when students occupied army barracks. Giant wall cartoons preach drugs and peace, but the inhabitants are less fond of cameras and picture-taking—which they forbid within the compound.

The **Arbejdermuseet** (Workers Museum; Rømersgade 22, tel. 33/13–01–52; admission DKr25 adults, DKr15 children; open Tues.–Fri. 10–3, weekends 11–4) chronicles the history of the working class from 1850 to the present, with life-size "day-in-the-life-of" exhibits.

W.Ø. Larsens Tobaksmuseet (the W.Ø. Larsen's Tobacco Museum; Amagertorv 9, tel. 33/12–20–50; admission free; open weekdays 9:30–5) exhibits pipes made in every conceivable shape from every conceivable material (including a tiny one not bigger than an embroidery needle), paintings, drawings, and an amazing collection of smoking accoutrements.

The former Danish Surgical Academy is now home of the **Medicinsk Historisk Museum** (Medical History Museum; Bredgade 62, tel. 33/15–25–01; admission free; open Tues., Thurs., and Sat. at 2 for tour in English) and has a small collection of human body parts, primitive surgical apparatus, and other exhibits.

Shopping

Copenhagen seems designed with shoppers in mind. Small, easy to explore on foot, and conveniently crammed with boutiques and specialty stores, the city's core is a showcase for world-famous Danish design and craftsmanship. The best buys are such luxury items as crystal, porcelain, silver, and furs. Look for sales (*tilbud* or *udsalg* in Danish) and check antiques and secondhand shops for classics at cut-rate prices.

Although prices are inflated by a hefty 25% Value Added Tax (Danes call it MOMS), non-EC citizens can receive about a 20% refund (*see* Shopping in Staying in Denmark, *above*). For more details and a list of all tax-free shops, ask at the tourist board for a copy of the *Tax-Free Shopping Guide*.

Shopping Districts/Streets/Malls The pedestrian-only **Strøget** and adjacent **Købmagergade** are *the* shopping streets, but wander down the smaller streets for lower priced, offbeat stores. You'll find the most exclusive shops at the end of Strøget, around **Kongens Nytorv,** and on **Ny Adelgade, Grønnegade,** and **Pistolstræde,** but remember that taxes and transportation costs push designer prices up in Denmark. **Scala,** the city's glittering café- and boutique-studded mall, is across the street from Tivoli and boasts a trendy selection of clothing stores. Farther down, on **Vesterbrogade,** you'll find discount stores—especially leather and clothing shops.

Department Stores **Illums** (Østergade 52, tel. 33/14–40–02), not to be confused with Illums Bolighus (*see* Design, *below*), is a well-stocked department store with a lovely rooftop café. **Magasin** (Kongens Nytorv 13, tel. 33/11–44–33), the largest department store in Scandinavia, occupies nearly an entire block and includes an excellent gourmet grocery.

Street Markets Check with the tourist board or the tourist magazine *Copenhagen This Week* for flea markets. Bargaining is expected. For a good overview of antiques and junk, visit the flea market at **Israels Plads** (near Nørreport Station; open May–Oct., Sat. 8–2). It is run by more than 100 professional dealers, and prices are steep, but there are loads of classic Danish porcelain, silver, jewelry, and crystal, plus books, prints, postcards, and more. Slightly smaller, with lower prices and more junk, are the markets behind **Frederiksberg Rådhus** (Saturday morning) and at **Lyngby Storcenter** near Lyngby Station (every Sunday morning), both in summer.

Specialty Stores For silver, porcelain, and crystal, the well-stocked shops on
Antiques **Bredgade** are upscale and expensive. Visit **Royal Copenhagen Antiques** (Bredgade 11, tel. 33/14–02–29), **Kaabers Antikvariat** (Skindergade 34, tel. 33/15–41–77) for old and rare books and prints, **Branner's Old Book Shop** (Bredgade 10, tel. 33/15–91–87), **Antik 14** (Læderstræde 14, tel. 33/14–41–58) for Oriental antiques, **H. Danielsens** (Læderstræde 11, tel. 33/13–02–74) for silver, Christmas plates, and porcelain, and **Danborg Gold and Silver** (Holbergsgade 17, tel. 33/32–93–94) for estate jewelry and silver flatwear. For furniture, **Ravnsborggade** has dozens of stores that carry traditional pine, oak, and mahogany furniture, in addition to such smaller items as lamps and tableware. (Most sell tax-free and can arrange shipping.) Call the **Association of Antique Dealers in Ravnsborggade** (tel. 35/37–55–33) for information.

Audio Equipment For high-tech design and acoustics, **Bang & Olufsen** (Østergade 3, tel. 33/15–04–22) is so renowned that its products are in the permanent design collection of New York's Museum of Modern Art. You'll find more B&O at **Fredgaard** (Nørre Voldgade 17, tel. 33/13–82–45), near Nørreport Station.

Clothing Retail clothing tends to be expensive and trendy, so stick to the best stores—where you can be sure of the quality. These include: **Brødrene Andersen** (Østergade 7–9, tel. 33/15–15–77), for Hugo Boss, Hermes, and Pringle sweaters for men; **Jens Sørensen** (Vester Voldgade 5, tel. 33/12–26–02) for fine men's and women's clothing and outerwear, and a Burberry's collection; **Petitgas Chapeaux** (Købmagergade 5, tel. 33/13–62–70) for old-fashioned men's hats; and the **Company Store** (Frederiksberggade 24, tel. 33/11–35–55) for trendy, youthful styles. If you are interested in the newest Danish designs, keep your eyes open for cooperatives and designer-owned stores. For inventive, handmade women's clothing by two of the city's best young designers, visit **Met Mari** (Vestergade 11, tel. 33/15–87–25) and **McVerdi** (St. Regnegade 22, tel. 33/15–10–14). Thick traditional patterned and solid Scandinavian sweaters are available at the **Sweater Market** (Frederiksberggade 15, tel. 33/15–27–73), while there's a smaller selection of more modern styles (and loads of gift ideas) at **Artium** (Vesterbrogade 1, tel. 33/12–34–88).

Crystal and Minus the VAT, such Danish classics as Holmegaard crystal and
Porcelain Royal Copenhagen porcelain are less expensive than they are back home. Signed art glass is always more expensive, but be on the lookout for seconds, secondhand, and unsigned pieces. Among the specialists: **Bing & Grøndahl** (a part of Royal Copenhagen) (Amagertorv 6, tel. 33/12–26–86), **Chicago** (Vimmelskaftet 47 on Strøget, tel. 33/12–30–31), **Skandinavisk Glas** (Ny Østergade 4, tel. 33/13–80–95), and **Holmegaards**

Glass (Østergade 15, tel. 33/12–44–77). Both the main Royal Copenhagen shop (Amagertorv 6, tel. 33/13–71–81) and the **Royal Porcelain Factory** (Smallegade 45, tel. 31/86–48–48) have firsts and seconds.

Design   Part gallery, part department store, **Illums Bolighus** (Amagertorv 6, tel. 33/14–19–41) shows off cutting-edge Danish and international design—art glass, porcelain, silverware, carpets, and loads of grown-up toys. **Lysberg, Hansen and Therp** (Bredgade 3, tel. 33/14–47–87), one of the most prestigious interior-design firms in Denmark, has sumptuous showrooms done up in traditional and modern styles. There's also an exquisite gift shop with silk, silver, and leather accessories. **Interieur** (Gothersgade 91, tel. 33/13–15–56) displays fresh Danish style as well as a chic kitchenware shop. Master florist **Tage Andersen** (Ny Adelgade 12, tel. 33/93–09–13) has a fantasy-infused shop and studio filled with one-of-a-kind gifts and arrangements. Browsers (who generally don't purchase the pricey items) are charged a DKr40 admission to the shop, which doubles as a gallery.

Fur   Because of a glut in the international market, fur prices—especially for mink—have dropped dramatically. A SAGA label means that the animals (often mink or fox) are ranched—never trapped in the wild. Furs are graded on a system of Xs, with a 4X being the best. **A.C. Bang** (Østergade 27, tel. 33/15–17–26) is Copenhagen's venerable furrier—and that of the Royal Court since 1817. **Birger Christensen** (Østergade 38, tel. 33/11–55–55) is just slightly less expensive. **Otto D. Madsen** (Vesterbrogade 1, tel. 33/13–41–10), not as chichi, has some of the best prices in town.

Silver   Check the silver standard of a piece by its stamp. Three towers and "925S" (which means 925 parts out of 1,000) mark sterling. Two towers are used for silver plate. The "826S" stamp was used until the 1920s. For the best, visit **Georg Jensen** (Amagertorv 4, tel. 33/11–40–80), an elegant, austere shop aglitter with velvet-cushioned sterling. (The same pieces are available at Royal Copenhagen, down the street, which owns Georg Jensen.) **Peter Krog** (4 Bredgade, tel. 33/12–45–55), **Ketti Hartogsohn** (Palægade 8, tel. 33/15–53–98), and the **English Silver House** (Pilestræde 4, tel. 33/14–83–81) are excellent for used silver at prices 20% to 40% lower. Also visit the city's largest (and brightest) silver store, **Sølvkælderen** (Kompagnistræde 1, tel. 33/13–36–34). The **Tin Centret** (Pewter Center; Ny Østergade 2, tel. 33/14–82–00) has a huge selection of mostly new Scandinavian and European pewter, and a small selection of secondhand pieces.

Sports and Fitness

Participant Sports   Copenhagen is a cyclist's city. Bike rentals (DKr100–DKr200
Bicycling   deposit and DKr30–DKr50 per day) are available throughout the city (*see* Getting Around, *above*), and most roads have bike lanes. Follow all traffic signs and signals; bicycle lights must be used at night. For more information, contact the **Dansk Cyclist Forbund** (Danish Cyclist Federation, Rømersgade 7, tel. 33/32–31–21).

Golf   Denmark's best course (where international tournaments are played) is the 18-hole **Rungsted Golf Klub** (Vestre Stationsvej 16, tel. 42/86–34–44), with a 24 handicap for men and 29 for

women. The 18-hole **Københavns Golf Klub** (Dyrehaven 2, tel. 31/63–04–83) is said to be Scandinavia's oldest. Admission (greens fees, DKr150–DKr200) must be reserved at least two days in advance—longer in the summer.

Health and Fitness Clubs A day pass for weights and aerobics at the **Fitness Club** is DKr65 (Vesterbrogade at Scala, tel. 33/32–10–02). **Form og Figur** (Form and Figure) offers one-hour aerobic classes for DKr80 at the SAS Globetrotter Hotel in Amager (Engvej 171, tel. 31/55–00–70), and weights, treadmill, and stationary bikes for DKr75 at the SAS Scandinavia Hotel (Amager Boulevard 70, tel. 31/54–28–88) and Øbro-Hallen (Ved Idrætsparken 1, tel. 35/26–79–39).

Horseback Riding You can ride at the **Dyrehavebakken** (Deer Forest Hills) in Lyngby, at the **Fortunens Ponyudlejning** (Pony Rental) (Ved-Fortunen 33, tel. 45/87–60–58). A 50-minute session, where both experienced and inexperienced riders go out with a guide, costs DKr75.

Jogging The 6-kilometer (4-mile) loop around the three swan-filled lakes just west of the center of the city—**St. Jorgens, Peblinge,** and **Sortedams**—is a runner's heaven. There are also paths at the **Rosenborg Have, Frederiksberg Garden** (near Frederiksberg Station, at the corner of Frederiksberg Allé and Pile Allé), and the **Dyrehaven** north of the city near Klampenborg.

Swimming Swimming is very popular and pools are crowded but well maintained. Separate bath tickets can also be purchased. Local pools (admission: DKr20–DKr40) include **Frederiksberg Svømmehal** (Helgesvej 29, tel. 38/88–00–71), **Øbro Hallen** (Ved Idrætsparken 3, tel. 31/42–30–65), **Vesterbro Svømmehal** (Angelgade 4, tel. 31/22–05–10), and **Lyngby Svømmehal** (Lundoftevej 53, tel. 45/87–44–56).

Tennis Courts for guests are very expensive, often including court rental (DKr75 per person) and a separate nonmembers' user fee (as high as DKr130). If you are still interested, courts (open to guests before 1 PM only) are available at **Københavns Boldklub** (PeterBangs Vej 147, tel. 31/71–41–50), **Hellerup Idræts Klub** (Hartmannsvej 37, tel. 31/62–14–28), the **Skovshoved Idræts Forening** (Krørsvej 5A, tel. 31/64–23–83), and the **Gentofte Tennis Club** (Skolevej 36, tel. 31/68–26–63).

Spectator Sports *Soccer* Danish soccer fans call themselves *Rolegans* (which loosely translates as well-behaved fans), as opposed to hooligans, and idolize the national team's soccer players as superstars. When the rivalry is most intense (especially against Sweden and Norway), fans don face paint, wear head-to-toe red-and-white, incessantly wave the *Dannebrog* (Danish flag), and have a good time whether or not they win. The biggest stadium in town for national and international games is **Parken** (P.H. Lings Allé 2, tel. 35/27–81–00). Tickets (DKr100 for standing room, DKr200 for seats) can be bought at the gates.

Beaches

North of Copenhagen along the old beach road, **Strandvejen,** there's a string of lovely old seaside towns and beaches. The **Bellevue beach** (across the street from Klampenborg Station) is packed with locals and also has cafés, kiosks, and surfboard rentals, while **Charlottelund** (Bus 6 from Rådhusplads) is a bit

more private. **Vedbæk,** farther north, is less crowded. The summer water temperature along this coast is 65°–68°F.

Dining

Food is one of the great pleasures of a stay in Copenhagen, a
city with more than 2,000 restaurants. Traditional Danish fare
spans all price categories: You can order a light lunch of traditional *smørrebrød* (sandwiches), munch alfresco from a street-
side *pølser* (sausage) cart, or dine out on Limfjord oysters and
local plaice. Even the most upscale restaurants have moderate-
price fixed menus, but the cost of wine increases totals enor-
mously. Happily, the local Tuborg and Carlsberg beers complement the traditional fare better than wine.

The Danes are Francophiles when it comes to fine dining, and
many restaurants are fond of combining fresh, local ingredients with French preparation. The city's more affordable ethnic restaurants are concentrated in Vesterbro, Nørrebro, and
the side streets off Strøget.

Highly recommended restaurants are indicated by a star ★.

Very Expensive   **Gyldne Fortun's Fiskekælderc.** Among the city's finest seafood
restaurants, this "fish cellar" is brightly decorated with sea-
shell-shaded halogen lamps and aquariums. Across the street
from Christiansborg (the Parliament), it is popular with politi-
cians as well as businesspeople. Specialties include fillets of
Scandinavian sole poached in white wine, stuffed with salmon
mousseline, served with prawns—and finally glazed with hollandaise. *Ved Stranden 18, tel. 33/12–20–11. Reservations required. Dress: casual but neat. AE, DC, MC, V. No weekend
lunch. Closed Dec. 24–26 and 30, Jan. 1, Easter.*
Kong Hans. Five centuries ago this was a Nordic vineyard, but
now it's one of Scandinavia's finest restaurants. Chef Daniel
Letz's French-inspired cuisine uses the freshest local and
French ingredients, while the setting is subterranean and mysterious, with whitewashed walls and arched ceilings. Try the
airy duck-liver mousse, surrounded by fresh tomato purée, or
the oysters Charentaise. *Vingårdstræde 6, tel. 33/11–68–68.
Reservations advised. Jacket advised. AE, DC, MC, V. No
lunch. Closed mid-July–mid-Aug., Dec. 24–25, and Sun.*
Krogs. This elegant canal-front restaurant commands a loyal
clientele—both foreign and local. It is decorated with mirrored
ceilings and paintings of old Copenhagen on the pale-green
walls. The menu (printed in five languages) includes such specialties as Canadian lobster flambé, as well as poached Norwegian salmon served with spinach, cranberries, and saffron.
*Gammel Strand 38, tel. 33/15–89–15. Jacket advised. Reserva-
tions required. AE, DC, MC, V. Closed Dec. 24–Jan. 1.*

★ **Skt. Gertrudes Kloster.** The history of this medieval monastery
goes back 600 years, when even then, its vaulted stone interiors welcomed tradesmen and wayfarers. The dining room
is bedecked with hundreds of icons, the only light provided
by 1,500 candles. The French menu is extensive, with such
specials as fresh fillet of halibut steamed in oyster sauce and
l'Alsace duck breast in sherry vinaigrette. *32 Hauser Plads,
tel. 33/14–66–30. Reservations required. Jacket and tie
advised. AE, DC, MC, V. No lunch. Closed Dec. 24–Jan. 1
and Easter.*

Dining

Bacchullus, **9**
Café Restaurant
Philippe, **8**
Els, **11**
Fiskekælderen, **24**
Flyvefisken, **21**
Gyldne Fortun's
Fiskekældere, **24**
Havfruen, **16**
Ida Davidsen, **7**
Kasmir, **2**
Kommandanten, **10**
Kong Hans, **25**
Krogs, **23**
La Brasserie, **15**
L'Alsace, **14**
Pakhuskælderen, **26**
Peder Oxe, **13**
Quattro Fontane, **1**
Riz Raz, **22**
Skt. Gertrudes
Kloster, **6**

Lodging

Ascot, **19**
Copenhagen
Admiral, **17**
Copenhagen Star, **30**
D'Angleterre, **15**
Hotel Cab-Inn, **3**
Kong Frederik, **20**
Missionhotellet
Nebo, **29**
Neptun, **12**
Nyhavn 71, **25**
Plaza, **28**
SAS Scandinavia, **31**
Sheraton, **18**
Skovshoved, **4**
Triton, **27**
Viking, **5**

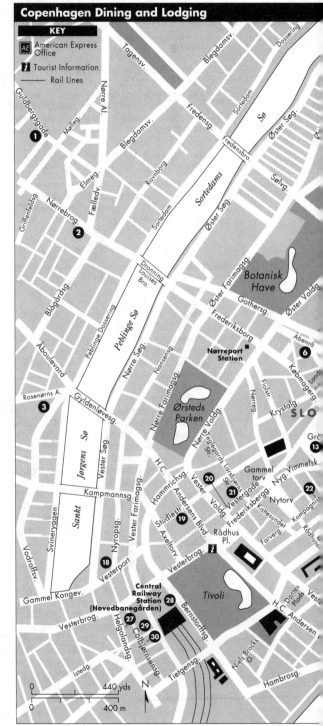

Copenhagen Dining and Lodging

KEY

🅰🅴 American Express Office

ℹ️ Tourist Information

— Rail Lines

Expensive **Els.** When it opened in 1853, the intimate Els was the place to be seen before the theater, and the painted muses on the walls still watch diners rush to make an eight o'clock curtain. The antique wooden columns and furniture complement owner and chef Ole Mathiesen's nouvelle Danish/French menu. It changes daily and incorporates game, fish, and market produce. *Store Strandestræde 3, tel. 33/14–13–41. Reservations advised. Jacket advised. AE, DC, MC, V. Closed Dec. 24 and 31.*

Kommandanten. Fancifully decorated by master florist Tage Andersen, with brushed iron and copper furniture, down pillows and foliage-flanked lights, this is among the city's most chic dinner spots, attracting well-heeled businesspeople and local celebrities. The adventuresome international fare includes rabbit with bouillon-cooked lentils, herbs, and bacon, and marinated salmon with oysters and parsley. *Ny Adelgade 7, tel. 33/ 12–09–90. Reservations advised. Jacket advised. AE, DC, MC, V. Closed Sat. lunch, Sun.*

★ **L'Alsace.** Set in the cobbled courtyard of Pistolstræde and hung with paintings by Danish surrealist Wilhelm Freddie, this restaurant is peaceful and quiet, attracting such diverse diners as Queen Margrethe, Elton John, and Pope Paul II. The hand-drawn menu lists oysters from Brittany, terrine de foie gras, and choucrôute à la Strasbourgeois (a hearty mélange of cold cabbage, homemade sausage, and pork, among other specialties). Ask to sit in the patio overlooking the courtyard. *Ny Østergade 9, tel. 33/14–57–43. Reservations advised. Dress: casual but neat. AE, DC, MC, V. Closed Sun. and holidays.*

La Brasserie. This is where Copenhagen's see-and-be-seen set come to eat, drink, and mingle. Diners enjoy French-inspired food in charming bistro surroundings under a giant illuminated clock. During lunch there's a smørrebrød menu, while at night the vivacious crowds relish such à la carte items as antipasto, salads, escargot, sautéed duck liver, and more substantial entrées. *Hotel D'Angleterre, Kongens Nytorv 34, tel. 33/32–01– 22. Reservations advised. Dress: casual but neat. AE, DC, MC, V. Closed Sun.*

Pakhuskælderen. Surrounded by thick white walls and raw timbers, Nyhavn 71 hotel's intimate restaurant attracts a mix of business and holiday guests. Known for his fresh seafood classics, Chef Finn Lytje often accompanies fresh fish with light cream sauces. Baked red mullet soufflé with lobster meat, and roast venison with homemade herb noodles and horseradish cream are among his best creations. There's also an excellent Danish buffet at lunch. *Nyhavn 71, tel. 33/11–85–85. Reservations required. Dress: casual but neat. AE, DC, MC, V.*

Moderate **Cafe Restaurant Philippe.** Checkered tablecloths and corny
★ French music, Francophiles and love-struck couples supply this cozy restaurant with Gallic ambience. The Franco-Danish kitchen serves hearty warm salads, fresh fish, and meat. Try the warm goat-cheese salad followed by duck thigh stuffed with truffles in a cognac sauce. *Gråbrødretorv 2, tel. 33/32–92–92. Reservations advised. Dress: casual but neat. AE, DC, MC, V. Closed Sun. lunch and Dec. 23–Jan. 1.*

Havfruen. A life-size wooden mermaid swings decorously from the ceiling in this small, rustic fish restaurant in Nyhavn. Natives love the cozy, maritime-bistro air and come for the daily changing French-and-Danish menu, which utilizes cream

sauces and fresh salmon, turbot, and cod. *Nyhavn 39, tel. 33/11–11–38. Reservations advised. Dress: casual. DC, MC, V.*

Ida Davidsen. Five generations old, this world-renowned lunch spot is synonymous with smørrebrød. Dimly lit, with worn wooden tables and photographs of famous visitors, it's usually packed. Creative sandwiches include the H. C. Andersen with liver pâté, bacon, and tomatoes and the airplane clipper—steak tartare shaped like a plane and topped with caviar, smoked salmon, and egg yolk. *Store Kongensgade 70, tel. 33/91–36–55. Reservations required. Dress: casual. DC, MC, V. No dinner. Closed weekends, July, and Dec. 24–Jan. 1.*

Peder Oxe. Located on a historic square, this lively bistro is countrified, with rustic antiques and 15th-century Portuguese tiles. All entrées, which include grilled steaks and fish—and the best burgers in town—come with an excellent self-service salad bar. Damask-covered tables are set with heavy cutlery and opened bottles of hearty Pyrenées wine. A clever call-light for the waitress is above each table. *Gråbrødretorv 11, tel. 33/11–00–77. Reservations advised. Dress: casual. D, MC, V. Closed Dec. 24–26 and Jan. 1.*

Inexpensive **Bacchullus.** Located off Strøget on a small courtyard, Bacchullus is fashionably rustic and a mecca for the health-conscious. Well-dressed bohemians duck in here for the classical music and the vegetarian choices such as hummus and warm pita bread, organic pizza, stuffed eggplants, and other healthful options from a buffet that relies heavily on grains, natural sweeteners, fresh fruit, and vegetables. *Grønnegade 12–14, tel. 33/15–16–90. No reservations. Dress: casual. AE, DC, MC, V. Closed Sun. lunch.*

Flyvefisken. Silvery stenciled fish swim along blue-and-yellow walls in this funky vegetarian eatery. More experimental than Bacchullus (*see below*), the constantly changing daily menu makes use of salads, nuts, legumes, and fish. Popular specialties include an apple-beet salad, vegetable burgers, and salmon with shiitake mushrooms. *Lars Bjørnstræde 18, tel. 33/14–95–15. No reservations. Dress: casual. No credit cards. Closed Sat. evening, Sun., and holidays.*

Kasmir. This quiet, carpet-shrouded Indian restaurant is a favorite with locals, who come for the unusual vegetarian and fish menu. Specialties include tandoori-fried salmon, a hearty lentil soup, and the basic side dishes—such as *bhajis* (fried vegetables in a tomato sauce), *raita* (yogurt and cucumbers), and *nan* (thick round bread). *Nørrebrogade 35, tel. 35/37–54–71. Reservations advised on weekend. Dress: casual but neat. AE, MC, V. Closed Dec. 24–25.*

Quattro Fontane. On a corner west of the lakes, one of Copenhagen's best Italian restaurants is a busy, noisy, two-story affair, packed tight with marble-topped tables and a steady flow of young Danes. Served by chatty Italian waiters, the homemade food includes cheese or beef ravioli or cannelloni, linguine with clam sauce, and thick pizza. Leave room for the totally immoral ice cream or take some with you from the carry-out in Frederiksberg (Falkonér Allé 42, tel. 31/39–49–82). *Guldbergsgade 3, tel. 31/39–39–31. Reservations advised. Dress: casual. No credit cards.*

★ **Riz Raz.** Located on a corner off Strøget, this Middle Eastern restaurant hops with young locals, who pack it to bursting on weekends. The all-you-can-eat buffet is heaped with lentils, tomatoes and potatoes, olives, hummus, warm pita bread, *kufte*

(Middle Eastern meatballs), yogurt and cucumbers, pickled vegetables, bean salads, and occasionally pizza. *Kompagnistræde 20, tel. 33/15–05–75. Reservations advised (required on weekend). Dress: casual. DC, MC, V. Closed Dec. 24–25 and Jan. 1.*

Lodging

Copenhagen is well served by a wide range of hotels, but overall, they are among Europe's most expensive. The hotels around the seedy red-light district of Istedgade (which looks more dangerous than it is) are the least expensive. During summer, reservations are recommended, but should you arrive without one, try the hotel booking desk in the tourist office. This service will also locate rooms in private homes, with rates starting at DKr140 for a single. Young travelers should head for **Huset** (Rådhusstræde 13, tel. 33/15–65–18); after hours, check the bulletin board outside for suggestions on accommodations. Breakfast is included in the room rate at the following hotels unless otherwise indicated.

Highly recommended establishments are indicated by a star ★.

Very Expensive **D'Angleterre.** Just off Kongens Nytorv, the city's finest hotel
★ welcomes royalty and rock stars in palatial surroundings. Behind its imposing New Georgian facade is an English-style sitting room, while standard guest rooms are furnished in pastels, with overstuffed chairs and modern and antique furniture. The spit-and-polish staff accommodates every wish. *Kongens Nytorv 34, 1050 KBH K, tel. 33/12–00–95, fax 33/12–11–18. 130 rooms with bath, 28 suites. Facilities: 2 restaurants, bar, 24-hour room service, concierge, meeting rooms, shops, parking. Breakfast not included. AE, DC, MC, V.*

Nyhavn 71. Located in a 200-year-old warehouse, this quiet hotel is a good choice for privacy-seekers. It overlooks the old ships of Nyhavn and the maritime interiors have been preserved with the original thick plaster walls and exposed brick. The rooms are tiny but cozy, with warm woolen spreads, dark woods, soft leather furniture, and crisscrossing timbers. *Nyhavn 71, 1051 KBH K, tel. 33/11–85–85, fax 33/93–15–85. 82 rooms with bath, 6 suites. Facilities: restaurant, bar, room service, concierge, small meeting rooms, parking. Breakfast not included. AE, DC, MC, V.*

SAS Scandinavia. Near the airport, this is one of northern Europe's largest hotels, and Copenhagen's token skyscraper. An immense lobby, with cool, recessed lighting and streamlined furniture, gives access to the city's first (and only) casino. The guest rooms are large and somewhat institutional but offer every modern convenience: It is a good choice if you prefer convenience to character. *Amager Blvd. 70, 2300 KBH S, tel. 33/11–24–23, fax 31/57–01–93. 543 rooms with bath, 52 suites. Facilities: 3 restaurants, bar, casino, health club, pool, sauna, solarium, room service, concierge, meeting rooms, shops, parking. Breakfast not included. AE, DC, MC, V.*

Expensive **Copenhagen Star.** One of the city's newest, this hotel looks as trendy as Danish hotels can get. A few steps from the main train station, its frescoed and neon exterior stands out in the dingy neighborhood. Inside, the reception area and the nearby bar are art-directed with streamlined teak tables, leather

chairs, and granite pillars. Cool purple spreads and furniture are in the slick rooms. Downstairs there's a sunny breakfast restaurant. *Colbjørnsensgade 13, 1652 KBH V, tel. 31/22–11–00, fax 31/22–21–99. 134 rooms with bath, 3 suites. Facilities: bar, meeting rooms. AE, DC, MC, V. Closed Dec. 24–Jan. 2.*

Kong Frederik. West of Rådhus Pladsen and a two-minute walk from Strøget, this intimate hotel has the same British style as its sister hotels, the D'Angleterre and Plaza. The difference is the sun-drenched Queen's Garden restaurant, where a hearty hot and cold morning buffet is served in addition to lunch and dinner. The rooms are elegant, with Oriental vases, mauve carpets, and plain blue spreads. Ask for a top room, with a view of the city's towers. *Vester Voldgade 25, 1552 KBH V, tel. 33/12–59–02, fax 33/93–59–01. 110 rooms with bath, 13 suites. Facilities: restaurant, bar, room service, meeting rooms, parking. Breakfast not included. AE, DC, MC, V.*

★ **Neptun.** Recently expanded, this elegant, centrally situated hotel was bought years ago with the intention of making it the bohemian gathering place of Copenhagen, but proprietress Bente Noyens has also made it practical. The lobby and lounge are light, with slender furnishings and peach schemes, and next door there's a fine restaurant. The rooms are posh, with thoughtful details—such as pivotal desk and bed lights and bathroom-floor heating. *Skt. Annæ Plads 14–20, 1250 KBH K, tel. 33/13–89–00, fax 33/14–12–50. (In the United States, call Best Western, at 800/528–1234.) 137 rooms with bath, 14 suites. Facilities: restaurant, solarium, 24-hour room service, meeting rooms, parking, AE, DC, MC, V. Closed Dec. 22–Jan. 2.*

Plaza. The smallest of Copenhagen's three Royal Classic hotels, the Plaza is more modest than the D'Angleterre or Kong Frederik but attracts the likes of Tina Turner and Keith Richards. Close to Tivoli and the main station, the building opens with a stately lobby and the adjacent Russian restaurant, Alexander Nevski. The older rooms are scattered with antiques, while newer ones are furnished in a more modern style. *Bernstorffsgade 4, 1577 KBH V, tel. 33/14–92–62, fax 33/93–93–62. 93 rooms with bath, 6 suites. Facilities: restaurant, bar, room service, concierge, small meeting rooms, parking. Breakfast not included. AE, DC, MC, V. Closed Dec. 23–Jan. 2.*

Sheraton. Near the Tycho Brahe Planetarium and Lake District, this 18-story hotel offers impeccable service and standard Sheraton-style decor. The lobby is modern and vast, with dim lighting, plants, and leather sofas, while the rooms are generous and bright, done up in mint and peach and furnished with modern, gray wooden furniture. *Vester Søgade 6, 1601 KBH V, tel. 33/14–35–35, fax 33/32–12–23. 471 rooms with bath, 35 suites. Facilities: 2 restaurants, piano bar, massage and beauty services, sauna, solarium, 24-hour room service, nonsmoking floor, concierge, meeting rooms, shops, parking. AE, DC, MC, V.*

Moderate **Ascot.** Recently renovated, this charming downtown building features a wrought–iron staircase and an excellent breakfast buffet. The lobby has been classically remodeled in marble and columns, while the recently refurbished guest rooms remain cozy, with modern furniture and bright colors; a few have kitchenettes. *Studiestræde 61, 1554 KBH V, tel. 33/12–60–00, fax 33/14–60–40. 133 rooms with bath, 5 suites, 10 apartments.*

Facilities: restaurant, bar, meeting rooms, parking. AE, DC, MC, V.

Copenhagen Admiral. A five-minute stroll from Nyhavn, overlooking old Copenhagen and Amalienborg, the monolithic Admiral was once a grain warehouse but now affords travelers nononsense accommodation. With massive stone walls, broken by rows of tiny windows, it's one of the less expensive top hotels, cutting frills and prices. The guest rooms are spare, with jutting beams and modern prints. *Toldbodgade 24–28, 1253 KBH K, tel. 33/11–82–82, fax 33/32–55–42. 365 rooms with bath, 52 suites. Facilities: restaurant, bar, nightclub, sauna, solarium, meeting rooms, shop, parking. Breakfast not included. AE, MC, V.*

Triton. Despite its seedy surroundings, this streamlined hotel attracts a cosmopolitan clientele thanks to a central location in Vesterbro. The large rooms, in blond wood and warm tones, have all been updated with new bathrooms and state-of-the-art fixtures. The buffet breakfast is exceptionally generous, the staff friendly. There are also family rooms, with separate bedroom and foldout couch. *Helgolandsgade 7–11, 1653 KBH V, tel. 31/31–32–66, fax 31/31–69–70. 123 rooms with bath, 2 suites, 4 family rooms. Facilities: bar, meeting room. AE, DC, MC, V.*

Inexpensive **Hotel Cab–Inn.** This bright hotel is just west of the lakes and Vesterport Station. Guests enter an artful stenciled foyer and are checked in by a young and helpful staff. The impeccably maintained rooms are consciously small but are designed with superefficiency to include ample showers, stowaway and bunk beds, and even electric water kettles. The hotel is popular with business travelers in winter and kroner-pinching backpackers and families in summer. *Vodroffsvej 55–57, 1900 Frederiksberg C, tel. 35/36–11–11, fax 35/36–11–14. 201 rooms with shower. Facilities: breakfast restaurant, snack shop, meeting rooms. AE, DC, MC, V.*

★ **Missionhotellet Nebo.** This budget hotel is located between the main train station and Istedgade's seediest porn shops. The dubious location has no effect on the prim hotel, which is comfortable and well maintained by a friendly staff. The dormlike guest rooms are furnished with industrial carpeting, polished pine furniture, and gray-striped duvet covers. There are baths, showers, and toilets at the center of each hallway, and downstairs there's a breakfast restaurant with a tiny courtyard. *Istedgade 6, 1650 KBH V, tel. 31/21–12–17, fax 31/23–47–74. 96 rooms, 40 with bath. AE, DC, MC, V.*

Skovshoved. A delightful inn 8 kilometers (5 miles) north of town, the Skovshoved is neighbors with a few old fishing cottages beside the yacht harbor. Licensed since 1660, it has retained its provincial charm, though it is fully modernized. Rooms differ—some overlook the sea, while small ones rim the courtyard. *Strandvejen 267, 7920 Charlottelund, tel. 31/64–00–28, fax 31/64–06–72. 20 rooms with bath. Facilities: restaurant, bar, meeting room. AE, DC, MC, V.*

Viking. A comfortable, century-old former mansion near Amalienborg, Nyhavn, and Langelinie, this hotel is close to most sights and Strøget—making it a favorite for inner-city guests. Though the halls are decorated with antiques, the rooms are filled with '60s and '70s furniture. Despite the dated decor, they are clean, comfortable, and spacious. *Bredgade 65, 1260 KBH K, tel. 33/12–45–50, fax 33/12–46–18. 90 rooms, 22*

with shower. Facilities: breakfast restaurant, 24-hour bar, small meeting room, parking. AE, DC, MC. Closed Dec. 22– Jan. 2.

There are also two **hostels** in the Copenhagen area. The **Bellahøj Hostel** (tel. 31/28–97–15) is 4.5 kilometers (3 miles) outside of town. Take Bus 2 from Rådhusplads, marked either "Bellahøj" or "Brønshoj." The **Amager Hostel** (tel. 32/52–29– 08), which is the same distance out of town, is close to the airport. From Rådhusplads, take Bus 16 and change to Bus 37 at Mozartplads.

The Arts and Nightlife

The Arts The most complete English calendar of events is included in the tourist magazine *Copenhagen This Week* and includes musical and theatrical events, as well as films and exhibitions. Concert and festival information is available from the **Dansk Musik Information Center** (Vimmelskaftet 48, tel. 33/11–20–66). The free newspaper *Neon Guiden* is available in most record shops, cafés, and the tourist office, and lists rock, pop, and jazz concerts, as well as restaurants and events. Copenhagen's main theater and concert season runs from September through May, and tickets can be obtained either directly from theaters and concert halls or from ticket agencies. Box offices include **Arte** (64 Hvidkilevej, tel. 38/88–49–00), **Scala** (2 Axeltorv, no tel.), **Fiolstræde/Nørregade Kiosk** for half-price tickets on the day of the performance (opposite Norreport Station, no tel.), **Montmartre** (Nørregade 41, tel. 33/13–69–66), and **Tivoli Billetcenter** (Vesterbrogade 3, tel. 33/15–10–12).

Opera, Ballet, and Theater Tickets at the **Kongelige Teater** (Royal Theater, tel. 33/14–10– 02) are reasonably priced at DKr140–DKr230; the season is October to May. It is home to the Royal Danish Ballet, one of the premier companies of the world. Not as famous but also accomplished are the Royal Danish Opera and the Royal Danish Orchestra, the latter of which performs in all productions. Plays are exclusively in Danish. For information and reservations, call the theater. For English-language theater, attend a performance at the **Mermaid Theater** (27 Skt. Peder Stræde, tel. 33/11–43–03).

Film Films open in Copenhagen a few months to a year after their U.S. premier. Nonetheless the Danes are avid viewers, willing to pay DKr60 per ticket, wait in lines for premiers, and read subtitles. Monday nights are traditionally half price, but tickets go fast. Call the theater for a reservation and pick up tickets (which include a seat number) an hour before the movie. Most theaters have a café, so it's not hard to sit back and people-watch before the show. Among the city's alternative venues are **Vester Vov Vov** (Absalonsgade 5, tel. 31/24–42–00) and the **Grand** (Mikkel Bryggersgade 8, 33/15–16–11), all of which tend to include arty and foreign films—which are naturally subtitled in Danish.

Nightlife Most nightlife is concentrated in the area in and around **Strøget,** though there are student and "left" cafés and bars in **Nørrebro,** and more upscale and alternative spots in **Østerbro.** Many restaurants, cafés, bars, and clubs stay open after midnight, a few until 5 AM. Copenhagen used to be famous for jazz, but unfortunately that has changed over the past couple of years, with many of the best clubs closing down. However, you'll find

night spots catering to almost all musical tastes, from bop to ball-room music—and for the younger crowd, house and rap clubs soundtracked by local DJs. The area around Nikolaj Kirke boasts the highest concentration of trendy discos and dance spots, with cover prices averaging DKr40.

Bars and Lounges　Business travelers flock to **Fellini** (SAS Royal Hotel, 1 Ham-merichsgade, 33/93–32–39) to dance, mingle, drink outra-geously expensive booze, and ogle the not-so-risqué dancers. **Peder Oxe's** basement (Gråbrødretorv 11, tel. 33/11–11–93) is much more casual and young, though nearly impossible to squeeze into on late weekends. The **Library,** located in the Pla-za Hotel (4 Bernstorffsgade, tel. 33/14–92–62), is an elegant and romantic spot for a quiet drink, whereas the more than 270-year-old **Hviids Vinstue** (Kongens Nytorv 19, 33/15–10–64) at-tracts all kinds, young and old, single and coupled, for a glass of wine or cognac. **Vin & Ølgod** (Skindergade 45, tel. 33/13–26–25) is where the same crowd goes to sing, drink vast quantities of beer, and link arms for old-fashioned dancing to corny swing bands.

Cafés　Café life appeared in Copenhagen in the '70s and quickly be-came a compulsory part of its urban existence. The cheapest sit-down eateries in town, with a cappuccino and sandwich of-ten costing less than DKr40, cafés are lively and relaxed at night. **Café Sommersko** (Kronprinsensgade 6, tel. 33/14–81–89) is the granddaddy, attracting an eclectic crowd during the day and night. **Krasnapolsky** (Vestergade 10, tel. 33/32–88–00) packs a young, hip, and excruciatingly well-dressed audience at night, a more mixed group for its quiet afternoons. **Café Dan Turrell** (Skt. Regnegade 3, tel. 33/14–10–47), another old café, is as mixed as Sommersko and a favorite with students and in-tellectuals. **Victors Café** (Ny Østergade 8, tel. 33/13–36–13) is all brass and dark wood, lovely for a light lunch. Among the newer cafés is the very chic **Europa** (Amagertorv 1, tel. 33/14–28–09), where the people-watching and coffee far surpass the fare.

Casinos　Casinos are new to Denmark, having just opened in 1991. The **Casino Copenhagen** is at the SAS Scandinavia (Amager Boulevarden 70, tel. 33/11–51–15), with American and French roulette, blackjack, baccarat, and slot machines. Admission is DKr40 (and you must show a photo I.D.), and the casino is open 4 PM to 2 AM.

Discos and Dancing　Most discos open at 11 PM, have a cover charge (about DKr40), and pile on steep drink prices. Among the popular clubs: **Anna-bel's** (Lille Kongensgade 16, tel. 33/11–20–20) is young and up-scale, while **Jarlen** (Kompagnistræde 18) is more casual, with an English-style bar downstairs, a disco upstairs. At **Axel's** (in Scala on Vesterbrogade, tel. 33/13–03–78), which has three bars and a large dance floor, chic attendees run tabs on cards that work like temporary credit cards, then pay up when they exit. **Privé** (Ny Østergade 14, tel. 33/13–75–20) attracts a hip, young, well-dressed (tie included) crowd who come for the rock and disco. At **Woodstock** (Vestergade 12, tel. 33/11–20–71) a mixed audience grooves to music of the '60s. **Søpavillionen** (Gyldenløvesgade 24, tel. 33/15–12–24) between St. Jørgen's and Peblinge lakes glows white on the outside, with pop and disco for an older crowd inside. There's also the **Røde Pimpernel** (Hans Christian Andersen Blvd. 7, tel. 33/12–20–32), where an

adult audience gathers for dancing to live orchestras, trios, and old-time music.

Gay Bars For more information, call or visit the **Lesbiske og Bøsser Landsforening** (Lesbian and Gay Association; Knabostræde 3, Box 1023, 1007 KBH K, tel. 33/13–19–48), which also has a café, bookshop, and more than 45 years of experience. Check the local free paper *Pan* for listings of nightlife events and clubs, or call the **Gay and Lesbian Information Hotline** (tel. 33/13–01–12).

The **Amigo Bar** (Schønbergsgade 4, tel. 31/21–49–15) serves light meals and is popular with men of all ages but shouldn't be confused with the mammoth **Club Amigo** (Studiostræde 31A, tel. 33/15–33–32), which includes a sauna, solarium, and cinema as well as two discos, **After Dark** and **Metro**. The **Pan Club** (Knabrostræde 3, tel. 33/32–49–08) is the biggest gay disco in town, with two dance floors. The **Stable Bar** (Teglgårdsstræde 3, tel. 33/12–73–03) and the **Cosy Bar** (Studiestræde 24, tel. 33/12–74–27) are the motorcycle and leather clubs. **Sebastian Bar Café** (Hyskenstræde 10, tel. 33/32–22–79) is laid back for a drink or coffee. **Babooshka** (Turesensgade 6, tel. 33/15–05–36) is a cozy lesbian café that welcomes men.

Jazz Clubs Hard times have thinned Copenhagen's once-thriving jazz scene. Among the clubs still open, most headline local names, though European and international artists also perform, especially in June, when the Copenhagen Jazz Festival spills over into the clubs. **Copenhagen Jazz House** is upscale (Niels Hemmingsens Gade 10, tel. 33/15–26–00), while **La Fontaine** (Kompagnistræde 11, tel. 33/11–60–98) is more local in terms of both artists and audience. **Tivoli's Jazzhus Slukefter** (Bernstorffsgade 1, tel. 33/11–11–13) attracts some of the biggest names in the world, but it's only open during the summer.

Rock Clubs Copenhagen has a good selection of rock clubs, most of which cost less than DKr40. Almost all are filled with young, fashionable crowds. **Montmartre** (Nørregade 41, tel. 33/12–78–36) attracts international and Scandinavian rock and occasionally jazz greats, often at ticket prices of upwards of DKr145. **Cafe'en Funk** (Blegdamsvej 2, tel. 31/35–17–41) plays hardcore funk, while **Pumpehuset** (Studiestræde 52, tel. 33/93–19–60) plays rap and rock. **Huset** (Rådhusstræde 13, tel. 33/32–00–66) has two venues under the same roof: **Musikcafeen** hosts international rock, soul, reggae, and funk groups; **Bar Bue** is the place for experimental Danish and European rock.

Sjælland and Its Islands

The goddess Gefion is said to have carved Sjælland (Zealand) from Sweden. If she did, she must have wrestled with the north, slicing it deep with a fjord, while she chopped the south to pieces and left the sides bowing west. Though the coasts are dramatically serrated, Gefion's myth is more dramatic than the flat, fertile land of rich meadows and beech stands.

Slightly larger than the state of Delaware, Sjælland is the largest of the Danish islands. From Copenhagen, almost any point on it can be reached in an hour and a half, making it the most traveled portion of country. To the north of the capital, the ritzy beach towns line up between Hellerup and Humlebæk. Helsingør's Kronborg, which Shakespeare immortalized in

Hamlet, and Hillerød's stronghold of Frederiksborg, considered one of the most magnificent Renaissance castles in Europe, are also north. To the west of Copenhagen is Roskilde, medieval Denmark's most important town, which boasts an eclectic cathedral that was northern Europe's spiritual center 1,000 years ago.

West and south, rural towns and farms edge up to beach communities and fine white beaches, often surrounded by forests. Even more unspoiled are the lilliputian islands around southern Sjælland, virtually unchanged over the past century.

Important Addresses and Numbers

Tourist Information Tourist offices in the chief towns covered in this chapter are at **Helsingør** (Havnepladsen 3, tel. 49/21–13–33), **Hillerød** (Slotsgade 52, tel. 42/26–28–52), **Køge** (Vestergade 1, tel. 53/65–58–00), **Lolland** (at Nykøbing Falster) (Østergårdgade 7, tel. 54/85–13–03), **Roskilde** (Fondens Bro 3, tel. 42/35–27–00), **Sakskøbing** (in summer, Torvegade 4, tel. 53/89–56–30; in winter, tel. 53/89–45–72); and **Stege** and **Møn** (Storegade 2, Stege, tel. 55/81–44–11).

Emergencies For **police, fire,** or **ambulance,** dial 112.

Hospital Emergency Rooms Emergency care is available at **Helsingør** (Esrumvej 145, tel. 49/21–61–00) and **Roskilde** (Roskilde Amtssygehus, Køgevej 7, tel. 46/32–32–00).

Late-Night Pharmacies **Helsingør** (Axeltorvs, Groskenstræde 2A, tel. 49/21–12–23; Stengades, Stengade 46, tel. 49/21–86–00) and **Roskilde** (Dom Apoteket, Algade 8, tel. 42/35–40–16, and Svane Apoteket, Skomagergade 12, tel. 42/35–83–00) have pharmacies that are open late. In each town, pharmacies rotate 24-hour service, so call first to see which is open.

Arriving and Departing by Plane

Copenhagen's **Kastrup Airport** is Sjælland's only airport (*see* Arriving and Departing by Plane in Copenhagen, *above*).

Arriving and Departing by Car and Train

By Car There are several **DSB** car ferries from Germany. They connect Kiel to Bagenkop, on the island of Langeland (from there, drive north to Spodsbjerg and take another ferry to Lolland, which is connected to Falster and Sjælland by bridges); Puttgarden to Rødbyhavn on Lolland; Travemünde and Warnemünde to Gedser on Falster. Sjælland is connected to Fyn, which is connected to Jylland, by bridges and frequent ferries. If you are driving from Sweden, take a car ferry from either Helsingborg to Helsingør or Limhamn to Dragør. Or sail directly to Copenhagen (*see* Arriving and Departing by Car, in Copenhagen, *above*). In Denmark, call **DSB** (tel. 33/14–88–80); in Sweden, call **Scandlines** (tel. 46/42/18–60–00).

By Train Most train routes to Sjælland, whether international or domestic, are directed to Copenhagen. Routes to north and south Sjælland usually require a transfer at Copenhagen's main station. For timetables, call **DSB** (tel. 33/14–17–01).

Getting Around

By Car Highways and country roads throughout Sjælland are excellent, and traffic—even around Copenhagen—is manageable most of the time.

By Train and Bus The **Copenhagen Card,** which affords free train and bus transport, as well as admission to museums and sights, is valid within the HT-bus and rail system, which extends north to Helsingør, west to Roskilde, and south to Køge (*see* Getting Around in Copenhagen, *above*). Every town in Sjælland has a central train station, usually within walking distance of hotels and sights. (For long distances, buses are not convenient.) The only part of the island not connected to the DSB network is the sliver of northwestern peninsula known as **Sjællands Odde** (Zealand's Tongue). Trains leave from Holbæk to Højby, where you can bus to the tip of the point. For information, call the private railway company, **Odsherrede** (tel. 53/41–00–03). Two vintage trains (dating from the 1880s) run from Helsingør (tel. 42/30–89–35) and Hillerød (tel. 48/30–00–30 or 42/12–00–98) to Gilleleje.

Guided Tours

Check with the local tourism boards for general sightseeing tours in the larger towns or for self-guided walking tours. The following tours begin in Copenhagen: The Roskilde **Vikingland Tour** (6 hours) includes the market and cathedral, Christian IV's Chapel, and the Viking Ship Museum. The **Afternoon Hamlet Tour** (4½ hours) includes Frederiksborg Castle and Fredensborg Palace, while the **Castle Tour of North Zealand** (7 hours) also stops at Kronborg Castle. For additional information, call **Vikingbus** (tel. 31/57–26–00) or **Copenhagen Excursion** (tel. 31/54–06–06).

Boat Tours The turn-of-the-century *Saga fjord* (the Viking Ship Museum, Vikingeskibshallen, tel. 42/35–35–75) plies the waters of the Roskildefjord from April through September, and meals are served. Schedules vary.

Exploring Sjælland and Its Islands

Numbers in the margin correspond to points of interest on the Sjælland and Its Islands map.

Most of Sjælland can be explored in day trips from Copenhagen. The exceptions are the northwestern beaches around the Sejerø Bugt (Sejerø Bay) and those south of Møn, all of which require at least a night's stay and a day's loll.

Tour 1: North Sjælland

North of Copenhagen on Route 152, the Strandvejen (Beach Road), Sjælland's east coast is lined with upscale seaside neighborhoods. In **Rungsted,** between Copenhagen and Helsingør, is **Rungstedlund,** the former manor of Baroness Karen Blixen. The author of *Out of Africa* and several accounts of aristocratic Danish life, Blixen wrote under the pen name Isak Dinesen. The manor, where she lived as a child and returned in 1931, recently opened as a museum and includes manuscripts, photographs, and memorabilia documenting her years in Africa

Sjælland and Its Islands

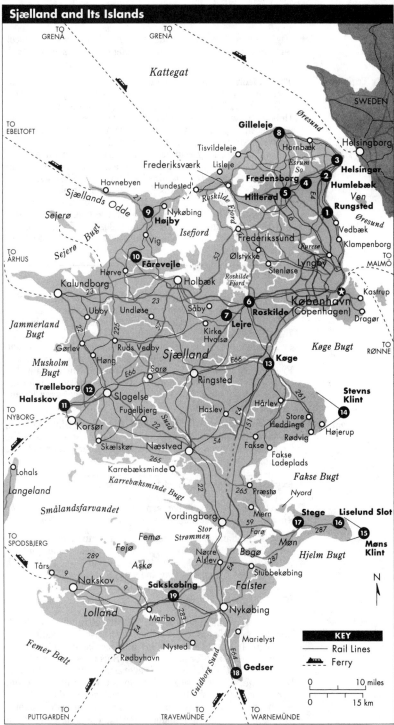

Kattegat

SWEDEN

TO GRENÅ

TO GRENÅ

TO EBELTOFT

Gilleleje **8**

Tisvildeleje

Hornbæk

Øresund

Helsingborg

Esrum Sø

3

Helsingør

Frederiksværk

Lisleje

Fredensborg

2

Havnebyen

Hundested

5 **4**

Humlebæk

Hillerød

Rungsted

Roskilde Fjord

1

Sjællands Odde

Nykøbing

9

Højby

Vedbæk

Øresund

Sejerø

Vig

Iseford

Frederikssund

Furesø

Klampenborg

Sejerø Bugt

10

Fåreveile

Ølstykke

Lyngby

TO MALMÖ

Hørve

Holbæk

Stenløse

TO ÅRHUS

Kalundborg

Roskilde Fjord

Kastrup

23

Ubby

Undløse

23

Såby

6

Roskilde

København
(Copenhagen)

Dragør

Jammerland Bugt

7

Lejre

Kirke Hvalsø

Musholm Bugt

Gørlev

Ruds Vedby

225

Sjælland

E66

13

Køge

Køge Bugt

TO RØNNE

Høng

Sorø

E66

Ringsted

Trælleborg **12**

Halsskov

Slagelse

Haslev

Hårlev

261

Store Heddinge

Stevns Klint

14

Højerup

TO NYBORG

11

Fugelbjerg

Susa

151

E4

Korsør

22

Rødvig

Skælskør

Næstved

54

Fakse

Lohals

265

Karrebæksminde

Fakse Ladeplads

Langeland

Karrebæksminde Bugt

22

265

Præstø

Fakse Bugt

Smålandsfarvandet

Vordingborg

Mern

Nyord

Stege

Liselund Slot

Femø

Stor Strømmen

Farø

17 **16**

15

TO SPODSBJERG

Fejø

Nørre Alslev

Bogø

Møn

287

Møns Klint

Tårs

Askø

E4

287

Hjelm Bugt

9

289

Stubbekøbing

Nakskov

Sakskøbing

Falster

9

19

Lolland

Maribo

283

Nykøbing

Femer Bælt

E4

Nysted

Marielyst

Rødbyhavn

E64

18 **Gedser**

Guldborg Sund

N

KEY

— Rail Lines

⛴ Ferry

0   10 miles

0   15 km

TO PUTTGARDEN

TO TRAVEMÜNDE

TO WARNEMÜNDE

and Denmark. *Rungstedlund, tel. 42/57–10–57. Admission: DKr30 adults, children free (for combined train-and-admission tickets, call DSB, tel. 33/14–17–01). Open May–Sept., daily 10–5; Oct.–Apr., Wed.–Fri. 1–4, weekends 11–4.*

② Another 10 kilometers (6 miles) northward is **Humlebæk** and the must-see **Louisiana** museum. Housed in a pearly 19th-century villa, surrounded by dramatic views of the Øresund waters, the permanent collection includes modern American paintings and Danish painting from the COBRA (a northern European painting trend that took its name from its active locations: Copenhagen, Brussels, Amsterdam) and Deconstructivism movements. Be sure to see the haunting collection of Giacomettis backdropped by picture windows overlooking the sound. *Gammel Strandvej 13, tel. 42/19–07–19. Admission: DKr45 adults, DKr35 senior citizens and students, children under 16 free (for combined train-and-admission tickets, call DSB, tel. 33/14–17–01). Open daily 10–5, Wed. until 10.*

③ At the northeastern tip of the island is **Helsingør,** the departure point for ferries to Helsingborg, Sweden, and the site of **Kronborg Slot.** William Shakespeare based *Hamlet* on Danish mythology's Amleth, and—never having seen the castle—used it as the setting nonetheless. Built in the late 16th century, it's 600 years younger than the Elsinore we imagine from the tragedy and was built as a Renaissance tollbooth. From its cannon-mounted bastions, forces collected Erik of Pomerania's much-hated Sound Dues, a tariff charged to all ships crossing the sliver of water between Denmark and Sweden. Well worth seeing are the 200-foot-long dining hall and the dungeons, where a brooding statue of Holger Danske sits. According to legend, the Viking chief sleeps, but will awaken to defend Denmark when it is in danger. *Helsingør, tel. 49/21–30–78. Admission: DKr20 adults, DKr10 children. Open May–Sept., daily 10:30–5; Oct. and Apr., daily 11–4; Nov.–Mar., daily 11–3.*

Thanks to the hefty tolls, the town prospered. Stroll past the carefully restored medieval merchants' and ferrymen's houses in the middle of town, and on the corner of Stengade and Skt. Annæ Gade near the harbor, you'll come to **Skt. Olai's Kirke** (St. Olai's Church), the country's largest town-church, which is worth poking into for its elaborately carved wooden altar. Next door is the 15th-century **Carmelite Kloster** (Carmelite Convent), one of the most well-preserved examples of medieval architecture in Scandinavia. After the Reformation, it was used as a hospital, and by 1630, a poor house. *Admission: DKr10 adults, DKr5 children. Guided tours year-round, daily 2 PM.*

Beside it is the **By Museum** (Town Museum), with exhibits of 19th-century handicrafts, dolls, and a model of the town. *Skt. Annæ Gade 36, tel. 49/21–00–98. Admission: DKr10 adults, children free. Open daily 12–4.*

If you are interested in castles, visit the Louis XVI–style **Marienlyst Slot,** about 1 kilometer (½ mile) north of Helsingør. Built in 1587 at the queen's behest, it provided her with a delicate change of scenery from the militant Kronborg. Today the gardens have been replanted, and the interiors contain paintings by north Sjælland artists. *Marienlyst Allé, tel. 49/21–16–27. Admission: DKr20 adults, DKr10 students and senior citizens, children free. Open daily 12–5.*

4 Southwest 15 kilometers (9 miles) is the town of **Fredensborg** and the **Fredensborg Slot** (Castle of Peace), built by Frederik IV to commemorate the 1720 peace treaty with Sweden. The Castle of Peace was originally inspired by French and Italian castles, with a towering domed hall in the center; however, 18th-century reconstructions conceal the original design and instead serve as a review of domestic architecture. The castle became a favorite of Frederik V, who lined the marble gardens with sculptures of ordinary people. It is now the summer residence of the royal family; interiors are closed except during July. The neatly trimmed park around the palace, connecting with Lake Esrum, is a lovely spot for a stroll. *Tel. 42/28–00–25. Palace open July, daily 1–4. Park open year-round.*

5 **Hillerød** and the **Frederiksborg Slot** (castle) lie another 10 kilometers (6 miles) south. Acquired and rebuilt by Frederik II, the fortress was demolished by his son, king–cum–architect Christian IV, and rebuilt as one of Scandinavia's most magnificent castles. With three wings and a low entrance portal, the moated Dutch-Renaissance structure covers three islets. It is peaked with dozens of gables, spires, and turrets. The interiors include a two-storied marble gallery known as the Great Hall. Audaciously festooned with drapery, paintings, and reliefs, it's atop the vaulted chapel, where 17th- to 19th-century monarchs were crowned. Devastated by a fire in 1859, the castle was reconstructed with the support of the Carlsberg Foundation, and it now includes a museum of Danish history. *Tel. 42/ 26–04–39. Admission: DKr30 adults, DKr5 children. Open Apr. and Oct., daily 10–4; May–Sept., daily 10–5; Nov.– Mar., daily 11–3.*

Forty kilometers (24 miles) south of Hillerød (on Rte. 6) and 32 kilometers (20 miles) west of Copenhagen (on Rte. 156) is **6** **Roskilde,** Sjælland's second-largest town and one of its oldest. Over a weekend at the end of June, it's filled with the rock music of the **Roskilde Festival,** said to be the largest outdoor concert in northern Europe, attracting 75,000 people.

Roskilde was the royal residence in the 10th century and became the spiritual capital of Denmark and northern Europe in 1170, when Bishop Absalon built the **Roskilde Domkirke** (Roskilde Cathedral) on the site of a church erected 200 years earlier by Harald Bluetooth. Overwhelming the center of town, the current structure took more than 300 years to complete and thus provides a one-stop crash course in Danish architecture. Inside there's an ornate Dutch altarpiece, as well as the sarcophagi, ranging from opulent to modest, of 38 Danish monarchs. Predictably, Christian IV is interred in a magnificent chapel with a massive painting of himself in combat, as well as a bronze sculpture by Thorvaldsen. In modest contrast is the newest addition, the simple brick chapel outside the church, of King Frederik IX, who died in 1972. On the interior south wall above the entrance is a 16th-century clock that depicts St. George charging a dragon, which hisses and howls, echoing throughout the church and causing Peter Døver, "The Deafener," to sound the hour. A squeamish Kirsten Kiemer, "The Chimer," shakes her head in fright but manages to strike the quarters. *Domkirkestræde 10, tel. 42/35–27–00. Admission: DKr5 adults, DKr2 students and senior citizens, DKr1 children. Hours vary; call first.*

Less than a kilometer (½ mile) north of the cathedral, on the fjord, is the **Vikingeskibshallen** (Viking Ship Museum), a modern museum that contains five Viking ships sunk in the fjord 1,000 years ago to block enemy ships. They were discovered in 1957. The painstaking recovery involved building a watertight dam and then draining the water from that section of the fjord. The splinters of wreckage were then preserved and reassembled in an ongoing process. A deep-sea trader, a warship, a ferry, a merchant ship, and a fierce 92½-foot man-of-war attest to the Vikings' sophisticated and aesthetic boat-making skills. *Strandengen, tel. 42/35–65–55. Admission: DKr28 adults, DKr18 children. Open Apr.–Oct., daily 9–5; Nov.–Mar., daily 10–4.*

7 Another 10 kilometers (6 miles) west of Roskilde in **Lejre** is the **Lejre Forsøgscenter** (Lejre Archaeological Research Center). Within the 50-acre compound, a village dating from the Iron Age and two 19th-century farmhouses have been reconstructed and during the summer are inhabited by a handful of hardy Danish families. Under the observation of researchers, the inhabitants go about their daily routine—grinding grain, herding goats, wearing skins—and give a clearer picture of ancient ways of life. In Bodalen (the Fire Valley), visitors (especially children) can grind corn, file an ax, and sail in a dugout canoe. *Slangæleen, tel. 42/38–02–45. Admission: DKr40 adults, DKr20 children; DKr60 combined family ticket (2 adults and 2 children). Open May–Sept., daily 10–5.*

Time Out There are picnic tables but no cafeteria at the archaeological center, so bring your lunch, or head back to **Druedahl's Konditori** (Skomagergade 40, tel. 42/35–01–13) in Roskilde, which has freshly baked pastries and bread. There's also a cafeteria at the Viking Ship Museum, overlooking the fjord.

Tour 2: West and South Sjælland

Sjælland's northwest coast is characterized by level land and summerhouse communities. Within this pastoral setting is **8** **Gilleleje,** at the very top of the island. Once a small fishing community, it experiences a population explosion every summer, when northern Europeans take to its woods and fine, sandy beaches. It was a favorite getaway of philosopher Søren Kierkegaard, who wrote: "I often stood there and reflected over my past life. The force of the sea and the struggle of the elements made me realize how unimportant I was." The less existential will go for a swim and visit the philosopher's monument on a nearby hill. The old part of town, with its thatched-roofed and colorfully painted houses, is also good for a walk.

Farther west is the hammer-shaped **Odsherred,** which is curved by the Sejerø Bugt (bay) and dotted with hundreds of burial mounds. If you are a devotee of ecclesiastical art, make a pilgrimage to explore the frescoes of several 12th- to 15th-century churches, among them the Roman/Gothic/Renaissance **Højby** **9** **kirke** (in the town of **Højby,** near Nykøbing Sjælland) and the **10** Gothic **Fårevejle kirke** (in the town of **Fårevejle**), with the earl of Bothwell's chapel. Alternatively, you can simply bask on the powdery beaches.

While the England–France Chunnel is creating a stir on the
Continent, Europe's second-biggest tunnel-bridge (18-kilome-
⑪ ters/11¼-miles) is in the process of linking **Halsskov**, on west
Sjælland, to Nyborg, on east Fyn. The **Storebælt Udstillings
Center** (Great Belt Exhibition Center), detailing the roadwork,
which will be completed sometime in the mid-'90s, includes
videos and models and makes for an informative stop while
you're waiting for a ferry. *Halsskov, tel. 58/35–01–00. Admission: DKr30 adults, DKr15 children. Open Oct.–Apr., Tues.–
Sun. 10–5; May–Sept., daily 10–8.*

If you are a Viking enthusiast, head instead 14 kilometers (8½
⑫ miles) northeast, just outside Slagelse, to **Trælleborg**, an excavated Viking encampment with a reconstructed army shelter.
No longer content to rely on farmer warriors, the Viking hier-
archy designed the geometrically exact camp within a circular,
moated rampart, thought to be of Oriental inspiration. The 16
barracks, of which there is one model, could accommodate
1,300 men. *Trælleborg Allé, tel. 53/54–95–06. Admission:
DKr15 adults, DKr10 children. Open Apr.–Sept., daily 10–6.*

On the east coast, 40 kilometers (24 miles) south of Copenha-
⑬ gen, is the well-preserved medieval town of **Køge,** which used to
be a witch-hunting town. In the **Køge Museum,** a 17th-century
merchant's house, you will see souvenirs from Hans Christian
Andersen, costumes, local artifacts, an executioner's sword,
and a 13th-century stone font. A story is told that the font had
to be removed from the town church after a crippled woman
committed an unsavory act into it, hoping her bizarre behavior
would cure her. Also on exhibit are 16th-century silver coins
from a buried treasure of more than 2,000 coins found in the
courtyard of Langkildes Gård. *Nørregade 4, tel. 53/65–02–62.
Admission: DKr10 adults, DKr5 children. Open Sept.–May,
weekdays 2–5, Sat.–Sun. 1–5; June–Aug., daily 10–5.*

On a calmer scale, the old part of Køge is filled with 300 half-
timbered houses, all protected by the National Trust; it's a
lovely area for a stroll. At the end of Kirkestræde, the 15th-
century **Skt. Nikolai Kirke** (St. Nicholas Church) was the hanging tower for pirates, while the floor is covered with more than
100 tombs of Køge VIPs. Carved angels line the church's walls,
but most have their noses cut off—a favorite pastime of drunk-
en Swedish soldiers in the 1700s. *Kirkestræde, tel. 53/65–13–
59. Admission free. Open Sept.–May, weekdays 10–12; June–
Aug., weekdays 10–4.*

Nearby the **Køge Kunst Museet Skitsesamling** (Køge Art Museum) has changing exhibitions and an extensive permanent collection of Queen Margrethe's artistic works. Among them:
silver spoons designed for Georg Jensen and porcelain figures
for Royal Copenhagen, in addition to embroidery, watercolor
paintings, and sketches. *Nørregade 29, tel. 53/66–24–14. Admission: DKr10 adults, children free. Open Tues.–Sun. 11–3.*

Near **Rødvig,** 24 kilometers (15 miles) south of Køge, are the
⑭ chalk cliffs of **Stevns Klint,** a third smaller than those farther
south at Møn but interesting because of the 13th-century
Højerup Kirke (church) that was built on their plateau. As the
cliffs eroded, first the cemetery, then the choir toppled into the
sea. In recent years the church has been restored and the cliffs
below bolstered by masonry to prevent further damage.

*Højerup Church, Stevns Klint, no tel. Admission: DKr5
adults, children free. Open Apr.–Sept., daily 11–5.*

Continuing south to the southeastern tip of Sjælland, Route 59
east crosses a bridge to the island of **Møn,** bumped throughout
with nearly 100 Neolithic burial mounds, but most famous for
its dramatic chalk **Møns Klint** (Møn's Cliffs). Rimmed by a
beech forest, the milky-white 75-million-year-old bluffs plunge
120 meters (400 feet) to a small, craggy beach—accessible by a
path and 560 steps. Once there, Danish families usually spend
their time hunting for blanched fossils of cuttlefish, sea ur-
chins, and other sea life. The cliffs are an important navigatio-
nal marker for ships, defining south Sjælland's otherwise flat
topography.

You can walk to a delightful folly of the 18th century, **Liselund
Slot** (not to be confused with a hotel of the same name), which is
4 kilometers (2.4 miles) north of the cliffs. Antoine de la Cal-
mette, the island's sheriff and a royal chamberlain, took his inspiration from Marie Antoinette's Le Hameau (the Hamlet) in
Versailles and built the classical structure in 1792 for his beloved wife. The thatched palace, complete with English gardens, combines a Norwegian country facade with elegant
Pompeian interiors. In this lovely setting, Hans Christian Andersen wrote his fairy tale *The Tinder Box.* The palace has
been open to the public since 1938; visitors must wear the slippers provided to enter the house. *Tel. 55/81–21–78. Admission: DKr20 adults, DKr5 children. Tours May–Oct., Mon.–
Sat. 10:30, 11, 1:30, and 2; Sun. 10:30, 11, 1:30, 2, 4, and 4:30.
Tours are in Danish and German.*

The island's capital, **Stege,** received its town charter in 1268.
Take time to explore its medieval churches, including **Stege,
Elmelunde, Keldby,** and **Fanefjord,** which are famous for their
naïve frescoes. Thought to have been completed by a collaborative group of artisans, the whimsical paintings include peda-
gogic and biblical doodlings.

Connected to Møn by Route 59 is the tiny northeastern island of
Nyord (New Word), which has a sanctuary for rare birds, including hen harriers, rough-legged buzzards, and snow bunt-
ings. The island has been divided among the same 20 farms,
unchanged, for the past 300 years. Cars are not allowed in the
island's central town. **Bogø** (Book Island) is southwest on Route
287. Relatively unchanged for the past several centuries, the islands are inhabited by a handful of families who continue to
farm and sail.

Next is the island of **Falster,** accessible from Bogø directly on
the E–47's striking Farø Bridge. Shaped like a tiny South
America, the island has excellent blond beaches, especially
southeastern **Marielyst** and southernmost **Gedser.** The island is
also one of the country's major producers of sugar beets.

West on the E–47 is the island of **Lolland,** which has a history
going back more than 1,000 years to when a man named Saxe
sat at the mouth of the fjord and collected a toll. He later
cleared the surrounding land and leased it. It became known as
Saxtorp, and eventually **Sakskøbing,** the island's capital.
Though most people head straight for the beaches, the area has
a few sights, including an excellent **car museum** in the 13th-cen-
tury **Ålholm Slot** (castle), with more than 240 vehicles and a water tower with a smiling face. *Parkvej 7, Nysted, tel. 53/87–15–*

*09. Admission to car museum: DKr40 adults, DKr20 children.
Open mid-Apr.–May and early Sept.–mid-Oct., weekends and
holidays; June–Aug., daily 11–6. Admission to castle: DKr40
adults, DKr20 children. Open June–Aug., daily 11–6.*

What to See and Do with Children

The **Knuthenborg Safari Park** on Lolland has a drive-through
range where you can rubberneck at tigers, zebras, rhinoceroses, and giraffes, and pet camels, goats, and ponies. Besides
seeing 20 species of animals, children can also play in
Miniworld, which has a jungle gym, a minitrain, and other
rides. *Knuthenborg Safaripark, DK–4930 Maribo, tel. 53/88–
80–89. Admission: DKr58 adults, DKr29 children. Open May–
Sept. 15.*

Off the Beaten Track

West of Gilleleje, on the northwestern coast of Sjælland between Tisvilde and Liseleje, is the **Troldeskoven** (Trolls' Forest), where gnarled evergreens were planted 250 years ago to
control the drifting sands. When you want to escape the
beaches, this woodland provides a magical respite.

Shopping

Shops are concentrated in the center of each town, along the
pedestrian street. Between Roskilde and Holbæk is **Kirke
Sonnerup Kunsthåndværk** (Art Handicrafts, Englerupvej 62,
Såby, tel. 42/39–25–77), which has a good selection of pottery,
glass, clothing, and woodwork produced by more than 50 Danish artists. Farther south in Næstved is the **Holmegaards
Glasværker** (Holmegaards Glass Workshop, Glasværksvej
52, Fensmark, tel. 55/54–62–00), with seconds of glasses,
lamps, and occasionally art glass and savings of up to 40% off
the "perfect" cost. The **Danish Amber Gallery** (Skodsborgparken 21, Skodsborg, tel. 42/80–71–62), 18 kilometers (11
miles) north of Copenhagen, has a good selection of jewelry and
a workshop.

Sports and Outdoor Activities

Bicycling Every town in Sjælland has a bicycle rental, and most roads
have cycle lanes. Ask the tourist board for maps and local
routes, especially along coastal roads.

Canoeing Though there aren't any rapids, there are several calm lakes
north of Copenhagen, especially in the Lyngby area on the
Mølleå (Mølle River) and the **Bagsværd, Lyngby,** and **Furesø**
(Bagsværd, Lyngby, and Fur lakes). Contact **Frederiksdal
Kanoudlejning** (canoe rental; Nybrovej, Lyngby, tel. 42/85–
67–70), which offers hourly, daily, and package tours and rentals. In south Sjælland, for trips on the **Suså** (Sus River), call
Susåen Kanoudlejning (canoe rental; tel. 53/64–61–44).

Fishing A license, which costs DKr250 and can be purchased from any
post office, is required to fish along Sjælland's coast. Elsewhere, along lakes, streams, and the ocean, check with the local tourism office for license requirements, which vary from
one area to another. Remember, it is illegal to fish within 500
meters (1,650 feet) of the mouth of a stream.

Golf There are more than 20 golf courses in Sjælland. Among them: the 18-hole **Korsør Course** (Ørnumvej 8, Korsør, tel. 53/57–18–36), the 18-hole **Sydsjælland Golf Klub** on Falster (Præstolandevej 39, Mogenstrup, tel. 53/76–15–03), **Roskilde's** 18-hole course (Kongemarken 34, tel. 42/37–01–80), and the 18-hole **Helsingør Golf Klub** (Gamle Hellebækvej, Helsingør, tel. 42/21–29–70).

Beaches

The beaches on the northern tip of Sjælland, especially **Hornbæk** and **Gilleleje,** are full of summer cottages, white dunes, and calm waters. **Tisvildeleje,** farther west, is quieter and close to woods; while **Sjællands Odde** (Zealand's Tongue), the tiny strip of land north of the Sejerø Bay, is marshier and more private. Inside the bay, the beaches are once again smooth and blond. **Nykøbing Falster,** especially around **Marielyst** and **Gedser,** is lined with woods and great beaches but can get crowded. Almost everywhere, you'll find cafés, facilities, and water-sports rentals.

Dining and Lodging

Dining and lodging throughout Sjælland is more moderately priced than in Copenhagen. Keep in mind, however, that many restaurants close early (some by 8 PM) and that some hotels expect you to check in before 7 PM.

Highly recommended establishments are indicated by a star ★.

Fredensborg **Hotel Store Kro.** Built by King Frederik IV, this magnificent
Dining and Lodging Renaissance annex to Fredensborg Castle is the archetypal
★ stately inn. Inside it's appointed with European antiques and paintings, while outside glass gazebos and classical statues look over a lovely garden. The recently renovated rooms are equally sumptuous, with delicate patterned wallpapers and antiques. *Slotsgade 6, DK–3480, tel. 42/28–00–47, fax 42/28–45–61. 49 rooms with bath. Facilities: restaurant, bar, sauna, room service, meeting rooms, parking. AE, DC, MC, V. Very Expensive.*

Helsingør **Bøf og Grønt.** Across from the harbor, this arty restaurant has
Dining peach walls covered with old photos of Danish movie stars. In the summer there's outdoor seating in the square and inside a hefty salad bar that comes with the steaks and a few vegetarian dishes. A Mexican and Chinese restaurant as well as a basement bar are under the same management. *Stengade 81 in Færgegaarden, tel. 49/21–39–46. Reservations advised. Dress: casual but neat. AE, DC, MC, V. Closed Mon.–Tues. Jan.–Feb. Moderate.*

Dining and Lodging **Marienlyst.** Flashy neon, bolts of drapery, and glass architec-
★ ture make this grown-up playground look airlifted from Atlantic City. A large casino, endless lounges, and two resident orchestras drive the point home, but when guests tire of gambling, there's a huge second-floor "Swinging Pool" with a water slide. The rooms are plush, done up in pastels, with every convenience. *Nordre Strandvej 2, DK–3000, tel. 49/20–20–20, fax 49/26–26–26. 203 rooms with bath, 24 suites. Facilities: 2 restaurants, 2 bars, nightclub, casino, indoor pool, sauna, solarium, room service, meeting rooms, parking. AE, DC, MC, V. Very Expensive.*

Hotel Hamlet. A few minutes from the harbor, this overly reno-vated hotel has lost some of its charm but makes an attempt at character with raw timbers and deep-green walls. The rooms are furnished in rose schemes and dark-wood modern, all com-fortable if nondescript. Downstairs there's a cozy bar and the Ophelia Restaurant, which serves traditional Danish seafood, steaks, and open-face sandwiches. *Bramstrædet 5, DK-3000, tel. 49/21–28–02, fax 49/26–01–30. 36 rooms with bath. Facili-ties: restaurant, bar, small meeting room. AE, DC, MC, V. Closed Dec. 24–Jan. 1. Expensive.*

Hillerød
Dining

Slotsherrenskro. Under the shadow of the Frederiksborg Cas-tle, this busy family restaurant used to be the castle stables. Antique on the outside, it's bright orange inside, with prints and paintings of royalty and the castle. Popular with visitors who come to the castle, the Danish menu ranges from quick open-face sandwiches to savory stews, soups, and steaks. *Slotherrens Kro, tel. 42/26–75–16. Reservations advised. Dress: casual. DC, MC, V. No dinner Thurs., Nov.–Mar. In-expensive.*

Klampenborg
Dining
★

Strandmollekroen. This 200-year-old beachfront inn is bur-nished with deep-green walls and filled with antiques and hunting trophies, but the best views are of the Øresund from the back dining room. The fare is seafood and steaks served ele-gantly. For a bit of everything, try the seafood platter, with lobster, crab claws, and Greenland shrimp. *Strandvejen 808, tel. 31/63–01–04. Reservations advised. Dress: casual but neat. AE, DC, MC, V. Moderate.*

Lolland
Dining and Lodging

Lalandia. This massive water-park hotel has an indoor palm-studded pool, a beach-side view, and lots of happy families. Lo-cated on the southern coast of Lolland, about 27 kilometers (16 miles) southwest of Sakskøbing, its modern, white apart-ments, with full kitchen and bath, accommodate 2, 4, 5, 6 or 8 people. *Røbdy Havn, DK-4970 Rødby, tel. 54/60–42–00, fax 54/60–41–44. 300 apartments. Facilities: restaurant, bar, health club, indoor-and-outdoor pool, tennis, golf, sauna, so-larium, meeting rooms, shops, parking, baker, hairdresser, playground. AE, DC, MC, V. Moderate.*

Hotel Saxkjøbing. Behind its yellow half-timbered facade, this comfortable hotel doesn't offer character or frills, but the rooms are bright, sunny, and modern, if very simply furnished. Located in the center of town, it is convenient to everything. *Torvet 9, Saxkjøbing, DK-4990, tel. 53/89–40–39, fax 53/89–53–50. Facilities: restaurant, bar, nightclub, meeting room, parking. AE, DC, MC. Inexpensive.*

Møn
Dining and Lodging
★

Liselund Ny Slot. Set in a grand old manor on an isolated estate, this bright, modern hotel offers stately accommodations minus stodginess. The square staircase and painted ceilings have been preserved, while the renovated rooms are fresh and sim-ple, with wicker and pastel schemes, half of which overlook a swan-filled pond and the forest. Downstairs there's an excel-lent restaurant that relies heavily on natural ingredients. *Liselund Ny Slot, DK-4791 Børre, tel. 55/81–20–81, fax 55/81–21–91. 25 rooms with bath, 1 suite. Facilities: restaurant, meeting rooms. AE, DC, MC, V. Moderate.*

Nykøbing Falster
Dining

Czarens Hus. This stylish old inn dates back more than 200 years, when it was a guest house and supply store for area farmers and merchants. Deep-green walls, gold trim, and

chandeliers provide a background for antique furnishings. The specialty of the house is Continental Danish cuisine, which translates as creative beef and fish dishes, often served with cream sauces. Try the *Zar Beuf* (calf tenderloin in a mushroom-and-onion cream sauce). *Langgade 2, Nykøbing Falster, tel. 54/ 85–28–29. Reservations advised. Jacket advised. AE, DC, MC, V. Expensive.*

Steenhus. Done up in bright pastels, this central and very popular restaurant is touted as one of the best in the area. The menu includes traditional Danish dishes, such as schnitzel and fresh fish, as well as more daring French specialties, such as blackened chicken. Located in the middle of town, it's dimly lit, with high-back striped booths and benches and dark wood. *Torvet, Nykøbing Falster, tel. 54/85–82–82. Reservations advised. Dress: casual. DC, MC, V. Closed Dec. 24–Jan. 2. Expensive.*

Lodging **Hotel Falster.** This sleek and efficient hotel accommodates conference guests as well as vacationers, with an ambience that's comfortable and businesslike. Rustic brick walls and Danish antiques mix with sleek Danish-design lamps and sculpture, while the rooms are comfortably done up with dark wood and modular furniture. *Skovalleen, Nykøbing Falster, DK-4800, tel. 54/85–93–93, fax 54/82–21–99. 70 rooms with bath. Facilities: restaurant, bar, meeting room, whirlpool. AE, DC, MC, V. Moderate.*

Roskilde **Spise Loftet.** Despite the name, Eating Loft, this charming res-
Dining taurant is popular with locals who come for the mix-and-match
★ menu: appetizer, entrée and dessert, and salad bar for DKr120. Choices range from vegetable quiche and steaks to Calvados or apple pie for dessert. The double-decker interior has two tables downstairs and a dozen upstairs beneath a gleaming white cathedral ceiling. *Algade 42, tel. 42/35–15–46. Reservations advised. Dress: casual. AE, DC, MC, V. Closed lunch. Moderate.*

Toppen. A half-hour walk from Roskilde Cathedral, this circular restaurant high above the water tower looks frayed, with covered metal tables and dozens of round paper lamps hanging from the ceiling. The fish and steak menu, though somewhat institutional, includes a family Colorado Steak for up to four people. Ask to sit in the smaller dining room overlooking the fjord. *Bymarken 37, tel. 42/36–04–12. Reservations advised. Dress: casual. DC, MC. No weekend lunch. Inexpensive.*

Dining and Lodging **Hotel Prindsen.** Centrally located in downtown Roskilde, this convenient hotel is popular with business guests. Built 100 years ago, it's been recently renovated with an elegant dark-wood lobby and nondescript rooms that are nonetheless homey and comfortable. Downstairs, the restaurant La Bøf serves up grill and fish fare, and next door there's a cozy bar. *Algade 13, tel. 42/35–80–10, fax 42/35–81–10. 38 rooms with shower. Facilities: restaurant, bar, meeting room. AE, DC, MC, V. Moderate.*

Roskilde Vandrehjem Hørgården. In front of a grassy yard, this youth hostel is perfect for families and budget travelers. In a former schoolhouse 2 kilometers (1.2 miles) east of the Roskilde Domkirke, everything looks straight out of third grade, and the rooms, with bunks, look like camp. *Hørhusene 61, DK-4000, tel. 42/35–21–84, fax 46/32–66–90. 21 rooms with 4 beds each, 8 showers. Facilities: kitchen. No credit cards. Open*

May–Sept., but call at other times to check room availability. Inexpensive.

The Arts and Nightlife

The Arts   Sjælland's cultural center is Copenhagen; however, many towns do have free outdoor concerts and theater in the summer, most notably Roskilde, Køge, and Helsingør. Check with the local tourist offices for details. Some summers, **Kronborg Castle** is the site of outdoor performances of *Hamlet* by internationally renowned theater groups. The schedule varies from year to year, but check with the tourism board for current details.

Nightlife   Outside of Roskilde and Helsingør, most islanders go to Copenhagen for a big night out. In the smaller towns you'll find local bars, outdated discos, and quiet cafés and wine cellars. In Roskilde, the young head to **Gimle** (Ringstedgade 30, tel. 42/35–12–13) for live rock on the weekends, followed by the **Exima** disco (Algade 25A, tel. 46/32–06–92). **Kloster Kælderen** (Store Gråbrødrestræde 23, tel. 42/37–20–33) is a beer basement with a slightly older crowd. The **Bryggerhesten** (Algade 15, tel. 42/35–01–03) is where adults have a late supper and beer in cozy surroundings. During the summer **Mullerudi** (Djalma Lunds Gord 7, tel. 42/37–03–25) is an arty spot with indoor and outdoor seating and live jazz. In Helsingør, **New York, New York** (Hovedvagtsstræde 2, tel. 49/26–42–21) draws the young to disco.

Casinos   The **Marienlyst Casino** (Ndr. Strandvej 2, tel. 42/20–20–20) is a big, glitzy affair located in the Marienlyst Hotel, with several bars, blackjack, baccarat, and slot machines.

Fyn and the Central Islands

Christened the Garden of Denmark by its most famous son, Hans Christian Andersen, Fyn (Funen) is the smaller of the country's two major islands. Lined with plumb-straight vegetable fields and flower gardens, the flat-as-a-board land is relieved by beech glades and swan ponds. Manor houses and castles that seem to pop up from the countryside like magnificent mirages include some of northern Europe's best preserved: the 12th-century Nyborg Slot, travel pinup Egeskov Slot, and the lavish Valdemars Slot. The fairytale cliché often attached to Denmark really does spring from this provincial isle, where the only faint pulse emanates from Odense, its capital. Trimmed with thatched-roof houses and green parks, the city makes the most of the Andersen legacy but surprises with a rich arts community at the Brandts Klædefabrik, a former textile factory turned museum compound.

It's quick and easy to reach the smaller islands of Langeland and Tåsinge—both are connected to Fyn by bridges. Slightly more isolated is Ærø, where the town of Ærøskøbing, with its painted half-timbered houses and winding streets, seems caught in a delightful time warp.

Important Addresses and Numbers

Tourist Information Most city tourism offices are open weekdays 10–4 and Saturday 9–noon during the fall and winter, and Monday through Saturday 9–5 in spring and summer. **Odense Tourist Office** (City Hall, tel. 66/12–75–20) has information for all of Fyn, including the helpful "Tourist Information on Fyn" brochure. There are also offices in **Kerteminde** (Strandgade 5A, tel. 65/32–11–21), **Svendborg** (Centrumpladsen, tel. 62/21–09–80), **Nyborg** (Torvet 9, tel. 65/31–02–80), and **Ærøskøbing** (Torvet, tel. 62/52–13–00).

Emergencies For **police, fire,** or **ambulance** service, dial 112.

Hospital Emergency Room There is an emergency room at **Odense Hospital,** (J. B. Winsløws Vej, tel. 66/11–33–33).

Doctors and Dentists From 4 PM to 7 AM, call 65/90–60–10 for a doctor. For dental or other emergencies, call **Falck** (tel. 66/11–22–22).

Late-Night Pharmacy **Ørnen Apoteket** (Vestergade 80, Odense, tel. 66/12–29–70) is open late.

Arriving and Departing by Plane

Airport and Airlines **Odense Airport** (tel. 65/95–50–72), 11 kilometers (7 miles) north of Odense, is served by **Mærsk Air** (tel. 65/95–53–55) and **Muk Air** (65/95–50–20 or 98/19–03–88). There are nine daily flights between Copenhagen and Odense. The 25-minute flight costs DKr550.

Between the Airport and Center City Metered airport taxis charge DKr120 for the 15-minute drive downtown. A **Mærsk Airbus** meets each flight and stops at the Grand Hotel, Hans Christian Andersen Hotel, and the main railway station. The fare is DKr40.

Arriving and Departing by Car and Train

By Car From Copenhagen, take the E20 west to Halskov, near Korsør, and drive aboard **Storebælt Færgen** (the Great Belt ferry; DKr275 per car, with up to five passengers and a reservation; unreserved tickets are DKr250, with a possible wait of several hours). For reservations, call **DSB** (tel. 33/14–88–00). The ferry departs daily every 40 minutes. You'll arrive in Knudshoved, near Nyborg, which is a half hour from Odense or Svendborg.

By Train Trains from Copenhagen's main station depart for the three-hour trip to Odense hourly, every day. Stations in both towns are central, close to hotels and sights. The one-way fare is DKr104 on Tuesday, Wednesday, Thursday, and Saturday; DKr130 Sunday, Monday, and Friday. A reservation is an additional DKr30 (tel. 33/14–17–01).

Getting Around

By Car The highways are excellent, while small roads meander beautifully on two lanes through the countryside. There is little traffic.

By Train and Bus Large towns are served by intercity trains. These include a Nyborg–Odense–Middelfart and Odense–Svendborg route. The only other public transportation is by bus. Timetables are

posted at all bus stops and central stations (rutebilstation). Passengers buy tickets on board and pay according to the distance traveled (tel. 66/11–71–11). For central Odense, the **Odense Eventyrpas** (Adventure Pass), available at the tourism office, affords admission to sights and museums and free city bus and train transport. The cost is DKr100 adults, DKr50 children.

By Bicycle With their level landscape and short distances, Fyn and the central islands are perfect for cycling. Pick up maps from the tourism offices and rent bikes throughout the islands at **CykelCentret** (Allegade 72, Odense, tel. 66/13–88–94), **Cykel Biksen** (Nedergade 14–16, tel. 66/12–40–98), or **Fåborg Sportshandel** (Havnegade 40, Fåborg, tel. 62/61–28–22).

Guided Tours

The Odense Tourist Office (*see above*) oversees the **Odense City Tour** (two hours), which includes a visit to St. Knuds Cathedral and Hollufgård, and ends in the Hans Christian Andersen area, at 11 weekdays and at 2 Saturday from the end of June through August. Most other towns do not have organized tours, but check the local tourist office for step-by-step walking brochures. Full-day **Hans Christian Andersen** tours to Odense depart from Copenhagen's Rådhuspladsen mid-May–mid-September, Sunday at 8:45 AM, and cost DKr460. (Six out of 11 hours are spent in transit.)

Tour 1: Northern Fyn

Numbers in the margin correspond to points of interest on the Fyn and the Central Islands map.

❶ Most visitors disembark from the ferry in **Nyborg**, a 13th-century town that was Denmark's capital during the Middle Ages. The city's major landmark, the moated 12th-century **Nyborg Slot** (castle), was the seat of the Danehof, the Danish parliament from 1200 to 1413. It was here that King Erik Klipping signed the country's first constitution, the Great Charter, in 1282. Besides geometric wall murals and an armory collection, the castle houses changing art exhibits. *Slotspladsen, tel. 65/31–02–07. Admission: DKr20 adults, DKr10 children. Open Mar.–May and Sept.–Oct., Tues.–Sun. 10–3; June–Aug., daily 10–5.*

Cross Gammel Torv and walk down the street to the **Nyborg Museum**, which is housed in a half-timbered merchant's house from 1601, for a picture of 17th-century life. Besides furnished rooms, there's a small brewery. *Slotsgade 11, tel. 65/31–02–07. Admission: DKr5 adults, DKr2 children. Open Mar.–May and Sept.–Oct., Tues.–Sun. 10–3; June–Aug., Mon.–Sun. 10–5.*

Take Route 160 northwest to the Avnslev junction and turn north to Route 165; then drive the 15 kilometers (9 miles) along
❷ the coast to **Kerteminde**, an important fishing village and picturesque summer resort. On Langegade, walk past the neat half-timbered houses to Møllebakken and the museum of the Danish painter **Johannes Larsen** (1867–1961). Across from a crimson strawberry patch and a 100-year-old windmill, the artist built a modest country cottage that has been perfectly preserved, right down to the teacups. In front, there's a sculpture

Fyn and the Central Islands

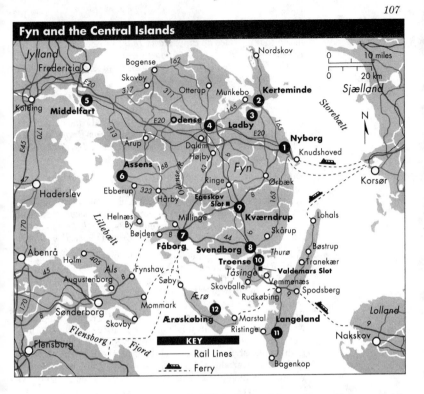

of a woman by Kai Nielsen. Local legend goes that one night, after a particularly wild party in Copenhagen, its legs were broken off. An ambulance was called, but once it arrived, the enraged driver demanded the artists pay a fine. A chagrined Larsen paid, and in return kept the wounded sculpture. *Møllebakken, tel. 65/32–37–27. Admission: DKr25 adults, children free. Open Mar. 25–May and Sept.–Oct., Tues.–Sun. 10–4; Nov.–Feb., Wed. and Sun. noon–4; June–Aug., Tues.–Sun. 10–5.*

3 If you are a Viking enthusiast, head a few kilometers south to the village of **Ladby** and the 1,100-year-old remains of the **Ladbyskibet,** a Viking chieftain's ship burial, complete with hunting dogs and horses for his trip to Valhalla—the afterlife. *Vikingsvej 12, tel. 65/32–16–67. Admission: DKr15 adults, DKr3 children. Open May–Sept., daily 10–6; Oct.–Apr., daily 10–3.*

4 Twenty kilometers (12 miles) southwest on Route 165 is **Odense,** Denmark's third-largest city and the birthplace of fairy-tale author Hans Christian Andersen.

Begin at the flourishing **Kongens Have** (King's Garden) and 18th-century Odense Castle, now a government building, and walk east on Stationsvej to Thomas B. Thriges Gade and Hans Jensens Stræde, where the **Hans Christian Andersen Hus** (H.C. Andersen Museum) stands in a manicured neighborhood of half-timbered houses and cobbled streets. Inside, the storyteller's life is chronicled through his photographs, drawings, letters, and personal belongings. There's also a library with

Andersen's works in more than 100 languages, where you can listen to fairy tales on tape. *Hans Jensenstræde 37, tel. 66/13–13–72. Admission: DKr20 adults, DKr10 children. Open Apr.–May and Sept., daily 10–5; June–Aug., daily 9–6; Oct.–May, daily 10–3.*

At the end of Hans Jensens Stræde is the sleek **Carl Nielsen Museum,** which has multimedia exhibits of the life and work of Denmark's most famous composer (1865–1931) and of his wife, the sculptor Anne Marie Carl-Nielsen. *Claus-Bergs Gade 11, tel. 66/13–13–72. Admission: DKr15 adults, DKr5 children. Open daily 10–4.*

Take a left on Claus Bergsgade to **Møntergården,** Odense's museum of urban history, which occupies four 17th-century row houses in a shady, cobbled courtyard. Exhibits range from interiors of the Middle Ages to Denmark's Nazi occupation to an impressive coin collection. *Overgade 48–50, tel. 66/13–13–72. Admission: DKr15 adults, DKr5 children. Open daily 10–4.*

Toward the pedestrian street on St. Knuds Kirkestræde, just in front of the Andersen Park, is the stately **St. Knuds Kirke,** built from the 13th to the 15th century, the only purely Gothic cathedral in Denmark. Inside there's an intricate wooden altar covered with gold leaf, carved by German sculptor Claus Berg. Beneath the sepulcher are the bones of St. (King) Knud, who was killed during a farmers' uprising in 1086, and his brother. Continue west on St. Knuds Kirkestræde and take a left on Munkemøllestræde for a quick look at the diminutive **H. C. Andersens Barndomshjem** (Andersen's Childhood Home), where the young boy and his parents lived in a room barely five feet by six feet.

Next, take a left from St. Knuds Kirkestræde on Filosofgangen to the takeoff point for the **Odense River Cruises** (tel. 65/95–79–96). Here you can catch a boat (June–mid-August, daily 1, 3, and 5) downriver to the **Fruens Bøge** (the Lady's Beech Forest) and then walk down Erik Bøghs Sti (Erik Bøgh's footpath) to **Den Fynske Landsby** (the Fyn Village). Among the country's largest open-air museums, it includes 25 farm buildings and workshops, a vicarage, a water mill, and a theater, which in summer stages adaptations of Andersen's tales. *Sejerskovvej, tel. 66/13–13–72. Admission: DKr20 adults, DKr10 children. Open Apr.–May and Sept.–Oct., daily 10–4; June–Aug., daily 10–6:30; Nov.–Mar., Sun. and holidays 10–4.*

Cruise back to the town center or catch Bus 21 or 22, and walk down the boutique- and café-lined pedestrian street, which in summer is abuzz with street performers, musicians, and brass bands.

North of the river and parallel to Kongensgade is the artistic compound of **Brandt's Klædefabrik.** A former textile factory, the four-story building now houses **Museet for Fotokunst** (the Museum of Photographic Art), **Danmarks Grafiske Museum** (the Danish Graphics Museum), **Dansk Presse museum** (the Danish Press Museum), and **Kunsthallen** (an art gallery). Exhibits vary widely from national to international offerings, but the Photography Museum and the art gallery especially show experimental work. *Brandt's Passage 37, tel. 66/13–78–97. Admission: DKr15–25 for each museum, DKr40 for all; children about half price. Open Tues.–Sun. 10–5.*

Time Out The **Cafe Biografen** (Brandt's Passage, tel. 66/13–16–16) next door is a popular—and inexpensive—meeting place for locals to have a cup of coffee or snack.

Among the newest museums is **Hollufgård,** a former 16th-century manor. Although it remains closed, the grounds include 19th-century buildings that house Fyn's archaeological museums. Special exhibits include the archaeological find of the month, as well as ecology displays. Nearby is a sculpture center where you can see an artist at work, as well as a sculpture garden. *Hestehaven 201, tel. 66/13–13–72. Admission: DKr15 adults, DKr5 children. Open Jan.–Apr., Sun. 11–4; May–Oct., Tues.–Sun. 10–5; Nov.–Dec., Tues.–Sun. 11–3.*

If you continue west on E20, you'll reach the westernmost point ⑤ of Fyn, the town of **Middelfart,** where you can cross the country's only suspension bridge to Jylland and the European continent.

Tour 2: Southern Fyn and the Archipelago

Continue south from Odense on Route 168 and you'll reach the ⑥ quiet town of **Assens.** The local gem is Tove Sylvest's sprawling **Seven Gardens,** just south on the Strandvej (Beach Road) off Route 323 in the town of Å. A privately owned botanical United Nations, the gardens represent the flora of seven European countries, including many plants rare to Denmark. *Å Strandvej 62, Ebberup, tel. 64/74–12–85. Admission: DKr30 adults, DKr15 children. Open May–Oct., daily 10–5.*

Thirty kilometers (18 miles) south of Odense on Route 43 is ⑦ **Fåborg,** a lovely 12th-century town whose surrounding beaches are invaded by sun-seeking Germans and Danes in summer. Four times a day you can hear the dulcet chiming of **Klokketårnet's** (the Belfry's) carillon, the island's largest. In the center of town is the controversial **Ymerbrønden** sculpture by Kai Nielsen, depicting a naked man drinking from an emaciated cow while it licks a baby.

On the more traditional side, the 18th-century **Den Gamle Gård** (the Old Merchant's House), of 1725, chronicles local history through furnished interiors, as well as exhibits of glass and textiles. *Holkegade 1, tel. 62/61–33–38. Admission: DKr20 adults, children free. Open May–Sept., daily 10:30–4:30.*

Next, follow Grønnegade and you'll pass the local **Familie og Ungdoms Vandre hjem** (Family and Youth Hostel), which is housed in a charming white half-timbered building that used to be a poorhouse (tel. 62/61–12–03).

Next door the **Fåborg Museum for Fynsk Malerkunst** (Art Gallery for Fyn Paintings) has a good collection of turn-of-the-century paintings and sculpture by the Fyn Painters, a school of artists whose work captures the dusky light of the Scandinavian sun. *Grønnegade 75, tel. 62/61–06–45. Admission: DKr20 adults, children free. Open Apr.–May and Sept.–Oct., daily 10–4; Nov.–Mar., daily 11–3; June–Aug., daily 10–5.*

From Fåborg, take Route 44 east 25 kilometers (15½ miles) to ⑧ **Svendborg,** Fyn's second-largest town. Svendborg celebrates its 800-year-old maritime traditions in July, when old Danish wooden ships congregate in the harbor for the circular **Fyn rundt** (regatta). (There's even the chance to get on board and

shuttle between towns. Contact the tourist board or any agreeable captain.) With many charter-boat options and good marinas, use Svendborg as a base to explore the hundreds of islands of the South Fyn Archipelago.

From the harbor, walk down Frederiksgade, cross Møllergade to Torvet, the market square. To the left on Fruestræde is the black-and-yellow **Anne Hvides Gård,** the oldest secular house in Svendborg and one of the four branches of **Svendborgs Omegns Museum** (the Svendborg County Museum). Inside you'll see 18th- and 19th-century interiors and glass and silver collections. *Fruestræde 3, tel. 62/21–02–61. Admission: DKr15 adults; children free. Open May–mid-June, daily 10–4; mid-June–Oct., daily 10–5.*

Take a left on Teatergade and cross Skolegade to **Bagergade,** (Baker's Street), which is lined with some of Svendborg's oldest half-timbered houses. On the left, at the corner of Grubbemøllevej and Svinget is the **Viebæltegård,** the headquarters of the Svendborg County Museum, a former poorhouse. You can wander through dining halls, washrooms, and the "tipsy clink," where inebriated citizens were left to sober up as recently as 1974. *Grubbemøllevej 13, tel. 62/21–02–61. Admission: DKr15 adults, DKr5 children, senior citizens, and students. Open May–mid-June, daily 10–4; mid-June–Oct., daily 10–5; Nov.–Apr., daily 1–4.*

North of Svendborg 15 kilometers (9 miles) on Route 9 is the town of **Kværndrup** and the moated Renaissance **Egeskov Slot,** one of the best-preserved island-castles in Europe. Peaked with copper spires and surrounded by Renaissance, Baroque, English, and peasant gardens, the castle has an antique vehicle museum and the world's largest maze, designed by the Danish scientist turned poet Piet Hein. Visitors can see a few of the rooms, including the great hall, the hunting room, and the Riborg Room, where the daughter of the house was locked up from 1599 to 1604 after giving birth to a son out of wedlock. *Kværndrup, tel. 62/27–10–16. Admission: DKr45 for maze, gardens, and car museum; for castle additional DKr40 adults; children half price. Open June–Aug., daily 9–6; May and Sept., daily 10–5.*

In the opposite direction, a few miles south of Svendborg, are the lilliputian islands of Thurø and Tåsinge. Admittedly, there are no major sights on **Thurø,** but it does offer a lovely embodiment of an unspoiled, provincial Danish isle. To the west, across the Svendborg Sound Bridge, is **Tåsinge,** where the local 19th-century drama involves Elvira Madigan (recall the movie?) and her married Swedish lover, Sixten Sparre. Preferring heavenly union to earthly separation, they shot themselves and are now buried in the central Landet churchyard. It's a tradition for brides to throw their bouquets on the lovers' grave.

With half-timbered buildings and hand-carved doors, the island's main town of **Troense** is one of the country's best-preserved maritime villages. South of town is **Valdemars Slot,** dating from 1610, which is one of Denmark's oldest privately owned castles. Visitors have free passage to almost all the sumptuously furnished rooms (everything is under electronic surveillance), the libraries, and the candle-lit church. (There's also an X-rated 19th-century cigar box that shouldn't be missed.) *Troense, tel. 62/22–61–06 or 62/22–50–04. Admis-*

sion: DKr40 adults, DKr15 children. Open May–Sept., daily 10–5.

⑪ Tåsinge is connected to nearby **Langeland** by a causeway bridge. The largest island of the southern archipelago, Langeland is rich in relics, and the beaches are worth scouting out. Bird-watching is excellent on the southern half of the island, where migratory birds roost before setting off on their cross-Baltic journey. To the south are **Ristinge** and **Bagenkop,** two towns with good beaches; at Bagenkop you can catch the ferry to Kiel, Germany.

From either Svendborg, Langeland, or Fåborg, you can take a car ferry to the island of **Ærø**, the "Jewel of the Archipelago," where country roads wend through fertile fields and past thatched farmhouses. About 27 kilometers (16 miles) southeast of Søby, the port town where the ferry from Fåborg arrives, is

⑫ the storybook town of **Ærøskøbing**, on the island's north coast. Established as a market center in the 13th century, it did not flourish until it became a sailing town in the 1700s, but every night when the gas lights illuminate the cobbled streets, time seemingly has stood still.

What to See and Do with Children

Fyn's **Terrarium** has all kinds of slippery and slithery creatures, including snakes, iguanas, alligators, and the nearly extinct blue frog. *Kirkehelle 5, Vissenbjerg, tel. 64/47–18–50. Admission: DKr30 adults, DKr15 children. Open May–Aug., daily 9–6; Sept.–Apr., daily 9–4.*

Off the Beaten Track

History is recorded in miniature at the **Flaskeskibssamlingen** (Bottle Ship Collection), thanks to curator Peter Jacobsen. A former ship's cook known as "Peter Bottle," he has built nearly 2,000 bottle ships in his day. *Smegade 22, Ærøskøbing, tel. 62/ 52–29–51. Admission: DKr10 adults, DKr5 children. Open July–mid-Aug., daily 9–5; mid-Aug.–July, daily 9–4.*

Covered wagons (which sleep two adults and two children), complete with a horse and feed, are available for a week of old-fashioned transportation, following preset routes and overnighting at designated camps, from **Destinations Langeland.** At DKr3,600 per week, it's an inexpensive and unique holiday. *DK–5935 Bagenenkop, tel. 62/51–14–44.*

Shopping

Antiques · Many of Fyn's manor houses and castles now double as antiques emporiums. The largest is at **Hindemae** (near Rte. 315, 12 km/7 mi west of Nyborg, exit 46 or 47, tel. 65/35–22–05), which has one of Fyn's most extensive European antiques collections. Smaller collections are also available at **Hønnerup Hougård** (Hougårdsvej 6, Gelsted, tel. 64/49–13–00).

Crafts Studios · As elsewhere in Denmark, crafts and handmade items in Fyn and Shops · are well designed and functional. At the **Bjørnholt Keramik** (Risingevej 12, Munkebo, tel. 65/97–40–90), you can watch ceramics in the making. **Mogens Eigenbrod** (Adelgade 40, Bogense, tel. 64/81–18–81) produces endearing handmade wood carvings and Christmas ornaments. **Uromagerens Hus** (the mo-

bile maker's house, tel. 66/12–70–44) is in a half-timbered house across from the H.C. Andersen Museum. Inside, hand-made mobiles range from simple paper hangings to intricate ceramic balloons. For hand-blown glass, visit **Glasmagerne** (Vemmenæsvej 10, Tåsinge, tel. 62/54–14–94).

Produce Markets Wednesday and Saturday mornings throughout the summer are market days in towns across Fyn. Often held in the central square, these markets offer fresh produce, flowers, and cheeses. Check with the local tourism office for details.

Sports and Outdoor Activities

Bicycling Flat and smooth, Fyn is perfect for bikes. Packages with bike rental, hotel accommodations, and half-board are available from **Hotel Svendborg** (Centrumpladsen, 5700 Svendborg, tel. 62/21–17–00). For maps and tips, contact local tourism boards (*see* Important Addresses and Numbers, *above*).

Fishing A state license is required to angle anywhere on **Fyn's** 1,130-kilometer (680-mile) coast. It costs DKr100 and can be purchased at any post office. A separate municipal license from the tourist bureau is required to fish the Odense River. **Langeland** has particularly rich waters, with cod, salmon, flounder, and gar. For package tours, contact **Erling Olsson** (Ristinge Fæled 4, DK–5932 Humble, tel. 62/57–20–23) or **Ole Dehn** (Søndergade 22, Lohals, DK–5953 Tranekær, tel. 62/55–17–00).

Golf Fyn has three 18-hole courses that are open to the public— **Odense** (which has recently opened a 9-hole course as well), St. Knud's (in Nyborg), and **Svendborg.** You can also visit the new driving range (tel. 65/96–80–08) in Blommenlyst, 12 kilometers (7 miles) from Odense, west toward Middelfart. For information, fees, and tee-off times, call the **Odense Golf Klub** (tel. 65/95–90–00).

Water Sports For smooth **windsurfing,** head to the Little Belt and southern shores; windier conditions can be found on the east and north coasts. The **Middelfart Tourism Office** (tel. 64/41–17–88) rents sailboards to windsurfers.

Beaches

The golden **beaches** of southern Fyn are among the gentlest in Denmark and very popular with northern Europeans. Public facilities, kiosks, and cafés are always nearby.

Dining and Lodging

Fyn boasts a wide range of hotels, inns, and restaurants. You can make arrangements to stay in one of Fyn's many *kroer* (inns) by purchasing a packet of coupons valid at 79 inns (*see* Inns under Lodging in Before You Go, *above*). The islands also have numerous campsites and hostels, all clean and attractively located, but make your reservations early. Europeans book well in advance, leaving few rooms for last-minute travelers.

Highly recommended establishments are indicated by a star ★.

Ærøskøbing **Ærøhus.** A half-timbered building with a steep red roof, the
Lodging Ærøhus looks like a rustic cottage on the outside, an old aunt's house on the inside. Hanging pots and slanted interiors fill the

living areas, while pine furniture and cheerful duvets keep the guest rooms simple and bright. The garden's five cottages have small terraces. *Vestergade 38, DK–5970, tel. 62/52–10–03, fax 62/52–21–23. 30 rooms, 17 with bath; 5 cottages. Facilities: restaurant, garden. AE, V. Closed Dec. 27–Jan. 20. Moderate.*

Fåborg **Vester Skerninge Kro.** Midway between Fåborg and Svendborg,
Dining this traditional inn is cluttered and comfortable. Pine tables are polished from years of serving hot stews and homemade *mediste pølse* (mild grilled sausage) and *æggkage* (fluffy omelet made with cream, smoked bacon, chives, and tomatoes). *Krovej 9, Vester Skerninge, tel. 62/24–10–04. Reservations advised. Dress: casual. No credit cards. Closed Tues. Inexpensive.*

Dining and Lodging **Falsled Kro.** Once a smuggler's hideaway, the 500-year-old
★ Falsled Kro is now among Denmark's most elegant inns. A Relais et Châteaux member, it has appointed its cottages sumptuously with European antiques and stone fireplaces. The restaurant combines French and Danish cuisines, using ingredients from its garden and markets in Lyon. *Assensvej 513, DK–5642 Millinge, tel. 62/68–11–11, fax 62/68–11–62. 14 rooms with bath, 3 apartments. Facilities: restaurant, helicopter pad, 3-hole golf course, room service, sailing, horseback riding. AE, DC, MC, V. Closed mid-Dec.–Feb. Very Expensive.*

Steensgaard Herregårdspension. A long avenue of beeches leads to this 700-year-old moated manor that's tucked 7 kilometers (4½ miles) northwest of Fåborg. The rooms are elegant, with antiques, four-poster beds, and yards of silk damask. In the fine restaurant, wild game is served from the manor's own reserve. *Steensgaard 4, 5642 Millinge, tel. 62/61–94–90, fax 62/61–78–61. 15 rooms, 13 with bath. Facilities: restaurant, tennis, horseback riding, helicopter pad. AE, DC, MC, V. Closed Jan. Very Expensive.*

Kerteminde **Rudolph Mathis.** This busy harbor-side restaurant is topped by
Dining two chimneys venting open grills that broil popular fish dishes such as catfish with butter, fennel, and Pernod sauce, and grilled turbot in a green-pepper and lime sauce. *Dosserengen 13, Munkebo, tel. 65/32–32–33. Reservations accepted. Dress: casual. AE, MC, V. Closed Jan.–Mar.; Mon.–Sun. Sept.–Dec. Moderate.*

Nyborg **Danehofkroen.** Outside Nyborg Slot, this family-run restau-
Dining rant does a brisk lunch, serving traditional Danish meals to tourists who enjoy a view of the castle and its tree-lined moat. The menu is meat-and-potatoes, featuring such dishes as *flæskesteg* (sliced pork served with the crisp rind). *Slotsplads, tel. 65/31–02–02. Reservations required. Dress: casual but neat. No credit cards. Closed Mon. Moderate.*

Lodging **Hesselet.** This modern hotel looks like a brick slab outside, a refined English-cum-Oriental sanctuary inside. The guest rooms are furnished with cushy, modern furniture, and most have a splendid view of the Storebælt (Great Belt). *Christianslundsvej 119, 5800 Nyborg, tel. 65/31–30–29, fax 65/31–29–58. 46 rooms with bath and shower, 3 suites. Facilities: restaurant, room service, meeting rooms, indoor pool, sauna. AE, DC, MC, V. Very Expensive.*

Odense **Marie Louise.** Near the pedestrian street, this elegant white-
Dining washed dining room glitters with crystal and silver. The daily
★ Franco-Danish menu typically offers such specialties as salmon

scallop with bordelaise sauce and grilled veal with lobster-cream sauce. Business and holiday diners are sometimes treated to gratis extras—such as quail's egg appetizers or after-dinner drinks. *Lottrups Gaard, Vestergade 70–72, tel. 66/ 17–92–95. Reservations advised. Jacket and tie advised. AE, DC, MC, V. Closed Sun. Expensive.*

Under Lindetræt. Once a bakery, this award-winning restaurant is now done up in linen and lace and frequented by well-heeled tourists. Classic French cuisine, such as medallions of beef with lemon-mushroom sauce and poached smoked salmon with green herbs, are served in a private parlor atmosphere, in the glow of low-hanging lamps and a fireplace. *Ramsherred 2, tel. 66/12–92–86. Reservations advised. Jacket advised. DC, MC, V. Expensive.*

Den Gamle Kro. Built within the courtyards of several 17th-century homes, this popular restaurant has an ancient stone decor sliced by a sliding glass roof. The Franco-Danish menu includes fillet of sole stuffed with salmon mousse, and chateaubriand with garlic potatoes, but there's also inexpensive smørrebrød. *Overgade 23, tel. 66/12–14–33. Reservations advised. Dress: casual. DC, MC, V. Moderate.*

★ **Frank A.** Guarded by a meter-tall wooden bulldog named Tobias, this merry meeting place is dominated by high-kitsch curios and paintings and an enormous collection of bric-a-brac. Friendly waiters serve drinks and French-inspired Danish dishes, such as ham schnitzel with creamed potatoes and pepper steak flambé, to a mostly local crowd. *Jernbanegade 4, tel. 66/12–27–57. Reservations accepted. Dress: casual. DC, MC, V. Moderate.*

★ **Den Grimme Ælling.** The name of this restaurant means the Ugly Duckling, but inside it's simply homey, with pine furnishings and family-style interiors. It's also extremely popular with tourists and locals alike, thanks to an all-you-can-eat buffet heaped with cold and warm dishes. *Hans Jensens Stræde 1, tel. 65/91–70–30. Reservations advised. DC, MC. Inexpensive.*

Målet. A lively crowd calls this sports club their neighborhood bar, and, next to steaming plates of schnitzel served in a dozen ways, soccer is the other delight of the house. *Jernbanegade 17, tel. 66/17–82–41. Reservations not accepted. Dress: casual. No credit cards. Inexpensive.*

Lodging **Reso Grand Hotel.** A century old, with renovated fin-de-siècle charm, this imposing four-story brick-front hotel greets guests with old-fashioned luxury. The original stone floors and chandeliers lead to a wide staircase and upstairs guest rooms that are modern, with plush furnishings and sleek marble bathrooms. *Jernabanegade 18, 5000 Odense C, tel. 66/11–71–71, fax 66/14–11–71. 134 rooms, 79 with bath, 59 with shower; 13 suites. Facilities: sauna, solarium, room service. AE, DC, MC, V. Expensive.*

★ **Hotel Ydes.** Newly remodeled, this bright, colorful hotel is a good bet for students and budget-conscious travelers tired of barracks-type accommodations. The plain, white hospital-style rooms are clean and comfortable. *Hans Tausensgade 11, 5000 Odense C, tel. 66/12–11–31. 30 rooms, 24 with shower. Facilities: café. MC, V. Inexpensive.*

Svendborg **Sandig.** This austere white eatery near the harbor is spartan,
Dining but food, not decor, is owner-chef-waiter-dishwasher Volkert
★ Sandig's priority. His daily-changing French-Danish menu in-

cludes inventive fish and beef specialties. Try the cod served with mussel and garlic sauce or the roast veal in a creamy mushroom ragout. *Kullinggade 1b, Svendborg, tel. 62/22–92–11. Reservations advised. Dress: casual. DC, MC, V. Closed daily 2–6 and Sun. Moderate.*

Ærø. A dim hodgepodge of ship parts and maritime doodads, this harbor-side restaurant is peopled by brusque waitresses and serious local trenchermen. The menu is old-fashioned, featuring *frikadeller* (fried meatballs), fried *rødspætte* (plaice) with hollandaise sauce, and dozens of smørrebrød options. *Brøgade 1 ved Ærøfærgen, tel. 62/21–07–60. Reservations advised. Dress: casual. DC, MC, V. Closed Sun. Inexpensive.*

Lodging **Margrethesminde.** The Fyn equivalent of a bed-and-breakfast, this manor house/art gallery is 16 kilometers (10 miles) west of Svendborg. Many things in the house, including European antiques, are for sale by owners Mogens and Britte Laursen. Sunlight fills the five guest rooms, which are largely decorated in beige and overlook the surrounding countryside. *Fåborgvej 154, 5762 Vester Skerninge, tel. 62/24–10–44, fax 62/24–10–62. 5 rooms with bath. Facilities: bicycle rental. MC, V. Moderate.*

Tåsinge **Restaurant Valdemars Slot.** Beneath the castle, this domed res-
Dining taurant is ankle-deep in pink carpet and aglow with candlelight. Fresh ingredients from France and Germany and wild game from the castle's preserve are the essentials for an ever-changing menu. Wild venison with cream sauce and duck breast à l'orange are typical of the French-inspired cuisine. A less expensive annex, Den Grå Dame, serves traditional Danish food. *Slotsalleen 100, Troense, tel. 62/22–59–00. Reservations advised. Jacket and tie advised. AE, DC. Closed Mon. Very Expensive.*

Lodging **Thurø Røgeriet.** Set on the water's edge, this friendly family-
★ owned and -run pension offers homespun hospitality and dramatic views of Tåsinge Sound. Although the living room is filled with antiques and paintings by grandfather Niels Hansen, the rooms are spare, with plain white beds and cane chairs; a few have balconies and slanted ceilings. *Måroddevej 22, Thurø, tel. 62/20–50–84. 16 rooms, 14 with bath. Facilities: restaurant. MC, V. Closed Dec.–Jan. Moderate.*

The Arts and Nightlife

The Arts **Castle Concerts** are held throughout the summer at **Egeskov,** **Nyborg,** and **Valdemar** castles and the rarely opened **Krengenrup** manor house, near Assens. Check with local tourism offices for schedules. In summer the **Odense Street Theater**'s *Hans Christian Andersen Happenings* are presented from the end of July until the first week in August, daily at 4 and 5, with living history and fairy-tale performances just outside the Andersen Museum.

Nightlife Fyn nightlife revolves around the major towns of Odense and Svendborg, while the smaller towns make do with local bars and quiet nights.

Bars and Lounges Odense's central Arcade is an entertainment mall, with bars, restaurants, and live music, ranging from corny sing-alongs to hard rock. For a quieter evening, stop by **Café Biografen** (Brandts Passage, tel. 66/13–16–16). In Svendborg, the very

mixed **Banjen Bar** (Frederiksgade 11C, tel. 62/22–25–46) often has live rock and blues.

Casinos   Fyn's sole casino is in the slick glass atrium of the **SAS Hans Christian Andersen Hotel** (Claus Bergs Gade 7, Odense, tel. 66/14–78–00), with blackjack, roulette, and baccarat.

Discos   In Odense, the popular **All Night Boogie Dance Café** (Nørregade 21, tel. 66/14–00–39) plays pop, disco, and '60s music to a laid-back crowd. The **Atlantic Night Club** (Overgade 45, tel. 65/91–05–27) is more chic, with revolving mirror balls and strobe lights. Svendborg's **Chess** (Vestergade 7, tel. 62/22–17–16) is popular with a young crowd that comes for the live bands.

Jazz Clubs   **The Cotton Club** (Pantheonsgade 5C, tel. 66/12–55–25) in Odense is a venue for old-fashioned jazz. Though Svendborg doesn't have a permanent jazz club, the **Orangi** (Jessens Mole, tel. 62/22–82–92), an old sailing ship that's moored in the harbor, is a popular summer restaurant where jazz musicians often perform.

Jylland

Denmark's western peninsula is the only part of the country naturally connected to mainland Europe; its southern boundary is the frontier with Germany. Compared with the smooth, postcard-perfect land of Fyn and Sjælland, this Ice Age–chiseled peninsula is bisected at the north by the craggy Limfjord and spiked below by the Danish "mountains." Himmelbjerget, the zenith of this modest range, peaks at 438 feet, while farther south the Yding Skovhøj plateau measures 568 feet—modest hills just about anywhere else.

The first inhabitants of Denmark were hunters who lived in southern Jylland (Jutland) 250,000 years ago. You can see flint tools and artifacts from this period locked away in museums, but the land holds more stirring relics from a later epoch: After 1,000 years, Viking burial mounds and stones still swell the land, some in protected areas, others lying in farmers' fields, tended by grazing sheep.

The windswept landscapes filmed in *Babette's Feast*, the movie version of Isak Dinesen's novel, trace the west coast northward to Skagen, a luminous, dune-covered point (geographically not unlike the Outer Banks of North Carolina), while to the east coast, facing Fyn, lie deep fjords rimmed with forests. The center is dotted with castles, parklands, and the famed Legoland. Ribe, Denmark's oldest town, lies to the south, while the east coast is anchored by Århus and Aalborg, respectively Denmark's second- and fourth-largest cities, with nightlife and sights to rival Copenhagen's.

Important Addresses and Numbers

Tourist Information   Tourism offices, open weekdays 10–4, Saturday 9–noon in winter and 9–6 weekdays and Saturday in the summer, are in **Aalborg** (Østerå 8, tel. 98/12–60–22), **Århus** (Rådhuset, tel. 86/12–16–00), **Billund** (c/o Legoland A/S, Åstvej, tel. 75/33–19–26), **Randers** (Hellingandhuset, Erik Menveds Plads 1, tel. 86/42–44–77), **Ribe** (Torvet 3–5, tel. 75/42–15–00), **Silkeborg** (Godthåbsvej 4, tel. 86/82–19–11), and **Viborg** (Nytorv 5, tel. 86/62–16–17).

Emergencies For **ambulance, fire,** or **police** emergencies, call 113.

Doctors After normal hours (4 PM–7 AM), in **Aalborg**, call 98/13–62–11. In **Århus**, call 86/20–10–22. Fees (DKr300–DKr400) must be paid in cash. Elsewhere, call directory assistance at 118 and ask for the number for the local **night doctor.**

Late-Night Pharmacies Try **Århus** (Løve Apoteket, Store Torv 5, tel. 86/12–00–22) or **Aalborg** (Budolfi Apotek, corner of Vesterbro and Algade, tel. 98/12–06–77). Pharmacies elsewhere rotate 24-hour emergency service and will fill only prescriptions that have been called in by doctors.

Arriving and Departing by Plane

Billund Airport, 2 kilometers (1.2 miles) southwest of downtown, receives flights from London, Stockholm, Brussels, Amsterdam, and Stavanger on **Mærsk Air** (tel. 75/33–28–44) and on the Norwegian carrier **Braathens** to Oslo, which continues to Århus. Several domestic airports, including **Aalborg, Århus,** and **Esbjerg,** are served by **Mærsk, Cimber Air** (tel. 74/42–22–77), and **SAS** (75/33–14–11), all of which have good connections to Copenhagen.

Arriving and Departing by Car, Train, and Ferry

By Car Two bridges link Middelfart on Fyn to Fredericia on Jylland. The older, lower bridge (1.7 kilometers/1 mile) follows Route 161, while the newer suspension bridge (1.2 kilometers/¾ mile) on E20 is faster.

By Train DSB (tel. 33/14–17–01) makes hourly links between Copenhagen and Fredericia. The 3½-hour trip includes train passage aboard the ferry, which crosses the Store Bælt between Korsør, on west Sjælland, and Nyborg, on east Fyn.

By Ferry Ferries from Hundested, Sjælland, to Grena in east Jylland take 2½ hours, while those from Kalundborg to Århus take 3 hours. For information, call **DSB** (tel. 33/14–17–01). **Scandinavian Seaways** (tel. in Esbjerg, 75/12–48–00; in Copenhagen, 33/15–63–00) also links Harwich and New Castle to Esbjerg in the southwest. There are also ferries from Göteborg (3¼ hours), on Sweden's west coast and Oslo, Norway (10 hours), to Frederikshavn in the northeast. Call **Stena Line** (tel. 96/20–02–00) for both.

Getting Around

By Car Although train and bus connections are excellent, sights and towns are widely dispersed, so this tour is best made by car. Whether you decide to take speedy, modern highways or winding old roads, traffic is virtually nonexistent.

By Train For long trips, the **DSB** (tel. 86/13–17–00) trains are fast and efficient, with superb views of the countryside. Smaller towns do not have inner-city trains, so you'll have to switch to buses once you arrive.

By Bus Intercity buses are punctual but slower than trains. Passengers can buy tickets on the bus and pay according to destination. For schedules and fares, call **DSB** weekdays (tel. 86/12–67–03). For inner-city travel, schedules are posted at all bus stops and fares are usually under DKr10.

By Bicycle Jylland has scores of bike paths. In the west, the **Vestkyst-stien** (west-coast path) goes from Skagen in the north to Bulbjerg in the south. On the east, the **Vendsyssel-stien** (winding path) goes from Frederikshavn to the mouth of the Limfjord. The **Østkyst-stien** (east-coast path) follows, and leads to the south of, the Limfjord. In the south, much of the 1,000-year-old **Hærvejen** (Old Military Road) has been converted into a network of picturesque cycling lanes. It's sign-posted for all 240 kilometers (145 miles) through the center of Jylland, from Padborg in the south to Viborg in the north. Many auto routes also have cycle lanes. Bike rentals are available in most towns from the tourism board, which can also supply maps and brochures. Among the tourist offices that can help with bike tips are the Viborg and Silkeborg (*see* Tourist Information, *above*) and the Vejen tourist boards (tel. 75/36–26–96).

Guided Tours

Guided tours are few and far between, but check with the local tourism offices for tips and reservations. Some carry brochures that describe walking tours. The **Århus Round the City** tour (2½ hours) begins at the tourist office and includes Den Gamle By, Domkirke, the concert hall, the university, and the harbor. **Aalborg's City Tour** (2 hours) departs from Adelgade and includes most of the town museums, the Budolfi Cathedral, Monastery of the Holy Ghost, the Town Hall, Jens Bang Stenhus, and Jomfru Ane Gade.

Exploring Jylland

Numbers in the margin correspond to points of interest on the Jylland map.

Nearly three times the size of the rest of Denmark, with long distances between towns, the peninsula of Jylland rewards several days or even weeks of exploring. If you are pressed for time, concentrate on one tour or a couple of cities. Delightful as they are, the offshore islands are suitable only for those with plenty of time, as many require an overnight stay.

The **Jutland Pass** coupon booklet (DKr35) is available from tourist offices and Statoil gas stations throughout Jylland. However, Scandic Hotels and the Stena Line Ferries between Denmark and Sweden often distribute the pass free of charge. It's packed with nearly 200 coupons, affording restaurant, museum, and sightseeing deals.

Tour 1: South Jylland

❶ Most travelers arrive from **Middelfart** to **Fredericia,** Jylland's main rail junction, and 350 years ago a defense center. There's not much to see, so continue 20 kilometers (12 miles) southwest **❷** to **Kolding** and the well-preserved **Koldinghus.** The massive stonework structure was a fortress and then a royal residence in the Middle Ages and is a historical museum today. In the winter of 1808, during the Napoleonic Wars, Spanish soldiers set fire to most of it as they tried to keep warm. *Rådhusstræde, tel. 75/50–15–00, ext. 5400. Admission: DKr25 adults, children free. Open Apr.–Sept., daily 10–5; Oct.–Mar., weekdays noon–3, weekends 10–3.*

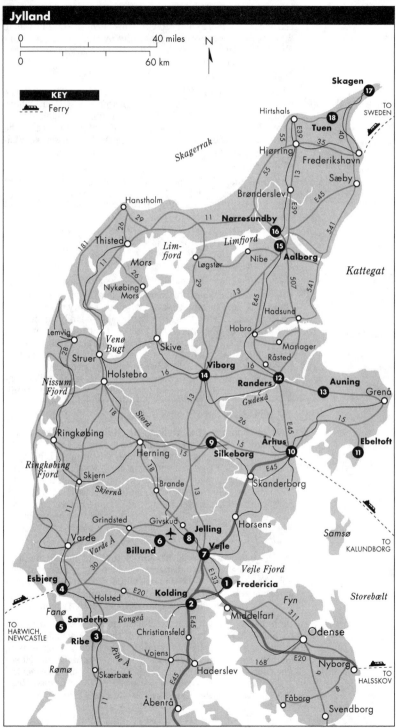

In the south of town is **Den Geografiske Have** (Geographical Garden), with more than 120 varieties of roses as well as some 2,000 plants arranged geographically by continent. *Christian Fjerde Vej, tel. 75/50–38–80. Admission: DKr22 adults, children free. Open June and Aug., daily 9–7; July, daily 9–8; Sept.–May, daily 10–6.*

About 60 kilometers (36 miles) southwest, but well worth the extra driving time, is **Ribe**, the country's oldest town, whose medieval center is preserved by the Danish National Trust. From May to mid-September, a night watchman circles the town telling of its history and singing traditional songs. Visitors can accompany him nightly by gathering at the main square at 10 PM.

The **Ribe Domkirke** (Cathedral) stands at the site of one of Denmark's earliest churches, built around AD 860. The present structure dates from the 12th century, with a 14th-century bell tower. Note the Cat Head Door, said to be for the exclusive use of the devil. *Torvet, tel. 75/42–06–19. Admission: DKr5 adults, DKr1 children. Open May, Mon.–Sat. 10–5, Sun. noon–5; June–Aug., Mon.–Sat. 10–6, Sun. noon–6; Sept., Mon.–Sat. 10–5, Sun. noon–5; Oct.–Apr., Mon.–Sat. 11–3, Sun. noon–3.*

On Route 24, 23 kilometers (14 miles) to the northwest, is **Esbjerg,** arrival point for ferries coming from Harwich and Newcastle, and terminus for the 20-minute ferry to the tiny island of **Fanø.** During the 19th century, the island had an enormous shipbuilding industry and a fleet second only to Copenhagen's. The shipping industry deteriorated, but the proud maritime heritage remains. From the ferry port in Nordby, take a bus south to **Sønderho.** Along the tiny winding lanes are thatched cottages decorated with ships' relics, figureheads, painted doors, and brass lanterns. Even the traditional costume is still in use, especially on *Sønderhodag,* a town fest held on the third Sunday in July.

Next in south-central Jylland is **Billund** and the famed **Legoland.** It's filled with scaled-down versions of cities and villages, working harbors and airports, a Statue of Liberty, a statue of Sitting Bull, Mount Rushmore, a safari park, and a Wild West saloon—all constructed from 35 million toy, plastic Lego bricks. There are also exhibits of toys from pre-Lego days, the most exquisite of which is **Tatania's Palace,** a sumptuous dollhouse built in 1907 by Sir Neville Wilkinson for his daughter. *Billund, tel. 75/33–13–33. Admission: DKr95 adults, DKr75 children. Open May–Sept. 15, daily 10–7.*

On the east coast, **Vejle,** 20 kilometers (12 miles) north of Kolding, is beautifully positioned on the fjord, amid forest-clad hills. You can hear the time of day chiming on an old **Dominican monastery clock;** the clock remains, but the monastery long ago gave way to the town's imposing 19th-century city hall.

In the center of town, at Kirke Torvet, is **Skt. Nicolai Kirke** (St. Nicholas Church). In the left arm of the cross-shaped church, lying in a glass Empire-style coffin, is the body of a **bog woman,** found preserved in a peat marsh in 1835, that dates to 500 BC. The church walls also conceal the skulls of 23 thieves executed in the 17th century. *Kirke Torvet, tel. 75/82–41–39. Open May–Sept., Mon.–Fri. 9–5, Sat. 9–noon, Sun. 9–11:30.*

8 From Vejle there's a **vintage steam train** to **Jelling** every Sunday in July and the first Sunday in August. Otherwise, take Route 18 10 kilometers (6 miles) north through the pastoral Grejs Valley to Jelling. There, two 10th-century burial mounds mark the seat of King Gorm and his wife, Thyra. Between the mounds are two **Runestener** (runic stones), one of which is Denmark's certificate of baptism, showing the oldest known figure of Christ in Scandinavia. The inscription explains that the stone was erected by Gorm's son, King Harald Bluetooth, who brought Christianity to the Danes in AD 960.

Time Out   There are few eateries in Jelling, so go 2 kilometers (1.2 miles) west to **Skovdal Kro** (Fårupvej 23, tel. 75/87–17–81), a traditional inn that serves old-fashioned meals.

Tour 2: The Lake District and Central Jylland

9 North toward **Silkeborg,** on the banks of the River Gudena, is Jylland's **lake district.** Stretching from Silkeborg in the west to Skanderborg in the east, it contains some of Denmark's loveliest scenery, as well as some of the country's meager mountains, including the 438-foot Himmelbjerget. The best way to explore the area is by water, as the Gudena winds its way some 160 kilometers (100 miles) through lakes and wooded hillsides down to the sea. Take one of the excursion boats or, better still, the world's last coal paddle steamer, *Hjejlen,* which runs in the summer and is based in Silkeborg. *Havnen, Silkeborg. Reservations: tel. 86/82–07–66. Admission: round-trip tickets DKr29–66 adults; children half price. Departs Silkeborg Harbor 10 and 1:45 Sun. in June; daily mid-June–beginning of Aug.*

Since 1861, it has paddled its way through narrow stretches of fjord, where the treetops meet overhead, to the foot of the **Himmelbjerget** at Julsø (Lake Jul). From that point you can climb the narrow paths through the heather and trees to the top, where an 80-foot tower stands sentinel, placed there on Constitution Day in 1875 in memory of King Frederik VII.

Silkeborg's main attractions are housed in the **Kulturhistoriske Museum** (Museum of Cultural History): the 2,200-year-old **Tollund Man** and **Elling Girl,** two more bog people, preserved by natural ingredients in the soil and water. *Hovedgådsvej, tel. 86/82–15–78. Admission: DKr20 adults, DKr5 children. Open Apr. 15–Oct. 23, daily 10–5; Oct. 24–Apr. 14, Wed. and weekends 12–4.*

10 On the coast, 40 kilometers (24 miles) east of Silkeborg, is **Århus,** Denmark's second-largest city. The town is liveliest during the 10-day Århus Festival in September, which combines everything from concerts, theater, and exhibitions to beer tents and sports. In addition, the **Århus International Jazz Festival** in mid-June gathers international and local greats. During the last week of July, the **Viking Moot** draws aficionados to the beach below the Museum of Prehistory at Moesgård. Activities and exhibits include market booths, ancient defense techniques, and rides on Viking ships. Finally, Århus has a tradition of supporting uniquely women's arts, particularly at the beginning of July, when the **International Women's Theater and Cultural Festival** sweeps into town.

A good starting point is the **Århus Rådhus,** probably the most unusual city hall in Denmark. Built in 1941 by noted architects Arne Jacobsen and Erik Møller, the pale Norwegian-marble block building is controversial but cuts a startling figure when illuminated in the evening. *Park Allé, tel. 86/40-20-00. Free tours June-mid-Sept., weekdays at 4.*

Not to be missed is the town's open-air museum, known as **Den Gamle By** (the Old Town), which features 70 half-timbered houses, a mill, and a millstream, all carefully moved from locations throughout Jylland and meticulously re-created, inside and out. *Viborgvej, tel. 86/12-31-88. Admission: DKr35 adults, children free. Open Jan.-Mar. and Nov., daily 11-3; Apr. and Oct., daily 10-4; May and Sept., daily 10-5; June-Aug., daily 9-6; Dec., Mon.-Sat. 10-3, Sun. 10-4.*

In a 250-acre forest in a park south of Århus is the indoor-outdoor **Moesgård Forhistorisk Museum** (Prehistoric Museum), with exhibits on ethnography and archaeology, including the famed **Grauballe Man,** a 2,000-year-old corpse so well bog-preserved that scientists could determine his last meal. Also, take the **Forhistoriskvej** (Prehistoric Trail) through the forest, which leads past Stone and Bronze Age displays to reconstructed houses from Viking times. *Moesgård Allé, tel. 86/27-24-33. Admission: DKr25 adults, children free. Open Jan.-Apr. and mid-Sept.-Dec., Tues.-Sun. 12-4; May-mid-Sept., daily 10-4.*

If you have time, drive northeast to the tip of what Danes call ⑪ Jylland's nose, **Ebeltoft,** a town of crooked streets, sloping row houses, and local crafts shops. Danish efficiency is showcased beside the ferry, at the **Vindmølleparken,** one of the largest windmill parks in the world, where 16 wind-powered mills on a curved spit of land generate electricity for 600 families. *Færgehaven, tel. 86/34-12-44. Admission free. Open daily.*

Tour 3: North Jylland

North 21 kilometers (15 miles) from Århus is the medieval town ⑫ of **Randers,** where in 1340 the Danish patriot Niels Ebbesen killed the German oppressor, Count Gert the Bald of Holstein, whose army was then occupying most of Jylland. To the east of Randers is the **Djursland Peninsula,** a popular vacation area, with fine manor houses that are open to the public.

If time permits, visit **Gammel Estrup Slot,** a grand 17th-century ⑬ manor in the tiny village of **Auning;** it's filled with rich period furnishings, including an alchemist's cellar. *Randersvej 2, tel. 86/48-30-01. Admission: DKr20 adults, DKr5 children. Open Apr.-Sept., daily 10-5; Oct.-Mar., Tues.-Sun. 11-3.*

⑭ About 60 kilometers (36 miles) west of Randers is **Viborg,** whose history predates the 8th century, when it was a trading post and a place of pagan sacrifice. Later it became a center of Christianity, with monasteries and an episcopal residence. The 1,000-year-old **Hærvejen,** the old military road that starts near here, was once Denmark's most important connection with the outside world. Legend has it that in the 11th century, King Canute set out from Viborg to conquer England; he succeeded, of course, and ruled from 1016 to 1035. Today you can buy reproductions of a silver coin minted by the king, embossed

with the inscription "Knud, Englands Kong" (Canute, King of England).

Built in 1130, Viborg's **Domkirke** (Cathedral) was once the largest granite church in the world. Today only the crypt remains of the original building, which was restored and reopened in 1876. The dazzling early 20th-century biblical frescoes are by Danish painter Joakim Skovgard. *Mogensgade, tel. 86/62–10–60. Admission free. Open June–Aug., Mon.–Sat. 10–4; Sun. noon–5; Sept. and Apr.–May, Mon.–Sat. 11–4, Sun. noon–4; Oct.–Mar., Mon.–Sat. 11–3, Sun. noon–3.*

There's terrific walking country 8 kilometers (5 miles) south of Viborg, beside **Hald Sø** (Hald Lake) and on the heather-clad **Dollerup Bakker** (Dollerup Hills).

Another 80 kilometers (50 miles) north are the gentle waters of the **Limfjord,** the great waterway that severs Jylland. ⑮ Clamped to its narrowest point is **Aalborg,** Denmark's fourth-largest community, which celebrated its 1,300th birthday in 1992 with a year of festivities. The gateway between north and south Jylland, the city is a charming combination of new and old: twisting lanes filled with medieval houses and, nearby, broad modern boulevards. The only Fourth of July celebrations outside the United States annually blast off in nearby Rebild Park, a salute to the United States for welcoming 300,000 Danish immigrants that has continued since 1912.

Among the sights, the local favorite is the magnificent 17th-century **Jens Bangs Stenhus** (Jens Bang's Stone House), built by a wealthy merchant. Chagrined that he was never made a town council member, the cantankerous Bang avenged himself by caricaturing his political enemies in gargoyles all over the building and then adding his own face, its tongue sticking out at town hall. A five-story building dating from 1624, it has a vaulted Gothic stone beer and wine cellar (*see* The Arts and Nightlife, *below*). *Østerå 9.*

A short walk to Gammel Torv takes you to the Baroque cathedral, **Budolfi Kirke,** dedicated to the English saint Botolph, and the 15th-century **Helligandsklosteret** (Monastery of the Holy Ghost). One of Denmark's best-preserved monasteries—and perhaps the only one that allowed both nuns and monks—it is now a home for the elderly. During World War II the monastery was the meeting place for the Churchill Club, a group of Aalborg schoolboys who became world-famous for their sabotage of the Nazis.

In the center of the old town is **Jomfru Ane Gade,** named, as the story goes, for an aristocratic maiden who was accused of being a witch then beheaded. Now the street's fame is second only to Copenhagen's Strøget. Despite the flashing neon and booming music of about 30 discos, bars, clubs, and eateries, the street remains old-fashioned, appealing to all ages.

⑯ Just north of the city, at **Nørresundby,** is **Lindholm Høje,** a Viking and Iron Age burial ground where stones placed in the shape of a ship enclose many of the site's 682 graves and sheep often outnumber tourists. At its entrance there's a brand-new museum that chronicles the Viking civilization, as well as recent excavations. *Hvorupvej, tel. 98/17–55–22. Museum admission: DKr20 adults, DKr10 children; burial-ground admission free. Open Sept.–mid-Oct. and Apr.–May, daily*

10–5; June–Aug., daily 10–7; mid-Oct.–mid-Apr., daily 10–4.

17 At the desolate northern tip of Jylland is **Skagen** (pronounced Skane), where long beaches and luminous light have inspired painters and writers alike. The 19th-century Danish artist Holger Drachmann (1846–1908) and his friends, including the very popular P. S. Kroyer, founded the Skagen School of painting, which captured the special quality of northern light; you can see their efforts on display in the **Skagen Museum.** *4 Brøndumsvej, tel. 98/44–64–44. Admission: DKr25 adults, children free. Open Apr. and Oct., Tues.–Sun. 11–4; May and Sept., daily 10–5; June–Aug., daily 10–6; Nov.–Mar., Wed.–Fri. 1–4, Sat. 11–4, Sun. 11–3.*

Danes say that here you can "stand one foot in the Kattegat [the strait between Sweden and eastern Jylland], the other in the Skagerrak [the strait between western Denmark and Norway]." The point is so thrashed by storms and clashing waters that the 18th-century **Tilsandede Kirke** (Sand Buried Church), 2 kilometers (1 mile) south of town, is completely covered by dunes. Equally dramatic is the west coast's **Råbjerg Mile,** a protected migrating dune that moves about 33 feet a year and is accessible on foot from the Kandestederne.

18 Another 30 kilometers (18 miles) south, at **Tuen,** is **Bindslev Ørne Reservat** (the Bindslev Eagle Sanctuary, the only place in the world where golden- and white-tailed eagles and large falcons are raised in close contact with people. In summer educational exhibits include feedings and aerial acrobatics. *107 Skagensvej, Tuen, tel. 98/93–20–31. Admission: DKr50 adults, DKr25 children. Showtimes: Apr., Wed. 10; May, Tues. and Wed. 10, Sun. 3; June, Tues. and Wed. 10, weekends 5; July, Tues.–Fri. 10 and 5, weekends 5; Aug., Wed. 10 and 5, Tues. 10, Fri.–Sun. 5; Sept., Tues. and Wed. 10, Sat. 3.*

What to See and Do with Children

Besides Legoland, there's the **Fårup Sommerland** (Summer Land) recreation center in Saltum, about 30 kilometers (18 miles) west of Aalborg, with a massive water park, moon buggies, trampolines, and rides. *147 Pirupvejen, tel. 98/88–16–00. Admission: DKr75–DKr90. Opening times vary; call for current hours.*

Aalborg's **Tivoliland** has a boomerang roller coaster, buggies, and gardens. *Karolinelundsvej, tel. 98/12–58–74. Admission: DKr40 adults, DKr20 children. Open May–Sept.; hours vary.*

In Århus there is yet another **Tivoli,** with rides, music, and lovely gardens. *Skovbrynet, tel. 86/14–73–00. Admission: DKr22 adults, DKr10 children. Open mid-Apr.–May, daily 1–9; May–mid-June, daily 1–10; mid-June–mid-Aug., daily 1–11.*

Off the Beaten Track

A thousand years ago the Vikings mined their chalk from the caves of **Mønsted Kalkgruber** (Chalk Mines), but now the cool, multipurpose grottoes store 220 tons of cheese and a Museum of Bats. Occasional classical concerts are also held in the mine. *Kalkværksvej, Mønsted (15 km w of Viborg), tel. 86/64–60–02.*

Admission: DKr30 adults, DKr10 children. Open mid-May–mid-June and mid-Aug.–mid-Sept., Tues.–Sun. 1–4; mid-June–mid-Aug., daily 10–5.

See exactly how small the world can be at the **Verdenskort** (World Map Garden), near Klejtrup Lake in the north of the peninsula. For 25 years Søren Poulsen has been digging, moving and sculpting dirt along the southern shore of the lake into the exact shape of the continents. Leaps and bounds can take you around the world—and you can even putt on a miniature golf course. *Klejtrup Lake, 10 km (6 mi) southwest of Hobro and tip of Mariager Fjord, tel. 98/54–61–32. Admission: DKr12 adults, DKr6 children. Open Sept.–May, daily 9–6; June–Aug., daily 9–8.*

Shopping

Ask at the tourism offices about local potters, glassblowers, and craftspeople, as well as antiques dealers, and stroll through the central pedestrian streets, which are full of shops.

Sports and Outdoor Activities

Bicycling Package holidays range from island day trips to eight-day excursions. Information is available from any tourism board or the **County of North Jylland** (Niels Bohrsvej, Box 8300, DK–9220 Aalborg, tel. 98/15–62–22). (*See also* Getting Around by Bicycle, *above*.)

Canoeing Canoe rentals (about DKr180 per day) are available in the lake district, Limfjord, and on almost all lakes and rivers. One- to three-day package tours are available with either camping or hostel accommodations. For more information, contact the **Randers Tourist Bureau.**

Fishing There's great angling (trout, perch, pike, and others), especially along the **Limfjord, Karup River** near Skive, and south along the **Lake District.** License requirements vary and package tours are also available; contact any tourism board for details.

Golf There are 21 18-hole courses, all of which are open to guests. For greens fees and tee times, call **Holstebro Golf Club** near Randers (4 Brandsbjergvej, Råsted 7570 Vemb, tel. 97/48–51–55), the **Aalborg Golf Club** (Jægersprisvej 35, tel. 98/34–14–76), or the **Esbjerg Golf Club** (Sønderhedevej Marbæk, tel. 75/26–92–19).

Beaches

Jylland is famous among northern Europeans for its wide beaches and shifting dunes. Facilities and cafés are almost always nearby, and the beaches and water are clean. The east coast has calm waters, good for children and windsurfing, while western and northern waters are rougher, with expansive beaches. In these areas you'll need to rent or buy a wind tarp as protection from the blowing sands.

Dining and Lodging

Dining in Jylland ranges from homespun *kro* (inns) serving huge country meals to snazzy restaurants offering French nouveau. As the area is mostly frequented by Danes, national spe-

cialties are almost always homemade, and prices tend to be substantially lower than those in the rest of the country. As elsewhere in the Danish countryside, hotels, and especially family restaurants, expect guests to arrive early (say, by 7 PM). (For price-category definitions, *see* Dining and Lodging in Staying in Denmark, *above*.)

Highly recommended establishments are indicated by a star ★.

Aalborg
Dining

Cafeen og Dufy. Light and bright on an old cobbled street, these are among the most popular eateries in town. Downstairs, bistro-style Cafeen has a French-style ambience, with marble-topped tables, engraved mirrors, and windows over Jomfru Ane Gade, while upstairs, Dufy is more elegant and quiet. The French menu is the same in both, including lobster-and-cognac soup for two, sliced roast duck with Waldorf salad, and beef fillet. *Jomfru Ane Gade 8, tel. 98/16–34–44. Reservations advised. Dress: casual but neat. DC, MC, V. Moderate.*

★ **Spisehuset Kniv og Gaffel.** In a 400-year-old building parallel to Jumfru Ane Gade, this busy restaurant is crammed with oak tables, crazy slanting floors, and candlelight, while a year-round courtyard is a veritable greenhouse. Young waitresses negotiate the mayhem to deliver inch-thick steaks, the house specialty. *Maren Turisgade 10, tel. 98/16–69–72. Reservations advised. Dress: casual but neat. DC, MC, V. Closed Sun. Moderate.*

Dining and Lodging

Helnan Phønix. Centrally located in a sumptuous old mansion, this hotel is popular with international and business guests. The rooms are luxuriously furnished with plump chairs and polished dark-wood furniture; in some the original raw beams are still intact. The Brigadier serves excellent French and Danish food. *Vesterbro 77, DK–9000, tel. 98/12–00–11, fax 98/16–31–66. 185 rooms: 120 with bath and shower, 57 with shower; 3 suites. Facilities: restaurant, bar, café, sauna, solarium, room service, meeting center, parking. AE, DC, MC, V. Very Expensive.*

Århus
Dining
★

Restaurant Mahler. Located on a busy street lined with ethnic restaurants, this representative of French cuisine is elegant, with swagged drapes, hanging clusters of dried spices, and gem-colored flasks of oils. The ever-changing menu of co-owners Hanne Hesseldal and Lene Gabel is classical, with new dishes also included. Every two weeks they feature the gastronomy of another region of France, while using only the freshest Danish ingredients. *Vestergade 39, tel. 86/19–06–96. Reservations advised. Dress: casual but neat. AE, DC, MC, V. Closed Mon., Sat. lunch, Sun., holidays, and Dec. 24–Jan 2. Expensive.*

Lodging

Royal Hotel. Open since 1838, Århus's grand hotel has welcomed such greats as Artur Rubinstein and Marian Anderson. Well-heeled guests are welcomed into a stately lobby appointed in Chesterfield sofas, modern paintings, and a winding staircase that leads to the rooms above. The plush rooms vary in style and decor, but all boast rich drapery, velour and brocade furniture, and marble bathrooms. *Store Torv 4, 8100 Århus C, tel. 86/12–00–11, fax 86/76–04–04. 111 rooms with shower, 7 suites. Facilities: restaurant, bar, casino, sauna, solarium, business center. AE, DC, MC, V. Expensive.*

Ansgar Missions Hotel. This old hotel is simple and dated, with

used Danish furniture, but the staff is agreeable and helpful. Despite drab halls and worn carpets, the rooms are adequate and comfortable, with laminated furniture, old-fashioned wallpaper, and bright lighting. Downstairs there's a cafeteria-style restaurant where you can choose from a large smørrebrød table and nonalcoholic beverages. *Banegårdsplads 14, DK–8100, tel. 86/12–41–22, fax 86/20–29–04. 170 rooms, 137 with shower, 20 with shower and bath. Facilities: restaurant. DC, MC, V. Inexpensive.*

Fanø
Dining and Lodging
★

Sønderho Kro. Just 13 kilometers (8 miles) from Fanø's main town of Norrebro, this 270-year-old thatched-roof inn is one of Jylland's finest, its charm preserved with a beamed foyer, painted doors, and timbered ceilings. The rooms are gussied up with four-poster beds, elegant tapestries, and gauzy curtains. The Franco-Danish restaurant serves excellent seafood on its old tables. *Kropladsen 11, DK–6720, Sønderho, tel. 75/16–40–09. 7 rooms with bath, 1 suite. Facilities: restaurant, parking. AE, DC, MC, V. Closed Jan. 8–Feb. 7. Moderate.*

Kolding
Dining and Lodging
★

Hotel Koldingfjord. An impressive neoclassical building, this vast hotel was refurbished a few years back, and fitted with mahogany floors and pyramid skylights. Five minutes from town, it faces the Kolding Fjord and 50 acres of countryside. The rooms vary in size (with 39 in a separate annex), but all have mahogany beds, bright prints, and views of fjord or forest. There's also an excellent French-Danish restaurant. *Fjordvej 154, Strandhuse, 6000, tel. 75/51–00–00, fax 75/51–00–51. 115 rooms, 7 suites. Facilities: restaurant, bar, health club, indoor pool, tennis courts, sauna, solarium, breakfast included. AE, DC, MC, V. Closed Dec. 27–30. Expensive.*

Ribe
Dining

Sælhunden. This 300-year-old canal-side tavern barely accommodates a dozen tables, but its cozy atmosphere makes it popular with wayfarers and locals. Its name means "male seal"; the only seal mementos left are a few skins and pictures, but you can still order a "seal's special" of cold shrimp, sautéed potatoes, and scrambled eggs or—an old Danish favorite—fat strips of bacon served with cream gravy and boiled potatoes. *Skibbroen 13, tel. 75/42–09–46. No reservations. Dress: casual. DC, MC, V. Closed for dinner after 8:45. Inexpensive.*

Dining and Lodging
★

Hotel Dagmar. In the midst of Ribe's quaint center, this cozy half-timbered hotel encapsulates the charm of the 16th century—with stained-glass windows, sloping wooden floors, and carved chairs. The lavish rooms are all appointed with antique canopy beds, fat armchairs, and chaise longues. The fine French restaurant serves such specialties as fillet of salmon in sorrel cream sauce and marinated foie gras de Canard. *Torvet 1, DK–6760, tel. 75/42–00–33, fax 75/42–36–52. 48 rooms with bath. Facilities: restaurant, bar, parking, meeting rooms. AE, DC, MC, V. Closed Dec. 24–Jan. 1. Expensive.*

Lodging

Ribe Family and Youth Hostel. Located in the center of town, this plain, redbrick hostelry is run by helpful wardens. Six- and four-bed dorm rooms are arranged in clusters of four, each sharing a shower, toilet, and small hallway. They are functional and child-proof, with pine bunks and industrial carpeting. *Ribehallen, Skt. Pedersgade 16, tel. 75/42–06–20, fax 75/42–42–88. 26 rooms, 12 communal showers and toilets. Facilities: cafeteria, kitchen, parking, sports hall. No credit cards. Closed Dec.–Jan. Inexpensive.*

Silkeborg **Spisehuset Christian VIII.** Divided from Silkeborg's center by a
Dining highway, this tiny crooked building seems transported from
another time. Inside it's elegant—and busy, with an international group of diners occupying the dozen cramped tables. The
inventive menu includes such meat and poultry dishes as veal
medallion stuffed with wild-duck breast and lamb chops stuffed
with feta cheese and rosemary. *Christian VIII Vej 54, tel. 86/
82–25–62. Reservations advised. Dress: casual but neat. AE,
DC, MC, V. Closed Sun. and 2 weeks in July. Moderate.*

Skagen **Brøndums Hotel.** A few minutes from the beach, this 150-year-
Dining and Lodging old gabled inn is furnished with antiques and Skagen School
★ paintings. The 21 guest rooms in the main building, without
TVs or phones, are old-fashioned, with wicker chairs and Oriental rugs, pine and four-poster beds. The 25 annex rooms are
more modern. The hotel has a fine Danish-French restaurant
with a lavish cold table. *Anchersvej 3, DK–9990, tel. 98/44–15–
55, fax 98/45–15–20. 46 rooms, 11 with bath, 1 suite. Facilities:
restaurant, conference rooms, parking. AE, DC, MC, V.
Closed Dec. 24–Jan. 1. Expensive.*

Vejle **Munkebjerg Hotel.** Seven kilometers (4 miles) southeast of
Dining and Lodging town, surrounded by a thick beech forest and majestic views of
the Vejle Fjord, this elegant hotel attracts guests who prefer
privacy. The rooms overlook the forest and are furnished in
blond pine and soft green, while the lobby is rustic. There are
also two top-notch French-Danish restaurants and a swank
new casino. *Munkebjergvej 125, DK–7100, tel. 75/72–35–00,
fax 75/72–08–86. 145 rooms with bath, 2 suites. Facilities: 2
restaurants, casino, health club, indoor pool, tennis court,
sauna, solarium, room service, business center, parking, heli-
port. AE, DC, MC, V. Closed Dec. 20–28. Very Expensive.*
Bredal Kro. Eight kilometers (5 miles) north of Vejle, this
street-side inn is an essential stop for travelers. Behind the
green gables, the traditional menu of hearty Danish omelets
and stews probably hasn't changed in 250 years, but for the
health-conscious there's a list of low-fat and cholesterol-free
fish and game. Modest, motel-style rooms are in a separate annex. *Horsensvej 581, DK–7100, tel. 75/89–57–99. Reservations
accepted. Dress: casual. AE, DC, MC, V. Closed Dec. 24–Jan.
1. Inexpensive.*

The Arts and Nightlife

The Arts Cultural activities are concentrated in Århus and Aalborg,
both of which have local symphonies and concert halls and free
events throughout the summer. There's no better time to visit
Århus than during the **10-day music festival** in September,
when jazz, classical, and rock concerts are nonstop (*see* Exploring Jylland, Århus, *above*).

Nightlife Nightlife in Århus, and especially Aalborg, is as glittery as
anything in Copenhagen. Much of it is geared toward young au-
diences, but there are late-night cafés and bars for an older
crowd.

Bars, Lounges, Besides dozens of bars on **Aalborg's** Jomfrue Ane Gade, **Duus**
and Discos **Vinkjælder** (Østerå 9, tel. 98/12–50–56), the atmospheric wine
cellar of the Jens Bangs Hus, is extremely popular. Among the
discos, **Gaslight** (tel. 98/10–17–50), **New York** (tel. 98/16–45–
44), and **Over and Under the Clock** (tel. 98/10–30–22) on
Aalborg's Jomfrue Ane Gade all draw young crowds, while

Ambassadeur (Vesterbro 76, tel. 98/12–62–22), with four dance restaurants and live music, is popular with a more mature audience.

In **Århus, Café Mozart** (Vesterport 10, tel. 86/18–55–63) features classical music, while **Den Sidste Café** (Paradisegade 9, tel. 86/13–71–11) rocks until 5 AM. **Down Town** (Store Torv 4, tel. 86/13–95–77) is packed with youngsters, but the new **Beach Club** in the Hotel Marselis (Strandvejen 25, tel. 86/14–44–11) attracts all ages for dancing to a trio every night except Sunday and Monday, when the music is country-western. The **Alexis Night Club** (Frederiksgade 72, tel. 86/12–77–55) is all shiny neon, with a well-dressed crowd of all ages. **Edison** (Frederiksgade 76, tel. 86/12–25–88) caters to all ages.

Casinos   There are three new casinos on Jylland, all with blackjack, roulette, baccarat, and slot machines. They are in **Limsfjordshotellet** (Ved Stranden 14–16, **Aalborg,** tel. 98/16–43–33), **Munkebjerg Hotel** (Munkebjergvej 125, **Vejle,** tel. 75/72–35–00), and the **Royal Hotel** (Store Torv 4, **Århus,** tel. 86/12–00–11).

Jazz Clubs   In **Århus, Bent J's** (Nørre Allé 66, tel. 86/12–04–92) is a small club with free-admission jam sessions three times a week and occasional big-name concerts. On a larger scale there's **Glazz Huset** (Åboulevarden 35, tel. 86/12–13–12). **Aalborg** doesn't have a regular club, but local musicians get together at least once a week for **jam sessions.** Ask the tourist board for details.

Bornholm

Called the Pearl of the Baltic for its natural beauty and winsomely rustic towns, Bornholm, 177 kilometers (110 miles) southeast of Sjælland, is geographically unlike the rest of Denmark. A temperate climate has made this 363-square-kilometer (225-square-mile) jumble of granite bluffs, clay soil, and rift valleys an extravagance of nature. Rich plantations of fir bristle beside wide dunes and vast heather fields, while lush gardens and meadows bear fig, cherry, chestnut, and mulberry trees—even grape vines. Denmark's third-largest forest, the Almindingen, crowns the center, while the southern tip is ringed with some of Europe's whitest beaches.

During the Iron and Bronze ages, Bornholm was inhabited by seafaring and farming cultures that dotted the land with their burial dolmens and engravings. From the Middle Ages to the 18th century, the Danes battled the Swedes for ownership of the island, protecting it with strongholds, battlegrounds, and fortified churches, many of which still loom over the landscape.

Today Bornholmers continue to draw their livelihood from the land and sea—and increasingly from tourism. The towns are peaked with chalk-white chimneys, the harbors are abob with carefully painted fishing boats, and, in spring and summer, the fields blaze with amber mustard and grain—all of which can best be seen from a bicycle.

Important Addresses and Numbers

Tourist   **Bornholm's** information center in **Rønne** (Ndr. Kystvej 3, tel.
Information   56/95–95–00) has brochures and maps that cover the entire island. Local tourist offices can be found in **Allinge** (Kirkegade

4, tel. 56/48–00–01), **Åkirkeby** (Jernbanegade 1, tel. 56/97–45–20), **Gudhjem** (Åbogade 9, tel. 56/48–52–10), **Nexø** (Åsen 4, tel. 56/49–32–00), and **Svaneke** (Storegade 24, tel. 56/49–63–50).

Emergencies For **ambulance, accident,** or **fire,** call 112.

Hospital Emergency **Bornholm's Central Hospital,** Sygehusvej, Rønne, tel. 56/95–
Room 11–65

Late-Night The **Rønne Apotek** (Store Torvegade 12, Rønne, tel. 56/95–01–
Pharmacy 30) is open until 8 on weeknights. At night a phone number is left in the window for emergency calls.

Arriving and Departing by Plane

The airport is 5 kilometers (3½ miles) south of Rønne at the island's southwestern tip. **DanAir** (tel. 56/95–11–11) makes several daily flights only from Copenhagen.

Arriving and Departing by Car Ferry, Hydrofoil, and Bus

By Car Ferry The car ferry from Copenhagen's Kvæsthusbro Harbor (near
and Hydrofoil Nyhavn) departs at 11:30 PM year-round and June through August, Friday, Saturday, and Sunday at 8:30 AM. The trip takes 7 hours. To avoid delays, make a reservation. Comfortable sleeping bunks in a massive hall are also available for an extra cost. Additional summer ferries link Neu Mukran (3½ hours) and Sassnitz (4 hours; both on the island of Rügen) in Germany. There is also a boat between Swinoujscie, Poland, and Rønne (7 hours). Call **Bornholms Trafikken** (tel. 33/13–18–66). Germany's TT Line (tel. 040–3601–442–446) runs a ferry between Rostock and Rønne (7 hours). A hydrofoil from Nyhavn goes to Malmö, Sweden, where it connects with a bus to Ystad and a ferry to Rønne. The 4-hour voyage runs twice daily, usually in the morning and again in the late afternoon. Call **Flyve Bådene** (tel. 33/12–80–88).

By Bus A **Gråhund** (Greyhound) No. 866 bus from Copenhagen's Main Station travels to Dragør, boards a ferry to Limhamn, and then continues to Ystad, where it connects with a ferry to Rønne. Buses depart twice daily, once in the morning and again in late afternoon. Call **Bornholm Bussen** (tel. 44/68–44–00).

Getting Around

By Car There are excellent roads on the island, but be alert for cyclists and occasional wandering cows.

By Bus Bus service is good, with regular connections between towns. Schedules are posted at all stations, and you can usually pick one up on board. The fare is DKr7.50 per zone, or you can buy a *klip-kort* (punch ticket) of 10 *klips* for DKr60 (tel. 56/95–21–21). A 24-hour bus pass costs DKr90.

By Bicycle The island has a network of more than 600 kilometers (360 miles) of cycle roads, including an old railway converted to a cross-island path. There are more than 20 places to rent sturdy two-speeds and tandems, for about DKr50 a day. Rentals are available near the ferry, the airport, Allinge, Gudhjem, Hasle, Pedersker (near Åkirkeby), Rønne, Svaneke, and most other towns. Try **Bornholms Cykleudlejning** (Havnegade 11, tel. 56/

95–13–59) and **Cykel-Centret** (Søndergade 7, tel. 56/95–06–04), both in Rønne.

Guided Tours

The **Bornholmrund** (Round Bornholm) bus tour (8½ hours), at 9:30 Tuesday and Thursday, includes Rønne, Hammershus, Allinge, Gudhjem, Østerlars Church, Svaneke, Nexø, Balka, Åkirkeby, and the Almindingen Forest. To make reservations, call the Bornholm Tourist Center. An aerial tour in a Cessna or Piper plane (20–45 min.) covers either the entire coast or the northern tip. Call **Klippefly** (tel. 56/95–35–73 or 56/48–42–01). From mid-June to mid-September, boats to **Helligdomsklipperne** (the Sanctuary Cliffs) leave Gudhjem at 10:30, 1:30, and 2:30, with extra sails mid-June to mid-August. Call **Thor Båd** (tel. 56/48–51–65). Boats to **Christiansø** depart Svaneke at 10 daily; May to September daily at 10:20 from Gudhjem and at 1 from Allinge. From mid-June to August, boats also leave Gudhjem weekdays at 9:40 and 12:15. Call **Christiansø Farten** (tel. 56/48–51–76) for additional information.

Special-Interest   The **Kunst og håndværk** (Arts and Crafts) bus tour (5 hours) runs Monday through Thursday at 10 and includes six glass and pottery studios. The **Pelle the Conqueror Tour** (6 hours) follows the history of Swedish immigrants as portrayed in Martin Andersen Nexø's novel *Pelle the Conqueror*, which was made into an Oscar-winning film. The tour is at 10 Wednesday and includes the Moseløkken Quarry Museum, Vang, Almindingen Forest, the Paradise Hills, and the Agricultural Museum at Melstedgård. For reservations, call 56/95–21–21.

Exploring Bornholm

Numbers in the margin correspond to points of interest on the Bornholm map.

❶ The island's capital, port, and largest town is **Rønne,** a good starting point for exploring northward or southward on the island. East of Nørrekås Harbor on Laksegade, you'll find an enchanting area of rose-clad 17th- and 18th-century houses, among them the terra-cotta-roofed **Erichsens Gård** (farm). The home of the wealthy Erichsen family, whose daughter married the Danish poet Holger Drachmann, it is preserved with paintings by Danish artist Kristian Zahrtmann, period furnishings, and a lovely garden. *Laksegade 7, tel. 56/95–87–35. Admission: DKr10 adults, children free. Open May–mid-Oct., Mon.–Sat. 1–4, Sun. 1–5.*

Down the street, off Store Torv (Town Center), you'll come to the **Bornholm Museum,** which features local geologic and archaeological exhibits, in addition to more than 4,500 pieces of ceramics and glass. Antiques and clock lovers shouldn't miss the 25 18th-century *Bornholmure* (Bornholm Clocks), which are as characteristic of the island as smoked herring. In 1744, a Dutch ship was wrecked on Bornholm, and the English grandfather clocks aboard it became the model for the island's clocks. There's also an annex of Bornholm paintings. *Skt. Mortensgade 29, tel. 56/95–07–35. Admission: DKr20 adults, DKr5 children. Open Apr.–Oct., Mon.–Sat. 10–5, Sun. 1–5; Nov.–Apr., Tues., Thurs., and Sun. 2–5.*

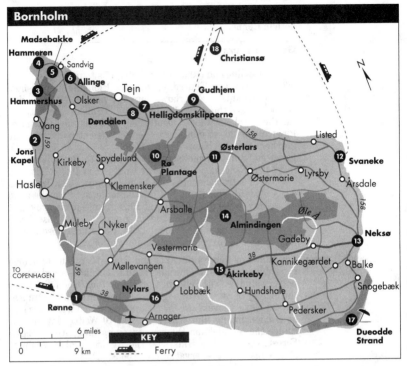

Bornholm

2 Another 14 kilometers (8½ miles) north is **Jons Kapel** (Jon's Chapel), where a medieval legend has it that a monk, Brother Jon, lived in a cave here and used the treacherous sea cliffs as a pulpit for his sermons. Wear rubber-soled hiking boots and climb the stairs that lead to the pulpit, where the agile friar stood atop a dramatic 72-foot-high cliffs that loom over the crashing waves.

3 You can drive or bike northward on Route 159 to **Hammershus** fortress, but it's lovely (though mildly strenuous) to hike from the town of **Vang** up the rocky coast to the ruins of northern Europe's largest stronghold. The fortress, begun in 1255 by the archbishop of Lund (Sweden), became the object of centuries of struggle between Denmark and Sweden. In 1648 Danes under Jens Kofoed killed its Swedish governor, and the castle was given back to Denmark. Used until 1743, it became a ruin when it was quarried for stone to fortify Christiansø and that island's buildings. The government finally intervened in 1822, and the site is now an impressive mass of snaggletoothed walls and juggernaut-shaped towers atop a grassy knoll. During restoration work in 1967, 22 gold German guilders were found. *No tel. Admission free.*

4 Bornholm's northern tip is called **Hammeren** (The Hammer) and is nearly separated from the island by a deep rift valley and the **Hammer Sø** (Hammer Lake). Despite constant Baltic winds, rare plants and trees grow on the warm, granite-scattered land, including bright anemones. Look across the water south of the tip to the stone formation called the Camel Heads.

⑤ South of the tip, outside the town of **Sandvig,** is **Madsebakke,** the largest collection of Bronze Age rock carvings in Denmark. They are presumed to be ceremonial carvings, which ancient fishermen and farmers hoped would bring good weather and bountiful crops. The most interesting of them depicts 11 ships, including one with a sun wheel.

⑥ To the northeast are the twin towns of Sandvig and **Allinge.** Here you'll find centuries-old neighborhoods and, particularly in Allinge, half-timbered houses and herring smokehouses sprouting tall chimneys. Just south is a wood the islanders call the **Trolleskoe** (Troll Forest). Legend says trolls live in the woods, and when they brew fog, they escape the heat in the kitchen and go out looking for trouble. The most mischievous is the littlest troll, Krølle Bølle.

Another 8 kilometers (5 miles) south on the coastal path are the
⑦ grottoes and granite cliffs of **Helligdomsklipperne** (the Cliffs of Sanctuary), a well-known rock formation best seen from boats that ply the nearby waters in summer. There is also a pastoral
⑧ coastal path that leads to the tiny, preserved **Døndalen** forest. The fertile ground bears Mediterranean vegetation such as fig and cherry trees, and during rainy periods there's a waterfall at the bottom of the dale.

⑨ Southeast of the forest is the town of **Gudhjem** (God's Home). Tiny half-timbered houses with lace curtains and clay roofs are built atop steep stone streets that loop around the harbor and the island's first smokehouses, which still produce alder-smoked golden herring.

Time Out Gudhjem has bakeries and cafés; the favorite local snack is a Sol over Gudhjem (Sun Over Gudhjem): a slice of dark buttered bread, topped with filleted herring (that's the Gudhjem), a raw egg (that's the sun), onions, chives, and rock salt, from **Niels Hansens Rogeri** (Ejnar Mikkelsenf. vej 6, tel. 56/48–50–64) near the harbor. For something sweet, try the ice cream named after the impish **Krølle Bølle** that's available at cafés and kiosks.

Before you leave Gudhjem, walk down Brøddegade, which turns into Melstedvej. Here you'll find the **Landsbrugs Museum** (Agricultural Museum) and a working farm with cows, horses, sheep, and the house and garden of a 19th-century farm family. *Melstedvej 25, tel. 56/48–55–98. Admission: DKr15 adults, DKr5 children. Open mid-May–mid-Oct., Tues.–Sun. 10–5.*

⑩ Five kilometers (3 miles) inland is the **Rø Plantage** (Rø Plantation). A century ago it was a heather-covered grazing area, but after stone dikes were erected to keep the cattle out, spruce, pine, larch, and birch were cultivated. The cool refuge now consists mostly of saplings and new growth—the result of devastating storms in the late '50s and '60s.

Southeast of the plantation 5 kilometers (3 miles) is the town of
⑪ **Østerlars** and the **Østerlars Kirke** (Østerlars Church). The largest of the island's four round churches, it was built in about 1150; extensions, including the buttresses, were added later. Constructed from boulders and slabs of limestone, the whitewashed church was part spiritual sanctuary, part fortification, affording protection from enemy armies and pirates. Inside is the island's only painted tympanum, with a faded im-

age of a cross and decorative foliage. Several Gothic wall paintings—including images of the Annunciation and the Birth of
Christ—have survived from the 1300s. *Gudhjemsvej 28, tel. 56/
49–82–64. Admission: DKr3 adults, children free. Open Apr.–
mid-Oct., Mon.–Sat. 9–5.*

⓬ The coastal town of **Svaneke,** Denmark's easternmost settlement, is an enchanting hamlet of 17th- and 18th-century
houses, winding cobbled streets, and a harbor that was sliced
from the rocky earth. Once a fishing village, it is now immacu-
lately preserved and boasts a thriving artists' community.

⓭ Next is **Neksø** (or Nexø), 9 kilometers (5½ miles) south of
Svaneke. Though it looks like a typical 17th-century town, it
was rebuilt almost completely after World War II, when the
Russians bombed it to dislodge stubborn German troops who
refused to surrender—three days after the rest of Denmark
had been liberated. The Russians also lingered on the island,
until March 1946.

The **Neksø Museum** has a fine collection of fishing and local history exhibits, including photographs and memorabilia of Danish author Martin Andersen Hansen (1909–1955), who changed
his last name to Nexø after his beloved town. A complicated and
vehement socialist, he wrote, among other works, *Pelle the
Conqueror,* which is set in Bornholm at the turn of the century,
when Swedish immigrants were exploited by Danish landowners. *Havnen, tel. 56/49–25–56. Admission: DKr10 adults,
DKr5 children. Open mid-June–mid-Sept., Tues.–Sun. 9–
noon.*

⓮ In the center of the island is the **Almindingen,** Bornholm's largest and Denmark's third-largest forest. Filled with ponds,
lakes, evergreens, and well-marked trails, it blooms with lily of
the valley in spring. Within it, the oak-lined **Ekkodalen** (Echo
Valley) is networked with trails leading to smooth rock faces
soaring up 72 feet. At the northern edge, near the road to
Østermarie, is one of Bornholm's most famous sights: seven
evergreens growing from a single trunk.

⓯ Five kilometers (3 miles) south is **Åkirkeby,** the oldest town on
the island, with a municipal charter from 1346. The town's
church, **Åkirke,** is Bornholm's oldest and largest, dating from
the mid-13th century. Though it is not a round church, both
walls and tower were well suited for defense. The altarpiece
and pulpit are Dutch Renaissance from about 1600, but the engraved sandstone font is as old as the church itself. *Torvet, tel.
56/97–41–03. Admission DKr5. Open daily 9–5.*

⓰ Next, 8 kilometers (5 miles) west, is **Nylars** and the **Nylars
Kirke,** another round church. Like the Østerlars Church, it
dates from 1150, but the chalk paintings from the Old Testament on the central pillar are the oldest on the island, possibly
dating from 1250. Even older are the runic stones on the
church's porch. Both are of Viking origin. *Kirkevej, tel. 56/97–
20–13. Donation: DKr3. Open mid-May–mid-Sept., Mon.–
Sat. 9–5.*

⓱ At the southern tip of the island is the **Dueodde Strand,** which
can be reached by walking through a pine, spruce, and winter-
green forest. The dunes crest up to 46 feet, and locals claim that
the sand, which was once used to fill hourglasses, is the finest in
the world.

Before leaving Bornholm, take the 45-minute boat ride to the ⑱ island of **Christiansø**. It was originally a bastion, but the Storetårn (Big Tower) and Lilletårn (Little Tower) are all that remain of the fort, which was built in 1684 and dismantled in 1855. The barracks, street, and gardens, for which the earth was transported in boats, have hardly changed since and remain under the jurisdiction of the defense ministry, making it a tiny tax-free haven for the 100 inhabitants. Nearby, the rocky, uninhabited island of **Græsholmen** is an inaccessible bird sanctuary—the only place in Denmark where the razorbill and guillemot breed.

What to See and Do with Children

Brændesgårdshaven is an old-fashioned amusement park with a rowboat pond, miniature golf, a toy factory, and Vandland (Waterland), with several water rides and swimming pools, about 6 kilometers (3½ miles) south of Svaneke. Bring a bathing suit and a towel. *Ibsker, tel. 56/49–60–76. Admission: DKr40 Sept.–June, DKr45 July–Aug. Open May–June and Aug.–Sept., daily 10–6; July–Aug., daily 9–8.*

Bornholms Dyre og Naturpark (Deer and Nature Park) is filled with tame goats, donkeys, ponies, and fenced-in ostriches, llamas, camels, and other animals. *Borrelyngvej, 2 km (1 mi) south of Allinge in Hasle, tel. 56/48–15–65. Admission: DKr30 adults, DKr10 children. Open May–Sept., daily 10–5.*

Off the Beaten Track

At least one night, do as the Danes do: Climb the **Dueodde Fyr** (lighthouse) for a panoramic view, then watch the lingering indigo-and-purple sunset. Or just sit on a beach, near **Pedersker,** and watch the swallows dive. Afterward, trudge up the dunes to the beach-side kiosks—where children and grown-ups patiently queue up for bags of handpicked candy and jam-topped ice-cream cones.

Shopping

Bornholm is famous in Scandinavia for its craftspeople, especially the glassblowers and ceramicists, whose work is often pricier in Copenhagen and Stockholm. In the center of each town (especially Gudhjem and Svaneke), you'll find crafts shops and *værksteder* (workshops). When you're on the road, watch for *keramik* (ceramics) signs, which direct you to artists working from home.

Ceramics and Glass The **Kampeløkken** (Havnegade 45, Allinge, tel. 56/48–17–66) gallery shop stocks the work of 24 potters and four glassblowers. Also stroll through the ateliers and boutiques in the central **Glastorvet** in Allinge. Among them is the studio of **Pernille Bülow,** one of Denmark's most famous glassblowers. Her work is sold in Copenhagen's best design shops. Even if you buy directly from her studio (Glastorvet, Brænderigænget 8, tel. 56/49–66–72), don't expect bargains, but do expect colorful, experimental work. **Baltic Sea Glass** (Melstedvej 47, Gudhjem, tel. 56/48–56–41) offers high-quality bright, imaginative decanters, glasses, candlesticks, and one-of-a-kind pieces. In Gudhjem you can see the delicate porcelain bowls of **Per Rehfeldt** (Kastenievej 8, tel. 56/48–54–13) and the unique,

hand-thrown pieces of **Julia Manitius** (Holkavej 12, tel. 56/48–55–99).

Specialty Stores   A *Bornholmur* is a type of grandfather clock handmade on the island. Antique versions cost from DKr5,000 to DKr9,000 and more. New clocks modeled from museum originals are custom-made by **Bornholmerure** (Torneværksvej 26, Rønne, tel. 56/95–31–08). The clocks often have round faces but can be rectangular as well and are completely handmade and painted. On the hour, the modern clocks sound the hour with music—which ranges from Mozart and Verdi to Sondheim and Andrew Lloyd Webber. A handmade custom clock can cost as much as DKr25,000 ($4,166). For **leather,** visit **Askepot** (Postgade 5, Svaneke, tel. 53/99–70–42) for handmade hats, jackets, and wallets. For exquisite **woodwork,** see **Bernard Romain** (Rønnevej 54, Neksø, tel. 56/48–86–66), and for **hand-printed textiles, Bente Hammer** (Nyker Hovedgade 32, Rønne, tel. 56/96–33–35).

Street Markets   There is a large vegetable and fruit market on Wednesday and Saturday mornings in Stor Torv, the main square in **Rønne.**

Sports and Outdoor Activities

Bicycling   *See* Getting Around, *above.*

Camping   There are more than 15 excellent campsites on the island, including **Galløkken Camping** (Strandvejen 4, DK–3700 Rønne, tel. 56/95–23–20, **Sandvig Familie Camping** (Sandlinien 5, DK–3770 Allinge, tel. 56/48–04–47 or 56/48–00–01), and **Dueodde Camping** (Skrokkegårdsvej 3730 Neksø, tel. 56/48–81–19).

Fishing   Cod, salmon, and herring fishing are excellent in season, though better from a boat than onshore. Licenses cost DKr25 per day, DKr75 per week, and DKr100 for a year. Contact the tourist board for details and information on charter trips. Among the handful of charter companies is **Per Andersen** (Holkavej 22, Gudhjem, tel. 56/48–55–54).

Golf   There are three courses on the island; the **Rønne Golfbane** near Rønne (tel. 56/95–68–54), **Rø Golfbane** up north (tel. 56/48–40–50), and **Dueodde Golfbane** (tel. 56/48–89–87) near the southern forest. Admission to each green is about DKr140.

Hiking   Marked trails crisscross the island, including three 4-kilometer (2½-mile) hikes through the Almindingen forest and several more through its Ekkodalen. The northern coastline is beautiful but a rocky and more strenuous walk. Ask for a map, routes, and tips from any tourism office. The *Bornholm Green Guide,* which is available in shops and tourism offices, offers suggestions for walking and hiking tours.

Windsurfing   The winds are strongest and most constant on the sandy southern coast, especially during spring and fall. The shores are rockier north of Neksø. There are several board rentals and classes on the island, including **Windsurfing ved Balke Strand** (tel. 56/95–00–77), south of Neksø.

Beaches

The northern beaches are rocky and narrow, better suited for hiking and walking, though some people like to dive from the rocks. On the road from Gudhjem to Svaneke on the east coast,

there's a lovely rocky beach, but the swimming and sunning are best farther south, between Pedersker and Snogebæk, where the dunes are tall, the beaches wide. As elsewhere in Denmark, topless bathing is acceptable and nude bathing is tolerated.

Dining and Lodging

Most of the island's finest restaurants are in hotels, while inexpensive smokehouses and cafés provide Bornholm's "fast food." The island is popular with returning Europeans, who book accommodations up to a year in advance. In summer space is scarce and expensive, but if you arrive without a hotel, the tourist office can sometimes find a room or a campsite.

Highly recommended establishments are indicated by a star ★.

Allinge **Strandhotellet.** Completely renovated after a fire, this old hotel
Dining and Lodging still has its romantic, Old World charm. Located on a corner
★ across from the harbor, it has a white, arched entry into a stone-and-whitewashed lobby. The rooms are furnished in plain beech furniture with woolen covers and pastel colors. *Strandpromenaden 7, DK–3770, tel. 56/48–03–14, fax 56/48–02–09. 50 rooms with shower, 1 suite. Facilities: restaurant, bar, health club, sauna, solarium, steam room, parking. AE, DC, MC, V. Closed mid-Oct.–mid-Apr. Moderate.*

Dueodde **Bornholm.** In the midst of the Dueodde woods, this hotel has
Dining and Lodging simple double rooms, apartments, and very sought-after bungalows, which have a living room, a terrace, two to three bedrooms, a kitchenette, and a shower. All are furnished in pre-1970 pivot chairs and Formica. The entire compound faces the white beaches of the island's southern tip. *Pilegårdsvej 1, Dueodde, DK–3730, tel. 56/48–83–83, fax 56/48–85–37. 27 rooms, 16 apartments, 7 bungalows. Facilities: restaurant, laundry, sauna, solarium, indoor and outdoor pools, tennis, car and bicycle rental. No credit cards. Closed 1 week in mid-Feb. Expensive.*

Gudhjem **Skt. Jørgens Gård Vandrehjem.** In a 100-year-old former manor
Lodging house, this half-timbered hostel in the middle of Gudhjem offers one- to eight-bed rooms with standard Danish hostel style: pine bunks and industrial carpeting. *Gudhjem Vandrehjem, DK–3760, tel. 56/48–50–35, fax 56/48–56–35. 52 rooms, 26 with bath. Facilities: restaurant, 6 kitchens. No credit cards. Inexpensive.*

Pedersker **Bakkarøgeriet.** In the middle of a quiet neighborhood, this
Dining smokehouse looks like a garage but has a brisk carryout herring business. There is also a laid-back patio where guests munch on local seafood or hamburgers. *Østre Sømarksvej 29, tel. 56/97–71–20. Reservations not accepted. Dress: casual. No credit cards. Closed Sept.–Apr. Inexpensive.*

Rønne **Rådhuskroen.** With exposed timbers, comfortable armchairs,
Dining and close-set tables, this restaurant provides a softly lit change from Rønne's busy streets. The menu is Bornholm continental, with such specialties as poached Baltic salmon with salmon roe and lobster sauce and grilled fillet of rosefish (redfish) with curry sauce. Beef choices include pepper steak with wine and cream sauce. *Nørregade 2, tel. 56/95–00–69. Reservations accepted. Dress: casual. AE, D, MC, V. Moderate.*

Dining and Lodging **Fredensborg.** On a curve of forest near a small beach, this hotel sets the island's standard for luxury. The glass and clay-tile lobby is spare and sunny, the staff pleasant and eager. The dozen ample apartments have full kitchens, while the guest rooms are in pastel schemes, with modern furniture and balconies overlooking the sea. The timbered restaurant, De Fire Ståuerne, serves traditional Danish food. *Strandvejen 116, DK-3700, tel. 56/95-44-44, fax 56/95-03-14. 72 rooms with bath, 12 apartments. Facilities: restaurant, bar, whirlpool, tennis court, sauna, solarium, 24-hour room service, meeting rooms, parking. AE, DC, MC, V. Expensive.*

Hotel Griffen. Just off a busy street and the Rønne harbor, this is one of Bornholm's largest and most modern hotels. It's three stories tall, with plenty of windows and views of the sea on one side and Rønne on the other. The rooms, done in deep-brown tones, have every modern convenience. *Kredsen 1, DK-3700, tel. 56/95-51-11, fax 56/95-52-97. 140 rooms with bath, 2 suites. Facilities: restaurant, bar, disco, indoor pool, sauna, room service, meeting rooms, parking. AE, DC, MC, V. Closed mid-Dec.–Jan. 7. Expensive.*

Snogebæk **Den Lille Havefrue.** This busy fish restaurant is lined with the
Dining paintings and ceramics of local artist Kirsten Kleman. Dine in-
★ side or out in the ample garden (with a play area for kids), which faces the Baltic. The menu includes steaks, soups, and salads, but the specialty is fresh, traditional fish, such as boiled or fried plaice, grilled cod with lobster gravy, and salmon with cream-and-chive sauce. *Hovedgaden 5, tel. 56/48-80-55. Reservations advised. Dress: casual but neat. AE, DC, MC, V. Moderate.*

Svaneke **Glas Caféen.** The name of this lunch café means sunshine, and
Dining everything is healthful—from hot veggie plates to occasional meat dishes, quiche, excellent brownies, and iced cappuccino. Like the food, the atmosphere is fresh, with posters and art on the walls and, true to its name, lots of sunlight. *Glastorvet 3, tel. 56/49-65-86. No credit cards. No dinner. Closed Oct.–Apr. Inexpensive.*

Dining and Lodging **Siemsens Gaard.** Built in a 400-year-old merchant house, this U-shaped hotel with a gravel-courtyard café overlooks the harbor. Inside it's cushy with Chesterfield sofas beneath severe black-and-white prints and antiques. The rooms differ, but all are done up in stripped pine and soft colors. The bright, modern restaurant serves Franco-Danish food, with a menu of 125 options—from club sandwiches to smoked Baltic salmon to smørrebrød. *Havnebryggen 9, DK-3740, tel. 56/49-61-49, fax 56/49-61-03. 50 rooms with shower. Facilities: restaurant, café, health club, sauna. AE, DC, MC, V. Moderate.*

Lodging **Hotel Østersøen.** Across from the harbor, this newly renovated
★ hotel has a provincial facade and a Key West courtyard with palm trees and a swimming pool. Industrial carpets and century-old beams line the modern lobby, and the stark apartments (rented by the week) are furnished with leather sofas, swanky teak dinette sets, and streamlined furniture. The hotel is well suited for families and couples traveling in pairs. *Havnebryggen 5, DK-3740, tel. 56/49-60-20, fax 56/49-72-79. 21 apartments. Facilities: outdoor pool, business facilities. AE, DC. Moderate.*

The Arts and Nightlife

The Arts   Check with the tourist board for information on church and park concerts and special events at Hammershus.

Nightlife   Bornholm nightlife is limited to a handful of discos and clubs in Rønne. The largest disco is **Annabelle's** (Kredsen 1, tel. 56/95–51–11) in the Griffen Hotel, which draws a mixed crowd, while **Sølvknappen** (Store Torv, tel. 56/95–48–01) is smaller, with lots of young locals. **Vise Vesth Huset** (Brøddegade 24, tel. 56/48–50–80) is popular for light meals and live folk music. For a rowdier time there's **Sørens Værthus,** near the harbor in Snogebæk (Hovedgaden 1G, tel. 56/48–80–20), a popular pizza place with live rock, and a rowboat hanging from the ceiling— into which daring guests often climb.

Greenland

When Eric the Red discovered Greenland (Kalaallit Nunaat in Greenlandic, Grønland in Danish) a thousand years ago, his Norsemen thought they had reached the edge of the world. After it, there was only *Ginnungagap,* the endless abyss.

Greenland still commands awe from the handful of visitors who venture off the usual Scandinavian path to explore the world's largest island. Measuring more than 1.3 million square kilometers (840,000 square miles), it's larger than Italy, France, Great Britain, unified Germany, and Spain combined. The coastal regions are sparsely populated with 55,000 Danes and Inuit—the local people, whose roots can be traced to the people native to Canada's Arctic. More than 80% of the land is eternally frozen beneath an ice cap that, at its deepest, reaches 3 kilometers (2 miles). If it melted, sea levels around the world would rise nearly 20 feet.

By its nature, Greenland is far more difficult to explore than dwarfed mother Denmark, but the southern and western towns, which are trimmed with building-block red-and-green houses and well-traveled harbors, have adequate hotels, airfields and helicopter pads, and some summertime ferry service. (Greenland has few roads and no railroads.) Man-made luxuries are few, but the rewards of nature are savagely beautiful. Below the Arctic Circle, the draws include Norse ruins, Ice Age–gouged mountains, and jagged fjords, while farther north, dogsleds whip over icy plains and ferries glide past icebergs as big as city blocks.

Greenland's first inhabitants probably arrived 4,000 years ago from North America but had mysteriously disappeared, apparently migrating westward to Canada by 500 BC, when the climate grew colder. Recorded history began in AD 982, when Eric and his Norse settlers claimed the land, but after 400 years of colonization they, too, disappeared mysteriously. During this period Denmark and Norway joined under the Danish crown, a union that muddled ownership of Greenland until 1933, when the International High Court awarded Denmark complete sovereignty. (Because of this dual heritage, almost every town has a Greenlandic and a Danish name.) Geographically isolated and increasingly politically independent, Greenlanders are intent on redefining their ethnic identity in a modern world. They refer to themselves as Inuit, in solidarity

with natives of Canada, Alaska, and the former Soviet Union, and most people speak the native language in addition to Danish.

In 1978 Denmark granted Greenland home rule, investing its tiny *Landsting* (Parliament), located in the capital, Nuuk/Godthåb, with power over internal affairs. Though Denmark continues to devolve power, it still administers foreign policy and provides large doses of financial aid to bolster an economy based on fishing, animal husbandry, construction, and, increasingly, tourism. As of press time (summer 1993), plans were under way to improve the infrastructure and introduce charter travel to the island, with the intention of reducing astronomical transportation costs.

With so few tourists (numbering under 5,000 annually), the ways of the isolated Greenlander can seem blissfully nonchalant. When things appear hopeless (as you will often be told they are), you'll do better if you remain calm and polite. Just be sure to do your research, arrange as much of your itinerary as possible before leaving home, and bring your own guidebooks.

When to Go

The loveliest time to visit is May to early August, when the sun hardly sets. Summer temperatures average 53°–65°F in the south (Nanortalik to Paamiut) and 50°–60°F in the center (Nuuk to Qeqertarsuaq), but it feels warmer due to low humidity. The temperature drops dramatically in the afternoon and evening, and the winds never die down completely. Sudden ice, rain, and snow squalls are common in the central and northern regions. Winter is harsh, dark, and extremely windy, with temperatures dipping below 32° to 5°F in the south, –22°F and far below in the center and north, which also experiences polar night from November to March.

What to Pack

Pack light, as you'll have to tote your own luggage and because of cargo and weight considerations on small planes and helicopters.

Clothing   Bring durable, wind- and waterproof sportswear, sturdy hiking or moon boots or rubber-heeled walking shoes, a cap (one that won't fly off in the wind), and gloves or mittens. Woolen sweaters, cotton T-shirts, and neat trousers are about as dressy as you'll need.

Miscellaneous   The northern summer sun is blinding. Bring a pair of ultraviolet (UVA and UVB) filter sunglasses and a waterproof UVA/UVB sunscreen of at least SPF15. Greenland's midges and mosquitoes are vicious, especially at the height of summer, so pack a good repellent and carry it with you at all times. (An even better solution is a netted cap.) For your camera, bring a UV filter to compensate for the glare that will otherwise tint your photos blue.

Language

Take along a Danish-English phrase book. Though most Greenlanders speak Danish, English is not common.

Important Addresses and Numbers

Tourist Information There is a tourism office in almost every town, but brochures, maps, and specific information may be limited. The following are small, often mobile offices, so call first for an exact location (a 299 access code must be dialed before all phone numbers when calling from outside Greenland): **Ilulissat/Jacobshavn** (Kussangajaannguaq B 447, Box 272, DK–3952 Ilulissat, tel. 4–42–22, fax 4–39–33), **Narsaq** (Box 148, DK–3921 Narsaq, tel. 3–13–25, fax 3–13–98), **Nuuk/Godthåb** (Box 199, DK–3900 Nuuk, tel. 2–27–00, fax 2–27–10), **Qaqortoq/Julianehåb** (Box 128, DK–3920 Qaqortoq, tel. 3–84–44, fax 3–84–95), **Qasigiannguit/Christianhåb** (Box 160, DK–3951 Qasigiannguit, tel. 4–50–81, fax 4–55–24), and **Uummannaq** (c/o Hotel Uummannaq, DK–3961 Uummannaq, tel. 4–85–18, fax 4–82–62). Tourist information offices in **Søndre Strømfjord** (tel. 1–10–98) and **Narsarsuak** (tel. 3–52–53) open when planes arrive. In Copenhagen, the staff at **Greenland Travel** (Gammel Mønt 12, tel. 33/13–10–11) and **Greenland Tourism** (Pilestræde 52, tel. 33/13–69–75) are helpful.

Emergencies Every community has its own fire, ambulance, and police numbers, and dentist and doctor, all of which are available from your hotel. The best way to handle emergencies is to avoid danger in the first place. Don't take risks, ask for advice, and give your travel agent and hotel your itinerary so that they can reach you in case of emergencies—or if you don't show up when you're due.

Hospital Emergency Room **Sana (Dronning Ingrids) Hospital,** DK–3900 Nuuk, tel. 2–11–01

Late-Night Pharmacies If you are on a medication, bring enough to last throughout your visit. For emergencies, the local hospital can fill prescriptions.

Arriving and Departing by Plane and Helicopter

Icelandair has flights from New York, Baltimore, Fort Lauderdale, and Orlando to Keflavik, Iceland, daily in summer. **Greenlandair** (Grønlandsfly in Danish) makes two flights a week between Keflavik and Narsarsuak, also in summer. It's more expensive to go by way of Copenhagen, with **SAS,** which flies three times a week to Søndre Strømfjord/Kangangerlussuaq. Even pricier are connections through Canada, where you can catch an early morning flight from Montreal to Frobisher Bay on Baffin Island, then cross the Davis Strait to Nuuk on Greenlandair. Because of Greenland's highly variable weather, delays are frequent. Helicopters and small planes connect small towns.

Getting Around

By Plane and Helicopter **Greenlandair** is the only airline licensed for domestic flights on the island. Its modest fleet of helicopters and small planes are booked year-round, so make reservations very early.

By Boat The most beautiful passage between towns is by water. Every town has a harbor, where private boats can be hired for connections or excursions. Some coastal boats as well as the government-run *Disko* ferry ply the waters of the west coast, making frequent stops, but space is limited and booked months in ad-

vance by locals. Again, reserve early. Plans are also under way to begin circumnavigations of the island with a Russian icebreaker. Though the trip is expected to be expensive and rough, it will be an option for those who want to travel on the wild side. Contact **KNI** (Greenland Trade, DK–3900 Nuuk, tel. 2–52–11) or Greenland Travel in Copenhagen (tel. 31/13–10–11).

Guided Tours

Because transportation and accommodations are limited, have all details of your trip—connections, accommodations, sightseeing, and meals—arranged by an experienced travel agent, tour organizer, or airline. (It's also helpful to bring a copy of your tour contract and all confirmations.) Tour packages range from one- to four-day east-coast excursions from Reykjavík by Icelandair to month-long nature expeditions, which can include sailing, hiking, hunting, dogsledging (March to May), whale safaris, and iceberg-watching. On-the-spot excursions are available in most towns and range from about DKr250 for a half day to DKr350 for a full day, more for dogsledging (as it is called in Greenland), boat and helicopter trips. Among the travel agencies most experienced with Greenland are: **Bennett of Scandinavia** (270 Madison Ave., New York, NY 10016, tel. 212/532–5060), **Eurocruises** (303 W. 13th St., New York, NY 10014, tel. 212/691–2099), **Icelandair** (360 W. 31st St., New York, NY 10001, tel. 212/330–1470), **Quark Expeditions** (980 Post Rd., Darien, CT 06820, 203/656–0499), **Scanam** (933 Highway 23, Pompton Plains, NJ, 07444, tel. 800/545–2204), **Scantours Inc.** (1535 6th St., Suite 209, Santa Monica, CA 90401, tel. 800/223–7226), and **Travcoa** (4000 McArthur Blvd. E, Suite 650, Newport Beach, CA 92660, tel. 714/476–2800). In Denmark, contact **Arctic Adventure** (Reventlowsgade 30, DK–1651 KBH V, tel. 33/25–32–21) and **Greenland Travel** (*see* Tourist Information, *above*).

Exploring Greenland

Numbers in the margin correspond to points of interest on the Greenland map.

Most museums and sights in Greenland do not have street addresses. To check for opening hours, ask at your hotel.

Tour 1: Southern Greenland

A convenient place to start exploring is near the island's southwestern tip because most towns in this area have harbors and airstrips connecting them via Copenhagen, Reykjavík, and Montreal to the United States, Europe, and domestic routes.

❶ If you begin in **Nanortalik,** take a stroll past the Ice Age granite, the old harbor, and the paint-box-color 19th-century buildings, a vestige of the Danish colonial past. During May and June, the normally quiet town bustles with local whale and seal hunters, who install themselves in tents and makeshift huts.

❷ Northward 90 kilometers (54 miles) is **Qaqortoq/Julianehåb.** With a population of 3,000, this is the largest town in southern Greenland and one of the loveliest. In the town square you'll see the island's only fountain, surrounded by half-timbered build-

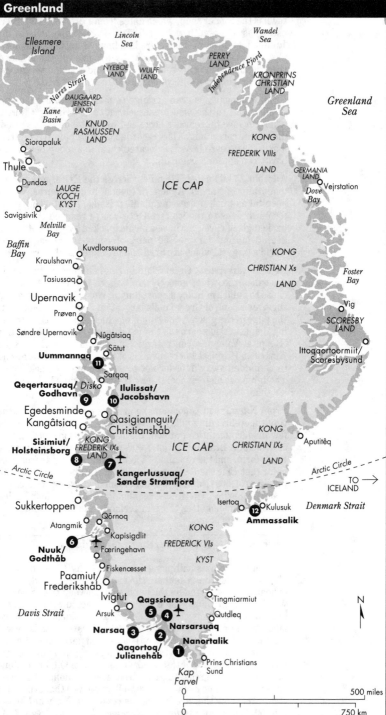

Greenland

Ellesmere
Island

*Lincoln
Sea*

*Wandel
Sea*

*NYEBOE
LAND*

*WULFF
LAND*

*PERRY
LAND*

Independence Fjord

*KRONPRINS
CHRISTIAN
LAND*

Nares Strait

*DAUGAARD-
JENSEN
LAND*

*Kane
Basin*

*KNUD
RASMUSSEN
LAND*

Greenland
Sea

Siorapaluk

Thule

Dundas

*LAUGE
KOCH
KYST*

ICE CAP

*KONG
FREDERIK VIIIs
LAND*

*GERMANIA
LAND*

Vejrstation

*Dove
Bay*

Savigsivik

*Melville
Bay*

*Baffin
Bay*

Kuvdlorssuaq

Kraulshavn

Tasiussaq

*KONG
CHRISTIAN Xs
LAND*

*Foster
Bay*

Upernavik

Prøven

Vig

*SCORESBY
LAND*

Søndre Upernavik

Nûgâtsiaq

Sätut

Uummannaq ⑪

Sarqaq

Ittoqqortoormiit/
Scoresbysund

**Qeqertarsuaq/
Godhavn** ⑨ *Disko*

**Ilulissat/
Jacobshavn** ⑩

Egedesminde

Kangâtsiaq

Qasigiannguit/
Christianshåb

*KONG
CHRISTIAN IXs
LAND*

Aputitêq

**Sisimiut/
Holsteinsborg** ⑧

*KONG
FREDERIK IXs
LAND* ✈ ⑦

ICE CAP

Arctic Circle

**Kangerlussuaq/
Søndre Strømfjord**

Arctic Circle

TO →
ICELAND

Sukkertoppen

Isertoq

Kulusuk ⑫

Denmark Strait

Ammassalik

Atangmik

Qôrnoq

Kapisigdlit

*KONG
FREDERIK VIs
KYST*

⑥
**Nuuk/
Godthåb**

✈

Færingehavn

Fiskenæsset

Paamiut/
Frederikshåb

Ivigtut

Qagssiarssuq ✈
⑤ ④

Davis Strait

Arsuk

Narsaq ③

② **Narsarsuaq**

Tingmiarmiut

Qutdleq

**Qaqortoq/
Julianehåb**

① **Nanortalik**

N

Prins Christians
Sund

*Kap
Farvel*

0 _____ 500 miles

0 _____ 750 km

ings and crayon-colored houses. Though the oldest building in town is the cooper shop, which dates from 1797, the most interesting is the smithy, from 1871, which now houses the **Julianehåb Museum.** Inside are handmade hunting tools, kayaks, Inuit clothing, and a furnished sod house you can enter. A traditional dwelling, it remained cozy and warm even during the harsh winter. *Admission free. Open Mon.–Fri. 11–4.*

From this point, you can arrange to make the 14.5-kilometer (9-mile) sail to the well-preserved ruins of **Hvalsey Church,** where in 1408 there was a large and well-attended Norse wedding—the community's last recorded activity before it mysteriously disappeared. As it is located close to a rocky beach, the hardy can opt for a frigid dip.

Another 25 kilometers (15 miles) across the Ericsfjord are the mountains of **Narsaq.** A modern town of bright houses, with a hospital and fish-processing plant, it is also the starting point for excursions to the ice cap. Once you've reached the humpbacked glacier, you can have a picnic (packed by your hotel) and keep a lookout for the 150 pairs of white-tailed eagles, the world's largest, which are bred and protected in the area.

Next is **Narsarsuaq,** Great Plain in English, a name that aptly describes the wide, smooth land where the U.S. Air Force chose to build a military airport during World War II—one that survives as one of Greenland's largest civil airports. Not far is the edge of the glacier, the runoff of which is collected for making drinks. Also nearby is the point locals call **Hospitalsdalen** (Hospital Valley), a controversial area named for the alleged American Hospital where invalids of the Korean War were said to be hidden away in order not to weaken morale back home. Though most history books deny the story, many locals swear it's true.

From Narsarsuaq you can make arrangements to explore the tiny sheep-breeding village of **Qagssiarssuq.** Though there are few modern facilities in town, the Norse ruins are fascinating and include **Brattahlíð,** the 1,000-year-old ruins of Eric the Red's farm, and the remains of **Tjodhilde Kirke.** It was from this point that Eric the Red's son, Leif Ericsson, began his expedition in AD 1,000 to discover Vinland, somewhere on the coast of North America. The first Greenlandic *Ting* (Outdoor Parliament), fashioned after those in Iceland, was also held here at about the same time.

Tour 2: Central and Northern Greenland

An hour or so by small plane, or 15 hours by ferry, north of Narsarsuaq is **Nuuk/Godthåb,** the capital of Greenland, which is beautifully situated on the peninsula between two fjords. It was founded in 1728 by the Norwegian missionary Hans Egede; his harbor-side home is now the private residence of the island's home-rule premier. The centrally located **Landsmuseet** (National Museum of Greenland) has a good permanent display that includes kayaks, costumes, and hunting weapons, an art exhibit, and the five 15th-century mummies of Qilakitsoq, one of Greenland's archaeological treasures. Among the most striking are a woman and child so well preserved that even their 500-year-old clothes are in pristine condition. *National Museum, tel. 22611. Admission free. Open weekdays and Sun. 1–4.*

7 Next (about one hour by plane from Nuuk) is **Kangerlussuaq/ Søndre Strømfjord,** which is at the head of one of the longest and deepest fjords in the world. The airport, the island's most vital, lies just 20 kilometers (13 miles) from the ice cap. Until World War II, nobody lived here permanently, but Greenlanders would come in the spring to hunt reindeer. During the war, the U.S. Air Force chose its dry, stable climate for an air base, called Bluie West Eight. The military moved out in fall 1992, selling all the facilities to the local government for the sum of $1.

8 Farther west, on the Davis Strait, is **Sisimiut/Holsteinsborg,** which means Burrow People. This hilltop town boasts many Danish-style wooden houses, a local luxury, as all wood is imported. A favorite area for dogsledging, it is also the southernmost boundary for walrus hunting; the walrus is a popular game animal because of its valuable tusks.

Another 110 kilometers (70 miles) north is **Disko Bugt** (Bay) and the island of **Qeqertarsuaq/Disko,** where the main town is **Qeqertarsuaq/Godhavn.** Until 1950 it was the capital of northern Greenland, while Nuuk/Godthåb was the southern capital. The task was divided because it was too difficult to rule the entire island from one town. Accessible by helicopter and ship, it's often booked to capacity by French and German tourists who come for the organized dogsledding trips.

10 In the center of Disko Bay is **Ilulissat/Jacobshavn,** which lies 300 kilometers (185 miles) north of the Arctic Circle. The tip of its fjord boasts the Northern Hemisphere's most productive iceberg, calving 130 million tons of floes each day (which the tourist board says is equivalent to the amount of water New York City uses in a day). For a humbling experience, take one of the helicopter tours that circle the glacier. A violent land of floating ice giants and dazzling panoramas, it's been inhabited by the Inuit for as long as 4,000 years. The town was founded in 1741 by a Danish merchant, Jakob Severin. Today the largest industry is shrimping, though in the winter halibut is fished from dogsleds along the fjord. You can also visit the **Knud Rasmussens Fødehjem** (Childhood Home of Knud Rasmussen) (1879–1933). The Danish-Greenlandic explorer initiated the seven Thule expeditions, which enlarged the knowledge of Arctic geography and Inuit culture. At the museum you can follow his explorations through photographs, equipment, and clothing. *Open daily 10–4.*

11 About 240 kilometers (150 miles) north, and less than an hour by helicopter, is the island of **Uummannaq** and the town of the same name. Maintaining Greenlandic traditions in step with modern European life, inhabitants range from hunters to linguists, and dogsleds are as apt to cruise through town as four-wheel drives. The town is situated beneath the magnificent hues and double humps of the granite Uummannaq Mountain, which rises 1,175 meters (3,855 feet). Because the village is also situated on uneven stone cliffs, housing largely consists of brightly painted, freestanding cottages rather than the ugly Danish barracks that line most villages.

The local museum gives a good impression of life on the island, with photographs and costumes of local hunters and the now-defunct mines of the area. Exhibits also detail the doomed 1930 expedition of German explorer Alfred Wegener, and a bit on

the Qilaqitsoq mummies (*see* Tour 2, Nuuk/Godthåb, *above*), which were found in a nearby cave in 1977. *Uummannaq Museum. tel. 4–81–04. Open weekdays 8–4. Admission free.*

The town's stone church, dating from 1937, is the only one in Greenland and is made from local granite. Next door to it are three sod huts, typical Inuit dwellings until just a couple of decades ago.

Though there is plenty of dogsledging north of the Arctic Circle, including in Ilulissat, the trips from Uummannaq are the most authentic. Visitors sit comfortably on fur-lined sledges that tear across the frozen fjord in the hands of experienced Inuit drivers. Trips can be arranged by the tourist board or at the Hotel Uummannaq and range from a few hours to several days. The terrifying beauty and brilliance of this trip, racing on the frozen bay and sleeping beneath the shadow of icebergs, instill consummate humility.

The northern reaches of Greenland are sparsely populated, with few hotels. The American air base at Thule used for monitoring the Northern Hemisphere can be visited only by members of groups with special permits (check with the tourist office in Ilulissat), who should be prepared for delays. Much of the east coast is also empty, though a recent gold rush, along the southeast coast, has given rise to some makeshift accommodations. The only truly accessible towns on the east side are ⑫ **Ammassalik,** 831 kilometers (470 miles) northwest of Reykjavík, and **Kulusuk,** a tiny village slightly farther northeast. Both towns welcome most of Greenland's visitors, who are day-trippers from Iceland. Though tours (which are arranged through Icelandair) are usually short, they are very well organized, offering an accurate (and relatively affordable) peek into Greenlandic culture, as well as stunning Arctic nature.

Shopping

Clothing Most clothing is expensive and comparable to what is available in provincial Danish towns. The exception is the intricate—and expensive—**Greenlandic national costume.** It generally consists of a red pullover, an intricately worked pearl and embroidery collar, embroidered sealskin trousers, and boots. Individual parts of the costume may be bought for prices starting at DKr2,200 (for the boots). Thick hand-knit woolen turtlenecks, in traditional beige, brown, and gray patterns, are more common.

Furs **Seal** and **fox fur** are widely available. You can find both raw skins and finished coats, jackets, slippers, and other outerwear. It's expensive, but impenetrable to cold. The **Great Greenland** tannery in Qaqortoq/Julianehåb is a good place to watch the furs being sewn and to shop. Bargaining is not done.

Handicrafts In most towns you can buy handmade folk art and crafts. Among the most unusual items are **tupilaks,** carvings the Inuit once believed would bring bad luck to enemies. These very collectible pieces were once made from fur, bones, peat, and other materials but are now carved from wood, antler, tusk, and teeth. **Soapstone,** a soft, gray or green stone, is carved into small figures depicting humans and animals from Greenlandic mythology. Trees are scarce and precious in Greenland, so driftwood is often carved into utilitarian bowls and baskets.

Street Markets Every town has an outdoor market called *brædttet* (the plank, or board). Here locals buy and trade game, fish, and occasionally skins (a medium-size sealskin costs less than DKr500). Prices are set by the government, so there's no bargaining.

Sports and Outdoor Activities

Dogsledding The huskies that traverse the ice-covered land are only allowed north of the Arctic Circle. They are half-wild, so don't try to play with or pet them. For rides, contact the local tourist office or your hotel.

Fishing and Hunting The right to fish and hunt in Greenland is reserved for residents; however, visitors can buy fishing and hunting licenses from the local police, major hotels, and tourism offices. A fishing license costs DKr500, a small game license DKr1,000, and a large game license DKr3,000.

Hiking It's wiser to join an organized hike with an experienced guide than to attempt a solo expedition. (It's not uncommon for rescue crews to go out in search of lost hikers.) Organized excursions are available in Nuuk/Godthåb, Narsaq, and Narsarsuak for about DKr150 for a half day, DKr300 for a full day. The tourist offices of Qaqortoq/Julianehåb, Nanortalik, and Sisimiut/Holsteinsborg arrange hikes upon request and charge according to the number of participants.

National Parks Most of Greenland's ice cap is protected as the world's largest national parkland and is as big as Great Britain and France combined—yet it's only 25% of the island. Some portions of the area can be visited either by private charter from Iceland or by other special arrangements made well in advance.

Dining and Lodging

Good hotels are available with very plain rooms and few or no extras. Most restaurants are located in hotels and feature both Danish and Greenlandic fare. Expect a lot of fresh cod, flounder, salmon, and reindeer, as well as occasional whale and seal meat. Delicacies include large shrimp and the local lamb.

Ilulissat/Jacobshavn **Hotel Arctic Ilulissat.** This modern hotel is in the mountains on *Dining and Lodging* the edge of town, with adequate rooms, most of which have TV, phone, and views of the ice fjord and the mountains. *Box 501, DK–3952, tel. 4–41–53, fax 4–39–24. 40 rooms with shower. Facilities: restaurant, conference rooms, sauna, billiards. AE, DC, MC. Very Expensive.*
Hotel Hvide Falk. All rooms in this centrally located moderate-size two-story building have a magnificent view of the glacier and the Disko mountains. The restaurant, which offers Danish, Greenlandic, and French specialties, looks out over the bay and the Vistafjord, which is abob with icebergs. *Box 20, DK–3952, tel. 4–33–43, fax 4–35–08. 21 rooms with bath. Facilities: restaurant, guided tours, billiards. DC. Expensive.*

Narsarsuaq **Hotel Narsarsuaq.** This large hotel boasts comfortable rooms, *Dining and Lodging* with functional Danish furniture, TVs, telephone, and private bath. The restaurant, which gets its ingredients from Denmark, overlooks Eric the Red's Farm. A few hundred yards from the airstrip, the hotel organizes tours to the surrounding fjord and mountains and has its own excursion boats. *DK–3923, tel. 3–52–53, fax 3–53–70. 90 rooms with bath. Facilities: res-*

taurant, bar, pub, sauna, solarium, laundry service. AE, DC, MC, V. Moderate.

Nuuk/Godthåb
Dining and Lodging

Hans Egede. This hotel, built in 1986, is the largest in Greenland. The rooms are plain and functional but have such extras as minibars, TVs, videos, and phones. The sixth-floor Sky Top restaurant, known for its lovely view of the fjords and its inventive nouveau Greenlandic menu, combines local fish with French methods. *Box 289, DK–3900, tel. 2–42–22, fax 2–44–87. 110 rooms with bath. Facilities: restaurant, conference rooms, discothèque, pub. DC, MC, V. Very Expensive.*

Qaqortoq/Julianehåb
Lodging

Hotel Qaqortoq. Built in 1987, this hotel is among the more modern on the huge island. Its glass and white facade atop a hill overlooks the surrounding fjord and picturesque center of town. The rooms are simple but comfortable, all with private bath. *Box 155, DK–3920, Qaqortoq, tel. 3–85–05, fax 3–72–34. 21 rooms with bath. Facilities: restaurant. DC, MC, V. Very Expensive.*

Qasigiannguit/
Christianhåb
Lodging

Hotel Igdlo Qasigiannguit. This simple three-story wood-and-concrete hotel sits on a mountainside with views of the harbor and Disko Bay. *Box 160, DK–3951, tel. 4–50–81, fax 4–55–24. 15 rooms. Facilities: restaurant, café, disco, conference rooms. AE, DC, MC, V. Very Expensive.*

Nightlife

There's not much in the way of tourist nightlife, especially bars and discos, except in the finest hotels, and on weekends even these get rowdy.

The Faroe Islands

The 18 Faroe Islands (Føroyar in Faroese; Færøerne in Danish) striate the North Atlantic in an extended knuckle of volcanic archipelago. All but one are inhabited, by 47,000 people and 80,000 sheep. They live by fishing, fish farming, and shepherding and carefully maintain their own pace of life.

Located 290 kilometers (180 miles) northwest of Scotland, 450 kilometers (280 miles) southeast of Iceland, and 1,500 kilometers (940 miles) northwest of Denmark, the fjord-chiseled islands are sparsely vegetated, with a bristle of short grasses and moss. The climate is oceanic: humid, changeable, and stormy, with surprisingly mild temperatures—52°F in the summer, and 40°F in the winter, with a heavy annual rainfall of 63 inches.

Of its 1,399 square kilometers (540 square miles), 7% is fertile, the rest rough pasture—an Eden for 70 breeding and 120 migratory species of birds, among them thousands of guillemots, gannets, auks, and puffins. Beneath azure skies and rugged, mossy mountains, villages of colorful thatched houses cling to hillsides and harbors, while drying fish flap like laundry in the breeze. Religious and proud, the Faroese have built churches in nearly every settlement.

Catholic monks from Ireland were the first to settle the islands but died out and were replaced by Norwegian Vikings, who settled the land in about AD 800. It was here that the *Løgting* (Parliament) met for the first time in AD 1200 in Tórshavn—and still

does. Though under the Danish crown, the islands have had a home-rule government since 1948, with their own flag and language.

The roots of the Faroese language are in old west Norse. The young people know some English, but a Danish dictionary can be helpful to the visitor; Danish is the second language.

It's difficult for visitors to understand the isolation or the practical relationship the Faroese have with the natural world. Dubious outsiders, for example, accuse locals of cruelty during the traditional pilot whale harvests. An essential foodstuff, the islands' national sea mammals are killed in limited numbers and permit less dependence on imported meat. The hunt is also an important part of Faroese society, involving the youngest to the eldest.

In 1993 the islands plunged into a severe depression, with unemployment, formerly an unknown phenomenon, surging from below 3% to more than 30%. The hard times are the result of a changing global fishing industry, coupled with an intensive overdevelopment of the local infrastructure that left island coffers empty. Hard times are compelling islanders to eye tourism as a salvation; they are eager to draw more visitors to spend time and money on their shores. Depending upon how they fare, the next few years will tell whether the traditional Faroese can meet the demands of a changing world.

Important Addresses and Numbers

Tourist Information In Copenhagen, call the **Faroese Government Office** (Højbroplads 7, tel. 33/14–08–66). Locally, the tourist offices are **Strandferdslan Tourist Information** (á Stongunum, FR 700 Klaksvík, tel. 298/56006) and **Aldan Tourist Information** (Reyngøta 17, FR 100 Tórshavn, tel. 298/19391). The brochure "Around the Faroe Islands" is particularly helpful. The **Danish Tourist Board** (branches in Denmark and abroad) can also supply information.

Emergencies Dial 000 for any emergency.

Pharmacies Try **Tórshavn** (by SMS shopping center, tel. 298/11100), **Klaksvík** (Klaksvíksvegur, tel. 298/55055), or **Tvøroyri** (tel. 298/71076).

Arriving and Departing by Plane

From Copenhagen there are daily connections to the western island of Vágar that take about two hours. From there, count another 2½ hours to get to Tórshavn by bus and ferry. Delays due to heavy fog are common. For reservations on either **Danair** or **Atlantic Airways,** call **SAS** (tel. 33/5–52–66) in Copenhagen or **Flogfelag Føroya** (tel. 298/32755) in the Faroe Islands. Two weekly flights are also available from Reykjavík (tel. 91–25100) and one a week from Bergen, Norway (tel. 05/31–26–00), on **Icelandair,** which also flies once a week from Glasgow to the Faroes and on to Iceland.

Arriving and Departing by Ferry

There is frequent ferry service to all islands, with the most remote areas served by helicopter as well. Once a week in summer

there are car ferries from Esbjerg (33 hours) to Tórshavn. Call **DFDS** (tel. 33/11–22–55). Year-round ferries depart from Hirtshals, Jylland, on Friday and arrive in Tórshavn on Monday (48 hours). Call **Faroeship** (tel. 31/29–26–88) for more information.

Getting Around

By Bus, Ferry, and Helicopter The main islands are connected by regular ferries, while smaller ones are linked by mailboat and helicopter. For ferries, call **Strandfaraskip Landsins,** Tórshavn (tel. 298/14550 or 298/16450, fax 298/16000). **Helicopter Service** is in Tórshavn (tel. 298/16450). In towns, and between islands that are connected by bridges, there is regular bus service. For schedules and reservations, call **Bygdaleiðir** in Tórshavn (tel. 298/14366).

By Car Driving laws are the same as in Denmark. Car rentals are available in the larger towns, such as Tórshavn and Klaksvík. A network of two-lane asphalt roads has been built between towns, using tunnels and bridges. The roads are best on the nine main islands. Speed limits are 50 kilometers per hour (30 miles per hour) in urban areas, 80 kph (50 mph) outside. Once outside towns, beware of untethered animals. The islanders are extremely strict about drunk driving.

Guided Tours

There are two main tour operators on the islands: **Kunningarstovan** (Vaglid, Tórshavn, tel. 298/15788) and **Tora Tourist Travel** (N. Finsensgøta, Tórshavn, tel. 298/15505), which offer angling, city, and bird-watching tours. Among them are **Boat tours of Nolsoy and Hestur** (Kunningarstovan), which leave from Tórshavn harbor (3 hours) and include coastal sails through the Kapilsund strait and Hestur's west coast to see puffins and other seabirds. Tora Tourist Travel organizes a tour to **Gjógv,** the northernmost village on Eysturoy (5 hours), including a view of mountains and a local village, and the **Vestmanna Birdcliffs Tour** (6 hours), which includes a look at bird colonies and nearby caves. Many hotels also offer tours within their vicinity.

Exploring the Faroe Islands

Numbers in the margin correspond to points of interest on the Faroe Islands map.

Most visitors who arrive by plane begin on the largest and most traveled island of **Streymoy,** which, though carved by sheer cliffs and waterfalls, has good roads and tunnels. On the northern end of the island are bird sanctuaries and a NATO base. On its southeastern flank is one of the world's tiniest capitals, **❶ Tórshavn,** named for the Viking god Thor.

Centrally located among the islands, it has a population of 16,000. The Viking *Alting* (Parliament) met here on St. Olav's Day, AD 825, and founded the *Løgting* (legislative body). All that's left of it is the **Tinganes,** a rocky ridge that divides the harbor. St. Olav's Day, July 29, is now the Tórshavn Festival, Ólavsøka, with celebrations that include rowing competitions, chain dancing, and, in a land of temperance, drinking.

The Faroe Islands

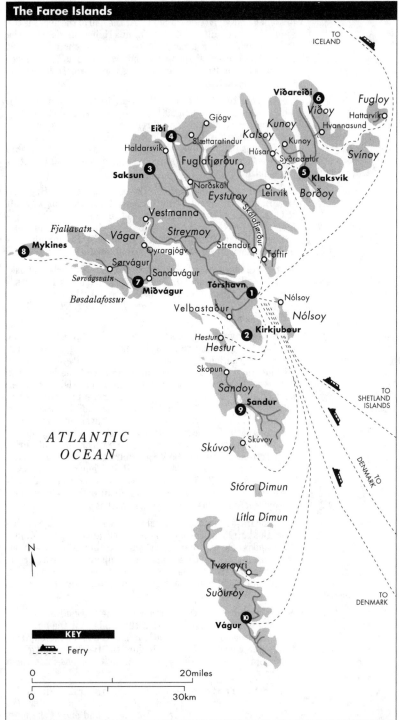

TO ICELAND

Viðareiði ⑥

Fugloy

Viðoy

Hattarvík

Kunoy

Kalsoy

Hvannasund

Gjógv

Eiði ④

Slættaratindur

Kunoy

Haldarsvík

Húsar

Svínoy

Saksun ③

Fuglafjørður

Syðradalur

⑤ Klaksvík

Norðskáli

Eysturoy

Leirvík

Borðoy

Vestmanna

Streymoy

Fjallavatn

Vágar

Strendur

Oyrargjógv

Skálafjørður

Toftir

Mykines ⑧

Sørvágur

Sandavágur

Tórshavn ①

Nólsoy

Sørvágsvatn

Miðvágur ⑦

Nólsoy

Bøsdalafossur

Velbastaður

② Kirkjubøur

Hestur

Hestur

Skopun

Sandoy

Sandur ⑨

Skúvoy

Skúvoy

ATLANTIC
OCEAN

TO
SHETLAND
ISLANDS

Stóra Dimun

TO DENMARK

Lítla Dímun

Tvøroyri

Suðuroy

TO
DENMARK

Vágur ⑩

N

KEY

🚢 Ferry

0		20miles
0		30km

On the rugged Tinganes are several buildings, including the present **Landsstýri** (Government). At the end of the docks is the **Skansin,** a fort built in 1580 by Magnus Heinason to fortify the town against pirate attacks. After many reconstructions, it reached its present shape in 1790 and was used as Faroe headquarters by the British Navy during World War II. Two guns from that period remain.

Down from the Tinganes is the **Gongin** (Old Main Street), which is lined with small 19th-century houses and crossed by twisting streets. In the same direction, you'll come to the slate **Havnar Kirkja** (Tórshavn's Church), which has been rebuilt many times in its 200-year history. Inside is a model of a ship salvaged from an 18th-century wreck, its bell, and an altarpiece dating from 1647.

As there are very few trees on the islands, walk up Hoyviksvegur and get your fill at the **Tórshavn Park.** On your way, off R.C. Effersøes Gøta, you'll come to the **Kongaminnið** (King's Memorial) on Norðrari Ringvegur, a basalt obelisk commemorating the visit of King Christian IX in 1874. Standing atop a hill, it commands a good view of the old town.

At the northern tip of town is the modern **Norðurlandahúsið** (Nordic Culture House), built in 1983, which hosts an international jazz festival in mid-August, as well as theater and concerts throughout the year. *Norðrari Ringvegur, tel. 298/17900. Call for event schedules.*

2 From Tórshavn, take a bus to the town of **Kirkjubøur** or follow the Landavegur road west to the small town of Velbastaður, where you can follow a mountain path (opposite Rte. 536) to **Kirkjubøur.** Located on the southern part of the island, the town was the spiritual and cultural center of the islands as well as the bishop's seat during the 12th century. A particularly ambitious priest, Bishop Erland, attempted to build a cathedral in the town in the 13th century, but it was never completed, and the ruins of the Gothic **Magnus Cathedral** still stand. Inside the church is a large stone tablet engraved with an image of Christ on the cross, flanked by the Virgin Mary and Mary Magdalene, and an inscription to St. Magnus and St. Thorlak. During restoration work in 1905, the tablet was removed to reveal well-preserved relics of the saints. In 1538, after the Reformation, the episcopal see was dissolved, and with it the town's power.

Also in Kirkjubøur, the restored **St. Olav's Church,** which dates from the late 13th century, was a cathedral during the Middle Ages and is now the only church from that time still in use. Most of the sculptures have been moved to Copenhagen, leaving little to see, but there's a hole on the north wall that, until 1740, was used by lepers to watch the mass and receive the Eucharist.

Near the church are two farmhouses, the **Roykstovan** and the **Stokkastovan.** Legend has it that the lumber for the buildings came drifting to the town, neatly numbered and bundled, from the Sogne Fjord in Norway. Inside, the two buildings give a good impression of traditional Faroese living in one-main-room cottages.

3 The northern end of the island is sliced by fjords. Within this rugged setting is the tiny town of **Saksun,** 30 kilometers (18 miles) northwest by bus from Tórshavn, and one of the most

popular excursions on the island. Set around a pastoral lake in the midst of a deep valley are scattered sod-roof houses and lovely views. The town also swarms with great skuas, a large brown seabird that's prone to low dives.

The next island, **Eysturoy,** is connected by bridge and buses to Streymoy. The center of activity is the town of **Eiði,** which lies to the northwest within a spectacular landscape of steep cliffs. Looking northwest, you can see two 250-foot cliffs, a part of local mythology: One night an Icelandic giant and his wife came to carry the islands to Iceland, but she dropped them, giving the islands their cracked geography. Once the sun rose, the giants were petrified and transformed into the bluffs.

Due east of the town is the highest point of the islands, the 2,910-foot **Slættaratindur** mountain. The island also has the longest fjord, the southern **Skálafjørður,** around which most of the population of 10,500 live.

The island of **Borðoy** is next, accessible by boat from eastern Eysturoy. On its southwest coast, nearly divided by two fjords, is the Faroes' second-largest town, **Klaksvík.** Within this scattering of islands, Borðoy, Viðoy, and Kunoy are connected by causeways. The other three islands, Fugloy, Svinoy, and Kalsoy, are accessible by passenger boat or helicopter.

Klaksvík is the most important fishing harbor in the Faroes, with a fleet of sophisticated boats that harvest cod, haddock, herring, and other fish. The local church, **Christianskirkjan** (Christian's Church), has a 4,000-year-old granite baptismal font thought to have had pagan origins in Denmark. Also under the church roof, you can see a 24-foot boat used by a former vicar to visit nearby towns.

The island of **Viðoy** is among the wildest, most alpine and beautiful of the islands, with mountains of 2,800 feet and sheer cliffs plunging into extremely rough, unnavigable waters. Amazingly, 600 people live here. From the town of **Viðareiði** (call Tora Tourist) you can take a boat tour to see many seabirds nesting on cliff walls, including guillemots, kittiwakes, and puffins—endearing little black-and-white birds with enormous orange beaks. The Faroese have a remarkable relationship with the puffins, harvesting them by the thousand for food and yet not endangering their numbers.

To the west, the name of **Vágar,** the third-largest island, means fjords, and it is cut by three of them, as well as by the **Fjallavatn** and **Sørvágsvatn** lakes, the last of which boasts the **Bøsdalafossur,** a 100-foot waterfall. The main town here is **Miðvágur,** an excellent perch for auk- and gannet-watching.

West of the town, you can see a tall pointy cliff, called the **Trøllkonufingur** (Witch's Finger), which was climbed only once, in 1844, with tragic results. On the occasion of a royal visit, a young local climbed the monolith's sheer face to wave to Crown Prince Frederik VIII. The second time he scaled it, to retrieve a glove, he slipped and fell to his death.

It's rough sailing to the tiny atoll of **Mykines** and only manageable when weather permits. Accessible by helicopter or by traversing the island northward on foot about 2 kilometers (1.2 miles) from the boat landing is the isolated town of the same name, **Mykines,** population 30, where the few dwellings are

roofed with sod. The town was sited here to be close to the **Mykineshólmur,** an islet swarming with thousands of puffins, which must be harvested for food.

 Sandoy, the fifth-largest island, lies to the south. Relatively fertile, it's named for the sandy white beaches of the town of **Sandur,** which lies in its bay. Amid green hills sheep graze, while the lakes north and west of town swell with auks, purple sandpipers, and great skuas. This is great land for walking or cycling (bike rentals are available in town).

The southernmost island, **Suðuroy,** is milder than the others, with cultivated green fields at its center and mountains along the coast. It is reachable by ferry from Tórshavn; the arrival docks are in **Vágur** and the quieter village of **Tvøroyri.**

Dining and Lodging

Accommodations and hotels are minimal, though summer cottages are available through the Tora and Kunningarstovan tour operators (*see* Guided Tours, *above*). Most restaurants are located in hotels. Faroese cuisine consists mainly of fish, mutton, and lamb, and you can also find Danish open-face sandwiches. Because some islands have few shops and restaurants, it's a good idea to pack sandwiches and water when you go exploring.

Eiði/Eysturoy
Dining and Lodging

Hotel Eiði. Perched on a hilltop village near the sea, about an hour by bus from Tórshavn, this slightly dated hotel is small and clean, with TVs and refrigerators in all rooms. *FR–470 Eiði, tel. 298/23456, fax 298/23200. 31 rooms. Facilities: restaurant. DC, MC, V. Moderate.*

Eysturoy
Lodging

Gjáargarður. This youth hostel, built in traditional Faroese style, is located in a beautiful area, on the north end of the island, near the ocean and the mountains. *FR–476, tel. 23171, fax 23505. 100 beds. No credit cards. Inexpensive.*

Klaksvík/Borðoy
Dining and Lodging

Klaksvíkar Sjómansheim. This big white sailors' hotel has comfortable rooms. *Vikavegur, tel. 55333. 68 beds. No credit cards. Moderate.*
Ibuð Youth Hostel. This youth and family hostel, the only one on the northern islands, is in a former hotel, built in 1945. It is near a ferry slip and surrounded by hiking trails. *Garðavegur 31, FR–700 Klaksvík, tel. 55403 or 57555. 67 beds. No credit cards. Inexpensive.*

Suðuroy
Dining and Lodging

Hotel Tvøroyri. In the middle of town, this old hotel has simple, clean rooms and minimal service. *FR–800 Tvøroyri, tel. 71171, fax 71394. 32 beds. AE. Moderate.*

Sörvágur/Vágar
Dining and Lodging

Hotel Vágar. A standard small hotel, this one is modern. *FR–380 Sørvágur, tel. 32955, fax 32310. 50 rooms. Facilities: restaurant. AE, DC, MC. Moderate.*

Tórshavn/Streymoy
Dining and Lodging

Hotel Föroyar. Five minutes from the center of Tórshavn, this hotel has a view of the old town. The rooms all have TVs, refrigerators, and phones, and there's a good restaurant that features island specialties. *Oyggjarvegur, tel. 17500, fax 16019. 108 rooms with bath. Facilities: restaurant. AE, DC, MC. Expensive.*
Hotel Hafnia. Close to the pedestrian streets of town, this modern business hotel offers a good buffet and big-city ambience.

The rooms have TV, refrigerator, and phone. *Áarvegur 4, tel. 11270, fax 15250. 103 rooms with bath. Facilities: restaurant. AE, DC, MC. Expensive.*

Skansin Guesthouse. This modern, two-story guest house has only been open for a year, and it has already become a favorite among travelers and business guests. Showers are available on both floors, and breakfast is included in the price of a room. The obliging staff can also help with travel or tour arrangements. *Jekaragøta 8, Box 57, FR–110 Tórshavn, tel. 12242, fax 10657. 22 beds. No credit cards. Moderate.*

Summarhotel. Open as a hotel from July to September, this is a school during the winter. *Vesturgøta 15, tel. 18900, fax 15707. 106 rooms with shower and toilet. AE, DC, MC. Moderate.*

Tórshavnar Sjómansheim. This sailors' hotel has comfortable rooms and a good restaurant. *Tórsgøta 4, tel. 13515, fax 13286. 84 beds. Facilities: restaurant. No credit cards. Inexpensive.*

Vágur/Suðuroy
Dining and Lodging

Hotel Bakkin. This plain lodging is usually booked by fishermen and local workers. *FR–900 Vágur, tel. 73961. 24 beds. No credit cards. Inexpensive.*

Viðoy
Dining and Lodging

Hotel Norð. In a small town of 300 inhabitants on the northern end of the island, this simple business hotel has beautiful surroundings and great bird-watching. *FR–750 Vidareisi, tel. 51061, fax 51144. 10 rooms. No credit cards. Closed Oct.–May. Moderate.*

3 Finland

*Updated by
Enrique Tessieri*

If you like majestic open spaces, fine architecture, and civilized living, Finland is for you. The music of Jean Sibelius, Finland's most famous son, tells you what to expect from this Nordic landscape. Both can swing from the somber nocturne of mid-winter darkness to the tremolo of sunlight slanting through pine and birch, or from the crescendo of a blazing sunset to the pianissimo of the next day's dawn. The architecture of Alvar Aalto and the Saarinens, Eliel and son Eero, visible in many U.S. cities, bespeaks the Finnish affinity with nature too, with soaring spaces evocative of Finland's moss-floored forests. In fact, Eliel and his family moved to the United States in 1923 and became American citizens—but it was to a lonely Finnish sea-shore that Saarinen had his ashes returned.

Until 1917, Finland was under the domination of its nearest neighbors, Sweden and Russia, who fought over it for centuries. After more than 600 years under Swedish rule and 100 under the czars, the country inevitably bears many traces of the two cultures, including a small (6%) Swedish-speaking population and a scattering of Russian Orthodox churches.

But the Finns themselves are neither Scandinavian nor Slavic. All that is known of their origins—they speak a Finno-Ugrian tongue, part Finnish, part Hungarian—is that they are descended from wandering tribes who probably originated west of Russia's Ural Mountains before the Christian era and settled on the Gulf of Finland's swampy shores.

There is a tough, resilient quality to the Finn. Finland is one of the very few countries that shared a border with the Soviet Union in 1939 and retained its independence. Indeed, no country has fought the Soviets to a standstill, as the Finns did in the grueling 105-day Winter War of 1939–40. This resilience stems from the turbulence of the country's past and from the people's determination to work the land and survive the long, brutal winters. No wonder there is a poet-philosopher lurking in most Finns, one who sometimes drowns the darker, melancholic side in a bottle. The Finn lives in a constant state of confrontation—against the weather and the land. Finns are stubborn, patriotic, and self-sufficient, yet not aggressively nationalistic. On the contrary, rather than boasting of past battles, Finns are proud of finding ways to live in peace with their neighbors. They are trying to cling to their country's neutrality and their personal freedom even as they apply for membership in the European Community (EC).

The average Finn volunteers little information, but that's due to reserve, not indifference. Make the first approach and you may have a friend for life. Finns like their silent spaces, though, and won't appreciate backslapping familiarity—least of all in the sauna, still regarded by many as a spiritual as well as a cleansing experience.

Before You Go

Government Tourist Offices

In North America **Finnish Tourist Board,** 655 3rd Ave., New York, NY 10017, tel. 212/949–2333; 1900 Avenue of the Stars, Suite 1070, Los Angeles, CA 90067, tel. 310/277–5226.

Finland

In the **Finnish Tourist Board,** 66–68 Haymarket, London SW1Y 4RF,
United Kingdom tel. 071/839–4048.

When to Go

Finland is delightful in the summer, with its clear clean air and phenomenally long sunny days. In the extreme north, the sun doesn't set at all during June and July, and even in Helsinki, where the sun often doesn't set before 10:30 PM, the night sky never becomes truly black. In the winter, not only is it very cold, but many of the tourist facilities are scaled down or even closed completely. The hotels are also less expensive in summer (and on weekends year-round), and so are domestic airfares. Finns tend to travel heavily during Christmas, Easter, and July—the peak summer-vacation month—so book ahead if you must fly during these times.

Climate In summer Finland is the warmest of the Scandinavian countries. Temperatures are surprisingly high, often in the 80s and 90s. In winter Helsinki averages about 25° F. Average temperatures in central Finland are 5° lower, and in Lapland, 10° lower. The following are average daily maximum and minimum temperatures for Helsinki.

Helsinki	**Jan.**	27F	− 3C	**May**	57F	14C	**Sept.**	57F	14C
		18	− 8		43	6		46	8
	Feb.	27F	− 3C	**June**	66F	19C	**Oct.**	48F	9C
		16	− 9		52	11		39	4
	Mar.	34F	1C	**July**	70F	21C	**Nov.**	37F	3C
		23	− 5		55	13		30	− 1
	Apr.	43F	6C	**Aug.**	66F	19C	**Dec.**	32F	0C
		32	0		54	12		21	− 6

Festivals and Seasonal Events

January: The **Arctic Rally** gets into gear yearly in Rovaniemi, Lapland.
February: Shrove Tuesday Celebrations, throughout Finland, include skiing, skating, and tobogganing events; **Finlandia Ski** is a 75-kilometer (47-mile) Hämeenlinna–Lahti ski event.
March: The **Tar Skiing Race** in Oulu is the oldest cross-country ski trek (75 kilometers/47 miles) in the country.
The Tampere International Short Film Festival features some of the best film in its category in Finland's second-largest city.
April: April Jazz/Espoo features foreign and Finnish performers in a Helsinki suburb; the **Porokuninkuusajot Reindeer Races** are run in Inari; and the **Vermo Cup Horse Event** is held at the Helsinki trotting track.
May: Vapunaatto and Vappu (May Day Eve and May Day) celebrations occur nationwide and include picnicking and drinking; **Kainuu Jazz** means four days of listening to native and foreign musicians jamming in Kajaani.
June: The **Kuopio Music and Dance Festival** is on stage in Kuopio, while the **Naantali Music Festival** soothes the ears of chamber-music lovers; **Juhannus** (Midsummer Eve and Day) is celebrated nationwide with bonfires and all-night boat cruises.
July: The **Savonlinna Opera Festival,** on a grand scale and a month long, is a festival of international opera staged at Olavinlinna Castle, Savonlinna; **Pori Jazz,** Finland's premier interna-

tional jazz festival, is set in Pori; the **Kuhmo Chamber Music Festival** means a week of chamber music in eastern Finland; and the **Kaustinen Folk Music Festival** is based in Kaustinen, western Finland.

August: The **Turku Music Festival** has Baroque to contemporary performances; the **Tampere International Theater Festival** includes plays staged by Finnish and foreign troupes; the **Helsinki Festival** means two weeks of dance, music, drama, and children's shows in the capital and its environs.

October: The **Baltic Herring Festival** is the premier fishermen's fish market, for one weekend on the quayside in Helsinki.

November: Tampere Jazz, a modern jazz event, holds court in Tampere; the **Children's Festival** in Helsinki consists of performance art of all kinds; **Kaamos Jazz** is a festival of jazz in Lapland's winter twilight, at Saariselkä/Tankavaara, near Ivalo.

December: Independence Day (December 6) means a parade to the candlelit Senate Square in Helsinki; the **International Jean Sibelius Violin Competition** is held every fifth year (the next one is in 1995) in Helsinki; **New Year's Celebration** varies, but fireworks can be seen from Senate Square in Helsinki.

For further information, contact **Finland Festivals** (00100 Helsinki).

Finnish Currency

The unit of currency is the Finnmark (FM), also abbreviated as FIM and FMK. The Finnmark is divided into 100 pennies (penniä) in denominations of 10- and 50-penniä and 5- and 10-mark coins. Bills begin with the FM20 note and progress to FM50, 100, 500, and 1,000. At press time (summer 1993) the exchange rate was FM5.40 to the U.S. dollar, FM8.33 to the pound sterling, and FM4.30 to the Canadian dollar. There are exchange bureaus in all bank branches; some post offices, which also function as banks (Postipankki); major hotels; and at Helsinki-Vantaa Airport. Some large harbor terminals also have exchange bureaus, and international ferries have exchange desks. Banks give the best exchange rates, however. Extended exchange and banking hours at Kansallis-Osake-Pankki (KOP) bank booths at the airport are 6:30 AM–11 PM daily. The Postipankki bank booth is open daily 6:30 AM–8:30 PM.

What It Will Cost

The devaluations of its currency in November 1991 and September 1992 have made Finland's exchange rate quite reasonable in comparison with the rest of Europe. If you opt for campsites or cabin rentals rather than hotel rooms and shop for meals carefully, you can cut costs considerably. Helsinki is Finland's most expensive city for lodging. Food costs tend to be standardized across the country, however.

Taxes   There is a 22% sales tax on most consumer goods. Nonresidents can recover much of this by going through the "tax-free for tourists" procedure (*see* Tax-Free Shopping, *below*). Restaurants and hotels include a 15% service charge in their bills.

Sample Costs   Cup of coffee, FM5; soda, FM7; Continental breakfast in hotel, FM32–60; bottle of beer, FM15–FM20; 1-mile taxi ride, around FM20.

Passports and Visas

Citizens of the United States, Great Britain, Canada, and most European countries need a valid passport to enter Finland; a visa is necessary only if your total stay in the Nordic countries will be longer than three months (*see* Chapter 1 for additional information).

Customs and Duties

On Arrival Travelers aged 20 years and older may bring in two liters of beer, one liter of alcohol under 22% volume and one liter of alcohol over 22% volume; or two liters of beer plus two liters of alcohol under 22% volume. Travelers between 18 and 20 cannot bring in any alcohol in excess of 22% volume but can bring beer or wine. Non-European residents may bring in 400 cigarettes or a little over a pound (500 grams) of tobacco. European residents have a 200-cigarette, ½-pound-plus (250-gram) tobacco limit. A permit for firearms and ammunition must be obtained on arrival from airport or harbor police.

On Departure A license is required to export the following: handicrafts and works of art more than 50 years old; any object more than 50 years old that has cultural or historic value; valuable Finnish coins, medals, or postage stamps.

Language

Finnish, the principal language, is not Scandinavian in origin but is a Finno-Ugric tongue related to Estonian with distant links to Hungarian. The country's second official language is Swedish, although only about 6% of the population speaks it. In the south, most towns have Finnish and Swedish names; if the Swedish name is listed first, it indicates more Swedish than Finnish speakers in that area. The third language is Saame, the language of the Laplanders. English is spoken in most cities and resorts.

Car Rentals

Car rental in Finland is not cheap, but a group rental might make it worthwhile. Be on the lookout for weekend and summer discounts. It is cheaper to rent directly from the United States before coming to Finland. Some Finnish service stations also offer car rentals at reduced rates. Regular daily rates range from FM190 to FM400 ($37–$74), and per-kilometer surcharges from FM2.00 to FM4.00 (37¢–74¢). Insurance is sold by the rental agencies. Some centrally located agencies are: **Avis** (Pohjoinen Rautatiekatu 17, Helsinki, tel. 90/441 114; airport office, tel. 90/822–833 or 9800/2828), **Budget** (Hotel Inter-Continental, tel. 90/497–477; airport office, tel. 90/870–1606 or 9800/2535), Hertz (Mannerheimintie 44, tel. 90/446–910; airport office, tel. 90/821–052 or 9800/2012), and **InterRent-Europcar** (John Stenberginranta 6, tel. 90/758–3354; airport office, tel. 90/826–677 or 9800/2154).

Rail Passes

The **Finnrail Pass** gives unlimited first- or second-class travel within a set time; the one-week pass costs FM470 (FM705 for

first-class), the two-week pass FM730 (FM1,095, and the three-week pass FM920 (FM1,380). Children pay half fare. These passes can be bought in the United States and Canada by calling Rail Europe (tel. 914/682–2999); in the United Kingdom from Finlandia Travel (tel. 071/409–7334); and from the Finnish State Railways (VR).

Finland also participates in the following rail programs: **EurailPass, Eurail Youth Pass** (for travelers under 26), **ScanRail Pass** (unlimited travel in Scandinavia for 21 days), **InterRail** (for travelers under 26 who are not residents of Scandinavia), and **Rail Europe Senior Card** (for men and women older than 60). (*See also* Getting Around by Train, *below.*)

Traveling with Children

Finland's is a child-oriented society. Visitors have no problem finding such amenities as changing rooms, and almost all hotels welcome children. Helsinki's city tourist office has a list of qualified baby-sitters in the capital area.

In Finland, families of three or more traveling by bus over distances of at least 47 miles receive a 20% discount. **Finnrail** offers savings of 50% to all Finnrail Pass holders under 17 and savings of 20% to groups of three or more. Children ages 2 to 16 also get a 50% reduction on Finnair's Holiday Ticket, which offers 15 days of unlimited air travel in Finland.

Young people ages 17 to 24 qualify for a **Finnish Youth Holiday Ticket** that is good for up to 15 days of unlimited air travel within Finland. For further information, contact Finnair (tel. 800/950–5000). (*See also* Traveling with Children in Chapter 1.)

Farmhouse Holidays In Finland more than 150 farmhouses provide full-board, half-board, or bed-and-breakfast accommodations; many also have children's rates and offer handicrafts classes, farm tours, and other organized activities for children. Contact the Tourist Office for listings.

Hints for Travelers with Disabilities

In Finland, information on facilities for disabled visitors can be obtained from **Rullaten ry** (Malminkatu 38, 00100 Helsinki, tel. 90/694–1155), an organization that specializes in assisting the disabled in planning their travels. Special tours for the disabled of Helsinki and the surrounding area are organized by **Area Travel Agency** (Kaisanienmenkatu 13A, 00100 Helsinki, tel. 90/185 5368).

Hints for Older Travelers

Finland is a generally safe place with good public transportation, and visiting should be a pleasant experience for all. Carry some proof of your age whenever you buy tickets for events, museums, and especially for travel: There are significant discounts to be had for those who are older than 65—and sometimes for those over 60.

Arriving and Departing

From North America by Plane

Airports and Airlines All international flights arrive at Helsinki-Vantaa International-al Airport, 20 kilometers (12 miles) north of the city center. For arrival and departure information, call 90/818–500 (6:15 AM–11:45 PM) or 9700/8100 (24 hours).

Finnair (tel. 800/950–5000) offers domestic and international flights, with daily direct service from New York. **Delta** (tel. 800/221–1212) has direct service from New York. **British Airways** (tel. 800/247–9297), **Lufthansa** (tel. 800/645–3880), and **Scandinavian Airlines System** (SAS) (tel. 800/221–2350) also fly to Helsinki.

Flying Time Flying time from New York to Helsinki is about 8 hours, 9 hours for the return trip.

From the United Kingdom by Plane and Ship

By Plane **Finnair, British Airways,** and some charter companies fly from London to Helsinki. Ask the **Finnish National Tourist Board** for names of companies specializing in travel packages to Finland. All international flights land at Helsinki-Vantaa International Airport, 20 kilometers (12 miles) north of the capital. Finnair in the United Kingdom is located at 14 Clifford Street, London W1X 1RD (tel. 071/629–4349).

Flying Time Flying time from London to Helsinki is 2 hours, 45 minutes.

By Ship **DFDS Scandinavian Seaways** (Scandinavia House, Parkeston Quay, Harwich, Essex, tel. 225/240–234) sails from Harwich to Göteborg, Sweden, with overland (bus or train) transfer to Stockholm; from there, Silja and Viking Line ships cross to the Finnish Åland Islands, Turku, and Helsinki. Traveling time is about two days (*see also* Getting Around by Boat, *below*).

Staying in Finland

Getting Around

By Plane Finland's flagship air carrier, **Finnair,** runs an extensive domestic service and the charter companies **KarAir** and **Finnaviation.** Domestic flights are relatively cheap, and as some planes have a set number of discount seats allotted it's best to reserve early. Finnair's "Fly and Save" and "Super Fly and Save" offer 40% and 60% discounts, respectively, on domestic flights. Finnair's main office is at Helsinki-Vantaa Airport, Tietotie 11, 01530 Vantaa (tel. 90/81–881).

By Train **The Finnish State Railways,** or VR, serve southern Finland well, but connections in the central and northern sections are scarcer and are supplemented by buses (*see* Getting Around by Bus, *below*). Helsinki is the main junction, with Riihimäki to the north a major hub. You can get as far north as Rovaniemi and Kemijärvi by rail, but to penetrate farther into Lapland, you'll need to rely on buses, domestic flights, or local taxis.

First- and second-class seats are available on all express trains. Children (ages 6–16) travel half fare, and there is a 20% reduc-

tion when three or more people travel together. You must make a seat reservation on special fast trains (FM15–FM30). For FM50, senior citizens (over 65) can buy a special pass entitling them to 50% discounts on train fares. Car and passenger trains leave daily for northern Finland. Passenger trains leave Helsinki once daily for St. Petersburg (8 hours) and once daily on an overnighter to Moscow (15 hours). Travel to Russia requires a visa. To get to northern Sweden or Norway, you must combine train/bus or train/boat travel.

Inquiries on train travel can be made to the Finnish State Railways at the main railroad station in Helsinki, or to the **Information Service** at Vilhonkatu 13, PB 488, 00100 Helsinki (tel. 90/101 0115).

By Bus The Finnish bus network, **Matkahuolto** (Lauttasaarentie 8, 00200 Helsinki, tel. 90/692–2088), is extensive and the fares reasonable. You can also travel by bus between Finland and Norway, Sweden, or Russia. Full-time students can purchase a discount card for FM30 that translates into a 50% discount on longer trips. Senior citizens will get good discounts with the **65 Card** for FM30; it's available at Matkahuolto offices. Adults in groups of three or more are entitled to a 25% discount.

A **Coach Holiday Ticket** (FM300) is good for up to 1,000 kilometers (650 miles) of travel for two weeks.

By Car Driving is pleasant on Finland's relatively uncongested roads. At press time gasoline cost FM4.90 per liter. Driving is on the right. You must always use low-beam headlights outside of built-up areas. Seat belts are compulsory for everyone. You must yield to cars coming from the right at most intersections where roads are of equal size. There are strict drinking and driving laws.

Speed limits range from 40 to 80 and sometimes 100 kilometers per hour (25 to 50 and sometimes 65 miles per hour), depending on road size and proximity to settled areas. Late autumn and spring are the most hazardous times to drive. Roads are often icy in autumn (*kelivaroitus* is the slippery road warning), and the spring thaw can make for *kelirikko* (heaves). The **Automobile Touring Club of Finland** (Autoliitto ry, Kansakoulukatu 10, 00100 Helsinki, tel. 90/694–0022) has a wealth of information, including where to rent studded tires, which are mandatory from October through April.

Foreigners involved in road accidents should immediately notify the **Finnish Motor Insurers' Bureau** (Bulevardi 28, 00120 Helsinki, tel. 90/680401) as well as the police.

By Boat Finland is one of the world's largest shipbuilding nations, and the ferries that cruise the Baltic to the Finnish Åland islands and Sweden seem more like luxury liners. The boat operators make so much money selling duty-free alcohol, perfume, and chocolate that they spare no expense on facilities, which include saunas, children's playrooms, casinos, a host of bars and cafés, and often superb restaurants.

The Stockholm–Turku run takes about 10 hours; Stockholm–Helsinki takes about 14 hours, and all classes of sleeping accommodations are available on board. Other connections are Vaasa–Sundsvall and Umeå (Sweden), Kokkola–Skellefteå (Sweden), Helsinki–Travemünde (Germany), Helsinki–Tallinn (Estonia), and Helsinki–Gdansk (Poland).

By Taxi Taxis travel everywhere in Finland. The meter starts at FM12, with surcharges at certain times and on certain days. In cities people generally go to one of the numerous taxi stands and take the first available taxi. You can hail a cab, but most are on radio call. To order taxis by phone, look up "Taksi" in the white pages, then try to find one located nearby—they start the meter when leaving their station. Many taxi drivers take credit cards. Tipping is unnecessary; if you want to leave something, round up to the nearest FM5–FM10. A receipt is a *kuitti*.

By Bicycle Finland is a wonderful place to bicycle, with its easy terrain, light traffic, and wide network of bicycle paths. You can get bike-route maps for most major cities. In Helsinki, cycling is a great way to see the main peninsula as well as some of the surrounding islands, linked by bridges. Rentals average FM40–FM60 per day. **Suomen Retkeilymajajärjestö** (Finnish Youth Hostel Association, Yrjönkatu 38B, 00100 Helsinki, tel. 90/694–0377) offers a free brochure with information on long-distance cycling trips and hostels; the youth hostel at the Helsinki Olympic stadium rents bikes for FM40 per day.

Telephones

Local Calls Although Finland is gradually moving to the phone-card system, public phones charge FM2 and take coins up to FM5. Kiosks often have phones. Airport and hotel phones take credit cards. Ringing tones vary but are distinguishable from busy signals, which are always rapid. Most pay telephones have picture instructions illustrating how they operate.

Calls within Finland can be made from any phone. Remember that if you are dialing out of the immediate area, you must dial 9 first, followed by the region code (example: 9–0 for Helsinki), then the number. Drop the 9 when calling Finland from abroad. Finland's country code is 358.

International Calls You can call overseas at the post and telegraph office, in the "Lennätin" section, where you also may send faxes, telegrams, and telexes. In Helsinki, at Mannerheimintie 11B, the section is open weekdays 8 AM–10 PM, Saturday 10 AM–4 PM, and is closed on Sunday. The "Finland Direct" pamphlet tells you how to reach an operator in your own country for collect or credit-card calls. Use any booth that has a green light, and pay the cashier when you finish. You can also ask for a clerk to set up a collect call; when it is ready, the clerk will direct you to a booth. The access code for AT&T USA direct calls is 9800–100–10. The MCI access code is 9800–102–80.

The front of the phone book has overseas calling directions and rates. You must begin all direct overseas calls with 990 plus country code (1 for the United States/Canada, 44 for Great Britain). Finnish operators can be reached by dialing 92020 for overseas information or for placing collect calls.

Important Numbers For an operator in the United States, dial 9800–1–0010; in Canada, dial 9800–1–0011; and in the United Kingdom, dial 9800–1–0440. Other important numbers are as follows: 112, general emergency; 10040, news in English; 100151, wake-up call; 118, Helsinki information; 118, information elsewhere in Finland; 92020, international information.

Mail

Post offices are open weekdays 9–5; stamps, express mail, registered mail, and insured mail service are available. There is no Saturday delivery. Airmail letters to destinations outside Europe cost FM3.40; to central Europe and the United Kingdom, FM2.90; to other Scandinavian countries and within Finland, FM2.30. Postcards outside Europe are FM3.40. You may receive letters care of the Poste Restante anywhere in Finland; the Poste Restante address in the capital is Mannerheimintie 11C, 00100 Helsinki, at the side of the rail station. It is open Monday to Friday 8 AM to 9 PM, Saturday 9 AM to 6 PM, and Sunday 11 AM to 9 PM. You can also post mail 24 hours a day at Finland Post's Express Service (Läkkisepäntie 11, 00620 Helsinki; tel. 9800/70784, 8 AM–5 PM).

Tipping

Tipping is not the norm in Finland, but it is not unheard of, so use your own discretion. Finns normally do not tip cab drivers, but if they do they round up to the nearest FM5. Give FM5 to train or hotel porters if you wish. Coat-check fees are usually posted, and tips above this amount are not expected. Restaurant and hotel bills include a 10%–15% service charge, so an additional tip is unnecessary unless you want to reward good service. For all other services, no tip or FM5 is acceptable.

Opening and Closing Times

Banks Most banks are open weekdays 9–9:15 to 4–5; the bank at Helsinki Airport has extended hours (*see* Where to Change Money in Helsinki, *below*).

Shops Stores are generally open weekdays 9–6, Saturday 9–1 or 2, and are closed on Sunday. In Helsinki and other major cities, some large stores and malls remain open until 8 (on Saturday until 6 PM). Kiosks, with basic items such as milk and toilet paper, are open daily—usually from 7 AM until 9 or 10 PM—and are found throughout the country.

Shopping

Finland is known for design. Helsinki has the widest selection of goods and the highest prices. Most larger manufacturers and design firms set standard prices throughout the country. Furs, called *turkki* in Finland, are a good buy. You might also want to take home some of the delicious smoked or marinated fish found here—available vacuum-packed at Helsinki Airport.

Tax-Free Shopping The total sales tax is 22%. Depending on the size of the purchase, tax refunds range from 10% to 16%.

When you ask for your tax rebate, you'll get a tax-free voucher and your goods in a sealed bag. Present the voucher and unopened bag at tax-free cashiers when leaving the country. These are located at most major airports, on board most long-distance ferries, and at major overland crossings into Sweden, Norway, and Russia. Refunds are available only in Finnish marks. For a high fee, the tax refund can also be sent to your home country.

Sports and Outdoor Activities

Bicycling Bicycling is popular as both transport and sport. Route maps are available from local tourist offices and from the **Finnish Youth Hostel Association** (*see* Getting Around by Bicycle, *above*).

Boating Finns love all kinds of boating, and there are good facilities for guests' boats in most ports. Contact the **Finnish Yachting Association** or the **Finnish Motorboating Association** (Radiokatu 20, 00240 Helsinki, tel. 90/158–2110 and tel. 90/158–2561, respectively).

Canoeing Lapland is one of the most popular canoeing areas. **Lapptreks** (Ranta-Antintie 1, 99870 Inari, tel. 9697/51–375) offers a combined canoeing/hiking/gold-panning trip, or contact the local tourist board or the **Finnish Canoe Association** (Radiokatu 20, 00240 Helsinki, tel. 90/158–2363).

Cross-Country Skiing This is the most Finnish of all sports, and there are ski centers and resorts nationwide, many with equipment to rent. Any tourist board can advise you; or contact **Suomen Latu** (Fabianinkatu 7, 00130 Helsinki, tel. 90/170–101). Finnair has fly/ski packages to the north; Vuokatti, Ylläs, Saariselkä, and Kiilopää are Lapland's leading ski centers.

Find out about ski events, including the February Hämeenlinna–Lahti Finlandia Race from the **Finlandia Ski Race Office** (Urheilukeskus, 15110 Lahti, tel. 918/49–811); the March Salpausselkä Ski Games and jumping events are also in Lahti.

Downhill Skiing The best skiing is in Lapland and Oulu provinces. Major resorts include Levi (Levin Matkailu, Teletalo, 99100 Kittilä, tel. 9694/13466), Pyhä (Hotelli Pyhätunturi, 98540 Kultakero, tel. 9692/12081), and Ruka (Rukakeskus, Höy läämöntie 14, 00380 Helsinki, tel. 90/5060551). Contact the Finnish Tourist Board (Töölönkatu 11, 00100 Helsinki, tel. 90/403011) for detailed information.

Fishing The fish-rich waters of the Baltic archipelago and innumerable inland lakes and streams assure that you will never run out of fishing opportunities. A fishing license can be obtained from any post office (FM38) and is valid for one year. In addition to this general fishing license, a regional fishing permit must also be obtained. The Finnish Tourist Board has a "Finland Fishing" brochure and "A Guide to Angling," with information on 600 fishing spots. The **Finnish Forest and Parks Service** (Vernissäkatu 4, 01300 Vantaa, tel. 90/857841) will provide guidance, too.

Hiking The country is full of hiking trails, both in the wilds and near large towns. Most towns have a network of paths through the omnipresent forest. For those with rougher treks in mind, ask at local tourist boards or if you want to hike on state-owned land in eastern and northern Finland, write to the Finnish Forest and Parks Service (*see* Fishing, *above*).

Orienteering This has a big following in Finland, and you can find out about routes and events from the **Finnish Orienteering Association** (Radiokatu 20, 00240 Helsinki, tel. 90/158–2453).

Waterskiing At both lake- and seaside there are many water-ski clubs; contact the **Finnish Water-Ski Association** (Radiokatu 20, 00240 Helsinki, tel. 90/158–2595).

Beaches

For beaches with sand, you must look on the southern coastline and archipelago: for example, on the west coast of the Hailuoto Sands, a low, sandy island about 40 kilometers (25 miles) from Oulu. A car ferry runs there in summer. The nearly 40-kilometer-long (25-mile-long) Hankoniemi Cape is bordered by sandy beaches. The peninsula is part of the Salpausselkä ridge and forms Finland's southern tip.

Dining

Finnish food is known for freshness rather than variety, although recent years have seen major improvements in restaurant cuisine. Ironically, the hardest meal to find is the authentic Finnish meal—products from the forest, lakes, and sea. It is far easier to find pizza, which Finns prefer with many toppings.

However, search and you will find the stunning meals Finns make with game—pheasant, reindeer, hare, and grouse—accompanied by wild-berry compotes and exotic mushroom sauces. The chantarelle grows wild in Finland, as do dozens of other edible mushrooms, such as the tasty morel.

Other specialties are *poronkäristys* (reindeer casserole), *lihapullat* (meatballs in sauce), *uunijuusto* (oven cheese), and *hiilillä paistetut silakat* (charcoal-grilled Baltic herring). *Voileipäpöytä*, the Finnish cousin to smørgåsbord, is a cold table served at breakfast or lunch where you are free to take as little or as much food as you like.

Fish is, of course, popular, especially smoked fish. Crayfish season begins on July 21. Finnish baked goods are renowned. *Mämmi*, a dessert made of wheat flour, malt, and orange peels and served with cream and sugar, is served at Easter. More nourishing are *karjalan piirakka*, thin, oval wheat-bread pirogi filled with rice or mashed potatoes and served warm with a mixture of egg and butter. *Kalakukko* is seen most often in Savolax and consists of wheat bread with small pieces of meat and onions baked inside the dough, served warm with melted butter.

Hearty meat dishes include *karjalan paisti*, in which pork, lamb, and beef are mixed and baked for many hours. *Maksalaatikko* is a dish combining liver, rice, and raisins, served with melted butter.

Helsinki and other cities offer a decent variety of foreign restaurants, the dominant ones being Russian and Chinese. Home-cooked meals tend to be beef or pork accompanied by potatoes. Yogurt and other dairy products are extremely good. The Finns like to make pizza at home. Pancakes with filling, homemade bread, and sweet buns are other at-home favorites.

The prices of alcohol are legendary. A "cheap" bottle of wine (all wine is imported, though some is domestically bottled) will cost FM100 in a restaurant. The Finns make good beer, with a large brew costing around FM20. Cocktails usually start at about FM25. Spirits and liqueurs are pricey, too, but you'll fare a little better at **Alko,** the state liquor monopoly, open Monday–Thursday 10–5, Friday 10–6, Saturday 9–2. Some Alko stores are also open until 8 on Friday and 6 on Saturday.

Category	Helsinki*	Other Areas*
Very Expensive	over FM180	over FM150
Expensive	FM130–FM180	FM110–FM150
Moderate	FM80–FM130	FM65–FM110
Inexpensive	under FM80	under FM65

per person for dinner, excluding drinks and including appetizer, main course, dessert, and service charge.

Lodging

Every class of lodging exists in Finland, from five-star urban hotels to rustic cabins on lake shores and in the forest. Cleanliness is the rule, as is modern decor and plumbing. The standard setup includes a bathroom in each room with toilet and shower; only exceptions to this standard (for example full bathroom with bathtub, shared bath) will be mentioned in reviews in this chapter.

The **Hotel Booking Center** (00100, tel. 90/171133) in Helsinki, at the Railway Station, will make reservations for you anywhere in Finland for FM10 (telephone reservations are free). Some national hotel chains to contact are **Best Western Hotels Finland** (Annankatu 29, 00100 Helsinki, tel. 90/694–7755) or **Arctia Hotel Partners** (Iso Roobertinkatu 23–25, 00120 Helsinki, tel. 90/694–8022).

Lomarengas (Malminkaari 23C, 00700 Helsinki, tel. 90/3516–1321 or Eteläesplanadi 4, 00130 Helsinki, tel. 90/170611) arranges stays at a range of facilities, including *mökki* (cabin) holidays. **Suomen 4H Liitto** (Abrahaminkatu 7, 00180 Helsinki, tel. 90/642–233) arranges farm vacations.

Bed-and-Breakfasts **Lomarengas** and **Toyota Rent-a-Car** have lists of reasonably priced B&Bs, holiday cottages, farm accommodations, and car-rental services. Information and brochures are available from most offices of the Finnish Tourist Board (*see* Government Tourist Offices in Before You Go, *above*).

Summer Dormitories During the summer season (June 1–August 31) many university residence halls in Finland open their doors to visitors. Prices (usually from $42 per night in Helsinki and $30 elsewhere in Finland) are much lower than those in ordinary hotels, and meals are generally available. Ask the Finnish Tourist Board for its brochure on budget accommodations.

Camping Finland is prime camping territory because of the great wealth of open space. If you camp outside authorized areas, you must get the landowner's permission if you are in a settled area, and you cannot camp closer than 300 feet to anyone's house. You may also swim anywhere that is not clearly marked as private property.

Finncamping Cheque (FM68) is a coupon system for campers. For more information, contact the **Finnish Travel Association** (Camping Department, Mikonkatu 25, Box 776, 00101 Helsinki, tel. 90/170–868). The group also sells the National Camping Card, a useful ID card. The annually updated list of campsites, including classifications and English-language summary, is sold at large bookstores and R-kiosks.

The price categories below are based on weekday rates. Greater discounts are available on weekends and in summer months, especially between midsummer and July 31, when prices are usually 30% to 50% lower.

Category	Helsinki*	Other Areas*
Very Expensive	over FM750	over FM650
Expensive	FM550–FM750	FM440–FM650
Moderate	FM350–FM550	FM270–FM440
Inexpensive	under FM350	under FM270

Prices are for two people in a double room and include service charge and taxes.

Helsinki

Helsinki is a city of the sea, built on peninsulas that stab into the Baltic. Streets and avenues curve around bays, bridges arch across to nearby islands, and ferries reach out to islands farther offshore.

Like other European capitals, Helsinki has expanded its boundaries, now absorbing about one-sixth of the Finnish population, and the suburbs sprawl from one peninsula to another. However, most of the city's sights, hotels, and restaurants cluster on one peninsula, forming a compact hub of special interest for the traveler.

Unlike most other European capitals, Helsinki is "new." About 400 years ago, King Gustav Vasa of Sweden decided to woo trade from the Estonian city of Talinn and thus challenge the monopoly of the Hanseatic League. To do this, he commanded the people of four Finnish towns to pack up their belongings and relocate at the rapids on the River Vantaa. This new town became Helsinki.

For three centuries, Helsinki had its ups and downs as a trading town. Turku, to the west, remained the capital and the country's intellectual center. Ironically, not until Finland fell under Russia's dominance did Helsinki's fortunes improve. Czar Alexander I wanted Finland's political center closer to Russia and, in 1812, selected Helsinki as the new capital. Shortly after the capital was moved from Turku, Turku suffered a monstrous fire. Such was the damage that the university was also moved to Helsinki. From then on, Helsinki's future was secure.

Fire was indeed fortuitous for the city's future. Just before the czar's proclamation, a fire had gutted the town, permitting the construction of new buildings suitable for a nation's capital. The German-born architect Carl Ludvig Engel was commissioned to rebuild the city, and as a result, Helsinki has some of the purest neoclassical architecture in the world. Add to this foundation the modern buildings designed by talented Finnish architects and the result is a European capital city that is as architecturally eye-catching as it is distinct from other Scandinavian and European capitals.

Important Addresses and Numbers

Tourist Information The **Helsinki City Tourist Office** (Pohjoisesplanadi 19, 00100 Helsinki, tel. 90/169–3757) is open September 16–May 15, Monday 8:30–4:30 and Tuesday–Friday 8:30–4; and May 16–September 15, weekdays 8:30–6 and Saturday 8:30–1. The **Finnish Tourist Board's Information Office** (Eteläesplanadi 4, tel. 90/4030–1211 or 90/4030–1300) nearby is open June–August, weekdays 8:30–5, weekends 10–2; September–May, weekdays 8:30–4, closed weekends.

Embassies **U.S. Embassy,** Itäinen Puistotie 14A, 00140 Helsinki, tel. 90/171–931. **Canadian Embassy,** Pohjoisesplanadi 25B, 00100 Helsinki, tel. 90/171–141. **U.K. Embassy,** Itäinen Puistotie 17, 00140 Helsinki, tel. 90/661–293.

Emergencies The general emergency number is 112, which you can call for any emergency situation. Coins are not needed to make this call on pay phones.

Police Dial 112.

Ambulance Dial 112. Specify whether the situation seems life-threatening so that medical attendants can begin immediate treatment in the ambulance.

Hospital Emergency Rooms **Töölön Sairaala** (Töölönkatu 40, tel. 4711) is a centrally located hospital (about 2 kilometers/1 mile from city center) with a 24-hour emergency room and first-aid service.

Doctors Dial 10003.

Dentists Töölö Dental Care Center (Pohjoinen Herpseriankatu 17, tel. 90/431–4500; Mon.–Tues. 8–6, Wed.–Fri. 8–3).

Where to Change Money Banks give the best exchange rates; banks with exchange facilities at the airport remain open late. The KOP or Postipankki bank booths at Helsinki Airport offer extended-hours exchange and banking service and are open daily 6:30 AM to 11 PM. Elsewhere banks are open weekdays 9–9:15 to 4–5 and sometimes until 6 (post offices that offer Postipankki services). Major ferries, harbors, and rail stations have exchange facilities, too. You can also buy Finnmarks at the Post Restante in the main post office (on Railway Square, at the back of the Main Post Office at Mannerheimintie 11; open Mon.–Fri. 8–9, Sat. 9–6, Sun. 11–9). There is an automatic money-exchange machine on the ground floor of the Forum shopping center (corner Mannerheimintie and Simonkatu), but it does not offer the best rates. A passport is the preferred form of ID with traveler's checks, which can be cashed only at American Express (Area Travel Agency, Pohjoisesplanadi 2, 00170 Helsinki, tel. 90/18551, or Kanavaranta 9, 00160 Helsinki, tel. 90/125–1600) or Thomas Cook (Finland Travel Bureau, Kaivokatu 10 A, 00100 Helsinki, tel. 90/18261).

English-Language Bookstores **Akateeminen Kirjakauppa** (Academic Bookstore, Pohjoisesplanadi 39, tel. 90/12–141) and **Suomalainen Kirjakauppa** (The Finnish Bookstore, Aleksanterinkatu 23, tel. 90/651–855) both sell English-language books, newspapers, and magazines. Akateeminen is larger and more expensive.

Late-Night Pharmacy **Yliopiston Apteekki,** Mannerheimintie 5, tel. 90/179–092, is open daily 7 AM–midnight.

Travel Agencies **Area** (Kaisaniemenkatu 13A, 00100, tel. 90/18–551), **Finnish Travel Bureau** (Kaivokatu 10A, 00100, tel. 90/18261), **FinnSov Tours Ltd.** (Eerikinkatu 3, 00100 Helsinki, tel. 90/694–2011), **Kaleva Travel Agency** (Mannerheimintie 2, 00100 Helsinki, tel. 90/61–811), **Lomarengas** (accommodation service, Eteläesplanadi 4, 00130 Helsinki, tel. 90/170–611), and **Kilroy Travels** (Kaivokatu 10D, Kaivopiha, 00100 Helsinki, tel. 90/6807811) are the leading agencies.

Arriving and Departing by Plane

Airports and Airlines All domestic and international flights to Helsinki use Helsinki-Vantaa International Airport, 20 kilometers (14 miles) north of the city. Helsinki is served by most major European airlines, including: **SAS** (Keskuskatu 7A, Helsinki, tel. 90/175–611), **Lufthansa** (Yrjönkatu 29A, Helsinki, tel. 90/694–9900), **Swiss-Air** (Mikonkatu 7, tel. 90/175–300), **British Airways** (Keskuskatu 7, Helsinki, tel. 90/650–677), **Air France** (Pohjoisesplanadi 27C, Helsinki, tel. 90/625–862), and several East European carriers. North American service is available from **Delta** (Salomonkatu 17B, Helsinki, tel. 90/694–2422).

Between the Airport and Downtown
By Bus A local bus, the No. 615, runs three to four times an hour between the airport and the main railway station. The fare is FM15, and the trip takes about 40 minutes. Local Bus 614 runs three times a day between the airport and the main bus station; the trip takes approximately 40 minutes and the fare is FM15. Finnair buses carry travelers to and from the railway station (Finnair's city terminal) two to four times an hour, with a stop at the InterContinental hotel. Request stops along the route are also made. Travel time from the Inter-Continental hotel is about 30 minutes and about 35 minutes from the main railway station; the fare is FM20.

By Taxi There is a taxi stop at the arrivals building. A cab ride into central Helsinki will cost between FM100 and FM120. Driving time is 20 to 35 minutes, depending upon the time of day. Check to see if your hotel has a shuttle service, although this is not common here. **Airport Taxi Service** (tel. 90/2200 2500; cost FM50, FM90 for two passengers, FM110 for three; reserve two hours before flight departure; for flights departing before 7 AM, reserve before 7 PM) operates shuttles between the city and the airport.

By Limousine **International Limousine System** (Alkutie 32H, 00660 Helsinki, tel. 90/744–577 or 949/421–801). A limousine ride into central Helsinki will cost about FM480.

Getting Around

The center of Helsinki is compact and best explored on foot. However, the City Tourist Office provides a free Helsinki route map that shows all public transportation. Your best fare buy is the **Helsinki Card**, which gives unlimited travel on city public transportation as well as free entry to many museums, a free sightseeing tour, and a variety of other discounts. It's available for one, two, or three days (FM80, FM105, and FM125 adults; FM45, FM55, and FM65 children ages 7–16) and can be bought at most hotels or at the City Tourist Office.

By Car Ring Roads One and Three are the two major highways that encircle the city. Mannerheimintie and Hämeentie are the major

trunk roads out of Helsinki. Mannerheimintie feeds into High-way E79, which travels west and takes you to the Ring roads. Hämeentie leads you to Highway E4 as well as roads 4 and 7. From either route, you will find directions for Road 137 to the airport. For specific route information, contact the **Automobile and Touring Club of Finland** (Autoliitto ry, Kansakoulukatu 10, 00100 Helsinki, tel. 90/694–0022) or the City Tourist Office (*see* Tourist Information, *above*).

By Train Helsinki's suburbs as well as most of the rest of southern, west-ern, and central Finland are well served by trains. Travel on trains within the Helsinki city limits costs the same as all public transport, FM9 or less if you use the 10-trip tickets (*see below*). A 10-trip **Helsinki Area Ticket,** or *Seutulippu,* for FM125 also provides a small discount for travel back and forth to adjacent areas such as Espoo and Vantaa.

By Bus, Tram, and Metro The bus and tram networks are extensive and service is fre-quent. Be sure to pick up a route map at the tourist office—many stops do not have them. If you have a one-trip ticket, or *Kertalippu,* (cost: FM9) or a 10-trip ticket (*Kymmenen matkan kortti*) (cost: FM75); you must cancel it yourself. The metro system is small but has fast and frequent service from around 5:45 AM to 11:05 PM Monday through Saturday and infre-quent service on Sunday; the cost is the same as for buses and trams.

By Taxi There are numerous taxi stands; central stands are at Railway Square on the west side of the station, the main bus station, and in the Esplanade. Taxis can also be flagged, but this can some-times be difficult because many are on radio call.

Opening and Closing Times

Banks are open weekdays 9–9:15 to 4–5. Many offices and em-bassies close at 3 PM June–August. Stores are open weekdays 9–6 and Saturday 9–1 or 2 and are closed on Sunday. Some stores in malls remain open until 8 PM on weekdays and until 4 on Satur-day. In the Asematunneli (train station tunnel), stores are open weekdays 10–10 and weekends noon–10.

Guided Tours

Orientation Bus tours are a good way to get your orientation here. There is a 1½-hour tour of central Helsinki sights that comes free with the Helsinki Card; otherwise the cost is FM60 adults, FM30 children (ages 4–11). The tour leaves from Railway Square (Asema-aukio) on Sunday at 11 AM throughout the year; it also runs Tuesday and Thursday in September. For more information, contact **Suomen Turistiauto** (tel. 90/588–5166).

There is a year-round two-hour tour that leaves from the Olym-pic Harbor and Katajanokka Terminal daily at 9:30 AM. The cost is FM85 for adults and FM45 for children (under 12), not including lunch. For more information, call **Ageba Travel** (tel. 90/669–193). From April through October, Ageba also has a daily 2½-hour tour at 11 AM from the Olympic Harbor costing FM95 for adults and FM45 for children, excluding lunch).

Tram No. 3T around Helsinki, with a short recorded commentary in English, provides a good orientation to the city for the price of a regular tram ride (FM8 adults, FM4 children). You can get on

board in front of the railway station on Kaivokatu for the 60-minute round-trip.

The Guide Booking Center (Lönnrotinkatu 7, 00120 Helsinki, tel. 90/601–966) will arrange personal tour guides.

Boat Tours All boat tours depart from the Market Square. The easiest way to choose one is to go to the square in the morning and read the sandwich boards describing the tours. The city tourist office will have the most current information, however. Most tours run in the summer only. You can go as far afield as Porvoo (*see* Short Excursions from Helsinki, *below*) or take a short jaunt to the zoo.

A ferry to the Suomenlinna fortress island runs about twice an hour, depending on time of day. The ferry to the zoo island, Korkeasaari, runs from Hakaniemen Market Square.

Walking Tours The city tourist office has an excellent brochure, "See Helsinki on Foot," with six walks covering most points of interest.

Highlights for First-Time Visitors

Kaivohuone (Spa Restaurant) (*see* Tour 2)
Market Square (*see* Tour 1)
Senate Square (*see* Tour 3)
Seurasaari Island Outdoor Museum (*see* Tour 5)
Suomenlinna Fortress Island (*see* Tour 4)
Temppeliaukio Church (*see* Tour 5)
Uspenski Cathedral (*see* Tour 3)

Exploring Helsinki

Numbers in the margin correspond to points of interest on the Helsinki map.

Tour 1: From Market to Market

❶ The **Kauppatori** (Market Square) outdoor market is a Helsinki institution—and a charming one. Wooden stands with orange and gold awnings bustle in the mornings when everyone, tourists and townspeople alike, comes to check out what's available. Fish, produce, flowers, hot coffee and doughnuts, and a plethora of possible souvenirs such as fur pelts are sold here Monday through Saturday between 7 AM and 2 PM. In the summer there is also an evening market from 3:30 to 8. In the square's center is Helsinki's first public monument—**Czarina's Stone,** an obelisk with a double-headed golden eagle symbolizing Imperial Russia. Erected in 1835, it was toppled during the Russian Revolution in 1917 but fully restored in 1972.

Across from the market, on the other side of **Pohjoisesplanadi**
❷ (north esplanade) is the **Presidentinlinna** (President's Palace). Originally built as a private residence for a German businessman, it was redesigned in 1843 as a palace for the czars. Now it is the home of Finland's president. The most interesting part of the house is said to be its hall of mirrors, but the uniformed guards will prevent you from entering. Next to the palace is **Kaupingintalo** (City Hall) and various administrative offices, and across from it is the waterfront, where ferries and sightseeing boats set out into the bay.

Cross the thoroughfare carefully (watching for trams) to the west, where you'll pass the **Kappeli Café Brasserie.** Notice the restaurant's intricate lead-pane windows and the towers that **❸** allow ample views of the **Havis Amandan Patsas** (Havis Amanda Statue and Fountain). The fountain's brass centerpiece, a mermaid-woman perched on rocks and surrounded by dolphins, was commissioned by the city fathers as a symbol of Helsinki. Sculptor Ville Vallgren completed her in 1908—using a Parisian girl as his model. Partying university students crown her with their white caps on the eve before Vappu, the May 1 holiday.

On the Pohjoisesplanadi between Unioninkatu and Fabianinkatu is the **Kaupungin Matkailutoimisto** (City Tourist Office), where you can stop in for information or to pick up a map. It was **❹** originally built in 1816 as a private house for a Russian businessman and was rebuilt—with the exception of the facade—in 1968. A few yards west is the entrance to the Art Nouveau **Jugendsali** (Helsinki Information Office). Originally designed as a bank in 1906, it now serves as a cultural information office and temporary exhibition hall for Finnish photography. *Pohjoisesplanadi 19, tel. 90/169–3757. Open Sept. 16–May 15, Mon. 8:30–4:30, Tues.–Fri. 8:30–4; May 16–Sept. 15, Mon.– Fri. 8:30–6, Sat. 8:30–1.*

One block west along Pohjoisesplanadi (past the Arabia ceramics and Marimekko clothing stores) and across from the park is the elephantine **Gröngvistin Talo** (Grönqvist's block), designed by architect Theodor Höijer. Built in 1883, it was then Scandinavia's largest private apartment building.

Continue west on the Esplanade, which terminates at Mannerheimintie. On the right are Akateeminen Kirjakauppa and Stockmann's, respectively Finland's largest bookstore and department store (*see* Shopping, *below*). The bookstore was designed by Alvar Aalto, probably Finland's most famous architect.

Time Out The new **Aalto Café** (Pohjoisesplanadi 39) on the bookstore's mezzanine makes for a pleasant lunch or snack stop; you can also peer down at the tranquil hordes of book browsers.

❺ The round **Svenska Teatern** (Swedish Theater) on Mannerheimintie at the head of the Esplanadi has been rebuilt many times since its creation in 1827. The original wooden theater was replaced by a stone building in 1866 because of its vulnerability to fire. Ironically, the stone building, too, was nearly destroyed by a fire. The theater's last renovation was in 1936 by a group of architects that included Eero Saarinen and Jarl Eklund, but the red and gold auditorium dates from the 19th century. The theater has its own company, which performs plays in Swedish year-round. *Pohjoisesplanadi 2, tel. 90/171– 244. Box office open daily 10 AM–performance time.*

Turn left on Mannerheimintie and take a right onto broad, tree-shaded Bulevardi, passing **Vanha Kirkkopuisto** (Old Church Park), usually called Ruttopuisto (plague park), a tree-filled square that has a few 18th-century plague victims buried **❻** under it. Continue on to the **Sinebrychoffin Taidemuseo** (The Museum of Foreign Art, Sinebrychoff). Named after the Russian family who started the Sinebrychoff breweries, the museum houses a staid collection of Dutch and Swedish 17th- and

Cygnæuksen
Galleria, **13**

Finlandiatalo, **21**

Havis Amandan
Patsas, **3**

Helsingin
Taidehalli, **23**

Hietalahden Tori, **7**

Kaivohuone, **11**

Kauppatori, **1**

Kaupungin
Matkailutoimisto, **4**

Mannerheim
Museo, **12**

Merenkulkijoiden
Muistomerkki, **10**

Mikael Agricolan
Kirkko, **8**

Pörssitalo, **18**

Presedentinlinna, **2**

Senaatintori, **17**

Seurasaaren
Ulkomuseo, **25**

Sinebrychoffin
Taidemuseo, **6**

Suomen
Kansallismuseo, **22**

Suomen
Rakennustaiteen
Museo, **15**

Suomenlinna, **20**

Svenska Teatern, **5**

Taideteollisuus-
museo, **14**

Tamminiemi, **26**

Temppeliaukion
Kirkko, **24**

Uspenskin Kirkko, **16**

Valtion
Taidemuseo, **19**

Villa Johanna, **9**

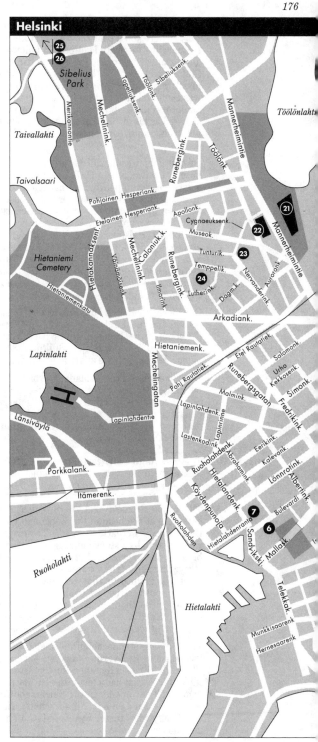

Helsinki

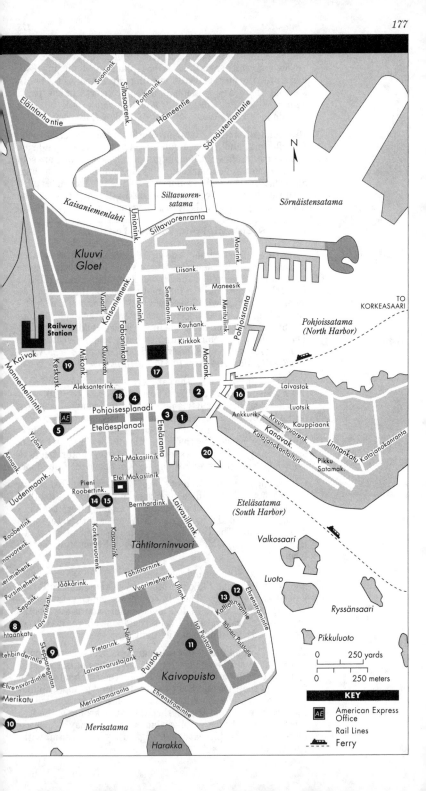

18th-century portraits, as well as a livelier collection of land-scapes, miniatures, porcelain, and decorative furniture. The yellow-and-white neo-Renaissance mansion, built in 1840, looks over the once-private Punavuori Park and its tower. In summer there are occasional outdoor concerts in the park. *Bulevardi 40, tel. 90/1733–6360. Admission: FM10. Open weekdays (except Tues.) 9–5 (until 8 on Wed.), weekends 11–5.*

7 **Hietalahden Tori** (the Hietalahti Market) across the street sells fish, flowers, and produce outside and meat inside the brick market hall. Coffee and doughnuts as well as meat pies are sold in the market. A flea market (open year-round Monday through Saturday 8–noon and in summer also 4–8 PM) has tables piled with the detritus of countless Helsinki attics and cellars. The market is popular with the Russian community.

Tour 2: Residential and Seaside Helsinki

From Bulevardi, turn south down Albertinkatu until you reach a small park, Tehtaanpuisto, where you'll see the sharp spire and tall brick steeple of the **Mikael Agricolan Kirkko** (Mikael Agricola Church). Built in 1935 by Lars Sonck, this church was named for the man who is credited with promoting Finnish as a national language by translating the New Testament into Finnish in 1548 and by creating the first Finnish children's speller. The inside of the church is quite bare, and no visitors are allowed except during Sunday services. *Tehtaankatu 23A, tel. 90/633–654. Services Sun. 10 AM–1 PM and 6 PM–9 PM.*

From the opposite side of the park, cross Tehtaankatu and walk down Laivurinkatu past **Eiran Sairaala** (Eira Hospital), with its witch-hat towers and triangular garret windows. Just south of the hospital is the Art Nouveau **Villa Johanna,** designed by Selim A. Lindqvist in 1906 and named for his wife. The villa is now privately owned by the Post Office Bank of Finland and is used for corporate dinners and events. You can't enter, but take a quick look at the carved roaring serpent above the front door.

Continuing south on the right side of Laivurinkatu, just before you reach Merikatu and an open view of the Baltic, is another Lindqvist creation (this time named for his daughter), the **Villa Ensi.** The white-and-pale-gray structure is a private apart-ment building. The two bronze statues in front of it are *Au Revoir* and *La Joie de la Maternité* by J. Sören-Ring, dating from 1910.

As you come to the end of Laivurinkatu, with the sea surround-ing you, the **Merenkulkijoiden Muistomerkki** (Seafarers Torch) will be on your right. The city commissioned the statue (fin-ished in 1968) as a tribute to Finnish sailors and as a symbol of hope for their safe return. The eternal flame above this tall ce-ment tripod is most dramatic at night.

Turn east to walk along **Merisatamanranta,** the seaside prome-nade. Out at sea is a handful of the thousands of islands that make up the Gulf of Finland archipelago. On your land side, the facades of the Eira and Kaivopuisto districts' grandest build-ings form a parade of architectural splendor. One tradition that remains, even in this neighborhood, is rug washing in the sea. The process looks incredibly arduous, and you may also be as-tounded to see people leave their rugs to dry in the sea air with-out fear of theft.

Time Out Continue east along the shoreline to the **Ursula Café** (Kaivopuisto, tel. 90/652-817) a favorite among locals for coffee, ice cream, pastry, and light lunches.

Kaivopuisto (Well Park) is a shady park with pleasant paths, surrounded by opulent private residences and embassies. The park was once the site of a popular spa that drew people from St. Petersburg, Tallinn, and all of Scandinavia until its popularity faded during the Crimean War. All of the spa structures were eventually destroyed except one, which is now **Kaivohuone**, a renowned and refined bar-restaurant.

Take Kaivohuoneenrinne through the park past a grand Empire-style villa built by Albert Edelfelt, father of the famous Finnish painter who bore the same name. Built in 1839, it is the oldest preserved villa in the park. Follow the eastward loop of Kalliolinnantie through the embassy district to the **Mannerheim Museo** (Marshal Mannerheim Museum). It exhibits the letters and personal effects of the great Finnish military leader Gustaf Mannerheim (1867–1951), who fought for Finnish freedom and later became president. The collection, set in his well-preserved family home, includes European furniture, Asian art, and military medals and weaponry. *Kalliolinnantie 14, tel. 90/635-443. Admission: FM20 adults, FM10 children. Open Fri.–Sun., 11–4; Mon.–Thurs. by appointment.*

On the same street is the tiny **Cygnaeuksen Galleria** (Cygnaeus Gallery) with its lookout tower. Inside is a display of works by a variety of Finnish painters, sculptors, and folk artists. This cottage overlooking the harbor was once the summer home of the poet and historian Fredrik Cygnaeus (1807–1881). When he died, he left the cottage and all the art inside to the Finnish public. *Kalliolinnantie 8, tel. 90/656-928. Admission: FM6 adults, FM3 children. Open Thurs.–Sun. 11–4, Wed. 11–4 and 6–8.*

Follow Itäinen Puistotie to Tehtaankatu 1, where you'll see Finnish police guarding the enormous fenced-in Russian Embassy complex. Then walk up Ullankatu and Ullanpuistikko to **Tähtitorninvuori**, the park named for the astronomical observatory on the hill. The observatory belongs to the astronomy department of Helsinki University and is closed to the public.

From here it is just a short hop (take any street to the left from the west side of the park, from Kasarmikatu to Korkeavuorenkatu) to one of Finland's finest museums, the **Taideteollisuusmuseo** (Museum of Applied Arts). All types of Finnish design can be seen here in permanent and temporary displays: furnishings, jewelry, and ceramics, as well as temporary exhibits of international design, frequently Italian and Japanese. *Korkeavuorenkatu 23, tel. 90/174-455. Admission: FM20 adults, FM5 children. Open Tues.–Fri. 11–5, Sat. 11–4, Sun. noon–6.*

From here you can go on to the **Suomen Rakennustaiteen Museo** (Museum of Finnish Architecture). The exhibits include Alvar Aalto furniture, the language of wood, the home as art, and visiting collections. The museum also provides a list of buildings by Aalto in Helsinki (also available from the tourist board), the most famous of which is Finlandiatalo (*see Tour 5, below*). *Kasarmikatu 24, tel. 90/661-918. Admission: FM10 adults, FM5 children. Open Tues.–Sun. 10–4.*

Tour 3: Katajanokka and Senate Square

The Katajanokka headland (separated from the mainland by a canal) begins just east of the market square and is a charming residential quarter as well as a busy cargo and passenger-ship port.

16 The first sight on Katajanokka is the **Uspenskin Kirkko** (Uspenski Cathedral) with its glistening onion domes. The main cathedral of the Russian Orthodox religion in Finland, it was built and dedicated in 1868 and is an example of the Byzantine-Slavonic style. The ornate interior of this imposing redbrick edifice was decorated by 19th-century Russian artists. *Kanavakatu 1, tel. 90/634-267. Open May 1–Sept. 30, Tues. 9:30–6, Wed.–Fri. 9:30–4, Sat. 9–noon, Sun. noon–3; Oct. 1–Apr. 30, Tues. and Thurs. 9–2, Wed. noon–6, Fri. 2–6, Sun. noon–3.*

Time Out On the north flank of Katajanokka, near the end of Katajanokan Pohjoisranta, you'll see the **Katajanokka Casino,** built in 1911. Set on its own headland, it was first a warehouse, then a naval officers' casino. It has a summer terrace from which you can gaze across the North Harbor to the Kruunuhaka district while sipping cold beer.

Take a right onto Linnankatu and a left onto Pikku Satamakatu to the **Wanha Satama** (the "W" pronounced as a "V") (Old Harbor complex). From the outside it looks like nothing more than an old brick warehouse, but inside it's a small shopping center with several food stores, restaurants, and cafés; there's even an art gallery in the left (north) wing.

Turn right and continue to Ankkurikatu toward the seafront. On your left will be some of the giant liners bound for Stockholm. Cross the wooden bridge back over to Market Square and
17 take any street north to **Senaatintori** (Senate Square). The north side of the square is dominated by **Tuomiokirkko** (the Lutheran Cathedral of Finland), finished in 1852 and designed, as was most of the area, by C. L. Engel, a Berliner and the architect who designed much of Tallinn and St. Petersburg. The crypt of the church, at its rear, is a site for historic and architectural exhibitions.

On the square's west side is one of the main buildings of **Helsingin Yliopisto** (Helsinki University), and up the hill is the university library. On the east side is **Valtionneuvosto** (the Council of State), completed in 1822 and once the seat of the autonomous Grand Duchy's Imperial Senate. At the lower end of the square are former merchants' homes now occupied by stores and restaurants, and the Senaatintori shopping hall. Many scenes from the film *Reds* were shot in and around this square.

Walk two streets west to Fabianinkatu to the Lars Sonck-de-
18 signed **Pörssitalo** (Stock Exchange), built in 1911. Although trading is fully automated, the beautiful interior of the building is worth seeing; be sure to notice the bullet-shaped chandeliers. *Fabianinkatu 14, tel. 90/650-133. Open weekdays 8–5.*

Time Out **Cafe Adlon** (Fabianinkatu 14, below the Stock Exchange, tel. 90/664-611) is a plush, busy bar that attracts Helsinki's young crowd.

⑲ Finish up this tour at the **Valtion Taidemuseo** (Finnish National Gallery), which is made up of two museums: the Ateneum (Finnish art from the 18th century to the 1960s) and the Museum of Contemporary Art (national and contemporary art since the 1960s). Housed in a splendid neoclassical building adorned with Greek statues, it features some major European works, but the outstanding attraction is the Finnish art, particularly the works of Akseli Gallen-Kallela, inspired by the national epic *Kalevala*. The rustic portraits by Albert Edelfelt are enchanting, and many contemporary Finnish artists are well represented. *Kaivokatu 2–4, tel. 90/173–361. Admission: FM20 adults, children free. Open Tues. and Fri. 9–5, Wed. and Thurs. 9–9, weekends 11–5.*

Tour 4: Suomenlinna

⑳ A former island fortress now taken over by resident artists, **Suomenlinna** (Finland's Castle; tel. 90/668–341) is a quirky, perennially popular collection of museums, parks, and gardens. In early summer it is engulfed in mauve-and-purple mists of lilacs, the trees introduced from Versailles by the Finnish architect Ehrensvärd. In 1748 the Finnish army helped build this fortress, which grew so over the years that today Suomenlinna is a series of interlinked islands. The impregnable fortress was long referred to as the "Gibraltar of the North." Although it has never been taken by assault, its occupants did surrender twice without a fight—once to the Russians in 1809 and again to the British in 1855 during the Crimean War.

There are no street names on the island, so be sure to get a map from the Helsinki tourist office before you go or buy one at the information kiosk on the island. From June 1 to August 31, there are guided tours in English that leave from the information kiosk daily at 12:30 and 2:30. To book a group tour, call 90/668–154. It is reached by public ferry (FM9) or round-trip private boat tour (FM20) from the Market Square.

Although the fortification of Suomenlinna involved six islands, the main attractions are concentrated on two, **Susisaari** and **Kustaanmiekka.** When you first land at Suomenlinna you will be facing the **Pohjoismainen Taidekeskus** (Nordic Arts Center) on Susisaari, with its changing exhibitions of contemporary Scandinavian art including sculpture, video art, painting, and more. *Suomenlinna (at ferry dock), tel. 90/688–148. Admission free. Open Tues.–Sun. 11–6.*

When you come out of the arts center, the church-lighthouse that you will see as you continue uphill through the archway is **Suomenlinna Kirkko** (Suomenlinna Church), built in 1854. The former Orthodox church is now Lutheran, open to the public on Sunday from noon to 4.

Walk past the church and the pastel-colored private wooden homes to explore Susisaari further. The **Ehrensvärd Museo** (Ehrensvärd Museum) is named for Augustin Ehrensvärd, who directed the fortification of the islands and whose tomb is also here. Among the historical museum's exhibits are a model-ship collection and officers quarters dating from the 18th century. *Tel. 90/668–154. Admission: FM10 adults, FM5 children. Open Jan. 2–May 7, weekends 11–4:30; May 8–Aug. 31, daily 10–5; Sept. 1–30, daily 10–4:30; Oct. 1–Nov. 30, weekends 11–4:30.*

On the coast of Susisaari island is the submarine *Vesikko,* which you'll be able to board. The submarine, which took part in World War II, was built in Turku in 1931–33. *Admission: FM5 adults, FM2.50 children. Open May 8–Aug. 31, daily 10–5; Sept. 1–30, daily 11–3.*

Time Out If possible, try to plan your visit around lunchtime so that after investigating the ramparts and visiting the museums you can make your way to the old fort near the historic King's gate for a meal at **Walhalla** (tel. 90/668–552), located deep within the fort on Kustaanmiekka.

On Kustaanmiekka, visit **Rannikkotykistömuseo** (Coastal Artillery Museum), an arms museum set in a vaulted arsenal. The items on display here are from World Wars I and II. *Tel. 90/68–601. Admission: FM5 adults, FM2.50 children. Open May 8–Aug. 31, daily 10–5; Sept. 1–30, daily 11–5.*

Five furnished rooms and a china collection make up the **Armfelt-Museo** (Armfelt Museum) in a reconstructed 19th-century upper-class home in a former barracks. *Tel. 90/668–132. Admission: FM6 adults, FM3 children. Open May 12–Aug. 31, daily 11–5:30; Sept., weekends 11–5:30.*

The information kiosk alongside Tykistolahti Bay is open May 5 through August 31, daily 10–5.

Tour 5: Töölö and Seurasaari

㉑ A short walk up Mannerheimintie from the train station will bring you to **Finlandiatalo** (Finlandia Hall), the concert hall that was one of Alvar Aalto's last creations. Its white, winged appearance is especially impressive on foggy days or at night. If you can't make it to a concert there, try to take a guided tour. *Karamzininkatu 4, tel. 90/40–241. Tickets cost: FM50–80. Concerts usually held Wed. and Thurs. nights.*

㉒ Behind the hall lies the inland bay of Töölönlahti, and across the street is the **Suomen Kansallismuseo** (National Museum). If you feel like you've seen it before, you probably have; its spired outline was the backdrop for televised reports on the 1990 U.S.-Soviet summit. The museum's exhibits take you from Finnish prehistory through medieval church art to contemporary Lapp exhibitions. One exhibit concentrates on Finland from the 16th century to the present; another focuses on Finno-Ugric cultures. *Mannerheimintie 34, tel. 90/40–501. Admission: FM10 adults, FM5 children. Open May–Sept., daily 11–4, Oct.–Apr., Mon.–Sat. 11–3, Sun. 11–4; also 6–9 Tues. (year-round).*

㉓ Take a left off Mannerheimintie onto Cygnaeuksenkatu (next street north), then a left onto Nervanderkatu, where you'll reach the **Helsingin Taidehalli** (Helsinki Art Hall). Here you'll see the best of contemporary Finnish art, including painting, sculpture, architecture, and industrial art and design. *Nervanderinkatu 3, tel. 90/444–855. Admission varies according to exhibition but is usually FM20. Open June–mid-Aug., weekdays 11–5, Sun. 12–4; mid-Aug.–Dec. and Jan.–May, Tues.–Sat. 11–6, Sun. 12–5.*

㉔ A few steps farther (take the small street directly across from the art hall) is the modern **Temppeliaukion Kirkko** (Temple

Square Church), carved into the rock cliffs at the square's center. Topped with a copper dome, it looks like a half-buried spaceship from the outside. The sun shines in from above, illuminating the stunning interior with its birch pews, tapestry seat cushions, modern pipe organ, and cavernous walls. Ecumenical and Lutheran services in various languages are held here throughout the week. *Lutherininkatu 3, tel. 90/494-698. Open June-Aug., weekdays 10-8, weekend hours vary; Sept.-May, Mon. 10-8, Tues. 10-12:45 and 2:15-8, Wed.-Fri. 10-6, weekend hours vary.*

㉕ The **Seurasaaren Ulkomuseo** (Seurasaari Outdoor Museum) is on an island about 3 kilometers (2 miles) northwest of the city center. You can walk there in about 30 minutes from the church (follow Lutherininkatu out of the square, turn left onto Runeberginkatu, right onto Arkadiankatu and follow to its end; then follow the coast and signposts); or you can take Bus 24, which you can board downtown in front of the Swedish theater at the west end of Esplanadi.

Seurasaari Island is connected to land by a pedestrian bridge and is a restful place for walking throughout the year, with its forest trails and ocean views. It was founded in 1909 with the intention of preserving Finnish rural architecture. The old farmhouses and barns that were brought to Seurasaari are mainly from Karelia in eastern Finland. Many are rough-hewn log buildings dating from as far back as the 17th century; these were of primary inspiration to architects of the late-19th-century national revivalist movement in Finland. All exhibits are marked by signposts along the trails. Be sure not to miss the church boat and the gabled church. *Seurasaari, tel. 90/484-712 or 90/484-562. Admission to outdoor museum: May-Aug., FM10 adults, FM5 children (ages 7-15); closed Sept.-Apr.*

The grand house overlooking Seurasaari from the mainland is **㉖ Tamminiemi** (President Urho Kekkonen's home), originally known as Villa Nissen. Inside are the scores of gifts to the late president donated by leaders from around the world. The house was built in 1904 and Kekkonen lived here from 1956 to 1986. His study is the most fascinating room, with its Hungarian pewter urn and gift from the United States of a cupboard full of *National Geographic* maps of the world. To assure an English-speaking guide, phone ahead (you cannot visit unguided). All large groups should call ahead. *Seurasaarentie 15, 00250 Helsinki, tel. 90/480-684. Admission: FM10 adults, FM5 children. Open May 2-Sept. 15, daily 11-4, also 6-8 Thurs. (year-round); Sept. 16-Apr. 30, Mon.-Sat. 11-3, Sun. 11-4.*

Time Out   Tamminiementie, the road leading straight inland from the bridge to Seurasaari, has three cafés within five minutes' walk of one another.

Short Excursions from Helsinki

Tarvaspää/ Gallen-Kallela Estate   This turreted brick-and-stucco mansion was the self-designed studio and home of the Finnish Romantic painter Akseli Gallen-Kallela. It is set at the edge of the sea and surrounded by towering, windbent pines. Gallen-Kallela (1865–1931) lived in the mansion on and off from its completion in 1913 until his death. Inside, the tremendous open rooms of the painter's former

work spaces make the perfect exhibition hall for his paintings. Also displayed are some of his posters and sketches of the ceiling murals he made for the Paris Art Exhibition at the turn of the 20th century. There is a café on the grounds. *Gallen-Kallelan tie 27, tel. 90/513–388. Admission: FM30 adults, FM10 children. Open May 15–Aug. 31, Mon.–Thurs. 10–8, Fri.–Sun. 10–5; Sept.–May 14, Tues.–Sat. 10–4, Sun. 10–5.*

Getting There To get to Tarvaspää from central Helsinki, take Tram 4 to Munkkiniemi and transfer to Bus 33; request the Tarvaspää stop. If you prefer, walk the kilometer (⅔ mile) from Munkkiniemi.

Porvoo **Porvoo,** only 48 kilometers (30 miles) outside Helsinki, has much to offer. Visit the 15th-century stone-and-wood cathedral, where the diet of the first duchy of Finland was held in the 1800s. There are a number of artisan boutiques around the Old Town Hall Square, and you'll want to be sure and take a stroll into the Old Quarter to see the multicolored old wooden houses. The **Walter Runebergin Kulttuuri, Kokoelma** (Walter Runeberg Sculpture Collection) (Aleksanterinkatu 5) and the **Porvoo and Edelfelt-Vallgren Museo** (Välikatu 11) feature exhibits of Edelfelt's art and the region's cultural history. Places of interest near Porvoo include the painter **Albert Edelfeltin Atelje** (Albert Edelfelt's studio) in Haikko, the nearby **Ruskis Luonnonsuojelualue** (Ruskis bird sanctuary), and the **Ilola Mäkitupalaiskylä** (Ilola Village Open Air Museum).

Tourist Information Porvoo City Tourist Office, Rauhankatu 20, 06100 Porvoo, tel. 915/580–145, also at old Town Hall Square in summer, June 1–August 15, tel. 915/130–747.

Getting There The most pleasant way to travel to Porvoo is by boat. (There are also bus and road connections.) In the summer (June 13–Aug. 16), there are daily cruise departures from Helsinki's South Harbor (average round-trip cost is about FM135; travel time depends on the boat; the *J. L. Runeberg* takes 3½ hours, the *Queen* 1½ hours each way). You will be taken westward through dozens of islands before landing at Porvoo, which is small enough to cover on foot.

Vantaa Although it is not a remarkable city, **Vantaa,** the municipality just north of Helsinki proper (and home to the international airport) has some attractions well worth seeing. There is also a welcome surplus of open green space in Vantaa, and trails for biking, hiking, and jogging. It may also be a place to keep in mind as a base if your trip to Helsinki coincides with a convention and you can't find a room there. Vantaa is reached easily by public transport (a regional Helsinki ticket includes Vantaa and Espoo), and the airport is easily accessible.

The **Heureka Suomalainen Tiedekeskus** (Heureka, the Finnish Science Center) opened in 1989 and features exhibits on robotics, solar energy, and interactive computers; there is also the Jules Verne Planetarium; taped commentary is available in English. *Tiedepuisto 1, Tikkurila, Vantaa, tel. 90/85–799. Admission: FM55–FM75 adults, FM35–FM45 children (ages 6–15). Open Mon.–Wed. 10–6, Thurs. 10–8, Fri.–Sun. 10–6.*

Near the Myyrmäki train station on the Helsinki–Martinlaakso suburban line (M train) is the **Myyrmäki Kirkko** (Uomatie 1, Myyrmäki Vantaa), an evocative example of Finnish contemporary church architecture. It has brilliant white

walls, columns of tall windows, and vivid tapestries hung out to mark events in the Lutheran calendar.

Other Vantaa attractions are the 15th-century **Helsingin Pitajan Kirkko** (Parish Church Village; Kirkkoaukio) and the **Viherpaja, Icelandic, Japanese and Cactus Gardens** (Meiramitie 1, tel. 90/822–628). *Admission to Japanese Garden: FM5; admission to other gardens free. Open June–Aug., weekdays 8–6, weekends 9–2; Sept.–May, weekdays 8–7, weekends 9–5.*

Also visit the **Finnish Aviation Museum.** *Tietotie 3, tel. 90/821870. Open daily noon–6.*

Tourist Information Vantaa Tourist Office (Unikkotie 2, Tikkurila, 01300 Vantaa, tel. 90/839–3134).

Getting There Easiest access is by local bus or train; ask at airport information.

Helsinki for Free

Several Helsinki parks, notably Kaivopuisto, have gigantic **outdoor chess boards** with life-size pieces you move around a grid painted on asphalt; games are free to all comers.

Also free are some of the **outdoor concerts** at the band shell (summertime) in Esplanadi at the side of the Kappeli restaurant, and in Kaivopuisto Park, near the sea.

All cross-country ski trails around Helsinki are free, as are the many nature, bike, and jogging trails. The tourist board's Ulkoilukartta (outdoor activities map) shows you where to find these **outdoor trails.**

In winter **Seurasaari,** the outdoor island museum, is free, mainly because access to the island is open to anyone who crosses the ice to get to it.

What to See and Do with Children

The two-week Helsinki Festival of performing arts in late August–early September includes **children's shows** in Helsinki and environs.

The **Suomenlinna** fortress island makes a good excursion for travelers with children (*see* Exploring Helsinki, *above*), and includes a **Doll and Toy Museum** designed with children in mind.

The daily ferry to **Korkeasaari Elaintarha (Helsinki Zoo)** runs from the North Harbor, just above the juncture of the Katajanokka Peninsula to the mainland; the zoo is small, but children will like it anyway. You can also take the metro to the Kulosaari stop, cross under the tracks, and then follow the signs to the zoo (about a 20-minute walk). *Tel. 90/19981. Admission: FM20 adults, FM10 children 7–16, under 7 free. Open Jan.–Feb., daily 10–4; Mar.–Apr., daily 10–6; May–Sept., daily 10–8; Oct.–Dec., daily 10–4.*

Linnanmäki, Helsinki's best-known amusement park, can be reached by Trams 3B and 3T from in front of the railway station. *Tivolikuja 1, tel. 90/750–391. Admission: FM10 adults, FM5 children. Open mid-May–mid-June, Tues.–Fri. 4–10, Sat. 1–10, Sun. 1–9; mid-June–mid-Aug., daily 1–10.*

Off the Beaten Track

Located in **Espoo,** Helsinki's next-door neighbor, is the garden city of **Tapiola,** one of Finland's architectural highlights. Designed by Aalvar Aalto, the urban landscape of alternating high and low residential buildings, gardens, fountains, and swimming pools blends into the natural surroundings. Guides and sightseeing tours are available from the Espoo City Tourist Office. *Itätuulenkuja, 11, Espoo, tel. 90/460–311.*

Shopping

Helsinki's shopping facilities are improving all the time. Although many international stores are still missing, there are several malls and shopping districts where you can shop thoroughly and in comfort. Stores are generally open weekdays 9–6 and Saturday 9–1. The **Forum** (*see* Shopping Malls, *below*) and **Stockmann's** (*see* Department Stores, *below*) are open weekdays 9–8 and Saturday 9–6.

Kiosks remain open late and on weekends; they sell such basics as milk, juice, and tissues. Stores in **Asematunneli,** the train-station tunnel, are open weekdays 10–10 and weekends noon–10.

Shopping Malls The three largest shopping complexes are the **Forum** (Mannerheimintie and Simonkatu), **Kaivopiha** (Kaivokatu 10, across from the train station); and **Kluuvi** shopping center (Kluuvikatu and Aleksanterinaktu). The large **Itäksekus** shopping complex in east Helsinki can be reached by metro. All have a good mix of stores plus several cafés and restaurants.

Shopping Districts **Pohjoisesplanadi** on the north side of the Esplanade has most of Helsinki's trademark design stores—including Arabia, Marimekko, and Aarikka—and a wide array of other goods.

Senaatintori, the south side of Senate Square, has a host of souvenir and crafts stores (open weekdays 10–6, Sat. 10–3), with several antiques shops and secondhand bookstores on the adjoining streets. Next to Senate Square is the **Kiseleff Bazaar Hall,** an attractive shopping gallery.

There are many smaller boutiques in the streets **west of Mannerheimintie** (Fredrikinkatu and Annankatu, for example), and there is one pedestrian shopping street a few blocks south of the Esplanade, on **Iso Roobertinkatu;** stores here are conventional, but the atmosphere is more relaxed.

Department Stores **Stockmann's** (Esplanade and Mannerheimintie, tel. 90/1211), is Helsinki's premier department store. **Aleksi 13** (Aleksanterinkatu 13, tel. 90/131–441) is less expensive than Stockmann's.

Street Markets The **Market Square, Hietalahdentori Market,** and **Hakaniemi** are the main street markets. They specialize in food, but all have some clothing (new and used) and household products. The Market Square also sells some fur products. Hours are Monday–Saturday 6:30–2; in summer they reopen from 3:30 to 8. Almost adjacent to the Market Square is the **Old Market Hall** (open weekdays 8–6, Sat. 8–3), where you can browse and shop for anything from flowers to vegetables, meat, and fish. **Hietalahti's flea market** is open Monday–Saturday 8–2; in summer it reopens 3:30–9.

Specialty Stores
Antiques

The **Kruunuhaka** area (north of Senate Square) is the best bet for antiques. Some stores to try are **Antik Oskar** (Rauhankatu 7, tel. 90/135–7410), **Antiikkiliike Karl Fredrik** (Mariankatu 13, tel. 90/630–014), **Punavuoren Antiikki** (Mariankatu 14, tel. 90/662–682), and **Atlas Antiques** (Rauhankatu 8, tel. 90/628–186) if you are interested in coins, bank notes, medals, and silver. Other shops mix china, furniture, and art. Some of the old farm furniture is pretty but hard to find. Most stores are loaded with old china and cut glass, however. Also try **Kamppi** and **Punavuori districts,** between Eerikinkatu and Tehtaankatu; many here also sell secondhand books (usually a small selection in English).

Ceramics and Accessories

Firms like **Hackman Arabia** (which also sells Iittala and Nuutajärvi) (Pohjoisesplanadi 25, tel. 90/170–055), **Pentik** (Pohjoisesplanadi 27C, tel. 90/625–558), and **Aarikka** (Pohjoisesplanadi 25–27, tel. 90/652–277) offer ceramics, leather, accessories, and wooden toys; the Arabia factory, at the end of the Tram 6 line, also exhibits older designs.

Clothing

Marimekko (Pohjoisesplanadi 31, tel. 90/177–944, and Eteläesplanadi 14, tel. 90/170–704), on the Esplanade in Helsinki and with outlets in other cities, has bright, modern, unusual clothes for men, women, and children in quality fabrics, at a price. Take a look even if you don't plan to spend.

Jewelry

Kaunis Koru (Aleksanterinkatu 28, tel. 90/656–850) and **Lapponia Jewelry** (Mäkelänkatu 60A, tel. 90/146–4600) produce avant-garde silver and gold designs, while **Kalevala Koru** (Unioninkatu 25, tel. 90/171–520) is more traditional.

Sports and Fitness

Bicycling

Helsinki and environs make for good biking because there is a decent network of trails, many running through parks, forests, and fields. The free area sporting map (Ulkoilukartta) gives details of all trails. Daily rentals start from FM40 at the **Olympic Stadium Youth Hostel** (Pohjoinen Stadiontie 3B, 00250 Helsinki, tel. 90/496–071, fax 90/496–466).

Golf

For full information on golf in Helsinki and environs, contact the **Finnish Golf Union** (Radiokatu 20, 00240 Helsinki, tel. 90/158–2244). There are 18- and 9-hole and par-3 (FM50) courses in Helsinki and surroundings, with greens fees from FM120 to FM200.

Swimming

Among Helsinki's indoor swimming pools and saunas, the oldest and one of the most famous is **Yrjönkatu Uimahalli** (Yrjönkatu 21B, tel. 90/60–981), where swimming is in the nude. The best beaches in Helsinki are **Pihlajasaari, Mustikkamaa, Uunisaari,** and **Hietaniemi** (especially for young people).

Tennis

There are some six tennis centers and 31 clubs in Helsinki. For specifics, contact the **Finnish Tennis Association** (Radiokatu 20, 00240 Helsinki, tel. 90/158–2268). It's best to bring your own equipment, although rentals are available.

Dining

Helsinki is home to some of the best Finnish eating establishments. Although the Russian restaurants are the star attraction, try to seek out Finnish specialties such as game—

pheasant, reindeer, hare, and grouse—accompanied by wild-berry compotes and exotic mushroom sauces.

Highly recommended restaurants are indicated by a star ★.

Very Expensive **Alexander Nevski.** Helsinki is reputed to have the best Russian
★ restaurants in the Nordic region, and the Nevski is foremost among these. It sets high standards in the preparation of czarist-era dishes such as lamb steak in mint-and-rosemary sauce, traditional roe-filled blintzes, or ox fillet with wild mushrooms. Among the more extraordinary offerings is roast bear in a pot. Set at the edge of the harbor and marketplace, Nevski has all the trappings you'd expect to find in a czar's dining hall—heavy draperies, glistening samovars, potted palms, and crisp linen tablecloths. *Pohjoisesplanadi 17, tel. 90/639–610. Reservations advised. Dress: casual but neat. AE, DC, MC, V. Closed Christmas, all national holidays except Easter, and Sun.; July, closed Sun., Mon., and lunch.*

★ **Amadeus.** The elegant decor in this old town house between Senate Square and the South Harbor matches the czarist architecture of the neighborhood. The game, reindeer, and mushroom dishes have made it a favorite of Helsinki gourmets. The two dining rooms are tinted in soft browns and pinks. As an appetizer, try the salmon with mustard and sour cream, and as a main course, the deer chops in champagne sauce. *Sofiankatu 4, tel. 90/626676. Reservations required. Dress: casual but neat. AE, DC, MC, V. Closed Sun., Christmas, Easter, Midsummer.*

Galateia. The white grand piano and paintings of languid mermaids lend a classy, serene ambience to Helsinki's best seafood restaurant. Located on the top floor of the Hotel Inter-Continental, Galateia offers a nighttime panorama that takes in the city lights and an illuminated Finlandia Hall reflected in Töölo Bay. Fresh Continental-style seafood is featured, along with caviar and roe specialties. If you are in Helsinki during the crayfish season, this is one of the best places to sample it. Attentive and knowledgeable waiters offer an impressive selection of appropriate wines. *Mannerheimintie 46, tel. 90/405–5900. Reservations suggested. Jacket and tie advised. AE, DC, MC, V. Closed July, Dec. 21–Jan. 2, and weekends. No lunch.*

Palace Gourmet. This outstanding hotel restaurant has a magnificent view of the South Harbor. Chef Markku Taimi's specialty is French and Finnish fare, including such creations as smoked brook trout with champagne sauce and caviar and curry of reindeer with cranberry sauce. *Palace Hotel. Eteläranta 10, tel. 90/134561. Reservations advised. Dress: casual but neat. AE, DC, MC, V. Closed weekends, last 4 weeks of July, Christmas, Easter, Midsummer.*

Savoy. With its airy, Alvar Aalto–designed, functionalist dining room overlooking the Esplanade gardens, the Savoy is a frequent choice for business lunches and was also Finnish statesman Marshal Karl Gustaf Mannerheim's favorite. He is rumored to have introduced the *Vorschmack* (minced-lamb-and-anchovies) recipe. The Savoy's menu includes such delicacies as pheasant breast with walnuts and warm orange sauce as well as such old-fashioned Finnish home-cooked dishes as meatballs, grilled herring, and *läski soosi* (fried fatty pork in brown sauce). *Eteläesplanadi 14, 90/176571. Reservations advised. Dress: casual but neat. AE, DC, MC, V. Closed Sun. and national holidays.*

Expensive **Bellevue.** The spare lines of Bellevue belie its real age—it has been around since 1917, serving imaginative dishes inspired by Russian cuisine of yore and Finnish country fare. The tremendous modern paintings on the wall are set off by pale table linens and wood-and-plush seats. Particularly noteworthy are the innovative meat dishes. The Bellevue is also famous for blinis—small pancakes topped with roe, onions, and sour cream. The plush interior of this elegant town house has many shining samovars, but only some of them are functional; each table has lighted candles. Appropriately, the restaurant is tucked behind the Russian Orthodox Uspensky Cathedral. *Rahapajankatu 3, tel. 90/ 179–560. Reservations advised. Dress: casual but neat. AE, DC, MC, V. Closed Christmas and Midsummer. No lunch weekends.*

Katariina. Next to Senate Square is one of Helsinki's most popular restaurants, specializing in traditional Finnish fare, such as reindeer fillet with cooked vegetables or perch fillet. In summer you can also dine on the terrace surrounded by the neighborhood's czarist architecture. The cellar used to be a police detention center where drunks and criminal suspects were locked up. Some vestiges of this period are still visible. *Aleksanterinkatu 22–24, tel. 90/656722. Reservations accepted. Dress: casual but neat. AE, DC, MC, V. Closed weekends and national holidays.*

Kosmos. Just a short walk from Stockmann's, this cozy restaurant has become a lunchtime favorite among businesspeople who work nearby. In the evenings the restaurant is frequented by artists and journalists. Its high ceilings and understated decor give it a Scandinavian atmosphere of simplicity and efficiency. Among the specialties are sweetbreads with curry, cream, and port sauce, and mutton chops stuffed with ground veal and olives and served with garlic potatoes. *Kalevankatu 3, tel. 90/ 607603. Reservations advised. Dress: casual. AE, DC, MC, V. Closed weekends and national holidays.*

★ **Piekka Finnish Restaurant.** One of the few restaurants in Finland that explicitly promote the national cuisine, Piekka provides the perfect setting. Designed in birchwood from floor to ceiling, with handwoven table linens in rich blues, this restaurant offers delicately prepared reindeer and other game and seasonal fish dishes, and makes a superb pork gravy. *Sibeliuksenkatu 2, tel. 90/493–591. Reservations advised. Dress: casual but neat. AE, DC, MC, V. Closed Christmas, Easter, and Midsummer.*

Ritarisali. Focused on a medieval theme, this restaurant serves a very hearty French cuisine influenced by locally caught seafood. Lunch includes such daily specials as veal meatballs with caper sauce or braised salmon with cucumber sauce. Dinners are grand. The annually changed "Menu du Chevalier" is a tremendous—and very expensive—gastronomic venture that might include a sole and crab starter and a main course featuring supremes of pheasant Catalan style with grapefruit sorbet served between courses. Regular dinner choices are expensive and include fillet of pike perch and rabbit soup with chanterelles. Large-paned windows shed light on immaculate, embossed white table linens, wood paneling, warm creamy-orange walls, and parquet floors with Oriental rugs. *Kalevankatu 5 (Hotel Torni), tel. 90/131–131. Reservations advised. Dress: casual but neat. AE, DC, MC, V.*

Dining
Alexander Nevski, **32**
Amadeus, **33**
Bellevue, **37**
Galateia, **4**
Katariina, **34**
Kosmos, **16**
Kynsilaukka, **19**
Omenapuu, **18**
Palace Gourmet, **36**
Parrilla Torni, **15**
Perho Mechelin, **6**
Piekka Finnish
Restaurant, **2**
Pizzeria Dennis, **13**
Ritarisali, **14**
Savoy, **31**
Sukothai, **5**
Svenska Klubben, **35**
Wellamo, **39**

Lodging
Airport Hotel
Rantasipi, **9**
Anna, **22**
Aurora, **11**
Erottajanpuisto
Matkailukoti, **21**
Finn Apartments, **28**
Hesperia, **3**
Hospitz, **24**
Hostel Academica, **7**
Hotel Pilotti, **10**
Inter-Continental
Helsinki, **4**
Kalastajatorppa, **1**
Lordhotel, **12**
Martahotelli, **20**
Merihotelli, **27**
Olympia, **30**
Palace, **36**
SAS Royal Hotel, **8**
Seurahuone, **17**
Skatta, **38**
Strand Inter-
Continental, **26**
Teatterimajatalo
Omapohja, **23**
Torni, **14**
Ursula, **25**
Vantaa Hostel, **29**

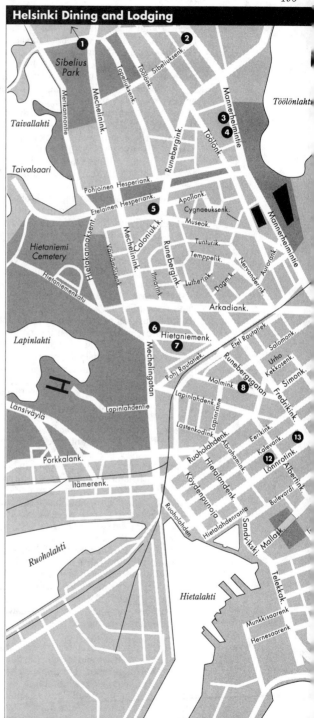

Helsinki Dining and Lodging

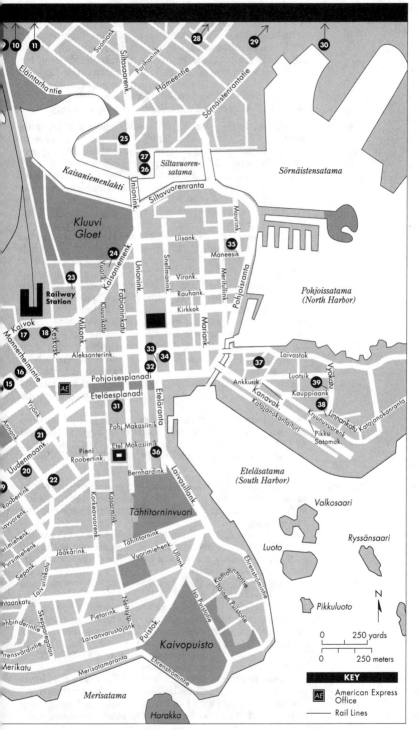

KEY

AE American Express Office

— Rail Lines

Closed weekends, Christmas, Easter, and Midsummer–early Aug.

Svenska Klubben. This stately turn-of-the-century house resembles an old-fashioned, exclusive gentleman's club. You can enjoy an aperitif at the lobby bar, which has a fireplace and big, comfortable armchairs. Local fish, roe, game, and fowl predominate on the à la carte menu. *Maurinkatu 6, tel. 90/ 1354706. Reservations advised. Dress: casual but neat. AE, DC, MC, V. Closed Sun., Christmas, Easter, and July.*

Moderate **Omenapuu.** In the heart of the busy shopping district on the second floor of a large office building, this convenient restaurant specializes in Finnish and international fare. During periodic theme weeks it features various assortments of game and fish. The generous windows overlook the downtown bustle. Live piano music adds to the pleasant atmosphere in the mirrored, red-carpeted room. *Keskuskatu 6, 2nd floor, tel. 90/ 630205. Reservations accepted. Dress: casual. AE, DC, MC, V. Closed Christmas.*

Parrilla Torni. The chef of Helsinki's oldest Spanish restaurant (opened in 1960), Juhani Lindroos, spends part of his holidays in Spain searching out new recipes. Along with its extensive Spanish wine list, Parrilla offers grilled chicken with chocolate sauce and chestnuts, herb-fried red snapper with garlic mayonnaise, olive chicken, paella marinara, and an assortment of omelets. Starters include a vegetable omelet and a shrimp-and-garlic casserole. For dessert, try the almond surprise with figs. Small and intimate, the restaurant has an authentic Iberian atmosphere, with dark-wood tables, leather seat backs, iron grillwork, and a bull's head on the wall. *Kalevankatu 5/Yrjönkatu 26 (through Hotel Torni lobby), tel. 90/131–131. Reservations advised. Dress: casual but neat. AE, DC, MC, V. Closed Mon. and Christmas.*

Pizzeria Dennis. This attractive New York-style Italian restaurant with white walls and dark pizza wood tables serves the best pizza and home-made pasta in town. *Fredrikinkatu 36, tel. 90/ 694–5271. Reservations advised. DC, MC, V. Closed Midsummer and Christmas.*

Inexpensive **Kynsilaukka.** This is one of Helsinki's most imaginative restaurants. Dominated by garlic (there's even garlic beer), the food
★ is fresh and beautifully presented, and often served by the three young owner-chefs themselves. The seafood bouillabaisse is superb, as is the cold marinated beef, the avocado salad, and the lamb pot. For dessert, the pancakes with cloudberry sauce and ice cream are a must. The decor is rustic and comfortable with a maritime accent. The set lunch menu is a good buy. *Fredrikinkatu 22, tel. 90/651–939. Reservations advised. Dress: casual. AE, DC, MC, V.*

Perho Mechelin. Helsinki's catering school operates this brasserie-style restaurant decorated in pine. In summer the emphasis is on Finnish food, particularly salmon and reindeer. Its low prices and good location are the draw. *Mechelininkatu 7, tel. 90/493–481. Reservations advised. AE, DC, MC, V. Closed Midsummer and Christmas.*

Sukothai. Opened in 1989, this is one of Helsinki's first ethnic restaurants; it specializes in Thai food. The small space is sparsely decorated with handmade Thai curios. Shrimp soup, curries, and fried noodles are on the extensive menu, which

also offers dishes flavored with fresh coriander. *Runebergin-katu 32, tel. 90/446774. Reservations advised. Dress: casual. MC, V. Closed Christmas and Midsummer.*

Wellamo. Decorated with changing exhibitions by new artists, Wellamo specializes in Russian-style fare, featuring roast mutton with mint sauce or garlic butter. *Vyökatu 9, tel. 90/663139. No reservations. Dress: casual. AE, MC, V. Closed Mon., Christmas, Easter (Good Friday), and Midsummer.*

Lodging

Helsinki's hotels are notoriously expensive, and most cater to the business traveler. The standards of cleanliness are high, though, and the level of service usually corresponds to the price.

Highly recommended hotels are indicated by a star ★.

Very Expensive **Hesperia.** The marble floor and dark-brown wood paneling of the lobby renovated in 1992 give the hotel a renewed elegance. Close to the city center, the Hesperia is modern in the best Finnish tradition. The lobby's convenient semicircle of service booths includes a travel agent, a car-rental service, and even an airport helicopter booth. The relatively spacious contemporary rooms are well equipped but unmemorable except for those with king-size beds—a rarity in Helsinki hotels. Some rooms overlook Töölö Bay and the main avenue, Mannerheimintie; the back rooms face a quieter street. *Mannerheimintie 50, 00260, tel. 90/43-101, fax 90/431-0995. 376 rooms, 4 suites. Facilities: restaurant, bar, café, cable TV, 21-hour room service, minibars, health club, saunas, indoor pool, solarium, golf-course simulator, rooms for nonsmokers and allergy sufferers. AE, DC, MC, V. Sometimes closed Christmas.*

Hotel Torni. The original part was built in 1903, and its towers and internal details reflect some of the more fanciful touches of Helsinki's Jugendstil period. The functionalist-style newer section was added in 1931. The original section has striking views of Helsinki from the higher floors—the Torni is one of the city's tallest buildings—and some of the rooms have large windows. As of mid-1991 all the rooms were redone. The old-section rooms on the courtyard are recommended, however. Some have high ceilings with original carved-wood details and wooden writing desks; many have little alcoves or other pleasing design oddities. There is a conference room and bar atop the tower, with art exhibitions that change monthly. *Yrjönkatu 26, 00100, tel. 90/131-131, fax 90/131-1361. 154 rooms with bath or shower, 9 suites. Facilities: 2 restaurants, 3 bars, saunas, cable TV, room service, conference rooms. AE, DC, MC, V. Closed Christmas.*

★ **Inter-Continental Helsinki.** This modern, centrally located hotel is one of the most popular in the city—particularly with American business travelers. It's a virtual Helsinki institution. Decor in the rather small rooms is pleasant and light—oatmeal carpets, birch paneling and closets, subtle floral-print bedspreads and curtains. Services for business travelers are excellent. Galateia (*see* Dining, *above*) offers good seafood and a wonderful view. *Mannerheimintie 46, 00260, tel. 90/405-51, fax 90/405-5255. 555 rooms, 12 suites. Facilities: saunas, indoor pool, cable TV, 24-hour room service, rooms for nonsmokers and allergy sufferers. AE, DC, MC, V.*

Kalastajatorppa. Located in the plush western Munkkiniemi neighborhood, this hotel catered to U.S. presidents Ronald Reagan in 1988 and George Bush in 1990 and 1992. A 15- to 25-minute ride by taxi from the city center, the hotel has also been a favorite of international artists seeking anonymity. The best rooms are in the seaside annex, but all are large and airy, decorated in fresh pastel colors with clear pine and birchwood paneling, and have furniture designed by architect Alvar Aalto. Rooms in the main building may be equipped with bath and terrace or with showers only, and prices vary accordingly. *Kalastajatorpantie 1, 00330, tel. 90/458–152 or 90/458–11, fax 90/458–1668. 235 rooms, 8 suites. Facilities: 2 restaurants, nightclub, 2 bars, 2 indoor pools, sauna, rooms for nonsmokers, solarium. AE, DC, MC, V. Sometimes closed Christmas.*

Palace. Built for the 1952 Olympic games, this small hotel is located on the 9th and 10th floors of a waterfront commercial building with a splendid view of the South Harbor. The hotel attracts a faithful clientele of largely British, American, and Swedish patrons who appreciate the personal service that comes with its small size and such intimate touches as daily afternoon tea. The decor is nondescript, except for the wood paneling and plush carpet, and amenities in the guest rooms are few. The hotel's restaurants (especially Palace Gourmet, *see* Dining, *above*) are among Helsinki's best. All rooms were renovated in 1991. *Eteläranta 10, 00100, tel. 90/134–561, fax 90/654–786. 34 rooms, 14 junior suites, 2 suites. Facilities: 2 restaurants, bar, saunas, cable TV, 24-hour room service. AE, DC, MC, V. Closed Dec. 24–26.*

SAS Royal Hotel. Opened in the summer of 1991, this hotel was conceived and built to serve the business traveler. Set in a residential section of the central city, the hotel is right on the metro line. Two floors are made up of Royal SAS Club rooms, including several suites and conference areas. The decor varies with the rooms; some are elegant Scandinavian (light colors and wood), others are Oriental (light and warm colors and silk bedcovers), and some are Italian (modern, with primary colors). The Johan Ludvig restaurant specializes in meat dishes such as prime rib of beef. Størget is cheaper and offers Danish sandwiches. *Runeberginkatu 2, 00100, tel. 90/69–580. 260 rooms, 7 suites. Facilities: restaurants, bar, SAS service center, SAS check-in counter, saunas, room service, conference and banquet rooms. AE, DC, MC, V.*

★ **Strand Inter-Continental.** You will want for nothing at one of Helsinki's newest and most expensive big hotels—from the tastefully furnished rooftop saunas and the large, crisply decorated rooms to the bathrooms with heated floors and the carwash service in the basement garage. The hotel's distinctive use of granite and Finnish marble in the central lobby is accentuated by a soaring atrium. Choose from a lobby bar and two restaurants—the superb Pamir (haute-cuisine seafood, steak, or game) or the Atrium Plaza (light meals). An entire floor is reserved for nonsmokers. Locals smile knowingly at the situating of this luxurious executive retreat in a traditionally socialist, working-class neighborhood; but the location is central, the waterfront vistas a pleasure. Five of the eight suites have panoramic views of the sea. *John Stenberginranta 4, 00530, tel. 90/39–351, fax 90/761–362. 200 rooms, 10 suites. Facilities: 2 restaurants, bar, saunas, indoor pool, cable TV, room service. AE, DC, MC, V. Sometimes closed Christmas.*

Expensive **Airport Hotel Rantasipi.** This fully equipped, modern accom-
★ modation satisfies Helsinki's need for an airport hotel that
meets the highest international standards. Convenient for lay-
overs, the hotel borders the airport commercial zone but has
pleasant views of surrounding fields and forest. A standard
room includes a large sofa and king-size bed and has such soft
touches as paisley bedspreads and wicker furniture; all rooms
are soundproof and air-conditioned. *Robert Hubertintie 4,
01510 Vantaa, tel. 90/87–051, fax 90/822–846. 300 rooms, 4
suites. Facilities: 3 restaurants, music bar, conference center,
minibar, TV, disabled access, indoor pool, free shuttle to airport, rooms for nonsmokers and allergy sufferers. AE, DC,
MC, V. Closed Christmas.*

Anna. Pleasantly situated in a central, residential neighborhood, the Anna is in a seven-story apartment building dating
from the 1930s. The room fittings are modern, however, with
light, comfortable furniture. The room price includes a buffet
breakfast. *Annankatu 1, 00120, tel. 90/648–011, fax 90/602–
664. 60 rooms, 1 suite. Facilities: coffee shop, sauna, floor for
nonsmokers. AE, DC, MC, V. Closed Christmas, Easter, and
New Year's Day.*

★ **Lordhotel.** Located on a quiet side street, this small luxury hotel has set itself apart. The front section is a handsome stone
castle, built in 1903, whose wood-beamed, medieval-style
rooms have been converted into restaurants, lounges, a cavernous banquet hall, conference rooms, a sauna lounge, and an airy
breakfast room. A walkway across a dreary inner court brings
you to the modern building housing the guest rooms. Each
of the rooms exhibits fine attention to detail: The desks and
lighting are excellent; the contemporary-style furnishings, in
soothing pastel blue and gray tones, comfortable; and the
storage space ample. For its rare combination of character,
consistency, and service, this is a fine choice. There are
discounts on weekends and in summer. *Lonnrotinkatu 29,
00180, tel. 90/680–1680, fax 90/680–1315. 48 rooms with
shower or bath, 1 suite (17 rooms are equipped with a Jacuzzi). Facilities: restaurant, bar, saunas, banquet hall,
conference rooms, free parking. AE, DC, MC, V. Sometimes
closed Christmas.*

Merihotelli. Located next to Hakaniemi Market Square,
Merihotelli is only a 10-minute walk from the heart of Helsinki.
The smallish guest rooms were fully renovated in 1991, deco-
rated in shades of pale blue, and the ambience is serene. *John
Stenbergin ranta 6, 00530, tel. 90/708–711, fax 90/760–271. 87
rooms with shower. Facilities: café, bar. AE, DC, MC, V.*

Olympia. There's fine ambience in the public areas of this hotel, with their stone floors, dark walls, and sturdy furniture.
By contrast, the rooms are light, with white walls and blue-
green textiles and upholstery. The hotel dates from 1977; the
most recent redecoration was in 1990. *Läntinen Brahenkatu
2, 00510, tel. 90/750–801 (fax same as switchboard number).
98 rooms, 1 suite. Facilities: restaurant, sauna, rooms for
nonsmokers, nightclub. AE, DC, MC, V. Sometimes closed
Christmas.*

Seurahuone. This Viennese-style town house was built in 1914
and renovated in 1992, and has a loyal clientele won over by
its ageless charm and cosmopolitan atmosphere. Well-worn
elegance emanates from the grand main stairway; the
chandeliered Art Nouveau café; the ornate, skylit Socis pub;

and the traditionally furnished rooms (brass beds, high ceilings, chandeliers, teak cabinets) in the old section. The new section has sleek, modern rooms, so specify your preference. Many of the rooms, even the modern ones, are furnished with Victorian antiques. As the hotel faces the railway station and houses a popular disco in addition to a café and a pub, the lobby and public area are among the busiest in town. *Kaivokatu 12, 00100, tel. 170–441, fax 90/664–170. 118 rooms, 5 suites. Facilities: restaurant, bar, pub, café, saunas, cable TV. AE, DC, MC, V. Sometimes closed Christmas.*

Moderate **Aurora.** Built in 1970 and renovated from 1989 to 1991, this redbrick hotel has small modern rooms decorated in pale blues, greens, and peach. Larger rooms have brown wood paneling. Located across from the Linnanmäki Amusement Park, it has become a favorite for families. It is a 10-minute bus ride from the city center. *Helsinginkatu 50, 00530, tel. 90/717400, fax 90/714–240. 68 rooms with shower or bath. Facilities: restaurant, sauna, pool, squash courts, health spa, solarium. AE, DC, MC, V. Closed 2 weeks following Dec. 23.*

Hospitz. Owned by the Helsinki YMCA, the Hospitz is centrally located. Unpretentious and comfortable, the hotel has a restaurant, but no alcohol is served. *Vuorikatu 17B, 00100, tel. 90/173441, fax 90/626–8807. 161 rooms with shower or bath. Facilities: restaurant, sauna. AE, DC, MC, V. Closed Christmas week.*

Hotel Pilotti. In a quiet suburban setting but within five minutes' drive of the airport, the Pilotti is also about 5 kilometers (3 miles) from Hureka (The Finnish Science Center). Built in 1989, it is modern inside and out; each compact room has a large round porthole-style window. *Veromäentie 1, 01510 Vantaa, tel. 90/870–2100, fax 90/870–2109. 104 rooms, 8 suites. Facilities: restaurant, sauna, free airport shuttle. AE, DC, MC, V. Sometimes closed Christmas.*

Marttahotelli. Centrally located, it is small and cozy, with simply decorated, fresh, white rooms. The hotel was fully renovated in 1990. *Uudenmankatu 24, 00120, tel. 90/646211, fax 90/680–1266. 40 rooms with shower and 5 with bath. Facilities: sauna. AE, DC, MC, V. Closed Christmas, Midsummer, and sometimes Easter.*

Ursula. The furnishings in this hotel's rooms are much like those you'd find in a typical Finnish home: simple, clean lines, a plethora of wood tones, duvets with covers in bright, primary colors. Located in a traditional Helsinki working-class neighborhood but near the center and Hakaniemi market and Market Square, the Ursula is also near the airport bus stop and the Hakaniemi metro stop. *Paasivuorenkatu 1, 00530, tel. 90/750–311, fax 90/701–4527. 40 rooms, 3 suites. AE, DC, MC, V. Closed Christmas.*

Inexpensive **Finn Apartments.** Located on a side street north of Hakaniemi Square, 10 minutes by tram from the city center, this apartment hotel offers clean, reasonably priced rooms. One option for guests, many of whom are businesspeople, is a private studio apartment with kitchenette and bathroom; an even less expensive choice is an unpretentious, light-colored economy room. The cheapest rooms must be shared with another guest. *Franzeninkatu 26, 00530 Helsinki, tel. 90/773–1661, fax 90/701–6889. 135 rooms. Facilities: sauna. AE, DC, MC, V.*

Hostel Academica. This summer hotel is made up of what are, during the rest of the year, university students' apartments.

Each floor has a small lounge; the rooms are sturdy, modern, and have their own small kitchens. Family rooms and extra beds are also available, and there are special family rates. Guests can eat reduced-price meals at the nearby Perho restaurant. The central location is good for shopping and transport. *Hietaniemenkatu 14, 00180, tel. 90/402-0206, fax 90/441-201. 217 rooms (115 with bath/shower, 102 with bath and use of hall shower). Facilities: sauna, pool, tennis court. AE, DC, MC, V. Closed Sept. 2–May 31.*

Skatta. Located in the quiet Katajanokka island neighborhood 2 kilometers (1.2 miles) from the railway station, this modest hotel began as a home for sailors at the turn of the century. It was converted into a hotel in 1960. The bright, brown and red rooms offer good views of the south harbor. *Linnankatu 3, 00160, tel. 90/659233, fax 90/631-352. 24 rooms with shower, kitchenette. Facilities: sauna, gym, solarium. AE, DC, MC, V. Sometimes closed Christmas.*

Teatterimajatalo Omapohja. Dating from 1906, this inn used to be a base for actors performing at the state theater next door. The rooms are cozily old-fashioned, with wood-paneled walls and handwoven bedspreads; they also have tremendous windows. You'll find this hotel at the bear sign in a mint-green Jugend-style building. *Itäinen Teatterikuja 3, 00100, tel. 90/ 666-211. 15 rooms, 4 with shower. Facilities: TV, breakfast served in room. MC, V. Closed Dec. 23–26, Easter, Midsummer holiday.*

Vantaa Hostel. This hostel was built in 1980 and extended in 1989. As hostels go, it is one of the cleanest and brightest you'll ever find. The old wing of the hostel is cheaper than the rooms in the new extension. *Valkoisenlähteentie 52, 01300 Vantaa, tel. 90/839-3310, fax 90/839-4366. 7 rooms with shared baths and showers (old wing); 24 rooms with toilet and shower (new wing). Facilities: use of sports center, washing machine. Sometimes closed Christmas.*

The Arts and Nightlife

The Arts For a list of events, pick up *Helsinki This Week*, available in hotels and tourist offices. Two ticket agencies are **Lippupalvelu** (Mannerheimintie 5, in the Bio-Bio cinema arcade, tel. 9700/ 4700 or 90/664-466) and **Tiketti** (Yrjönkatu 29C, tel. 90/693-2255).

In summer plays and music are performed at many outdoor theaters such as Keskuspuisto, Suomenlinna, and Mustikkamaa, and Seurasaari islands, and also at the Rowing Stadium. The Helsinki Festival, a performance and visual-arts celebration set in venues around the city, is held yearly in early autumn.

Concerts **Finlandiatalo** (Finlandia Hall) (Karamzininkatu 4, tel. 90/40–241), the home of the Helsinki Philharmonic, also hosts many visiting world-class orchestras. Finland has produced many fine conductors, and because many of them are based abroad—Esa-Pekka Salonen and Paavo Berglund, for example—it is an event when they come home. Concerts are generally held from September through May on Wednesday and Thursday evenings. Just a few hundred feet from Finlandia Hall is the splendid **Suomen Kansallisoopera** Opera House (Helsinginkatu 58, tel. 90/403021), which opened in 1993 in a waterside park by Töölönlahti. There is much original Finnish opera performed

here, as well as international favorites. The rock-hewn **Temppeliaukio Kirkko** (Lutherinkatu 3, tel. 90/494–698) is a favorite venue for choral and chamber music.

Film There are about 50 cinemas in Helsinki. Foreign films have Finnish and Swedish subtitles. Movie listings are in most daily papers and are also posted at the kiosk near the eastern entrance of the main train station. Most cinemas have assigned seats. Tickets cost FM25–35.

Theater Though the recession has forced the state to cut back on its generous financing, private support of the arts continues strong— especially for the theaters, the best-known of which are the **National Theater, City Theater, Swedish Theater,** and the **Lilla Teatern.** However, unless you are fluent in Finnish or Swedish, you'll have a difficult time understanding the performances.

Nightlife At night, street life in restrained Helsinki consists mainly of youths hanging out at the train station or driving around in vintage American cars. The range of clubs is limited to quiet places for a chat or discos and hotel nightclubs with loud music. Cover charges average FM15–FM50.

The Helsinki City Tourist Office has a "Clubs and Music Bars" listing of venues' music nights and cover-charge details.

Bars and Lounges A stylish crowd mingles in whimsical postmodern surroundings at the new **Cincin Bar** (Marski Hotel, Mannerheimintie 10, tel. 90/680–6648). The **Socis Pub** (Kaivokatu 12, tel. 90/170–441) at the Seurahuone Hotel offers turn-of-the-century European ambience. **Säkkipilli** (Kalevankatu 2, tel. 90/605–607) is an English-style pub. Several other pubs, restaurants, and discos are located in the **Säkkipilli/Old Baker's complex** (Mannerheimintie 12, tel. 90/605–607), especially popular with young professionals after work. **Angleterre** (Fredrikinkatu 47, tel. 90/647–371), another English-style pub, attracts a fair share of foreigners, and the beer is slightly cheaper. For a taste of Ireland, visit one of Helsinki's most popular pubs, **O'Malley's** (Hotel Torni, Yrjönkatu 28, tel. 90/131–131).

Bar Restaurants **Café Nouveau** (Keskuskatu 3, tel. 90/602–003) offers live music *with Music* (including jazz and blues) (Tues.–Sat. 10:30 PM–2 AM). **Cantina West** (Kasarminkatu 23, tel. 90/622–1500) is a lively spot for enjoying country, country-rock, and Tex-Mex music.

Rock Clubs Friday and Saturday nights at **Botta** (Museokatu 10, tel. 90/446–940) are strictly disco. **Tavastia** (Urho Kekkosenkatu 4–6, tel. 90/694–3066) is university-owned and one of the best clubs for top Finnish talent as well as some solid imports.

Nightclubs The **Hesperia Hotel Nightclub** (Mannerheimintie 50, tel. 90/43–101), Helsinki's largest and most famous club, occasionally hosts big-name acts. Enjoy gorgeous city views and the cabaret-style floor shows at the ninth-floor **Sky Bar** (Hotel Vaakuna, Asemaaukio 2, tel. 90/131–181). Also popular is the **Bar & Night Club Fizz** at the Hotel Marski (Mannerheimintie 10, tel. 90/68–061), **Fennia** (Mikonkatu 17, tel. 90/666–355), **Café Adlon** (Fabianinkatu 14, tel. 90/664–611), and **Kaivohuone** (Kaivohuone Kaivopuisto, tel. 90/177–881).

Casinos On the third floor of the Ramada Presidentti Hotel, **Casino Ray** (Eteläinen Rautatie 4, tel. 90/694–2900), opened in 1991, offers roulette, blackjack, and slot machines.

Jazz Clubs Helsinki's newest and most popular jazz club is **Storyville** (Museokatu 8, tel. 90/408–007), which offers live jazz every night. **Jumo Jazzclub** (Keskuskatu 6, tel. 90/171–585) offers pleasant evenings of jazz, usually on Tuesday, Wednesday, and Friday. It's conveniently located in the railway-station tunnel. **Kaksi Kanaa** (Kanavakatu 3, tel. 90/669–260) is a bistro supper club with jazz usually on Thursdays. The interior is cabaretlike but spanking clean. Reservations are advised.

Gay Bars **Gay Disco Triangle**, at **Botta** (*see* Rock Clubs, *above*) has gay nights every Monday; for details, contact the gay switchboard SETA (Wed.–Sun. 6–9 PM, tel. 90/769–642). Other gay clubs in Helsinki are **H₂O** (Eerikinkatu 14, tel. 90/604–077) and **Don't Tell Mama** (Annankatu 32, tel. 90/694–1122).

South Coast and Ålands

Anyone with a weakness for islands will be thrilled to see their magical world stretching along Finland's coastline. There, in the Gulf of Finland and the Baltic, more than 30,000 islands form a magnificent archipelago. The rugged and fascinating Åland Islands group rides westward from Turku, forming an autonomous province of its own. Turku, the former capital, was also the main gateway through which cultural influences reached Finland over the centuries.

The southwest is a region of flat, often mist-soaked rural farmlands. The larger villages are highly scenic because of their traditional wooden houses, but except for summer, when the cultural life of the region briefly comes alive, the southwest is pastoral and quiet.

Turku remains a busy harbor, from which you can sail for the Åland islands and points in Sweden. Historic seabound Naantali, with its 15th-century cloister and riot of boat harbors, makes a particularly pleasant detour from Turku.

The Ålands, a collection of small rocky islands, are inhabited in large part by families that fish or run small farms. Their connection with the sea is inevitable, and their tradition of being at sea is a revered one. Some of the greatest grain ships sailing the seas were built by the Gustav Eriksson family in Mariehamn.

Important Addresses and Numbers

Tourist The main tourist offices in the area are located at **Åland**
Information (Storagatan 11, 22100 Mariehamn, tel. 928/27–310), **Hanko** (Bulevardi 15; Bulevardi 10 after June 1994, 10900, tel. 911/280–3411), **Naantali** (Kaivotori 2, 21100, tel. 921/850–850), **Tammisaari** (Ekenäs) (Raatihuonentori, 10600, tel. 911/263–2100), and **Turku** (Kasityöläiskatu 3, 20100, tel. 921/233–6366).

Emergencies The nationwide emergency number is 112; it can be used to call police and ambulance services. A major medical center in the region is the **Turun Yliopistollinen Keskusairaala** (University of Turku Central Hospital, Kiinamyllynkatu 4–8, Turku, tel. 921/611611). For dentists, call the Turun Hammaslääkärikeskus (Turku Dental Center, Hämeenkatu 2, Turku, tel. 921/233–3778).

Late-Night Late-night pharmacies are found only in large towns. Look un-
Pharmacies der *Apteekki* in the phone book; listings include pharmacy
hours.

Arriving and Departing by Plane

The region's airports are at **Mariehamn** and **Turku.** Both have
connections to Helsinki and Stockholm, with service by Finnair and its charter company Karair.

Arriving and Departing by Car,
Train, Bus, and Boat

By Car The Helsinki–Turku trip is 165 kilometers (100 miles) on Route
E3; signs on E3 will tell you where to turn off for the south-
coast towns of Tammisaari and Hanko. Most of southwestern
Finland is well served by public transport, so a car is not really
necessary.

By Train Trains leave Helsinki for Turku several times a day; however,
for most smaller towns, you must stop at stations along the Helsinki–Turku route and change to a local bus. Bus fares are usually a bit cheaper than train fares.

By Bus There is good bus service connecting the capital to the southwest from Helsinki's long-distance bus station, just west of
the train station off Mannerheimintie. Information from **Matkahuolto** (Head office, Lauttasaarentie 8, 00200 Helsinki, tel.
692–2088).

By Boat Åland is most cheaply reached by boat from Turku and
Naantali. Call **Silja Line** in Turku (tel. 921/652–244 or 9800/
174552), or Helsinki (tel. 90/180–4422); or call **Viking Line** in
Helsinki (tel. 90/12–351), Turku (tel. 921/63–311), or Tampere
(tel. 931/140–511). Tickets can also be purchased at the harbor.

Guided Tours

Orientation Available through the Tammisaari tourist office are **Tammisaari Archipelago Tours** (1½ to 7 hours), by boat, which take
in the national park. The cost for the shortest tour is FM50
adults, FM20 children (6–12 years).

Special-Interest **Ageba Special Travel Service** (Pohjoisranta 4, Helsinki, tel. 90/
661–123) arranges a variety of tours in the region.

The **Seven Churches** 100-kilometer (65-mile) tour from Turku,
taking in the area's major medieval churches and a country
manor house, lasts about 7 hours and is arranged (for groups of
25 or more only) through **Varsinais-Suomen Matkailuyhdistys**
(L. Rantakatu 13, 20100 Turku, tel. 921/517–333). The cost is
FM100.

Exploring the South Coast and Ålands

*Numbers in the margin correspond to points of interest on the
South Coast and Ålands map.*

Turku and the A trip to Turku via **Hanko** and Tammisaari will give you a taste
Hanko Peninsula of Finland at its most historic and scenic. Moving southwest
from Helsinki along the Hanko road for about 77 kilometers (48
❶ miles), you'll arrive in **Snappertuna,** a small farming town with
a proud hilltop church, a charming homestead museum, and the

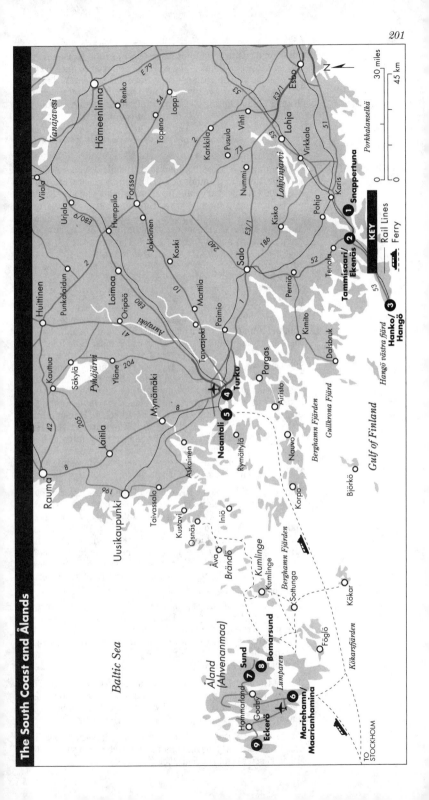

The South Coast and Ålands

Baltic Sea

Gulf of Finland

Åland (Ahvenanmaa)

1 Snappertuna
2 Tammisaari/Ekenäs
3 Hanko/Hangö
4 Turku
5 Naantali
6 Mariehamn/Maarianhamina
7 Sund
8 Bomarsund
9 Eckerö

KEY
Rail Lines
Ferry

Hämeenlinna
Esbo
Porkkalanselkä
30 miles
45 km

Renko
Loppi
Topeno
Karkkila
Vihti
Pusula
Lohja
Virkkala
Karis
Kaija
Pohja
Tenala
Snappertuna

Viiala
Forssa
Humppila
Jokioinen
Koski
Salo
Pertteli
Kimito
Dalsbruk

Urjala
Nummi
Kisko

Huittinen
Loimaa
Oripää
Marttila
Paimio
Pargas
Airisto
Berghamn Fjärd
Gullkrona Fjärd

Punkalaidun
Tarvasjoki
Turku
Nauvo

Kauttua
Säkylä
Yläne
Mynämäki
Rymättylä
Korpo
Björkö

Pyhäjärvi
Laitila
Taivassalo
Askainen
Iniö
Kumlinge
Sottunga
Kökar

Rauma
Uusikaupunki
Osnäs
Kustavi
Åva
Brändö
Kumlinge
Berghamn Fjärden
Kökarsfjärden

Hammarland
Godby
Sund
Bomarsund
Föglö

Eckerö
Mariehamn/Maarianhamina
Lumparen

TO STOCKHOLM

Vanajavesi
Aurajoki
Lohjanjärvi
Hangö västra fjärd

handsome restored ruin of **Rasaseporin Linna** (Raseborg Castle), set in a small dale. The castle is believed to date from the 13th century. One 16th-century siege left the castle damaged, but restorations have given it a new face. In summer, concerts, dramas, old-time market fairs, and mock medieval duels are staged here. *Tel. 911/34–015. Admission: FM5 adults, FM2 children. Open May 1–Aug. 31, daily 10–8. Guides arranged by Tammisaari tourist office (see Important Addresses and Numbers, above).*

Continuing south for 16 kilometers (10 miles), you will find the historic town of **Tammisaari** (Ekenäs), with its colorful old quarter, 19th-century buildings, and a lively marina. The scenery is dazzling in summer when the sun glints off the water and marine traffic is at its peak. The three-part **Tammisaaren Museo** (Ekenäs Commoners' Museum) provides a taste of the town's culture and history. *Kustaa Vaasan katu 13, tel. 911/263–3161. Admission: summer, FM10 adults; children under 7 free; FM5 senior citizens over 65 and full-time university students with ID. Open May 15–Aug. 2, Tues.–Sun. 11–4; Aug. 3–May 14, open for special exhibitions only; call for a special tour.*

An hour's drive farther west is the popular seaside resort of **Hanko** (Hango), with its long stretch of sandy beach. This customs port has some of the largest and most fanciful private homes in Finland. Their porches are edged with gingerbread iron- and woodwork, and crazy towers sprout from their roofs. There are several beaches and good cycling paths, but the best pastime is a stroll along the main avenue past the great wooden houses with their wraparound porches. A popular sailing center, Hanko has Finland's largest guest harbor. Hanko is historically rich, too. Fortified in the 18th century, the Hanko defense was destroyed by the Russians in 1854, during the Crimean War. Later it became a popular spa town for Russians, then the port from which more than 300,000 Finns emigrated to North America between 1880 and 1930.

Northwest of Hanko at the mouth of the Aura River is **Turku,** the center of Finland's southwest. Turku is the nation's oldest city, founded at the beginning of the 13th century, and the original capital. With a population of more than 160,000, it is the fifth-largest city and is often called "the cradle of Finnish culture." Commercially, its significance lies in its year-round harbor; *turku* means "trading post." It is also known for its shipyards and for being the site of the first Finnish university.

The 700-year-old **Turun Tuomiokirkko** (Turku Cathedral) remains the seat of the archbishop of Finland. Although it was partially gutted by fire in 1827, the cathedral has been completely restored. In the choir can be seen R. W. Ekman's frescoes portraying Bishop Henry (an Englishman) baptizing the then-heathen Finns, and Mikael Agricola offering the Finnish translation of the New Testament to Gustav Vasa of Sweden.

Where the Aura flows into the sea stands **Turun Linna** (Turku Castle), one of the city's most important historical monuments. The oldest part of the fortress was built at the end of the 13th century, and the newer part dates from the 16th century.

Turku seems a staid town at first glance, but there is a lively artistic community here. It is most active during the August Music Festival and the Ruisrock Festival in July.

Time Out The **Hamburg Börs Hotel** (Kauppiaskatu 6, tel. 921/637–381) has a pleasant German-style tavern for drinks or meals; it's next to the market square.

A recommended stop 16 kilometers (10 miles) from Turku is the coastal village of **Naantali,** an artists' town lining a snug harbor. Many of the buildings in Naantali date from the 17th century, following a massive rebuilding after the Great Fire of 1628. There are also a number of 18th- and 19th-century buildings, and these form the basis of the Old Town, a settlement by the water's edge. These shingled wooden buildings were originally built as private residences, and many remain so, although a few now house small galleries.

The town's extremely narrow cobblestone lanes gave rise to a very odd law. During periods when economic conditions were poor, Naantalians earned their keep by knitting socks and exporting them by the tens of thousands. Men, women, and children all knitted so feverishly that the town council forbade groups of more than six from meeting in narrow lanes with their knitting—and causing road obstructions.

A major attraction in the village is **Kultaranta,** the summer residence for Finland's presidents, with its more than 3,500 rosebushes. Guided tours can be arranged through the Naantali tourist board (*see above*) year-round. *Luonnonmaasaari. Call tourist board to check opening times; they vary greatly.*

Naantalin Luostarikirkko, Naantali's Vallis Gratiae/Order of St. Birgitta Convent, was founded in 1443. The convent, which alternately housed nuns then monks, operated under the aegis of the Catholic church until it was dissolved by the Reformation in the 17th century. The church is all that remains of the convent. *Nunnakatu, Naantali, tel. 921/850–109. Admission free for nonguided visits. Open Sat. 9–4; May 2–May 31 and Aug. 16–31, daily 12–3; June 1–Aug. 15, daily 12–6; Sept. 1–Apr. 30, Sun. 12–3. Group tours available through Naantali tourist office (see Tourist Information, above).*

Time Out Near Naantali's marina, a footbridge leads to **Kailo** Island, a popular summer activity center with a theater; beach, sports and picnic facilities; and a snack bar.

The Åland Islands From Turku there are air and sea connections to the **Åland** (Ahvenanmaa) Islands (approximately 5½ hours by boat), where rural calm combines with striking coastal scenery. In all, there are more than 6,500 islands and skerries; virtually all the inhabitants are Swedish-speaking and very proud of their largely autonomous status.

Åland is particularly well organized for cycling and fishing packages, motor tours (you can go island-hopping on the fleet of car or passenger ferries), and rental cottages (there are more than 7,000 scattered throughout the islands). These are also marvelous sailing waters for experienced mariners.

Nearly half the population lives in the tiny capital of **Mariehamn** (Maarianhamina), the hub of Åland life and the main port, on the main island of Åland. The *Pommern* **Museefartyget** (*Pommern* Museum Ship), situated in Mariehamn West Harbor at the center of town, is one of the last existing grain ships in the world. She belonged to the sailing fleet of the Mariehamn

shipping magnate Gustav Erikson; the *Pommern* carried wheat from Australia to England from 1923 to 1939. *Tel. 928/ 531–421. Admission: FM15 adults, FM8 children. Open Apr.– Oct., daily.*

Time Out The marina café, just down the quay from the *Pommern* Museefartyget, allows you to relax near the water.

In prehistoric times the islands were, relatively speaking, heavily populated, as shown by traces of no less than 10,000 ancient settlements, graves, and strongholds. While in **Sund,** visit the island's only medieval **castle,** which was built by the Swedes to strengthen their presence on Åland. *Admission (castle tour with guide): FM20 adults, FM14 children. Guided tours May–June, daily 10, 11, 11:30, 1, 1:30, 2:30, 3, and 4; July, 9:30, 10, 10:30, 11:30, 12, 12:30, 1:30, 2, 2:30, 3:30, 4, and 4:30; Aug.–Sept., 10, 11:30, 1, 2:30, 4. Closed Oct.–Apr.*

Adjacent to the medieval castle is **Jan-Karls Gardenin Ulkoilmamuseo** (Jan-Karl's Garden Outdoor Museum), a very popular open-air museum with buildings and sheds from the 18th century that portray farming life on the island 200 years ago. *Admission: FM10 adults, FM7 children. Open.*

About 10 kilometers (8 miles) from Sund are the scattered ruins of **Bomarsund Fort,** a huge naval fortress built by the Russians in the early 19th century and only half finished when it was destroyed by Anglo-French forces during the Crimean War. It is in **Bomarsund,** about 30 kilometers (22 miles) north of Mariehamn on Route 2. The fishing community of **Eckerö** (37 kilometers/23 miles northwest) and its small bathing beach also make for a good day's outing.

What to See and Do with Children

In Mariehamn, the *Pommern* Museefartyget (*see above*) is likely to fascinate children, big or small. Nearby is **Lilla Holmen,** a small island with long sandy beaches and an open-air animal park.

Through the telescope of **Vesitorni** (Hanko's Watch Tower), you can follow the comings and goings of the town's marine traffic and get a grander view of some of the very small islands sprinkled around the peninsula's edges. *Vartiovuori. Admission: FM5 adults, FM2 children. Open June–Aug., daily 10–noon and 3–5.*

In Karjaa, **Lystiland** (Amusement Land) includes a miniature train tour on an enchanted forest path. *Karjaantie, tel. 911/36– 565. Prices and hours were being changed at press time. Call ahead.*

Off the Beaten Track

Ninety-two kilometers (57 miles) northwest of Turku is **Rauma,** the third-oldest city in Finland. The city, which is widely known for its tradition of lace making and its annual event, Lace Week, held every year at the end of July, is also known for the beauty of its old wooden houses painted in distinctive 19th-century colors. The colors are so extraordinary, in fact, that no house can be repainted before the Old Rauma Association approves the color. UNESCO has chosen Rauma's

old town as a world-heritage site. For further information, contact the Rauma City Tourist Office (Valtakatu 2, 26100, tel. 938/344551).

Shopping

If you are in the market for **nautical knickknacks,** this area has them in abundance. Otherwise, there are no products unique to the region, though the tendency among Finnish artists to summer in coastal towns probably accounts for an inordinate number of **galleries, art exhibitions,** and **handicraft boutiques.** In Naantali you'll find the workshop of a famous Finnish contemporary jewelry designer, **Karl Laine** (Mannerheiminkatu 10B, tel. 921/751–648). His use of brass and Lappish gold, and his combinations of starkly geometric and richly clustered metals, sometimes studded with tiny precious stones, are singular in their creativeness.

Sports and Outdoor Activities

Bicycling Most towns have bikes for rent from about FM35 per day (FM150 per week). The fine scenery and the terrain, alternately dead-flat and gently rolling, make for ideal cycling. The roads are not busy once you leave the highway. The **Suomen Retkeilymajajärjestö** (Finnish Youth Hostel Association, Yrjönkatu 38B, 00100 Helsinki, tel. 90/694–0377) has bicycle trips varying in length from four days to two weeks (with overnight stops at hostels if you wish). For Åland bicycle routes, contact **Ålandsresor Ab** (PB 62, Storagatan 9, 22101 Mariehamn, tel. 928/28–040). Both organizations also rent bikes.

Boating A variety of boats can be rented through the Tammisaari, Hanko, and Mariehamn tourist offices (*see* Tourist Information, *above*); or at the guest harbor Info-Point in Hanko. Whenever the annual **Hanko Regatta** takes place, on a weekend at the end of June/beginning of July, the population of the city doubles to 20,000.

Tennis Mariehamn, Eckerö, Turku, Tammisaari, and Hanko have outdoor public tennis courts, many of which rent equipment. Contact local tourist offices for information.

Beaches

Hanko has Finland's best beaches, about 30 kilometers' (21 miles') worth, some sandy and some with sea-smoothed boulders. The islands tend to have small but pleasant beaches, and Naantali has several bathing areas.

Dining and Lodging

Åland **Arkipelag.** Set on the bay and right in the middle of Ma-
Dining and Lodging riehamn, Arkipelag Hotel is known for its fine marina and lively disco/bar. The rooms are modern and comfortable, with huge picture windows. The restaurants, set in long, wood-paneled rooms with wide windows overlooking an ocean inlet, are a good place to sample Åland seafood at its best. Try the crayfish when it's in season. In the Terrace restaurant, the fresh-shrimp sandwiches with dill mayonnaise are a treat. *Strandgatan 31, 22100 Mariehamn, tel. 928/24–020, fax 928/24384. 86 rooms, 8 suites. Facilities: restaurant, nightclub, bar, casino,*

sauna, indoor/outdoor pool, solarium, conference rooms. DC, MC, V. Very Expensive.

Lodging **Björklidens stugby.** The appeal here are the snug, redwood cabins in the timeless style of Finnish summer cottages. They're small, but you are meant to be outdoors. Enjoy the free rowboats, grassy lawns, and trees with swings. It is 25 kilometers (17 miles) from Mariehamn. *22240 Hammarland, tel. 928/38-908, fax 928/37801. 17 cabins. Facilities: beach, TV room, outdoor grill, fishing, playground, washing machines. MC, V. Closed late Aug.–May. Inexpensive.*

Hanko **Hanko Camping, Silversand.** There are various facilities on the
Lodging grounds, including eight-person cabins and full hookups for trailers, as well as trailers and tents for rent. *Hopeahietikko, 10960 Hanko, tel. 911/248-5500, fax 911/713713. Facilities: cafeteria, store, cooking facilities, sauna, showers, bathrooms. Open May 25–Aug. 16. Inexpensive.*

Naantali **Tavastin Kilta.** This summer restaurant with a view of the boat
Dining harbor has a fresh cold table where the herring and marinated beef are especially good. Broiled steaks and fish are the featured hot dishes; vegetarian dishes are also offered. There is the Old World bishop's dining room, a nautical bar, and a tapas bar decorated in 19th-century style. Lemon pastries are a dessert specialty. *Mannerheimintie 1, tel. 921/751-066. Reservations advised. Dress: casual but neat. AE, DC, MC, V. Moderate.*

Lodging **Naantali Spa.** The emphasis here is on pampering, with foot massages, shiatsu physical therapy, mud packs, and spa-water and algae baths. Activities include gymnastics and a special seven-day fasting program offered twice a year under medical supervision. All kinds of health packages can be arranged, including health-rehabilitation programs. It is set on a peninsula in a grandiose building (1984) that replaced the original spa on the site and was expanded once again in 1992. *Matkailijantie 2, 21100, tel. 921/857-711, fax 921/857790. 209 rooms. Facilities: beauty salon, massage, physiotherapy solarium, Turkish bath, Roman pools, swimming pools. AE, DC, MC, V. Expensive–Very Expensive.*

Tammisaari **Ekenäs Stadshotell and Restaurant.** This modern, airy hotel is
Dining and Lodging set among fine lawns and gardens. The rooms, each with its own balcony, have wide picture windows and comfortable modern furnishings, all in pale and neutral colors. The location, near the sea and the old town, is one kilometer (.6 miles) from the town center. The restaurant offers Continental food and Swedish-Finnish seafood specialties prepared by a veteran chef. *Pohjoinen Rantakatu 1, 10600 Tammisaari, tel. 911/241-3131, fax 911/61550. 16 rooms, 2 suites. Facilities: restaurant, bar, 2 cafés, cable TV, room service, indoor pool, dance floor. AE, DC, MC, V. Closed Dec. 24–25. Expensive.*

Strand Hotel and Restaurant. Right in the heart of Tammisaari, this modern hotel stretches along the shoreline. The exterior is handsomely rendered in the style of turn-of-the-century wooden manor houses. The rooms are modern, with sea-green carpet and spreads and old-fashioned nautical prints. The large restaurant in the round, with views over the sea, serves classic French-style cuisine. Choose between the game-bird dishes and the fresh seafood. There's an adjacent dance floor. *Pohjankatu 2, 10600 Tammisaari, tel. 911/246-1500, fax 911/*

61505. 20 rooms, 1 suite. Facilities: restaurant, bar, boat dock, sauna, cable TV, meeting rooms. AE, DC, V. Closed Dec. 24–26. Moderate.

Turku **Julia.** Here the specialty is French country fare. In this infor-
Dining mal and cozy restaurant you can enjoy a tasty meal by the
warmth of a fireplace. *Eerikinkatu 4, tel. 921/503–300. Reservations advised. Dress: casual but neat. AE, DC, MC, V.
Expensive. Closed Sun., Midsummer, Christmas, and sometimes Easter. Expensive.*

Lodging **Park Hotel.** Park Hotel, two blocks from the main market
square, is one of the most unusual hotels in Finland. Built in
1904 in Art Nouveau style for a British executive who ran the
local shipyard, the building resembles a castle. The hotel's
rooms have high ceilings and are decorated with antique furniture. *Rauhankatu 1, 20100 Turku, tel. 921/519–666, fax 921/
617750. 21 rooms. Facilities: sauna, restaurant, minibar. AE,
DC, MC, V. Very Expensive.*

The Arts

Each town hosts concerts and art exhibitions in summer, often
in outdoor venues. The best way to find out about arts happenings is through local tourist boards. The **Scandinavian Guitar
Festival** comes to Tammisaari in July. The **Naantali Music Festival** offers chamber music at the beginning of June.

Lapland

Lapland is often called Europe's last wilderness, a region of
endless forests, fells, and great silences. Often the arrival of
settlers obliterates all that existed before, but here humans
have walked gently and left the virgin solitude almost unspoiled. Now easily accessible by plane, train, or bus, this Arctic outpost offers comfortable hotels and modern amenities, yet
you won't have to go very far to find yourself in an almost pri-
mordial setting.

The oldest traces of human habitation in Finland have been
found in Lapland, and hordes of Danish, English, and even Ara-
bian coins indicate the existence of trade activities many centuries ago. The origins of the Lapps themselves are lost in the
mists of history. There are only about 4,000 pure Lapps still
living here; the remainder of the province's population of
200,000 are Finns. Until the 1930s, Lapland remained largely
unexploited, a region where any trip was an adventure. Then
the Canadian-owned Petsamo Nickel Company completed the
great road that connects Rovaniemi with the Arctic Sea. Building activities increased along this route (later to be known as
the Arctic Highway), the land was turned and sown, and a few
hotels were built to cater to an increasing number of visitors.

The Lapps, a proud, sensitive, and intelligent people, prefer
their own name for themselves, Saame (also spelled Sami or
Same). Some of them can be resentful toward visitors who regard them as only tourist attractions put there for photo opportunities. Modern influences (among them intermarriage) have
regrettably changed many aspects of the traditional Saame
way of life; for example, their attractive costumes are rarely
seen, except on festive occasions. The young especially have

been affected by the changes, and many of them are now far more interested in becoming teachers, lawyers, or engineers than in breeding reindeer or hunting from their remote homesteads. Others profit from selling souvenirs to tourists, but most prefer to go about their daily life minding their own business.

Summer has the blessing of round-the-clock daylight and often beautiful weather to go with it. In early fall the colors are so fabulous the Finns have a special word for it: *ruskaa*. If you can take the intense (but dry) cold, winter is a fascinating time in Lapland, not only for the northern lights but for such experiences as the reindeer roundups. Depending on how far north of the Arctic Circle you travel, the sun might not rise for several weeks around midwinter. But it is never pitch-black; light reflects from the invisible sun below the horizon even during midday, and there is luminosity from the ever-present snow.

But Finns cherish the outdoors no matter what the light. Here it is the wilderness that's the draw. For although the cities have fine facilities and much going on culturally, it is the lonely fells with the occasional profile of a reindeer herd crossing, the gin-clear forest streams, and the bright trail of the midnight sun reflected on a lake's blackest waters that leave the indelible impressions.

Important Addresses and Numbers

Tourist Information The main offices are in **Inari** (99870, tel. 9697/51193), **Ivalo** (Piiskuntie 5, 99800, bus station, tel. 9697/12521), **Kemijärvi** (Kemijärven Kehitys Oy, Matkailutoimisto, Kuumaniemenkatu 2 A, 98100, tel. 9692/13777), **Kuusamo** (Kaiterantie 22, 93600, tel. 989/850–2202), **Oulu** (Torikatu 10, 90100, tel. 981/314–1294), **Rovaniemi** (Aallonkatu 1, 96200, tel. 960/346–270, and **Sodankylä** (Sodankylä Matkailu Oy, Jäämerentie 9, 99600, tel. 9693/13–474).

Emergencies The nationwide emergency number is 112; it can be used for police and ambulance services. Lapland's leading hospital is **Lapin Keskussairaala** (Lapland Central Hospital, Ounasrinteentie 22, Rovaniemi, tel. 960/3281). Dentists can be reached at **Hammashoitola Viisaudenhammas** (Koskikatu 9 B, Rovaniemi, tel. 960/347620).

Late-Night Pharmacies You will find late-night pharmacies only in large towns. Look under *Apteekki* in the phone book; the listings include pharmacy hours.

Arriving and Departing by Plane

The airports serving Lapland are at **Enontekiö, Ivalo, Kemi, Kittilä, Kuusamo, Oulu, Rovaniemi,** and **Sodankylä**. Finnair serves all these airports with flights from Helsinki; not all flights are nonstop, though. You can also fly to the north from most of southwestern Finland's larger cities and from the lakes region.

Arriving and Departing by Car, Train, and Bus

By Car If you are driving north, follow Arctic Highway No. 4 (national highway) to Kuopio–Oulu–Rovaniemi, or go via the west coast to Oulu, then to Rovaniemi. From Rovaniemi, the national

highway continues straight up to Lake Inari via Ivalo. The roads are generally good, but some in the extreme north may be rough.

By Train Train service will get you to Rovaniemi and Kemijärvi. From there you must make connections with other forms of transport.

By Bus Bus service into the region centers on Rovaniemi; from there, you can switch to local buses.

Getting Around

By Plane There is service every day but Sunday between Rovaniemi and Ivalo. You can also fly between Oulu or Rovaniemi to Ivalo, Enontekiö, Kemi, Kittilä, and Sodankylä, all on Finnair domestic services (Air Botnia). Finnair also has daily flights directly from Helsinki to Kuusamo. There are seasonal schedules.

By Car A car is necessary only if you want to reach remote places.

By Bus Buses leave five times daily from Rovaniemi to Inari (five hours), and five times a day to Ivalo (four hours). You can take countryside taxis to your final destination; taxi stands are at most bus stations.

Guided Tours

Guided tours in towns are arranged through city tourist offices. The national tourist board's "Lappi à la Carte" booklet suggests gourmet trails through the north.

Orientation There is a large variety of Lapland tours, catering to both general and special interests. Finnair arranges many tours from Helsinki, including the Midnight Sun Flight Tour (one day, one night); the Arctic Safari to Lapland (one day, one night); and the 120-kilometer Hiking Tour (eight days, seven nights). Reservations and itinerary details are available from **Finnair** (Mannerheimintie 102, 00250, tel. 90/81–881, fax 90/818–8736). **Finland Travel Bureau** (Kaivokatu 10A, 00100 Helsinki, tel. 90/18261) offers a Polar Safari Adventure Tour (four days, three nights). **Lapptreks** (99870 Inari, tel. 9697/51375) arranges reindeer, canoe, and snowmobile safaris; ski treks; and fishing trips. Tours to Lapland can be also purchased through **Area Travel** (Pohjoisesplanadi 2, 00130 Helsinki, tel. 90/18551). Travel agencies also offer a variety of white-water rafting and nature-photography tours. For independent travelers, the **Finnish Youth Hostel Association** (*see* Getting Around, By Bicycle, in Staying in Finland, *above*) can suggest trekking routes and hostel/cabin/camping accommodations.

From Rovaniemi, the tourist board (*see* Important Addresses and Numbers, *above*) has a 2½-hour evening Arctic Circle tour. From Inari, **Feelings Unlimited** runs two-hour Lake Inari tours that leave from the Saame (Lapp) Museum and visit a Saame stone altar and burial island. Reservations are available from **Raimo Mustkangas** (Inari, June–Sept., tel. 9697/51352; Rovaniemi, year-round, tel. 960/181–701).

Exploring Lapland

Numbers in the margin correspond to points of interest on the Lapland map.

1 Your best base for traveling around the Arctic area is **Rovaniemi,** where the Ounas and Kemi rivers meet almost on the Arctic Circle. Rovaniemi is the "gateway to Lapland" and the administrative and communications center of the province.

If you're expecting an Arctic shantytown, you're in for a surprise. Rovaniemi was nearly razed by the retreating German army in 1944, and today its modern appearance is strongly influenced by Alvar Aalto's architecture. During rebuilding, the population rose from 8,000 to more than 33,000, so be prepared for a contemporary city on the edge of wilderness. If the street layout seems capricious, it's because Aalto planned the town so it would look like reindeer antlers from the air.

One of the best ways to tune in to the culture of Finland's far north is to visit **Arktikum** (the Arctic Research Center), which also houses the Lapland Provincial Museum. Its riveting exhibit on Saame (Lapp) life, giving the full story of their survival, opened in December 1992. *Pohjoisranta 4, tel. 960/322-2483.*

Rovaniemi's real claim to fame, though, is that Santa Claus lives in its suburbs. Take the Arctic Highway (E75) 8 kilometers (5 miles) north toward the Arctic Circle to **Joulupukin Pajakylä** (Santa Claus Village). Lapps in native dress and reindeer hauling sleighs enhance its feeling of authenticity. At Santa Claus's Workshop, gifts can be bought in midsummer for shipping at any time of year. For most visitors the main attraction is to mail postcards home from the special Arctic Circle post office. There's also a complete souvenir shopping complex, and the impressive sight of the mountains of mail that pour in from children all over the world. Yes, all of it gets answered! *Admission free. Open June–Aug., daily 8–8; Sept.–May, daily 9–5.*

Time Out Take the 3-kilometer (2-mile) hike to Ounasvaara hill for midnight-sun viewing from on high, and stop at the **Sky Hotel** for coffee and pastries at the café.

2 After driving north for a couple of hours, you may want to take a short detour to the modern tourist center at **Luostotunturi,** in the fell district of southern Lapland. Turn right off the main road onto a secondary road about 16 kilometers (10 miles) south of Sodankylä, and follow it 22 kilometers (13 miles) to the cen-
3 ter. There is also a daily bus from **Kemijärvi** (reached via local
4 train from Rovaniemi) to the **Pyhätunturi** and **Luostotunturi** fell districts; these areas are superb hiking territory.

5 Back on the main road at **Sodankylä** there is a Northern Lights Observatory (for professionals only) and an ancient wooden church.

6 Continue north through the village of Vuotso to **Tankavaara,** 230 kilometers (143 miles) north of Rovaniemi and 60 kilometers (37 miles) south of Ivalo, the most accessible and the best-developed of several gold-panning areas. The **Kultamuseo** (Gold Museum) tells the century-old story of Lapland's hardy fortune seekers. For a small fee, authentic prospectors will show you how to pan gold dust and tiny nuggets from the silt of

Lapland

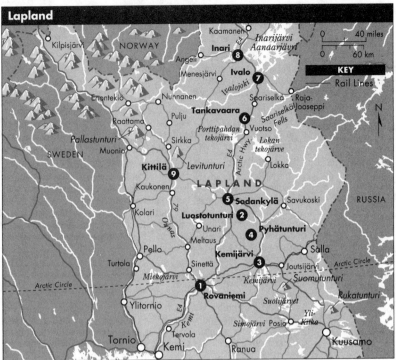

an icy stream. *Arctic Highway 4, Kultakylä, Tankavaara, tel. 9693/46–158. Admission: FM20 adults, FM5 children under 12, discounts for groups of 10 or more. Open June–Aug. 16, daily 9–6; Aug. 17–Sept. 30, daily 9–5; Oct.–May, opening hours vary—check locally.*

7 The village of **Ivalo** is the main center for northern Lapland. With its first-class hotel, airport, and many modern amenities, it offers little to the tourist in search of a wilderness experience, but the huge island-studded expanses of **Inarijärvi** (Lake Inari), north of Ivalo, offer vast possibilities for wilderness exploration with its seemingly limitless boating, fishing, hiking, and hunting opportunities. It is a beautiful 40-kilometer (24-**8** mile) drive northwest from Ivalo, along the lakeshore, to **Inari.** The **Saamelaismuseo** (Saame Museum), on the village outskirts, covers all facets of Lapp culture. *Inari, tel. 9697/51107. Admission: FM12 adults, FM5 children. Open June–Aug. 10, daily 8–10, Aug. 11–31, daily 8–8; Sept. 1–20, weekdays 9–3:30.*

The **Inarin Porofarmi** is a working **reindeer farm** 14 kilometers **9** (9 miles) from Inari in the direction of **Kittilä.** The farm trains racing reindeer. You can drive a reindeer sled or be pulled on skis by reindeer. From here, take Route 79 back to Rovaniemi. *Kaksamajärvi, Inari, tel. 9697/56512.*

What to See and Do with Children

Lapland abounds with possibilities for children. **Gold panning** (*see* Exploring Lapland, *above*) is an activity children of all ages

enjoy; most of Finland's gold comes from the region. A seven-hour trip up the Lemmenjoki River from Ivalo can be arranged by **Lemmenjoen Lomamajat** (Lemmenjoki, tel. 9697/57–135).

Tunturikeskus Kiilopää (*see* Lodging, *below*) has a multi-activity center for children, including snow-castle building, centrifuge sledding, special ski tracks, and reindeer and dogsled trips; there are summer activities, too.

During the winter at **Salla Reindeer Farm** (PL 7, 98901 Salla, tel. 9692/37771), 150 kilometers (93 miles) east of Rovaniemi and 67 kilometers (42 miles) from Kemijärvi, children can obtain a reindeer driver's license (FM40) and feed the animals.

Santa Claus Village (Joulupukinpajakylä, 96930 Arctic Circle, tel. 960/62096), 8 kilometers (5 miles) north of Rovaniemi, is closed when Santa is abroad on December 25. Accessible by car and bus, it is the most famed attraction in the region, and apart from all Santa's paraphernalia, it is likely to be the only place where your children will be able to pet a reindeer—the ones you'll see in the wild are shy. There is also a working reindeer farm near Inari (*see* Exploring Lapland, *above*) that is fun for everyone.

Off the Beaten Track

There are hundreds of hiking and skiing trails throughout the north that you could travel for days without seeing another soul. Thirty kilometers (18 miles) north of Tankavarra is **Saariselkä,** which has a variety of accommodations and makes a central base from which to set off on a trip into the true wilderness. There are marked trails through forests and over fells, where nothing much has changed since the last Ice Age. More than 1,556 kilometers (965 square miles) of this magnificent area has been named the **Uhrokekkosen Kansallispüisto** (Urho Kekkonen National Park). The park guide center is at Tankavaara.

Shopping

Lapp **handicrafts** are not only useful but artistically attractive. Keep an eye out for the **camping knives** with beautifully carved bone or wooden handles; products made from **reindeer pelts;** colorful **weavings** and **embroidered mittens** and **gloves; felt shoes;** and **birchbark baskets** and **rucksacks.**

Sports and Outdoor Activities

Bicycling There are numerous planned cycling "safaris" offered in Lapland; for details contact the Finnish Youth Hostel Association (*see*, Getting Around, By Bicycle, in Staying in Finland, *above*).

Canoeing From canoe trips on Lake Inari to a foray over the rapids of the Ivalojoki River, choices for canoers are bountiful. Contact the **Finnish Canoe Association** (Radiokatu 20, 00240 Helsinki, tel. 90/158–2363) or local tourist boards.

Fishing Fly-fishing and combined canoe/fishing trips are readily available. Contact **Lapland Travel Ltd.** (Maakuntakatu 10, 96100 Rovaniemi, tel. 960/346–052).

Golf Lapland's uncrowded courses offer such unusual experiences as snow golf and midnight-sun golf. Contact the **Finnish Golf Union** (Radiokatu 20, 00240 Helsinki, tel. 90/158–2244).

Hiking Maps of marked trails through Lapland's national parks can be ordered through **Karttakeskus Pasila** (Opastinsilta 12, 00520 Helsinki, tel. 90/154–521) or **Karttakeskus** (Hallituskatu 1–3C, 96100 Rovaniemi, tel. 960/294517). For organized hiking tours for families with children, as well as beginners, contact **Suomen Latu ry** (Fabianinkatu 7, 00130 Helsinki, tel. 90/170–101), or **Tunturikeskus Kiilopää** (*see* Dining and Lodging in Ivalo/ Kiilopää, *below*).

Skiing Cross-country and downhill skiing, although found at numerous locales, are best at **Saariselkä** resort, 30 kilometers (20 miles) south of Ivalo, as well as **Tunturikeskus Kiilopää** (*see* Hiking, *above*). Note that Finland does not have any very long downhill trails.

Swimming Lapland's waters are exceptionally clean and good for swimming. Many hotels have pools, and **Saariselkä Spa** at Saariselkä features an indoor water world.

Dining and Lodging

Inari/Saariselkä
Dining and Lodging

Hotelli Riekonlinna. The pinewood and blue-textile decor of this contemporary Lappish hotel, built in 1987 and renovated in 1990, goes well with its natural setting. It has a meeting center, a multisport complex, and it is only 30 minutes from Ivalo Airport. The restaurant serves fresh local specialties. *Saariseläntie, 99830 Saariselkä, tel. 9697/81601, fax 9697/81602. 124 rooms, 2 suites. Facilities: restaurant, cable TV, pools, aerobics room, squash and tennis courts, massage. AE, DC, MC, V. Very Expensive.*

Ivalo
Dining and Lodging

Hotelli Ivalo. Modern and well-equipped for business travelers and families, the hotel hugs the Ivalo River. The lobby has marble floors, and there's a brick fireplace in the sauna lounge. The rooms are spacious and modern, with burlap woven wallpaper, oatmeal carpets, and lots of blond birchwood trimming; ask for a room by the river. It is a kilometer (½ mile) from Ivalo. The restaurant offers local and Continental fare, and delicious "Lappi à la Carte" meals. *Ivalontie 34, 99800, tel. 9697/21911, fax 9697/21905. 94 rooms. Facilities: restaurant, saunas, TV, baby-sitting, playroom, pool, boating. AE, DC, MC, V. Moderate.*

Ivalo/Kiilopää
Dining and Lodging

Tunturikeskus Kiilopää. This "Fell Center" is in the midst of a hikers' and cross-country skiers' paradise in the Urho Kekkonen National Park district, 45 kilometers (30 miles) south of Ivalo Airport. Accommodation is in beautifully crafted log cabins, apartments, or individual hotel rooms, all of wood and stone; cabins have picture windows and some have individual fireplaces. The casual restaurant serves reindeer and other game entrées. *Arctic Hwy. 4, 99800 Ivalo, tel. 9697/87101, fax 9697/87121. 77 rooms. Facilities: restaurant, disabled access, ski rentals and trails, exercise rooms, gift store, rooms for nonsmokers. AE, DC, MC, V. Moderate–Expensive.*

Rovaniemi
Dining and Lodging

Hotel Gasthof. Set in the center of Rovaniemi, the Gasthof has rooms that are extremely homey and bright, with parquet floors and soft, subtle lighting; the furniture is modern, but with soft edges, especially the waterbeds. The saunas have

skylights, and the restaurant features Finnish cuisine. *Koskikatu 41, 96200, tel. 960/23–222, fax 960/23226. 142 rooms. Facilities: restaurant, saunas, indoor pool, seminar room, TV. AE, DC, MC, V. Expensive.*

Hotel Pohjanhovi. Stretched along the shore of the Kemijoki River, this hotel combines modern amenities with quick access to the fells. The rooms are large, with low ceilings and big windows. The decor varies from white-walled rooms with autumn-toned upholstery and wood trim to black walls with light upholstery—for those who have trouble sleeping during the days of the midnight sun. *Pohjanpuistikko 2, 96200, tel. 960/33711, fax 960/313997. 216 rooms, 4 suites. Facilities: restaurant, bar, café, casino, tennis courts, fishing, saunas, boat rental, conference rooms. AE, DC, MC, V. Expensive.*

Hotel Lapponia. Opened in 1992, this hotel is in the heart of Rovaniemi. The decor is modern, with light blue, gray, and brown color schemes in the rooms. Some have individual saunas and some are equipped with Jacuzzis. *Koskikatu 23, 96200, tel. 960/33–661, fax 960/313770. 167 rooms. Facilities: 5 restaurants, nightclub, bar, saunas, rooms for nonsmokers. AE, DC, MC, V. Expensive.*

Hotelli Oppipoika. Attached to one of Finland's premier hotelier and restaurateur schools, good service and an especially fine restaurant are prime attractions here. The modern rooms have pressed birch paneling and large windows. *Korkalonkatu 33, 96200, tel. 960/20321, fax 960/346969. 40 rooms. Facilities: restaurant, TV, indoor pool, gymnasium, sauna, conference room. AE, DC, MC, V. Moderate.*

Saariselkä
Dining

Riekonkieppi. Fully renovated in 1992, this family restaurant serves regional and Continental fare. The specialties are reindeer and fish. Two menus offer either inexpensive or moderate prices. *Hotel Riekonkieppi, Raitopolku 2, tel. 9697/81711. Reservations accepted. Dress: casual. AE, DC, MC, V. Closed May. Moderate.*

Dining and Lodging

Saariselkä Spa. Finished in 1990, this hotel features a luxurious spa center. The glass-domed swimming area is crammed with foliage, fountains, water slides, wave machines, and a Jacuzzi; the solarium, saunas, and Turkish baths are adjacent. The guest rooms' decor includes pressed blond and dark wood, slate-blue carpet, and textile bedspreads in muted blues, purples, and pinks. Moderately priced cabin accommodations also are available. Note that the breakfast and spa facilities are included in prices. Children 7–14 stay at half price; children under seven for free. The bus stops at the hotel. *99830 Saariselkä, tel. 9697/8121, fax 9697/812328. 37 rooms, 36 apartment cabins. Facilities: restaurant, tennis, squash, bodybuilding gym, weight-lifting equipment, table tennis, field sports, conference rooms. AE, DC, MC, V. Expensive–Very Expensive.*

Hotelli Riekonkieppi. The piney comfort of the rooms and the quietude of the setting make this a good Lapland base. *Lutontie, 99830, tel. 9697/81711. 104 rooms. Facilities: saunas, health center, tennis and squash courts, pools. AE, DC, MC, V. Closed Oct., May. Moderate.*

Tankavaara
Dining

Wanha Waskoolimies. In the tradition of the old gold prospectors, the rustic simplicity of the three rooms hewn from logs makes a pleasant change. Daily specials "Fish in the Gold Pan" and "Prospectors Beef" will give you a taste of simple Lapland fare; the restaurant has received the Lappi à la Carte gourmet

citation. *Tankavaara, tel. 9693/46158. Reservations accepted. Dress: casual. AE, DC, MC, V. Moderate.*

Dining and Lodging **Hotel Korundi.** In a quiet setting just off the Arctic Highway, this hotel has cozy, contemporary rooms for two to five people, each with its own fireplace. The restaurant is in a separate building. *99695 Tankavaara, tel. 9693/46158, fax 9693/46261. 8 rooms (7 with shower). Facilities: saunas. AE, DC, MC, V. Moderate.*

The Lakelands

Nearly 200,000 lakes dimple Finland's gentle topography, according to recent counts. Nearly every lake, big or small, is fringed with tiny cabins. The lake cabin is a Finnish institution, and until the recent advent of cheap package tours abroad, nearly every Finnish family vacationed in the same way—in their cabin on a lake.

In general, the larger towns of this region are much less appealing than the smaller lake locales. But Savonlinna stands out among the towns, not only for its stunning, waterbound views—it is hugged by gigantic Lake Saimaa—but for its cultural life. The month-long Savonlinna Opera Festival in July is one of Finland's greatest. The quality of the opera, ballet, drama, and instrumental performance here during the annual festival weeks is world-class. Most events are staged at the 14th-century Olavinlinna Castle, splendidly positioned just offshore.

For centuries the lakeland region was a buffer between the warring empires of Sweden and Russia. After visiting the people of the Lakelands, you should have a basic understanding of the Finnish word *sisu* (guts), a quality that has kept Finns independent.

Important Addresses and Numbers

Tourist Information The main offices are in **Heinola** (Torikatu 8, 18100, tel. 918/158–444), **Hämeenlinna** (Sibeliuksenkatu 5, 13100, tel. 917/142–877), **Imatra** (Liikekeskus Mansikkapaikka, PL 22, 55121, tel. 954/681–2505), **Joensuu/North Karelia** (Koskikatu 1, 80100, tel. 973/167–5300), **Jyväskylä** (Vapaudenkatu 38, 40100, tel. 941/624–903), **Kuopio** (Haapaniemenkatu 17, 70100, tel. 971/182–590), **Lahti** (Torikatu 3B, PL 175, 15111, tel. 918/818–2580), **Lappeenranta** (Linja-auto asema, PL113, 53101, tel. 953/415–6860), **Mikkeli** (Hallituskatu 3A, 50100, tel. 955/151–444), **Savonlinna** (Puistokatu 1, 57100, tel. 957/273–492), and **Tampere** (Verkatehtaankatu 2, PL 87, 33211, 33100, tel. 931/126–652).

Emergencies The nationwide emergency number is 112; it can be used to call police and ambulance services. A major hospital is **Tampere Keskussairaala** (Tampere Central Hospital, Teiskontie 35, Tampere, tel. 931/247–5111). For dental care call Hammaslääkäri Päivystys (Dentists' 24-Hour Service, tel. 931/100178).

Late-Night Pharmacies Late-night pharmacies are found only in large towns. Look under *Apteekki* in the phone book; listings include pharmacy hours.

Arriving and Departing by Plane

Airports in the Lakelands are at **Tampere, Mikkeli, Jyväsky-lä, Varkaus, Lappeenranta, Savonlinna, Kuopio,** and **Joensuu.**
Flight time to the Savonlinna area from Helsinki is 40 minutes.
All the airports are served by Finnair's domestic service, in-cluding the KarAir charter company.

Arriving and Departing by Car, Train, and Bus

By Car   The region is vast, so the route you choose will depend on your
destination. Consult the **Finnish Automobile Association** (*see*
Getting Around, By Car, in Staying in Finland, *above*) or tour-ist boards for route advice.

The Joensuu–Kuopio–Lahti–Tampere road belt will transport
you quickly from one major point to the next, but if you are go-ing to be taking a lake vacation you will usually finish your jour-ney on small roads. The last stretch to the *mökki* (cabin) may be
unpaved. You will need a detailed map to find most mökkis,
which tend to be tucked away in well-hidden spots.

By Train Trains run from Helsinki to Lahti, Mikkeli, Imatra, Lappeen-ranta, Joensuu, and Jyväskylä. There is sleeping-car service to
Joensuu and Kuopio, and in summer only, to Savonlinna. The
trip from Helsinki to Savonlinna takes 5½ hours.

By Bus   Buses are the best form of public transport into the region,
with frequent connections to lake destinations from most major
towns. It is a six-hour ride from Helsinki to Savonlinna.

Guided Tours

Orientation   The Lakelands are well served by tours, most of which employ
boat service. Try some of these boat tours: **Western Lakeland
Silverline and Poets' Way Tour** (Verkatehtaankatu 2, 33100 Tam-pere, tel. 931/124–803), **Western Lakeland and Lake Päijänne
Tour** (Lake Päijänne Cruises, Pellonpää, 40820 Haapaniemi,
tel. 941/618–885), and **Saimaa Lakeland** (Roll Line Ltd.,
Matkustajasatama, 70100 Kuopio, tel. 971/262–6744). There
are dozens of other boat-tour companies operating in the
Lakelands; contact the **Finnish Tourist Board Head Office**
(Suomen Matkatoimisto, Töölönkatu 11, PL265, 00101 Helsin-ki, tel. 90/403–011) or local tourist offices in the region for a
complete list as well as details of routes.

Special-Interest   Avid canoers should contact the **Finnish Canoe Association**
(Radiokatu 20, 00240 Helsinki, tel. 90/158–2363); almost all of
its 66 clubs arrange guided tours; canoes are rented at about
FM100 per day. **Lomaväline Ky** (Seminaarinraitti 9, 18100
Heinola, tel. 918/143–523) arranges numerous lakeland canoe
tours ranging in length from 2 to 15 days.

Two agencies that do white-water trips and canoe safaris in the
region are **Ikaalinen Tourist Service** (Valtakatu 7, 39500, tel.
933/450–1221) and **Lieksan Matkailu Oy** (Pielisentie 7, 81700
Lieksa, tel. 975/520–1500).

Many sailing schools operate in the lakes region, with courses
for sailors of all levels. Contact either the **Finnish Yachting As-sociation** (Radiokatu 20, Helsinki, tel. 90/158–2326) or the
Nautic Center (Lautkankaile, 21570 Sauvo, tel. 921/730–192).

Guided fishing tours are offered by **Heinola Matkailupalvelu** (Torikatu 8, 18100 Heinola, tel. 918/158–444).

Exploring the Lakelands

Numbers in the margin correspond to points of interest on the Lakelands map.

Savonlinna
❶ The center of **Savonlinna** is a series of islands linked by bridges. First, stop in at the tourist office for information; then cross the bridge east to the open-air market that flourishes alongside the main passenger quay. It's from here that you can catch the boat to Kuopio. In days when waterborne traffic was the major form of transportation, Savonlinna was the central hub of the passenger fleet serving Saimaa, the largest lake system in Europe. Now the lake traffic is dominated by cruise and sightseeing boats, but the quayside still bustles with arrivals and departures every summer morning and evening.

A 10-minute stroll from the quay to the southeast brings you to Savonlinna's most famous sight, the castle of **Olavinlinna.** First built in 1475 to protect Finland's eastern border, the castle retains its medieval character and is one of Scandinavia's best-preserved historic monuments. Still surrounded by water that once formed part of its defensive strength, the fortress rises majestically out of the lake. The Savonlinna Opera Festival (tel. 957/514700 or 957/273492) is held in the courtyard each July. The combination of music and setting is spellbinding. You will need to make reservations well in advance, for both tickets and hotel rooms, as Savonlinna becomes a mecca for music lovers. And music is not the only activity; arts and crafts are also strongly featured in exhibits around town. *Admission (castle): FM14 adults, FM7 children; includes a guided tour. Open June–Aug., daily 10–5; Sept.–May, daily 10–3.*

Close to the castle are the 19th-century steam schooners, *Salama*, *Mikko*, and *Savonlinna*, which house an excellent museum on the history of lake traffic, including the fascinating floating timber trains that are still a common sight on Saimaa today. *Admission: FM12 adults, FM6 children. Open June–Aug., daily 10–8; Sept.–May, Tues.–Sun. 11–5.*

❷ The most popular excursion from Savonlinna is to **Retretti.** You can take either a 2-hour boat ride or a 30-minute, 29-kilometer (18-mile) bus trip. The journey by bus takes you along the 8-
❸ kilometer (5-mile) ridge of **Punkaharju.** This amazing ridge of pine-covered rocks, which rises out of the water and separates the lakes on either side, predates the Ice Age. At times it narrows to only 25 feet, yet it still manages to accommodate a road and train tracks. Retretti itself is a modern art complex of unique design, which includes a new cavern section built into Punkaharju ridge. It's also a magnificent setting for concerts in summer. *Admission: FM60 adults, FM55 senior citizens and students, FM25 children. Open May 21–June and Aug., daily 10–6; July, daily 10–7.*

Kuopio
❹ The 12-hour boat trip from Savonlinna to **Kuopio** is probably the best opportunity you'll get to feel the soul of the Finnish Lakelands. Meals are available on board. The boat arrives at Kuopio passenger harbor, where you'll find a small evening market in action daily from 3 to 10.

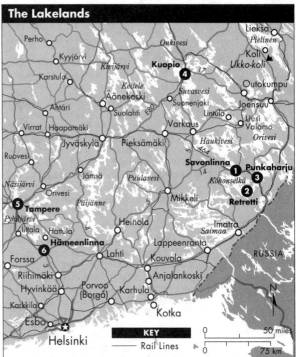

The Lakelands

The Kuopio tourist office is located close to the **Tori** (market-place). The Tori should be one of the places you visit first, for it is one of the most colorful outdoor markets in Finland. *Open May–Aug., Mon.–Sat. 7–3; Sept.–Apr., Mon.–Sat. 7–2. Closed national holidays.*

The **Ortodoksinen Kirkkomuseo** (Orthodox Church Museum) has one of the most interesting and unusual collections of its kind in the world. When Karelia was ceded to what was then the Soviet Union after World War II, the religious art was taken out of the monasteries and brought to Kuopio. The collection is eclectic and, of its type, one of the rarest in the world. *Karjalankatu 1, Kuopio, tel. 971/261–8818. Open May–Aug., Tues.–Sun. 10–4; Sept.–Apr., weekdays noon–3, weekends noon–5.*

Visitors who are fascinated by the treasures in the museum will want to visit the Orthodox convent of Lintula and the **Valamon Luostari** (Monastery of Valamo). The monastery is a center for Russian Orthodox religious and cultural life in Finland. The precious 18th-century icons and sacred objects are housed in the main church and in the icon conservation center. The Orthodox library is the most extensive in Finland and is open to visitors. Church services are held daily. *Uusi Valamo, tel. 972/ 61911 (972/61959 for hotel reservations). Guided tours: FM20 adults, FM5 children. Open May and Aug. 11–Sept. 30, daily 10–6; June and Aug. 1–10, daily 9 AM–10 PM; July, daily 9 AM– midnight.*

The **Lintulan Luostari** (Convent of Lintula) can be reached by boat from Valamo, or you can visit both the convent and the monastery by boat on scenic day excursions from Kuopio (tourist office; tickets: FM240 adults, FM125 children; June 10–Aug. 13).

Puijon Näkötorni (Puijo Tower) is best visited at sunset, when the lakes shimmer with reflected light. The slender tower is located 3 kilometers (2 miles) northwest of Kuopio. It has two observation decks and a revolving restaurant on top where you can enjoy the marvelous views. *Open June 1–Aug. 15, daily 9 AM–10 PM; Aug. 16–May 31, daily 10–6.*

Tampere ❺ The 320-kilometer (192-mile) journey from Kuopio to **Tampere** will take four to five hours, whether you travel by car or bus. The train ride from Helsinki to Tampere takes about two hours.

Tampere, the country's second-largest city, is an industrial center with a difference. From about the year 1000, this part of Finland was a base from which traders and hunters set out on their expeditions to northern Finland and even to Lapland. But it was not until 1779 that a Swedish king, Gustav III, actually founded Tampere. Eighty-three years later, Scotsman James Finlayson came to the infant city and established a factory for spinning cotton. This was perhaps the beginning of "big business" in Finland. The firm of Finlayson exists today and is still one of the country's major industrial enterprises.

Artful location is the secret of Tampere's many factories. An isthmus little more than half a mile wide at its narrowest point separates the lakes Näsijärvi and Pyhäjärvi, and at one spot the Tammerkoski Rapids provide an outlet for the waters of one to cascade through to the other. Called the "Mother of Tampere," these rapids once provided the electrical power on which the town's livelihood depended. Their natural beauty has been preserved in spite of the factories on either bank, and the well-designed public buildings of the city grouped around them enhance their general effect. Also in the heart of town is **Hämeensilta Bridge,** with its four statues by the well-known Finnish sculptor Wäinö Aaltonen.

Close to the Hämeensilta bridge, near the high-rise Hotel Ilves, are some old factory buildings that have been restored as shops and boutiques. Nearby, at Verkatehtaankatu 2, is the city tourist office.

Parts of the ridge of **Pyynikki** separating the two lakes form a natural park, including the Särkänniemi peninsula, about a 20-minute walk northwest of the city center. On the way there, visit one of Tampere's best small museums, Amurin **Työläiskort-telimuseo** (The Amuri Museum of Workers' Housing). It consists of a block of old timber houses, with descriptions and illustrations of how the original tenants lived; it is so well done that you half expect them to return at any minute. *Makasiininkatu 12. Admission: FM10 adults, FM3 children. Open May 11–Sept. 19, Tues.–Sat. 9–5, Sun. 11–5.*

A 1.5-kilometer (1-mile) walk from the heart of Tampere is the **Särkänniemen Huvikeskus** (Särkäniemi Amusement Center). The seven attractions at the Center include Finland's tallest structure, the 168-meter (550-foot) **Näsinneulan Näkötorni** (Näsinneula Observatory Tower), the aquarium, the

planetarium, the dolphinarium, the children's zoo, and the Sara Hildén Art Museum, a striking example of Finnish architecture where the works of modern Finnish and international artists (including Miró, Leger, Picasso, and Chagall) are on display. *Särkäniemi, tel. 931/248–8111. Admission: Särkäniemi Passport (dolphinarium and 3 other attractions) FM60 adults, FM30 children 4–11; individual attractions FM10–30 adults, FM3–15 children. Check locally for museum hours and exhibitions; children's zoo open May–Aug., daily 10–6 or 7; other attractions open Apr.–Aug., daily 10–10 (check locally).*

At the foot of the Pyynikki Ridge is the **Pynnikin Kesäteatteri** (Pyynikki Open Air Theater), with a revolving auditorium that can be moved, even with a full load of spectators, to face any one of the sets.

On the east side of the town is the modern **Kalevan Kirkko** (Kaleva Church). What may appear from the outside to be a grain elevator is in fact, as seen from the interior, a soaring monument to space and light. *Open May–Aug., daily 10–6; Sept.–Apr., daily 11–1.*

Most buildings in Tampere, including the cathedral, are comparatively modern. However, though the cathedral was built only in 1907, it is worth a visit to see some of the best-known masterpieces of Finnish art, including Magnus Encknell's frescoes, *The Resurrection*, and a few by Hugo Simberg, including *Wounded Angel* and *Garden of Death*.

It was in Tampere that Lenin and Stalin first met, and this fateful occasion is commemorated with displays of photos and mementoes in the **Lenin-Museo** (Lenin Museum). *Hämeenpuisto 28. Admission: FM10 adults, FM3 children. Open Mon.–Fri. 9–5, weekends 11–4.*

Only 3 kilometers (2 miles) from the city center is the **Haiharan Nukke ja Pukumuseo** (Haihara Doll and Costume Museum), which exhibits thousands of dolls from all over the world dating from the 12th to the 20th century. Costumes are mainly Finnish from the 19th century. *Hatanpää valtatie 34, D 403, tel. 931/22626. Admission: FM10 adults, FM3 children. Open June–Aug., weekdays noon–4; Sept.–May, Sun.–Fri. noon–4; closed Sat.*

One of the most popular excursions from Tampere is the **Runoilijan Tie** (Poet's Way) boat tour along Lake Näsijärvi. The boat passes through the agricultural parish of Ruovesi, where J. L. Runeberg, Finland's national poet, used to live. Shortly before the boat docks at Virrat, you'll pass through the straits of Visuvesi, where many artists and writers spend their summers. *Finnish Silverline and Poet's Way, Verkatehtaankatu 2, 33100 Tampere, tel. 931/124–804. Round-trip fare: FM220.*

Not far north of Virrat is **Ähtäri**, where Finland's first wildlife park has been established in a beautiful setting, with a holiday village, a good hotel, and recreation facilities.

Hämeenlinna
❻
The Silverline's white motor ships leave Tampere for **Hämeenlinna** from the Laukontori terminal. If you're traveling by car, take Highway 3 and stop en route at the famous **Iittalan Lasikeskus** (Iittala Glassworks), which offers guided tours and has a museum and shop. The magnificent glass is produced by

top designers, and the "seconds" are bargains you won't find elsewhere. *Open Jan.–Apr., daily 10–6; May–Aug., daily 9–8; Sept.–mid-Nov., daily 10–6; mid-Nov.–Dec., weekdays 10–8, weekends 10–6.*

Hämeenlinna's secondary school has educated many famous Finns, among them composer Jean Sibelius (1865–1957). The only surviving timber house in the town center is the **birthplace of Sibelius,** a modest dwelling built in 1834. Here you can listen to tapes of his music and see the harmonium he played when he was a child. *Hallituskatu 11. Admission: FM10 adults, FM5 children. Open May–Aug., daily 10–4; Sept.–Apr., Sun. noon–4.*

The much-altered medieval **Hämeen Linna** (Häme Castle), on the lakeshore half a mile north of the town center, doesn't compare with Savonlinna's, but it has seen a lot of action in its time and has also been used as a granary and a prison. *Admission (includes guided tour): FM14 adults, FM7 children. Open May–Aug., daily 10–6; Sept.–Apr., daily 10–4.*

Hattulan Kirkko (Hattula Church), 6 kilometers (3½ miles) to the north, is the most famous of Finland's medieval churches. The interior is a fresco gallery of biblical scenes whose vicious little devils and soulful saints are as clear and fresh as when they were first painted around 1510. There is regular bus service from the town center. *Admission: FM10 adults, FM5 children. Open mid-May–mid-Aug., daily 10–4.*

Rail and bus schedules to Helsinki are frequent. If you're traveling by car, take Highway 3. As you pass by **Riihimäki,** you'll see signs to the **Suomen Lasimuseo** (Finnish Glass Museum). Follow them! It's an outstanding display of the history of glass from early Egyptian times to the present, beautifully arranged in an old glass factory. *Tehtaankatu 21, Riihimäki, tel. 914/741–494. Admission: FM10 adults, FM5 children. Open Apr.–Sept., daily 10–6. Closed Oct.–Mar.*

What to See and Do with Children

In **Outokumpu,** directly north of Savonlinna, is the **Vuoren Peikon Leikkipuisto** (Land of the Mountain Troll), with an amusement park, a mining museum, and a mineral exhibition. *Kiisukatu 6, tel. 973/54795.*

Retretti Taidekeskus (the Retretti Art Center) at Punkaharju near Savonlinna has over 40 different indoor and outdoor activities scheduled for children throughout the summer.

In **Mikkeli,** the **Visulahden Matkailukeskus** (Visulahti Tourist Center), 5 kilometers (3 miles) from town, includes a waxworks, an old car museum, and an amusement park.

Shopping

Wild mushrooms and berries are abundant in this region, and Finns make use of all of them. The various **preserves**—jams, compotes, and sauces included—are all delicacies and make good gifts; Finns eat them with thin pancakes.

Many towns in this region have **textile** workshops or factories, called *Tekstiilitehdas* or *Tekstiilimyymälä,* featuring woven **wall hangings** and **rya rugs** (*ryijy* in Finnish). **Ceramics** (*Kera-*

miikkamyymälä) works selling dishes and pottery are also scattered throughout the region; the soil here produces a rich clay.

If you want to go to the source of one of Finland's biggest manufacturers of **cross-country skis,** you'll find it right off Hartola's main street, at **Peltosen Suksitehdas** (Peltonen Ski Factory, Rajatie 1, tel. 918/161–601). Call ahead for a guided tour.

Many lake towns have traditional **outdoor markets,** usually on Saturday. Most sell produce. In the autumn you'll find slightly larger markets when towns have their September fairs. These vestiges of harvest festivals are now mostly excuses to hold fun fairs and consume coffee and doughnuts.

Sports and Outdoor Activities

Canoeing The Finlandia Canoe Relay lasts for a week in mid-June. During a grueling seven days, the 400–500-kilometer (250–310-mile) relay is a real test of endurance. For information on where in the Lakelands region the race will kick off, contact the **Finnish Canoe Association** (tel. 90/1582363). **Kymen Matkailu ry** (Varuskuntakatu 11, 45100 Kouvola, tel. 951/312–1763) offers special canoe tours (*see also* Special-interest Tours, *above*).

Golf **Karelia Golf** (80780 Kontioniemi, tel. 973/732–411) is one of Finland's best 18-hole golf courses. If you want to play on an 18-hole lakeside course, ask at Hämeenlinna's **Hotel Vaakuna** (Possentie 7, 13200 Hämeenlinna, tel. 917/5831).

Sailing **Saimaa Sailing Oy** (Kimpisenkatu 22, 53100 Lappeenranta, tel. 953/411–8560) has four-day courses for groups of four to five that are worked into all-inclusive vacation packages. The base is the handsome, historic coastal town of **Lappeenranta.** Sailing vacation packages are also organized by **Joensuun Pursiseura** (Joensuu Sailing Club, Box 227, Joensuu). For other areas contact the **Finnish Yachting Association** (Radiokatu 29, Helsinki, tel. 90/158–2326). (*See* Special-interest Tours, *above*.) Europe's biggest inland sailing race, the Päijänne Regatta, takes place yearly in July. Contact the Finnish Yachting Association for details.

Windsurfing There are numerous windsurfing centers on the shores of Lakes Saimaa and Paijanne. Contact the **Finnish Windsurfing Association** (c/o the Finnish Yachting Association, Radiokatu 29, Helsinki, tel. 90/158–2326).

Dining and Lodging

For details and price category definitions, *see* Dining in Staying in Finland, *above*. Highly recommended establishments are indicated by a star ★.

Hämeenlinna **Fransmanni.** Located in one of the city's foremost hotels
Dining (Vaakuna), this country-French-style restaurant specializes in dishes such as grilled chicken or pepper steak. *Possentie 7, Hämeenlinna, tel. 917/5831. Reservations accepted. AE, DC, MC, V. Expensive.*
Piiparkakkutalo. Located in a renovated old timber building, Piiparkakkutalo has a restaurant upstairs, a pub downstairs. The menu offers fine Finnish fare. *Kirkkorinne 2, tel. 917/121–606. Reservations advised. AE, DC, MC, V. Expensive.*

Lodging **Rantasipi Aulanko.** One of Finland's top hotels sits on the lake-
★ shore in a beautifully landscaped park 6.4 kilometers (2 miles)
from town. *14999, tel. 917/58–801, fax 917/21922. 245 rooms.
Facilities: nightclub, saunas, pool, tennis, golf, riding, boating, tax-free shop. AE, DC, MC, V. Very Expensive (Moderate
in July).*

Kuopio **Mustalammas.** Located near the passenger harbor, Mustalam-
Dining mas has been attractively adapted from a beer cellar and features steaks and basic fish dishes. *Satamakatu 4, tel. 971/262–
3494. Reservations advised. AE, DC, MC, V. Expensive.*
Sampo. Situated in the town center, Sampo specializes in ven-
dace *(muikku)*, a kind of whitefish. Try the smoked variety.
The atmosphere is unpretentious and lively. *Kauppakatu 13,
tel. 971/261–4677. AE, MC, V. Moderate.*

Lodging **Arctia.** Completed in 1987, the Arctia is the most modern and
best equipped of local hotels. It has all the advantages of a lake-
front location and is close to the center of town. *Satamakatu 1,
70100, tel. 971/195–111, fax 971/195170. 141 rooms. Facilities:
sauna, swimming pool, Jacuzzi, solarium, boat rental. AE,
DC, MC, V. Expensive.*
Rauhalahti. About 5 kilometers (3 miles) from the town center,
Rauhalahti is set near the lakeshore and has a number of amenities catering to sportsmen and families. The hotel has three
restaurants, including the tavern-style Vanha Apteekkari—a
local favorite. *Katiskaniementie 8 70700, tel. 971/311–700, fax
971/311843. 106 rooms (Expensive), 15 apartments (Moderate), 5 youth-hostel rooms (Inexpensive). Facilities: saunas,
swimming pool, solarium, tropical spa, gymnasium, children's playroom, tennis, horseback riding, squash, boat rental, rock climbing. AE, DC, MC, V. Expensive.*
Hotelli Iso-Valkeinen. On the lakeshore only 5 kilometers (3
miles) from the town center, this hotel has large, quiet rooms.
*Päiväranta, 70420, tel. 971/341444, fax 971/341344. 100 rooms
with shower. Facilities: 4 restaurants, 2 saunas, swimming
pool, minigolf, tennis, swimming beach, fishing, boat rental,
nightclub. DC, MC, V. Moderate.*

Savonlinna **Rauhalinna.** This romantic turn-of-the-century timber villa
Dining was built by a general in the Imperial Russian Army. From
town it's 16 kilometers (10 miles) by road, 40 minutes by boat.
Both food and atmosphere are old Russian, but some Finnish
specialties are also available. *Lehtiniemi, tel. 957/523–119 (for
special bookings in winter tel. 957/57–500). Reservations required during festival season. AE, DC, MC, V. Closed Sept.–
May. Expensive.*
Ravintola Hopeasalmi. Right on the market square is a 100-
year-old steamboat that has been converted into a restaurant, a
pizzeria (Moderate), and a pub. The restaurant specializes in
generous portions of local fish such as *muikku* (a small local
freshwater fish). *Kauppatori, tel. 957/21701. Reservations advised. DC, MC, V. Closed mid-Sept.–Apr. Expensive.*
Snellman. This small 1920s-style mansion is in the center of
town. Meals are served against a quiet background of classical
music. Among the specialties of the house are cold-salted salmon and steak with morel sauce. *Olavinkatu 31, tel. 957/273104.
Reservations advised. AE, DC, MC, V. Expensive.*
Majakka. Centrally located, Majakka goes in for home cooking
and a family atmosphere. *Satamakatu 11, tel. 957/21456. Res-*

ervations required during festival season. AE, DC, V. Moderate.

Paviljonki. Just 1 kilometer (½ mile) from the city center is Paviljonki, the restaurant of the Savonlinna restaurant school. It serves homemade Finnish dishes. *Rajalahdenkatu 4, tel. 957/520960. V. Inexpensive.*

Lodging **Casino Spa.** Built in the 1960s and renovated in 1986, the Casino Spa has a restful lakeside location on an island linked to the center of town by a pedestrian bridge. *Kylpylaitoksentie, Kasinonsaari, 57130, tel. 957/57–500, fax 957/272524. 80 rooms. Facilities: restaurant, saunas, pool, marina, spa treatment. AE, DC, MC, V. Expensive.*

Savonlinna Seurahuone. This old town house is located near the market and passenger harbor. A new extension opened in 1989. Some older rooms are small. *Kauppatori 4, 57130, tel. 957/5731, fax 957/273918. 84 rooms. Facilities: 2 restaurants, bar, nightclub, saunas. AE, DC, MC, V. Expensive.*

Punkaharju Valtion Hotelli. A manor house with small rooms decorated in the old Finnish country style, the hotel is located a half hour's drive from Savonlinna. *58450 Punkaharju, tel. 957/441761, fax 957/441784. 30 rooms. Facilities: restaurant. DC, MC, V. Closed Sept.–mid-May. Moderate.*

Vuorilinna Summer Hotel. The simple white rooms of this modern student dorm become a hotel in summer. Guests may use the facilities, including the restaurant, of the nearby Casino Spa hotel. *Kasinonsaari, 57130, tel. 957/57500, fax 957/272524. 230 rooms, with shower, toilet, and kitchenette for every 2 rooms. AE, DC, MC, V. Closed mid-Aug.–late June. Moderate.*

Hospits. In the heart of Savonlinna overlooking Saimaa lake, this YMCA hotel has small, unpretentious rooms, many of which were refurbished in 1992. *Linnankatu 20, 57130, tel. 957/22443, fax 957/515120. 20 rooms. Facilities: breakfast room, sauna. V. Inexpensive.*

Tampere **Natalie.** Russian in atmosphere, cuisine, and background mu-
Dining sic, the Natalie is housed in the old Workers' Theater near the center of town. *Hallituskatu 19, tel. 931/232–040. Reservations advised. AE, DC, MC, V. Moderate.*

Salud Bodega. The Salud has a well-earned reputation for Spanish specialties, though it also features a few Finnish dishes. *Otavalankatu 10, tel. 931/235–996. Reservations advised. DC, MC, V. Moderate.*

Silakka. Although its atmosphere is casual and unpretentious, the Silakka has earned an excellent reputation for its Finnish fish specialties. *Hätänpään valtatie 1, tel. 931/149–740. DC, MC, V. Moderate.*

Lodging **Ilves.** This hotel soars above a newly gentrified area of old warehouses near the city center. It is favored by Americans. *Hätänpään valtatie 1, 33100, tel. 931/121–212, fax 931/132565. 336 rooms. Facilities: 3 restaurants, gymnasium, nightclub, saunas, pool, Jacuzzi, rooms for nonsmokers. AE, DC, MC, V. Very Expensive.*

Cumulus Koskikatu. Overlooking the tamed rapids of Tammerkoski, Cumulus Koskikatu is central and modern. The Finnair terminal is in the same building. *Koskikatu 5, 33100, tel. 931/242-4111, fax 931/242-4399. 230 rooms with shower. Facilities: restaurant, bar, nightclub, saunas, pool. AE, DC, MC, V. Expensive.*

Domus Summer Hotel. About 3 kilometers (2 miles) from the center of town, in the Kaleva district, this hotel is a good value. *Pellervonkatu 9, 33540, tel. 931/550–000, fax 931/225409. 200 rooms, 85 with shower. Facilities: disco, saunas, pool. MC, V. Closed Sept.–May. Inexpensive.*

The Arts and Nightlife

The Arts These are limited in the Lakelands to the museums and galleries in the larger towns, and the occasional visiting exhibition or act in summer. For more information, consult local tourist boards.

Nightlife Hotels and restaurants usually serve alcohol until midnight, and almost every town has its basic tavern or pub. In the larger towns, look for such chain-restaurant establishments as **Rosso** and **Martina** for a relaxed eating and drinking atmosphere.

4   Iceland

*By Jon Asgeir
Sigurðsson*

*Updated by Anne
Yates*

On the highway from Keflavík Airport into Iceland's capital, Reykjavík, the traveler is met by an eerie moonscape under a steel-gray sky. The flat terrain is barely covered by its thin scalp of luminescent green moss. Here and there columns of steam rise from hot spots in the lava fields. While trees are few and far between, an occasional scrawny shrub clings to a rock outcropping. The very air smells different—clean and crisp—and it's so clear here you can see for miles.

Welcome to Iceland, one of the most dramatic natural spectacles on this planet. It is a land of dazzling white glaciers and rugged black lava fields, of red sulfur, blue hot springs, and green, green valleys. This North Atlantic island offers insight into the ferocious powers of nature, ranging from the still-warm lava of the Vestmannaeyjar volcanic eruption in 1973 to the chilling splendor of the Vatnajökull glacier. Generally the country is barren, with hardly a tree to be seen, but its few birches, wildflowers, and delicate vegetation are all the more lovely in contrast. Contrary to the country's forbidding name, the climate is surprisingly mild.

Located so far north—parts of the country touch the Arctic Circle—Iceland has the usual Scandinavian long hours of darkness in winter. This may be why Icelanders are such good chess players (Iceland played host to the memorable Fischer-Spassky chess match of 1972). These long nights may also explain why, per capita, more books are written, printed, bought, and read in Iceland than anywhere else in the world. The birth rate is unusually high for Europe, too!

Another reason for this near-universal literacy may be Iceland's long tradition of participatory democracy, dating from AD 930, when the first parliament met at Þingvellir. Today it's a modern Nordic (most would find the term "Scandinavian" too limited) society with a well-developed social welfare system. Women have a unique measure of equality: Because children are given a surname created from their father's first name, Magnús, son of Svein, becomes Magnús Sveinsson, while Guðrún, daughter of Pétur, becomes Guðrún Pétursdóttir, and Guðrún keeps her maiden name even after she marries, though her children will take a patronymic from their father's first name. Perhaps there is no connection, but it is interesting to note that in 1980 Iceland also elected the first woman president in Europe, Vigdís Finnbogadóttir.

Iceland was settled by Vikings and Celts more than a thousand years ago (the first Norse settlers arrived in AD 874, but there is some evidence that Irish monks landed even earlier). The Norse Sagas, describing the adventures of life in the Viking era, were written by Icelanders, and modern Icelandic is remarkably close to Old Norse. The Norsemen brought to the island sturdy horses, robust cattle, and Celtic slaves, which is why you'll see so many redheads here today. Perhaps Irish tales of the supernatural spawned Iceland's traditional lore of the *huldufólk*, or "hidden people," said to reside in splendor in rocks and crags. Even today some roads and construction projects may be changed to accommodate elfin homes.

Iceland is the westernmost outpost of Europe, 800 kilometers (500 miles) from the nearest European landfall (in Scotland) and nearly 1,600 kilometers (1,000 miles) from Copenhagen, which was its administrative capital during Danish rule from

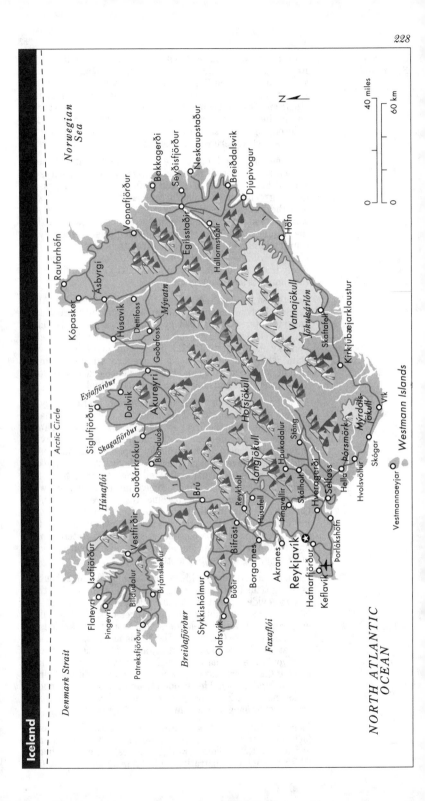

Iceland

Denmark Strait

Norwegian Sea

Raufarhöfn

Arctic Circle

Kópasker

Ásbyrgi

Vopnafjörður

Bakkagerði

Seyðisfjörður

Neskaupstaður

Breiðdalsvik

Djúpivogur

Húsavik

Dettifoss

Mývatn

Egilsstaðir

Hallormsstaður

Höfn

Goðafoss

Eyjafjörður

Siglufjörður

Dalvik

Akureyri

Vatnajökull

Jökulsárlón

Skaftafell

Kirkjubæjarklaustur

Skagafjörður

Blönduós

Hofsjökull

Húnaflói

Sauðárkrókur

Brú

Vestfirðir

Ísafjörður

Bíldudalur

Brjánslækur

Þingeyri

Flateyri

Patreksfjörður

Langjökull

Haukadalur

Stöng

Myrdalsjökull

Vik

Þórsmörk

Skógar

Reykholt

Húsafell

Þingvellir

Skálholt

Hveragerði

Selfoss

Hella

Hvolsvöllur

Bifröst

Borgarnes

Akranes

Reykjavik

Hafnarfjörður

Keflavik

Þorlákshöfn

Breiðafjörður

Stykkishólmur

Búðir

Ólafsvik

Faxaflói

Vestmannaeyjar

Westmann Islands

NORTH ATLANTIC OCEAN

N

40 miles

60 km

0

0

1380 to 1944. Located in the middle of the North Atlantic, where the warm Gulf Stream from the south confronts the icy Arctic currents from the north, it also straddles the mid-Atlantic ridge, where the edges of two tectonic plates, the North American and the European, meet. As the plates slowly move apart, they create the volcanic activity by which Iceland is still being formed. (There has been an eruption in Iceland on an average of every five years during the past few centuries, the latest being that of Mt. Hekla in January 1991.) Beneath the snowy glaciers and rugged lava are fires that heat hot springs and geysers all over the island, and the resourceful Icelanders have harnessed this thermal energy to heat their homes, power industry, and warm their outdoor swimming pools year-round. Swift glacial rivers produce abundant hydroelectricity.

More than 80% of the island's 103,000 square kilometers (40,000 square miles) remains uninhabited. Ice caps cover 11% of the country, more than 50% is wasteland, and 6% consists of lakes and rivers. Less than 2% of land in Iceland is cultivated, although another 23% is grazing land of varying quality. Surrounded by the sea, the Icelanders have become great fishermen, and fish remains the cornerstone of the Icelandic economy. Seafood exports pay for all the imported foodstuffs and other goods that today's Icelanders require, and which cannot economically be produced in such a small society (population 250,000). Partly because so much has to be imported, prices are steep in Iceland. Hotel and restaurant prices are relatively high, but you can always find a number of inexpensive alternatives for lodging, food, and travel—provided you look.

While the cosmopolitan capital, Reykjavík, is a good place to start your visit, any traveler who wants to know Iceland should venture out into the countryside, where rainbow-arched waterfalls cleave mountains with great spiked ridges and snow-capped peaks. Climb mountains, ford rivers, watch birds, catch trout or salmon, even tend sheep and cattle at a typical Icelandic farm. Although the majority of visitors opt to see the country in the warmest months of June, July, and August, a growing minority choose the winter season, when attractions include downhill and cross-country skiing, snowmobiling, and tours by specially equipped 4×4 vehicles across the snow-blanketed landscape. The ocean here is always too cold for swimming, but the country is full of hot springs and naturally heated pools where Icelanders from all walks of life—from cabinet ministers on down—congregate for a soak or a swim all year round.

Before You Go

Government Tourist Offices

The main office of the **Iceland Tourist Board** is at Gimli, Lækjargata 3, 101 Reykjavík (tel. 1/27488, fax 1/624749). For serious exploring or hiking, you can obtain good up-to-date maps from **Landmælingar Íslands** (the Icelandic Geodetic Survey) at Laugavegi 178, 105 Reykjavík (tel. 1/680999).

In the United States **Icelandic Tourist Board,** 655 3rd Ave., New York, NY 10017, tel. 212/949-2333, fax 212/983-5260.

In the **Icelandair,** 172 Tottenham Court Rd., 3rd floor, London W1P
United Kingdom 9LG, tel. 071/388–5599, fax 071/387–5711, distributes information on behalf of the Iceland Tourist Board.

When to Go

The traditional time to visit is in June, July, and August, and
most travel services are geared to this period. During these
months there is perpetual daylight—in Reykjavík the sun dips
below the horizon for only a couple of twilight hours, and in the
northernmost reaches of the island the sun never sets. Even
during these peak months, traffic on the roads remains light by
international standards, but accommodations at popular destinations may become fully booked, especially if the weather
turns nasty and holidaymakers flee the campsites for better
shelter. Summer prices tend to be higher, but on the other
hand a far wider range of accommodations is available during
these months.

If you visit in the winter, be prepared for long hours of darkness. In December, Iceland enjoys daylight for only three
hours daily, but as a consolation you can watch a spectacular
show of the aurora borealis, the northern lights.

Climate Considering its northerly latitude, Iceland has a surprisingly
temperate climate—Reykjavík's average winter temperature
is one degree Fahrenheit *above* that of New York. The warm
Gulf Stream flows along the western and southern coasts, although this is counteracted by the Arctic current that circles
along the northern and eastern coasts. As a result, conditions
are very changeable and you can get a sampling of all types of
weather in a single afternoon. Paradoxically, the climate is
more stable in the north, with less rain and wind, and in summer it's often warmer there. June, July, and August can be
expected to be partly sunny, breezy, with intermittent
light showers. Summer temperatures seldom rise above 70°F
(20°C). Winters can bring anything from brilliant sunshine and
a crisp frost (ideal for sightseeing by car or bus) to blizzards,
gales, and deluges. You can even experience them all in one
day. The following are average daily maximum and minimum
temperatures for Reykjavík.

Jan.	36F	2C	May	50F	10C	Sept.	52F	11C
	28	– 2		39	4		43	6
Feb.	37F	3C	June	54F	12C	Oct.	45F	7C
	28	– 2		45	7		37	3
Mar.	39F	4C	July	57F	14C	Nov.	39F	4C
	30	– 1		48	9		32	0
Apr.	43F	6C	Aug.	57F	14C	Dec.	36F	2C
	34	1		46	8		28	– 2

Festivals and Seasonal Events

Shops, museums, and businesses are closed on national holidays: Maundy Thursday (March 31), Good Friday (April 1),
Easter Monday (April 4), First Day of Summer (April 21), Labor Day (May 1), Ascension Day (May 12), Whit Monday (May
23), National Day (June 17), Summer Bank Holiday (August 1),
after midday on Christmas Eve (December 24), Christmas Day
(December 25), Boxing Day (December 26), after midday on

New Year's Eve (December 31), and New Year's Day (January 1).

January 21–mid-February: Þorri Banquets around the country feature traditional Icelandic foods and drinks.

March 31–April 4: Easter Weekend sees skiing competitions in Akureyri and Isafjordur.

June 1–19: The Reykjavík Arts Festival, held in even-numbered years, features a wide variety of music and visual arts.

June 12: Sjómannadagur (Seamen's Day) is celebrated in many coastal towns; in Reykjavík there are rowing and swimming competitions, speeches, and an awards ceremony.

June 17: Iceland National Day is a nationwide party, with parades and outdoor dancing downtown in Reykjavík, Akureyri, and other towns. This year the nation celebrates the 50th anniversary of the republic, so events should be particularly memorable.

June 23–26: The Arctic Open Golf Tournament is held, in the Midnight Sun, on the 18-hole golf course at Akureyri.

July–August: The Skálholt Music Festival is held at Skálholt Cathedral in the south from the beginning of July to mid-August. Concerts of Baroque and contemporary music are held every weekend.

July 30–August 1: Bank Holiday Weekend draws large crowds for outdoor celebrations throughout the country.

July 30–August 1: Þjóðhátíð 1874 (National Festival) is celebrated in Vestmannaeyjar (the Westmann Islands).

August: Reykjavík Marathon sends world-class distance runners on their annual race around the city.

What to Pack

Clothing   Wherever and however you plan to travel, be prepared for sudden changes in the weather, and carry a waterproof coat or jacket, a woolen sweater, headgear, and gloves. If your itinerary includes any serious walking, forget the jeans and sneakers. Good walking boots and wool trousers are a must. For traveling in the highlands, proper clothing and equipment is essential, so seek expert advice.

Miscellaneous   The domestic electric supply in Iceland is 220 volts AC (50 cycles). Most hotels have built-in hair dryers. If you need a plug adapter or converter, buy it before leaving home.

Taking Money Abroad

You can bring in any amount of foreign currency and exchange it at any Icelandic bank, so don't go to the trouble of obtaining Icelandic currency before you go. Most hotels, shops, and restaurants accept common European currencies and U.S. dollars, but they may round up the daily exchange rate. VISA and MasterCard/Eurocard are widely accepted in Iceland. Most banks, hotels, and restaurants also accept other popular credit cards such as American Express and Diners Club.

Icelandic Currency

The unit of currency in Iceland is the króna (IKr). Icelandic notes come in denominations of IKr100, 500, 1,000, and 5,000. Coins are IKr1, 5, 10, and 50. The króna is divided into 100 *aurar*, which are as good as worthless. Icelandic money can be dif-

ficult to exchange back home, so exchange any last krónas you are carrying at the departure terminal in Keflavík.

At press time (summer 1993) the exchange rate of the króna hovered around IKr62 to the U.S. dollar, IKr98 to the pound sterling, and IKr49 to the Canadian dollar.

What It Will Cost

Iceland is an expensive destination, but the effect can often be softened by shopping around. For instance, a cup of coffee costs IKr100 at a cafeteria but IKr150 at a fine restaurant. An imported German beer or Icelandic brew costs IKr110–IKr150 (in six-packs only) at the state monopoly store (ÁTVR), but IKr500 at a bar. A can of soda costs IKr80 at the grocery, IKr150 at a restaurant or bar. A ready-made sandwich at the grocery costs IKr160–IKr200, and at a bakery you can buy a roll and butter for about IKr70. A short taxi ride within Reykjavík costs IKr500. A movie ticket costs IKr450—more for Icelandic-made films.

Hotels and restaurants cost up to 50% more in Reykjavík than elsewhere in the country.

Taxes A 24.5% value-added tax (VAT) applies to most goods and services, with the exception of lodging and transportation. Usually the VAT is included in a price; if not, that fact must be stated explicitly.

On domestic flights and on flights to Greenland and the Faroe Islands, the airport tax is IKr165; for all other destinations the international departure tax is IKr1,250, payable when buying the ticket.

Passports and Visas

U.S., Canadian, and British citizens are required to have a valid passport to enter Iceland for a stay of up to three months. Visas and health certificates are not required.

U.S. Citizens For more information, contact the **Embassy of Iceland** (2022 Connecticut Ave. NW, Washington, DC 20008, tel. 202/265–6653).

U.K. Citizens Contact the **Embassy of Iceland** (1 Eaton Terr., London SW1 W8EY, tel. 071/730–5131).

Canadian Citizens Contact the **Consulate General of Iceland** (1093 Taylor Ave., Suite 7, Winnipeg, Manitoba R3M 2K4, tel. 204/477–6588).

Customs

On Arrival Tourists can bring in 6 liters of imported or 8 liters of Icelandic beer, or 1 liter of wine, and 1 liter of liquor not exceeding 47% alcohol, and 200 cigarettes. Laws regarding drugs are strictly enforced. Iceland also stringently prohibits any imports of fresh meat, poultry, or other farm produce, as well as live animals.

On Departure *See* Customs and Duties in Chapter 1.

Language

The official language is Icelandic, a highly inflected Germanic tongue, brought to the country by early Norse settlers. It has changed little over the centuries, enabling Icelanders to read the ancient manuscripts of the Sagas without difficulty. English and Danish are widely spoken and understood, while many Icelanders also speak other Scandinavian languages or German, and some speak French.

The Icelandic alphabet contains two unique letters—þ, pronounced like the *th* in thin, and ð, pronounced like the *th* in leather.

Staying Healthy

Iceland has one of the best health-care services in the world. All Icelandic physicians further their education in some specialty, usually at a teaching hospital abroad. There are hospitals in all corners of the island, and doctors in most communities. Due to reciprocal agreements, Scandinavian nationals and British subjects have access to all health services at the same rates as Icelanders.

While there is little danger of disease, visitors should be careful of accidents when out in the countryside hiking, fishing, climbing, or horse trekking. Beware of the deceptive currents of Icelandic rivers, hidden crevasses in the glaciers, or sudden shifts in the weather. In the interior, NEVER travel alone, and ALWAYS leave details of your planned itinerary. People have lost their lives because they underestimated the perils of highland travel in Iceland. Travel with an organized tour; these range from easy-going bus tours requiring the minimum of effort to demanding guided backpacking and camping tours.

Car Rentals

Renting a car in Iceland is expensive. A typical price for a compact car is around IKr5,900 per day, with 100 kilometers (62 miles) free, plus IKr29 per kilometer. A four-wheel-drive vehicle for rougher roads will cost about IKr12,900 per day, with 100 kilometers (62 miles) included, plus IKr58 per kilometer. These prices do not include collision damage waiver. There are many car-rental agencies in Iceland, so it is worth shopping around for the best buy. You must also pay for the gasoline, which is very expensive, IKr65 to IKr70 per liter depending on octane rating. If you plan to explore the interior, make sure you rent a four-wheel-drive vehicle.

Hertz (tel. 2/29577), **Avis** (tel. 2/50760), and **Icelandair** (tel. 1/690200) operate offices in the Leifur Eiríksson Terminal at Keflavík Airport. In other areas, rental agencies are usually close to airports.

Hints for Travelers with Disabilities

For information on provisions for the disabled in Iceland, contact the **Iceland Tourist Board** in New York or, in Iceland, the **Sjálfsbjörg** (Hátún 12, 105 Reykjavík, tel. 1/29133).

Further Reading

The Icelandic Sagas, the Nordic countries' most valuable contribution to world literature, have been translated into many languages. They tell of the lives, characters, and exploits of Icelandic heroes in the 10th and 11th centuries in an intricate combination of fantasy and history. The best-known are *Grettis Saga*, about the outlaw Grettir the Strong; *Laxdæla Saga*, a tragedy spanning four generations in which women play a prominent role; *Egil's Saga*, about the truculent Viking-poet Egill Skallagrímsson; and *Njal's Saga*, generally considered the greatest, about two heroes, one young and brave, the other old and wise. Told in simple language, with emphasis on dialogue, these epic poems are about love and hatred, family feuds and vengeance, loyalty and friendship, and tragic destiny.

Snorri Sturluson (1179–1241), counted among the greatest historians of the Middle Ages, wrote the history of the kings of Norway up to 1184 in his *Heimskringla* (Orb of the World). His *Edda*, the only surviving document of the beliefs, cosmology, and outlook of the Germanic peoples in pre-Christian times, influenced Richard Wagner in writing his epic Ring Cycle of operas.

In 1936 two young poets, W. H. Auden and Louis MacNeice, summering in Iceland, wrote a miscellany of poetry and prose that were later collected in Auden's *Letters from Iceland*. Full of insights on the country, its people, and its politics, they are an unorthodox and witty introduction to Iceland even 50 years later. Another modern work of at least peripheral interest to those traveling to Iceland is Jules Verne's classic science-fiction novel *Journey to the Center of the Earth*, in which the heroes begin their subterrannean adventure with a descent into Iceland's majestic Snæfellsjökull glacier.

More than 50 different volumes on Iceland—including poetry, biographies, travel guides, and picture books in English—can be ordered from *Iceland Review* (Box 8576, 128 Reykjavík, Iceland, tel. 1/675700, fax 1/674066). The review itself is a quarterly magazine with a lively mix of culture, current affairs, and some of the best color photos from Iceland. It is well worth subscribing to *News from Iceland*, a monthly newspaper published by *Iceland Review*, prior to your trip.

Arriving and Departing

From the United States by Plane

Airports and Airlines All international flights originate from and arrive at **Keflavík Airport** (tel. 2/50600) in the southwestern corner of Iceland, 50 kilometers (30 miles) south of Reykjavík. On arrival you may spot some military aircraft, for Keflavík is also a NATO military installation, manned by the U.S. Navy. However, the Leifur Eiríksson terminal is completely separate from the base.

Icelandair (610 5th Ave., New York, NY 10020, tel. 800/223-5500 or 212/967–8888) operates regular direct flights daily from New York City's JFK airport; service from Baltimore, Maryland, flies five times a week in summer, three times a week in winter; service from Orlando, Florida, runs twice a

week in winter. The flight from New York to Keflavík takes 5½ hours.

Discount Flights Iceland is a good destination to combine with a trip to continental Europe. The full round-trip fare from New York to Iceland in June 1993 was $1,416 midweek (APEX fare $678), but the full round-trip fare from New York to Luxembourg, Icelandair's main European gateway, cost only $819 midweek and allowed a stopover in Iceland for up to one week. If you stop over in Iceland for three days or less, the round-trip to Luxembourg would cost $778 midweek (weekend fares are slightly higher). Various special discount offers may be available at different times, for limited-validity and prebooked seats, so check on your options. Icelandair also makes various special offers on its domestic services for passengers on international flights to Iceland. These must, in general, be booked in advance, when you book your trip. *See* details of the Air Rover and other special deals in Staying in Iceland, below.

From the United Kingdom by Plane

Icelandair (172 Tottenham Court Rd., 3rd floor, London W1P 9LG, tel. 017/388–5599) flies daily from London's Heathrow to Keflavík. There are two flights a week from Glasgow, and once a week Icelandair flies from Glasgow via the Faroe Islands to Iceland. The full round-trip fare from London in summer 1993 was £820 (APEX fare £304). The flight from London takes three hours.

From Scandinavia by Plane

Icelandair and **SAS** both operate between mainland Scandinavia and Iceland. Hitherto in competition, the two airlines have now made a collaborative agreement, which means that schedules will be coordinated by summer 1994. For information on services, contact Icelandair in Copenhagen (tel. 33/12–33–88), Stockholm (tel. 08/310240), or Oslo (tel. 02/42–39–75), or SAS in Copenhagen (tel. 33/15–48–77).

From Scandinavia by Ship

It is possible to sail to Iceland on the car-and-passenger ferry *Norröna* operated by **Smyril Line** (Box 370, 3800 Tórshavn, Faroe Islands, tel. 1/5900, fax 1/5707; Engelgarden, Nye Bryggen, N–5023 Bergen, Norway, tel. 5/320970, fax 5/960272; or in Iceland, **Norröna Travel,** Laugavegur 3, 101 Reykjavík, tel. 1/626362, fax 1/29450).

The *Norröna* plies between the Faroes, Esbjerg in Denmark, Bergen in Norway, and Seyðisfjörður on the east coast of Iceland. Another Smyril Line ship, the *Smyril*, older and less luxurious than the *Norröna*, plies between the Faroes and Scotland. Depending upon your point of departure and where you are going, the trip may involve a stopover of some days in the Faroes. Special offers for accommodations may be available through Smyril Line, and special fly/cruise arrangements are available through Smyril Line and Icelandair. You can also sail between Iceland and Europe by freight vessel. **Eimskip,** Iceland's largest shipping company, offers limited passenger accommodations (plus the option of taking your own car along) on container vessels. You can sail from Immingham (England),

Hamburg (Germany), Antwerp (Belgium), or Rotterdam (Netherlands) to Reykjavík. Information and bookings are available from **ÚrvalÚtsýn Travel** (Álfabakki 16, Box 9180, 129 Reykjavík, tel. 1/699300).

Staying in Iceland

Getting Around

By Plane Because so much of Iceland's central region is uninhabited, domestic air transport has been well developed to link the coastal towns. It isn't particularly cheap—round-trip fares range between IKr7,990 and IKr16,070—but there are various discounts available. The longest domestic flight takes just over an hour.

In summer, **Icelandair** (tel. 1/690200) schedules daily or frequent flights from Reykjavík to most of the large towns, such as Akureyri, Egilsstaðir, Húsavík, Höfn, Ísafjörður, Patreksfjörður, Sauðárkrókur, and Vestmannaeyjar. Icelandair provides bus connections between airports outside Reykjavík and nearby towns and villages.

Íslandsflug (tel. 1/616060) flies daily to Vestmannaeyjar, Egilsstaðir, and Bíldudalur, and also flies regularly to Flateyri, Siglufjörður, Rif, Neskaupstaður, Hólmavík, and Gjögur. **Norlandair** (tel. 1/690200) serves the north from Akureyri, **Eastair** (tel. 1/690200) serves the east out of Egilsstaðir, and **Ernir Air** (tel. 1/24200) serves the western fjords from Ísafjörður. Apex tickets are available on domestic flights if booked two days in advance. These offer savings of 50% on the full airfare (e.g., round-trip Reykjavík to Akureyri IKr5,900 instead of IKr11,800).

Various special discount tickets are available on domestic air services, some valid only on Icelandair flights, others on the regional airlines as well.

The **Fly As You Please** pass is valid for unlimited travel on all Icelandair domestic routes for 12 days. Sold exclusively in advance, to Icelandair international passengers, it cost $270 in summer 1993. The **Four-Sector Iceland Air Pass** is valid for a month and can be used on any four sectors flown by Icelandair and Eastair, Norlandair, and Ernir. This air pass must also be booked before arrival in Iceland, and costs $176. The **Mini-Iceland Air Pass** is similar but is valid on two sectors instead of four and costs $112. The **Air Rover** is valid for a journey from Reykjavík to Ísafjörður, Akureyri, Egilsstaðir, Höfn and back to Reykjavík (or vice versa). Valid for a month, the Air Rover is sold in Iceland and abroad, and costs about IKr16,000. A mini **Air Rover** ticket, for the Reykjavík–Ísafjörður–Akureyri–Reykavík route, costs approximately IKr11,000.

By Bus An extensive network of buses serves most parts of Iceland; services are intermittent in the winter season, and some routes are operated only in summer. Fares range from IKr1,000 for a round-trip to Þingvellir to IKr6,600 for a round-trip to Akureyri. The bus network is operated from **Bifreiðastöð Íslands** (BSÍ, Vatnsmýrarvegur 10, tel. 1/22300, fax 1/29973); its terminal is located on the northern rim of Reykjavík Airport.

If you want to explore the island extensively, it's a good idea to buy the **Omnibus Passport,** which covers travel on all scheduled bus routes, with unlimited stopovers. A seven-day pass costs about IKr14,300, a two-week pass IKr19,700, a three-week pass IKr25,500, and a four-week pass IKr28,500. The **Full Circle Passport,** which costs IKr12,900, is valid for a circular trip on the Ring Road mid-July to mid-September; you can take as long as you want to complete the journey, as long as you keep heading in the same direction on the circuit (detours into the interior must be paid for separately).

The **Air/Bus Rover** ticket offered by Icelandair and BSÍ allows you to fly one-way to any domestic Icelandair destination and by bus in the other direction, so you can save some time and still have a chance to explore the countryside. Prices start at IKr9,000 for Reykjavík–Akureyri. The price rises to IKr14,000 if you take the mountain bus route by way of Sprengisandur instead of the Ring Road.

Holders of BSÍ Passport tickets are entitled to various discounts, for instance at campsites, Edda hotels, and on ferries. Mountain bikes can be rented from BSÍ at prices from IKr1,100 for a day to IKr20,500 for four weeks.

By Car The Ring Road, which generally hugs the coastline, stretches almost 1,400 kilometers (900 miles) around Iceland. It is paved from Reykjavík beyond Hella in the south and in large stretches between the capital and Akureyri on the north coast; the rest of the road has a gravel surface, which can be quite smooth or full of potholes. Do not expect to drive fast.

Service stations are spaced no more than half a day's drive apart, on both main roads and side roads. Service stations in the Reykjavík area are open Monday through Saturday 7:30 AM to 8 PM; opening hours outside Reykjavík vary, but gas stations are often open until 11:30 PM. For information on road conditions and availability of gas off the beaten track, call **Vegagerð Ríkisins** (Public Roads Administration; Borgartún 5–7, Reykjavík, tel. 1/21001).

Traffic outside Reykjavík is generally light, but roads have only one lane going in each direction, so stay within the speed limit: 70 kph (45 mph) on the open road, 50 kph (30 mph) in urban areas. Drivers are required by law to use headlights at all times. Seat belts are required for the driver and all passengers.

Be cautious when driving in the interior in Iceland. The terrain can be treacherous, and many roads can only be traversed in four-wheel-drive vehicles; always drive in the company of at least one other car. Unbridged rivers, which must be forded, constitute a real hazard and should never be crossed without the advice of an experienced Iceland highland driver. Most mountain roads are closed by snow in winter and do not open again until mid June or early July, when the road surface has dried out after the spring thaw.

By Boat There is daily scheduled ferry service year-round between Reykjavík and Akranes on the ferry *Akraborg* (tel. 1/16050), and between Þorlákshöfn on the southern coast, and Vestmannaeyjar (the Westmann Islands) on the ferry *Herjólfur* (tel. 1/686464, fax 8/12991). The *Baldur* car ferry (tel. 3/81120 or 4/2020, fax 3/81093) sails twice daily in summer from Stykkis-

hólmur, on the Snæfellsnes Peninsula, across Breiðafjörður Bay to Brjánslækur in the Western Fjords.

Telephones

The international country code for Iceland is 354. The city code for Reykjavík is 1; other regions have one-digit codes. When calling between telephone regions within Iceland, dial 9 and the regional digit before the actual telephone number.

Local Calls There is one telephone directory for the entire country, divided into eight regions; names are listed alphabetically by first name as a result of the patronymic system (men add *-son* to their father's first name, women add *-dóttir*). Jobs or professions are often listed together with names and addresses.

Pay phones are usually located indoors in post offices, hotels, or at transportation terminals. They accept IKr5, IKr10, or IKr50 coins, which are placed in the slot before dialing. The dial tone is continuous. A 10-minute call between regions costs between IKr50 and IKr75.

International Calls You can dial direct or use an international calling card. Avoid charging overseas calls to your hotel bills, as the surcharge can double the cost of the call. Card phones are becoming more common: 100-unit phone cards (price IKr500) can be purchased at all post offices and some other outlets. For overseas calls, dial the operator 09 (or 08 for directory assistance). Iceland's country code is 354.

Operators and Information For long-distance calls within Iceland, dial 02 for the operator or 03 for directory assistance.

Mail

Stamps for postcards to Europe cost IKr30, for airmail letters IKr35. Stamps for postcards to the United States cost IKr35, airmail letters IKr55. Mail to and from northern Europe and Scandinavia usually takes two to three days. Other services are slower. All post offices also have fax machines for public use.

Tipping

Tipping is not conventional in Iceland and may even be frowned upon. Service charges of 15% to 20% are included in prices when applicable.

Opening and Closing Times

Museums and other attractions are generally open regular hours June–August. (Individual listings below state hours of opening.) If you wish to visit a site that doesn't have regular hours September–May, call the listed telephone number and make an appointment for a private visit.

Banks All banks in Iceland are open weekdays 9:15–4. A few branches in major towns are also open Thursday 5–6.

Post Offices In most towns, post offices open at 8:30 or 9 and close at 4:30 or 5, weekdays only.

Shops Standard shopping hours are weekdays 9–6 and Saturday 10–4. In summer, some shops are closed on Saturday. But su-

permarkets are often open later on Friday, and many smaller food stores are open daily until 10 or 11 PM. Bakeries are open daily, as are florists and kiosks. Outside Reykjavík it is generally possible to find food stores that open seven days a week.

Restaurants Restaurants are usually open midmorning until midnight. Lunch is generally served from noon to 2; dinnertime is between 6 and 9.

Shopping

The classic gift to bring home from Iceland is the Icelandic sweater, hand-knit in traditional designs; no two sweaters are alike. The thick, soft Icelandic yarn makes a warm fabric that also breathes easily, just right for keeping sailors snug throughout long days at sea. The natural lanolin of the sheep is left in the yarn, which lightly mats its fibers for extra protection from cold and damp.

Like other Scandinavian countries, Iceland produces local ales and spirits, the most famous being *brennivín*, an 80-proof liquor similar to aquavit. All alcoholic beverages, including beer and table wine, are sold exclusively at state-run liquor stores (ATVR), which are few and far between and open Monday to Friday 9–6. They do not take credit cards, and prices are high.

Pickled herring and smoked salmon are the main delicacies from the sea. Choose between *graflax* (dill-cured salmon), sliced smoked salmon, or whole fillets of smoked salmon or trout. Herring bits come marinated in wine, garlic, and other sauces. You may also want to pick up a small jar of the red Icelandic lumpfish caviar, or some *harðfiskur* (dried fish), which is best eaten in small bits. Icelandic lamb is another delicacy; you can buy it frozen or smoked.

Jewelry is a popular souvenir of Iceland. For upwards of IKr600 you can buy silver replicas of Viking brooches, rings, necklaces, and religious symbols such as the *þórshamar* (Thor's hammer), runic letters, and pagan magical letters. A number of goldsmiths and silversmiths also design beautiful modern jewelry with Icelandic stones, such as agate, jasper, and black obsidian, as well as diamonds and other precious stones.

VAT Refund Foreign visitors can claim a partial refund on the value-added tax (*virðisaukaskattur,* commonly called VSK), which accounts for 19.68% of the purchase price of most goods and services. Fifteen percent of the purchase price is refunded, providing you buy a minimum of IKr5,000 at that store. Souvenir stores issue "tax-free checks" that allow foreign visitors to collect the VSK rebates directly in the duty-free store when departing from Keflavík Airport. To qualify, keep your purchases in tax-free packages (except woolens), and show them to customs officers at the departure gate along with a passport and the tax-free check. If you depart the country from somewhere other than Keflavík, have customs authorities stamp your tax-free check, then mail the stamped check within three months to Iceland Tax-Free Shopping, Box 1200, 235 Keflavík, Iceland. You will be reimbursed in U.S. dollars at the current exchange rate.

Sports and Outdoor Activities

Fishing Iceland abounds with rivers and lakes where you can catch salmon, sea trout, brown trout, or char. The **trout** season normally runs April 1–September 20; permits can be bought on the spot for a number of lakes and rivers, at prices varying from a couple of hundred kronas up to several thousand per day, depending upon the quality of the fishing. *The Icelandic Fishing Guide* and a special fishing voucher book available from **Icelandic Farm Holidays** (Bændahöllin við Hagatorg, 107 Reykjavík, tel. 1/623640 or 1/19200) can be used in 50 river and lake locations around the country. Fishing-rod rental can be arranged.

The normal **salmon** season runs from early June to September 10. At most rivers, guides as well as accommodations are provided. The most popular (and expensive) rivers must be booked at least a year in advance and you pay IKr51,000–IKr120,000 per fishing rod per day, not including travel, accommodations, or food. For other rivers you must make reservations at least two months in advance and expect to pay around IKr10,000 per rod per day. However, it is often possible to buy salmon-fishing permits during the summer at tackle shops or angling clubs. In Reykjavík, contact the **Angling Club of Reykjavík** (Háaleitisbraut 68, tel. 1/686050), the **Icelandic Fishing Association** (Bolholt 6, tel. 1/31510), or the **Angling Club Laxá** (Laugavegur 51, tel. 1/23931). Reykjavík tackle shops include **Veiðihúsið** (Nóatún 17, tel. 1/84085), **Veiðivon** (Mörkin 6, tel. 1/687090), **Veiðimaðurinn** (Hafnarstræti 5, tel. 1/16760), **Vesturröst** (Laugavegur 178, tel. 1/16770).

Sea angling enjoys growing popularity in Iceland as a leisure sport, and sea-angling cruises can be organized from many of the country's fishing towns and villages. For further information, contact the Tourist Information Center (Bankastræti 2, tel. 1/623044, fax 1/624749). Several weekend deep-sea fishing competitions are held each year: in May in **Vestmanneyjar** (contact Elínborg Bernódusdóttir, tel. 8/11279); in July at **Ísafjörður** (contact Kolbrún Halldórsdóttir, tel. 4/3103); in August at **Siglufjörður** (contact Viðar Otteson, tel. 6/71514) or **Akureyri** (contact Júlíus Snorrason, tel. 6/21173).

If you wish to bring your own fishing tackle, it must be disinfected either at home (certificate needed) or by customs at Keflavík Airport.

Golf There are more than 30 golf courses in Iceland. Most are rather rough nine-hole courses, but there are six 18-hole courses, the best in Reykjavík and Akureyri. Greens fees range up to IKr1,500 for nine-hole courses and IKr1,500–IKr2,500 for 18-hole courses.

Small golf courses are also operated privately on some farms. For information on golfing opportunities in Iceland, contact the **Golf Association** (tel. 1/686686).

The **Arctic Open Golf Tournament** is held each year at Akureyri (the most northerly 18-hole course in the world) around the longest day of the year (in the Midnight Sun, needless to say!). For details, contact the **Akureyri Golf Club** (tel. 6/22974, fax 6/11755) or **Iceland Tourist Bureau** (tel. 1/623300, fax 1/625895).

Hiking Many organized tours from Reykjavík and other towns include some days of hiking. You can also join special hiking tours

that are popular among Icelanders, arranged by the touring clubs **Ferðafélag Íslands** (Touring Club of Iceland, Mörkin 6, 108 Reykjavík, tel. 682533, fax 682535) and **Útivist** (Touring Club Útivist Hallveigarstígur 1, 101 Reykjavík, tel. 1/14606, fax 614606). In Akureyri contact **Ferðafélag Akureyrar** (Touring Club of Akureyri, Strandgata 23, 600 Akureyri, tel. 1/ 22720). Be aware of the considerable dangers of hiking alone. Lava covered with moss can be treacherous, with razor-sharp edges that can cut through clothes and skin. Around hot springs and sulfur springs, the ground may suddenly give way, leaving you standing in boiling water or mud. When hiking across country, follow paths made by sheep if footpaths are not available. Don't venture away from frequented areas unless you have researched the territory in advance. Always let someone know of your hiking plans, and avoid hiking alone.

Horseback Riding The Icelandic horse is a purebred descendant of its ancestors from the Viking age, small but strong, exceptionally sure-footed, intelligent, and easy to handle. It boasts a unique gait, the *tölt*, or "running pace," which yields an extraordinarily smooth ride. A number of firms offer a variety of tours, from short one-day trips to 12-day treks, for more experienced riders, across various regions.

Many equestrian events are held around the country during the summer months, from local races and contests to major regional championships. Contact **Landssamband hestamannafélaga** (Equestrian Federation) (Bændahöllin, Hagatorg, 101 Reykjavík, tel. 1/29899) for details of forthcoming horse events.

Skiing The winter season begins in January and usually lasts through April. There are about 90 ski lifts around the country, and at the larger resorts both alpine and cross-country skiing trails are available.

Snowmobiling An increasingly popular leisure pursuit in winter months, snowmobiling is also possible in summer on Iceland's glaciers, such as Mýrdalsjökull in the south, where **Snjósleðaferðir** (Dugguvogi 10, 104 Reykjavík, tel. 1/682310, fax 1/813102) operates.

In summer, the **Kerlingarfjöll Ski School** west of the Hofsjökull glacier runs five- to six-day courses; you can also get lift tickets without taking lessons, and there are accommodations and food at the school. Contact Úrval/Útsýn Travel Agency (Alfabakki 16, 109 Reykjavík, tel. 1/699300).

Swimming Almost every community in Iceland has at least one public outdoor swimming pool heated by thermal springs. Swimming is a compulsory subject in elementary schools and the country's most common sports activity.

Dining

The menu used to be very simple—boiled fish and roast leg of lamb. Now many restaurants offer gourmet cooking, and the best restaurants keep up with the latest culinary trends worldwide. Most offer menus that consist of a marriage of the best in traditional Scandinavian cooking and classic French cuisine.

You have not eaten in Iceland until you try the seafood: haddock, halibut, lobster, prawns, scallops, sole, monkfish, ocean perch, shrimp, turbot, *tindabikkja* (starry ray), salmon, and

trout caught in clear mountain rivers—the list can go on forever.

Icelandic lamb is another delicacy, its distinct wild taste resulting from the fact that the sheep roam free in the grasslands of the interior and feed on highland herbs. In addition to succulent cuts of fresh lamb, menus also offer traditional *hangikjöt* (smoked lamb) and a more lightly flavored alternative, London lamb. Game, such as duck and reindeer, are popular at the more expensive restaurants. Local beef is also of high quality.

Part of the culinary revolution of the last decade included a proliferation of new domestic cheeses, many modeled on European specialty cheeses. *Gouda* remains number one, but there are many excellent types—including *Búri*, *Flóa Camembert*, *Dala-Brie*, and blue cheese. *Skyr*, a delicious yogurtlike food made from skim milk, is especially good with fresh fruit; one of its by-products is a cool drink called *mysa* (whey).

There are fully licensed full-service restaurants in most large towns, especially in summer when the Edda Hotels (boarding schools open to tourists as lodgings in summer) are open. It's wise to make reservations on weekends. Most establishments accept informal attire, casual but neat, but restaurants that feature dancing and entertainment usually require men to wear a shirt and tie.

The following chart defines the price categories used in the restaurant reviews below.

Category	Cost*
Very Expensive	over IKr3,500
Expensive	IKr2,600–IKr3,500
Moderate	IKr1,500–IKr2,600
Inexpensive	under IKr1,500

*per person for a three-course meal, including taxes and service charge and excluding wine

More than 50 restaurants around the country participate in a tourist-menu scheme: a meal of soup or starter, fish or meat dish, and coffee costs IKr1,000 to IKr1,200 for lunch, or IKr1,300 to IKr2,000 for dinner, with discounts for children (children under five eat free). A leaflet listing all participating restaurants is available free from the **Icelandic Hotel and Restaurant Association** (Hafnarstræti 20, 101 Reykjavík, tel. 1/27410 or 1/621410, fax 1/27478). Details of restaurants all over the country and the services they offer are given in another booklet available free from the association, "Dining and Wining."

Wines and Spirits Most restaurants are licensed to serve the full range of alcoholic beverages—local or imported beer, German and French wines, cognac, and spirits. Wines, however, are very expensive. Like other Scandinavian countries, Iceland is renowned for its ales and spirits, the most famous being *brennivín*. Its nickname, "black death," alludes not only to the black labels on its bottles but also to the physical effects of drinking too much of it. Brennivín is associated with the midwinter celebrations of Þorrablót, when it is drunk ice-cold and undiluted; more com-

monly, it is drunk mixed with cola. Icelandic vodkas, such as *Elduris* and *Icy*, are also of high quality.

Lodging

The past few years have seen a concerted effort to upgrade the level of accommodations offered in Iceland; most of the better hotels were built or totally renovated in the past decade, and strict standards for good mattresses apply even to guest rooms at Icelandic farms. During the summer season, hotels or even youth hostels may be fully booked, so make reservations well in advance.

The following chart defines the price categories used in the hotel reviews below.

Category	Cost*
Very Expensive	over IKr12,000
Expensive	IKr9,600–IKr12,000
Moderate	IKr4,800–IKr9,600
Inexpensive	under IKr4,800

Prices are for a double room with bath.

Hotels and Guest Houses
Hotels in Reykjavík and larger towns offer the amenities typical of all good hotels: hair dryer, trouser press, telephone, and satellite TV in every room, with a Continental breakfast included in the room rate. Many travelers, however, find the simple guest houses adequate, while others prefer bed-and-breakfast at a private home. All types of lodging are regulated. The **Icelandic Hotel and Restaurant Association** (*see* Dining, *above*) publishes a brochure each year with details of hotels and guest houses throughout the country.

Farm Holidays
An increasingly popular mode of lodging in Iceland, even among Icelanders themselves, farm holidays are a fun way to get to know the country and its people, and to explore the magnificent natural surroundings. You can choose from about 130 locations around Iceland, about half of them real working farms. Know ahead of time what each farm offers, for they vary widely: You might stay in a separate cottage, in a bed in the farmhouse, or in a sleeping bag in an outbuilding. Breakfast is included in the price. Some farms have cooking facilities for guests, while others serve full meals if requested. Make reservations well in advance of your visit. A double room without breakfast costs IKr1,750 to IKr2,700 per night; sleeping-bag accommodation without breakfast costs IKr1,150 per night. Write to **Icelandic Farm Holidays** (Bændahöllinni við Hagatorg, 107 Reykjavík, tel. 1/19200 or 1/623640, fax 1/623644) for a booklet describing all farms and their facilities.

Campgrounds
Organized camping grounds are available throughout the country. Some are located on private property, others are owned and operated by local communities, and still others are located in protected areas supervised by the Nature Conservation Council. Look for signs reading *"Tjaldstæði bönnuð"* (camping prohibited) or *"tjaldstæði"* (camping allowed). It is forbidden to use scrubwood for fuel; bring paraffin or gas stoves for cooking.

Camping equipment can be rented in Reykjavík at **Tjaldaleigan Rent-a-Tent** (tel. 1/13072). Write to the **Association of Leisure**

Site Owners (c/o the Tourist Information Center, Bankastræti 2, 101 Reykjavík, tel. 1/623045, fax 1/624749) for a comprehensive listing of campgrounds. Even the most complete campgrounds cost about IKr500 per person per day, with a tent, trailer, or camper.

Mountain Huts You can also stay at one of 19 mountain huts owned by **Ferðafélag Íslands** (the Touring Club of Iceland; *see* Hiking, *above*) for IKr700–IKr1,050 depending upon facilities.

Youth Hostels At Iceland's 25 youth hostels, accommodations are inexpensive: about IKr1,250 per night, or IKr1,000 for members of the Youth Hostel Association. You get a bed, access to a kitchen and toilet, a pillow, and a blanket. Breakfast costs IKr550. Some hostels are crowded during the summer, so call ahead. Hostels outside Reykjavík permit you to use your own sleeping bag. For information, write to **Farfugladeild Reykjavíkur** (Sundlaugavegi 34, 105 Reykjavík, tel. 1/38110, fax 1/679201).

Summer Hotels Seventeen boarding schools around the country, which would otherwise stand empty during the long summer vacation, open up as Edda summer hotels, offering both accommodations with made-up beds and more basic sleeping-bag facilities. A double room costs $75, a single $55. You can sleep on a mattress in your own sleeping bag for $15 per night, and there is usually a restaurant offering good home-style cooking. Special package offers are often available. For information and bookings, contact the **Iceland Tourist Bureau** (Skógarhlíð 18, 101 Reykjavík, tel. 1/623300, fax 1/625895).

Reykjavík

The sprawling city of Reykjavík is the nation's nerve center, the seat of government, home to half of the island's population, and the main point of contact with the outside world. It's a relaxed casual city, where people enjoy having fun, even (or especially) throughout the dark days of winter.

The highlight of this summer in Reykjavík will doubtless be the Reykjavík Arts Festival, held every other year since 1970. Scheduled for June 1 to 19, the festival spans a wide variety of visual arts and musical events, which this year include a recital by famed pianist Vladimir Ashkenazy. This year's festival coincides with celebrations of the half centenary of the modern Icelandic republic, founded on June 17, 1944. Details are available from the Reykjavík Arts Festival Office (Box 88, 121 Reykjavík, tel. 1/612444, fax 1/622350).

Set on a fjord overlooked by proud Mt. Esja, with its ever-changing hues, Reykjavík presents a colorful sight, its concrete houses painted in light colors and topped by vibrant red, blue, and green roofs.

Any part of town can be reached by city bus, but take a walk around to get an idea of the present and the past. In the Old Town, lovely old wooden buildings rub shoulders with modern timber and concrete structures. Many once-neglected old houses in the Grjótaþorp and Þingholt districts have been lovingly restored to their former glory. Others have fallen prey to bulldozers, or been moved to the Árbær Museum of historic houses.

Reykjavík's name comes from the Icelandic words for steam, *reykur,* and for bay, *vík.* In AD 874, Norseman Ingólfur Arnarson saw Iceland rising out of the misty sea and came ashore at a bay eerily shrouded with plumes of steam from nearby hot springs. Today most of the houses in Reykjavík are heated by near-boiling water carried from the hot springs. Hot water is pumped 27 kilometers (16 miles) from Nesjavellir into the city. Natural heating means that there is little air pollution. You may notice, however, that the hot water brings a slight sulfur smell to the bathroom.

The latest landmark to be added to Reykjavík's skyline is Perlan (the Pearl), a monument to Iceland's invaluable geothermal water supplies, which opened in 1991. On the top of Öskjuhlíð, the hill overlooking Reykjavík Airport, up to 24,000 cubic meters of hot water are stored in six vast tanks. Between the tanks and atop them is Perlan, its silvery glass dome visible from all over the city. Perlan houses art exhibits and musical events, while the theme of hot water is emphasized by a fountain that spouts every few minutes like a geyser. Above the tanks, a circular viewing platform offers panoramic vistas, together with telescopes and multilingual recorded commentaries, plus a coffee bar and an ice-cream parlor. The crowning glory is a revolving restaurant under the glass dome; it's pricey, but the view is second to none.

In contrast to the treeless countryside, Reykjavík has many tall Icelandic birches, rowans, and willows, as well as imported pines and spruces. At the Tjörnin lake, near the city center, you can observe many of the 17 species of ducks that nest in the country.

Reykjavík is the logical starting point for any visit to Iceland. Prices for hotel rooms, restaurant meals, and short tours are easily on a par with those of Amsterdam, Copenhagen, London, and Paris, although you can walk around its historic areas and visit its museums free of charge or for a modest fee.

Important Addresses and Numbers

Tourist Information
The Reykjavík **Tourist Information Center** (Bankastræti 2, tel. 1/623045, fax 624749), located a few yards up the street from Lækjartorg square, is open June–August weekdays 8:30–6, Saturday 8:30–2, and Sunday 10–2; September–May it's open weekdays 10–4, Saturday 10–2. The **Iceland Tourist Board's** headquarters next door (Gimli, Lækjargata 3, tel. 1/27488) is open June, July, and August, weekdays 8–4; the rest of the year, 9–5.

Embassies
U.S. Embassy: Laufásvegur 21, tel. 1/29100. **British Embassy:** Laufásvegur 49, tel. 1/15883. **Canadian Consulate:** Suðurlandsbraut 10, tel. 1/680820.

Emergencies
Dial 1/11166 for **police** and 1/11100 for **ambulance** or **fire.**

Hospital Emergency Room
The emergency ward at **Borgarspítalinn city hospital** (tel. 1/696600) is open 24 hours a day.

Doctors and Dentists
Six health centers with officially appointed family doctors receive patients on short notice 8–5 weekdays. Call the **Reykjavík Health Centers** (tel. 1/22400) or look under *Heilsugæslustöð* in the phone book; at other times, call the Duty Doctors

(**Læknavakt;** tel. 1/21230). You can speak to a nurse, arrange to see a doctor, or ask for a house call.

Late-Night Reykjavík pharmacies take turns at staying open around the
Pharmacies clock. Signs are posted in all pharmacies indicating which one has the night watch (*næturvakt*). For information, call 1/18888.

Where to The **Tourist Information Center** at Bankastræti exchanges for-
Change Money eign currencies in June, July, and August 4:30–6 weekdays, 9–1 Saturday. At the **Hotel Loftleiðir,** a bank is open Monday– Saturday 8:15–4 and 5–7:15.

English-Language **Bókabúð Braga** (at Hlemmur bus station tel. 1/29311 or 1/
Bookstores 624202) and **Sigfús Eymundsson** (Austurstræti 18, tel. 1/27077; also at Kringlan mall) carry foreign books as well as foreign newspapers and magazines, but these are usually several days old. **Mál og menning** (Laugavegur 18, tel. 1/24240 and Síðumúli 6–7, tel. 1/688577), one of the largest bookstores in the city, has an extensive foreign section.

Travel Agencies Major agencies include **Guðmundur Jónasson** (Borgartún 34, tel. 1/683222), **Iceland Tourist Bureau** (Skógarhlíð 18, tel. 1/ 623300), **Icelandair** (Reykjavík Airport, tel. 1/690100), **Samvinn-Travel** (Austurstræti 12, tel. 1/691070), **Úrval-Útsýn** (Álfabakki 16, tel. 1/603060).

Arriving and Departing by Plane

Airports and **Keflavík Airport** (tel. 2/50600), 50 kilometers (30 miles) south of
Airlines the city, hosts all international flights. For reservations and information in Reykjavík, contact **Icelandair** (tel. 1/690300) or **SAS** (tel. 1/622211).

Reykjavík Airport (tel. 1/694100) is the central hub of domestic air travel in Iceland. For reservations and information, contact **Icelandair** (tel. 1/690200), **Íslandsflug** (tel. 1/616060), or **Ernir** (tel. 1/624200).

Between the The **Reykjavík FlyBus** (tel. 1/621011) leaves Keflavík (from di-
Airport and rectly outside the terminal building) and arrives in Reykjavík
Downtown at the **Loftleiðir Hotel** at Reykjavík Airport. From there you
By Bus can take a taxi or municipal bus to your destination. Buses are scheduled in connection with each flight arrival and departure. For departures catch the FlyBus at the Saga, Esja, and Loftleiðir hotels and the Holiday Inn. The FlyBus also leaves the youth hostel in Laugardalur at 5 AM daily June–August. The fare is IKr 500 per person. The drive takes 40–50 minutes.

From Reykjavík Airport, the municipal (SVR) Bus 5 leaves from the Icelandair terminal on the western side of the airport. Other airlines operate from the east terminal (behind the Loftleiðir Hotel), which is served by Bus 17.

By Taxi A taxi from the airport to Reykjavík is a little faster than the FlyBus and will cost IKr4,200, though if you share it with others you can split the cost. Taxi companies include **Aðalstöðin** (tel. 2/1515 or 2/52525) and **Ökuleiðir** (tel. 2/14141). From Reykjavík Airport, a taxi to your hotel will cost around IKr600; there are direct phones to taxi companies in the arrivals hall.

Getting Around

The best way to see Reykjavík is on foot. Many of the interesting sights are in the city center, within easy walking distance of one another. There is no subway system.

By Bus The municipal bus (**SVR**) system (tel. 1/12700) is extensive, cheap, and reliable. Buses run from 7 AM to midnight or 1 AM. On most routes, buses run every 20 minutes during the day and every half hour evenings and weekends. Bus stops are marked by signposts with an "SVR" on top, or by a bus shelter with a posted list of routes. The flat fare is IKr100 adults, IKr25 children, payable to the driver upon boarding. You can buy strips of tickets at a lower price from the drivers or at the main terminals. The fare allows you to travel any distance in town; if you have to change buses, ask for *skiptimiða* (*skiff*-tee-mee-thee), a transfer ticket that you give the second bus driver. The SVR system connects with AV the bus systems in the Kópavogur, Garðabær, and Hafnarfjörður municipalities south of Reykjavík. If you plan an extended stay in the Reykjavík area, it may be worthwhile to buy a monthly season ticket, the Green Card, valid on all SVR and AV routes.

By Taxi Most cabs are late-model fully equipped passenger sedans, including many Mercedes. They have small TAXI signs on top and can be hailed anywhere on the street; the sign LAUS indicates that the cab is available. All cars are radio-equipped and respond to calls within minutes. Some taxis accept major credit cards, but you must state that you want one when requesting the taxi. Fares are regulated by meter; rides around Reykjavík run between IKr500 and IKr800. Call **BSR** (tel. 1/611720), **Bæjarleiðir** (tel. 1/33500), or **Hreyfill** (tel. 1/685522). There is no tipping.

By Car The excellent bus system and quick, inexpensive taxis make automobiles unnecessary for getting around town, doubly so considering how expensive car rentals and gasoline are. Gas stations are usually open 7:30 AM–11 PM. Most have self-service pumps that accept IKr100, 500, and 1,000 notes. Among the car rentals in Reykjavík are **Icelandair** (tel. 1/690500), **Geysir** (tel. 1/688888), **Avis** (tel. 1/624433), and **InterRent** (tel. 1/686915).

Opening and Closing Times

Even though many Reykjavík citizens like to stay up late, most of the capital closes down early on weekdays, and Sunday remains largely a sabbatical day. **Bars, discotheques,** and **dance clubs** stay open until 1 AM Monday–Thursday and 3 AM Friday and Saturday. **Bus service** stops between midnight and 1 AM, but **taxis** run around the clock.

Post offices are open weekdays 8:30–4:30; a post office at the BSÍ bus terminal is open 1:30–6 weekdays and 8:30–3 Saturday, and the post office at the Kringlan shopping mall stays open until 6, Monday to Friday.

Museums and galleries are generally open Tuesday–Saturday 11–4 and Sunday 2–6. Monday is the usual closing day.

Shops are open weekdays 9–6. Most supermarkets stay open later on Friday and open 10–4 on Saturday. Some are open on Sunday afternoons. Many smaller food stores are open daily until 10 or 11 PM. Bakeries, souvenir shops, florists, and kiosks are open daily.

Guided Tours

Orientation **Kynnisferðir** (Reykjavík Excursions), owned by the Icelandic Tourist Bureau, is the main tour operator in and out of Reykjavík. Kynnisferðir has offices at the Loftleiðir Hotel (tel. 1/621011) and at the Esja Hotel (tel. 1/688922). "Reykjavík City-Sightseeing" is a daily 2½-hour tour that provides useful orientation for newcomers; it includes museums and art galleries, shopping centers, and so on.

Personal Guides Many travel agencies offer English-speaking personal guides for tours of the city and outlying areas. Contact **Úrval-Útsýn Travel** (Álfabakki 16, tel. 1/699300, fax 1/670202) or **Samvinn-Travel** (Austurstræti 17, tel. 1/691010, fax 1/27796). The **Association of Travel Guides** (Suðurlandsbraut 30, 108 Reykjavík, tel. 1/678670) can provide qualified guides who work in a variety of languages and have different specialties.

Highlights for First-Time Visitors

Alþingishús (House of Parliament), *see* Tour 1
Árbæjarsafn (Open-Air Municipal Museum), *see* Tour 1
Árni Magnússon Institute, *see* Tour 2
Dómkirkjan (Lutheran Cathedral), *see* Tour 1
Hallgrímskirkja church, *see* Tour 2
Þjóðminjasafn (National Museum), *see* Tour 2
Tjörnin Lake, *see* Tour 1

Tour 1: The Historic Downtown

Numbers in the margin correspond to points of interest on the Reykjavík map.

Most bus routes meet at **Hlemmur** square on the eastern edge of downtown. To the north is the tall, unimpressive central **Police Station**, housing the **Ministry of Foreign Affairs** on the top floor. The building on the west side houses the **Náttúru-fræðistofnun** (Museum of Natural History), which has an interesting though small collection. Exhibits include stuffed peacocks, giant sea turtles, and a specimen of the extinct great auk. *Hverfisgata 116, tel. 1/29822. Admission free. Open Sun., Tues., Thurs., Sat. 1:30–4.*

Walk west five blocks down Laugavegur, traditionally the city's main shopping street (although it now meets stiff competition from the Kringlan shopping mall uptown—*see* Shopping, *below*). You'll pass high-fashion clothing stores, jewelry and record shops, bookstores, bars, and restaurants on the way downtown.

Time Out Stop in at the **Tíu Dropar** coffeehouse (Laugavegur 27), which serves a tantalizing selection of homemade cakes, a variety of coffees, and chocolate with lots of genuine whipped cream.

Turning right on Klapparstígur and left again on Hverfisgata, you'll be in an area housing many government ministries. On the right, past the Danish Embassy, is the newly renovated Þjóðleikhús (National Theater), designed by architect Guðjón Samúelsson and built during the 1940s. Next door is the **Landsbókasafnið** (National Library), an impressive early 20th-century structure testifying to this nation's universal literacy

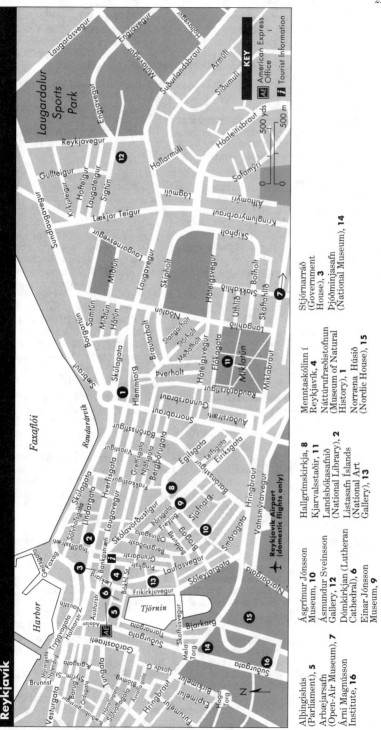

Reykjavik

KEY

AE American Express Office

i Tourist Information

500 yds

500 m

Faxaflói

Laugardalur Sports Park

Harbor

Brunnsf

Tjörnin

Reykjavik Airport (domestic flights only)

N

Alþingishús (Parliament), **5**

Árbæjarsafn (Open-Air Museum), **7**

Árni Magnússon Institute, **16**

Ásgrímur Jónsson Museum, **10**

Ásmundur Sveinsson Gallery, **12**

Dómkirkjan (Lutheran Cathedral), **6**

Einar Jónsson Museum, **9**

Hallgrímskirkja, **8**

Kjarvalsstaðir, **11**

Landsbókasafnið (National Library), **2**

Listasafn Íslands (National Art Gallery), **13**

Menntaskólinn í Reykjavík, **4**

Náttúrufræðistofnun (Museum of Natural History), **1**

Norræna Húsið (Nordic House), **15**

Stjórnarráð (Government House), **3**

Þjóðminjasafn (National Museum), **14**

and great interest in the printed word. The public reading room houses everything from current issues of *The New York Times Book Review* to myriad volumes on Icelandic genealogy. *Safnahús, western end of Hverfisgata, tel. 1/16864 or 1/13080. Admission free. Open weekdays 9–7, Sat. 10–12.*

On the west side of the library there is a grassy knoll known as Arnarhóll because it is topped by a **statue of Ingólfur Arnarson,** the first settler of Iceland and Reykjavík's founder. From here there's a fine panorama of Reykjavík's architectural mélange: 18th-century stone houses, 19th-century small wooden houses, office blocks from the '30s and '40s, and, to the north, the futuristic **Seðlabanki** (Central Bank).

❸ Just past the hill, turn left on Lækjargata. On the left at the corner of Bankastræti is the **Stjórnarráð** (Government House), a low white building constructed in the 18th century as a prison. Today it houses the offices of President Vigdís Finnbogadóttir (the first woman president in Europe) and the prime minister. Continue along Lækjargata; on your left is the historic **Bernhöftstorfa** district, a row of colorful two-story wooden houses from the mid-19th century. Alongside them stands **❹ Menntaskólinn í Reykjavík** (the Reykjavík Grammar School), Iceland's oldest educational establishment (corner of Amtmannsstígur and Lækjargata); its graduates have from the early days dominated the country's political and social life. Turn right off Lækjargata onto Vonarstræti; to your left you can look out across **Tjörnin** lake. Warm water flows into a corner of this pond, making it an attraction for birds year-round and a popular area for bird-watchers. It's also popular with ice skaters in winter. The new **Ráðhús** (City Hall), opened in 1992, is on the corner of Vonarstræti and Tjarnargata, overlooking the lake.

❺ Head up Templarasund away from the lake. At the next corner, on your left you'll see the 19th-century **Alþingishús** (Parliament House), one of Iceland's oldest stone buildings. When Parliament is in session (October–May), you can view the proceed- **❻** ings from the visitors' gallery. On your right is **Dómkirkjan** (the Lutheran Cathedral), a small, charming church erected in 1785. Directly ahead is **Austurvöllur,** the city's historic central square, with its **statue of Jón Sigurðsson** (1811–79), who led Iceland's fight for independence from Denmark. This is also where Ingólfur Arnarson built his residence back in the 9th century.

Time Out   If it is late afternoon, visit one of the historic area's old pubs: **Café Hressó** (Austurstræti 20, tel. 1/14353), with its summery back garden; **Fógetinn** (Aðalstræti 10, tel. 1/16323), an intimate spot with low ceilings; or arty **Cafe Solon Islandus** (Bankastræti 7a, tel. 1/12666), where you can see some modern art, eat a snack or a cake, and have a perfect view of the cultural avant-garde.

Leading west out of the square is Austurstræti, a pedestrian shopping street with the main post office on the right. From here you can take Bus 10 or 100 for a 20-minute ride to **❼ Árbæjarsafn** (Open-Air Municipal Museum), a "village" of 18th- and 19th-century houses furnished in old-fashioned style, displaying authentic household utensils and tools for cottage industries. The museum hums with life on summer weekends, when a variety of educational and ethnic events are organized,

from demonstrations of crafts to a taste of piping-hot *lummur* (chewy pancakes) from a peat-fired farmhouse stove. *Corner Höfðabakki and Rofabær, tel. 1/814412 or 814093, fax 1/ 673620. Admission: IKr300 adults, IKr150 senior citizens, children under 16 free. Open June–Aug., Tues.–Sun. 10–6; Sept., Sat.–Sun. 10–6; Oct.–May, open by request only.*

Tour 2: Museums and the University

8 Take bus No. 1 to the large **Hallgrímskirkja** (Hallgrim's Church), with its 210-foot stair-stepped gray-stone tower that dominates the city's skyline. The church, which was completed in 1986 after more than 40 years of construction, is named for the 17th-century hymn-writer Hallgrímur Pétursson. From the church tower, the city's highest vantage point, you can enjoy a panoramic view; note the compactness of the city center to the west, compared with the suburbs that sprawled outward with a tenfold increase in population after World War II. *Tel. 1/10745. Admission to tower: IKr200 adults, IKr50 children 5–12, children under 5 free. Open Tues.–Sun. 10–6, Mon. 1:30–5.*

In front of the church is a **statue of Leifur Eiríksson,** the Icelander who discovered America 500 years before Columbus did. (Leif's father was Eric the Red, who discovered Greenland.) The statue, by American sculptor Stirling Calder, was presented to the people of Iceland by the people of the United States in 1930, to mark the millennium of the Alþingi.

9 Across from the church is the **Einar Jónsson Museum** and **Sculpture Garden.** Jónsson (1874–1954) was a pioneer of Icelandic sculpture early in this century; his works explore a wide range of religious and mythical subjects. *Corner Njarðargata and Þórsgata, tel. 1/13797. Admission: IKr100 adults. Open June–Sept., Tues.–Sun. 1:30–4; Feb.–May, weekends 1:30–4.*

10 From here art lovers may want to visit three other art galleries. Follow Njarðargata to Bergstaðastræti for the **Ásgrímur Jónsson Museum,** which features the works of the popular neo-impressionist painter Ásgrímur Jónsson (1870–1968). *Bergstaðastræti 74, tel. 1/13644. Admission free. Open June–Aug., Tues.–Sun. 1:30–4; Sept.–May, weekends only 1:30–4.*

11 **Kjarvalsstaðir** (the Reykjavík Municipal Art Gallery), named in honor of Jóhannes Kjarval (1889–1972), the nation's best-loved painter, features work by Kjarval and others. It's a 10-minute walk uptown from Hallgrímskirkja, in the spacious **Miklatún** public park. *Tel. 1/26131. Free or small admission fee, depending on exhibitions. Open daily 10–6.*

12 Go north to Laugavegur and catch the No. 4 bus to reach the **Ásmundur Sveinsson Gallery.** Sveinsson (1893–1982), a social-realist sculptor, began his career in the 1920s. The surrounding garden, open at all times, contains many of his chunky, powerful sculptures. *Corner Sigtún and Reykjavegur, tel. 1/32155. Admission: IKr100. Open mid-May–Sept., daily 10–4; Oct.–mid-May, daily 1–4.*

From Hallgrímskirkja, walk downhill on Þórsgata (stay on it when it becomes Spítalastígur) to Þingholtsstræti, where you turn left. Pass the **Borgarbókasafn** (City Library), which has a selection of books on Iceland in English on the second floor, and turn right onto Laufásvegur. The United States Embassy is to the right, an unimpressive building, but opposite it is the en-

⑬ trance to the **Listasafn Íslands** (National Art Gallery). This interesting structure, originally built as an ice house, was Reykjavík's hottest night spot in the '60s and has now been adapted and extended as a temple to modern art. The gallery exhibits the works of Iceland's "old masters," Kjarval and Gunnlaugur Scheving, as well as those of contemporary Icelandic and visiting artists. There is a pleasant coffee shop with a view of the lake. *Fríkirkjuvegur 7, tel. 1/621000. Admission free. Open Jan. 4–early Dec., Tues.–Sun. 12–6.*

Walk between the gallery and the **Fríkirkjan** church (corner of Fríkirkjuvegur and Skálholtsstígur) toward Tjörnin lake and turn left onto Lækjargata. Follow the lakeshore to the bridge on your right; cross the bridge and continue to the end of Skothúsvegur. On the right lies the old Reykjavík cemetery, a peaceful, shady spot. On your left is a traffic circle, on the far ⑭ side of which stands the **Þjóðminjasafn** (National Museum). On display are Viking artifacts, national costumes, weaving, silver work, wood carvings, and some unusual whalebone carvings, as well as exhibits of agricultural and maritime history, and a replica of an old farmhouse interior. The small coffee shop offers refreshments. *Suðurgata 41, tel. 1/28888. Admission IKr200 adults, children free. Open mid-May–mid-Sept., Tues.–Sun. 12–4; Oct.–May, Tues., Thurs., and weekends 12–4.*

The museum is on the campus of the **University of Iceland,** founded in 1911. Leave the museum by walking between its main entrance side and **Félagsstofnun Stúdenta** (the Student Union). Continue along the sidewalk directly toward the main university building, in front of which is a large crescent-shaped lawn. On the lawn there is a **statue of Sæmundur Fróði,** a symbol of the value of book learning. Legend has it that after studying abroad, Sæmundur made a pact with the devil to change into a seal to carry him home. Just as they arrived, Sæmundur hit the seal on the head with the Bible and escaped unscathed.

⑮ Before you is the white-and-blue cultural center, **Norræna Húsið** (Nordic House), designed by Finnish architect Alvar Aalto. There's a gallery in the basement, and lectures in Scandinavian languages and concerts are often held upstairs. *Tel. 1/17030, fax 1/26476. Open daily 2–7.*

Time Out The **Nordic House cafeteria,** which offers a tempting selection of sandwiches and cakes, is a favorite haunt of university intelligentsia. A wide selection of Scandinavian newspapers is available.

Southwest of Nordic House, on Sturlugata, you pass **Oddi,** the Social Sciences Building (the **University Art Museum** on the third floor is open daily in summer 1:30–6; admission is free), and arrive at the Árnagarður Building, behind the Social Sciences Building, facing Suðurgata. The ground floor of Árna- ⑯ garður houses the **Árni Magnússon Institute,** which exhibits priceless original vellum manuscripts of many of the Sagas. *Tel. 1/25540. Admission free. Open mid-June–Aug., Mon.–Sat. 2–4; Sept.–early June, by request only.*

What to See and Do with Children

The most central supervised playgrounds are at **Njálsgata** (tel.
1/26568), **Vesturgata** (tel. 1/16830), **Frostaskjól** (tel. 1/23944),
and **Dunhagi** (tel. 1/23918). Children of all ages will want to visit one of the open-air, heated swimming pools, which have special shallow areas and water slides. All age groups would enjoy
a visit to **Laugardalur,** a park in the northeastern suburbs (take
Bus 2 east), with its large playground and swimming pool. It
also features the **Farm Zoo,** which includes goats, cows, horses,
and other domestic animals; seals and fish are also on view in
this handsomely laid-out park, opened in 1990. *Tel. 1/32533 or
1/32561. Admission: IKr200 adults, IKr100 students, senior
citizens, and 6–12 year-olds; children under 6 free. Open
Mon.–Tues. and Thurs.–Fri. 1–5, Sat. and Sun. 10–6.*

Adjacent to the Farm Zoo, a large new Family Park is scheduled to open by summer 1994.

Just opposite the Farm Zoo, also in Laugardalur, is the
Grasagarður (Botanical Garden), with its extensive outdoor
collection of plants from all over the world. *Tel. 1/38870. Admission free. Open June–Sept., weekdays 8 AM–10 PM, weekends
10–10. Open until dusk rest of year.*

Off the Beaten Track

Visit the harborfront for an impression of the smells, sounds,
and bustling activity of Iceland's basic export industry, fishing. Take Bus 2 to the end of its route at the beginning of
Grandagarður and walk 15 minutes along that street out onto
the **Örfirisey** peninsula. To the north you have a good view of
Esja, mountain of a thousand hues. On the eastern side of
Örfirisey is the city's largest and most modern fish-processing
plant. Walking past it, you eventually end up at one of the two
beacons at the entrance to Reykjavík Harbor.

Return along the waterfront, taking in the sights of a multitude
of fishing vessels, pleasure boats, and freighters. On weekdays
this is a bustling part of the city, with fishing boats coming in
all the time. Beyond the bus stop, past another fish-processing
plant, turn left on Mýrargata, heading downtown past small
shipyards. Walk out along the landing ramps, where Icelandic
youngsters like to hang out for some serious fishing.

At the **Tollstöðin** (Customs House) you may want to detour
around to the building's inland side, on Tryggvagata, where
you can see Iceland's largest mosaic mural, a harbor scene by
Gerður Helgadóttir. Return to the harbor's edge and walk
north along the eastern pier, past more freighters and fishing
vessels. Soon you come to **Ingólfsgarður pier,** with its distinctive yellow lighthouse at the end.

In good weather the verdant offshore island of **Viðey** is well
worth a visit: it is only accessible by ferry (tel. 1/681085, 1/
621632, or 985/20099) from its own pier at the modern
Sundahöfn freight harbor. A few minutes' crossing brings you
to an unspoiled island; it's a paradise for nesting birds and a
wonderful place for a walk and a picnic. Do not miss **Áfangar,**
Richard Serra's landscape art arrangement of basalt pillars on
the northern part of the island. The 18th-century governor's

residence, **Viðey House,** and the little church have been renovated. The House is now a classy restaurant/banquet hall.

Shopping

The main shopping streets **downtown** are on and around Laugavegur, Bankastræti, Austurstræti, Aðalstræti, and Hafnarstræti. The **Kringlan** mall is on the east side of town (intersection of Miklabraut and Kringlumýrarbraut; take Bus 3 or 6 from Lækjartorg, or Bus 8 or 9 from Hlemmur). There are also galleries and crafts workshops all around town.

Street Markets In summertime **Lækjartorg** fills with the stands of outdoor merchants offering anything from woolens, records, and books to vegetables, fruit, and bread. On Saturday and some Sundays the **Kolaport** car park (underneath the new Central Bank building—you can't miss it) is transformed into a lively flea market where you may find almost anything on sale and almost certainly something you fancy.

Specialty Stores **Gallery Borg** (Austurvöllur, tel. 1/24211, and Austurstræti 3,
Art Galleries tel. 1/11664), and **Gallery FÍM** (Garðastræti 6, tel. 1/25060) display the latest works by contemporary Icelandic artists.

Coins and Stamps **Hjá Magna** (Laugavegur 15, tel. 1/23011) offers a wide selection. Due to the limited size of the issues involved, a number of Icelandic stamps and coins are considered valuable items. For stamp collectors, the post office offers a special philatelic service, with subscription schemes for new issues. **Postphil** is located at the main post office (Pósthússtræti 5, Box 8445, 128 Reykjavík).

Crafts Long the staple purchase of visitors, woolens include both traditional hand knitted sweaters (a good sweater is priced at about IKr5,900 to IKr6,700) and stylish, multicolored new designs. Lava ceramics, sheepskin rugs, and Viking-inspired jewelry are also popular souvenirs. Shop at **Rammagerðin** (Hafnarstræti 19, tel. 1/17910; at the Kringlan mall, tel. 1/689960; at Hotel Loftleiðir, tel. 1/25460; at Hotel Esja, tel. 1/681124), **Handprjónasamband** (Skólavörðustígur 19, tel. 1/21890), and **Íslenskur heimilisiðnaður** (Hafnarstræti 3, tel. 1/11785). An arts-and-crafts market at **Hlaðvarpinn,** Vesturgata 3, offers original hand-made garments and jewelry. It's open Tuesday to Saturday.

Sports and Fitness

Participant Sports At the southern tip of Seltjarnarnes, the westernmost part of
Golf the Reykjavík area, **Golfklúbbur Ness** (Suðurnes, tel. 1/611930) offers a well-kept 9-hole course with a great view in all directions. **Golfklúbbur Reykjavíkur** (Grafarholti, tel. 1/82815) is the granddaddy of them all, a challenging 18-hole course located just east of Reykjavík. **Keilir** (Vesturkoti, Hvaleyrarbraut, tel. 1/53360) is another well-established 18-hole course, located in Hafnarfjörður, south of Reykjavík.

Horseback Riding Two stables in the Reykjavík area rent horses by the hour or by the day. **Laxnes Horse Farm** (Mosfellsdalur, tel. 1/666179 or 1/621011 at Reykjavík Excursions) offers three-hour riding tours for IKr2,800, including guides and transportation to and from Reykjavík. **Icelandic Riding Tours** (Bæjarhraun 2, Hafnarfjörður, tel. 1/653044) offers one- to five-hour rides for IKr1,900–

IKr2,800, which also includes guides and transportation from Reykjavík hotels.

Jogging In the crisp, clean air of the Reykjavík area, jogging is a pleasure on the wide sidewalks and in the parks. Favorite routes are around **Tjörnin** lake (*see* Tours 1 and 2, *above*), in **Laugardalur** park (*see* Swimming, *below*), and in **Miklatún** park (*see* Tour 2, *above*). For distance runners, there is the **Reykjavík Marathon** in August.

Skating The man-made skating rink in **Laugardalur,** adjacent to the Botanical Gardens and Farm Zoo, rents skates (October to April).

Skiing In wintertime, try the downhill and cross-country skiing at the **Bláfjöll** (tel. 1/78559) and **Skálafell** (tel. 1/666095) areas outside Reykjavík. Both are within a 30-minute drive of the capital and can be reached by BSÍ bus (tel. 1/22300).

Swimming There are nine swimming pools in the greater Reykjavík area, some with saunas. Rules of hygiene are strictly enforced—you must shower thoroughly, without a swimsuit, before entering the pool. The pools of **Vesturbær** at Hofsvallagata (Bus 4) and **Laugardalur** (Bus 2 going east) are favorite summer haunts. Both are open year-round, weekdays 7 AM–8:30 PM, Saturday 7:30–5:30, and Sunday 8–5:30. A locker and access to the swimming pool costs IKr120 or IKr60 for children (discount tickets available), but you must bring or rent a towel. Use of the sauna is extra. Swimwear and towels can be rented. *Note:* swimming pools are one of the few places in Iceland where you should be on your guard against petty theft. If you are wearing really snazzy running shoes, lock them up with your clothes in the locker.

For a unique swimming experience, the **Blue Lagoon** (tel. 2/68526) should not be missed. Located just 15 kilometers (10 miles) from Keflavík Airport and 50 kilometers (31 miles) from Reykjavík, the lagoon is a man-made wonder. Superheated water is pumped up from 2 kilometers (1¼ miles) beneath the earth's surface to power a geothermal energy plant; the run-off water collects in the lava to form a warm, salty, mineral-rich lagoon. Facilities at the lagoon are basic (communal changing rooms, no lockers). Buses run from the BSÍ bus terminal in Reykjavík to the Blue Lagoon twice daily—three times a day in July and August.

Spectator Sports Handball, a national obsession and a big crowd-puller, is *the*
Handball winter sport in Iceland. For fast, furious, and exciting matches between Iceland's leading teams, as well as thrilling confrontations with some of the world's best handball nations, contact the **Handball Federation** (tel. 1/685422).

Soccer The national sport is played in summer before thousands of fans. A number of Icelandic soccer players are with professional soccer teams in Europe, and most come home to participate in international matches. The most important matches are played at **Laugardalsvöllur Stadium** (tel. 1/33527; take Bus 2 going east). Buy tickets at the box office just before the game, or inquire at downtown bookstores for advance sales.

Dining

Most of the better Reykjavík hotels have gourmet restaurants that belong to the Chaine des Rotisseurs. There are also 11 ful-

ly licensed full-service restaurants with an international menu. In addition, there are 20 combination pub/restaurants in the capital offering less extensive menus at reasonable prices.

Highly recommended restaurants are indicated by a star ★.

Very Expensive **Argentína.** Come here for a change from seafood—there are 24 meat items on the menu. Located in a house set back off Barónsstígur, this steak house creates a South American atmosphere with white tiled walls, wooden benches and beams. Argentine wines are available, and there are some distinctly Argentine items on the menu, but Argentína also serves first-rate domestic Icelandic beef, basted with chicimurra sauce before being grilled. *Barónsstígur 11a, tel. 1/19555. Reservations advised. Dress: casual but neat. AE, DC, MC, V. No lunch.*

Grillið. Just off the university campus, atop the Saga Hotel, the Grillið offers a spectacular view of the capital and the surrounding hinterlands. Seafood specialties include blue ling with mild mustard sauce. An excellent dessert is chocolate ribbons with espresso mousse and angostura truffles. *Hagatorg, tel. 1/25033. Reservations advised. Dress: casual but neat. AE, DC, MC, V.*

★ **Holt.** Located at the Holt Hotel, within walking distance of downtown, this restaurant is decorated with one of the finest collections of paintings by Icelandic masters; the bar features drawings by Jóhannes Kjarval. Holt has long been in the forefront of Icelandic restaurants, offering impeccable service with the emphasis on mouth-watering seafood cuisine, as well as a wine list famed for its breadth (and price). Favorite dishes include: graflax as appetizer, grilled halibut, rack of lamb, or reindeer steak as entrées. *Bergstaðastræti 37, tel. 1/25700. Reservations advised. Dress: casual but neat. AE, DC, MC, V.*

Perlan. The rotating restaurant atop Reykjavík's hot-water storage tanks on Öskjuhlíð hill, opened in 1991. It is the city's trendiest eating place, with the most spectacular views in town (one revolution takes about an hour). The menu is international, with an emphasis on quality Icelandic ingredients, such as succulent lamb and lumpfish caviar. A special seafood menu changes from day to day to offer the best and freshest fish available. Specialties of the house include halibut cheeks, pan-fried with langoustine sauce or served on a bed of vegetables. Alfonsin *(Hoplostethus islandicus)*, a species of fish recently discovered by chefs and gourmets, is also featured on the seafood menu when it's available. Perlan's bakery produces fresh bread, cakes, and pastries. *Öskjuhlíð, tel. 1/620203. Reservations advised. Dress: casual but neat. AE, DC, MC, V. Closed lunch.*

Expensive **Óðinsvé.** Just east of downtown, this cozy restaurant is located on the first floor of the Óðinsvé Hotel. Decorated in pastel colors with pink tablecloths, half the dining area is under a covered porch. The chefs cook in a Scandinavian-French style, with an emphasis on seafood. Choice appetizers include the fish chowder; the best dessert is hot apple strudel. *Óðinstorg, tel. 1/25090. Reservations advised. Dress: casual but neat. AE, DC, MC, V.*

★ **Við Tjörnina.** This restaurant is simply the best in Iceland. The owner, epicure Rúnar Marvinsson, runs the kitchen himself, turning out classic Icelandic cuisine. Scallops in lobster sauce is a good choice for the appetizer; *tindabikkja* (starry ray with grapes, capers, and Pernod) is an unforgettable entrée. Lunch-

time can be a bargain, with a Dish of the Day (soup and a fish dish) for only IKr800. It's located just across Templarasund from the Parliament building and Dómkirkjan, on the second floor of a typical corrugated-iron-clad early 20th-century house. The old-fashioned decor remains true to the house, with a hand-carved bar and chairs, embroidered tablecloths, and crocheted drapes. *Templarasund 3, tel. 1/18666. Reservations advised. Dress: casual but neat. AE, MC, V.*

Moderate **Ítalía.** Crisp Italian decor, a wine list that includes most Italian wines available in Iceland, and Parmesan cheese on every table helps this small eatery live up to its name. Hors d'oeuvres include ragout of escargots and smoked salmon tartare. The Italian cook makes excellent pork tortellini in cream sauce and lasagna Bolognese with blue cheese. For dessert, try Italian ice cream stirred with Amaretto and chopped fruit. *Laugavegur 11, tel. 1/24630. Reservations advised. Dress: casual but neat. AE, DC, MC, V.*

Potturinn og pannan. Within walking distance of the uptown hotels, this is one of the city's best buys, offering an excellent selection of good-quality fish and meat dishes. There's an American-style open salad bar and plenty of fresh-baked whole-grain bread to choose from; fish or lamb entrées include juicy halibut steaks and lamb pepper steak with carrots and baked potatoes. Tiled floors, copper light fixtures, and tables with benches create a cozy, intimate setting. Service is pleasantly brisk and efficient, but it's a popular spot, so you may have a wait during peak hours of lunch and dinner. A good children's menu and a play corner for the youngest diners make this a popular place for families. *Brautarholt 22, tel. 1/11690. No reservations. Dress: casual. AE, DC, MC, V.*

Þrír Frakkar hjá Úlfari. This fine little restaurant is located in a residential area not far from downtown. Yellowish walls, wood paneling, wrought-iron tables, and comfortable chairs are set in a tasteful atmosphere. The menu features first-rate seafood as well as succulent beef dishes. Try the vegetable broth as an appetizer, butter-fried trout or Portuguese style bacalao (codfish stewed or fried with vegetables) as a main course, and apple pie for dessert. *Baldursgata 14, tel. 1/23939. Reservations advised. Dress: casual but neat. AE, DC, MC, V.*

Inexpensive **Bæjarins beztu.** The most famous, most popular fast-food place in Iceland may easily escape you. Facing the harbor, set in a parking lot at the corner of Tryggvagata and Pósthússtræti, this is the home of the original Icelandic hot dog; one person serves about a thousand hot dogs a day out the window of a tiny hut—watch how fast his hands move. Ask for *ayn-ah-mud-lou* (pronounced quickly in monotone with stress on "mud"), which means "one with everything": mustard, tomato sauce, mayonnaise, and chopped raw onion. Eat standing up at one of the small outdoor tables. It's open from 10 AM until midnight. *Tryggvagata/Pósthússtræti, no tel. No reservations. Dress: casual. No credit cards.*

Kaffivagninn. Favored by cabdrivers, fishermen, and stevedores, this unpretentious harbor-side restaurant serves traditional Icelandic fare. Sit at a table at the windows where you can have a nice view of the water. *Grandagarður 10, tel. 1/15932. No reservations. Dress: casual. MC, V.*

Lodging

Hotels and guest houses are located all around Reykjavík, with
the Holt and Óðinsvé hotels closest to downtown. Everything
from modern, first-class Scandinavian-style hotels to inexpensive bed-and-breakfasts is available. Breakfast is usually included in the price, and free parking is available at all hotels.
Inquire at the desk whether your hotel offers complimentary
admission tickets to the closest swimming pool.

Highly recommended hotels are indicated by a ★.

Very Expensive **Holiday Inn.** This international-class hotel built in 1987 is tastefully decorated in pastel colors with spacious rooms. Amenities
include hair dryers, direct-dial telephones, minibars, and color
TV. It's a 10-minute walk to Laugardalur park and pool, and
also is close to the Ásmundur Sveinsson Gallery. *Sigtún 38,
105, tel. 1/689000, fax 1/680675. 100 rooms with bath, 3 suites.
Facilities: restaurant, coffee shop, bars. AE, DC, MC, V.*

Ísland. This chunky, seven-story, post-modern blue hotel
opened in 1991, although the nightspot of the same name on the
ground floor has been open since 1987. Under the same management as Hotel Saga, the Ísland hotel is located close to
Laugardalur park and recreation area. The light and airy
rooms are decorated in pink and brown pastel floral prints,
with dark wood and smooth, curved shapes. There are terrific
views over the bay and Mt. Esja. *Ármúli 9, tel. 1/688999, fax
689957. 119 rooms with bath or shower, 5 with kitchenette, 3
suites. Facilities: restaurant, bar, nightclub. AE, DC, MC, V.*

Expensive **Borg.** Reykjavík's oldest hotel, built in 1930, has just been totally refurbished; restored to its original Art Deco glory, it also
has modern amenities such as satellite TV and direct fax to
your room on request. Room furnishings, with an emphasis on
tasteful prints, aim to combine good, old-fashioned quality
with modern comfort. The hotel is located at the heart of the
city, overlooking Austurvöllur and close to Parliament House.
Occasional dinner dances are held in the downstairs restau-
rant/ballroom. *Pósthússtræti 11, Box 200, 121 Reykjavík, tel.
1/11440, fax 1/11420. 29 rooms, 5 suites. Facilities: restaurant,
bar. AE, DC, MC, V.*

Holt. Excellent service and a gourmet restaurant make this
quietly elegant hotel a favorite among business travelers. The
main drawback is that the rooms are small, though luxuriously
decorated, many with works by leading Icelandic artists. The
location is in a pleasant neighborhood close to the center of
town. *Bergstaðastræti 37, 101, tel. 1/25700, fax 1/623025. 50
rooms with bath, 4 suites. Facilities: restaurant, bar, lounge,
conference room. AE, DC, MC, V.*

Loftleiðir. Recently redecorated in Scandinavian style, the hotel offers a wide range of amenities. The main drawback is its
location at Reykjavík Airport, which means that you cannot
easily walk anywhere and bus connections are difficult. The advantage is nearby Öskjuhlíð, where you can take pleasant
walks among the trees and shrubs, enjoy the superb view, and
perhaps stroll up to Perlan for an ice cream or a meal. *Reykjavík
Airport, tel. 1/22322, fax 1/25320. 211 rooms with bath, 9 deluxe rooms, 1 apartment suite. Facilities: restaurant, bar,
meeting rooms, pool, sauna, shops, bank, travel agency. AE,
DC, MC, V.*

★ **Saga.** Located just off the university campus, the hotel is a 10-

minute walk from most museums, shops, and restaurants. All rooms are above the fourth floor and have spectacular views. *Hagatorg, 107, tel. 1/29900, fax 1/623980. 216 rooms with bath, 8 suites. Facilities: 2 restaurants, bars, nightclub, conference rooms, health club, shops, bank, travel agency. AE, DC, MC, V.*

Moderate **Lind.** Quietly unpretentious, decorated in light pastel colors,
★ and located uptown close to the Hlemmur bus station, the Lind was fully renovated in 1987. Its clientele is largely Icelanders from the countryside attending conferences or cultural events in Reykjavík. *Rauðarárstígur 18, 105, tel. 1/623350, fax 1/ 623150. 44 rooms with bath. Facilities: restaurant, conference rooms. AE, DC, MC, V.*

Inexpensive There are several guest houses around town, offering basic accommodations at relatively low prices, and bed-and-breakfasts in private homes are also available. These accommodations can be booked in advance through your travel agent. The **Tourist Information Center** (Bankastræti 2, tel. 1/623045, fax 1/624749) has registers of guest houses (from about IKr4,000 a night) and B&B accommodation (about IKr3,700) in and around Reykjavík. The **Salvation Army** (Kirkjustræti 2, tel. 1/613203) charges IKr3,000 for a double room without bath or breakfast. The **Reykjavík Youth Hostel** (Sundlaugavegur 34, tel. 1/38110) has 104 beds, without breakfast, for around IKr1,500 per night.

The Arts and Nightlife

Consult the monthly *Around Reykjavík* or *News from Iceland* and the biweekly *What's on in Reykjavík*, all available at hotels, for events of interest. Most hotels offer satellite TV channels from Europe and the United States, in addition to the countrywide Channel 1 and local Channel 2.

The Arts Theater, music, and opera are all popular in Iceland, but for the summer visitor the problem is that everything closes down during June, July, and August, except for the odd concert or two. Most art galleries and many museums do put on special summer shows with the visitor in mind, however.

Film The eight movie houses around the capital have up to six screens each and for the most part show recent English-language films (with Icelandic subtitles). In summer, recent Icelandic films are screened with English subtitles for tourists. For listings, see the daily newspaper *Morgunblaðið*. The **University Cinemas** are on Hagatorg, near the university.

Folklore Traditional folklore entertainment in English, based on the Icelandic Sagas, is offered in summer by the **Light Nights** actors' show in various locations. Check with the Tourist Information Center (tel. 1/623045).

Music Visiting musicians play everything from the classics to jazz, opera to rock. The **Icelandic Opera,** a resident company, performs in winter at its home on Ingólfsstræti.

Theater In winter, the **National Theater** (Hverfisgata, tel. 1/11200) and **City Theater** (Listabraut, tel. 1/680680) offer plays by Icelandic writers, such as Nobel Prize winner Halldór Laxness, as well as works by such diverse dramatists as Henrik Ibsen, Tennessee Williams, and Rodgers and Hammerstein.

Nightlife Nightlife in Reykjavík essentially means two types of establishments: "night spots," offering dancing with live music or discothèque, where an entrance fee is charged, and pubs, where entrance is free. Night spots usually enforce some basic dress rules, so men should wear a jacket and tie, and women should avoid wearing jeans. Pubs make no such demands. Some pubs, however, also have small dance floors and often charge an entrance fee if a live band is playing. Both pubs and night spots charge high prices for drinks. The minimum age for entering such licensed premises is 18.

Plúsinn (Vitastígur 3, tel. 1/623137) is a terrific place for live music, even if conversation suffers for it. Jazz, rock, blues—anything goes here. The fashionable place to see and be seen is **Café Solon Islandus** (Bankastræti 7a, tel. 1/12666), where live music—everything from blues to classical—goes on into the small hours on weekends. An upstairs art gallery that doubles as an intimate theater completes the seductively arty ambience. **Hótel Ísland** (Ármúli 9, tel. 1/687111), the largest restaurant and dance hall in Iceland, swallows more than a thousand guests at a time. Offering live entertainment and music, it is popular with all ages.

Golden Circle Excursion

If you make only one foray outside Reykjavík, take this popular day trip to the lakes, waterfalls, and hot springs just inland from the capital. You'll begin at Þingvellir, ancient seat of the world's first parliament; then you will see the original Geysir (whence the term *geyser*) hot spring and stop at Gullfoss, the "Golden Waterfall" from which this tour takes its name.

Important Addresses and Numbers

Tourist General information is available in Reykjavík at the **Tourist In-**
Information **formation Center** (Bankastræti 2, tel. 1/623045) or the **Iceland Tourist Board** (Lækjargata 3, tel. 1/27488).

In Hveragerði, contact the **South Coast Travel Service and Information Center** (Breiðumörk 10, tel. 8/34280).

Emergencies In Hveragerði the **police** can be reached at tel. 8/31154.

Getting There

By Car This circuit should take seven or eight hours by car, allowing time for stops at the various sights. At the farthest point, Gullfoss, you'll only be 125 kilometers (78 miles) from Reykjavík, and most of the drive is along paved main roads.

By Bus It is possible to explore this area by BSÍ bus, but you must allow plenty of time and perhaps stay overnight en route. **BSÍ Travel** (tel. 1/22300) serves Þingvellir twice daily (June–mid-Sept.) and Gullfoss/Geysir twice daily (June 15–Aug.).

Guided Tours

Kynnisferðir (Reykjavík Excursions, tel. 1/621011 or 1/688922) offers an eight-hour guided Golden Circle tour May–September, daily at 9 AM, and October–April, daily except Tuesday and Thursday.

Exploring the Golden Circle

After an hour's drive from Reykjavík, along Route 36 across the Mosfellsheiði heath, the broad lava plain of Þingvellir suddenly opens in front of you. Located at the northern end of Iceland's largest lake, Þingvallavatn, this has been the nation's most hallowed place since AD 930, when the settler Grímur Geitskór chose it as the site for the world's oldest parliament, the Icelandic *Alþingi* (Congress of All). In July of each year delegates from all over the country camped for two weeks at Þingvellir, meeting to pass laws and render judicial sentences. Iceland remained a sovereign nation-state, ruled solely by the people without a personal sovereign or central government, until 1262, when it came under the Norwegian crown; even then, the Alþingi continued to meet at Þingvellir until 1798, when it was dissolved by Iceland's Danish rulers. Today Þingvellir is a national park and remains a potent symbol of the national heritage.

After you enter the Þingvellir park, but before you descend to the central plain, turn right at the sign for **Almannagjá** (Everyman's Gorge) and follow a short road to the rim, where there is a fabulous view from the orientation marker. You can go down a path into the Almannagjá, which leads straight east to **Lögberg** (Law Rock), where the person chosen as guardian of the laws would recite them from memory.

In AD 1000 the Alþingi decided that Iceland should become a Christian country, but the old heathen gods were still worshiped in secret. Those Viking gods remain part of everyday English: Týr (as in Tuesday), Óðinn (as in Wednesday), Þór (as in Thursday), and the goddess Frigg (as in Friday). The **Öxaráfoss** (Öxara Waterfall) is just north of Lögberg, with some beautiful, peaceful picnic spots north of it. Just below the waterfall in a deep stretch of the river lies the forbidding **Drekkingarhylur** pool, where unfaithful wives were drowned.

Besides its historic interest, Þingvellir has a special interest for naturalists: It is the geologic meeting point of two continents. At Almannagjá, on the west side of the plain, is the easternmost edge of the American tectonic plate, which is otherwise submerged in the Atlantic Ocean. Over on the plain's east side, at the Heiðargjá gorge, you are at the westernmost edge of the Eurasian plate. In the 9,000 years since the Þingvellir lava field was formed, the tectonic plates have moved 231 feet apart. And they are still moving.

Time Out The quaint **Valhöll Hotel and Restaurant** (in Þingvellir national park, tel. 8/22622) offers a fine menu. For a coffee break you might try the delicious *pönnukökur* (crepes filled with whipped cream and jam). Rather than the large common room, try to sit in one of the cozy corners of the restaurant, which are decorated with original Icelandic landscape paintings.

Seven kilometers (4 miles) east of the Þingvellir plain, Route 36 meets the road to **Laugarvatn** (Warm Springs Lake), Route 365, which climbs 16 kilometers (10 miles) through the high country. If you keep a close lookout halfway along this road, you'll see on the left the large opening of a cave in which people lived in the early 20th century. True to its name, Laugarvatn is a lake warm enough for bathing, its water naturally heated by

hot springs at the northern end. A cluster of buildings here houses a school in winter and Edda Hotels in summer. Drive around them to the lake's edge to a bathhouse where you can rent towels and take showers year-round. The entrance fee also covers a natural steam bath in an adjoining hut, where you actually sit atop a hissing hot spring.

A mile or so farther along Route 365, turn left onto Route 37, which leads 25 kilometers (16 miles) north to Route 35. A couple of kilometers east on Route 35 you'll come to the popular tourist spot Haukadalur, home of the **Geysir** and **Strokkur** geysers. Both are close to the road, near the Geysir restaurant and hotel (*see* Dining and Lodging, *below*). The famous Geysir hot spring used to gush a column of scalding water 130 to 200 feet into the air, but the old geyser has now gone into retirement. Strokkur is a more reliable performer, having been drilled open in 1964 after a quiet period of 70 years; it throws up boiling water to as high as 100 feet at five-minute intervals. In the same area there are small boreholes from which steam arises, as well as beautiful pools of blue water. Always be careful when approaching hot springs or mud baths—the ground may be treacherous, giving way suddenly beneath you.

A couple of kilometers farther east along Route 35 you will come to thundering **Gullfoss** (Golden Falls), the nation's most admired waterfall. Gullfoss, which is 105 feet high, is a double cascade in the Hvítá river, which turns at right-angles in mid-drop. Below Gullfoss on the western bank of the river, where the steep walls begin to slant more, is a beautiful hidden spot a short, steep climb from the road. Called **Pjaxi**, from the Latin *pax* meaning "peace," this is a restful nook of grassy knolls, natural springs, clear streams, and birch trees.

Return toward Reykjavík via Route 35 to the south. After 23 kilometers (14 miles), turn left onto Route 31, which takes you 5 kilometers (3 miles) past **Skálholt Cathedral.** This ancient place of worship was established in 1056, soon after Iceland converted to Christianity; the present exquisitely simple building, with its modern altarpiece, is the 11th church at this spot, consecrated in 1963. Beneath it lies the ancient crypt. Skálholt was the seat of the southern bishopric, the main center of learning and religion in Iceland until the 18th century. The modern memorial church at Skálholt houses many relics from the past. Works by two of Iceland's most important modern artists adorn the cathedral: a unique mosaic altarpiece by Nína Tryggvadóttir and stained-glass windows by Gerður Helgadóttir. Each summer the cathedral hosts the **Skálholt Music Festival** (for information, write to Helga Ingólfsdóttir, Strönd, Bessastaðahreppur), which brings together musicians from Iceland and abroad. Baroque music, performed on original instruments, is the central feature of the festival.

Continue 10 kilometers (6 miles) along Route 31, then turn right to go south on Route 30, rolling through one of the most prosperous agricultural regions in Iceland. After 17 kilometers (11 miles), take a right onto Route 1, heading west toward Reykjavík. It's about 70 kilometers (43 miles) back to the capital, but if you have time, stop halfway along in **Hveragerði**, home to a horticultural school, a large number of greenhouses heated by hot springs, and a fine swimming pool. From there it's a 40-kilometer (25-mile) drive to Reykjavík.

What to See and Do with Children

In Hveragerði the large **Tívolí** indoor amusement park is filled with activities for kids, including go-carts and motorized inflatable boats. *Austurmörk 24, tel. 8/34115.*

Horse rentals in the area (*see* Horseback Riding, *below*) offer special tours for children.

Sports and Outdoor Activities

Fishing Trout and char are plentiful in Þingvallavatn. Obtain fishing permits at the Valhöll Hotel at Þingvellir (tel. 8/22622).

Horseback Riding A number of stables offer guided trail rides in this area: **Íshestar** (Icelandic Riding Tours) at Miðdalur near Laugarvatn (tel. 8/61169); **Eldhestar** (Volcano Horses) in Hveragerði (Hveramörk 17, tel. 8/34212); the **Laxnes** Pony Farm (tel. 1/666179) on Route 36 to Þingvellir; and **Íshestar** in Hafnarfjörður (Bæjarhraun 2, tel. 1/653044) south of Reykjavík. Horses can be hired for short or longer rides at **Brattholt** farm (tel. 8/68941), adjacent to Gullfoss.

Swimming The region has numerous swimming pools, located wherever there is plenty of natural hot water. Opening times vary. The swimming pool in Hveragerði (tel. 8/34113) is open Monday–Friday 7 AM–8:30 PM, Saturday 9–5:30, and Sunday 9–4:30.

Water Sports At Þingvellir you can rent boats for rowing on Þingvallavatn (the rental facility is on the river by the Valhöll Hotel). Take extraordinary safety precautions: The shoreline drops off precipitously and the water is ice-cold. Rowboats and sailboards can be hired on Laugarvatn lake. At Svínavatn in Grímsnes, you can rent jet-skis (tel. 8/64437) for an exhilarating run on the lake.

White-Water Rafting An exciting way to see the Hvitá river canyon below Gullfoss Falls is at water level by rubber dinghy. Waterproof clothing and life jackets are supplied for an hour's thrilling journey down the churning glacial river. (**Hvítárferðir**, Háagerði 41, Reykjavík, tel. 1/682504.)

Dining and Lodging

Haukadalur **Hótel Geysir.** Located at a popular tourist stop, beside the famous Geysir and Strokkur springs, this hotel is small and basic, but it has a large restaurant. *Tel. 8/68915. 10 rooms with shared baths. MC, V. Closed Sept.–May. Moderate.*

Hveragerði **Hótel Örk.** Recently built in the contemporary style, this white-concrete, blue-roofed hotel features a spa and a swimming pool. The greenhouses, mud pools, and hot springs of Hveragarði are within a couple of blocks' walk. While accommodations are expensive, meals in the ground-floor restaurant are more moderately priced. *Breiðamörk 1, tel. 8/34700, fax 8/34775. 79 rooms with shower. Facilities: restaurant, pool, sauna, tennis. AE, MC, V. Expensive.*

Laugarvatn **Edda Hússtjórnarskóli.** This comfortable hotel and restaurant combination benefits from its location on the lake. *Tel. 8/61154. 27 rooms with bath or shower. MC, V. Closed Sept.–mid-June. Moderate.*
Edda Menntaskóli. This neighbor of the Edda Húsmæðraskóli

also has a lakeside location, although conditions are a little less plush. *Tel. 8/61118. 88 rooms with bath or shower. MC, V. Closed Sept.–mid-June. Moderate.*

Þingvellir **Valhöll.** This small, comfortable first-class hotel has an excellent location, right by the lake. Breakfast is included in the room rate. *Þingvellir National Park, tel. 8/22622, fax 1/621353. 37 rooms with bath or shower. Facilities: restaurant, fishing permits. MC, V. Closed Oct.–Apr. Expensive.*

Youth Hostels **Reykholt:** Biskupstungur, tel. 8/68831, 6/68936, fax 6/68709. 70 beds. Open June–Aug. **Hveragerði:** tel. 8/34198 or 8/34588. 24 beds. Open May–Aug.

The West and the Western Fjords

If you imagine the map of Iceland as the shape of a beast, two rugged western peninsulas—Snæfellsnes and Vestfirðir—would be its proudly rearing head, jaws open wide around the huge bay of Breiðafjörður. The North Atlantic just off this coast is one of the country's prime fishing grounds. Busy fishing villages abound in Vestfirðir (the Western Fjords), but there also are remote cliffs thick with seabirds, tall mountains and deep fjords carved out of basaltic rock. Snæfellsnes peninsula is crowned by the majestic Snæfells glacier.

Borgarfjörður, gateway to the west, is an area of rich farmland that attracted many early settlers. Traces of the Viking past still fire visitors' imagination here today.

Important Addresses and Numbers

Tourist In **Akranes,** the Tourist Information Center (Faxabraut 1, tel.
Information 3/13327) is open 1–3 PM. In **Borgarnes,** the Hótel Borgarnes (Egilsgata 14–16, tel. 3/71119) provides information 24 hours a day year-round. In **Ísafjörður** the Tourist Bureau (Aðalstræti 11, tel. 4/3557) is open 9–noon and 1–5.

Emergencies For local **police in** Borgarnes call tel. 3/71166, in Ísafjörður call tel. 4/4222, and in Stykkishólmur call 3/81008.

Arriving and Departing

By Plane Air travel is the best way to visit the Western Fjords. You can fly to Ísafjörður on **Icelandair** (tel. 1/690200) and **Ernir Air** (tel. 1/24200 or 4/4200), and from there fly on Ernir Air to Bíldudalur, Flateyri, Ingjaldssandur, Patreksfjörður, Reykjanes, Suðureyri, and Þingeyri.

By Car From Reykjavík and the north, you reach the West via the Ring Road (Route 1). Route 54 branches off to the Snæfellsness peninsula; Routes 60 and 68 branch off to the Western Fjords.

By Bus **BSÍ Travel** (Reykjavík Airport, tel. 1/22300) runs frequent daily service to most towns in the region. It's a two-hour trip to Borgarnes, four hours to Stykkishólmur. Bus travel is not the best way to visit the Western Fjords; service to Ísafjörður runs a couple of days a week in summer only, and it's a 12-hour trip.

By Boat The **Akranes** car ferry, *Akraborg* (tel. 1/16050), sails three or four times daily year-round between Reykjavík and Akranes. In summer the **Baldur** car ferry (tel. 3/81120 or 4/2020) links Stykkishólmur, on the Snæfellsnes peninsula, with Brjánslækur on the southern coast of the Western Fjords, calling at Flatey island.

From Ísafjörður, you can travel by the **Fagranes** ferry (tel. 4/3155 or 4/4655) around the Western Fjords.

Guided Tours

The **Iceland Tourist Bureau** (tel. 1/25855) operates a 12-hour day trip from Reykjavík to the Western Fjords, with a flight to Ísafjörður and then sightseeing by bus. The tour departs daily June–August.

Ísafjörður Travel Agency (Aðalstræti 11, tel. 4/3557) runs tours around the Western Fjords.

Boat Tours Sightseeing tours of Breiðafjörður, its innumerable islands and varied bird life, operate from **Stykkishólmur;** contact Eyjaferðir (tel. 3/81450). One-day sightseeing tours of the Western Fjords run in the summers from Ísafjörður (tel. 4/3155 or 4/4655).

Exploring the West

The starting point for this tour is **Borgarnes,** 116 kilometers (72 miles) from Reykjavík along the Ring Road (the Reykjavík–Akranes ferry is a convenient shortcut).

Borgarfjörður Drive northeast from Borgarnes on the Ring Road 11 kilometers (7 miles) until you come to Route 53 leading eastward. Turn right onto Route 53 and pass the **Ferjukot** wild salmon farm; cross the one-lane bridge over the muddy glacial Hvítá River. Take the first left turn onto Route 52 and in 10 minutes you come to the **Laxfoss** (Salmon Falls) on the Grímsá River, where salmon leap the rapids. Continue across the Grímsá north on Route 50 a little more than 10 kilometers (6 miles) until you come to the **Kleppjárnsreykir** horticultural center, with its many greenhouses heated by thermal water from the region's hot springs. Many kinds of fruit and vegetables are available at the greenhouses.

Route 518 leads eastward 8 kilometers (5 miles) to **Reykholt,** home of scholar/historian Snorri Sturluson (1206–41). Author of the *Edda*, a textbook of poetics, and the *Heimskringla*, a history of Norway's kings, Snorri was also a wealthy chieftain and political schemer. He was murdered in Reykholt in 1241 on the orders of the Norwegian king. A hot bathing pool believed to date from Snorri's time can be seen here, as well as part of the underground passage that once led from Snorri's homestead to the pool.

Continue for 15 minutes on Route 518 to the colorful **Hraunfossar** (Lava Falls). A multitude of natural springs under a birch-covered lava field above the Hvítá River creates a waterfall hundreds of feet wide, seemingly appearing out of nowhere. A little farther up the Hvítá (a few minutes along Route 518) is the **Barnafossar** (Children's Falls), which carves strange figures out of the rock. Tradition says that two children lost their lives when a natural stone bridge over the churning mael-

strom gave way. Today a trusty footbridge gives safe access to the opposite bank.

The **Húsafell** park a few hundred meters up the road is a popular summer camping site, with its birch trees, swimming pool, and chalets.

Return past Reykholt to the Ring Road and go north about 10 kilometers (6 miles) to Bifröst. Right by the road is the **Grábrók** volcanic cone, which you can easily scale for a panoramic view of the area. Grábrók's lava field, covered with moss, grass, and birches, offers many quiet spots for a picnic. Eight kilometers (5 miles) north is the distinctive pyramid-shaped **Mt. Baula,** a pastel-colored rhyolite mountain. In the 19th century, Icelanders enjoyed telling gullible foreign travelers fantastic stories of the beautiful green meadows and forests populated by dwarfs shepherding herds of fat sheep at Baula's summit.

Snæfellsnes Peninsula The southern shore of this peninsula begins about 40 kilometers (25 miles) north of Borgarnes. Begin the journey north from Borgarnes on Route 54. As you drive farther west on the peninsula, you'll pass through the Staðarsveit district, with its beautiful mountain range. Many small lakes abound with water flowers, and there are myriad sparkling springs. At **Lýsuhóll,** a few minutes north of Route 54, you can bathe in the warm water of a naturally carbonated swimming pool. About 10 kilometers (6 miles) farther west is the **Búðahraun** lava field, composed of rough, slaggy *apalhraun* lava. Its surface makes walking difficult, but it's more hospitable to vegetation than are most Icelandic landscapes; flowers, trees, herbs, and berries grow large here.

At **Búðir,** take a left turn onto the coastal road for a 50-kilometer (31-mile) drive circling the tip of the peninsula. On your right you'll see the majestic Snæfells glacier, **Snæfellsjökull,** which, like that on Fujiyama in Japan, caps a volcano. The glacier was featured in Jules Verne's novel *Journey to the Center of the Earth* as the spot where the explorers enter the depths of the world. The glacier plays a mystical role in Halldór Laxness's novel *Christianity at Glacier.*

The coastal drive will take you past many beautiful villages, such as **Arnarstapi** and **Hellnar.** About an hour's walk from the road at the western tip of the peninsula lie the **Svörtuloft Cliffs,** home to multitudes of seabirds in nesting season.

At **Ólafsvík** you can stop at the Hotel Nes (*see* Dining and Lodging, *below*) to arrange snowmobile tours or a hike to the top of the glacier. The main highway (now numbered Route 57) begins again at Ólafsvík; from there it's 67 kilometers (42 miles) along the peninsula's north coast to **Stykkishólmur,** home of the scallop fishery. A ferry sails from here to the sparsely populated islands of the Breiðafjörður. The island **Flatey,** where the ferry stops over on the way to the Western Fjords, is worth a visit. The now sleepy vacation village was an important center of commerce and learning in the 19th century; many classic houses still stand today.

Vestfirðir (Western Fjords) From Stykkishólmur, follow Route 57 for another 80 kilometers (50 miles) to Route 60. From the Ring Road, pick up Route 60 about 10 kilometers (6 miles) past Bifröst and drive 43 kilometers (27 miles) to the intersection with Route 57. From there it's a long drive north—340 kilometers (211 miles)—to **Ísa-**

fjörður, the main airport and cultural center of the Western Fjords. Ísafjörður itself is one of the most important fishing villages in Iceland, but for visitors its main use is as a jumping-off point for tours of Hornstrandir, the splendid, peaceful but desolate land north of the 66th parallel, uninhabited since the 1950s. Geologically the oldest part of Iceland, Vestfirðir offers spectacular views of mountains, fjords, and sheer cliffs. Hikers and mountaineers may want to hire guides to explore this unspoiled region, and anglers come here to catch trout in the rivers and lakes. The northernmost cliffs of **Hornbjarg** and **Hælavíkurbjarg** are home to large bird colonies; the largest colony, with millions of birds, is at **Látrabjarg,** an immense vertical cliff at Iceland's westernmost tip.

Sports and Outdoor Activities

Fishing Nearly 100 rivers and lakes offer trout and salmon fishing. Ask at local hotels and service stations, or consult the *Icelandic Fishing Guide* (*see* Sports and Outdoor Activities in Staying in Iceland, *above*).

Golf There are courses at **Ólafsvík** (at Froða, east of town) and **Stykkishólmur** (a 9-hole course by the Hotel Stykkishólmur).

Horseback Riding To rent horses for exploring the Borgarfjörður area, call **Hotel Bifröst** (tel. 3/50000 or 3/50005, fax 3/50003).

Swimming Swimming pools are plentiful in the geothermal areas of the west. There are swimming pools in **Borgarnes** (Skallagrímsgata, tel. 7/70027), **Ólafsvík** (Ennisbraut 9, tel. 3/61199), **Stykkishólmur** (tel. 3/81272), and **Ísafjörður** (Austurvegur 9, 4/3200).

Dining and Lodging

Bifröst **Hótel Bifröst.** Low white buildings with red roofs house this summer hotel beside the Ring Road in Borgarfjörður. *Hreðavatn, tel. 3/50000 or 3/50005, fax 3/50003. 26 rooms, 8 with bath. Facilities: restaurant, bar, horseback riding. MC, V. Expensive.*

Borgarnes **Hótel Borgarnes.** One of the biggest and most popular hotels on the west coast, this establishment offers both a cafeteria and an elegant restaurant. *Egilsgata 14–16, tel. 3/71119, fax 3/71443. 36 rooms, 20 with bath. AE, DC, MC, V. Moderate.*

Búðir **Hótel Búðir.** Under the magical Snæfellsjökull, and close to a golden beach, this hotel has an excellent restaurant. *Snæfellsnes, 311 Borgarnes, tel. 3/56700. 10 rooms with shared bath. Facilities: restaurant, boats, fishing. AE, DC, MC, V. Closed Oct.–Apr. Moderate.*

Ísafjörður **Hótel Ísafjörður.** This is a good family hotel, located in the heart of town. The restaurant offers a great variety of tasty seafood, and breakfast is included in the room rate. Sightseeing tours and boat trips are offered in summer. *Silfurtorgi 2, tel. 4/4111, fax 4/4767. 32 rooms with shower. AE, MC, V. Moderate.*

Ólafsvík **Hótel Nes.** This functional hotel is close to the harbor. Its cafeteria offers good food at moderate prices. There are many hiking paths in the vicinity, and tours to the Snæfellsnes glacier

leave from here. *Ólafsbraut 19, tel. 3/61300. 38 rooms with shared bath. No credit cards. Inexpensive.*

Reykholt **Edda.** Located in a scenic part of Borgarfjörður, this comfortable, modern building is a secondary school in winter and a hotel in summer. *Tel. 3/51260. 60 rooms with bath. Facilities: restaurant, pool. MC, V. Closed Sept.–mid-June. Moderate.*

Stykkishólmur **Hótel Stykkishólmur.** This hotel makes a convenient jumping-off point for excursions to the islands of Breiðafjörður and for the ferry to the Western Fjords. It includes a good restaurant. *Vatnàsi, tel. 3/81330, fax 3/81579. 33 rooms with shower. DC, MC, V. Moderate.*

Youth Hostels **Borgarnes:** Hamar, tel. 3/71663. 14 beds. Open June–Sept.
Borgarfjörður **Kleppjárnsreykir:** tel. 3/51262, 3/51185, fax 3/51437. 14 beds.

Snæfellsnes **Stykkishólmur:** tel. 3/81095. 50 beds.

Western Fjords **Breiðavík:** Rauðasandi, tel. 4/1575. 40 beds. Closed Oct.–Apr.
Patreksfjörður: tel. 4/1280 or 4/1275. 8 beds. Open June–Sept; other times of year by arrangement.

The North

From the Hrútafjörður (Rams' Fjord), which gouges deeply into the western end of the coast, to Vopnafjörður in the east, Iceland's north is a land created by the interplay of fire and ice. Inland, you can find the largest lava fields on earth, some with plants and mosses, others barren and bare. Yet valleys sheltered by the mountains are lush with vegetation and rich in color, and the deeply indented coast offers magnificent views north toward the Arctic, especially spectacular under the summer's midnight sun.

The commercial and cultural center, Akureyri, is Iceland's second-largest town; from there it's a pleasant drive to Lake Mývatn, where bird-watchers can spot vast numbers of waterfowl and hikers can explore weird lava formations. The weather is more stable here than in the south, and it's unusually mild around Mývatn, making it a pleasant outdoor destination.

Important Addresses and Numbers

Tourist In **Akureyri,** contact the Tourist Information Center (Coach
Information Terminal, Hafnarstræti 82, tel. 6/24442); it is open June–Aug., weekdays 8:30–7 PM. In **Húsavík,** Húsavík Travel (Stórigarður 7, tel. 6/42100) is open weekdays 9–noon and 1–5.

Emergencies To reach the local **police** in Akureyri, call 6/23222.

Arriving and Departing

By Plane **Icelandair** (tel. 1/690200) flies to Akureyri, Sauðárkrókur, and Húsavík. The flight to Akureyri takes about an hour. **Norlandair** and Icelandair (tel. 6/22000) share offices and operate flights from Akureyri to Grímsey, Húsavík, Kópasker, Ólafsfjörður, Raufarhöfn, Siglufjörður, Þórshöfn, and Vopnafjörður.

By Car It's a 432-kilometer (268-mile) drive from Reykjavík to Akureyri along the Ring Road (Route 1), a full day's journey. Branch off on Route 75 to Sauðárkrókur, or on Route 85 to Húsavík.

By Bus **BSÍ Travel** (tel. 1/22300) runs daily bus service from Reykjavík to the north. It's 4½ hours to Blönduós and 6½ hours to Akureyri. Bus service from Akureyri takes less than 1½ hours to Húsavík and two hours to Mývatn.

The **Akureyri Bus Company** (Gránufélagsgata 4, tel. 6/23510 or, at bus terminal, 6/24442) operates scheduled trips around the region, including a tour by bus and ferry to Hrísey Island, home of Galloway cattle, and to Grímsey Island on the Arctic Circle.

Guided Tours

The **Iceland Tourist Bureau** (tel. 1/25855) operates a 12-hour day trip from Reykjavík to Akureyri and Lake Mývatn by plane to Akureyri and then by bus to Mývatn. The tour departs daily June–mid-September.

Akureyri Travel Bureau (Ráðhústorg 3, tel. 6/25000) and **Nonni Travel** (Brekkugata 3, tel. 6/27922) run tours from Akureyri to Mývatn, historic sites, and the islands off the north coast.

Exploring the North

If you're driving the full Ring Road route, you'll enter the North at **Brú,** snuggled at the inland end of the long Hrútafjörð- ur. **Blönduós,** 90 kilometers (56 miles) farther west, makes a convenient stopping place. Another 50 kilometers (31 miles) west, Route 75 intersects the Ring Road. If you turn right and then take the next right a kilometer or so farther, you'll come to **Víðimýri,** where you can visit an 18th-century turf-roofed church. Returning north, cross the Ring Road and head north on Route 75 about 10 kilometers (6 miles) to the **Glaumbær Folk Museum.** Set in a turf-roofed farmhouse that originally be- longed to affluent farmers, the museum provides a glimpse of 18th- and 19th-century living conditions in rural Iceland. In the 11th century Glaumbær was the home of Guðríður Þorbjar- nardóttir and Þorfinnur Karlsefni, two of the Icelanders who attempted to settle in America after it was discovered by Leifur Eiríksson. Their son, Snorri, was probably the first Eu- ropean born in the New World. *Tel. 5/38266. Admission: IKR 120. Open June–Aug., daily 10–noon and 1–7.*

Another 17 kilometers (11 miles) north on Route 75 will bring you to **Sauðárkrókur,** a large coastal town. In summer boat trips from Sauðárkrókur to Drangey and Málmey islands pro- vide some striking views. On the eastern side of Skagafjörður, off Route 75, is the 18th-century stone cathedral of **Hólar,** which has recently been renovated and contains beautiful and priceless objects and works of art.

From the junction with Route 75, it's another 95 kilometers (59 miles) along the Ring Road to **Akureyri.** Though not as cosmo- politan as Reykjavík, Akureyri is a lively place. A century ago the farmers in the prosperous agricultural area surrounding Akureyri established KEA, a cooperative enterprise to combat the Danish businesses that dominated the area's economic life. Today KEA still runs most of the stores and industries in Akureyri.

Lying by the 64-kilometer-long (40-mile-long) Eyjafjörður, Akureyri is sheltered from the ocean winds and embraced by mountains on three sides. Late-19th-century wooden houses

give the city center a sense of history, while the twin spires of a modern Lutheran church, rising on a green hill near the waterfront, provide a focal point. The church is named for Akureyri native Matthías Jochumsson, the poet who wrote Iceland's national anthem in 1874.

From the church it's a short walk from the town center on Eyrarlandsvegur to the **Lystigarðurinn** (Arctic Botanic Gardens), which has been planted with more than 400 species of Icelandic flora, including some rare Arctic plants, and foreign flora. **Matthíasarhús,** (Eyrarlandsvegur 3), the house where Jochumsson once lived, is now open as a museum (daily 2–4). Akureyri has two other museums honoring Icelandic writers: **Davíðshús** (Bjarkastígur 6, open weekdays 3–5), the home of poet Davíð Stefánsson and **Nonnahús** (Aðalstræti 54b, open daily 2–4:30), the boyhood home of children's writer and Jesuit priest Jón Sveinsson.

Also near the church, on Hafnarstræti, is the **Náttúrugripasafnið** (Natural History Museum), which displays specimens of all the bird species that nest in Iceland. *Hafnarstræti 81. Open June and mid-Aug.–mid-Sept., Sun.–Fri. 1–4; July–mid-Aug., Sun.–Fri. 10–5; mid-Sept.–June, Sun. 1–3.*

The **Minjasafnið** (Folk Museum) displays a large collection of local relics and works of art, old farm tools, and fishing equipment. *Aðalgata 58, tel. 6/24162. Admission: IKr150. Open daily 1:30–5.*

During June and July, make a point of taking an evening drive north from Akureyri along Route 82. The midnight sun creates breathtaking views along the coast of Eyjafjörður.

Better still, take a cruise on the fjord: A ferry plies to and from the island of Hrísey in the waters of Eyjafjörður, and out to Grímsey island, 40 kilometers (25 miles) offshore, which straddles the Arctic Circle. Contact **Nonni Travel** (Brekkugata 3, Akureyri, tel. 6/27922, fax 6/26649).

From Akureyri you can see to the south the pyramid-shaped rhyolite mountain **Súlur** and, beyond it, **Kerling,** the highest peak in Eyjafjörður. Head toward them for a taste of history. Drive 10 kilometers (6 miles) south on Route 821 to **Kristnes,** where the area's first settler, Helgi Magri ("Helgi the Lean") from Ireland, lived on his farm, which no longer exists. Proceed 5 kilometers (3 miles) along Route 821 to **Grund,** where you can visit an attractive turn-of-the-century church. Another 13 kilometers (8 miles) south on Route 821 will bring you to **Saurbær,** with a church built in the 1850s from wood and turf; it's typical of Icelandic dwellings through the centuries. From Saurbær, turn left onto Route 829, which runs north parallel to Route 821. A couple of kilometers along, you pass the historic **Möðruvellir** farm. The Möðruvellir church has an English alabaster altarpiece dating from the 15th century. From here it is 25 kilometers (16 miles) north to the Ring Road.

If you drive east from Akureyri on the Ring Road, passing farms left and right, you'll soon cross the Vaðlaheiði (Marsh Heath) and enter the **Fnjóskadalur** (Tree-stump Valley), formed by glaciers only a few thousand years ago. Go a few hundred meters past Route 833, which leads south into the western part of the valley, and turn right onto the next road, which takes you to the **Vaglaskógur** (Log Forest), one of the largest

forests in this relatively treeless country. Vaglaskógur was probably even larger originally, but through the centuries trees were taken for building material and firewood. Its tallest birches today reach some 40 feet.

Return to the Ring Road and proceed east for about 12 kilometers (7 miles) to the beautiful **Goðafoss** (Waterfall of the Gods) in the Skjálfanda River. Its name derives from a historic event in AD 1000, when Þorgeir Ljósvetningagoði, ordered by the Icelandic Parliament to choose between paganism and Christianity, threw his pagan icons into the waterfall. Just before you reach Goðafoss, you'll pass the **Ljósavatn** church and farm where Þorgeir lived a millennium ago. Although the farm is long gone, you can visit the church, which houses among other relics some interesting runic stones recently unearthed. A new church and memorial will be built here before 2000, the millennial anniversary of Iceland's conversion to Christianity.

It's about 100 kilometers (62 miles) along the Ring Road from Akureyri to **Mývatn,** a gemlike lake set amid mountains and lava fields. This area deserves at least a day's exploration. Fed by cold springs in the lake bottom and from warm springs in the northeastern corner, the shallow lake, 15 square miles in area yet only three to 13 feet deep, teems with life—fish, birds, and insects, including the swarming midges for which the lake is named. Waterfowl migrate long distances to breed at Mývatn, where the duck population numbers up to 150,000 in summer. All Iceland's duck species except the eider (which prefers life on the ocean wave) nest at Mývatn. The lake is one of the major breeding grounds for waterfowl in Europe.

Turning off the Ring Road at Route 848, you pass **Skútustaðir,** a village on the lake's southern shore. Proceed along the eastern shore to the 1,300-foot-high **Hverfjall** ash cone, a few hundred meters from the road. Several paths lead to the top, where you can take in a sweeping view of the lake and surroundings. The outer walls of this volcanic crater are steep, but the ascent is easy. The walk around the top of the crater is about 4,300 feet. Southwest of Hverfjall is the **Dimmuborgir** (Dark Castles) lava field, a labyrinth of tall formations where you choose between short and longer signposted routes through the eerie landscape. Among its mysterious arches, gates, and caves, the best-known is the **Kirkja** (Church), resembling a Gothic chapel (it's marked by a sign, lest you miss it). Don't wander off the paths, as Dimmuborgir is a highly sensitive environment.

Time Out   At the northeastern corner of Mývatn, where Route 848 meets the Ring Road again, the modern **Reynihlíð Hotel** (tel. 6/44170) serves coffee and *kökur* (pastries), including traditional *kleinur* (deep-fried twists) and *pönnukökur* (thin pancakes).

Proceeding a few kilometers south from Mývatn on the Ring Road, you pass a factory that processes diatomite (tiny skeletons of algae) sucked from the bottom of the lake, where they have been deposited through the centuries. The diatomite factory at Mývatn is highly controversial; conservationists fear that it may endanger the ecosystem of the lake, yet it provides welcome employment for the local population. Research is now under way, and the plant may be closed down within a few years.

In the **Námaskarð** mountain ridge, on the eastern side of the Ring Road, are bubbling mud and purple sulfur, boiling like a witch's cauldron in the strange red and yellow valleys. Hike around this fascinating area, but remember to step carefully and avoid the noxious gases.

Route 87 branches off the Ring Road to **Húsavík,** an attractive port on the north coast. (From Akureyri, the drive is 90 kilometers/56 miles.) From there take Route 85 north along the coast to Tjörnes, ending up inland at the lush nature reserve of **Ásbyrgi** (Shelter of the Gods). The forest here is surrounded by steep cliffs on all sides except the north, making it a peaceful shelter from the wind. Legend says this horseshoe-shaped canyon was formed by the giant hoof of Sleipnir, the eight-footed horse of Óðinn. Contiguous with Ásbyrgi is the wild and magnificent **Jökulsárgljúfur National Park,** the rugged canyon of the glacial Jökulsá river. At the southernmost point of the park, on route 864, see Europe's most powerful waterfall, **Dettifoss,** where 212 tons of water cascade each second over a 44-meter (145-foot) drop. Farther inland at **Kverkfjöll,** hot springs rise at the edge of the Vatnajökull glacier, creating spectacular ice caves. Tours operate from Húsavík (BSH, Garðabraut 7, Box 115, Húsavík, tel. 6/42200, fax 6/42201).

Shopping

As Iceland's second-largest city, Akureyri offers better shopping than most towns outside of Reykjavík. Woolens, ceramics, and other gift items are available at **París** (Hafnarstræti 96, tel. 6/27744).

Sports and Outdoor Activities

Bicycling The **Hótel Reynihlíð** (Mývatnssveit, tel. 6/44170) in Mývatn offers bicycle rentals for exploring the area around the lake.

Fishing Near Hrútafjörður, **Arinbjörn Jóhannsson** (Brekkulækur, tel. 5/12938) offers lake trout fishing and 7- to 13-day fishing trips on specified dates.

Golf In **Akureyri,** enjoy golf at the world's northernmost 18-hole course, at Jaðar on the outskirts of town. The **Arctic Open Golf Tournament** is held around midsummer night each year on the Akureyri course. For information contact the Iceland Tourist Bureau, tel. 1/623300, fax 1/625895. There also are golf courses in Ólafsfjörður and Sauðárkrókur.

Hiking **Akureyri Travel Bureau** (Ráðhústorg 3, tel. 6/25000) and **Nonni Travel** (Brekkugata 3, tel. 6/27922) run mountain hiking tours from Akureyri.

Horseback Riding The **Hotel Reynihlíð** (tel. 6/44170) in Mývatn offers pony treks around the lake. Near Hrútafjörður, **Arinbjörn Jóhannsson** (tel. 5/12938) in Brekkulækur also organizes horseback treks. In Akureyri, contact **Pólarhestar** (Grýtubakki 11, tel. 6/33179).

Swimming There are open-air pools in **Blönduós** (tel. 5/24451), **Sauðárkrókur** (tel. 5/35226), **Ólafsfjörður** (tel. 6/62363), **Akureyri** (Þingvallastræti 13, tel. 6/23260), and **Húsavík** (tel. 6/41144).

Dining and Lodging

Akureyri
Dining
Fiðlarinn. The view is fabulous from this rooftop restaurant and bar overlooking Akureyri harbor and Eyjafjörður. The dining room is tastefully decorated in pale wood and paint. Danish haute cuisine is featured. *Skipagata 14, tel. 6/27100. Reservations advised. Dress: casual but neat. AE, DC, MC, V. Expensive.*

Höfðaberg. Located in the KEA Hotel (*see* Lodging, *below*), this fine restaurant has modern maroon-and-mauve Scandinavian decor. The cuisine is both international and Icelandic. *Hafnarstræti 87–89, tel. 6/22600. Summer reservations advised. Dress: casual but neat. AE, DC, MC, V. Expensive.*

Lodging
Hótel KEA. Mauve-and-maroon decor with dark-wood trim characterizes this recently renovated property, which is on a par with many of the capital's hotels. In addition to the Höfðaberg restaurant (*see* Dining, *above*), there is an inexpensive cafeteria on the ground floor. On weekends the KEA is one of the city's main dancing spots. *Hafnarstræti 87–89, tel. 6/22200, fax 6/21009. 72 rooms with bath, 1 suite. Facilities: restaurant, bar, lounge, conference and banquet rooms. AE, DC, MC, V. Expensive.*

Hótel Norðurland. Completely renovated in 1989, with Danish modern furniture, this hotel features all the amenities of the better Reykjavík hotels. On the ground floor is the separately run Hlóðir Restaurant, where hotel guests get a hearty breakfast. *Geislagata 7, tel. 6/22600, fax 6/27833. 28 rooms, 18 with bath. Facilities: restaurant, bar, satellite TV, minibars, telephones. AE, DC, MC, V. Expensive.*

Brú
Dining
Staðarskáli í Hrútafirði. At the inland end of Hrútafjörður, this neat and clean restaurant offers good cooking—grilled lamb is a specialty—at reasonable prices. *Corner Rtes. 1 and 68, tel. 5/11150. Reservations not necessary. Dress: casual. Moderate.*

Húsavík
Dining and Lodging
Hotel Húsavík. Popular with skiers, this solid hotel has a good restaurant and a cafeteria; breakfast is included in the room rate. *Ketilsbraut 22, tel. 6/41220, fax 6/42161. 21 rooms with shower. AE, DC, MC, V. Expensive.*

Mývatn
Dining and Lodging
Hotel Reynihlíð. This popular hotel has a helpful general information service for tourists and a restaurant. *Mývatnssveit, tel. 6/44170, fax 6/44310. 48 rooms with shower. Facilities: horseback riding, bicycle rentals. AE, DC, MC, V. Moderate.*

Hotel Reykjahlíð. Set in an exclusive location by the lake, this small hotel has a convenient restaurant. *Mývatnssveit, tel. 6/44142. 12 rooms with shared bath. AE, MC, V. Closed Sept.–May. Inexpensive.*

Sauðárkrókur
Dining
Dalakofinn. Reminiscent of a classic cozy American diner, complete with chrome chairs and plastic flowers, this restaurant serves somewhat standard food—overcooked Icelandic cuisine. *Aðalgata 15, tel. 5/36655. Reservations not necessary. Dress: casual. AE, MC, V. Inexpensive.*

Dining and Lodging
Mælifell. The restaurant serves good food at fair prices. There are six guest rooms for overnight stays. *Aðalgata 7, tel. 5/35265. 6 rooms with shared bath. AE, MC, V. Moderate.*

Youth Hostels
Akureyri: tel. 6/23657. 32 beds.
Lonsá (near Akureyri): tel. 6/25037. 35 beds. Open June–Oct.
Hvammstangi: tel. 5/12678, fax 5/12678. 15 beds.

Hrútafjörður: Sæberg, tel. 5/10015, fax 5/10015. 30 beds.
Fosshóll (near Mývatn): tel. 6/43318, fax 6/43108. 50 beds.
Lónkot: Skagafirði, tel. 5/37432. 20 beds. Closed Oct.–May 14.

The East

In 1974, when the final bridge was completed across the treacherous glacial rivers and shifting sands south of the Vatnajökull glacier, the eastern side of the island finally became accessible from Reykjavík. It is still a long journey by car, but you can watch ice floes gliding toward the sea while the great skuas, predatory seabirds, swoop across weird black volcanic beaches. Egilsstaðir, on the shore of Lake Lögurinn, is the hub of the Eastern Fjords, and the Norröna ferry from Europe arrives at Seyðisfjörður 25 kilometers (16 miles) to the east.

Important Addresses and Numbers

Tourist Information In **Egilsstaðir**, the Austurland Travel Bureau (Kaupvangur 6, tel. 7/12000) is open weekdays 9–noon and 1–5. In **Seyðisfjörður**, the Austfar Travel Agency (Fjarðargata 6, tel. 7/21111) is open weekdays 9–noon and 1–5. In **Höfn**, the campsite (tel. 7/81701) is open July–August, daily, 8–11 and 5–11.

Arriving and Departing

By Plane **Icelandair** (tel. 7/12000) and **Eastair** (tel. 7/11122) operate scheduled flights from Reykjavík to Egilsstaðir. From there, there are connections to Bakkafjörður, Borgarfjörður, Breiðdalsvík, Fáskrúðsfjörður, Hornafjörður, Norðfjörður, and Vopnafjörður. **Íslandsflug** (tel. 1/616060) flies to Neskaupstaður and Egilsstaðir.

By Boat The **Norröna** car ferry from Norway or Denmark, via the Faroe Islands, arrives in Seyðisfjörður. Contact Norröna Travel, Laugavegur 3, 101 Reykjavík (tel. 1/626362, fax 1/29450) or Austfar, 710 Seyðisfjörður (tel. 7/21111, fax 7/21105).

By Car The region is accessible by car on the Ring Road (Route 1). The drive from Reykjavík to Egilsstaðir is about 700 kilometers (434 miles), and from Akureyri 273 kilometers (170 miles).

By Bus The East is so far from Reykjavík that bus travel is recommended only if you are making the entire circuit. From Akureyri the six-hour trip to Egilsstaðir runs daily in summer, three times a week the rest of the year. From Egilsstaðir there's frequent service around the region; it takes about five hours to get to Höfn.

Guided Tours

The **Iceland Tourist Bureau** (tel. 1/623300) operates a day trip from Reykjavík to Höfn by plane, with a snowmobile tour of the Vatnajökull glacier and a boat tour on the Jökulsárlón lagoon. The tour runs daily mid-June–Aug. Glacier tours are operated from many different locations around Vatnajökull glacier: from Eskifjörður by **Tanni** (tel. 7/61399, fax 7/61599), and from Höfn by **Jöklaferðir** (tel. 7/81503, fax 7/81901).

Exploring the East

Egilsstaðir is located at the northern end of the long, narrow lake called **Lögurinn**. While the town itself has no particular sights to see, an easy 25-kilometer (15-mile) drive from town along the lake's southern shore, first on the Ring Road then onto Route 931, will take you to beautiful **Hallormsstaður Forestry Reserve**, which contains the country's largest forest; more than 40 varieties of trees grow here, mostly spruce and larch. This area is one of Iceland's most accessible paradises, and a visit is strongly recommended. The Atlavík campground on the lake south of Hallormsstaðaskógur is a popular vacation spot, although the lake is reputed to be home to a monster who lies on a chest of treasure. In the highlands west of Lögurinn you may be able to spot Icelandic reindeer. Though not native to the island (they were originally brought from Norway in the 18th century), the reindeer have thrived to the point that controlled hunting is allowed; some 600 animals can be killed every year.

Another excursion from Egilsstaðir will take you 71 kilometers (44 miles) north and east on Route 94 to **Bakkagerði** by Borgarfjörður (not to be confused with its larger namesake in the west). The Borgarfjörður road, though bumpy, is entirely safe, but do not be in a hurry. Savor the swooping descent from the Vatnsskarð mountain pass and the spectacular coast road along Njarðvíkurskriður. In a land of stunning mountain scenery, Borgarfjörður (east) is a natural masterpiece, where the changing tones in the landscape have to be seen to be believed. The painter Jóhannes Kjarval lived here and used many local features in his paintings.

At **Eiðar,** just north of Egilsstaðir on the Borgarfjörður road, an open-air dramatic and musical entertainment is scheduled weekly in summer. It is in Icelandic, but English summaries are available, and you don't have to understand the language to learn folk dances! Contact Philip Vogler (Dalskógar 12, 700 Egilsstaðir, tel. 7/11673, fax 7/12190) for information.

Head east from Egilsstaðir on Route 92 and you'll have a breathtaking drive over the highest mountain pass in the country. You'll pass through **Eskifjörður** (48 kilometers/30 miles from Egilsstaðir) and end up in **Neskaupstaður,** which is 71 kilometers (44 miles) from Egilsstaðir. Both are large towns dramatically perched below steep crags on the rims of their respective fjords.

To continue along the Ring Road, drive south from Egilsstaðir 150 kilometers (93 miles) to the rugged stretch of coast indented by the inlets of **Álftafjörður** (Swan Fjord) and **Hamarsfjörður.** Surrounded by majestic mountains, these shallow waters host myriad swans, ducks, and other birds that migrate from Europe in the spring and summer here.

Another 100 kilometers (62 miles) south is the town of **Höfn,** which is slowly being closed off from the ocean by silt washed by glacial rivers into the fjord. Spread out on a low-lying headland at the mouth of the fjord, Höfn offers a fine view of the awesome **Vatnajökull** glacier, which is not only Iceland's largest but is equal in size to all the glaciers on the European mainland put together. From Höfn you can arrange tours of the glacier. About 50 kilometers (31 miles) west of Höfn, at the **Jökulsárlón** lagoon, you can see large chunks of the glacier tum-

ble and float around in a spectacular ice show. Boat trips on the lagoon are operated throughout the summer. For details call Fjölnir Torfason (tel. 7/81065). Light meals and refreshments are available at a small coffee house at the lagoon. On the **Breiðamerkur sands** west of the lagoon is the largest North Atlantic colony of skua, large predatory sea birds that unhesitatingly "dive-bomb" intruders in the nesting season.

Another 50 kilometers (31 miles) west of Jökulsárlón bordering on Vatnajökull is **Skaftafell**, the largest of Iceland's three national parks. The surrounding glacier shelters Skaftafell from winds, creating a verdant oasis, and farther up is the highest mountain in Iceland, **Hvannadalshnúkur**, rising to 2,119 meters (6,300 feet). The famous **Svartifoss** (Black Falls) tumbles over a cliff whose sides resemble the pipes of a great organ. In the park you can walk for an hour or a day on beautiful trails through a rare combination of green forest, clear water, waterfalls, sands, mountains, and glaciers. Do not miss **Sel,** a restored gabled farmhouse high up on the slope. Guided walks in the National Park are organized daily.

Sports and Outdoor Activities

Fishing Near Seyðisfjörður, you can get fishing permits at Hotel Snæfell (Austurvegur 3, tel. 7/21460). Sea-angling and sight-seeing cruises are available from many villages on the east coast, such as Neskaupstaður (**Fjarðaferðir,** tel. 7/71321, fax 7/71322) and Seyðisfjörður (**Hotel Snæfell,** tel. 7/21460, fax 7/21570).

Horseback Riding Around Lake Lögurinn you can rent horses at **Guesthouse Egilsstaðir** (tel. 7/11114). In Seyðifjörður, rent horses at **Hotel Snæfell** (Austurvegur 3, tel. 7/21460). To rent ponies near the Jökulsá Lagoon, call **Fjölnir Torfason** (tel. 7/81065).

Swimming There are swimming pools in **Egilsstaðir** (tel. 7/11467), **Neskaupstaður** (Miðstræti 5, tel. 7/71243), **Eskifjörður** (Lambeyrarbraut 14, tel. 7/61238), and **Höfn** (Hafnarbraut, tel. 7/81157).

Dining and Lodging

Breiðdalsvík **Hótel Bláfell.** Though it's only a few years old, this small hotel in a fishing village on Route 96 has a cozily rustic exterior and an award-winning restaurant. Fishing permits are available for the area. *Sólvellir 14, tel. 7/56770. 15 rooms with shared bath. AE, MC, V. Moderate.*

Djúpivogur **Hótel Framtíð.** In an old fishing village where 19th-century Danish merchant homes still stand, this small wood-frame hotel is right by the harbor. In the dining room, home-style food is served in a friendly atmosphere; seafood is a specialty. *Vogalandi 4, tel. 7/88887. 10 rooms with shared bath. Facilities: restaurant, sauna. AE, MC, V. Inexpensive.*

Egilsstaðir **Hótel Valaskjálf.** Large and practical, this hotel has a restaurant and a cafeteria. Breakfast is included in the room rate, and there is dancing on weekends. *Skógarland, tel. 7/11500, fax 7/11501. 66 rooms with shower. AE, MC, V. Moderate–Expensive.*
Guesthouse Egilsstaðir. This charming farmhouse hotel is on

the outskirts of town. *Egilsstaðir 1, tel. 7/11114. 11 rooms with shared bath. No credit cards. Inexpensive.*

Hallormsstaður **Edda.** The hotel is adequate; the natural harmony of forest, lake, and quiet bays is the real attraction. The Edda has a good restaurant. *Hallormsstað, tel. 7/11705. 17 rooms with shared bath. AE, DC, V. Closed Sept.–mid-June. Moderate.*

Höfn **Hótel Höfn.** This newly built, modern-style hotel is clean and comfortable and has a good restaurant. The almond trout is excellent; fast food is also available at the grill. There's dancing on weekends. *Víkurbraut, tel. 7/81240, fax 7/81996. 40 rooms, 20 with shower. AE, MC, V. Expensive.*

Seyðisfjörður **Hótel Snæfell.** Set in an old wooden house, this new hotel serves good food in a glassed-in restaurant by a dramatic fjord. *Austurvegur 3, tel. 7/21460. 13 rooms, 9 with shower and 4 with shared bath. AE, MC, V. Moderate.*

Skaftafell **Freysnes Guesthouse.** This newly built guest house is situated a stone's throw from Skaftafell National Park. Most rooms have private bath. *Skaftafell, 781 Höfn, tel. 7/81945, fax 7/81946. Facilities: restaurant, snack bar. MC, V. Moderate.*

Youth Hostels **Bakkafjörður:** tel. 7/31686 or 7/31621. 17 beds. Closed Sept.–May.
Höfn: tel. 7/81736. 30 beds. Closed Oct. 16–May 14.
Húsey: tel. 7/13010. 20 beds. Closed Sept.–May.
Seyðisfjörður: tel. 7/21410, fax 7/21486. 28 beds.
Reyðarfjörður: tel. 7/41447 or 7/41419, fax 7/41454. 15 beds.
Berunes: tel. 7/88988. 20 beds. Open May–Sept.
Stafafell (near Höfn): tel. 7/81717. 45 beds. Open June–Sept.

The South

The power of volcanoes is all too evident on this final leg of the Ring Road tour. At Kirkjubæjarklaustur you can still see scars of the great Laki eruption of 1783. At Stöng you can visit excavated ruins of a farmstead buried in 1104 by the eruption of Mt. Hekla, which was known throughout medieval Europe as the abode of the damned; Hekla is still active, having erupted most recently in 1991. Off the coast, the Vestmannaeyjar (Westmann Islands) are still being formed by volcanic activity, and a 1973 eruption almost wiped out all habitation. The south also includes Þórsmörk (Thor's Forest), a popular nature reserve.

Important Addresses and Numbers

Tourist In **Kirkjubæjarklaustur,** the Community Center (tel. 8/74621) is
Information open June 15–August 15, daily 10–4. In **Vík,** the Camping Site and Víkurskáli (tel. 8/71345) will provide information.

Emergencies In **Kirkjubæjarklaustur,** contact the **police** at tel. 8/74694; in **Vík,** tel. 8/71176; in **Hvolsvöllur,** tel. 8/78434; and in **Selfoss,** tel. 8/21154.

Arriving and Departing

By Plane **Icelandair** (tel. 1/690200) and **Íslandsflug** (tel. 1/616060) fly daily from Reykjavík Airport to the Vestmannaeyjar (the Westmann Islands); flight time is about 30 minutes.

By Car Kirkjubæjarklaustur is 272 kilometers (169 miles) east of Reykjavík on the Ring Road. West from Höfn, it is 201 kilometers (125 miles) to Kirkjubæjarklaustur.

By Ferry The passenger and car ferry **Herjólfur** (tel. 8/11792 or 1/686464) sails daily to Vestmannaeyjar from Þorlákshöfn. Allow 3¼ hours for the journey. There are immediate bus connections to Reykjavík from the Westmann Islands ferry at Þorlákshöfn; the trip takes about 90 minutes.

By Bus BSÍ has daily service from Reykjavík, stopping in Hella, Hvolsvöllur, Selfoss, Vík, and Þorlakshöfn. The journey to Vík takes less than four hours; to Þorlakshöfn or Selfoss, one hour.

Guided Tours

The **Iceland Tourist Bureau** (tel. 1/623300) operates a 10-hour day trip from Reykjavík to the Vestmannaeyjar by plane, running daily all year. Arrangements can also be made for a three-hour sightseeing flight over Heimaey in the islands. **Austurleið** bus company (Austurvegi 1, Hvolsvöllur, tel. 8/78197) operates tours to Þórsmörk, Skaftafell, the Eastern Fjords, and the interior.

Exploring the South

Pick up the Ring Road in **Kirkjubæjarklaustur,** the site of an old convent from the 12th century to the Reformation. Just west of the village, turn right on the highland road leading north to see **Laki** volcano, with more than 100 craters dotting the landscape. The great lava field of the south coast was created by this volcano in a single eruption, in 1783–84. The worst in Iceland's history, it wiped out about 70% of the country's livestock and a fifth of the population. Jón Steingrímsson, then the priest at Kirkjubæjarklaustur, is said to have stopped the advance of the lava by prayer. About 30 kilometers (19 miles) east of Kirkjubæjarklaustur, don't miss the little chapel at **Núpsstaður,** one of a handful of extant turf churches. This well-preserved building has remained almost unchanged since the 17th century.

West from Kirkjubæjarklaustur 25 kilometers (15 miles) on Route 1, turn right onto Route 208 and continue for 20 kilometers (12 miles) on the mountain road Route F22 to **Eldgjá,** a 20-mile-long volcanic rift. Historic records suggest it erupted in 934 with a ferocity similar to that of the Laki eruption. The northwestern part of the gulch is most interesting, with Ófærufoss, a waterfall cascading under a natural basalt bridge.

Proceeding west along the Ring Road, you cross the Mýrdalssandur desert and arrive at the village of **Vík,** with its vast population of arctic terns. Twelve kilometers (7 miles) past Vík, turn left toward the ocean to reach the southernmost point of the country, the **Dyrhólaey** promontory, with its lighthouse. The ocean has worn the black basalt rock here into the shape of an arch, 394 feet high; ships can sail through it in calm weather. This headland is also a bird sanctuary, so expect it to be closed during the nesting period in early summer.

Another 15 kilometers (9 miles) west on Route 1, turn right to the tiny settlement of **Skógar,** where you can visit one of Iceland's best folk museums. Among the mementos of this re-

gion's past is one of the tiny, frail boats in which local fishermen once navigated this treacherous coast. *Tel. 8/78845. Admission free. Open May–Sept. 15, daily 9–noon, 1–6.*

Just west of Skógar is the impressive **Skógafoss,** a waterfall that's more than 197 feet high.

Another 30 kilometers (19 miles) along the Ring Road, you'll come to the powerful **Markarfljót River.** Route 249 on its east bank leads 15 kilometers (9 miles) east to some treacherous, dangerous streams into the **Þórsmörk** (Thor's Forest) nature reserve, a popular vacation area bounded on its eastern and southern sides by the Eyjafjalla and Mýrdals glaciers. Nestled in a valley surrounded by mountain peaks, Þórsmörk enjoys exceptionally calm and often sunny weather, making it a veritable haven of birch trees and other Icelandic flora. There are many excellent trekking routes (*see* Hiking and Camping, *below*), such as a day's trip over the **Fimmvörðuháls mountain pass** (a compass is a necessity) down to Skógar, or a three-day hike into the interior to visit **Landmannalaugar,** where hot and cold springs punctuate a landscape rich in pastel, yellow, brown, and red rhyolite hills carved by glacial rivers.

The road on the west bank of the Markarfljót leads 10 kilometers (6 miles) north into Saga country, to the site of **Hlíðarendi,** the farm where Gunnar Hámundarson, one of the heroes of *Njál's Saga,* lived and died. Exiled by the Alþingi for murdering Þorgeir Oddkelsson, he refused to leave "these beautiful slopes." In the lowlands to the southwest of the Markarfljót (turn left off the Ring Road onto Route 252 and drive 20 kilometers/12 miles) is another famous place from *Njál's Saga:* **Bergþórshvoll,** where Njál's enemies surrounded his farmhouse and burned it to the ground, killing all within.

Continuing west on the Ring Road, you'll come to **Hella,** 100 kilometers (62 miles) west of Vík. About 10 kilometers (6 miles) past Hella, turn right onto Route 26 and drive 40 kilometers (25 miles) or so until you see, on your right, the tallest peak in the region—the famous **Hekla volcano,** which has erupted nearly 20 times in recorded history and remains active. In the Middle Ages, Hekla was known throughout Western Europe as the abode of the damned. Some 25 kilometers (16 miles) farther, Route 26 intersects Route 32; turn left and go 15 kilometers (9 miles) to the right turn for **Stöng,** an ancient settlement on the west bank of the Þjórsá River, Iceland's longest. The original farm here dates back almost 900 years; it was buried in 1104 when Hekla erupted, but you can visit the excavated ruins. A complete replica has been built, using the same materials as the settlers used, located south of Stöng at Búrfell on Route 32. *Tel. 8/77713.*

From Hella it's 93 kilometers (58 miles) along the Ring Road back to Reykjavík. At Hveragerði (*see* Golden Circle Excursion, *above*), take a left turn onto Route 38 and drive 20 kilometers (12 miles) to **Þorlákshöfn**—gateway to **Vestmannaeyjar,** the Westmann Islands.

Vestmannaeyjar (Westmann Islands) This tiny cluster of 15 islands off the south coast was named for the Irish slaves—called Westmen—brought to Iceland by the Viking settlers after AD 874. After a rebellion in which some slaves killed their master, Hjörleifur, sworn brother of Reykjavík settler Ingólfur Arnarson, the Westmen fled to the

islands. Ingólfur avenged his brother by killing most of the slaves or driving them off the cliffs in Vestmannaeyjar.

The islands were formed by volcanic eruptions only 5,000 to 10,000 years ago, and there is still much volcanic activity here. **Surtsey,** the latest addition, was formed in November 1963 with an eruption that lasted 3½ years. In 1973 a five-month-long eruption on **Heimaey,** the only inhabited island in the group, wiped out part of the town of Vestmannaeyjar. The island's entire population was forced to flee in fishing boats, with only a few hours' notice. A few years later, however, the people of Vestmannaeyjar had removed tons of black lava dust from their streets and rebuilt everything. The lava, still hot, is used for heat by the resourceful islanders.

The main industry here is fishing, but another local occupation (nowadays more a sport than a job) is more unusual: egg hunting. Egg-pickers dangle from ropes over the sheer black volcanic cliffs to collect eggs from the nests of seabirds. The islands are rich in birds, especially puffins, which are used for food.

Sightseeing cruises run around Vestmannaeyjar, offering views of dramatic sea caves and neighboring islands. Sightseeing flights over Surtsey and the rest of the Westmann Islands group can be arranged from Reykjavík or from Heimaey. Every August, islanders celebrate the 1874 grant of Icelandic sovereignty with a huge festival in the town of Vestmannaeyjar, on Heimaey. The population moves into a tent city in the **Herjólfsdalur** (Herjolf's Valley) a short distance west of town for an extended weekend of bonfires, dancing, and singing.

Sports and Outdoor Activities

Golf | The Svarfhólsvöllur course, in **Selfoss,** is on the banks of the Ölfusá River. There also is a golf course in **Hella.**

Hiking and Camping | Both main Icelandic touring clubs, **Ferðafélag Íslands** (Mörkin 6, 108 Reykjavík, tel. 1/682533, fax 1/682535) and **Útivist** (Hallveigarstígur 1, Reykjavík, tel. 1/14606, fax 1/614606) maintain large cabins with sleeping-bag accommodations in Þórsmörk; many long-distance hikes are organized from there.

Horseback Riding | In Hvölsvollur contact **Saga Hestar** (tel. 8/78138); in Hella call **Heklu Hestar** (tel. 8/76598).

Snowmobiling | Snowmobiling is possible in summer on the Mýrdalsjökull glacier, overlooking Vík through **Snjósleðaferðir** (Dugguvògur 10, 104 Reykjavík, tel. 1/682310, fax 1/813102).

Swimming | There are swimming pools in **Hvolsvöllur** (tel. 8/78607), **Hella** (tel. 8/75334), **Þorlákshöfn** (tel. 8/33807), and **Selfoss** (Bankavegur, tel. 8/21227).

Dining and Lodging

Hvolsvöllur | **Hótel Hvolsvöllur.** Facilities at this hotel include a restaurant, bar, and swimming pool. *Hlíðarvegur 7, tel. 8/78187. 28 rooms. AE, MC, V. Moderate.*

Kirkjubæjarklaustur | **Edda.** Open year-round, this standard Edda facility in a modern building offers both a restaurant and a swimming pool. *Tel. 8/74799. 55 rooms with shower. AE, MC, V. Moderate.*

Skógar **Edda.** Close to the Skógafoss waterfall, this hotel is beautifully located, with views of the sea and the mountains and glaciers. It has a restaurant. *Skógum, tel. 8/78870. 36 rooms with shared bath. AE, MC, V. Closed Sept.–mid-June. Moderate.*

Youth Hostels **Fljótshlíð:** Fljótsdalur, tel. 8/78498. 15 beds. Closed Oct. 16–Apr. 14.
Mýrdalur: Reynisbrekka, tel. 7/71106, fax 8/71303. 25 beds. Closed Sept. 16–May.
Vestmannaeyjar: tel. 8/12915. 35 beds. Closed Sept. 16–May.
Leirubakki (near Selfoss): tel. 8/76591, fax 1/652113. 50 beds.

5 Norway

*By Melody Favish
and Karina
Porcelli*

Just north of Lillehammer there lives a Norwegian family on the banks of the Mjøsa River. Every year they pack their bags and drive to their holiday retreat, where they bask in the warmth of the long, northern sun for four full weeks—then they pack up and drive the 100 yards back home again.

While most Norwegians vacation a bit farther from home, their sentiments—attachment to, pride in, and reverence for their great outdoors—remain the same as the feelings of those who journey across the street. Whether in the verdant dales of the interior, the brooding mountains of the north, or the carved fjords and archipelagoes of the coast, their ubiquitous *hytter*, or cottages, dot even the most violent landscapes. It's a question of perspective: To a Norwegian, it's not a matter of whether or not to enjoy the land, but how to enjoy it at this very moment.

In any kind of weather, blasting or balmy, inordinate numbers are out of doors, to fish, bike, ski, hike, and, whether they know it or not, strike the pose many foreigners regard as larger-than-life Norwegian: ruddy-faced, athletic, reindeer-sweatered. And all—cherubic children to decorous senior citizens—bundled up for just one more swoosh down the slopes, one more walk through the forest.

Although it's a modern, highly industrialized nation, vast areas of the country, up to 95%, remain forested or fallow; and Norwegians intend to keep them that way—in part by making it extremely difficult for foreigners, who may feel differently about the land, to purchase property.

Norwegians like to say that if Oslo remained fixed and the northern part of the country were swung south, it would reach all the way to Rome. Perched at the very top of the globe, this northern land is long and rangy, 2,750 kilometers (1,700 miles) in length, with only 4 million people scattered over it—making it the least densely populated land in Europe except for Iceland. Knuckled by snow-topped mountains, and serrated by Gulf-Stream–warmed fjords, this country has an abundance of magnificent views. No matter how or where your approach, if you fly above the clean ivory mountains of Tromsø in the winter, or tear by in a heart-stopping train north of Voss in the spring, getting there is often as eye-popping as arriving.

Thanks to the Gulf Stream, the coastal regions enjoy a moderate, temperate climate in winter, keeping the country green, while the interior has a more typical northern climate. Of course, throughout the land, winter temperatures can dip far below zero, but that doesn't thwart the activities of the Norwegians. As one North Caper put it, "We don't have good weather or bad weather, only a lot of weather."

Norwegians are justifiably proud of their native land, and of their ability to survive the elements and foreign invasions. The first people to appear on the land were reindeer-hunters and fisherfolk, who migrated north, following the path of the retreating ice. By the Bronze Age, settlements began to appear and, as rock carvings show (and modern school children are proud to announce), the first Norwegians began to ski—purely as a form a locomotion—some 4,000 years ago.

The Viking Age has perhaps left the most indelible mark on the country. The Vikings' travels and conquests took them to Ice-

Norway

North Cape

TO SVALBARD

Vardø
Vadsø
Hammerfest
Kirkenes
Alta
Karasjok
Kautokeino

ATLANTIC
OCEAN

Tromsø

FINLAND

Norwegian
Sea

VESTERÅLEN
Harstad
LOFOTEN
Narvik
Vestfjord

Bodø
Fauske

Arctic Circle

Mo i Rana
Sandnessjøen
Mosjøen
E6
Brønnøysund

SWEDEN

Gulf of Bothnia

Rørvik
Namsos

Steinkjer

Trondheim
Meråker
Kristiansund
Støren
Molde
Oppdal
Røros
Ålesund
Andalsnes
Tynset
Geiranger
Dombås
Otta
Koppang
Nord fjord
Jostedalsbreen
Florø
Rena
Lillehammer
Sogne fjord
Lake
Mjøsa
Hamar
Voss
Geilo
Eidsvoll
Bergen
Hønefoss
Hardangerfjord
Drammen
Oslo
Kongsberg
Fredrikstad
Haugesund
Larvik
Halden
Porsgrunn
Oslofjord
Stavanger
Arendal
Baltic Sea
Sandnes
Evje
Grimstad
Mandal
Kristiansand
Skagerrak
Kattegat

N

0   200 miles
0   300 km

land, England, Ireland (they founded Dublin in the 840s), and North America. Though they were famed as plunderers, their craftsmanship and fearlessness is revered by modern Norwegians, who place ancient Viking ships in museums, cast copies of thousand-year-old silver designs into jewelry, and adventure across the seas in sailboats to prove the abilities of their forefathers.

Harald I, better known as Harald the Fairhaired, swore he would not cut his hair until he united Norway, and in the 8th century he succeeded in doing both. But a millennium passed between that great era and Norwegian independence. Between the Middle Ages and 1905, Norway remained under the rule of either Denmark or Sweden, even after the constitution was written in 1814.

The 19th century saw the establishment of the Norwegian identity and a blossoming of culture. This romantic period produced some of the nation's most famous individuals, among them, composer Edvard Grieg, dramatist Henrik Ibsen, expressionist painter Edvard Munch, polar explorer Roald Amundsen, and explorer/humanitarian Fridtjof Nansen. Vestiges of national lyricism spangle the buildings of the era with Viking dragonheads and scrollwork, all of which symbolize the rebirth of the Viking spirit.

Faithful to their democratic nature, in 1905, when independence from Sweden became reality, Norwegians held a referendum to choose a king. Prince Carl of Denmark became King Haakon VII. His baby son Alexander's name was changed to Olav, and he, and later his son, presided over the kingdom for more than 85 years. When King Olav died in January 1991, the normally reserved Norwegians stood in line for hours to write in the condolence book at the Royal Palace. Rather than simply sign their names, they wrote personal letters of devotion to the man they called the "people's king." Thousands set candles in the snow outside the palace, transforming the winter darkness into a cathedral of ice and flame.

Harald V, Olav's son, is now king, with continuity assured by his own young-adult son, Crown Prince Haakon. Norwegians continue to salute the royal family with flag-waving and parades on May 17, Constitution Day, a spirited holiday of independence that transforms Oslo's main boulevard, Karl Johans Gate, into a massive street party, when people of all ages, many in national costume, make a beeline to the Palace.

During both World Wars, Norway tried to maintain neutrality. World War I brought not only casualties and a considerable loss to the country's merchant fleet, but also financial gain through the repurchase of major companies, sovereignty over Svalbard (the islands near the North Pole), and the reaffirmation of Norway's prominence in international shipping. At the onset of World War II, Norway once again proclaimed neutrality and appeared more concerned with Allied mine-laying on the west coast than with national security. A country of mostly fisherfolk, lumber workers, and farmers, it was just beginning to realize its industrial potential when the Nazis invaded. Five years of German occupation and a burn-and-retreat strategy in the north finally left the nation ravaged. True to form, however, the people who had been evacuated returned to the embers of the north to rebuild their homes and villages.

In 1968, oil was discovered in the North Sea, and Norway was transformed from a fishing and shipping outpost to a highly developed industrial nation. Though still committed to a far-reaching social system, Norway developed in the next 20 years into a wealthy country, with one of the world's highest per capita standards of living and income, as well as long life expectancy.

Stand on a street corner with a map, and a curious Norwegian will show you the way. Visit a neighborhood, and within moments you'll be the talk of the town. As a native of Bergen quipped, "Next to skiing, gossip is a national sport." With one foot in modern, liberal Scandinavia and the other in the provincial and often self-righteous countryside, Norway, like her Nordic siblings, seems to be redefining her European identity. Famous for its social restrictiveness—smoking is frowned upon, liquor may not be served before 3 PM (and never on Sunday), and violence, even among cartoon characters, is closely monitored—Norway's government has applied to enter the European Community, thus paving the way for fewer limitations and more openmindedness. The next few years will define her course, as well as that of Scandinavia as a whole.

Before You Go

Government Tourist Offices

In the United States and Canada
Scandinavian Tourist Board, 655 3rd Ave., New York, NY 10017, tel. 212/949–2333.

The U.S. Department of State's **Citizens Emergency Center** issues Consular Information Sheets, which cover crime, security, and health risks as well as embassy locations, entry requirements, currency regulations, and other routine matters. For the latest information, stop in at any passport office, consulate, or embassy; call the interactive hotline (tel. 202/647–5225); or, with your PC's modem, tap into the Bureau of Consular Affairs' computer bulletin board (tel. 202/647–9225).

In the United Kingdom
Norwegian Tourist Board, 5 Lower Regent St., London SW1Y 4LX, tel. 071/839–6255, fax 071/839–4180.

When to Go

Every season has its charm and its enthusiasts. Winter means skiing at resorts in the country's midsection, where snow is abundant and facilities are first-rate. Winter in Oslo means evenings at the theater or at the concert house. Skiing on the lit trails surrounding Oslo is almost as good as that farther afield. On the down side, winter means little daylight, few organized tours, restricted opening hours at museums, and higher hotel rates except on weekends. At Christmas families retreat to the privacy of their own homes for much of the holiday, which begins on December 24, and, for many, does not end until January 2 or 3. Avoid Easter, the traditional "last ski trip of the year" for many Norwegians. May is one of the best times to visit Norway, for the days are long and sunny, the cultural life in the city is still going strong, tourists are few, and *Syttende mai* (Constitution Day, May 17), with all the festivities, is worth a trip for its own sake. For enjoying the outdoors, September is a

delightful time to hike in the hills. Most people come to Norway in the summer, and the months of July and August offer the most travel bargains. Hotels everywhere have special rates, and transportation packages of all kinds are available. In the far north, summer's main attraction is the midnight sun, visible at the North Cape from May 13 through July 29. In winter, the northern lights illuminate the sky.

Climate Coastal Norway enjoys mild winters, with more rain than snow in the southern areas. The temperature in Oslo seldom drops below 20°F, thanks to the Gulf Stream. It is dark, though, and if there's no snow, Oslo can look bleak. Summers in Norway are equally mild; days are relatively warm, but nights can be chilly. Inland and up north, winters are very long, cold, snowy, and dark, while summers are short, warm, intense, and endowed with an indescribably clear light.

What follows are average daily maximum and minimum temperatures for Oslo.

Oslo								
Jan.	28F	– 2C	**May**	61F	16C	**Sept.**	60F	16C
	19	– 7		43	6		46	8
Feb.	30F	– 1C	**June**	68F	20C	**Oct.**	48F	9C
	19	– 7		50	10		38	3
Mar.	39F	4C	**July**	72F	22C	**Nov.**	38F	3C
	25	– 4		55	13		31	– 1
Apr.	50F	10C	**Aug.**	70F	21C	**Dec.**	32F	0C
	34	1		54	12		25	– 4

Information Sources For current weather conditions for cities in the United States and abroad, plus the local time and helpful travel tips, call the **Weather Channel Connection** (tel. 900/932–8437; 95¢ per minute) from a touch-tone phone.

National Holidays

The following are national holidays in 1994: January 1, Easter (April 1–4), Labor Day (May 1), Constitution Day (May 17), Ascension (May 12), Whitmonday (May 23), December 25–26.

Festivals and Seasonal Events 1994

1994: 200th anniversary of the city of Tromsø.
January: Northern Light Festival, Tromsø, features classical, contemporary, and chamber music.
February 12–27: Winter Olympics at Lillehammer.
March: The **Holmenkollen Ski Festival** in Oslo features international Nordic events, including ski jumping. The **Birkebeiner Race** commemorates a centuries-old cross-country ski race from Lillehammer to Rena.
April: The **Karasjok Easter Festival** features traditional Sami entertainment and folklore and reindeer racing.
May 17: Constitution Day brings out every flag in the country and crowds of marchers for the parade in Oslo.
May: The **Grete Waitz Race,** a 5-kilometer street marathon in Oslo challenges women only.
June 23: Midsummer Eve, called "Sankt Hans," is celebrated nationwide with bonfires, fireworks, and outdoor dancing.
June: The annual **Bergen Music Festival** is customarily opened by the king. The **Emigration Festival.** Exhibitions and concerts in Stavanger commemorate the emigration to the United

States. The **North Norwegian Cultural Festival** at Harstad includes plays, concerts, ballet, and art exhibitions. The **North Cape March** brings hikers from around the world to walk the 70 kilometers from Honningsvåg to the North Cape and back. The **Great Endurance Test** is a bicycle race (560 km) from Trondheim to Oslo.

July: The **Bislett Games** attract the best international track and field stars to Bislett Stadium. The **Molde International Jazz Festival** is Norway's best-known jazz festival. The **Stiklestad Festivals** honor Olav the Holy (Haraldsson) with outdoor theater performances.

Mid-August: The **European Sea Fishing Championships** are held at Tananger, outside Stavanger.

August: Oslo Chamber Music Festival draws participants from around the world.

September: Oslo Marathon, 42 kilometers through the streets of Oslo, draws men and women.

December 1: The Christmas tree at University Square in Oslo is lit.

December 10: The **Nobel Peace Prize** is awarded in Oslo.

December: Christmas concerts, fairs, and crafts workshops are held at museums and churches throughout the country.

What to Pack

Clothing Casual clothing is the rule in Norway, although it is a good idea for men to pack a sport jacket for cool evenings. Women might want to bring a dress or suit, preferably with a jacket, for evenings. A jacket or neat casual dress might be required when going out at night. A windbreaker, good walking shoes, and sunglasses are a must. Summer in Norway can be both chilly and rainy, so bring a raincoat (with lining for the fringe seasons) and an umbrella. Winter weather demands heavy outerwear but normal indoor clothing, as Norwegian buildings are well heated. If you are traveling north in winter, bring heavy, impermeable boots and some kind of snow suit. However, if you're going on an organized outing (particularly dog- or reindeer-sledding), most outfitters provide both.

Miscellaneous Most hotels do not provide washcloths, so if you prefer them, bring your own. Many hotel bathrooms are equipped with converter outlets for shavers only, so if you bring a hair dryer, make sure that it is convertible. If you prefer decaffeinated coffee, bring some individual envelopes as many restaurants do not serve it. If you can't sleep when it is light and you are traveling during summer, bring a comfortable eye-mask, so you won't wake up automatically at the 4 AM sunrise. If you are going north in summer, bring along the best mosquito repellent you can find.

Because of the far northern latitude, the sun slants at angles unseen elsewhere on the globe, and a pair of dark sunglasses can prevent eyestrain. Bring an extra pair of eyeglasses or contact lenses. If you have a health problem that may require you to purchase a prescription drug, pack enough to last the duration of the trip, or have your doctor write a prescription using the drug's generic name, since brand names vary from country to country. And don't forget to pack a list of the addresses of offices that supply refunds for lost or stolen traveler's checks.

Taking Money Abroad

Traveler's Checks Although you will want plenty of cash when visiting small cities or rural areas, traveler's checks are usually preferable. The most widely recognized are **American Express, Citicorp, Thomas Cook,** and **Visa,** which are sold by major commercial banks. American Express also issues *Traveler's Cheques for Two,* which can be counter-signed and used by you or your traveling companion. Some checks are free; usually the issuing company or the bank at which you make your purchase charges 1%–2% of the checks' face value as a fee. Be sure to buy a few checks in small denominations to cash toward the end of your trip, when you don't want to be left with more foreign currency than you can spend. Always record the numbers of checks as you spend them, and keep this list separate from the checks.

Norwegian Currency

The unit of currency in Norway is the *krone* (plural: *kroner*), which translates as "crown," written officially as NOK. Price tags are seldom marked this way, but rather read "Kr." and then the amount, such as Kr10. (In this book, the Norwegian krone is abbreviated NKr.) One krone is divided into 100 øre, and coins of 10 and 50 øre, 1, 5, and 10 kroner are in circulation. Bills are issued in denominations of 50, 100, 500, and 1,000 kroner. In summer 1993, the exchange rate was NKr6.91 to U.S.$1, NKr10.70 to £1, and NKr5.45 to C$1. These rates fluctuate, so be sure to check them when planning a trip.

What It Will Cost

Sample Prices Cup of coffee, from $2 in a cafeteria to $3.50 or more in a restaurant; a 20-pack of cigarettes, $5.90; a half-liter of beer, $4.50–$6.50; the smallest hot dog (with bun plus *lompe*—a Norwegian tortilla—mustard, ketchup, and fried onions) at a convenience store, $2.10; cheapest bottle of wine from a government store, $8; the same bottle at a restaurant, $15–$25; urban transit fare in Oslo, $2.10; soft drink, from $2.75 in a cafeteria to $4 in a better restaurant; one adult movie ticket, $6; shrimp or roast beef sandwich at a cafeteria, $6; one-mile taxi ride, $6–$7 depending upon time of day.

Passports and Visas

If your passport is lost or stolen abroad, report it immediately to the nearest embassy or consulate and to the local police. If you can provide the consular officer with the information contained in the passport, they will usually be able to issue you a new passport. For this reason, it is a good idea to keep a copy of the data page of your passport in a separate place, or to leave the passport number, date, and place of issuance with a relative or friend at home.

Customs and Duties

Any adult can bring in duty-free ¾ liter of alcohol (not exceeding 60% alcohol by volume) and one liter of wine (not exceeding 21% alcohol by volume). As most liquor is sold in 1-liter bottles, the allowance is flexible on that point. Two liters of beer also can be imported duty-free. Anyone over 16 years old can import

200 cigarettes or 250 grams of other tobacco products duty-free. Importing alcohol over the above limit is not recommended.

Language

Every Norwegian receives at least seven years of English instruction, starting in the second grade. Norwegian has three additional vowels, æ, ø, and å. Æ is pronounced as a short "a." The ø, sometimes printed as *oe*, is the same as ö in German and Swedish, pronounced very much like a short "u." The å is a contraction of the archaic aa and sounds like long "o." These three letters appear at the end of alphabetical listings.

There are two officially sanctioned languages, Bokmål and Nynorsk. Bokmål is used by 84% of the population and is the main written form of Norwegian, the language of books, as the first half of its name indicates. Nynorsk, which translates as "new Norwegian," is actually a compilation of older dialect forms from rural Norway, which evolved during the national romantic period around the turn of this century. All Norwegians have to study both languages.

The Sami (incorrectly called Lapp) people have their own language, which is more akin to Finnish than to Norwegian.

Staying Healthy

Finding a Doctor The **International Association for Medical Assistance to Travellers** (IAMAT, 417 Center St., Lewiston, NY 14092, tel. 716/754–4883; 40 Regal Rd., Guelph, Ontario N1K 1B5; 57 Voirets, 1212 Grand-Lancy, Geneva, Switzerland) publishes a worldwide directory of English-speaking physicians whose qualifications meet IAMAT standards and who have agreed to treat members for a set fee. Membership is free.

Traveling with Children

Families visiting Norway in summer may enjoy renting an authentic *rorbu* (fisherman's shanty) at the seaside. Accommodations are simple yet adequate, and rowboats usually are available for rent. For more information contact **Borton Overseas** (5516 Lyndale Ave. S, Minneapolis, MN 55419, tel. 800/843–0602). Information on farming holidays in Norway is available from **Nortra** (Nortravel Marketing; Box 499, Sentrum, N-0105 Oslo, tel. 22/42–70–44).

Hints for Travelers with Disabilities

The Norwegian Association of the Disabled offers a leaflet detailing hotels with facilities for disabled visitors. (Norges Handikapforbund, Box 9217 Grønland N-0134, Oslo, tel. 22/17–02–55).

Hints for Older Travelers

Visitors over 67 are automatically entitled to a 50% reduction on all first- and second-class train tickets. Senior-citizen tickets can be purchased at all rail stations. For additional information on senior discounts and seasonal savings plans, contact the Scandinavian Tourist Board (*see* Government Tourist Offices,

above), and HT Reiser with Pensjonistenes Reisesenter (Travel Center for the Retired; tel. 22/36–20–40 in Oslo).

Arriving and Departing

From North America by Plane

Flights are either nonstop, direct, or connecting. A **nonstop** flight requires no change of plane and makes no stops. A **direct** flight stops at least once and can involve a change of plane, although the flight number remains the same; if the first leg is late, the second waits. This is not the case with a **connecting** flight, which involves a different plane and a different flight number.

Airports and Airlines **Oslo Fornebu Airport** is the gateway to Norway for most visitors. Once called a "cafeteria with a landing strip," it is currently being transformed into a modern airport worthy of a capital city. Other international airports include **Bergen, Kristiansand S., Sandefjord, Stavanger,** and **Trondheim.**

Scandinavian Airlines (SAS) (tel. 800/221–2350) has daily nonstop flights to Oslo from New York, daily connections to Oslo via Copenhagen from Chicago, Los Angeles, and Seattle, and twice-weekly connections (also via Copenhagen) from Toronto and Anchorage. During the summer months, **Delta Airlines** (tel. 800/221–1212) has daily nonstop flights from New York to Oslo. **Icelandair** (tel. 800/223–5500) flies from New York to Oslo via Reykjavik.

From the United Kingdom by Plane

SAS (tel. 071/734–6777, fax 071/465–0125) flies from Heathrow to Oslo and Stavanger, and from Aberdeen to Stavanger. **Braathens SAFE** operates flights from Newcastle to Stavanger and Oslo, and from London Gatwick to Oslo. **AirUK** has several flights weekly from Aberdeen to Stavanger and Bergen. Flying time from London to Oslo is about 1¾ hours and about 1½ hours to Stavanger.

British Airways (tel. 081/897–4000) offers nonstop flights from Heathrow to Bergen, Oslo, and Stavanger. **Aer Lingus** (tel. 0345/01–01–01; in Ireland, 0001/377–777), **Cimber Air** (tel. 0652/688491), **Business Air** (tel. 0382/66345), **Midtfly** (tel. 0224/723357), and **Icelandair** (tel. 071/388–5599; or 081/745–7051 at Heathrow Airport) all have flights between Great Britain or Ireland and major Scandinavian cities. The flying time from London to Oslo is about 1¾ hours.

From the United Kingdom by Train and Boat

By Train Traveling from Britain to Norway by train is not difficult. The best connection leaves London's Victoria Station at noon and connects at Dover with a boat to Oostende, Belgium. From Oostende there is a sleeping-car-only connection to Copenhagen that arrives the next morning at 8:25. The train to Oslo leaves at 9:45 AM and arrives at 7:42 PM. A number of special discounted trips are available, including the **InterRail Pass,** which is now available for European residents of all ages.

By Boat Only one ferry line serves Norway from the United Kingdom, **Color Line** (Tyne Commission Quay, North Shields [near Newcastle] LEN29 6EA, tel. 091/296–1313, or Skoltegrunnskaien, 5000 Bergen, tel. 55/32–27–80), which has three departures a week between Bergen, Stavanger, and Newcastle during the summer season (May 22–Sept. 10), two during the rest of the year. Crossings take about 20 hours. Monday sailings stop first in Stavanger and arrive in Bergen six hours later, while the other trips stop first in Bergen. **Scandinavian Seaways** has a crossing between Harwich and Göteborg, Sweden, a 4½-hour drive from Oslo.

Staying in Norway

Getting Around

The southern part of Norway can be considered fairly compact—all major cities are about a day's drive from one another (although Trondheim–Stavanger is pushing it). The distances make themselves felt on the way north, where Norway becomes narrower as it inches up to and beyond the Arctic Circle and hooks over Sweden and Finland to touch the Soviet Union. Because distances are so great, it is virtually impossible to visit the entire country from one base.

By Plane SAS (EuroClass, tel. 22/17–00–10; Tourist, tel. 22/17–00–20) serves most major cities, including Svalbard. **Braathens SAFE** (SAFE stands for the "South Asian and Far Eastern" routes of the parent shipping company; tel. 22/83–44–70) is the major domestic airline, serving cities throughout the country and along the coast as far north as Tromsø and Svalbard. It also has international routes from Oslo to Billund (Denmark), Malmö (Sweden), and Newcastle (England). **Widerøe** (tel. 22/73–65–00) serves smaller airports (with smaller planes), mostly along the coast, and in northern Norway. **Norsk Air** (tel. 33/46–90–00), a subsidiary of Widerøe, provides similar services in the southern part of the country. **Coast Air** (tel. 52/83–41–10) and **Norlink** (tel. 77/67–57–80), an SAS subsidiary, are commuter systems linking smaller and larger airports.

A number of special fares are available within Norway year-round, including air passes, family tickets, weekend excursions, youth (up to the age of 26), and senior (over 67). Youth fares are cheapest when purchased from the automatic ticket machines at the airport on the day of departure. All Norwegian routes have reduced rates from July through the middle of August, and tickets can be purchased on the spot. Outside of these times, a minifare during low traffic hours is probably the cheapest way to fly.

All flights within Scandinavia are nonsmoking, as are all airports in Norway, except in designated areas.

By Train NSB, the Norwegian State Railway System, has five main lines originating from the **Oslo S Station.** The longest runs north to Trondheim, then extends onward as far as Fauske and Bodø. The southern line hugs the coast to Stavanger, while the western line crosses some famous scenic territory on the way to Bergen. An eastern line through Kongsvinger links Norway with Sweden to Stockholm, while another southern line through Gothenburg is the main connection with Continental

There's only one airline that offers as many travel choices as Scandinavia itself.

Scandinavia is fjords, archipelagoes, rolling countryside, ancient castles, and quaint inns. It's lively capitals, gourmet restaurants, museums, first class hotels, opera and ballet. A region of wonderful contrasts and friendly, English-speaking people.

And SAS the airline with the most nonstop flights to Scandinavia, offers the most ways for you to enjoy your visit. Select from a full range of escorted tours as well as independent fly/drive and fly/cruise packages.

There's only one place like it. Scandinavia.

For information and reservations, contact your travel agent or call SAS at 800-221-2350.

Scandinavia

DENMARK · FINLAND · ICELAND · NORWAY · SWEDEN

BOO.

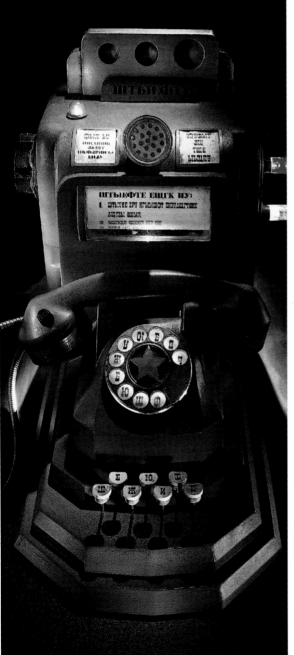

Europe. Narvik, north of Bodø, is the last stop on Sweden's Ofot line, which runs from Stockholm via Kiruna, the world's northernmost rail system. It is possible to take a five-hour bus trip between Bodø and Narvik to connect with the other train.

Discounted fares include family, senior citizen (including not-yet-senior spouses), and off-peak fares, which must be purchased a day in advance. NSB gives student discounts only to foreigners studying at Norwegian institutions.

NSB trains are clean, comfortable, and punctual. Most have special compartments for the disabled and for families with children under two years old. Both first- and second-class tickets are available. Both seat and sleeper reservations are required on long journeys. Prices vary according to one-, two-, or three-bunk cabins.

Most trains have food service, ranging from simple sandwiches and beverages to a buffet car selling hot dogs, pizza, and perhaps an entrée. Only the Oslo-Bergen route has a full-service dining car, where reservations are essential.

Train tickets can be purchased in railway stations or from travel agencies. NSB has its own travel agency in Oslo (Stortingsgt. 28, tel. 22/83–88–50).

NSB offers many kinds of passes, including the **Nordturist Card,** good for unlimited rail travel in Denmark, Sweden, Norway, and Finland and is valid on many ferries. The 21-day card costs about $380 (first class) or $285 (second class). Tickets can be bought at any train station in the four countries. Young people ages 12 to 25 pay about three-fourths, and children 4 to 11, half price. Rebates of up to 50% are granted on some other ferries and coaches and by some hotels. The Nordturist Card can also be purchased from NSB Travel Agency in London.

By Bus Every end station of the railroad is supported by a number of bus routes, some of which are operated by NSB, others by local companies.

Long-distance buses usually take longer than the railroad and fares are only slightly lower. Virtually every settlement on the mainland is served by bus, and for anyone with a desire to get off the beaten track, a pay-as-you-go open-ended bus trip is the best way to see Norway. **Nor-Way Bussekspress** (Bussterminalen, Galleri Olso, tel. 22/17–52–90, fax 22/17–59–22) has more than 40 different bus services, covering 10,000 kilometers (6,200 miles) and 500 destinations in its organization and can arrange any journey. One of its participating services, **Feriebussen** (Østerdal Billag A/S, 2560 Alvdal, tel. 62/48–74–00) offers five package tours with English guides.

Discounted tickets are available for children, people over 60, families, students, and military personnel.

By Boat Ferries and passenger ships remain important means of transportation. Along west-coast fjords, car ferries are a way of life. Once you know your route, buy tickets for those ferries that allow advance purchase—this lets you drive to the front of the line.

More specialized boat service includes hydrofoil/catamaran trips between Stavanger, Haugesund, and Bergen. There are also fjord cruises out of these cities and others in the north.

Color Line (Box 1422 Vika 0115, Oslo, tel. 22/94–44–00, fax 22/83–07–76) is a major carrier in Norwegian waters.

Norway's most renowned boat trip is **Hurtigruten,** or the Coastal Express, which departs from Bergen and stops at 36 ports in six days, ending with Kirkenes, near the Russian border, before turning back. Tickets can be purchased for the whole journey or for individual legs. Shore excursions are arranged at all ports. Tickets are available through travel agents or directly from the companies that run the service: FFR (9600 Hammerfest, tel. 78/41–10–00), OVDS (8501 Narvik, tel. 76/92–37–00), Nordenfjeldske Dampskibsselskab A/S (Kjøpmannsgt. 52, 7011 Trondheim, tel. 73/51–51–20, fax 73/51–51–46), and TFDS (9000 Tromsø, tel. 77/68–60–88).

By Car All vehicles registered abroad are required to carry international liability insurance and an international accident report form, which can be obtained from automobile clubs. Collision insurance is recommended. One important rule when driving in Norway: Yield to the vehicle approaching from the right.

Dimmed headlights are mandatory at all times, as is the use of seatbelts and children's seats (when appropriate) in both front and rear seats. All cars must carry red reflecting warning triangles to be placed a safe distance from a disabled vehicle.

Four-lane highways are the exception and are found only around major cities. Outside of main coastal routes, roads tend to be narrow and sharply twisting, with only token guardrails, and during the summer roads are always crowded. Along the west coast, waits for ferries can be significant.

Driving is on the right. Norwegian roads are well marked with directional, distance, and informational signs. Some roads, particularly those over mountains, can close for all or part of the winter.

The maximum speed limit is 90 kilometers per hour (55 miles per hour) on major motorways. On other highways, the limit is 80 kph (50 mph). The speed limit in cities and towns is 50 kph (30 mph), and 30 kph (18 mph) in residential areas.

Gas stations are plentiful, and unleaded gasoline and diesel fuel are sold virtually everywhere from self-service gas pumps. Those marked *kort* are 24-hour pumps, which take oil company credit cards or bank cards, either of which is inserted directly into the pump.

Norway has strict drinking and driving laws, and routine roadside checks, especially on Friday and Saturday nights, are common. The legal limit is a blood alcohol percentage of 0.05%, which corresponds to a glass of wine or a bottle of low-alcohol beer. If you are stopped for a routine check, you may be required to take a breath test. If that result is positive, you must submit to a blood test. No exceptions are made for foreigners, who can lose their licenses on the spot.

Speeding is also punished severely. Most roads are monitored by gray metal boxes equipped with radar and cameras. Signs warning of *Automatisk Trafikkontroll* (Automatic Traffic Monitoring) are posted periodically along appropriate roads. Norway has recently been in the process of changing the numbers of some of its routes and highways, especially those beginning

with "E." Make sure you double-check all directions and have an up-to-date map before you venture out.

By Taxi Even the smallest villages have some form of taxi service. Towns on the railroad normally have taxi ranks just outside the station. Look in the telephone book under "Taxi" or "Drosje." All city taxis are connected with a central dispatching office, so there is only one main telephone number, the taxi central.

Telephones

The telephone system is modern and efficient; international direct service is available throughout the country. Phone numbers are six digits in the cities, eight digits throughout the country.

Public telephones are of two types. Push-button phones, which accept NKr1, 5, and 10 coins, are easy to use: Lift the receiver, listen for the dial tone, insert the coins, dial the number, and wait for a connection. The digital screen at the top of the box indicates the amount of money in your "account."

Older rotary telephones sometimes have a grooved slope at the top for NKr1 coins, allowing them to drop into the phone as needed. Place several in the slope, lift off the receiver, listen for the dial tone, dial the number, and wait for a connection. When the call is connected, the telephone will emit a series of beeps, allowing coins to drop into the telephone.

Both types of telephones have warning signals (short pips) indicating that the purchased time is almost over.

Local Calls Local calls cost NKr2 (about 30 cents) from a pay phone and about NKr3 from hotel phones.

Long-Distance Calls All eight digits are required when dialing in Norway, both for local and long-distance calls. Rates vary according to distance and time of day.

International Calls Dial the international access code, 095, then the country code, and number. (Beginning in 1995, the new international access code will be 00.) All telephone books list country code numbers, including the United States and Canada (1), Great Britain (44), and Australia (61). Norway's code is 47. For operator-assisted calls, dial 117 for national calls and 115 for international calls. All international operators speak English.

Information Dial 180 for information for Norway and the other Scandinavian countries, 181 for international telephone numbers.

Mail

The letter rate for Norway is Nkr3.50, Nkr4 for the other Nordic countries, NKr4.40 for Europe, and NKr5.50 for outside Europe for a letter weighing up to 20g (¾ ounce).

Tipping

Tipping is kept to a minimum in Norway because service charges are added to most bills. It is, however, handy to have a supply of NKr5 or 10 coins for less formal service. Tip only in local currency.

Airport and railroad porters (if you can find them) have fixed rates per bag, so they will tell you how much they should be paid. Tips to doormen vary according to the type of bag and the distance carried—NKr5–10 each, with similar tips for porters carrying bags to the room. Room service usually has a service charge included already, so tipping is discretionary.

Round off a taxi fare to the next round digit, or anywhere from NKr5 to NKr10, a little more if the driver has been helpful with luggage.

All restaurants include a service charge ranging from 12% to 15% in the bill. It is customary to add an additional 5% for exceptional service, but it is not obligatory. Maitre d's are not tipped, and coat checks have flat rates, ranging from NKr5 to NKr10 per person.

Opening and Closing Times

Banks are open weekdays 8 to 3:30, Thursday until 6. Most shops are open 9 or 10 to 5 weekdays, Thursday until 7, Saturday 9 to 2, closed Sunday. Some large shopping centers are open until 8 weekdays. Supermarkets are open until 8 or 10 weekdays and until 6 on Saturdays. During the summer, most shops close weekdays at 4 and at 1 on Saturday, while banks open at 8:15 and close at 3, with a Thursday closing at 5. Most post offices are open weekdays 8 to 5:30, Saturday 8 to 1.

Shopping

Good buys include handicrafts, handknitted sweaters, yarn, embroidery kits, textiles, pewter, rustic ironwork, silverware, wooden bowls and spoons, hand-dipped candles, and Christmas ornaments made from natural materials. *Husfliden* (homecraft) outlets are located in almost every city. The **classic knitting designs,** with snowflakes and reindeer, have been bestsellers for years and can be bought at most Husfliden and specialty stores, while more modern sweaters, made of combinations of brightly colored yarns, can be purchased from yarn shops. *Juleduk* (Christmas tablecloths) with typical Norwegian themes, are for sale year-round at embroidery shops. **High-fashion textiles** include coats and jackets in wool blanket material with nature motifs. Other handmade items include **candlesticks** of both pewter and wrought iron, **handblown glass,** and handturned **wood bowls** and **platters** made of birch roots. All Husfliden stores and many gift shops sell **Christmas ornaments** handmade from straw and wood shavings. Other, more off-beat, items include **cheese planes** (*ostegvel* in Norwegian) and graduated forms for making almond ring cakes (*kransekakeformer*). Hobby gardeners will appreciate the *krafse,* a practical tool somewhere between a spade and a hoe, while the outdoor person will like the *supertrgye,* a gossamer thin, insulated undershirt. Because Norwegian children spend so much time out of doors, practical clothing is a must, and good buys include **Helly-Hansen rain gear** and **insulated boots.**

Norwegian silver companies produce a wide range of patterns. At 830 parts to 1,000, compared with 925 parts in sterling, Norwegian silver is stronger than English or American, and the price is very competitive.

Norwegian rustic antiques may not be exported. Even the simplest corner shelf or dish rack valued at $50 is considered a national treasure if it is known to be over 100 years old.

Value-Added Tax Refunds Value-added tax, MVA for short, but called *moms* all over Scandinavia, is a hefty 22% on all services and purchases except books; it is normally included in the prices of goods. All purchases of consumer goods totaling over NKr300 ($45) for export by nonresidents are eligible for value-added tax refunds.

Shops subscribing to "Norway Tax-Free Shopping" provide customers with vouchers, which they must present, together with their purchases, upon departure in order to receive an on-the-spot refund of 16.25% of the tax.

Shops that do not subscribe to this program have slightly more detailed forms, which must be presented to the Norwegian Customs Office along with the goods to obtain a refund by mail. This refund is closer to the actual amount of the tax.

It's essential to have both the forms and the goods available for inspection upon departure. Make sure that the appropriate stamps are on the voucher or other forms before leaving the country.

Sports and Outdoor Activities

Norway is a sports lover's paradise. Outdoor sports have always been popular, while indoor facilities have been built nationwide. Close to 100 recreational and competitive sports are recognized in Norway, each with its own national association, 57 of which are affiliated with the **Norges Idrettsforbund** (Norwegian Confederation of Sports, Hauger Skolevei 1, 1351 Rud, tel. 67/15–46–00). The tourist board's Norway brochure, which lists sporting- and active-holiday resources and contacts, is a more helpful starting point for visitors.

Bicycling Most cities have marked bike routes and paths. Bicycling on country roads away from traffic is a favorite national pastime, but as most routes are hilly, this demands good physical condition. All cyclists are required to wear protective helmets and use lights at night.

The **Norwegian Mountain Touring Association** (PB 1963 Vika N–0125 Oslo 1, tel. 22/83–25–50, fax 22/83–24–78) provides inexpensive lodging for cyclists planning overnight trips. You can also contact the helpful **Syklistens Landsforening** (Maridalsun. 60, N–0458 Oslo 4, tel. 22/71–92–93) for general information and maps, as well as the latest weather conditions.

Bird-Watching Northern Norway contains some of northern Europe's largest bird sanctuaries and teems with fantastic numbers of seabirds, including cormorants, razorbills, auks, guillemots, eider ducks, puffins, and even eagles. For organized tours, contact **Borton Overseas** (tel. 800/843–0602), **California Nature Tours** (tel. 619/241–2322), or, in Canada, **Quest Nature Tours** (tel. 800/387–1484).

Camping Norway offers more than 900 inspected and classified campsites, many with showers, bathrooms, and hookups for electricity. Most also have cabins or chalets to rent by the night or longer. For more information contact local tourist offices or the **Norwegian Automobile Federation** (Storgt. 2, N–0155, Oslo 1, tel. 22/34–14–00), the **National Camping Site Organization** (FOS,

Pilestredet 27, N–0164 Oslo 1, tel. 22/11–53–50), or, for a list of sites, the Norwegian Tourist Board.

Canoeing There are plenty of lakes and streams for canoeing in Norway, as well as rental facilities. Contact **Norges Kajakkforbund** (Hauger Skolevej 1, N–1351 Olso, tel. 67/13–77–00) for a list of rental companies and regional canoeing centers.

Fishing Whether it is fly-fishing for salmon or trout in western rivers or deep-sea fishing off the northern coast, Norway has all kinds of angling possibilities. Fishermen are required to buy an annual fishing tax card at the post office and a local license from the sporting goods store nearest the fishing site. Live bait is prohibited, and imported tackle must be disinfected before use.

Golf Golf came to Norway only recently, but the country has gone golf-crazy—there is even a course on arctic Spitsbergen! For information about guest privileges and greens fees, contact **Oslo Golfklubb** (Bogstad, 0740 Oslo 7, tel. 22/50–44–02); **Bergen Golfklubb** (Boks 470, 5001 Bergen, tel. 55/18–20–77); **Stavanger Golfklubb** (Longebakken 45, 4042 Hafrsfjord, tel. 51/55–54–31); or **Trondheim Golfklubb** (Boks 169, 7001 Trondheim, tel. 73–53–18–85).

Hiking Every city has surrounding trails and many have cabins where guests can rest, eat, and even spend the night. **Den Norske Turistforening** (**DNT**, Boks 1963 Vika, 0125 Oslo 1, tel. 22/83–25–50) and affiliated organizations administer cabins and tourist facilities in the central and northern mountainous areas of the country and will arrange group hikes. They have English brochures that can be ordered by mail.

Horseback Riding Most cities and resort areas have stables, which rent chunky Norwegian fjord ponies and horses. **Steinseth Ridesenter** (Sollivn. 74, 1370 Asker, tel. 66/78–75–46), is a 30-minute drive from Oslo. Many resorts specialize in mountain pack trips; riding camps are in operation every summer.

Mountaineering The mountains of the Lofoten Islands and the Lyngen area of Troms County offer Alpine-class mountaineering. The **DNT** (*see* Hiking, *above*) has information. Oslo rock climbers practice on the Kolsås cliffs, a 20-minute drive west of the city, while the pros go to the Trolltindene peaks in Romsdal, near Åndalsnes.

Orienteering Norway's top mass-participation sport is based on running or hiking over territory with a map and compass to find control points marked on a map. Special cards can be purchased at sports shops to be punched at control points found during a season. It's an enjoyable, inexpensive family sport, and gear can be purchased at any sports shop.

Rafting Rafting excursions are offered throughout Norway. For more information, contact: **Flåteopplevelser** (pb 227, 2051 Jessheim, tel. 63/97–29–04); **Norwegian Wildlife and Rafting** (2254 Lundersæter, tel. 62/82–97–24); **Dagali-Voss Rafting** (Dagali, 3580 Geilo, tel. 22/23–75–09 or 32/08–78–20); or **Schulstad Adventure** (Stabbursdal, 9710 Indre Billegjord, tel. 78/46–47–66).

Running Grete Waitz and Ingrid Kristiansen have put Norway on the marathon runners' map in recent years. The first national marathon championships were held in Norway in 1897 and the Oslo Marathon always attracts a large following. For the recreational runner, **Norges Friidretts Forbund** (Karl Johans Gate 2, 0104

Oslo, tel. 22/42–03–03) has information about local clubs and competitions.

Sailing Both the late King Olav V and the present King Harald V won Olympic gold medals in sailing. Sailing in Oslo fjord and among the islands of the southern coast is a favorite summer pastime. Contact **Norges Seilforbund** (Hauger Skolevei 1, 1351 Rud, tel. 67/15–46–00) about facilities around the country; for the Oslo region, contact **KNS** (The Royal Norwegian Sailing Association; Huk Aveny 1, 0287 Oslo 2, tel. 22/43–74–10).

Skating Norway had one of the first indoor rinks in the world in the early 20th century. Some rinks have a few hours of public figure skating on weekends and just about every school in the country floods its playground in winter.

Skiing The ski is Norway's contribution to the world of sports. Norway's skiing season lasts from November to Easter. In February the 1994 Winter Olympics will be held in Lillehammer, which, along with other Norwegian resorts, regularly hosts World Cup competitions. Cross-country skiing needs only basic equipment and rentals are readily available; every city has lit trails for evening skiing. In addition to downhill and cross-country, the 100-year-old **Telemark Style** is enjoying a revival across the country. It involves a characteristic deep knee bend in the turns and traditional garb, including heavy boots attached to the skis only at the toe. **Skiforeningen** (Kongevn. 5, 0390 Oslo 3, tel. 22/92–32–00) provides national snow condition reports. Ski centers in operation over the summer include: **Finse Skisenter** (3590 Finse, tel. 55/52–67–144); **Galdhøpiggen Sommerskisenter** (2687 Bøverdalen, tel. 61/01–21–42); and **Stryn Sommerskisenter** (6880 Stryn, tel. 57/87–19–95).

Swimming Most towns have indoor swimming pools, while larger cities have heated outdoor pools. Many resorts also have swimming pools.

Tennis Municipal courts are usually booked in advance for a season at a time, while private tennis clubs have covered courts that are in use year-round. Many resorts have tennis courts.

Windsurfing The best windsurfing (a new sport here) is in western Norway. Centers include: **BT Brettseilerskole** (Nygårdsgt. 5/11, 5015 Bergen, tel. 55/21–45–00); **Selje Sjøsportsenter** (6740 Selje, tel. 57/85–66–06); and **Stavanger Surfsenter** (Paradisvn. 33, 4012 Stavanger, tel. 51/52–31–08).

Sports for the Disabled Norway encouraged active participation in sports for the disabled long before it became popular elsewhere and has many Special Olympics medal winners. **Beitostølen Helsesportsenter** (2953 Beitostølen, tel. 61/34–12–00) has sports facilities for the blind and other physically challenged people as well as training programs for instructors. Sports offered include skiing, hiking, running, and horseback riding.

Beaches

Many Norwegians enjoy bathing in the summer, but low water temperatures, from 14°C to 18°C (57°F to 65°F), are enough to deter all but the most hardy. The beaches around **Mandal** in the south and **Sola** near Stavanger are the country's finest, with fine white sand, but all along the Oslo fjord there are many fine beaches. Be aware that some might have sharp pebbles and

broken mussel shells, making rubber bathing shoes a necessity. The western fjords are warmer and calmer than the open beaches of the south, and inland freshwater lakes are chillier still than Gulf Stream-warmed fjords.

Dining

For centuries, Norwegians regarded food as fuel, and their dining habits still bear traces of this.

Breakfast is a fairly big meal, usually with a selection of crusty bread, herring, cold meat, and cheese. *Geitost* (a sweet, caramel-flavored whey cheese made wholly or in part from goats' milk) is on virtually every table. It is eaten in thin slices, cut with a cheese plane or slicer, a Norwegian invention, on buttered brown bread.

Lunch is simple, usually open-faced sandwiches. Most businesses have only a 30-minute lunch break, so unless there's a company cafeteria, most people eat home-packed sandwiches. Big lunchtime buffet tables, *koldtbord*, where one can sample most of Norway's special dishes all at once, are primarily for special occasions and visitors.

Dinner, the only hot meal of the day, is early, from 1–4 in the country, 1–5 in the city, so many cafeterias serving home-style food close by six or seven in the evening.

Traditional, home-style Norwegian food is stick-to-the-ribs fare, served in generous portions and blanketed with gravy. The most popular meal is *kjøttkaker* (meat cakes), which resemble salisbury steaks, served with boiled potatoes and brown gravy. Almost as popular are *medisterkaker* (mild pork sausage patties), served with brown gravy and caraway-seasoned sauerkraut, and *reinsdyrkaker* (reindeer meatballs), served with cream sauce and lingonberry jam. Other typical meat dishes include *får i kål*, a great-tasting lamb and cabbage stew, and *stek* (roast meat), always served well-done. Fish dishes include poached *torsk* (cod) or *laks* (salmon), served with a creamy sauce called Sandefjord butter, *seibiff* (fried pollack and onions), and *fiskegrateng*, something between a fish souffle and a casserole, usually served with carrot slaw.

Norway is known for several eccentric, often pungent fish dishes, but these are not representative—both *rakfisk* (fermented trout) and *lutefisk* (dried cod soaked in lye and then boiled) are acquired tastes, even for natives.

Traditional desserts include the ubiquitous *karamellpudding* (creme caramel), and *rømmegrøt* (sour cream porridge served with cinnamon-sugar and a glass of raspberry juice). The latter, a typical farm dish, tastes rather like warm cheesecake batter—delicious. Christmas time brings with it a delectable array of light, sweet, and buttery pastries.

Norwegian restaurant food has undergone major changes in the last few years. Until recently, fine restaurants were invariably French, and fine food usually meant meat. Today, seafood and game have replaced beef and veal. Fish, from common cod and skate to the noble salmon, have a prominent place in the new Norwegian kitchen, and local cappelin roe, golden caviar, is served instead of the imported variety. Norwegian lamb, full of flavor, is now in the spotlight, and game, from birds to

moose, is prepared with sauces made from the wild berries that are part of their diet. These dishes are often accompanied by native root vegetables.

Desserts, too, often feature fruit and berries. Norwegian strawberries and raspberries ripen in the long early summer days and are sweeter and more intense than those grown farther south. Red and black currants are also used. Two berries native to Norway are *tyttebær* (lingonberries), which taste similar to cranberries but are much smaller, and *multer* (cloudberries), which look like orange raspberries, but which have an indescribable taste. These wild berries grow above the tree line and are a real delicacy.

Category	Cost
Very Expensive	over NKr450
Expensive	NKr300–NKr450
Moderate	NKr125–NKr300
Inexpensive	under NKr125

Prices are for a three-course meal, including tax and 12½% service charge.

Lodging

Norway is a land of hard beds and hearty breakfasts. Hotel standards are high, and even the simplest youth hostels provide good mattresses with fluffy down comforters and clean showers or baths. Breakfast, usually served buffet-style, is almost always included in the room price at hotels, while hostels often charge extra for the morning meal.

Norway has several hotel chains. **SAS**, which is a division of the airline, has a number of luxury hotels aimed at the business traveler. Many are above the Arctic Circle and are the "only game in town." **Rica** hotels, also a luxury chain, has expanded extensively in the last few years. The most interesting and individual hotel chain is **Home** hotels (Swedish-owned), which has successfully converted existing historic buildings into modern functional establishments in the middle price range. All Home hotels provide an evening meal, jogging suits, free beer, and other amenities designed to appeal to the single, usually business, traveler. As far as value for money is concerned, they are Norway's best buy. The **Farmer's Association** operates simple hotels in most towns and cities. These reasonably priced accommodations usually have **-heimen** as part of the name, such as Bondeheimen in Oslo. The same organization also operates cafeterias serving traditional Norwegian food, usually called **Kaffistova.** All these hotels and restaurants are alcohol-free.

Many hotels offer summer rates, although some require advance booking or hotel passes that also must be purchased in advance. **Inter Nor Hotels** (Dronningen Gate 40, 0154 Oslo, tel. 22/33–42–00, fax 22/33–69–06), a group of independently run hotels, offers a summer pass worth up to 50% off regular rates. It costs about $23 for two adults and two children and is valid at 250 hotels in Norway, 130 in the Nordic countries. **Fjord Pass** (Fjord Tours A/S PB 1752, 5024 Bergen, tel. 55/32–65–50, fax

55/31–86–56), which costs NKr50 (about $8) is valid at 298 establishments, from fancy hotels to simple mountain cabins.

Hostels Norway has 87 youth hostels, but in an effort to appeal to vacationers of all ages, the name has been changed to **vandrerhjem** (travelers' homes). Norwegian hostels are among the best in the world, squeaky clean and with excellent facilities—rooms sleep from two to six, and many have private showers. Membership can be arranged at any vandrerhjem, or you can buy a coupon book good for seven nights, which includes the membership fee. Linens are usually rented per night, so it's a good idea to bring your own—if you haven't, you can buy a *lakenpose* (sheet sleeping bag) at specialty stores. For more information and a list of vandrerhjem in Norway, contact **Norske Vandrerhjem** (Dronningensgt. 26, 0154 Oslo 1, tel. 22/42–14–10, fax 22/42–44–76).

Category	Cost
Very Expensive	over NKr1,300
Expensive	NKr1,000–NKr1,300
Moderate	NKr800–NKr1,000
Inexpensive	under NKr800

All prices are for a standard double room, including service and 22% V.A.T.

Oslo

Although it is one of the world's largest capital cities in area, Oslo has only about 475,000 inhabitants. Nevertheless, in recent years the city has taken off: Shops are open late; pubs, cafés, and restaurants are crowded at all hours; and theaters play to full houses every night of the week.

Even without nightlife, Oslo has a lot to offer—parks, water, trees, hiking/skiing trails (2,600 kilometers/1,600 miles in greater Oslo), and above all, spectacular views. Starting at the docks opposite City Hall, right at the edge of the Oslo Fjord, the city extends in great sweeps up the sides of the mountains that surround it, providing panoramic vistas from almost any vantage point.

Oslo has been Norway's center of commerce for 1,000 years, and most major Norwegian companies are based in the capital. The sea has always been Norway's lifeline to the rest of the world: The Oslo Fjord teems with activity, from summer sailors and shrimpers to merchant ships and passenger ferries heading for Denmark and Germany.

Oslo is an old city, dating from the mid-11th century. All but destroyed by fire in 1624, it was redesigned with wide boulevards and renamed Christiania by Denmark's royal builder, King Christian IV. An act of Parliament finally changed the name back to Oslo, its original Viking name, in 1925.

Important Addresses and Numbers

Tourist Information The main tourist office (**Norway Information Center,** tel. 22/83–00–50), located in the old Vestbanen railway station, is open

weekdays 9–6; weekends 9–4. The office at the main railway station, **Sentralstasjon** (Jernebanetorget, tel. 22/17–11–24) is open daily 8 AM–11 PM. Look for the big round blue-and-green signs marked with a white **i**. Information about the rest of the country can be obtained from **NORTRA** (Nortravel Marketing, Postboks 499, Sentrum, 0105 Oslo 1, tel. 22/42–70–44).

Embassies **U.S. Embassy,** Drammensvn. 18, tel. 22/44–85–50. **Canadian Embassy,** Oscarsgate 20, tel. 22/46–69–66. **U.K. Embassy,** Thomas Heftyesgate 8, tel. 22/55–24–00.

Emergencies **Police:** tel. 002 or 22/66–90–50. **Fire:** tel. 001 or 22/11–44–55. **Ambulance:** tel. 003 or 22/11–70–70. **Car Rescue:** tel. 22/23–20–85. After January 1, 1994, these numbers will change. **Police:** tel. 112 or 22/66–90–50. **Fire:** tel. 111 or 22/66–90–50. **Ambulance:** tel. 113 or 22/11–70–70. **Car Rescue:** tel. 22/23–20–85.

Hospital Emergency **Oslo Legevakt** (Storgt. 40, tel. 22/20–10–90), the city's public *Rooms* and thus less expensive hospital, is near the Oslo S Station and is open 24 hours.

Doctors **Volvat Medisinske Senter** (Borgenvn. 2A, tel. 22/95–75–00) is Norway's largest private clinic, located near the Borgen underground station. **Oslo Akutten** (N. Vollgt. 8, tel. 22/41–24–40) is an emergency clinic downtown, near Stortinget.

Dentists **Oslo Kommunale Tannlegevakt** (Kolstadgt. 18, tel. 22/67–30–00) is at Tøyen Senter. **Oslo Private Tannlegevakt** (Hansteens gt. 3, tel. 22/44–46–36) is a private clinic.

Late-Night **Jernbanetorvets apotek** (Jernbanetorget 4B, tel. 22/41–24–**Pharmacies** 82),across from Oslo S Station, is open 24 hours.

Where to After normal banking hours money can be changed at the fol-**Change Money** lowing places: The bank at **Oslo S Station** is open June–Sept., daily 8 AM–11 PM; otherwise, weekdays 8 AM–8:30 PM, Saturday 8–2. The bank at **Oslo Fornebu Airport** is open weekdays 6:30 AM–9 PM, Saturday 7–5, Sunday 7 AM–8 PM. All post offices exchange money. **Oslo Central Post Office** (Dronningensgt. 15) is open weekdays 8–8, Saturday 9–3.

English-Language The best selection of English books can be found at **Tanum**
Bookstores **Libris** (Karl Johans Gate 37, tel. 22/42–93–10) and at **Erik Qvist** (Drammensvn. 16, tel. 22/44–03–26 or 22/44–52–69).

Travel Agencies **American Express/Winge Reisebureau** (Karl Johans Gate 33/35, tel. 22/41–20–30); **Bennett Reisebureau** (Pilestredet 35, tel. 22/94–36–00); **Berg-Hansen** (agent for Thomas Cook, Arbiensgt. 3, tel. 22/55–19–01); and **Kilroy Travels Norway** (Universitetssenteret, Blindern, tel. 22/85–32–00), for student travel.

Arriving and Departing by Plane

Airports and **Oslo Fornebu Airport,** 20 minutes west of the city, has interna-**Airlines** tional and domestic services under the same roof. Nevertheless the walks between international arrivals, baggage claim, and passport control are long.

SAS (tel. 22/17–00–20) is the main carrier, with both international and domestic flights. **Braathens SAFE** (tel. 67/59–70–00) and **Widerøe** (tel. 22/73–65–00) are the main domestic carriers.

Other major airlines serving Fornebu include **British Airways** (tel. 22/33–16–00), **Air France** (tel. 22/83–56–30), **Delta Air Lines** (tel. 22/41–56–00), **Finnair** (tel. 22/42–58–56), **Icelandair**

(tel. 22/42–39–75), **KLM** (tel. 67/58–38–00), and **Lufthansa** (tel. 22/83–65–65).

Gardermoen Airport, 40 kilometers (25 miles) north of Oslo, is the only one in the area that can handle 747s and DC10s. It is used primarily for charter traffic.

Between the Airport and Downtown Oslo Fornebu Airport is a 10–15-minute ride from the center of Oslo at off-peak hours. At rush hour (7:30–9 AM from the airport and 3:30–5 PM to the airport), the trip can take more than twice as long. None of the downtown hotels provide free shuttle service, although some outside the city do.

By Bus **Flybussen** (tel. 67/59–62–20; tickets: NKr30 adults, children 15 and under free; weekdays 6 AM–9:45 PM, Sat. 6 AM–8:30 PM, Sun. 6 AM–9:45 PM) departs from its terminal under Galleri Oslo shopping center, three times per hour and reaches Fornebu approximately 20 minutes later. Another bus departs from the SAS Scandinavia Hotel 10 minutes after and 20 minutes before the hour and costs the same. Suburban bus No. 31, marked "Snarøya," stops outside the Arrivals terminal. On the trip into town, it stops on the main road opposite the entrance to the airport. The cost is NKr20.

By Taxi There is a taxi line to the right of the Arrivals exit. The fare to town is about NKr100. All taxi reservations should be made through the **Oslo Taxi Central** (tel. 22/38–80–80) no less than one hour before pickup time.

Arriving and Departing by Car, Train, and Bus

By Car Route E18 connects Oslo with Göteborg, Sweden (by ferry between Sandefjord and Strömstad, Sweden), Copenhagen, Denmark (by ferry between Kristiansand and Hirtshals, Denmark), and Stockholm directly overland. The land route from Oslo to Göteborg is E6. An electronic ring around Oslo requires all vehicles entering the city to pay NKr11. If you have the correct amount in change, drive through one of the lanes marked "Mynt." If you don't, or if you need a receipt, use the "Manuell" lane.

By Train Long-distance trains arrive at and leave from **Oslo S** (tel. 22/17–40–00), while suburban commuter trains use **Nationaltheatret** or **Oslo S.** Commuter cars reserved for monthly pass holders are marked with a large black "M" on a yellow circle.

By Bus The terminal, **Bussterminalen** (tel. 22/17–01–66), is located under Galleri Oslo, across from the Oslo S Station. Tickets for **Nor-Way Bussekspress** (long-distance routes tel. 22/17–52–90, fax 22/17–59–22) can be purchased here or at travel agencies. Local bus tickets can be bought at the terminal or on the bus. For local traffic information, call 22/17–70–30.

Getting Around

The **Oslo Card** offers unlimited travel on all public transport in greater Oslo as well as free admission to museums, theaters, sightseeing attractions, the amusement park Tusenfryd, and racetracks, and discounts at various stores, cinemas (May, June, July), sports centers, and hotels. The three-day adult card gives a 30% discount for trains to and from Oslo. A one-day Oslo Card costs NKr95, a two-day card NKr140, and a three-day card NKr170.

Tickets on all public transportation within Oslo cost NKr15 without transfer, while tickets that cross communal boundaries have different rates. It pays to buy a pass or a multiple travel card, which includes transfers. A one-day pass costs NKr35 and a seven-day pass costs NKr130. A Flexicard is good for eight trips with free transfer within one hour and costs NKr 130. Children 15 and under and senior citizens pay half price. These cards can be purchased at any post office, at tourist information offices, at subway stations, and on some routes. **Trafikanten** (Jernbanetorget, tel. 22/17–70–30), the information office for public transportation, is open weekdays 7 AM–11 PM, weekends 8–11.

Most public transportation starts running by 5:30 AM, with the last run just after midnight. On weekends there is night service on certain routes.

By Subway Oslo has eight subway lines, which converge at **Stortinget** station. The four eastern lines all stop at **Tøyen** before branching off, while the four western lines run through **Majorstuen** before emerging aboveground for the rest of their routes to the northwestern suburbs. Tickets can be purchased at the stations.

By Bus About 20 bus lines, including four night buses on weekends, serve the city. Most stop at **Jernbanetorget** opposite Oslo S Station. Tickets can be purchased from the driver.

By Tram/Streetcar Five tram lines serve the city. All stop at **Jernbanetorget** opposite Oslo S Station. Tickets can be purchased from the driver.

By Ferry A ferry to **Hovedøya** and other islands in the harbor basin leaves from **Vippetangen,** behind Akershus castle (take bus No. 29 from Jernbanetorget). From April through September, ferries run between **Rådhusbrygge 3,** in front of City Hall, and **Bygdøy,** the western peninsula.

By Car **Oslo Card** holders can park for free at all parking places run by the city (P-lots), but pay careful attention to time limits. Handicapped travelers with valid parking permits from their home country are allowed to park free and with no time limit in spaces reserved for the handicapped.

If you plan to do any amount of driving in Oslo, buy a copy of the *Stor Oslo* map, available at book stores and gasoline stations.

By Taxi All city taxis are connected with the central dispatching office (tel. 22/38–80–90), which can take up to 30 minutes to send one during peak hours. Cabs can be ordered from 1 to 24 hours in advance (tel. 22/38–80–80). Special transport, including vans and cabs equipped for the handicapped, can also be ordered (tel. 22/38–80–70). Taxi stands are located all over town, usually alongside Narvesen kiosks, and are listed in the telephone directory under "Taxi" or "Drosjer."

It is possible to hail a cab on the street. A cab with its roof light on is available, but cabs are not allowed to pick up passengers within 100 meters of a stand. Rates start at NKr8 for hailed or rank cabs, NKr30 to NKr40 for ordered taxis, depending upon the time of day.

Guided Tours

Tickets for all tours are available from Tourist Information at Vestbanen and at the Oslo S Station. Tickets for bus tours can

be purchased on the buses. All tours, except one, operate only during the summer.

Orientation   All bus tours leave from the harborside entrance to the City Hall (**Rådhuset**), while combination boat-bus tours depart from Rådhusbrygge 3, the wharf in front of City Hall.

H.M.K. Sightseeing (Hegdehaugsvn. 4, tel. 22/20–82–06) offers three bus tours. **Båtservice Sightseeing** (Rådhusbrygge 3, tel. 22/20–07–15) offers one bus tour, five cruises, and one combination tour.

Special-Interest   Tourist Information at Vestbanen can arrange four- to eight-
Forest Tours   hour motor safaris through the forests surrounding Oslo (tel. 22/83–00–50).

Sailing   **Norway Yacht Charter** (H. Hyerdahls gt. 1, tel. 22/42–64–98) can arrange sailing or yacht tours for groups of 5 to 200 people.

Sleigh Rides   During the winter it is possible to ride an old-fashioned sleigh through Oslomarka, the wooded area surrounding the city. **Vangen Skistue** (Laila and Jon Hamre, Fjell, 1404 Siggerud, tel. 64/86–54–81) or **Sørbråten Gård** (Helge Torp, Maridalen, tel. 22/42–35–79) can arrange this for you. In the summertime, they switch from sleighs to horses and buggies.

Dogsled Tours   For a faster and more exciting experience, tour the *marka* by dogsled. Both lunch and evening tours are available. Contact **Norske Sledehundturer** (Einar Kristen Aas, 1500 Moss, tel. 69/27–37–86).

Street Train   Starting at 11 AM and continuing at 45-minute intervals, the **Oslo Train** (tel. 22/42–23–64), which looks like a chain of dune buggies, leaves Aker Brygge for a 40-minute ride around the center of town.

Personal Guides   Tourist Information at Vestbanen can provide an authorized city guide for your own private tour. **OsloTaxi** (Trondheimsvn. 100, tel. 22/38–80–00) also offers private sightseeing.

Walking Tours   Organized walking tours are listed in *What's on in Oslo*, available from Tourist Information and at most hotels.

Highlights for First-Time Visitors

Frogner Park (Vigeland sculpture park) (*see* Tour 3)
Holmenkollen (*see* Tour 3)
Kon-Tiki Museum (*see* Tour 4)
Munch Museum (*see* Tour 3)
Norsk Folkemuseum (*see* Tour 4)
Polar Ship *Fram* (*see* Tour 4)
Rådhus (*see* Tour 1)
Viking ships (*see* Tour 4)

Exploring Oslo

Karl Johans Gate, starting at Oslo S Station and ending at the Royal Palace, forms the backbone of downtown Oslo. Many of Oslo's museums and most of its historic buildings lie between the parallel streets of Grensen and Rådhusgata. Just north of the center of town is a historic area with a medieval church and old buildings. West of downtown is Frogner, the residential area closest to town, with embassies, fine restaurants, antiques shops, galleries, and the Vigeland sculpture park.

Farther west is the Bygdøy Peninsula, with five museums and one castle. Northwest of town is Holmenkollen, with beautiful houses, a famous ski jump, and a restaurant. On the east side, where many new immigrants live, is the Munch Museum and the botanical gardens.

Numbers in the margin correspond to points of interest on the Oslo map.

Tour 1: Downtown, from the Royal Palace to the Harbor

Although the city is huge (454 square kilometers/175 square miles), downtown Oslo is compact, with shops, museums, historic sights, restaurants, and clubs concentrated in a small, walkable center—brightly illuminated at night.

Oslo's main promenade street, Karl Johans Gate, runs from **Slottet** (the Royal Palace). The neoclassical palace, completed in 1848, is closed to visitors, but the garden is open to the public. An equestrian statue of Karl Johan, king of Sweden and Norway, the street's namesake, stands in the square in front of the palace.

Down the incline and to the left are the three buildings of the old **Universitet** (university), which remains one of Norway's premier educational centers. The great hall of the center building is decorated with murals by Norwegian artist Edvard Munch, and is often the site of the Nobel Peace Prize award ceremony. *Aulaen, Karl Johans Gate 47, tel. 22/85–93–00, ext. 756. Admission free. Open July, weekdays noon–2.*

Around the corner from the university, with access from Universitetsgata, is the newly refurbished **Nasjonalgalleriet** (National Gallery). There are some excellent pieces in the 19th- and early 20th-century Norwegian rooms. Scandinavian impressionists, called the "Northern Light" artists, have recently been discovered by the rest of the world. The gallery also has an extensive Munch collection. *Universitetsgt. 13, tel. 22/20–04–04. Admission free. Open Mon., Wed., Fri., and Sat. 10–4; Thurs. 10–8; Sun. 11–3.*

Back-to-back with the National Gallery, across a parking lot, is a big cream-brick Art Nouveau–style building housing the **Historisk Museum** (History Museum). In addition to Asian and African ethnographic displays, the museum features a collection of Viking and medieval artifacts, including many intricately carved stave church portals. *Frederiksgt. 2, tel. 22/41–63–00. Admission free. Open May 15–Sept. 14, Tues.–Sun. 11–3; Sept. 15–May 14, Tues.–Sun. noon–3.*

Continue along Frederiksgate to the university and cross Karl Johans Gate to **Nationaltheatret** (the National Theater) and **Studenterlunden Park,** a few steps from the train station. In front of the theater are statues of Norway's great playwrights, Bjørnstjerne Bjørnsen (who wrote the words to the national anthem and won a Nobel Prize for his plays) and Henrik Ibsen, who wrote *A Doll's House* and *Hedda Gabler.*

Across the street on the other side of the theater is the **Hotel Continental,** owned by the same family since it was built in 1900. Take a quick tour around the lobby bar to see the collec-

Oslo

KEY

AE American Express Office

ℹ Tourist Information

—— Rail Lines

Akershus Slott, **11**
Domkirke, **8**
Fram-museet, **23**
Gamle Aker Kirke, **14**
Historisk Museum, **4**
Holmenkollbakken, **18**
Kon-Tiki Museum, **24**
Kunstindustri-museet, **13**
Munchmuseet, **19**

Museet for Samtidskunst, **9**
Nasjonalgalleriet, **3**
Nationaltheatret, **5**
Norsk Folkemuseum, **21**
Oscarshall Slott, **20**
Rådhus, **6**
Skogbrand Insurance, **12**

Slottet, **1**
Stortinget, **7**
Teatermuseet, **10**
Tryvannstårnet, **17**
Universitet, **2**
Vigelands anlegget, **15**
Vigelandsmuseet, **16**
Vikingskiphuset, **22**

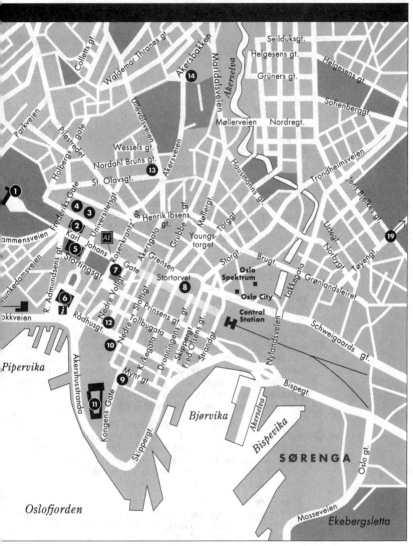

tion of Munch graphics. The hotel's Theatercafeen is one of Oslo's most fashionable restaurants.

6 Turn right on Universitetsgata to reach the redbrick **Rådhus** (City Hall), dedicated during Oslo's 900-year jubilee celebrations in 1950 and a familiar landmark with its two block towers. It took 17 years to build because construction was interrupted by World War II. Many sculptures outside, as well as murals inside, reflect the artistic climate in Norway in the 1930s—socialist modernism in its highest form. *Rådhusplassen, tel. 22/ 86–16–00. Admission: NKr15 adults, Nkr5 children. Open May–Sept., Mon.–Wed. and Fri.–Sat. 9–3:30; Thurs. 9–7; Sun. noon–3.*

Return to Stortingsgata and walk past Tordenskioldsgate to Rosenkrantz' Gate, both lined with specialty shops. Cross over Stortingsgata and along the short end of the park back to Karl Johans Gate. On the left is a refurbished news kiosk from the early years of this century. Across the street is the **Grand Hotel,** where many Norwegians check in on Constitution Day, May 17, in order to have a room overlooking the parades. The Grand Café was a favorite with Ibsen, who began his mornings with a brisk walk followed by a stiff drink here, in the company of local journalists.

Time Out Inside the Grand Hotel, in the informal **Palmen,** salads and light meals are served, as well as pastries and cakes.

7 Walk past the Lille Grensen shopping area and once again across Karl Johan to **Stortinget** (the Parliament), built in the middle of the 19th century. It's a classical building, magnificently perched on the top of the hill, and becomes a people-watching spot at night, with vendors, promenaders, and students. *Karl Johans Gate 22, tel. 22/31–30–50. Admission free. Open year-round when Parliament is not in session.*

8 Turn left on Kongens Gate from Karl Johans Gate to reach **Stortorvet,** Oslo's main square. On its west side is **Oslo Domkirke** (cathedral), completed in 1697, which includes an intricately carved Baroque pulpit. *Stortorvet 1, tel. 22/41–27–93. Admission free. Open June 1–Aug. 31, weekdays 10–3, Sat. 10–1; Sept. 1–May 31, weekdays 10–1.*

Behind the cathedral is a semicircular arcade housing many small artisans' shops, called **Kirkeristen** or Basarhallene. The building was constructed in the middle of the 19th century but was inspired by medieval architecture.

Time Out Order a cup of hot, foamy **cappuccino** at the **café** of the same name in the inner arcade. A copy of the *International Herald-Tribune* hangs from a rod inside for anyone to read.

9 From the cathedral, follow Kirkegata left past Karl Johan to Bankplassen and the 1902 Bank of Norway building, since 1990 **Museet for Samtidskunst** (the Museum of Contemporary Art). The building, a good example of geometric Norwegian Art Nouveau, houses a fine collection of international and Norwegian pieces, mostly in small rooms built around a large core. *Bankpl. 4, tel. 22/33–58–20. Admission free. Open Tues.–Fri. 11–7, weekends 11–4.*

Turn left onto Myntgata to reach Nedre Slottsgate, Oslo's oldest neighborhood, where the half-timber buildings on the left stable police horses. At the corner of Nedre Slottsgate and Rådhusgata is the old City Hall, housing **Gamle Rådhus** restaurant, which celebrates its 353rd anniversary this year. Upstairs

⑩ is **Teatermuseet** (the Theater Museum), a collection of old pictures and costumes, which sometimes holds an open house at which children can try on costumes and have makeup applied. The first public theater performance in Oslo took place here. *Nedre Slottsgt. 1, tel. 22/41-81-47. Admission: NKr10 adults, Nkr5 children. Open Wed. 11-3, Sun. noon-4.*

Diagonally across Rådhusgata are two 17th-century buildings that house art galleries and a café. Turn left on Rådhusgata and

⑪ walk over the grassy hill to the entrance of **Akershus Slott** (castle). It's a climb, but the views from the top are worth it. The oldest part of the castle was built around 1300 and includes an escape-proof room built for a thief named Ole Pedersen Høyland. In fact he broke out of this cell, robbed the Bank of Norway, was caught, and returned to jail. With no possibility of a second escape, he killed himself here. Today some of the building is used for state occasions, but a few rooms, including the recently restored chapel, are open to the public.

The castle became German headquarters during the occupation of Norway in World War II, and many members of the Resistance were executed on the castle grounds. Their memorial has been erected at the site, across the bridge at the harbor end of the castle precinct. In a building next to the castle, at the top of the hill, is **Norges Hjemmefrontmuseum** (the Norwegian Resistance Museum), which documents events that took place during the German occupation (1940-45). *Akershus Slott, Festningspl., tel. 22/41-25-21. Admission to castle grounds and concerts free. Open daily 6 AM-9 PM; concerts in chapel, May 20-Oct. 21, Sun. at 2. Admission to castle: NKr15 adults; NKr5 children, students, senior citizens. Open May 2-Sept. 15, Mon.-Sat. 10-4; year-round, Sun. 12:30-4. Norges Hjemmefrontmuseum, Akershus Festning, tel. 22/40-31-38. Admission: NKr15 adults; NKr5 children, students, senior citizens. Open Oct.-Apr. 14, Mon.-Sat. 10-3, Sun. 11-4; Apr. 15-June 14 and Sept., Mon.-Sat. 10-4 and Sun. 11-4; June 15-Aug., Mon.-Sat. 10-5, Sun. 11-5.*

Walk back to Rådhusgata to see another interesting building,

⑫ **Skogbrand Insurance** (Rådhusgt. 23B), in the block above the retaining wall. Architects Jan Digerud and Jon Lundberg have won awards for their innovative 1985 vertical addition to this 1917 building. Continue along to the harborside, where you can buy shrimp from one of the boats docked opposite City Hall and enjoy them on a bench overlooking the water.

Tour 2: St. Olavs Gate to Damstredet

This quiet, old-fashioned district is particularly well preserved. It features artisans' shops and Oslo's most historic cemetery.

⑬ At the corner of St. Olavs Gate and Akersgata is **Kunstindustrimuseet** (the Decorative Arts Museum), which houses a superb furniture collection as well as an entire floor of Norwegian decorative art. The most interesting collection is on the top floor—royal clothing, including Queen Maud's jewel-encrusted, waspwaist coronation gown from 1904—clothes worthy of any fairy-

tale. *St. Olavsgt. 1, tel. 22/20–35–78. Admission: NKr15 adults; NKr10 children, students, senior citizens. Open Tues.– Fri. 11–3, weekends noon–4.*

Across Akersgata is St. Olavs Kirke. Up the hill, on the right, is **Vår Frelsers Gravlund** (Our Savior's Cemetery), where many of Norway's famous, including Ibsen and Munch, are buried. At its northeastern corner is **Gamle Aker Kirke** (Old Aker Church), the city's only remaining medieval church, a stone basilica, which has undergone many changes since it was constructed around 1100. *Akersvn. 25, tel. 22/69–35–82. Admission free. Open Mon.–Sat. noon–2.*

Tour 3: Frogner, Holmenkollen, and the Munch Museum

Catch the No. 2 "Majorstuen og Frogner" streetcar, which stops on Stortingsgate at Nationaltheatret and runs along the Drammensveien side of the Royal Palace.

Opposite the southwestern end of the palace grounds is the triangular **U.S. Embassy,** designed by American architect Eero Saarinen and built in 1959. At Solli plass, the *trikk,* as Norwegians fondly call the streetcars, turns right onto Frognerveien.

Stay on the trikk and ride to Frogner Park or walk the seven short blocks, following Balders Gate to Arno Bergs plass with its central fountain. Turn left on Gyldenløves Gate (street of the golden lion) and walk through one of the city's most stylish neighborhoods. Most of the buildings were constructed in the early years of this century, and many have interesting sculptural decoration and wrought ironwork. Gyldenløves Gate ends at Kirkeveien. Turn right, past the Dutch Embassy, and cross the street at the light, which is next to the trikk stop. Frogner Park is just ahead.

There's nothing quite like **Vigelands anlegget** in Frogner Park anywhere else in the world. Sculptor Gustav Vigeland began his career as a wood-carver, and his talent was quickly appreciated and supported by the townspeople of Oslo. In 1921 they provided him with a free house and studio, in exchange for which, even during World War II and the German occupation, he began to chip away at his life's work, which he would ultimately donate to the city. After the war the work was unveiled, to the combined enchantment and horror of the townsfolk. Included was the 470-ton monolith that is now the highlight of the park, as well as hundreds of writhing, fighting, and loving sculptures representing the varied forms and stages of human life. The figures are nude, but they're more monumental than erotic—bullet-headed, muscular men and healthy, solid women with flowing hair.

Time Out Just before the sculpture bridge, on the left, is the park's outdoor restaurant, **Herregårdskroen,** where you can enjoy anything from a buffet lunch to a three-course dinner, depending on the time of day. It's a prime place for people-watching.

Frogner Park is a living part of the city—people walk dogs on the green and bathe chubby babies in the fountains, and they jog, ski, and sunbathe throughout. The park complex also includes the City Museum, a swimming pool, an ice rink and skat-

ing museum (tel. 22/46–68–50), several playgrounds, and a restaurant. *Kirkeveien. Admission free.*

⑯ **Vigelandmuseet** (the Vigeland Museum), across from the park, displays many of the plaster models for the sculptures, Vigeland's woodcuts and drawings, and mementos of his life. *Nobelsgt. 32, tel. 22/44–23–06. Admission: NKr20 adults; NKr10 children, students, senior citizens. Open May 1–Sept. 30, Tues.–Sat. 10–6, Sun. noon–7; Oct. 1–Apr. 30, Tues.–Sat. noon–4, Sun. noon–6.*

Continue on Kirkeveien to Majorstuen underground station, up the steps on the left, and take the Holmenkollen line to Frognerseteren, a 15-minute ride.

Time Out **Frognerseteren Restaurant,** built in the national romantic style, dates from 1909, when newly independent Norway sought inspiration from its earlier history.

As if the view from Frognerseteren weren't spectacular ⑰ enough, **Tryvannstårnet** TV tower, offering the best panoramic view of Oslo, is only a 15-minute, sign-posted walk away. *Voksenkollen, tel. 22/92–32–00. Admission: NKr50 adults; NKr25 children, students, senior citizens. Open July, daily 9 AM–10 PM; June and Aug., daily 10–8; May and Sept., daily 10–5; Jan.–Apr., weekdays 10–3, weekends 11–4.*

⑱ Downhill is **Holmenkollbakken** (the Holmenkollen Ski Museum and Ski Jump). The jump was built for the 1952 Winter Olympics and can be seen from many points in the city. At the base of the jump, turn right, past the statue of the late King Olav V on skis, to enter the museum. In addition to a collection of skis, the oldest dating from pre-Viking times, it displays equipment from the Nansen and Amundsen polar voyages and a model of a ski-maker's workshop. You can also climb (or ride the elevator) to the top of the jump tower. It's intimidating enough with a firm grip on the rail, but on skis and snow, it's mind-boggling. *Kongevn. 5, tel. 22/92–32–00. Admission: NKr50 adults; NKr25 children, students, senior citizens. Open July, daily 9 AM–10 PM; June and Aug., daily 10–8; May and Sept., daily 10–5; Jan.–Apr., weekdays 10–3, weekends 11–4.*

To catch the train back to town, walk downhill to Holmenkollen Station, less than a mile away. Leave the train at Majorstuen, cross the street, and catch the No. 20 bus, marked ⑲ "Galgeberg," which runs east to **Munchmuseet** (the Munch Museum). Edvard Munch, one of Scandinavia's leading artists, bequeathed an enormous collection of his work (about 1,200 paintings, 4,500 drawings, and 18,000 graphic works) to the city when he died in 1944. It languished in warehouses for nearly 20 years, until the city built a museum to house it in 1963. For much of his life Munch was a troubled man, and his major works, dating from the 1890s, with such titles as *The Scream* and *Vampire,* reveal his angst, but he was not without humor. His extraordinary talent as a graphic artist emerges in the print room, with its displays of lithographic stones and wood blocks. *Tøyengt. 53, tel. 22/67–37–74. Admission: NKr40 adults; NKr15 children, students, senior citizens. Open June 1–Sept. 15, Mon.–Sat. 10–6, Sun. noon–6; Sept. 16–May 31, Tues.–Sat. 10–4, Sun. noon–4.*

You can walk downhill from the Munch Museum to Tøyen Senter shopping area to catch the subway back downtown.

Tour 4: Bygdøy

Oslo's most important historical sights are concentrated on Bygdøy Peninsula. Take bus No. 30, marked "Bygdøy," from Stortingsgate at Nationaltheatret along Drammensveien to Bygdøy Allé, a wide avenue lined with chestnut trees. The bus passes Frogner Church and several embassies on its way to Olav Kyrres plass, where it turns left, and soon left again, onto the peninsula. If you see some horses on the left, they come from the king's stables (the dark red building with the monogram); the royal family's current summer palace, actually just a big white frame house, is on the right. Get off at the next stop, "Norsk Folkemuseum." Backtrack until you come to the narrow Oscarshallveien, which leads to **Oscarshall Slott,** an eccentric neo-Gothic palace built in 1852 for King Oscar I as a site for picnics and other summer pursuits. *Oscarshallvn., tel. 22/43–77–49. Admission: NKr15 adults, NKr5 children. Open June 1–Sept. 30, Sun. 11–4.*

㉑ Next is the **Norsk Folkemuseum** (Norwegian Folk Museum), which consists of some 140 structures from all over the country that have been reconstructed on site. The best-known and most important building is **Gol Stavkirke** (Gol Stave Church), constructed around 1200. In summer and on weekends, guides in the buildings demonstrate various home crafts, such as weaving tapestries, sewing national costumes, and baking flatbread. On one side of the museum is a reconstructed 19th-century village, with shops and houses. Among its exhibits are a pharmaceutical museum and a dentist's office, complete with turn-of-the-century braces—a real mouthful of springs and bands. Indoor collections in the main building include toys, dolls and dollhouses, a Sami (Lapp) collection, national costumes, and Ibsen's actual study. The museum puts on a special summer calendar of events, including daily activities from folk dancing to concerts with instruments from the museum's collection. *Museumsvn. 10, tel. 22/43–70–20. Summer admission: NKr35 adults, NKr25 students and senior citizens, NKr10 children. Winter: NKr20, NKr15, and NKr5. Open May 15–Sept. 14, daily 10–6; Sept. 15–May 14, daily noon–4.*

㉒ Around the corner to the right is **Vikingskiphuset** (the Viking Ship Museum), one of Norway's best-known attractions. It looks like a cathedral from the outside, and inside the feeling of reverence is very real. It's hard to imagine that the three ships on display, all found buried along the Oslo Fjord, are nearly 1,200 years old. The richly carved *Oseberg* ship, thought to have been the burial chamber for Queen Åse, is the most decorative, while the *Gokstad* ship is a functional longboat, devoid of ornament. The small *Tune* ship has been left unrestored. Items found with the ships, including sleds with intricately carved decoration, tools, household goods, and a tapestry, are also on view. *Huk aveny 35, tel. 22/43–83–79. Admission: NKr20 adults; NKr10 students, senior citizens, children. Open May 2–Aug. 31, daily 9–6; Sept., daily 11–5; Apr. and Oct., daily 11–4; Nov. 1–Mar. 31, daily 11–3.*

Time Out Besides a collection of model ships and small boats, the nearby **Maritime Museum** has an outdoor café, **Najaden,** overlooking the Oslo Fjord.

㉓ Just beyond the Maritime Museum is the **Fram-museet,** an A-frame structure in the shape of a traditional Viking boathouse. This museum, with its matter-of-fact displays of life on board ship, vividly depicts the history of polar exploration. The *Fram* was constructed in 1892 by Scottish-Norwegian shipbuilder Colin Archer. Fridtjof Nansen led the first *Fram* expedition across the ice surrounding the North Pole; the ship's most famous voyage took Roald Amundsen to Antarctica, the first leg of his successful expedition to the South Pole in 1911. Visitors board the ship by gangplank and are allowed to walk all over the vessel. *Bygdøynes, tel. 22/43-83-70. Admission: NKr15 adults; NKr8 students, children, senior citizens. Open May 16–Aug. 31, daily 9–5:45; May 1–15 and Sept., daily 10–4:45; Apr. and Oct., daily 11–2:45; Mar., weekends 11–2:45; closed Dec.–Feb.*

㉔ Across the parking lot from the *Fram* is the older **Kon-Tiki Museum,** which houses the raft, along with the papyrus boat, *Ra II.* Thor Heyerdahl continued the Norwegian tradition of exploration in his 1947 voyage from Peru to Polynesia on the *Kon-Tiki,* a balsa raft, to confirm his theory that the first Polynesians originally came from Peru. The *Kon-Tiki,* now showing its age, is suspended on a plastic sea. The *Ra II* sailed from Morocco to the Caribbean in 1970. *Bygdøynesvn. 36, tel. 22/43-80-50. Admission: NKr20 adults; NKr10 students, children, senior citizens. Open May 18–Aug. 31, daily 10–6; Apr. 1–May 16 and Sept., daily 10:30–5; Oct. 1–Mar. 31, daily 10:30–4.*

From May to September 30, you can take a 15-minute ferry ride from the dock in front of the *Fram* to the City Hall docks.

Short Excursions from Oslo

Numbers in the margin correspond to points of interest on the Oslo Excursions map.

The Henie-Onstad It's been more than 20 years since Sonja Henie died, but she
Center still skates her way through many a late-night movie. The three-time Olympic gold medal winner was the first to realize the potential of the ice show, and her technical assistant, Frank Zamboni, has been immortalized in skating rinks around the world by the ice-finishing machine he developed just for her, the Zamboni. Henie had a shrewd head for money and marriage, and her third, to Norwegian shipping magnate Niels

❶ Onstad, resulted in the **Henie-Onstad Center,** about 12 kilometers (7 miles) from Oslo. They put together a fine collection of early 20th-century art, with important works by Leger, Munch, Picasso, Bonnard, and Matisse.

Bus Nos. 151, 153, 161, 162, 251, and 252 from the old university on Karl Johans Gate stop at the entrance to the museum grounds. To drive, follow E18 (toward Drammen) 12 kilometers (about 7 miles) from Oslo. *1311 Høvikodden, tel. 67/54-30-50. Admission: NKr30 adults, NKr20 students and senior citizens, and NKr10 children. Open Mon. 11–5, Tues.–Fri. 9–7; also June–Aug., weekends 11–7 and Sept.–May, weekends 11–5.*

Oslo Excursions

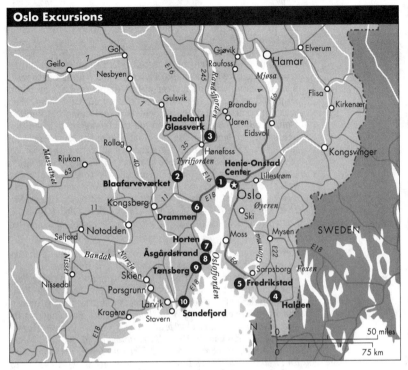

The Cobalt Works **Blaafarveværket** (the Cobalt Works), founded in 1776 to extract
❷ cobalt from the Modum mines, is about 70 kilometers (45 miles)
from Oslo, in Åmot i Modum. The mineral was used to make
dyes for the world's glass and porcelain industries. Today the
complex is a museum and a national park. The main building
houses a one-man/woman show of works by a different Scandinavian artist every year. There is also a permanent collection of
old cobalt-blue glass and porcelain. For the children, there's a
petting farm. Up the hill from the art complex is **Haugfossen,**
the highest waterfall in eastern Norway. Beside the falls is an
old-fashioned country store. Restaurants serve Norwegian
country dishes. Outdoor concerts are held on the grounds
throughout the summer.

Take E18 to Drammen, then Route 11 west to Hokksund, and
Route 35 to Åmot, turning onto Route 287 to Sigdal. The bus to
Modum leaves from the old university on Karl Johan at 9:45 AM
on Tuesday, Thursday, and Saturday. *Tel. 32/78–28–00. Admission to special exhibitions: NKr35 adults, NKr10 children;
cobalt works: NKr60 adults, children free with adults. Open
May 28–Aug. 29, daily 10–8; Aug. 29–Sept. 30, daily 10–4.*

Hadeland A day trip to **Hadeland** combines a drive along the Tyrifjord,
where you can see some of the best fjord views in eastern Norway, with a visit to a glass factory that has been in operation
❸ since 1762. **Hadeland Glassverk** (Rte. 241, toward Jevnaker,
tel. 61/31–10–00) produces both practical table crystal and one-
of-a-kind art glass. You can watch artisans blowing glass and
buy their handiwork (first quality and seconds) at the gift shop.
The museum and gallery have a collection of 15,000 items, with

about 800 on display. Take E18 west to Sandvika, turn right onto E16 and follow the signs to Hønefoss. At the Route 241 intersection, take the road to Jevnaker, which passes the glass factory. You can also take bus No. 71, marked Hønefoss, which leaves the old university on Karl Johan at seven minutes after the hour. Change in Hønefoss for the Jevnaker bus (no number). The total trip takes about two hours.

What to See and Do with Children

Bygdøy (*see* Tour 4, *above*) is a good place to take children. The Viking Ship, *Fram,* and *Kon-Tiki* museums are also good choices; the **Norsk Folkemuseum** has special exhibitions of old toys and doll houses. Live events, changing daily all summer, include old-fashioned bicycle races and sheep shearing.

The **Barnekunst** (Children's Art) **Museum** was the brainchild of Rafael Goldin, a Russian immigrant, who has collected children's drawings from more than 150 countries. Materials are provided for children to create on the spot. *Lille Frøensvn. 4, tel. 22/46–85–73. Admission: NKr30 adults; NKr15 children, students, senior citizens. Open June 25–Aug. 15, Tues.– Thurs., Sun. 11–4; Sept. 10–Dec. 15, Jan. 1–June 23, Tues.– Thurs. 9:30–2, Sun. 11–4.*

One stop closer to town on the subway is **Sporveismuseet** (the Transport Museum), with old buses and trains, including a horse-drawn streetcar. Take the subway to Majorstuen. *Gardevn. 15, tel. 22/60–94–09. Admission: NKr10 adults, NKr5 children. Open Apr.–Sept., weekends noon–3; Oct.– Aug., Sun. noon–3.*

Oslo is proud of its **Teknisk** (Technical) **Museum,** located about 20 minutes north of the city. Exhibits include the first airplane to fly over the North Sea, classic cars and motorcycles, and the development of computers, waterpower, and communication, all accompanied by demonstrations and films. *Kjelsåsvn. 143, tel. 22/22–25–50. Admission: NKr30 adults, NKr15 children. Open June–Aug., Tues.–Sun. 10–7; Sept.–May, Tues. 10–9, Wed.–Sat. 10–4, Sun. 10–5.*

Everyone enjoys **Tusenfryd,** Oslo's amusement park, a 20-minute ride east of the city. There are carnival rides, such as a merry-go-round, a Ferris wheel, and a roller coaster with a loop, and a water slide. *Vinterbro, tel. 64/94–63–63. Admission: NKr50. Open June 1–Aug. 20, daily 10:30–8; May and Aug. 21–Sept. 15, weekends 10–7:30.*

Off the Beaten Track

Oslo was founded by Harald Hårdråde (hard ruler) in 1048, and the earliest settlements were near what is now Bispegata, a few blocks behind Oslo S Station. The ruins at **Minneparken** are all that is left of the city's former spiritual center: **Korskirken** (Cross Church; Egedes Gate 2), a small stone church dating from the end of the 13th century; **Olavs kloster** (cloister; St. Halvards plass 3), built around 1240 by Dominican monks; and the foundations of **St. Halvards Kirke,** named for the patron saint of the city and dating from the early 12th century. The latter remained the city's cathedral until 1660. Stones from its walls were used to build Akershus Slott. Take trikk 9, marked "Ljabru," to Bispegata, where signs point to the various ruins.

Once you have your fill of history, you can get in touch with something a bit more corporeal at the **Emanuel Vigeland Museum.** Although he never gained the fame of his brother Gustav, the creator of Vigeland Park, the younger Emanuel is an artist of some notoriety. His alternately saucy, natural, and downright erotic frescoes make even the sexually liberated Norwegians blush. Take commuter train 15 to Slendal. *Grimelundsveien 8, tel. 22/14–23–28. Admission free. Open Sun. noon–3.*

Shopping

Oslo is the best place to buy anything Norwegian. Prices of handmade articles, such as knitwear, are controlled, making comparison shopping unnecessary. Otherwise, shops have both sales and specials—look for the words *salg* and *tilbud.* Sales of seasonal merchandise, combined with the value-added tax refund, can save you more than half the original price. Norwegians do like au courant skiwear, so there are plenty of bargains in last season's winter sportswear.

Two shopping districts stand out—downtown, in the area around **Karl Johans Gate;** and **Majorstuen.** starting at the subway station with the same name and proceeding down Bogstadveien to the Royal Palace.

Shopping Centers **Aker Brygge,** Norway's first major shopping center, is right on the water across from the Tourist Information office at Vestbanen. Shops are open until 8 most days, and some even on Sundays. **Oslo City,** at the other end of downtown, with access to the street from Oslo S station (Stenersgt. 1E, tel. 22/44–44–44), is the largest indoor mall, but the shops are run-of-the-mill, and the food is mostly fast. **Paleet Karl Johan** (Karl Johans Gate 39–41, between Universitetsgt. and Rosenkrantz Gate), the newest downtown development, opens up into a grand atrium lined with supports of various shades of black and gray marble. Upstairs are familiar chain stores and specialty shops, while in the basement is a food court.

Department Stores **Christiania GlasMagasin** (Stortorvet 9, tel. 22/11–63–50) is not a true department store, but it has a much more extensive selection of merchandise than a specialty shop. The best buys are glass and porcelain: Hadeland, Magnor, Randsfjord, and Severin glass, and Porsgrunn and Figgjo porcelain and stoneware. Christmas decorations reflecting Norway's rural heritage are easily packed. There is also a wide selection of pewter ware. **Steen & Strøm** (Kongensgt. 23, tel. 22/41–68–00) consists of several individually organized shops, including **Årstidene,** which offers a fine selection of Norwegian souvenirs.

Street Markets The best flea market is on Saturday at **Vestkanttorvet,** near Frogner Park. Check the local paper for others.

Specialty Stores Norwegian rustic antiques cannot be taken out of the country,
Antiques but just about anything else can with no problem. **Kaare Berntsen** (Universitetsgt. 12, tel. 22/20–34–29) sells paintings, furniture, and small items, all very exclusive, and priced accordingly. **Blomqvist Kunsthandel** (Tordenskiolds Gate 5, tel. 22/41–26–31) has a good selection of small items and paintings, with auctions six times a year. **West Sølv og Mynt** (Niels Juels Gate 27, tel. 22/55–75–83) has the largest selection of silver, both old and antique, in town. The Frogner district is dotted

with antiques shops, especially Skovveien and Thomas Heftyes Gate between Bygdøy Allé and Frogner Plass. **Esaias Solberg** (Dronningens Gate 27, tel. 22/42–41–08), behind Oslo Cathedral, has exceptional small antiques.

Books **Tanum Libris** (Karl Johans Gate 37, tel. 22/42–93–10) and **Erik Qvist** (Drammensveien 16, tel. 22/44–52–69) have the best selections of English books in Oslo. **Bjørn Ringstrøms Antikvariat** (Ullevålsvn. 1, tel. 22/20–78–05), across the street from the Museum of Decorative Art, has a wide selection of used books and records. For new and used paperbacks, go to **Pocketboka** (Ole Vigs Gate 25, tel. 22/69–00–18), at Majorstuen.

Embroidery **Husfliden** (*see* Handicrafts, *below*) sells embroidery kits, including do-it-yourself *bunader* (national costumes), while traditional yarn shops also sell embroidery. **Randi Mangen** (Jac Aalls Gate 17, tel. 22/60–50–59), near Majorstuen, sells only embroidery.

Food Take back a smoked salmon or trout for a special treat. Most grocery stores sell vacuum-packed fish. **W. Køltzow**, at Aker Brygge (Stranden 3, tel. 22/83–00–70), specializes in fish and can arrange for just about anything to be packed for export.

Fur Look for the Saga label for the best-quality farmed Arctic fox and mink. The most exclusive designs are found at **Studio H. Olesen** (Karl Johans Gate 31, enter at Rosenkrantz Gate, tel. 22/33–37–50, and Universitetsgt. 20, tel. 22/42–99–49). Another shop with an excellent selection is **Hansson Pels** (Kirkevn. 54, tel. 22/69–64–20), near Majorstuen.

Furniture Norway is well known for both rustic furniture and orthopedic, yet well-designed, chairs. Starting at **Tannum** (Stortingsgt. 28, tel. 22/83–42–95), Drammensveien and Bygdøy allé have a wide selection of interior-design stores.

Glass, Ceramics, If there's no time to visit a glass factory (*see* Short Excursions *and Pewter* from Oslo, *above*), go to **Christiania GlasMagasin** (Stortorvet 9, tel. 22/11–63–50) or to **Norway Designs** (Stortingsgt. 28, tel. 22/83–11–00) for the best items. The shops at Basarhallene behind the cathedral also sell glass and ceramics. Behind the Royal Palace is **Abelson Brukskunst** (Skovvn. 27, tel. 22/55–55–94), with a shop crammed with the best modern designs.

Handicrafts **Heimen** (Rosenkrantz Gate 8, tel. 22/41–40–50) has small souvenir items and a specialized department for Norwegian *bunader* (national costumes). **Husfliden** (Møllergt. 4, tel. 22/42–10–75), has an even larger selection, including pewter, ceramics, knits, handwoven textiles, furniture, handmade felt boots and slippers, hand-sewn loafers, sweaters, national costumes, wrought-iron accessories, and Christmas ornaments, all made in Norway. For individual pieces, visit **Format Kunsthandverk** (Vestbanepl. 1, tel. 22/83–73–12) or **Basarhallene**, the arcade behind the cathedral.

Jewelry Gold and precious stones are no bargain, but silver and enamel jewelry, along with reproductions of Viking pieces, are. Some silver pieces are made with Norwegian stones, particularly pink thulite. **David-Andersen** (Karl Johans Gate 20, tel. 22/41–69–55), Norway's best-known goldsmith, has the widest selection in Oslo. Other good jewelers are **Heyerdahl** (Stortingsgt. 18, tel. 22/41–59–18), near City Hall, and **Expo-Arte** (Drammensvn. 40, tel. 22/55–93–90), who specialize in custom pieces. (*See also* Antiques, *above*.)

Knitwear and Norway is famous for its handmade multicolored ski sweaters,
Clothing but even mass-produced models are of top quality. The prices
are regulated, so buy what you like when you see it. Sweaters
are sold at **Heimen** and **Husfliden** (*see* Handicrafts, *above*) and
at special sweater shops. **Maurtua** (Fr. Nansens pl. 9, tel. 22/
41–31–64), near City Hall, has a huge selection of both sweaters and blanket coats. **Oslo Sweater Shop** (SAS Scandinavia Hotel, Tullinsgt. 5, tel. 22/11–29–22) has one of the city's widest
selections. **Siril** (Rosenkrantz Gate 23, tel. 22/41–01–80), near
City Hall, is a small shop that offers personal service. **Rein og
Rose** (Ruseløkkvn. 3, tel. 22/83–21–39) has a good selection of
knitwear, yarn, and textiles. **William Schmidt** (Karl Johans
Gate 41, tel. 22/42–02–88), founded in 1853, is Oslo's oldest
shop specializing in sweaters and souvenirs.

Sportswear Look for the Helly-Hansen brand. The company makes everything from insulated underwear to rainwear, snow gear, and
great insulated mittens. **Sportshuset** (Ullevålsvn. 11, tel. 22/
20–11–21, and Frognervn. 9C, tel. 22/55–29–57) has the best
prices; **Gresvig** (Storgt. 20, tel. 22/17–39–80) and **Sigmund
Ruud** (Kirkevn. 57, tel. 22/69–43–90) have the best selections.

Watches For some reason, Swiss watches are much cheaper in Norway
than in many other countries. **Bjerke** (Karl Johans Gate 31, tel.
22/42–20–44, and Prinsensgt. 21, tel. 22/42–60–50) has the
largest selection in town.

Sports and Fitness

Surrounding Oslo's compact center are a variety of lovely and
unspoiled landscapes, including forests, countrysides, and, of
course, the fjord. Just 15 minutes north of the city center by
tram is the **Oslomarka,** where locals ski in winter and hike in
summer. The area is dotted with 27 small cottages, or *hytter*,
which can be reserved through **Den Norske Turistforening**
(Stortingsgt. 28, tel. 22/83–25–50), which has maps of the
marka as well. The **Oslo Archipelago** is also a favorite with sunbathing urbanites, who hop ferries to their favorite isles.

Bicycling **Den Rustne Eike** (The Rusty Spoke, Enga 2, tel. 22/83–72–31)
rents bikes and equipment, including helmets (required by
law). **Sykkeldelisk** (Fridtjof Nansens pl. 7, tel. 22/42–60–20)
and **Oslo Sykkelutleie** (Kjelsåsvn. 145, tel. 22/22–13–46) also
rent a full range of bikes. The latter are located just on the edge
of Oslomarka, and they specialize in arranging routes covering
that territory. **Syklistenes Landsforening** (National Organization of Cyclists; Maridalsvn. 60, tel. 22/71–92–93) sells books
and maps for cycling holidays in Norway and abroad and provides friendly, free advice.

Fishing A national fishing license (NKr60, available in post offices) and
a local fee (NKr60 from local sports shops) are required in order
to fish in the Oslo Fjord and the surrounding lakes. Ice fishing
is also popular in the winter, but you'll have a hard time finding
an ice drill—truly, you may want to bring one from home.

Golf Oslo's international-level golf course, **Oslo Golfklubb** (Bogstad,
tel. 22/50–44–02) is private, and heavily booked, but will admit
members of other golf clubs if the space is available. There are
also one 18-hole and several nine-hole courses, with expansions
planned.

Hiking and Jogging Head for the woods surrounding Oslo, the **marka,** for jogging or walking; there are thousands of kilometers of trails, hundreds of them lit. Frogner Park has many paths, and you can jog or hike along the Aker River, but a few unsavory types may be about late at night or early in the morning. Or you can take the Sognsvann tram to the end of the line and walk or jog along the Sognsvann stream. Den Norske Turist forening (*see above*) has many maps of trails around Oslo and can recommend individual routes.

Skiing The **Skiforeningen** (Storgt. 20, tel. 22/92–32–00) can provide tips on the multitude of cross-country trails. Among the flood-lighted trails in the Oslomarka are the **Bogstad** (3.5 kilometers/ 2.1 miles, marked for the disabled and blind), the **Lillomarka** (about 25 kilometers/15.6 miles), and the **Østmarken** (33 kilometers/20.6 miles).

For downhill, which usually lasts from mid-December to March, there are 15 local city slopes, and organized trips to several outside slopes, including **Norefjell** (tel. 32/14–92–79), 110 kilometers (69 miles) north of the city, are also available.

The Skiforeningen also offers cross-country classes for young children (3- to 7-year-olds), downhill for older children (7- to 12-year-olds) and both, in addition to Telemark-style and racing techniques for adults. For details, call the Skiforeningen.

Swimming **Tøyenbadet** (Helgesensgt. 90, tel. 22/68–24–23) and **Frogner Park** have large outdoor swimming pools that are open from May 18 through August 25 (open weekdays 7–7 and 10–7, weekends 10–5). Tøyenbadet also has an indoor pool (open weekdays 7–7 and 10–7, weekends 10–2:30). All pools cost NKr35 adults, NKr15 children.

Dining

Food once was an afterthought in Oslo, but no longer. Its chefs are winning contests all over the world, and Norwegian cuisine, based on the products of its pristine waters and countryside, is firmly in the culinary spotlight. Eating out is a luxury for many Norwegians. Oslo is also a place where bad food is expensive and good food doesn't necessarily cost more—it's just a matter of knowing where to go.

Highly recommended restaurants are indicated by a star ★.

Very Expensive
★ **Bagatelle.** Oslo's best restaurant is a short walk from downtown. Paintings by contemporary Norwegian artists accent the otherwise subdued interior. Internationally known chef/owner Eyvind Hellstrøm's cuisine is modern Norwegian with French overtones. His grilled scallops with a saffron-parsley sauce, and the marinated salmon tartare with an herbed *crème fraîche* sauce are extraordinary. Bagatelle has a wine cellar to match its food. *Bygdøy allé 3/5, tel. 22/44–63–97. Reservations advised. Jacket and tie required. AE, DC, MC, V. Closed Sun., 1 week at Christmas and Easter. Dinner only.*

D'Artagnan. Freddie Nielsen's restaurant, right off Karl Johan, recently underwent a facade refurbishment, but inside it's still the same. The stairs lead to a comfortable lounge, while another floor up is the dining room. The decor is eclectic, but the food is classic and pure. The saffron-poached pike with asparagus is a good way to start a meal, while the boned fillet of salmon with lobster-cream sauce seasoned with dill is attract-

Oslo Dining and Lodging

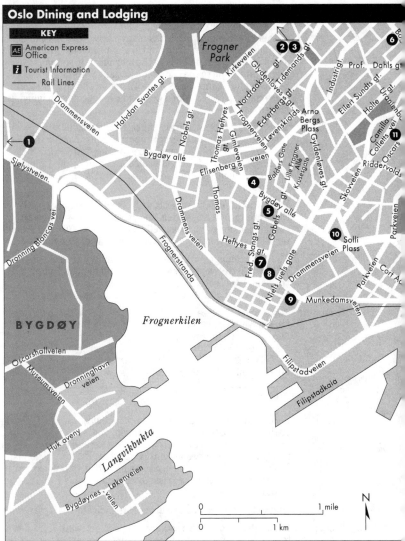

KEY

AE American Express Office

i Tourist Information

— Rail Lines

Frogner Park

BYGDØY

Frognerkilen

Langvikbukta

Arno Bergs Plass

Solli Plass

0   1 mile

0   1 km

N

Dining

Bagatelle, **10**
D'Artagnan, **26**
De Fem Stuer, **2**
Den Grimme
Ælling, **16**
Dinner, **24**
Dionysos Taverna, **29**
Feinschmecker, **4**
Fiskekroken, **3**
Fuji, **9**
Gamle Rådhus, **25**

Holberg's
Årstidene, **12**
Hos Thea, **8**
Kaffistova, **22**
Kastanjen, **5**
LaMer, **13**
Quatro Amigos, **14**
Sabroso, **11**
Shalimar, **32**
Theatercafeen, **15**
Tysk City Grill, **28**

Lodging

Ambassadeur, **11**
Bondeheimen, **22**
Bristol, **21**
Cecil, **20**
Gabelshus, **7**
Grand Hotel, **23**
Gyldenløve, **6**
Haraldsheim, **31**
Holmenkollen Park
Hotel Rica, **2**
Hotel Continental, **15**

Munch, **17**
Oslo Plaza, **30**
Rica Victoria, **19**
Royal Christiania, **27**
SAS Park Royal, **1**
SAS Scandinavia, **12**
Stefan, **18**

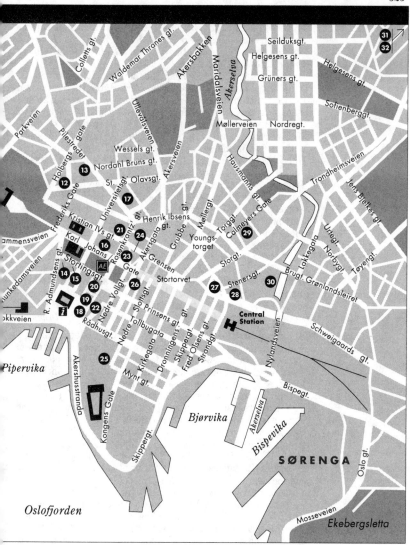

Seilduksgt.
Helgesens gt.
Grüners gt.
Helgesens gt.
Sofienberggt.
Collets gt.
Waldemar Thranes gt.
Akersbakken
Maridalsveien
Akerselva
Møllerveien
Nordregt.
Trondheimsveien
Jens Bjelkes gt.
Parkveien
Pilestredet
Holbergs Gate
Ullevålsveien
Wessels gt.
Nordahl Bruns gt.
Akersveien
St. Olavsgt.
Hausmanns gt.
Urtegt.
Norbygt.
Tøyengt.
Universitetsgt.
Henrik Ibsens
Møllergt.
Torggt.
Calmeyers Gate
Kristian IVs gt.
Akersgata gt.
Grubbe
Youngs-
torget
Brugt. Grønlandsleiret
Frederiks Gate
Karl Johans
Rosenkrantz' gt.
Grensen
Storgt.
Lakkegata
Stortingsgt.
Gate
Stortorvet
Stenersgt.
Nylandsveien
R. Admundsens gt.
Nedre Vollgt.
Prinsens gt.
Central
Station
Schweigaards gt.
Rådhusgt.
Nedre Slotsgt.
Tollbugata
Kirkegata
Dronningens gt.
Skippergt.
Fred Olsens gt.
Strandgt.
Bispegt.
Akersveien
Kongens Gate
Akershusstranda
Skippergt.
Mynt gt.
Bjørvika
Akerselva
Bispevika
SØRENGA
Oslo gt.
Pipervika
Oslofjorden
Mosseveien
Ekebergsletta

ive and flavorful. The dessert cart is loaded with jars of fruit preserved in liqueurs, which are served with various sorbets and ice creams. *Øvre Slottsgt. 16, tel. 22/41–74–04. Reservations advised. Jacket and tie required. AE, DC, MC, V. Closed weekends and July. No lunch.*

De Fem Stuer. Located near the famous Holmenkollen ski jump, in the historic Holmenkollen Park Hotel, this restaurant has first-rate views and food. Bent Stiansen has won an assortment of prizes for his cooking; the latest is the 1993 Bocuse d'Or medal. His modern Norwegian dishes have strong classic roots. Well worth trying is the three-course "A Taste of Norway," with salmon, reindeer, and cloudberries. *Holmenkollen Park Hotel, Kongevn. 26, tel. 22/92–20–00. Reservations advised. Jacket and tie required. AE, DC, MC, V.*

★ **Feinschmecker.** The name is German, but the food is modern Scandinavian. The atmosphere is friendly and intimate, with green rattan chairs, yellow tablecloths, and floral draperies. The owners are Lars Erik Underthun, one of Oslo's foremost chefs, and Bengt Wilson, one of Scandinavia's leading food photographers, so the food at Feinschmecker looks as good as it tastes. The roast rack of lamb with crunchy fried sweetbreads on tagliatelle and the chocolate-caramel teardrop with passion-fruit sauce are two choices on a menu that also makes fascinating reading. *Balchensgt. 5, tel. 22/44–17–77. Reservations advised. Dress: casual but neat. AE, DC, MC, V. Closed Sun., 1 week Christmas and Easter, last 3 weeks of July. No lunch.*

Expensive **Ambassadeur.** This cozy restaurant serving modern Scandinavian food is in the cellar of the Ambassadeur Hotel. It has one of the best bars in town, comfortable and well stocked. Huge swaths of fabric, dark colors, and baroque-style paintings of food create a plush, cocoonlike ambience. The food itself stands in contrast to the decor—it's light, in both concept and color. The seafood salad in a light vinaigrette with plump mussels and shrimp is a winner, while the scallops in lemon buerre blanc are delicate and subtle. *Hotel Ambassadeur, Camilla Collets vei 15, tel. 22/55–25–31. Reservations advised. Dress: casual but neat. AE, DC, MC, V. Closed Sat., Sun., and July. No lunch.*

Babette's Gjesthus. This tiny restaurant is hidden in the shopping arcade by City Hall. The atmosphere is warm and intimate. Bright blue walls, starched white tablecloths, and lace curtains against paned windows create a rustic, homey feel. The food is Scandinavian with a French touch. The dishes vary according to season but are always well prepared. Chef Ortwin Kulmus and his friendly staff know how to make their guests feel at home. *Rådhuspassasjen, Olav V's Gate 6, tel. 22/41–64–64. Reservations required. Dress: casual but neat. AE, DC, MC, V. Closed Sun. No lunch.*

Hos Thea. This gem has only 36 seats. It's located at the beginning of Embassy Row, a short distance from downtown. The decor is beige and blue, with a homey, old-fashioned look. The small menu offers four or five choices in each category, but every dish is superbly prepared, from the venison in a sauce of mixed berries to the orange-flavored crème caramel. Owner Sergio Barcilon, originally from Spain, is one of the pioneers of the new Scandinavian cooking. The noise and smoke levels can be high late in the evening. *Gabelsgt. 11, entrance on Drammensvn., tel. 22/44–68–74. Reservations required. Dress: casual but neat. AE, DC, MC, V. Closed 1 week at Christmas and Easter. No lunch.*

American Express offers Travelers Cheques built for two.

American Express® Cheques *for Two*. The first Travelers Cheques that allow either of you to use them because both of you have signed them. And only one of you needs to be present to purchase them.

Cheques *for Two* are accepted anywhere regular American Express Travelers Cheques are, which is just about everywhere. So stop by your bank, AAA* or any American Express Travel Service Office and ask for Cheques *for Two*.

Le Canard. This oasis in Frogner is furnished with antiques and Oriental rugs; fresh, white crocheted tablecloths and silver candlesticks contrast with the somber stone walls. The specialty is, of course, duck, but Chef Lucien Mares is known to conjure up sumptuous treats for his guests. The wine list is extensive. *Oscars Gate 81, tel. 22/43–40–28. Reservations advised. Dress: casual but neat. AE, DC, MC, V. Closed Sun., Christmas, Easter. No lunch.*

Moderate **A Touch of France** At this clean, inviting brasserie where the tables sit close together, the French ambience is further accented by the waiters' long, white aprons. The tempting menu includes a steaming hot bouillabaisse. *Øvre Slottsgt. 16, tel. 22/42–56–97. Reservations advised weekends. Dress: casual but neat. AE, DC, MC, V.*

★ **Dinner.** Though its name is not the best for a restaurant specializing in Szechuan-style cuisine, this is the only place for Chinese food, both hot and not so pungent. The mango pudding for dessert is wonderful. Don't bother with the other Chinese restaurants. *Arbeidergt. 2, tel. 22/42–68–90. Reservations advised. Dress: casual. AE, DC, MC, V. No lunch.*

★ **Dionysos Taverna.** Nicola Murati gives his guests a warm welcome in this unpretentious little Greek restaurant. The hors d'oeuvre platter, which includes stuffed vine leaves, meatballs, feta cheese, tzatziki, tomatoes, and cucumbers, is a meal in itself. The souvlaki and moussaka are authentically prepared, as are the more unusual casserole dishes. A bouzouki duo provides live music on Friday and Saturday. *Calmeyersgt. 11, tel. 22/60–78–64. Dress: casual. AE, MC, V. No lunch.*

Gamle Rådhus. Oslo's oldest restaurant, which celebrated its 350th birthday in 1991, is in the old City Hall. Don't let the beer signs and dirty windows put you off. The dining room is straight out of Ibsen, with dark brown wainscoting, deep-yellow painted walls, old prints, and heavy red curtains. Famous for its *lutefisk*, a Scandinavian specialty made from dried fish that has been soaked in lye and then poached, the restaurant's menu allows ample choice for the less daring. Try the fresh cod in season. *Nedre Slottsgt. 1, tel. 22/42–01–07. Dinner reservations advised. Dress: casual but neat. AE, DC, MC, V.*

★ **Kastanjen.** This casual Frogner bistro is the kind every neighborhood needs. The style of food is new traditional, with modern interpretations of classic Norwegian dishes. The three-course meal is good value for the money, but check out the "dish of the day" (*husmannskost*) at an unbeatable price. *Bygdøy allé 18, tel. 22/43–44–67. Reservations advised. Dress: casual. AE, DC, MC, V. Closed Sun., 1 week at Christmas and Easter.*

Shalimar. This Pakistani restaurant is off the beaten track but worth the trip, for the food, prepared by chefs imported from Karachi, is delectable. Try the tandoori mixed grill, which includes chicken, lamb, and kebab, or the chicken biryani with aromatic rice. Vegetarians have ample choices, and the naan bread is addictive. *Konghellegt. 5, tel. 22/37–47–68. Dress: casual. AE, DC, MC, V. No lunch.*

★ **Theatercafeen.** This Oslo institution, on the ground floor of the Hotel Continental, is jammed day and night. Built in 1900, the last Viennese-style café in northern Europe retains its Art Nouveau character. The menu is small and jumbled, with starters and main dishes interspersed; the only hint of the serving size is the price column. From 1 to 7, there's a reasonably priced two-course "family dinner." Pastry chef Robert

Bruun's *konfektkake* (a rich chocolate cake) and apple tart served with homemade ice cream are reasons enough to visit. *Stortingsgt. 24–26, tel. 22/33–32–00. Reservations advised. Dress: casual but neat. AE, DC, MC, V.*

Inexpensive **Den Grimme Ælling.** Dane Bjarne Hvid Pedersen is well established with his popular Copenhagen restaurant in the food court at Paleet. His *smørbrød* are the best buy in town: lots of meat, fish, or cheese on a small piece of bread. He also has daily dinner specials, such as *hakkebøf* (Danish Salisbury steak) with gravy, onions, and potatoes, or *frikadeller* (Danish meat cakes), all homemade. *Paleet, Karl Johans Gate 41B, tel. 22/42–47–83. Dress: casual. No credit cards.*

★ **Kaffistova.** Norwegian country cooking is served, cafeteria style, at this downtown restaurant. Everyday specials include soup and a selection of entrées, including a vegetarian dish. *Kjøttkaker* (meat cakes rather like Salisbury steak) served with creamed cabbage is a Norwegian staple, and the steamed salmon with Sandefjord butter is as good here as in places where it costs three times as much. Low-alcohol beer is the strongest drink served. *Rosenkrantz' Gate 8, tel. 22/42–99–74. Dress: casual. AE, DC, MC, V.*

Lofotstua. This rustic fish restaurant has a cozy atmosphere and personal service right out of Norway's far north. Good, moderately priced food includes fresh cod and seafood from Lofoten. *Kirkevn. 40, tel. 22/46–93–96. Reservations advised. Dress: casual. AE, DC, MC, V. Closed Sat.*

Quatro Amigos. A favorite among young Oslonians, this simple restaurant is the place to hit when you crave spicy Mexican fare and big portions. The menu has all the standards, including enchiladas, tacos, and burritos, which are served alongside rice, black beans, and salad. *Stortingsgt. 16, tel. 22/42–48–30. Dress: casual. AE, MC, V.*

★ **Tysk City Grill.** In the midst of the Oslo City shopping mall's food court is a tiny, authentic German restaurant, complete with oompah music. The grilled bratwurst (with real German mustard and curry ketchup) with homemade potato salad is the best cheap meal in town, while the eisbein and the pea soup, both homemade, are hearty fare. *Stenersgt. 1, tel. 22/17–05–12. Dress: casual. No credit cards.*

Lodging

Most hotels are centrally located, a short walk from the top of Karl Johans Gate, the main street. The newest hotels are in the area around Oslo S Station, at the bottom end of Karl Johan. For a quiet stay, choose a hotel in Frogner, the elegant residential neighborhood just minutes from downtown.

Lodging in the capital is expensive. Prices for downtown accommodations are high, even for bed-and-breakfasts, although just about all hotels have weekend, holiday, and summer rates (25% to 50% reductions). Taxes, service charges, and, unless otherwise noted, a buffet breakfast are included.

Oslo usually has enough hotel rooms to go around, but it's always a good idea to reserve a room at least for the first night of your stay, especially if you arrive late. The hotel accommodations office at Oslo S Station is open from 8 AM to 11 PM and can book you in anything from a luxury hotel to a room in a private

home for a fee of NKr20 adults, NKr10 children, plus 10% of the room rate, which is refunded when you check in.

If you are interested in renting an apartment, contact **Bed & Breakfast** (Stasjonsvn. 13, Blommenholm, 1300 Sandvika, tel. 67/54–06–80, fax 67/54–09–70; open weekdays 8:30–4). Most are located in Bærum, 15 to 20 minutes from downtown Oslo. All addresses provided by the group are no more than a 10-minute walk from public transport.

Highly recommended lodgings are indicated by a star ★.

Very Expensive
★

Grand Hotel. Located right in the center of Karl Johan, the Grand has been the premier hotel since it opened in 1874. Ibsen and Munch were regular guests, and since their time, the Grand has hosted many famous people and all recipients of the Nobel Peace Prize. The lobby gives no idea of the style and flair of the redecorated (1989–90) rooms. Even standard rooms are large, looking more like guest quarters in an elegant home than hotel rooms. Those in the new wing are smaller, cheaper, and not as nice. *Karl Johans Gate 31, 0159, tel. 22/42–93–90, fax 22/42–12–25. 270 rooms with bath, 60 suites. Facilities: 3 restaurants, 2 bars, health club, pool, conference center, newsstand. AE, DC, MC, V.*

Hotel Continental. The Brockmann family, owners since 1900, have succeeded in combining the rich elegance of the Old World with modern, comfortable living. The Theatercafeen (*see* Dining, *above*) is a landmark, and the newest addition, LPP, a restaurant, café, and bar in one, is among Oslo's "in" places. The newly refurbished Dagligstuen (The Sitting Room) is a wonderful place in which to start or end the evening with an appetizer or nightcap. Munch graphics from the family's own collection adorn the walls. *Stortingsgt. 24–26, 0156, tel. 22/41–90–60, fax 22/42–96–89. 169 rooms with bath, 12 suites. Facilities: 3 restaurants, 2 bars, nightclub. AE, DC, MC, V.*

Oslo Plaza. Northern Europe's largest hotel, built in 1990, is a three-minute walk from Karl Johans Gate (not a safe place to walk to at night). Modern, decorated in Scandinavian style, it is favored by business travelers, who tend toward the pricier, deluxe suites in the tower. Below the 27th floor the standard rooms are decorated in red tones and have ample marble baths. The hotel has one of the city's best Japanese restaurants, and the wild rooftop nightclub offers spectacular views of the city. *Sonja Henies pl. 3, 0107, tel. 22/17–10–00, fax 22/17–73–00. 685 rooms with bath, 20 suites. Facilities: 3 restaurants, 2 bars, nightclub, health club, pool, business/conference center, shops. AE, DC, MC, V.*

Royal Christiania. It started out as bare-bones housing for 1952 Olympians. The original exterior has been retained, but inside it's a whole new hotel, remodeled in 1990 and built around a central atrium. The rooms, decorated in soft colors with light furniture, are large. The California-style restaurant serves tasty, colorful food. *Biskop Gunnerus' Gate 3, 0106, tel. 22/42–94–10, fax 22/42–46–22. 451 rooms with bath, 100 suites. Facilities: 3 restaurants, 3 bars, nightclub, health club, pool, business/conference center, newsstand. AE, DC, MC, V.*

SAS Scandinavia Hotel. Oslo's only downtown business hotel, built in 1974, is getting some competition, but it still can hold its own: There's a business-class airline check-in in the lobby; the lower-level shopping arcade features high-fashion clothing and leather goods shops. Most of the rooms were modernized in

1991 in four different styles, from high-tech to Oriental. Standard rooms are spacious and light. The SAS is across the street from the palace grounds (but don't walk through them at night). *Holbergs Gate 30, 0166, tel. 22/11–30–00, fax 22/11–30–17. 500 rooms with bath, 15 suites. Facilities: 2 restaurants, 2 bars, nightclub, health club, pool, business center, shopping arcade. AE, DC, MC, V.*

Expensive **Ambassadeur.** This comfortable and elegant hotel hides behind
★ a pale pink facade with wrought-iron balconies in a stylish residential area behind the Royal Palace, a few minutes from downtown. Originally built in 1889 as an apartment hotel, the Ambassadeur has practically no lobby, but the rooms make up for that. Apart from several singles, each room is individually furnished with thematic decors and good Norwegian art. The small, professional staff don't bother with titles because everyone does whatever task presents itself, from laundering a shirt on short notice to delivering room service. *Camilla Colletts vei 15, 0258, tel. 22/44–18–35, fax 22/44–47–91. 42 rooms with bath, 8 suites. Facilities: restaurant, bar, pool, conference room. AE, DC, MC, V.*

Bristol. In the past few years, the Bristol has begun catering to people who want a classy but quiet hotel in the center of town. The lobby, decorated in the 1920s with a Moorish theme, is a tribute to style, and the library bar is Oslo's most comfortable. Some of the newly refurbished rooms are decorated with lightly colored painted Scandinavian furniture, while others have a Regency theme. The banquet rooms have true Old World elegance, and at the restaurant, the Bristol Grill, red meat has not gone out of style. *Kristian IV's Gate 7, 0130, tel. 22/41–58–40, fax 22/42–86–51. 141 rooms with bath, 4 suites. Facilities: 2 restaurants, 2 bars, nightclub, conference center, newsstand. AE, DC, MC, V.*

Holmenkollen Park Hotel Rica. The magnificent 1894 building in the national romantic style commands an unequaled panorama of the city and is worth a visit even if you don't lodge there. The rather ordinary guest rooms are in a newer structure (1982) behind it. The ice-covered snowflake sculpture in the lobby is appropriate for a hotel that's a stone's throw from Holmenkollen ski jump. Ski and walking trails are just outside. *Kongevn. 26, 0390, tel. 22/92–20–00, fax 22/14–61–92. 191 rooms with bath. Facilities: 2 restaurants, bar, nightclub, pool, business/conference center. AE, DC, MC, V.*

Rica Victoria. Opened in May 1991, the hotel occupies a contemporary structure built around a center atrium. The rooms are furnished with Biedermeier reproductions and textiles in bold reds and dark blues, elegant and very stylish. Rooms with windows on the atrium may be claustrophobic for some. *Rosenkrantz' Gate 13, 0160, tel. 22/42–99–40, fax 22/42–99–43. 161 rooms with bath or shower, 5 suites. Facilities: restaurant, bar. AE, DC, MC, V.*

SAS Park Royal. Oslo Fornebu Airport's only hotel is somewhat anonymous, with long, narrow corridors and standard American-style motel rooms. The restaurant serves modern Scandinavian food. There are excellent business facilities, including a business-class airline check-in, and the airport bus stops outside. *Fornebuparken, 1324 Lysaker, tel. 67/12–02–20, fax 67/12–00–11. 254 rooms with bath, 14 suites. Facilities: restaurant, bar, health club, tennis court, newsstand. AE, DC, MC, V.*

Stefan. This hotel makes every aspect of a stay a positive expe-

rience, from hot welcome drinks for late arrivals to breakfast tables complete with juice boxes and plastic bags for packing a lunch. The top-floor lounge has books and magazines in English. The Stefan's kitchen still creates the best buffet lunch in town—but it's only open to guests. *Rosenkrantz' Gate 1, 0159, tel. 22/42–92–50, fax 22/33–70–22. 130 rooms with bath or shower. Facilities: restaurant, conference center. AE, DC, MC, V.*

Moderate **Bondeheimen.** Founded in 1913 for country folk visiting the city, Bondeheimen, which means "farmers' home," still gives discounts to members of agricultural associations. The lobby and rooms are decorated with pine furniture, handwoven rag rugs, soft blue textiles, and modern Norwegian graphics, just the way a Norwegian country home should look. Bondeheimen serves no alcohol, and the staff of country girls has a squeaky-clean look. *Rosenkrantz' Gate 8, 0159, tel. 22/42–95–30, fax 22/41–94–37. 76 rooms with shower. Facilities: restaurant, conference room. AE, DC, MC, V.*

★ **Cecil.** This bed-and-breakfast one block from Parliament was built in 1989. The second floor opens onto an atrium: the hotel's activity center. In the morning it's a breakfast room, with one of Oslo's best buffets, while in the afternoon it becomes a lounge, serving coffee, juice, and fresh fruit, plus newspapers in many languages. The single rooms have double beds, while doubles have queen-size beds. *Stortingsgt. 8, 0130, tel. 22/42–70–00, fax 22/42–26–70. 110 rooms with bath, 2 suites. AE, DC, MC, V.*

Gabelshus. With only a discreet sign above the door, this ivy-covered brick house in an international residential area is one of Oslo's most personal hotels. It has been owned by the same family for 45 years. The lounges are filled with antiques, some in the national romantic style, but the rooms, renovated in 1989, are plain. It's a short walk to several of Oslo's best restaurants and a short streetcar ride to the center of town. The Ritz Hotel, across the parking lot, is owned by the same family and takes the overflow. *Gabels Gate 16, 0272, tel. 22/55–22–60, fax 22/44–27–30. 45 rooms with bath (plus 42 rooms with bath in Ritz). Facilities: restaurant. AE, DC, MC, V.*

Inexpensive **Gyldenløve.** Located in the heart of a busy shopping area, this hotel, modernized in 1992, is one of the city's most reasonable bed-and-breakfast establishments. It is within walking distance of Vigeland park, and the streetcar stops just outside the door. Reproductions of city scenes from old Christiania (Oslo) hang in every room. *Bogstadvn. 20, 0355, tel. 22/60–10–90, fax 22/60–33–90. 156 rooms with shower. AE, DC, MC, V.*

Haraldsheim. Oslo's youth hostel is one of Europe's largest. Most of the rooms have four beds, and those in the new wing all have showers. Nonmembers of the International Youth Hostel organization pay a surcharge. Bring your own sheet sleeping bag or rent one here. It is 4 kilometers (2½ miles) from city center. *Haraldsheimvn. 4, tel. 22/15–50–43, fax 22/34–71–97. 270 beds. Breakfast. No credit cards.*

Munch. This modern bed-and-breakfast, about a 10-minute walk from Karl Johans Gate, is unpretentious, well run, clean, and functional. The rooms are of a decent size and are under renovation in 1994. The lobby, with Chinese rugs and leather couches, contrasts with the rest of the hotel. *Munchsgt. 5, 0165, tel. 22/42–42–75, fax 22/20–64–69. 180 rooms with shower. Facilities: breakfast room. AE, DC, MC, V.*

The Arts and Nightlife

The Arts The monthly *Oslo Guide* lists cultural events, as does section four of *Aftenposten*, Oslo's (and Norway's) leading newspaper. The information number at **Oslo Spektrum** congress and concert complex (tel. 22/17–80–10) gives a rundown of all scheduled events. Tickets to virtually all performances in Norway, from classical or rock concerts to a hockey games, can be purchased at any post office.

Nationaltheatret (Stortingsgt. 15, tel. 22/41–27–10.) performances are in Norwegian: bring along a copy of the play in translation, and you're all set.

Det Norske Teatret (Kristian IV's Gate 8, tel. 22/42–43–44) is a showcase for pieces in Nynorsk, musicals, and guest artists from abroad. **Bryggeteatret** (Aker Brygge, tel. 22/83–88–20), Oslo's newest theater, features musicals and dance events.

The **Norwegian Philharmonic Orchestra**, under the direction of Mariss Janssons, is among Europe's leading ensembles. Its house, **Konserthuset** (Munkedamsvn. 14, tel. 22/83–32–00), was built in 1977 in marble, metal, and rosewood. **Den Norske Opera** (*Storgt. 23, tel. 22/42–77–24*) and the ballet perform at Youngstorvet.

Oslo Spektrum (*Sonja Henies pl. 2, tel. 22/17–80–10*), a rounded brick building sprinkled with vignettes of glazed tile, is the most interesting piece of architecture in the area around Oslo S Station. The Spektrum is used as a congress/conference complex, a sports stadium, and a concert hall.

All **films** are shown in the original language with subtitles, except for some children's films, which are dubbed. If you plan to take children to see a film, check the age limits first. The Norwegian film censors set high and strictly enforced age limits on films they consider to be violent.

Nightlife For the past few years Oslo been the nightlife capital of Scandinavia. At any time of the day or night, people are out on Karl Johan, and many clubs and restaurants in the central area stay open until 4 or 5 AM. Night-lifers can pick up a copy of the free monthly paper *Natt og Dag*, which lists rock, pop, and jazz venues and contains a "barometer" listing the city's cheapest and most expensive places for a beer—a necessary column in a city where a draft, on the average, costs NKr33.

Bars and Lounges **Churchill Wine Bar** (Fr. Nansens pl. 6, tel. 22/33–53–43) and **Fridtjof's** (Fr. Nansens pl. 7, tel. 22/33–40–88) are yuppie favorites for pricey after-work imbibing. Both are near City Hall. For the serious beer connoisseur, **Oslo Mikrobryggeri** (Bogstadvn. 6, tel. 22/56–97–76) is the place, with beer brewed on the premises; for variety, go to **Lorry** (Parkvn. 12, tel. 22/69–69–04). Filled with a cast of grizzled old artists, the place advertises 81 brews. **Eilefs Landhandleri** (Kristian IV's gt. 1, tel. 22/42–53–47) is a pub cum disco, with a piano player and a dance floor. For a more refined venue, go to **3 Brødre** (Øvre Slottsgt. 14, tel. 22/42–39–00), with a beer and wine bar at street level and 1890s-style wall paintings of forest maidens and cherubs on the ceiling. If you're more partial to lounging than drinking, try the English-style bar at the **Bristol Hotel** (Kristian IV's gt. 7, tel. 22/41–58–40).

Cafés For cappuccino and a quiet conversation, many cafés are open practically around the clock, and they're the cheapest eateries as well. In the trendy area around Frogner and Homansbyen, try **Onkel Oswald** (Hegdehaugsvn. 34, tel. 22/69–62–50) and **Clodion Art Café** (Bygdøy allé 63, tel. 22/44–97–26). Downtown, **Kafe Celsius** (Rådhusgt. 19, 22/42–45–39) in a half-timber building from 1626, attracts an arty crowd, while **Sjakk Matt** (Haakon VII's Gate, tel. 22/83–41–56) appeals to a very hip set. If you prefer the '50s, go to **Teddy's Soft Bar** (Brugt. 3, tel. 22/17–71–83), complete with vinyl stools.

Discos and Most discos open late, and the beat doesn't really start until
Nightclubs near midnight. There's usually an age limit, and the cover charge is around NKr50. Thursday is student disco night at **Snorre-Kompagniet** (Rosenkrantz' Gate 11, tel. 22/33–46–40). Oslo's beautiful people congregate at **Barock** (Universitetsgt. 26, tel. 22/42–44–20) and **Lipp** (Olav Vs Gate 2, tel. 22/41–44–00), a restaurant, nightclub, and bar. Most of the big hotels have discos that appeal to the over-30 crowd. **Sky Bar**, on the top floor of the Oslo Plaza (Sonja Henies pl. 3, tel. 22/17–10–00), is the most bizarre, accessible only from the glass elevator outside. **Grotten** (Wergelandsvn. 5, tel. 22/20–96–04) is popular with well-heeled and well-dressed singles over 30.

Gay Bars For information about gay activities in Oslo, call **Homo-guiden** (tel. 02/07–80–46) or the information telephone (tel. 22/11–36–60), or read *Blikk*, the gay newsletter. **LLH** (The Union for Lesbian and Gay Liberation), the nationwide gay association, has offices at St. Olavs Pl. 2, and operates **Molina Pub and Eatery** at the same address. **Andy Capp Pub** (Fridtjof Nansens pl. 4, tel. 22/41–41–65) is popular with gays (later at night), but it reeks of old smoke. **London Bar og Pub** (C. J. Hambros pl. 5, tel. 22/41–41–26) is packed on weekends. **Den Sorte Enke** (The Black Widow, Møllergt. 23, tel. 22/11–05–60), **Coco Chalet** (Øvre Slottsgt. 8, tel. 22/33–32–66), and **Recepten Bar** (Prinsensgt. 22, tel. 22/42–65–00) are also popular meeting places for lesbians and gays.

Jazz Clubs Norwegians love jazz, and every summer the Oslo Jazz Festival, with a list of major international artists, attracts big crowds. **Oslo Jazzhus** (Toftesgt. 69, tel. 22/38–59–63) is in an out-of-the-way location, but the music is worth it. **Stortorvets Gjæstgiveri** (Grensen 1, tel. 22/42–88–63) often presents New Orleans and ragtime bands. **Gamle Christiania** (Grensen 1, tel. 22/42–74–93) features the New Orleans Jazz Workshop. **Smuget** (Rosenkrantz' Gate 22, tel. 22/42–52–62) has live jazz, blues, and rock every evening.

Rock Clubs At Oslo's numerous rock clubs, the cover charges are low, the crowds young, and the music loud. **Rockefeller** (Torggt. 16, tel. 22/20–32–32) presents a good mix of musical styles, from avant-garde to Third World; Thursday is student disco night. Its only real competitor is **Sentrum Scene** (Arbeidersamfunnets pl. 2, tel. 22/20–60–40). There's always music at **Cruise Cafe** (Aker Brygge, tel. 22/83–64–30). If your taste leans toward reggae and calypso, the **Afro International Night Club** (Brennerivn. 5, tel. 22/36–07–53) has frequent Caribbean evenings.

Excursions from Oslo

Halden and Fredrikstad

Tourist Information

Fredrikstad: Fredrikstad turistkontor (Turistsentret v/Østre Brohode, N–1632 Gamle Fredrikstad, tel. 69/32–03–30). **Halden:** Halden Reiselivskontor (Box 167, N–1751 Halden, tel. 69/18–24–87). **Moss:** Moss Turistkontor (Chrystiesgt. 3, N–1530 Moss, tel. 69/25–54–51).

Getting There
By Car

Follow the E18 southeastward from Oslo and turn south at Mysen to reach Halden. E6 takes you north to Sarpsborg, where you can turn left to Fredrikstad.

By Train

Trains for Halden leave from Oslo S Station and take two hours to make the 136-kilometer (85-mile) trip. There are regular train connections between Halden and Fredrikstad.

Exploring Halden and Fredrikstad

Numbers in the margin correspond to points of interest on the Oslo Excursions map.

❹ **Halden** is practically at the Swedish border, a good enough reason to fortify the town; **Fredriksten Festning** (Fredriksten Fort), built on a French star-shaped plan in the late 17th century, is perched on the city's highest point. Norwegians and Swedes had ongoing border disputes, and the most famous skirmish at Fredriksten resulted in the death of King Karl XII in 1718. Few people realize that slavery existed in Scandinavia, but until 1845 there were up to 200 slaves at Fredriksten, mostly workers incarcerated and sentenced to a lifetime of hard labor for trivial offenses. Inside the fort itself is **Fredriksten Kro,** a good, old-fashioned inn, with outdoor seating. *Tel. 69/18–24–87. Admission: NKr15 adults, NKr5 children.*

❺ North of Halden is **Fredrikstad,** at the mouth of the Glomma, Norway's longest river. The country's oldest fortified city, it has bastions and a moat that date from the 1600s. The old town has been preserved and offers museums, art galleries, cafés, artisans' workshops, antiques shops, and old bookstores, as well as the **Fredrikstad Museum,** which documents town history. *Tel. 69/32–09–01. Admission NKr20 adults, children free with an adult. Open June–Aug., Mon.–Sat. 11–5, Sun. noon–5.*

Just east is **Kongsten Festning** (Kongsten Fort), which mounted 200 cannons and could muster 2,000 men at the peak of its glory. *Tel. 69/34–20–62. Admission free. Open 24 hours. Guided tours.*

A 5-kilometer (3-mile) ride outside **Moss,** at **Jeløy,** is **Galleri F15,** an art center set in an old farm. *Tel. 69/27–10–33. Admission free. Open daily 11–7.*

Dining and Lodging
★

Refsnes Gods. The main building dates from 1770, when it was a family estate, but it did not become a hotel until 1938. In the back is a long, tree-lined promenade extending to the shores of the Oslo Fjord. Refsnes has one of Norway's best kitchens and a wine cellar with some of the oldest bottles of Madeira in the country. Chef Frank Baer, a member of Norway's Culinary Olympic team, makes a meal here a memorable experience. *Jeløy, 1500 Moss, tel. 69/27–04–11, fax 69/27–25–42. 60 rooms. Facilities: restaurant, sauna, pool, beach, boats, function rooms. AE, DC, MC, V. Expensive.*

Drammen, Tønsberg, and Sandefjord

The towns lining the western side of the Oslo Fjord are among Norway's oldest and wealthiest, their fortunes derived from whaling and lumbering. Although these activities no longer dominate, their influence remains in the monuments and in the wood architecture. This is summer-vacation country for many Norwegians, who retreat to cabins on the water during July.

Tourist Information **Drammen:** Drammen Kommunale Turistinformasjonskontor (Rådhuset, N–3017 Drammen, tel. 32/80–62–10). **Sandefjord:** Sandefjord Reiselivsforening (Torvet, N–3200, tel. 33/46–05–90). **Tønsberg:** Tønsberg og Omland Reiselivslag (Storgt. 55, N–3100, tel. 33/31–02–20).

Getting There
By Car Route E18 south from Oslo follows the coast to within reach of the towns of this region. Sandefjord is 125 kilometers (78 miles) south of Oslo.

By Train Drammen is about 40 kilometers (25 miles) from Oslo. Take a suburban train from Nationaltheatret or trains from Oslo S to reach Horten, Tønsberg, and Sandefjord.

By Bus Because train service to these towns is infrequent, bus travel is the best alternative to cars. Check with Nor-Way Bussekspress (tel. 22/33–01–91) for schedules.

By Boat The most luxurious and scenic way to see the region is by boat: There are guest marinas at just about every port.

Exploring Drammen, Tønsberg, and Sandefjord
❻ **Drammen,** an industrial city of 50,000 situated on the Simoa River at its outlet to a fjord, was a timber town and port for 500 years, the main harbor for silver exported from the Kongsberg mines. Today cars are imported into Norway through Drammen. The city's main attraction, **Spiralen** (The Spiral), is a corkscrew road tunnel that makes six complete turns before emerging about 600 feet above, on Skansen Plateau. It's open year-round and is free. The entrance is behind the hospital by way of a well-marked road.

Drammens Museum, on the grounds of Marienlyst manor (which dates from 1750), is across the river. Its new addition looks like a small temple set in the manor garden. Displays include glass from the Nøstetangen factory and a collection of rustic painted pieces. *Konnerudgt. 7, tel. 32/83–89–48. Admission: NKr20 adults, NKr10 senior citizens and students, NKr5 children. Open May–Oct., Tues. 11–7, Wed.–Sat. 11–3, Sun. 11–5; Nov.–Apr., Tues.–Sat, 11–5, Sun. 11–3.*

❼ Off the main route south, toward the coast, is **Horten,** which has some distinctive museums. The town was once an important naval station and still retains the officers' candidates school. **Marinemuseet** (the Royal Norwegian Navy Museum), built in 1853 as a munitions warehouse, has displays of relics from the nation's naval history. Outside is the world's first torpedo boat, from 1872, plus some one-man submarines from World War II. Mistletoe thrives in the trees, but don't pick it: It's protected by law. *Karl Johans Vern, tel. 33/34–20–81, ext. 452. Admission free. Open June–Sept., weekdays 10–3, weekends noon–4; Oct.–May, weekdays 10–3, Sun. noon–4.*

Redningsselskapets Museum (Museum of the Sea Rescue Association) traces the history of ship-rescue operations. The organization has rescued more than 320,000 people since it was

founded more than 100 years ago. *Strandpromenaden 8, tel. 33/ 34–70–66. Admission: NKr10 adults, NKr5 children. Open Apr. 1–Sept. 30, Fri.–Sun. noon–4.*

Preus Fotomuseum houses one of the world's largest photographic collections. Exhibits include a turn-of-the-century photographer's studio and a tiny camera that was strapped to a pigeon for early aerial photography. *Langgt. 82, tel. 33/04–27– 37. Admission: NKr10 adults, NKr5 children. Open weekdays 10–2, Sun. noon–2.*

Just beyond the town, between the road and the sea, is a Viking grave site, **Borrehaugene,** with five earth and two stone mounds. Continue past the 12th-century Borre church to **8** **Åsgårdstrand,** which was an artists' colony for outdoor painting at the turn of the century. Edvard Munch painted *Girls on the Bridge* here and earned a reputation as a ladies' man. He spent seven summers at **Munchs lille hus** (little house), now a museum. *Munchs gt., no tel. Admission: NKr5. Open June–Aug., Tues.–Sun. 1–7; May and Sept., weekends 1–7.*

Continuing south, you'll pass the site where the Oseberg Viking ship, dating from around AD 800 and on display in Oslo, was found at **Slagen,** on the road to Tønsberg, 105 kilometers (64 miles) from Oslo. Look for a mound where it was buried as you pass Slagen's church.

9 According to the sagas, **Tønsberg** is Norway's oldest settlement, founded in 871. Little remains of its early structures, although the ruins at **Slottsfjellet** (Castle Hill), by the train station, include parts of the city wall, the remains of a church from around 1150, and a 13th-century brick citadel. Other medieval remains are below the cathedral and near Storgata 17. Tønsberg lay dormant from the Reformation to the end of the 18th century, when shipping and later whaling brought it into prominence again.

Vestfold Fylkesmuseum (county museum), north of the railroad station, houses a small Viking ship, several whale skeletons, and some inventions. There's an open-air section, too. *Farmannsvn. 30, tel. 33/31–29–19. Admission: NKr15 adults, NKr8 groups over 10, NKr2 children. Open mid-May–mid-Sept., weekdays 10–5, Sun. noon–5; mid-Sept.–mid-May, weekdays 10–3:30.*

Time Out Take a break at **Seterkafe,** the museum's restaurant. Try *spekemat* (dried cured meats) served with sour cream and/or potato salad.

10 Continue 25 kilometers (16 miles) south of Tønsberg to **Sandefjord,** which, in 1900, was the whaling capital of the world and possibly Norway's wealthiest city. Now the whales are gone and all that remains of that trade is a monument to it. Thanks to shipping and other industries, however, the city is still rich.

Kommandør Christensens Hvalfangstmuseum (Commander Christensen's Whaling Museum) traces the development of the industry from small primitive boats to huge floating factories. An especially arresting display chronicles whaling in the Antarctic. *Museumsgt. 39, tel. 33/16–32–51. Admission: NKr10 adults, NKr5 children and senior citizens. Open May–Sept., Mon.–Sat. 11–4, Sun. 11–5, Thurs. also 4–7; Oct.–Apr., Sun. noon–4, Thurs. 4–7.*

Dining **Edgar Ludl's Gourmet.** It took an Austrian chef to show the
★ Norwegians that there's more in the sea than cod and salmon.
Ludl is a champion of the local cuisine, and a "catch of the day"
platter may include salmon, ocean catfish, stuffed sole, a fish
roulade, and lobster. Ludl's desserts are equally good, especially the cloudberry marzipan basket. *Rådhusgt. 7, Sandefjord, tel. 33/16–27–41. Reservations advised. Dress: casual
but neat. AE, DC, MC, V. Moderate–Expensive.*

Lodging **Rica Park Hotel.** It *looks* formal for a hotel built right on the
water in a resort town, but there's no dress code. The older
rooms are nicer than the new ones. The decor is 1960s style, but
it doesn't seem passé. Summer rates make the Park more affordable. *Strandpromenaden 9, 3200 Sandefjord, tel. 33/16–
55–50, fax 33/16– 79–00. 174 rooms with bath, 6 suites. Facilities: 2 restaurants, 4 bars, 2 nightclubs, pool, health club, marina, business/ conference center. AE, DC, MC, V. Moderate–
Very Expensive.*

Atlantic. The Atlantic was built in 1914, when Sandefjord was a
whaling center, and remodeled in 1990. The history of whaling
is traced in exhibits in glass cases and in pictures throughout
the hotel. There's no restaurant, but the hotel provides *aftens,*
a supper consisting of bread and cold cuts plus a hot dish, as
part of the room rate. *Jernbanealleen 33, 3200 Sandefjord, tel.
33/16–31–05, fax 33/16–80–20. 77 rooms with bath. Facilities:
supper. AE, DC, MC, V. Inexpensive–Expensive.*

Sørlandet

The coast bordering the Skagerrak is lined with small communities as far as Lindesnes, which is at the southernmost tip.
Sørlandet (Southland) towns are often called "pearls on a
string," and in the dusk of a summer evening, reflections of the
white painted houses on the water have a silvery translucence.

This is a land of wide beaches toasted by the greatest number
of sunny days in Norway, waters warmed by the Gulf Stream,
and long, fertile tracts of flatland. Not a people to pass up a
minute of sunshine, the Norwegians have sprinkled the south
with their *hytter* and made it their number-one domestic holiday spot. Nonetheless, even at the height of summer, you can
sail to a quiet skerry or take a solitary walk through the forest.

The two chief cities of Norway's south, Kristiansand on the
east coast and Stavanger on the west coast, differ sharply.
Kristiansand is a resort town, scenic and relaxed, while Stavanger, once a fishing center, is now the hub of the oil industry
and Norway's most cosmopolitan city. Between the two is the
coastal plain of Jæren, dotted with prehistoric burial sites and
the setting for the works of some of the country's foremost
painters.

Important Addresses and Numbers

Tourist The tourist information office in **Kristiansand** is at Dronnin-
Information gensgt. 2, Box 592, 4601, tel. 38/02–60–65, fax 38/02–52–55.
Stavanger's is at Stavanger Kulturhus, Sølveberget, tel. 51/53–
51–00.

Other tourist offices in the region are in **Horten** (Torget 6A,
3190, tel. 33/04–33–90), **Kvinesdal** (Vestre Vest-Agder Reise-

livslag, N–4480, tel. 38/35–00–42), **Larvik** (Storgt. 3250, tel. 33/13–01–00), **Mandal** (Mandalsregionens Reiselivslag, Bryggegt., N–4500, tel. 38/26–08–20), **Sandefjord** (Torvet, 3200, tel. 33/46–05–90), and **Tønsberg** (Storgt. 55, 3100, tel. 33/31–02–20).

Emergencies Police: tel. 112. Fire: tel. 111. Ambulance: tel. 113. Car Rescue: in Kristiansand, tel. 38/02–60–00, in Stavanger, tel. 51/58–29–00.

Hospital Emergency Rooms In Kristiansand, **Røde Kors** (Red Cross) **Legevakt** (Kirkegt. 3, tel. 38/02–52–20) is open weekdays 4 PM–8 AM *and* weekends 24 hours. In Stavanger, call **Rogaland Sentralsykehus** (tel. 51/51–80–00).

Doctors In Kristiansand, **Kvadraturen Legesenter** (Vestre Strandgt. 22, tel. 38/02–66–11) is open 8–4.

Dentists In Kristiansand, **Sentraltannklinikken** (Festningsgt. 40, tel. 38/02–19–71) is open 7–3. In Stavanger, the tourist office has a list of dentists available for emergencies.

Pharmacies **Elefantapoteket** (Gyldenløvesgt. 13, Kristiansand, tel. 38/02–20–12) is open Monday through Saturday 8:20–8 and Sunday 4–8. **Løveapoteket** (Olav V's gt. 11, Stavanger, tel. 51/52–06–07) is open daily 8 AM–11 PM.

Arriving and Departing by Plane

Kristiansand **Kjevik** Airport, 16 kilometers (10 miles) outside town, is served by **Braathens SAFE** (tel. 38/02–14–10), with nonstop flights from Oslo, Bergen, and Stavanger, and **SAS** (tel. 38/06–30–33) with nonstop flights to Copenhagen. **MUK Air** serves Aalborg, Denmark, while **Agder Fly** serves Göteborg, Sweden, and Billund, Denmark. Tickets on the latter two can be booked with Braathen or SAS.

The airport bus (tel. 94/67–22–42) departs from the Braathens SAFE office, Vestre Strandgate, approximately one hour before every departure and proceeds, via downtown hotels, directly to Kjevik. Tickets cost NKr30 for adults, NKr15 for children.

Stavanger **Sola** Airport is 14 kilometers (9 miles) from downtown. **Braathens SAFE** (tel. 51/51–10–00) has nonstop flights from Oslo, Sandefjord, Kristiansand, Haugesund, Bergen, and Trondheim. **SAS** (tel. 51/63–89–00) has nonstop flights from Bergen, Oslo, Copenhagen, Aberdeen, Göteborg, and London. **KLM** (tel. 51/65–10–22), and **British Airways** (tel. 51/65–15–33) have nonstop flights to Stavanger from Billund and London, respectively.

The **Flybussen** to town takes 15 minutes and stops at hotels and outside the railroad station. Tickets cost NKr30.

Arriving and Departing by Car, Train, Bus, and Boat

By Car From Oslo, it is 329 kilometers (203 miles) to Kristiansand and 574 kilometers (352 miles) to Stavanger. E18 parallels the coastline but stays slightly inland on the eastern side of the country and farther inland in the western part. Although seldom wider than two lanes, it is easy driving because it is so flat.

By Train The **Sørlandsbanen** leaves Oslo S Station four times daily for the approximately five-hour journey to Kristiansand and three times daily for the 8½- to nine-hour journey to Stavanger. Two more trains travel the 3½-hour Kristiansand–Stavanger route. Kristiansand's train station is at V. Strandgata (tel. 38/02–27–00). For information on trains from Stavanger call 51/52–61–37.

By Bus **Aust-Agder Trafikkselskap** (tel. 37/02–65–00), based in Arendal, has two departures daily in each direction for the 5½- to six-hour journey between Oslo and Kristiansand.

Sørlandsruta (38/02–43–80), based in Mandal, has two departures in each direction for the 4½-hour trip from Kristiansand (Strandgt. 33) to Stavanger.

For information about both long-distance and local bus services in Stavanger, call 51/52–26–00; the bus terminal is outside the train station.

By Boat **Color Line** (Strandkaien, Stavanger, tel. 51/52–45–45) has four ships weekly on the Stavanger–Newcastle route. High-speed boats to Bergen are based in Stavanger at **Hurtigbåtterminalen** (tel. 51/52–20–90). There is also a car ferry from Hirtshals, in northern Denmark, that takes about four hours to make the crossing. Another connects Larvik to Frederikshavn, on Denmark's west coast. In Denmark contact **DSB** (tel. 33/14–17–01); in Norway contact **Color Line** (tel. 51/52–45–45).

Getting Around

By Car Sørlandet is flat, so it's easy driving throughout. All the water makes the center of **Stavanger** difficult to maneuver by car. One-way streets are the norm downtown. Parking is limited, and streets are very crowded on Saturday.

By Bus Bus connections in Sørlandet are infrequent; the tourist office can provide a comprehensive schedule. Tickets on **Stavanger's** excellent bus network cost NKr12.

By Taxi All **Kristiansand** taxis are connected with a central dispatching office (tel. 38/03–27–00). Journeys are charged by the taximeter within the city, otherwise by the kilometer.

Stavanger taxis are also connected to a central dispatching office (tel. 51/52–60–40). The initial charge is NKr19, with NKr9 per kilometer during the day and NKr11 at night.

Passes A **Sommerpass Kristiansand,** which costs NKr50 for adults and *Kristiansand* NKr30 for children, gives free admission to many sights and a 25% discount on tickets to the zoo and the M/S *Maarten*. It can be purchased at the tourist office, the zoo, and at all hotels. If you stay at any hotel in the city for four nights, the pass is free.

Stavanger The **Stavanger card,** sold at hotels, post offices in the region, and Stavanger Tourist Information, gives discounts of up to 50% on sightseeing tours, museums, buses, car rentals, and other services and attractions.

Guided Tours

Kristiansand Tours of Kristiansand run only in the summer. The **City Train** (Rådhusgt. 11, tel. 38/03–05–24) runs a 15-minute tour of the center. The M/S *Maarten* (Pier 6 by Fiskebrygga, tel. 30/02–

60–65) offers two-hour tours of the eastern archipelago (mid-June–mid-Aug.) and a three-hour tour of the western archipelago (July).

Stavanger A two-hour bus tour leaves from the Marina at **Vågen** daily at 1 between June and August. **Rødne Clipperkontoret** (Skagenkaien 18, tel. 51/89–52–70) offers three different tours, including an eye-popping fjord tour of the Lysefjord and Pulpit Rock. **Rogaland Trafikkselskap** (tel. 51/51–65–90) does the same, in either high-speed boats or ferries.

Exploring Sørlandet

Numbers in the margin correspond to points of interest on the Sørlandet map.

Tour 1: The Coast

❶ **Larvik** is the last of the big whaling towns, 19 kilometers (12 miles) south of Sandefjord. It's still a port, but now the traffic is made up of passengers to Fredrikshavn, Denmark. Near the ferry quays is **Kong Haakon VIIs kilde** (King Haakon VII's spring), also called Farris kilde (Farris spring), Norway's only natural source of mineral water. A spa was built here in 1880, but now people drink the water rather than bathe in it. *Fjellvn. Guided tours in summer.*

Larvik is the site of **Herregården,** a large estate once owned by the noble Gyldenløve family. The main building was finished in 1677. Inside, the furnishings are masterful examples of trompe l'oeil: Scandinavian nobility had to make do with furniture painted to look like marble or carving rather than the real thing. *Herregaardssletta1, tel. 33/13–04–04. Admission: NKr15 adults, NKr5 children. Open mid-June–Aug., daily 1–5; May 27–Sept. 2, Sun 1–5; Apr.–Oct., open on request. Call to confirm times.*

From Larvik, it's only 8 kilometers (5 miles) along the coast to **Stavern,** a popular sailing center. On the water east of town is **Fredriksvern,** which was Norway's main naval station between 1750 and 1850, named for King Fredrik V. The church is a fine example of Scandinavian Rococo. Its pews were designed so their backs could be folded down to make beds in case the church had to be used as a field hospital in time of war. *Stavern Church, tel. 33/19–91–78. Guided tours.*

Farther down the coast about 35 kilometers (22 miles) comes ❷ **Kragerø,** a picturesque town with its own small archipelago. **Theodor Kittelsen** (1857–1914), famous for his drawings of trolls and illustrations of Norwegian fairy tales, lived in Kragerø, and his birthplace is now a museum. *Th. Kittelsens v. 5. Admission: NKr20 adults, NKr10 children. Open June 15–Aug. 15, weekdays 11–3.*

The next pearl on the southern string is **Risør,** east from E18 on the coast. On the first weekend in August the town holds a festival that fills the harbor with beautiful antique boats.

❸ **Lyngør,** on four tiny rocky islands off the coast, was recently chosen Europe's best-preserved village. In winter the population is 110, but every summer thousands descend upon it. Hardly changed since the days of sailing ships, it's idyllic and carless, lined with rows of white-painted houses bearing win-

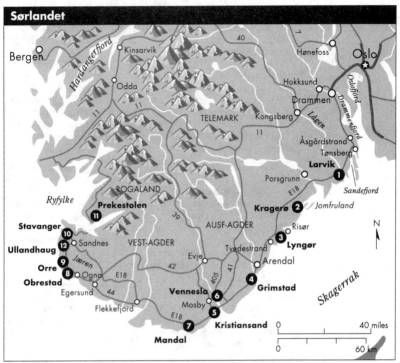

dow boxes filled with pink and red flowers. You'll find white houses all along the southern coast, a tradition that began about 100 years ago, when Dutch sailors traded white paint for wood. Up until that time, only red paint was available in Norway. To get to Lyngør follow E18 to the sign for Sørlandsporten (Gateway to the South). Turn off just after the sign and drive 26 kilometers (16 miles) to Lyngørfjorden Marina, where you can take a five-minute watertaxi (tel. 37/16–68–00) ride to the island. The only hotel books most of its rooms by the year to large firms, so don't count on staying overnight.

Time Out In a historic 100-year-old white house with blue trim, **Den Blå Lanterne** (tel. 37/16–64–80, reservations advised) is Lyngør's only restaurant. Although it's pricey, you can eat as much of their famous fish soup as you like, and there's often live music.

Arendal, a little farther south, has more tidy white houses. On the island of **Merdøy,** a 30-minute boat ride from Arendal's Langbrygga (wharf), is an early 18th-century sea-captain's home, now a museum, **Merdøgaard.** *Tel. 37/02–24–22. Admission: NKr10 adults, NKr5 children. Open June 15–Aug. 20, 11–4.*

❹ To the south is **Grimstad.** Its glory was also in the days of sailing ships—about the same time the 15-year-old Henrik Ibsen worked as an apprentice at the local apothecary shop. Grimstad Apotek is now a part of the **Ibsenhus** (Ibsen House) and has been preserved with its 1837 interior intact. Ibsen wrote his first play, *Catlina,* here. *Henrik Ibsensgt. 14, tel. 37/14–46–*

53. Admission: NKr15 adults, NKr5 children and senior citizens. Open May 15–Sept. 15, Mon.–Sat. 11–5, Sun. 1–5.

Tour 2: Kristiansand

⑤ Kristiansand, with 65,000 inhabitants, is one of Sørlandet's leading cities and the domestic summer-vacation capital of Norway. According to legend, King Christian IV in 1641 marked the four corners of the city with his walking stick, and within that framework the grid of wide streets was drawn. The center of the city, called the **Kvadrat,** still retains the grid, even after numerous fires.

Start at **Fisketorvet** (the fish market) at the southern corner of the grid right on the sea. Follow Strandpromenaden (the Beach Walk), and past Norwegian artist Kjell Nupen's interpretation of Kristiansand's roots more than 350 years ago to **Christiansholm Festning** (fortress), on a promontory opposite Festningsgata. Completed in 1672, the circular building with 15-foot-thick walls, has played more a decorative than a defensive role; it was used once, in 1807, to defend the city against British invasion. Now it contains art exhibits.

Six blocks inland is the Gothic Revival **Cathedral** from 1885. The third-largest church in Norway, it often hosts summertime concerts in addition to an annual week-long International Church Music Festival (beginning May 10) that includes organ, chamber, and gospel music. *Kirkegt., tel. 38/02–11–88. Admission free. Open May–Aug., Sun.–Fri. 10–2.*

Next, head north, across the Otra River, on Bus 22 or drive to Route E18 and cross the bridge over the Otra to Parkveien. Turn left onto Ryttergangen and drive to Gimleveien, where you'll turn right to **Gimle Gård** (Gimle Manor). Built by a wealthy merchant/shipowner around 1800 in the Empire style, it boasts period furnishings, paintings, silver, and decoration, including hand-blocked wallpaper. *Gimlevn. 23, tel. 38/09–21–32. Admission: NKr10 adults, NKr5 children (free with Summerpass). Open July 1–Aug. 15, Tues.–Sun. noon–3; May 1–June 30, Aug. 16–Nov. 1, Sun. noon–5.*

Eastward on Gimleveien is **Oddernes Church,** one of the oldest churches in Norway dedicated to St. Olav. The runestone in the cemetery tells that Øyvind, godson of St. Olav, built this church on property he inherited from his father. The altar and the pulpit are both in the Baroque style, and richly gilded. *Oddernesvn., tel. 38/09–01–87. Admission free. Open May–Aug., Sun.–Fri. 10–4.*

Continue to **Vest-Agder Fylkesmuseum** (County Museum), just south of Vigeveien. Here you can visit two *tun* (farm buildings traditionally set in clusters around a common area, which suited the extended families). A reconstructed city street features dwellings and workshops. *Vigevn., Kongsgård, tel. 38/09–02–28. Admission: NKr20 adults, NKr10 children (free with Summerpass). Open June 20–Aug. 20, Tues.–Sat. 10–6, Sun. noon–6; May 24–Sept. 13, Sun. noon–6.*

Once you've had your fill of museums, head back across the river and northwest of town to **Ravnedalen** (the Raven Valley), a lush park, filled in spring with flowers. It's a favorite with hikers and strolling nannies. Wear comfortable shoes and you can

hike the narrow, winding paths up the hills and climb 200 steps up to a 100-meter (304-foot) lookout.

East of town 11 kilometers (6 miles) is one of Norway's most popular attractions. **Kristiansand Dyrepark** is five separate parks, including a water park (bring bathing suits and towels), a forested park, an entertainment park, and a zoo, which contains an enclosure for Scandinavian wolves and Europe's (possibly the world's) largest breeding ground for Bactrian camels. Finally, the park contains **Kardemomme By** (Cardamom Town), named for a book by Norwegian illustrator and writer Thorbjørn Egner. His story comes alive here in a precisely replicated village, with actors playing townsfolk, shopkeepers, pirates, and a delightful trio of robbers. Families who are hooked can even stay overnight in one of the village's cozy apartments or nearby cottages (reserve at least a year in advance). *Kristiansand Dyrepark, 4609 Kardemomme by, tel. 38/04–97–00. Admission: NKr130 adults, NKr110 children; includes admission to all parks and rides. Open late May–mid-June, daily 10–3; mid-June–mid-Aug., daily 9–7; mid-Aug.–mid-Sept., daily 10-6.*

Excursions from Kristiansand ⑥ **Setesdalsbanen** (the Setesdal Railway) at **Grovane i Vennesla,** 20 kilometers (13 miles) north of Kristiansand, is a 4.7-kilometer- (3-mile-) long stretch of narrow-gauge track featuring a steam locomotive from 1894 and carriages from the early 1900s. Follow Route 39 to Mosby, veer right onto 405, and continue to Grovane. *Grovane, tel. 38/15–64–82. Fare: NKr40 adults, NKr20 children (50% discount with Summerpass). Open June 9–Aug. 25, Sun. at 11:30, 1, 2:30; July, Wed. at 6.*

Many rockhounds head for **Evje,** about 60 kilometers (36 miles) north of Kristiansand, to look for semiprecious stones. At **Evje Mineralsti,** you can hunt for blue-green amazonite. *No tel. Admission: NKr35, NKr70 family. Open daily 10–5:30. At other times, visitors pay by honor system.*

You can also visit **Fennefoss Museum** just south of Evje in Hornnes and look at the mineral collection. *No tel. Admission: NKr15 adults, NKr5 children. Open daily 10–2.*

Tour 3: The South

From Kristiansand you can go 28 kilometers (17 miles) south- ⑦ west to **Mandal,** with its historic core of well-preserved wood houses and its beautiful long beach, Sjøsanden.

Lindesnes Fyr, Norway's oldest lighthouse, was built on the southernmost point of the country. The old coal-fired light dates from 1822. Route E18 continues northward now along the rich agricultural coastal plain of **Jæren,** painted by many Norwegian artists. Ancient monuments are still visible here, nota- ⑧ bly the **Hå gravesite** below the Hå parsonage near **Obrestad** light on coastal Route 44, which connects with Route E18 by way of Route 504. It consists of about 60 mounds, including two star-shaped and one boat-shaped, dating from around AD 500, all marked with stones. **Hå parsonage,** built in the 1780s, is now a cultural center. *Admission: NKr15. Open May 1–Sept. 30, Sun.–Fri. noon–7, Sat. noon–5; Oct. 1–Apr. 30., Sat. noon–5, Sun. noon–7.*

9 Continue northward on Route 507 to **Orre,** site of a medieval stone church. Near Orre pond, slightly inland, is a bird-watching station.

Tour 4: Stavanger

10 **Stavanger** has always prospered from the riches of the sea. During the 19th century, huge harvests of brisling and herring established it as the sardine capital of the world. A resident is still called a Siddis, from S(tavanger) plus *iddis*, which means "sardine label," and the city symbol, fittingly enough, is the key of a sardine can.

During the past two decades, a different product from the sea has been Stavanger's lifeblood—oil. Since its discovery in the late 1960s, North Sea oil has transformed both the economy and the lifestyle of the city. In the early days of drilling, expertise was imported from abroad, chiefly from the United States. Although Norwegians have now taken over most of the projects, foreigners constitute almost a tenth of the inhabitants, making Stavanger the country's most cosmopolitan city. Though the population hovers around 100,000, the city has all the agreeable bustle of one many times its size.

In the center, next to a small pond called Breiavatnet, is **Stavanger Domkirke** (the cathedral), a large, well-preserved medieval church. Construction was begun about 1100 by Bishop Reinald of Winchester, probably assisted by English craftsmen. Largely destroyed by fire in 1125, it was rebuilt to include a Gothic chancery, the result of which is that its once elegant lines are now festooned with macabre death symbols and airborne putti. The cathedral often hosts organ recitals, with coffee served afterward in the crypt. *Admission free. Open mid-May–mid-Sept., Mon.–Sat. 9–8, Sun. 1–6; mid-Sept.–mid-May, Mon.–Sat. 9–2.*

Next to the cathedral is the **Kongsgård,** former residence of bishops and kings, but now a school and not open to visitors. A few streets to the left, on Eiganesveien, is an old patrician residential district. As the road angles to the left, it's only one long block to **Breidablikk** manor house, built by a Norwegian shipping magnate. An outstanding example of what the Norwegians call "Swiss style" architecture, it has been perfectly preserved since the '60s and feels as if the owner has only momentarily slipped away. In spite of its foreign label, the house is uniquely Norwegian, inspired by national romanticism. *Eiganesvn. 40A, tel. 51/52–60–35. Admission: NKr20 adults, NKr10 children. Open mid-June–mid-Aug., Tues.–Sun. 11–3; mid-Aug.–mid-June, Sun. 11–4.*

Across the road and through the park is **Ledaal,** a stately house built by the Kielland family in 1799 but now the residence of the royal family when they visit Stavanger. The second-floor library is dedicated to the writer Alexander Kielland, a social critic and satirist. *Eiganesvn. 45, tel. 51/52–60–35. Admission: NKr20 adults, NKr10 children. Open mid-June–mid-Aug., Tues.–Sun. 11–3; mid-Aug.–mid-June, Sun. 11–4.*

Exit toward Alexander Kiellands Gate, turn right, and walk around the stadium complex and several blocks farther until you reach Øvre Strandgate. Along with Nedre Strandgate, this forms the periphery of old Stavanger, where you can wind

down narrow cobblestoned streets past small, white houses with many-paned windows and terra-cotta roof tiles.

Tucked between the neighborhood and the harbor is the fascinating, albeit obscure, **Norsk Hermetikkmuseum** (Canning Museum), housed in a former canning factory. Exhibits document the production of brisling and sardines—the city's most important industry for nearly 100 years, thanks greatly to savvy turn-of-the-century packaging (naturally, the inventor of the sardine-can key was from Stavanger). Sundays between August and April, the museum hosts an iddis, or sardine-label, swap meet that draws a local crowd, many of whom have collected thousands of labels. *Øvre Strandgt. 88A, tel. 51/52–60–35. Admission: NKr20 adults, NKr10 children. Open June–Aug., Wed.–Sun. 11–3; Sept.–May, Sun. 11–4.*

Walk along Strandkaien to **Sjøfartsmuseet** (the Maritime Museum), in the only two shipping merchants' houses that remain completely intact. The warehouses face the wharf, while the shops, offices, and apartments face the street on the other side. Inside, the house is just as it was a century ago, complete with office furniture, files, and posters, while the apartments show the standard of living for the mercantile class at that time. *Nedre Strandgt. 17–19, tel. 51/52–60–35. Admission: NKr20 adults, NKr10 children. Open mid-June–mid-Aug., Tues.–Sun. 11–3; mid-Aug.–mid-June, Sun. 11–4.*

From all along the quay you can see **Valbergtårnet** (Valberget 4, tel. 51/52–21–95), built on the highest point of the old city. Once a fire watchtower, it is now a craft center.

If you are of Norwegian stock, you can trace your roots at **Det Norske Utvandrersenteret** (The Norwegian Emigrant Center). Bring along any information you have, especially where your ancestors came from in Norway and when they arrived in the United Kingdom, North America, or elsewhere. *Bergjelandsgt. 30, 4012 Stavanger, tel. 51/50–12–67. Admission is free, but each written request costs NKr 180. Open weekdays 9–3.*

Excursions from Stavanger

⑪ Not a good choice if you suffer from vertigo, but great for a heart-stopping view is **Prekestolen** (Pulpit Rock), a huge cube of rock with a vertical drop of 600 meters (2,000 feet). You can join a tour to get there (*see* Guided Tours, *above*) or you can do it on your own from June 16 to August 25 by taking the ferry from Fiskepiren to Tau. It takes 1½ to two hours to walk to the rock—the well-marked trail crosses some uneven terrain, so good walking shoes or boots are vital. Food and lodging are near the trail. The rock can also be reached by sightseeing boat.

⑫ About 5 kilometers (3 miles) west of Stavanger is **Ullandhaug,** a reconstruction of an Iron-Age farm. Three houses have been built around a central garden, and guides wearing period clothing demonstrate the daily activities of 1,500 years ago, spinning thread on a spindle, weaving, and cooking over an open hearth. *Ullandhaug, tel. 51/53–41–40. Admission: NKr10 adults, NKr5 children. Open June 15–Aug. 15, daily noon–5; May 8–June 14 and Aug. 16–Sept. 16, Sun. noon–5.*

What to See and Do with Children

Kristiansand **Kardemomme by** (Cardamom Town) and **Dyrehaven** (*see* Tour 2, *above*) are the big draws in Kristiansand.

Stavanger   At the **Canning Museum** (*see* Tour 4, *above*), children can collect
sardine-can labels and play marbles. **Kongeparken Amusement
Park** has an 85-meter (281-foot) -long figure of Gulliver as its
main attraction, and plenty of rides. *4330 Ålgård, tel. 51/61–
71–11. Admission: NKr25; rides and activities, NKr5–20.
Open mid-June–mid Aug., daily 11–7. Other spring and summer hours vary. Call the park for specific times.*

Shopping

Porsgrunn   Outside Porsgrunn, 27 kilometers (17 miles) west of Larvik, is
Porsgrunn Porselænfabrik (porcelain factory) (Porselensgt. 12,
tel. 35/55–00–40), where you can take a factory tour and visit
the seconds shop.

Stavanger   Outside of town are a ceramics factory and an outlet store:
Figgjo Ceramics (Rte. E18, 4333 Figgjo, tel. 51/67–00–00) was
started during World War II, when Norway was occupied by
German forces. A museum traces the history of the factory; the
seconds shop has discounts of around 50%. **Skjæveland
Strikkevarefabrikk** (4330 Ålgård, tel. 51/61–85–06) has a huge
selection of men's and women's sweaters in both Norwegian
patterns and other designs for around NKr200 less than prices
found in the shops.

Sports and Outdoor Activities

Southern Norway is an outdoor paradise, with a mild summer
climate and terrain varying from coastal flatland to inland
mountains and forests. There's plenty of fish in the rivers and
lakes, as well as along the coast. The region is particularly well
suited to canoeing, kayaking, and rafting, as well as hiking.
Southern Norway is home to beavers, deer, fox, and forest
birds, so bring binoculars if you like to see them more closely.

Bicycling   **Kristiansand** has 70 kilometers (43 miles) of bike trails around
the city. The tourist office can recommend routes and rentals.

From **Stavanger** you can take your bike onto the ferry that departs for Finnøy, one of the larger islands of the Ryfylke Archipelago. Spend the day or longer: Week-long cottage rentals are
available from **Finnøy Fjordsenter** (N–4160, Judaberg, tel. 51/
71–26–46). For more information about cottages in the archipelago and maps, contact the Stavanger Tourist Board. The
Department of the Environment can also provide information;
call their **Cycle Projects** (Sadnes Turistinformajon, Langgt. 8,
N–4300 Sadnes, Stavanger, tel. 51/65–03–19).

Bird-Watching   The **Jaerstrendene** in Jaeren, from Randabergvika in the north
to Ogna in the south, is a protected national park—and a good
area for spotting puffins, cormorants, and black guillemots, as
well as such waders as dunlins, little stints, and ringed plovers.
Some areas of the park are closed to visitors, and it is forbidden
to pick flowers, or for that matter, disturb anything.

Fishing   Both Sørlandet, around Kristiansand, and Rogaland, around
the Stavanger area, are famed for their fishing waters. For details on fishing holidays, contact the regional tourist boards.

Kristiansand   Just north of Kristiansand there is excellent trout, perch, and
eel fishing at Lillesand's **Vestre Grimevann** lake. You can get a
permit at any sports store or at the tourist office (tel. 37/27–21–
30). South of Kristiansand, in Mandal, sea trout run from mid-

May to mid-September. The daily fishing fee is NKr30. For details, contact the tourist office (tel. 38/26–08–20).

Stavanger Three of the 10 best fishing rivers in Norway, the **Ognaelva, Håelva,** and **Figgjo,** are located in Jæren, just south of Stavanger. Fishing licenses, which are sold in groceries and gas stations, are required at all of them.

The longest salmon river in western Norway, the **Suldalslågen,** is also nearby, made popular 100 years ago by a Scottish aristocrat, who built a fishing lodge there. **Lindum** still has cabins and camping facilities, as well as a dining room. Contact the **Lindum Ferie- og Kurssenter** (N–4240 Suldalsosen, tel. 52/79–91–61). The main salmon season is July through September (*see* also Water Sports, Stavanger, *below*).

Golf At Randesund, southeast of **Kristiansand,** is a nine-hole golf course. Contact **Kristiansand Golfklubb's** secretary (tel. 38/04–58–63) for details. The **Stavanger Golf klubb** (tel. 51/55–54–31) offers a lush, 18-hole, international-championship course and equipment rental.

Hiking In addition to the gardens and steep hills of **Ravnedalen** (*see*
Kristiansand Tour 2, *above*), the **Baneheia** forest, just a 15-minute walk north from the city center, is full of evergreens, small lakes, and paths that are ideal for a lazy walk or a challenging run.

Stavanger **Stavanger Turistforening** (Postboks 239, 4001 Stavanger, tel. 51/52–75–66) can plan a hike through the area, particularly in the rolling **Setesdalsheiene** and the thousands of islands and skerries of the **Ryfylke Archipelago.** The tourist board oversees 33 cabins for members (you can join on the spot) for overnighting along the way. Also in the Ryfylke area, thrill seekers can hike up to the **Kjerag,** a sheet of granite mountain that soars 3,555 feet, at the Lysefjord, near Forsand.

Hunting Throughout the Kristiansand and Stavanger areas, hunting laws are similar to those in the rest of Norway. For larger game, including elk, you must literally purchase a Norwegian's right, thereby ensuring that there is no overhunting. Beavers in the Kristiansand area and hare around Stavanger are numerous but still require the purchase of a permit. For information, contact **Info Sø** (Info South, Brokelandsheia, 4993 Sundrebru, tel. 37/15–85–60).

Water Sports **Kuholmen Marina** (Roligheden Camping, tel. 38/09–67–22) ar-
Kristiansand ranges rentals of boats, water skis, and water scooters. **Sail Scandinavia** (Tollbodgt. 8, tel. 38/07–07–49) rents sailboats by the day, weekend or week, with or without captain, while **Hamresanden Båtutleie** (Kirsti Stabel, Moneheia 4, tel. 38/04–68–25) rents out kayaks and rowboats. **Anker Dykkersenter** (Randesundsgt. 2, Kuholmen, tel. 38/09–79–09) rents scuba equipment, and **Blomberg Sport** (Skansen 24, tel. 38/02–98–08) rents windsurfers and holds classes. **Kristiansand Diving Club** (Myrbakken 3, tel. 38/01–03–32 between 6 PM and 9 PM) has information on local diving.

Combining history and sailing, the magnificent full-rig, square-sail school ship *Sørlandet* (Gravene 2, N–4610 Kristiansand, tel. 38/02–98–90, fax 38/02–93–34), built in 1927, takes on passengers ranging from senior citizens to college students and younger for two weeks, usually stopping for several days in a northern European port. Prices range from NKr6,500 for adults to NKr5,500 for students.

Stavanger Diving is excellent all along the coast—although Norwegian law requires all foreigners to dive with a Norwegian in order to ensure that wrecks are left undisturbed. Contact **Dive In** (Bergjelandsgt. 11, tel. 51/52–89–36), in the Ryfilke Archipelago, which rents equipment and offers a weekend rate.

On the island of **Kvitsøy**, in the archipelago just west of Stavanger, you can rent an apartment, complete with fish-smoking and -freezing facilities, and arrange to use a small sail- or motorboat. Contact **Kvitsøy Maritime Senter** (Box 35, N–4090 Kvitsøy, tel. 51/73–51–88).

Dining and Lodging

Dining Coastal Sørlandet is seafood country. Restaurants in this resort area are casual and unpretentious, and the cooking is simple. Better restaurants can usually be found in the hotels, especially in small towns.

Stavanger has many more good restaurants than other cities of comparable size, thanks to the influx of both foreigners and money to the city.

Lodging Hotels in the small towns along the coast are either modern and practical—suited for business guests—or quaint and old-fashioned. Prices are about the same regardless of style and are quite competitive during the low-season summer months.

Highly recommended establishments are indicated by a star ★.

Bryne **Time Station.** It's a 40-minute train ride from Stavanger to
Dining Bryne, and the restaurant is next to the station. The specialty of the house is a seafood platter with salmon, monkfish, ocean catfish, mussels, and ocean crayfish in a beurre-blanc sauce. For dessert, try the *krumkake*, a cookie baked on an iron, wafer thin, shaped into a cone, and filled with blackberry cream. *4340 Bryne, tel. 51/48–22–56. Reservations required. Dress: casual but neat. AE, DC, MC, V. No weekday lunch. Closed Sun. Moderate.*

Kristiansand **Sjøhuset.** Built in 1892 as a salt warehouse, this white-trimmed
Dining red building is furnished with comfortable leather chairs and accented with maritime antiques. The specialty is seafood, and the monkfish with Newburg sauce on green fettuccine is both colorful and delicious. *Østre Strangt. 12, tel. 38/02–62–60. Reservations advised. Dress: casual but neat. AE, DC, MC, V. Moderate–Expensive.*
Restaurant Bakgården. At this small and intimate restaurant the menu varies from day to day, but the seafood platter and rack of lamb are standard items. The staff is especially attentive to guests' wishes. *Tollbodgt. 5, tel. 38/02–79–55. Dress: casual but neat. AE, DC, MC, V. No lunch. Moderate–Expensive.*
Mållaget Kafeteria. At this cafeteria everything is homemade (except for the gelatin dessert). That includes such dishes as meatballs, brisket of beef with onion sauce, and trout in sour-cream sauce. It's the best deal in town, but it closes right around the time most people think about eating dinner. *Gyldenløves Gate 11, tel. 38/02–22–93. Reservations advised. Dress: casual. No credit cards. Inexpensive.*

Lodging **Ernst Park.** It was modernized in 1988, but a few clusters of chairs and sofas are left in nooks and crannies. The rooms are

decorated in light furniture, with chintz bedspreads and drapes. The corner rooms have a tower nook at one end. On Saturday the atrium restaurant is the local spot for a civilized tea and lovely cakes. *Rådhusgt. 2, 4611, tel. 38/02–14–00, fax 38/02–03–07. 113 rooms with bath or shower, 3 suites. Facilities: 3 restaurants, 2 bars, nightclub, conference rooms. AE, DC, MC, V. Moderate–Expensive.*

Hotel Norge. This recently refurbished hotel in the heart of town has an entrance more modern than that of the Ernst Park, but upstairs, the difference is negligible. Here the rooms are furnished in bright colors and dark woods. Get up for breakfast to taste the homemade breads and rolls. *Dronningens Gate 5, 4610, tel. 38/02–00–00, fax 38/02–35–30. 115 rooms with bath or shower. Facilities: restaurant, conference rooms; no alcohol. AE, DC, MC, V. Inexpensive–Moderate.*

Stavanger
Dining
★

Jans Mat & Vinhus. The cellar setting is rustic, with old stone walls and robust sideboards providing a nice counterpoint to the refined menu. Saddle of Rogaland county lamb is boned and rolled around a thyme-flavored stuffing, and the fillet is topped with a crunchy mustard crust. For dessert, there's a nougat parfait dusted with cocoa. *Breitorget, tel. 51/52–45–02. Reservations required. Jacket and tie required. AE, DC, MC, V. No lunch. Closed Sun. Expensive.*

Straen Fiskerestaurant. The city's chief fish restaurant, right on the quay, has two old-fashioned dining rooms. The three-course dinner of the day is always the best value. The house fish soup and the tournedos of monkfish with lobster sauce and a garnish of mussels and shrimp are excellent. *Strandkaien, tel. 51/52–62–30. Reservations advised. Dress: neat but casual. AE, DC, MC, V. Dinner only. Closed Sun. Expensive.*

City Bistro. This turn-of-the-century frame house with a tiled roof is furnished with massive oak tables and benches. Choose from reindeer medallions with rowanberry jelly, deer fillet with lingonberries and pears, or halibut poached in cream with saffron, garnished with shrimp, crayfish, and mussels. The dish of the day is served from 5 to 6. *Madlavn. 18–20, tel. 51/53–31–81. Reservations required. Dress: casual but neat. AE, DC, MC, V. No lunch. Moderate.*

Galeien Bistro. It used to be a sardine cannery, and the pictures on its wall illustrate the early history of the building. Ask for a window table overlooking the sea. Back in the kitchen, which you can visit, there are tanks filled with cod, flounder, oysters, mussels, crabs, and lobster. Simple preparations emphasize the natural flavor of the fish. *Hundvågvn. 27, tel. 51/54–91–44. Reservations advised. Dress: casual but neat. V. Moderate.*

Café Sting. It's a restaurant–gallery–concert hall–meeting place day and night. All food is made in-house and is less stodgy than most inexpensive fare in Norway. There's a skillet dish with crisp fried potatoes and bacon, flavored with leek and topped with melted cheese; and a meat loaf with mashed potatoes and sprinkled with cheese. The chocolate and almond cakes are good. *Valberggt. 3, tel. 51/53–24–40. Dress: casual. AE, DC, V. Inexpensive.*

Lodging

SAS Royal. Room styles include Scandinavian, American, Japanese, and Italian and lots of fashionable furniture that provides more good looks than real comfort. The Chicago Bar & Grill serves prime steaks. *Løkkevn. 26, 4008 Stavanger, tel. 51/56–70–00, fax 51/56–74–60. 204 rooms with bath, 8 suites. Facilities: 2 restaurants, bar, 24-hour room service, pool, fitness*

center, business/conference center. *AE, DC, MC, V. Moderate–Very Expensive.*

Skagen Brygge. This hotel incorporates three rehabilitated old
sea houses. Almost all rooms are different, from modern to old-
fashioned maritime with exposed beams and brick and wood
walls; many have harbor views. The hotel has an arrangement
with 15 restaurants in the area—they make the reservations
and the tab ends up on your hotel bill. *Skagenkaien 30, 4006,
tel. 51/53–03–50, fax 51/89–58–83. 110 rooms with bath, 2
suites. Facilities: bar, pool, fitness center, conference center.
AE, DC, MC, V. Moderate–Expensive.*

Grand Hotel. This hotel on the edge of the town center doesn't
aim to be fancy; rooms are comfortable and bright, done in light
pastels and white. In summer the rates drop significantly.
*Klubbgt. 3, Boks 80, 4001 Stavanger, tel. 51/53–30–20, fax 51/
56–19–42. 92 rooms with bath. Facilities: restaurant, bar. AE,
DC, MC, V. Inexpensive–Moderate.*

Hummeren. Built in 1986 in the style of old harborside buildings, Hummeren (The Lobster) is 15 kilometers (9 miles) from
Stavanger, at Tananger Harbor. Boats dock immediately outside, and it even has showers for people who otherwise live on
their boats. Many of the large rooms face the harbor, and some
have balconies. The restaurant serves fine, old-fashioned fare.
*4056 Tananger, tel. 51/69–04–33. 32 rooms with shower or tub.
Facilities: restaurant, bar, conference rooms. AE, DC, MC, V.
Inexpensive–Moderate.*

The Arts and Nightlife

The Arts **Stavanger Konserthus** (Concert Hall, Bjergsted, tel. 51/56–17–
Stavanger 16) features local artists and hosts free summertime foyer concerts. Built on an island in the archipelago in the Middle Ages,
today **Ulstein Kloster** is used for its superior acoustics and hosts
classical and jazz concerts on some weekday afternoons from
June to August.

Nightlife As in most smaller cities, Kristiansand's nightlife centers
Kristiansand around hotels.

Stavanger In summer people are out at all hours, and sidewalk restaurants stay open until the sun comes up. Walk along **Skagenkaien** and **Strandkaien** for a choice of pubs and nightclubs.
Among media junkies the place for a beer and a bit of CNN is
the **Newsman** (Skagen 14, tel. 51/53–57–09). The **Amadeus Disco,** at the Atlantik Hotel (Olav V's gt. 3, tel. 51/52–75–20) is for
the mid-twenties crowd.

Bergen

People from Bergen like to say they do not come from Norway
but from Bergen. Enfolded at the crook of seven mountains and
fish-boned by seven fjords, Bergen does seem far from the rest
of Norway.

Hanseatic merchants from northern Germany settled in Bergen during the 14th century and made it one of their four major
overseas trading centers. The surviving Hanseatic buildings on
Bryggen (the quay) are neatly topped with triangular cookie-
cutter roofs and scrupulously painted red, blue, yellow, and
green. A monument in themselves (they are on the UNESCO
World Heritage List), they now house boutiques, restaurants,

and museums. In the evening, when the harborside is illuminated, these modest buildings, together with the stocky Rosencrantz Tower, are reflected in the water—and provide one of the loveliest cityscapes in northern Europe.

During the Hanseatic period, this active port was Norway's capital and largest city. Boats from northern Norway brought dried fish to Bergen to be shipped abroad by the Dutch, English, Scottish, and German merchants who had settled here. By the time the Hansa lost power, the city had an ample supply of wealthy local merchants and shipowners to replace them. For years Bergen was the capital of shipping, and until well into the 19th century, it remained the country's major city.

Culturally, Bergen has also had its luminaries, including dramatist Ludvig Holberg, Scandinavia's answer to Molière—whom the Danes claim as their own. Bergensers know better. Norway's musical geniuses Ole Bull and Edvard Grieg also came from the city of the seven hills. In fact, once you've visited Troldhaugen, Greig's "Hill of Trolls," it's not difficult to see the source of his inspiration.

About 217,000 people live in the greater metropolitan area now, compared with nearly 500,000 in Oslo. Even though the balance of power has shifted to the capital, Bergen remains a strong commercial force, thanks to shipping and oil, and is a cultural center, with an international music and arts festival every spring. Although it's true that an umbrella and slicker are necessary in this town, the raindrops—actually 219 days per year of them—never obstruct the lovely views.

Important Addresses and Numbers

Tourist Information The **tourist information office** at Bryggen (tel. 55/32–14–80), by the wharf, has brochures and maps and can arrange for accommodations and sightseeing. There is also a currency exchange.

Emergencies **Police:** tel. 002. **Fire:** tel. 001. **Ambulance:** tel. 003. **Car Rescue:** tel. 55/29–22–22. After January 1, 1994, these numbers will change. **Police:** tel. 112. **Fire:** tel. 111. **Ambulance:** tel. 113.

Hospital Emergency Rooms The outpatient center at Lars Hillesgate 30 (tel. 55/32–11–20), near Grieghallen, is open 24 hours.

Dentists The dental emergency center, also at Lars Hillesgate 30 (tel. 55/32–11–20), is open daily 10–11 AM and 7–9 PM.

Pharmacies **Apotek Nordstjernen** (tel. 55/31–68–40), by the bus station, is open daily from 8:30 AM to midnight.

Where to Change Money Outside normal banking hours, the tourist information office on Bryggen can change money. Post offices exchange money and are open Monday through Wednesday 8 to 4:30, Thursday and Friday 8–6, and Saturday 9 to 2.

Arriving and Departing by Plane

Flesland Airport is 20 kilometers (12 miles) south of Bergen. **SAS** (tel. 55/99–76–10) and **Braathens SAFE** (tel. 55/23–23–25) are the main domestic carriers. **British Airways** and **Lufthansa** also serve Flesland.

Between the Airport and Downtown
By Bus Flesland is a 30-minute ride from the center of Bergen at off-peak hours. The **airport bus** departs three times per hour (less frequently on weekends) from the SAS Royal Hotel via Braathen SAFE's office at the Hotel Norge and from the bus station. Pickup prior to departure can be arranged. Tickets cost NKr36.

By Taxi A taxi rank is outside the Arrivals exit. The trip into the city costs around NKr200.

By Car Driving from Flesland to Bergen is simple, and the road is well marked. Bergen has an electronic ring surrounding it, so any vehicle entering the city weekdays between 6 AM and 10 PM has to pay NKr5. There is no toll in the other direction.

Arriving and Departing by Car, Train, Bus, and Boat

By Car Bergen is 485 kilometers (300 miles) from Oslo. Route 7 is good almost as far as Eidfjord at the eastern edge of the Hardangerfjord, but then deteriorates considerably. The ferry along the way, crossing the Hardanger Fjord from Main to Bruravik, runs continually 5 AM to midnight and takes 10 minutes. Route 7 from Kvanndal to Bergen hugs the fjord part of the way, making for spectacular scenery.

Driving from Stavanger to Bergen involves from two to four ferries and a long journey packed with breathtaking scenery. The Stavanger tourist information office can help plan the trip and reserve ferry space.

By Train The *Bergensbanen* has four departures daily, plus one more on Friday and two on Sunday, in both directions on the Oslo–Bergen route; it is widely acknowledged as one of the most beautiful train rides in the world. Trains leave from Oslo S Station for the 7½- to 8½-hour journey. For information about trains out of Bergen, call 55/96–60–50.

By Bus The summer-only bus from Oslo to Bergen, **Geiteryggekspressen** (literally, "Goat-Back Express"—does it refer to speed, comfort, or terrain?) leaves the Nor-Way bus terminal (Galleri Oslo, tel. 22/17–52–90) at 8 AM and arrives in Bergen 12½ hours later. Buses also connect Bergen with Trondheim and Ålesund. Western Norway is served by several bus companies, which use the station at Strømgaten 8 (tel. 55/32–67–80).

By Boat Boats have always been Bergen's lifeline to the world. **Color Line** (Skuteviksboder 1–2, 5023, tel. 55/56–86–60) ferries serve Newcastle. Others connect with the Shetland and Faroe islands, Denmark, Scotland, and Iceland. All dock at Skoltegrunnskaien.

Express boats between Bergen and Stavanger run three times daily on weekdays, twice daily on weekends, for the four-hour trip. All arrive and depart from **Munkebryggen.**

Getting Around

The best way to see the small center of Bergen is on foot. Most sights are within walking distance of the marketplace.

By Bus Tourist tickets for 48 hours of unlimited travel within the town boundaries cost NKr60, payable on the yellow city buses. All

buses serving the Bergen region depart from the central bus station at Strømgaten 8 (tel. 55/32–67–80).

By Taxi Taxi ranks are located in strategic places downtown. All taxis are connected to the central dispatching office (tel. 55/99–09–90) and can be booked in advance (tel. 55/99–13–00).

By Car Downtown Bergen is enclosed by an inner ring road. The area within is divided into three zones, which are separated by ONE-WAY and DO-NOT-ENTER signs. To get from one zone to another, return to the ring road and drive to an entry point into the desired zone. It's best to leave your car at a parking garage (the Birkebeiner Senter is on Rosenkrantz Gata, and there is a lot near the train station) and walk. You pay an NKr5 toll every time you drive into the city—but driving out is free.

Opening and Closing Times

Shops are open Monday–Wednesday and Friday 9–4:30. On Thursday, as well as Friday for some shops, the hours are 9–7. On Saturday shops are open 9–2. The shopping centers are open weekdays 9–8 and Saturday 9–4.

Guided Tours

Bergen is the guided-tour capital of Norway because it is the starting point for most fjord tours. Tickets for all tours are available from the tourist information office.

Orientation **HSD Busstrafikk** (tel. 55/23–87–00) offers two tours departing from Hotel Norge; one on Bergen sights, the other to Edvard Grieg's Home and the Fantoft Stave Church. **De Gule Bussene** (yellow buses, tel. 55/28–13–30) offers three tours departing from Torggaten by the Hotel Norge. The excellent **Bryggen Guiding** (1½ hours, June 1–Aug. 31) offers a historic tour of the buildings at Bryggen, as well as entrance to Bryggens Museum, the Hanseatic Museum, and Schøtstuene after the tour, conducted by knowledgeable guides. **Bergens-Expressen** (tel. 55/18–10–19), a "train on tires," leaves from Torgalmenningen for a one-hour ride around the center of town.

Fjord Tours Bergen is the much-acclaimed "Gateway to the Fjords," with dozens of fjord-tour possibilities. The following is only meant as a sampling. The ambitious all-day **"Norway-in-a-Nutshell"** bus/train tour (NSB, Strømgata 2, 50 15 Bergen, tel. 55/96–60–50) goes through Voss, Flåm, Myrdal, and Gudvangen—truly a breathtaking trip, especially if you're pressed for time.

Traveling by boat is an advantage because the contrasts between the fjords and mountains are greatest at water level, and the boats are comfortable and stable (the water is practically still), so seasickness is rare. Stops are frequent, and all sights are explained. *The White Lady* (tel. 55/31–43–20) offers a four-hour local fjord tour. **Fylkesbaatane** (County Boats) **i Sogn og Fjordane** (tel. 55/32–40–15) has several combination tours. Tickets are sold at the tourist information center (tel. 55/32–14–80) and at the quay. Students receive a 25% discount for most tours.

There are other combinations of tours through the Hardanger and Sogne fjords that include the surrounding countryside; some tours include options to fish or visit local villages or islands. The three-day **Panorama Fjord Cruise** plies the Har-

danger and Sognefjords but includes overnights in hotels. **Fjord Sightseeing** (tel. 55/31–43–20), offers boat tours leaving from Fisketorget. Both of these lines are operated by **Winge of Scandinavia** (Karl Johans Gate 35, Box 1705, Vika, N–0121 Oslo, tel. 02/41–20–20).

Highlights for First-Time Visitors

Bryggen (*see* Tour 1)
Bryggens Museum (*see* Tour 1)
Fantoft Stave Church (*see* Tour 3)
Fisketorget (*see* Tour 1)
Fløybanen (*see* Tour 1)
Hanseatisk Museum (*see* Tour 1)
Lysøen (*see* Tour 4)
Troldhaugen (Edvard Grieg's home) (*see* Tour 3)

Exploring Bergen

Numbers in the margin correspond to points of interest on the Bergen map.

Many of Bergen's sights are concentrated in a small area, so walking tours are the best way to see the city.

Tour 1: Historic Bergen

❶ Start at **Torget,** Bergen's marketplace, also called **Fisketorget** (fish market). At the turn of the century, pictures of this active and pungent square, with fishermen in Wellington boots and mackintoshes and women in long aprons, were popular post-card subjects. Times haven't changed, and it remains just as picturesque: Bring your camera. *Open Mon.–Sat. 8–3.*

❷ Look over toward **Bryggen,** the row of 14th-century painted wood buildings with pointed gables facing the harbor, built by Hansa merchants. The buildings, which are on the UNESCO World Heritage List, are mostly reconstructions, with the oldest dating from 1702. Several fires, the latest in 1955, destroyed the original structures.

❸ Follow the pier to the **Hanseatisk** (Hanseatic) **Museum** at Finnegården, which was office and home to an affluent German merchant. Apprentices lived upstairs, in boxed-in beds with windows cut into the wall, so the tiny cells could be made up from the hall. Although claustrophobic, they retained body heat, practical in these unheated buildings. *Bryggen, tel. 55/31–41–89. Admission: NKr15 adults, NKr8 children. Open June–Aug., daily 9–5; May and Sept., daily 11–2; Oct.–Apr., Sun., Mon., Wed., and Fri. 11–2.*

❹ Past the historic buildings, at the end of the Holmen promontory, is **Bergenhus Festning** (Bergenhus Fort), dating from the mid-13th century. **Håkonshallen,** a royal ceremonial hall used as early as 1261, was badly damaged by the explosion of a Dutch ship in 1944 but was restored by 1961. *Bergenhus, tel. 55/31–60–67. Admission: NKr10 adults, NKr5 children. Open May 15–Sept. 14, daily 10–4; Sept. 15–May 14, daily noon–3, also Thurs. 3–6. Closed during Bergen International Music Festival.*

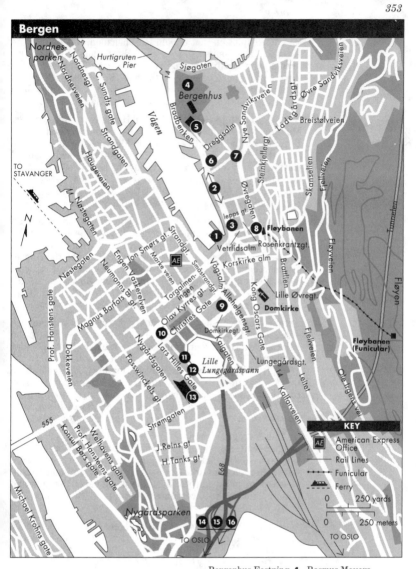

Bergen

Bergenhus Festning, **4**
Bryggen, **2**
Bryggen Museum, **6**
Fantoft Stavkirke, **15**
Fløybanen, **8**
Gamle Rådhuset, **9**
Grieghallen, **13**
Hanseatisk Museum, **3**
Lysøen, **16**
Mariakirken, **7**

Rasmus Meyers Samlinger, **12**
Rosenkrantztårnet, **5**
Stenersen Collection, **11**
Torget, **1**
Troldhaugen, **14**
Vestlandske Kunstindustri-museum, **10**

KEY

AE American Express Office
Rail Lines
Funicular
Ferry

0   250 yards
0   250 meters

❺ Nearby, **Rosenkrantztårnet** (Rosenkrantz tower), damaged in the same explosion that rocked Håkonshallen, was built in the 1560s by the Danish governor of Bergenhus, Erik Rosenkrantz, as a fortified official residence. It is furnished in the same formal, austere style as the hall. *Bergenhus, tel. 55/31–43–80. Admission: NKr10 adults, NKr5 children. Open May 15–Sept. 14, daily 10–4; Sept. 15–May 14, Sun. noon–3.*

❻ Retrace your steps to the SAS Royal Hotel. Nearby is **Bryggen Museum,** which houses artifacts found during excavations on Bryggen, including 12th-century buildings constructed on site from the original foundations. The collection provides a good picture of daily life before and during the heyday of the Hansa, down to a two-seater outhouse. *Bryggen, tel. 55/31–67–10. Admission: NKr15. Open May 1–Aug. 31, daily 10–5; Sept. 1–Apr. 30, weekdays 11–3, Sat. noon–3, Sun. noon–4.*

❼ The 12th-century **Mariakirken** (St. Mary's Church) is just up the street. Bergen's oldest building began as a Romanesque church but has gained a Gothic choir, richly decorated portals, and a splendid Baroque pulpit, much of it added by the Hanseatic merchants, who owned it from the 15th century. Organ recitals are held Tuesday and Thursday June 15 to August 26. *Dreggen, tel. 55/31–59–60. Admission: NKr10. Open May–Aug., weekdays 11–4; Sept.–Apr., Tues.–Fri. noon–1:30.*

From Øvregaten, the back boundary of Bryggen, you can look down toward the wharf along the narrow passages where the citizens of the city lived. Walk about four blocks to the popular
❽ **Fløybanen,** the funicular (a cable car that runs on tracks on the ground) to **Fløyen,** a lookout point 326 meters (1,050 feet) above the sea. Several marked trails lead from Fløyen in the surrounding wooded area, or you can walk back to town on Fjellveien. *Admission: NKr28 adults, NKr14 children; one-way tickets are half price. Rides every half hour 8 AM–11 PM.*

On Lille Øvregaten, and the area of crooked streets and hodge-podge architecture nearby, you'll find most of Bergen's antiques shops. On your left at the intersection with King Oscars Gate is Bergen **Domkirke** (the cathedral), another building constructed in a profusion of styles. The oldest parts, the choir and lower portion of the tower, date from the late 12th century. *Tel. 55/31–05–70. Open weekdays 11–2.*

❾ Walk down Domkirkegaten to Allehelgensgate, past the police station, and turn right. Across the street is **Gamle Rådhuset** (the old City Hall), built in the 16th century as the residence of the governor. The city council still meets there.

Tour 2: For Art Lovers

❿ From Torgalmeningen, walk to Nordahl Bruns Gate and turn left for the **Vestlandske Kunstindustrimuseum** (West Norway Museum of Decorative Arts). Seventeenth- and 18th-century Bergen silversmiths were renowned throughout Scandinavia for their heavy, elaborate Baroque designs. Tankards embossed with flower motifs or inlaid with coins form a rich display. The museum reopens in 1994 after major restoration. *Permanenten, Nordahl Bruns Gate 9, tel. 55/32–51–08.*

⓫ Follow Christies Gate along the park and turn left to reach the **Stenersen Collection,** which concentrates on Norwegian art since the mid-18th century but also houses an impressive collec-

tion of modern art, including works by Max Ernst, Paul Klee, Vassily Kandinsky, and Joan Miró, as well as Edvard Munch. *Rasmus Meyers allé, tel. 55/32–14–60. Admission: NKr15 adults, NKr8 children. Open May 15–Sept. 15, Mon.–Sat. 11–4, Sun. noon–3; Sept. 16–May 14, Tues.–Sun. noon–3.*

⑫ Just beyond is **Rasmus Meyers Samlinger** (collections). Meyer, a businessman who lived from 1858 to 1916, assembled a superb collection, with many names that are famous today but were unknown when he acquired them. You'll see the best Munchs outside Oslo, as well as major works by Scandinavian impressionists. The gallery also hosts summertime Grieg concerts. *Rasmus Meyers allé 7, tel. 55/97–80–00. Admission: NKr15 adults, NKr8 children. Open May 15–Sept. 15, Mon.–Sat. 11–4, Sun. noon–3; Sept. 16–May 14, Tues.–Sun., noon–3.*

⑬ Next is **Grieghallen** (the concert hall), named for the city's famous son, composer Edvard Grieg (1843–1907). Built in 1978, this home of the Bergen Philharmonic Orchestra is a conspicuous slab of glass and concrete, but the acoustics are marvelous. It is the stage for the annual International Music Festival.

Tour 3: Troldhaugen and Fantoft

Follow Route 1 (Nesttun/Voss) out of town about 5 kilometers (3 miles). Composer Edvard Grieg began his musical career under the tutelage of his mother, then went on to study music in Leipzig and Denmark, where he met his wife Nina, a Danish soprano. Even in his early compositions, his own unusual chord progressions fused with elements of Norwegian folk music.

⑭ Norway and its landscape were always an inspiration to him, and nowhere is this more clear than at his villa, **Troldhaugen** (Troll Hill) by Nordåsvannet, where he and Nina lived from about 1885. An enchanting white clapboard house, with restrained green gingerbread trim, it served as a salon and gathering place for many Scandinavian artists and brims with paintings, prints, and memorabilia. On Grieg's desk you'll see a small red troll—which, it is said, he religiously bade good night before he went to sleep. The house also contains his Steinway piano, which is still used for special concerts. Behind the grounds, at the edge of the fjord, you'll find a sheer rock face that was blasted open to provide a burial place for the couple. In 1985 **Troldsalen** (Troll Hall), which can seat 200 people, was built for concerts. *Tel. 55/91–17–91. Admission: NKr15 adults, NKr8 children. Open May 2–Oct. 1, daily 9:30–5:30.*

⑮ On the return trip, visit **Fantoft Stavkirke** (Fantoft Stave Church), which was completely rebuilt after a fire in 1992. It was originally built in the early 12th century in Sognefjord but was later moved to its present site. Stave churches are unique to Norway, a sort of first step, spiritually and architecturally, into Christianity, without complete relinquishment of pagan beliefs. They also parallel Viking ships, as they are built of strips of wood laid edge to edge rather than in log-cabin style. Peaked with what appears to be Oriental decoration, the Fantoft church is pure black, the result of ancient pitch waterproofing. You'll also see a hole at one end of the church that was used by lepers, who watched the service from outside. *Paradis, tel. 55/28–07–10. Admission: NKr10. Open May 15–Sept. 15, daily 10:30–1:30 and 2:20–5:30.*

Tour 4: Lysøen

Ole Bull, not as well known as some of Norway's other cultural luminaries, was a virtuoso violinist and patron of visionary dimension. In 1850, after failing to establish a "New Norwegian Theater" in America, he founded the National Theater in Norway. He then chose the young, unknown playwright Henrik Ibsen to write full-time for the theater and later encouraged and promoted another neophyte—15-year-old Edvard Grieg.

16 Getting to his villa, **Lysøen,** is a trek, but it's worth the effort. Take Route 1 or Route 553 to Fana, over Fanafjell to Sørestraumen. Follow signs to Buena Kai. The ferry, *Ole Bull,* leaves on the hour (Mon.–Sat. noon–3 and Sun. 11–4; last ferry leaves Lysøen Mon.–Sat. 4, Sun. 5; return fare is NKr30 adults, NKr15 children).

This Victorian dream castle, built in 1873, complete with an onion dome, gingerbread gables, curved staircase, and cutwork trim just about everywhere, has to be seen to be believed. Inside, the music room is a frenzy of filigree carving, fretwork, braided and twisted columns, and gables with intricate openwork in the supports, all done in knotty pine. Bull's descendants donated the house to the national preservation trust in 1973. *Tel. 56/30–90–77. Admission: NKr20 adults, NKr5 children. Open May 19–Aug. 29, Mon.–Sat. noon–4, Sun. 11–5.*

What to See and Do with Children

Akvariet (the Aquarium) has 50 tanks with a wide variety of fish, but the main attractions are penguins—several kinds, one of which has a platinum feather "hairdo," strangely appropriate in this land of blonds. There are also several seals. It's on Nordnes Peninsula, a 15-minute walk from downtown, or take bus No. 4. *Nordnes, tel. 55/32–04–52. Admission: Nkr30 adults, Nkr15 children. Open May–Sept., daily 9–8; Oct.–Apr., daily 10–6. Feeding times: 11, 2, and 6.*

Off the Beaten Track

Drum and crossbow drill teams are unique to Bergen. **Buekorpsmuseet** (the Crossbow Drill Corps Museum) is at "Muren," built in 1562. The exhibits include medals, banners, drums, and pictures. *Wall Gate. Admission free. Consult the tourist office for opening times, which vary.*

Shopping

Sundt City (Torgalmenningen 14, tel. 56/38–80–20) and **Kløverhuset** (Strandkaien 10, tel. 55/32–17–20) are traditional **department stores** with a wide selection of Norwegian sweaters and gifts. **Galleriet,** on Torgalmenningen, and **Bystasjonen,** by the bus terminal, are downtown **malls** with small shops. Shops specializing in Norwegian **crafts** are either near Torgalmenningen, on Bryggen, or just behind it. **Antiques** shops are concentrated in the area around Fløybanen.

Sports and Fitness

Below is a sampling of activities for the Bergen area, but outdoors lovers should be aware that the city is within easy reach

MCI brings Europe and America closer together.

Call the U.S. for less with MCI CALL USA®

It's easy and affordable to call home when you use MCI CALL USA!

- Less expensive than calling through hotel operators
- Available from over 80 countries and locations worldwide
- You're connected to English-speaking MCI® Operators
- Even call 800 numbers in the U.S.†

†Regular MCI CALL USA rates apply to 800 number calls.

Call the U.S. for less from these European locations.

Dial the toll-free access number for the country you're calling from. Give the U.S. MCI Operator the number you're calling and the method of payment: MCI Card, U.S. local phone company card or collect. Your call will be completed!

Austria	022-903-012	Hungary	00*-800-01411	Poland	0*-01-04-800-222
Belgium	078-11-00-12	Ireland	1-800-551-001	Portugal	05-017-1234
Czech/Slovak	00-42-000112	Italy	172-1022	San Marino	172-1022
Denmark	8001-0022	Liechtenstein	155-0222	Spain	900-99-0014
Finland	9800-102-80	Luxembourg	0800-0112	Sweden	020-795-922
France	19*-00-19	Monaco	19*-00-19	Switzerland	155-0222
Germany	0130-0012	Netherlands	06*-022-91-22	United Kingdom	0800-89-0222
Greece	00-800-1211	Norway	050-12912	Vatican City	172-1022

* Wait for 2nd dial tone.
Collect calls not accepted on MCI CALL USA calls to 800 numbers.
Some public phones may require deposit of coin or phone card for dial tone.

MCI®

Call 1-800-444-3333 in the U.S. to apply for your MCI Card® now!

Spend your
vacation
touring
castles.
Not train
stations.

Vacation Cars. Vacation Prices. Wherever your destination in Europe, there is sure to be one of more than 1,000 Budget locations nearby. Budget offers considerable values on a wide variety of quality cars, and if you book before you leave the U.S., you'll save even more with a special rate package from the Budget World Travel Plan.℠ For information and reservations, contact your travel consultant or call Budget in the U.S. at **800-472-3325.** Or, while traveling abroad, call a Budget reservation center.

THE SMART MONEY IS ON BUDGET.

We feature Ford and other fine cars.   *A system of corporate and licensee owned locations.*

of the Hardangervidda, the country's great plateau, which offers limitless outdoor possibilities (*see* Sports and Outdoor Activities in Mountains and Valleys of the Interior, *below*).

Fishing The **Bergen Angling Association** (Fosswinckelsgt. 37, tel. 55/32–11–64, closed July) can provide tips and information on permits. Among the many charters in the area, the *Fiskestrilen* (tel. 56/33–75–00 or 56/33–87–40) offers evening fishing tours from Glesvaer on the island of Sotra, about an hour's drive from Bergen, where you can catch coal fish, cod, mackerel, or haddock. On the sail home, they'll cook part of the catch.

Golf There is a nine-hole golf course at Åstveit (tel. 55/18–20–77), 15 minutes north of the city on E16. Or you can take the Åsane bus from the bus station.

Hiking Take the funicular up **Fløyen,** and minutes later you'll be in the midst of a forest. For a simple map of the mountain, ask at the tourist information office for the cartoon **"Gledeskartet"** map, which outlines 1.5- to 5-kilometer (1- to 3-mile) hikes. **Mount Ulriken** is also popular with walkers and can be best reached near the Montana Youth Hostel (Bus 4). Maps of the many walking-tour opportunities around Bergen are available from bookstores and from **Bergens Turlag** (touring club; Tverrgata 2–4, 5017-Bergen, tel. 55/32-22-30), which arranges hikes and maintains cabins for hikers.

The archipelago to the west of Bergen also offers many hiking options, ranging from the simple path between Morland and Fjell to the more rugged mountain climb at Haganes. For details, contact the Sund Cultural Office (tel. 56/33–75–00).

Skiing When there is snow on the ground, you can take the funicular up to the mountains for nearby cross-country skiing. Otherwise, Bergen is close to the major skiing center of Voss (*see* Sports under Central Fjord Country, *below*).

Yachting The **Bergen Yachting Club** (55/22–65–45) has its harbor at Hjellestad, about a half-hour bus ride from the city bus station. If you want to do more than ogle the boats, however, the 100-year-old Hardanger yacht, *Mathilde* (Stiftinga Hardangerjekt, Box 46, N–5601 Nordheimsund, tel. 56/55–22–77), with the world's largest authentic yacht rigging, does both one- and several-day trips, as well as coastal safaris.

Dining

Among the most characteristic of Bergen dishes is a fresh, perfectly poached, whole salmon, served with new potatoes and parsley-butter sauce. Then again, stroll among the stalls at Fisketorvet (the fish market), and you can munch bagsful of pink shrimp, heart-shaped fish cakes, and round buns topped with salmon—a typical Bergen repast, without the typical bill. Top it off with another local specialty, a *skillingsbolle*, a big cinnamon roll, sometimes with a custard center, but most authentic without.

Very Expensive **Bellevue.** Established in 1899, this restaurant is on a hill overlooking the city; it has an elegant and formal dining room, with 18th-century-style furnishings. Poached salmon in the traditional manner is a specialty, along with fillet of venison with chanterelle mushrooms, but more modern dishes are also on the menu. There's a limited choice at lunch. In good weather

the patio is open for less formal meals. *Bellevuebakken 9, tel. 55/31–02–40. Reservations required. Jacket and tie required. AE, DC, MC, V. Closed weekends.*

Lucullus. Although the decor seems a bit out of kilter—modern art matched with lace doilies and boardroom chairs—the food in this restaurant is always good. Sautéed monkfish with lobster sauce and rack of reindeer with blueberry sauce are two of many superb dishes. *Hotel Neptun, Walckendorfsgt. 8, tel. 55/90–10–00. Reservations required. Jacket and tie required. AE, DC, MC, V. No lunch. Closed Sun.*

Expensive **Fiskekrogen.** It's right on Fisketorvet, and in good weather you can sit outside for lunch. The fish soup is a meal in itself, and the appetizer plate is a sampling of specialties, from smoked shrimp to marinated moose. The fish symphony features two or three kinds of fish with lobster sauce and a garnish of shellfish. Meat lovers should try the grilled moose or venison rib-eye steak with herb butter. *Zachariasbryggen, Fisketorvet, tel. 55/31–75–66. Reservations required. Dress: casual. AE, DC, MC, V. No lunch Sept. 16–Apr.*

To Kokker. The name means "two cooks," and that's what there are. It's on Bryggen, in a 300-year-old building complete with crooked floors. Try the roasted reindeer or the marinated salmon. Desserts feature local fruit. *Enhjørningsgården, tel. 55/32–28–16. Reservations required. Dress: casual but neat. AE, DC, MC, V. No lunch. Closed Sun.*

Moderate **Bryggestuen & Bryggeloftet.** It's always full, upstairs and down. The menu's the same in both places, but only the first floor is authentically old. Poached halibut served with boiled potatoes and cucumber salad, a traditional favorite, is the specialty, but there's also sautéed ocean catfish with mushrooms and shrimp, and grilled lamb fillet. *Bryggen 11, tel. 55/31–06–30. Reservations advised. Dress: casual. AE, DC, MC, V.*

Munkestuen Café. With its five tables and red-and-white-check tablecloths this mom-and-pop place looks more Italian than Norwegian, but locals regard it as a hometown legend—make reservations as soon as you get into town. Try the monkfish with hollandaise sauce or the fillet of roe deer with morels. *Klostergaten 12, tel. 55/90–21–49. Reservations required. Dress: casual. AE, DC, MC, V. Closed Sat. and 3 weeks in July. No lunch.*

Inexpensive **Augusta** and **Augustus.** You can't beat these two cafeterias under the same management for lunch or for cake and coffee in the afternoon. Vegetarians will be impressed by the number of salads and quiches, in addition to pâté and open-face sandwiches. *Augusta: C. Sundtsgt. 24, tel. 55/23–00–25. No reservations. Dress: casual. Augustus: Galleriet, tel. 55/32–35–25. No reservations. Dress: casual. No credit cards.*

Banco Rotto. The fanciest café in town used to be a bank, and appropriately for Norway—a country where a cocktail costs a fortune—the liquor is still kept in the safe. Depending upon the time of day, it changes its identity from café to restaurant to piano bar; it functions best at either end—as a lunch café in the afternoon and as an evening spot with music and dancing on Friday and Saturday nights. *Vågsalmenning 16, tel. 55/32–75–20. No reservations. Dress: casual. AE, DC, MC, V.*

Børskafe. What began as a beer hall in 1894 is now more of a pub, with hearty homemade food at reasonable prices. The corned beef with potato dumplings is served only on Thursday

and Friday, while meat cakes with stewed peas and fried flounder plus the usual open-face sandwiches are always on the
menu. *Strandgt. 15, tel. 55/32–47–19. No reservations. Dress:
casual. No credit cards.*

Lodging

From June 20 through August 10, special summer double-room
rates are available in 21 Bergen hotels; rooms can only be reserved 48 hours in advance. In the winter, weekend specials
are often a fraction of the weekday rates, which are geared for
business travelers. All rates include breakfast. The tourist information office will assist in finding accommodations in hotels,
guest houses, or private houses.

Moderate–Very Expensive

Hotel Admiral. This dockside warehouse from 1906, right on
the water across Vågen from Bryggen, was converted into a hotel in 1987. The building is geometric Art Nouveau, and although the small rooms are ordinary, the larger rooms
overlooking the harbor have some of the best nighttime views
in town. The harborside restaurant, Emily, has a small but
good buffet table. *C. Sundts Gate 9–13, 5004, tel. 55/32–47–30,
fax 55/23–30–92. 95 rooms with bath or shower, 12 suites. Facilities: restaurant, bar. AE, DC, MC, V.*

Hotel Norge. Other hotels come and go, but the Norge stays.
It's a traditional luxury hotel in the center of town, right by the
park. The architecture is standard modern, with large rooms.
*Ole Bulls pl. 4, 5012, tel. 55/21–01–00, fax 55/21–02–99. 348
rooms with bath, 12 suites. Facilities: 4 restaurants, 2 bars,
nightclub, pool, fitness center, conference center, shops. AE,
DC, MC, V.*

SAS Royal Hotel Bryggen. The hotel is behind the famous buildings at Bryggen, one story taller, with the same width and roof
pitch, and very well designed. Finished in 1982, the smallish
guest rooms, with their subdued woven spreads and dark wood
beds, are beginning to look dated. More expensive rooms, on
the top floor, have been refurbished. *Bryggen, 5003, tel. 55/54–
30–00, fax 55/32–48–08. 267 rooms with bath, 7 suites. Facilities: 2 restaurants, 2 bars, nightclub, pool, fitness center, conference center. AE, DC, MC, V.*

Inexpensive–Moderate

Augustin Hotel. This small, family-run hotel, one block from
the harbor, is just off the main pedestrian shopping street. The
rooms are small but newly refurbished, and some overlook the
harbor. The first-floor bistro offers simple meals, and the coffee shop, Augusta (*see* Dining, *above*), serves wonderful cakes.
*C. Sundtsgate 24, 5004, tel. 55/23–00–25, fax 55/23–31–30. 38
rooms with shower. Facilities: 2 restaurants, conference room.
AE, DC, MC, V.*

Hotell Dreggen. Restored in 1990, this hotel is between
Bergenshus Fortress and Bryggen Museum. It's basically a
bed-and-breakfast, but other meals can be arranged. Virtually
every room is a different size or shape, but all are furnished in
light wood and pale-colored textiles. *Sandbrugt. 3, 5003, tel.
55/31–61–55, fax 55/31–54–23. 21 rooms with bath. Facilities:
restaurant, bar, conference room. AE, DC, MC, V.*

Hotel Park Pension. Near the university, this small family-run
hotel is in a well-kept Victorian building. Both the public rooms
and the guest rooms are furnished with antiques. It's a 10-min-
ute walk from downtown. *Harald Hårfagres Gate 35, 5000, tel.*

55/32–09–60, fax 55/31–03–34. 21 rooms with bath. Facilities: breakfast room, conference room. AE, V.

Inexpensive **Fantoft Sommerhotell.** This student dorm, 6 kilometers (3½ miles) from downtown, becomes a hotel from May 20 to August 20. Family rooms are available. Accommodation is simple but adequate. Take a bus from gate No. 18, 19, or 20 to Fantoft. *5036 Fantoft, tel. 55/27–60–10, fax 55/27–60–30. 72 rooms with shower. Facilities: restaurant. AE, DC, MC, V.*

The Arts and Nightlife

The Arts Bergen is known for its **Festspillene** (International Music Festival), held each year during the last week of May and the beginning of June. It features famous names in classical music, jazz, ballet, the arts, and theater. Tickets are available from the Festival Office at **Grieghallen** (Lars Hillesgt. 3, 5015, tel. 55/31–09–54).

During the summer, twice a week, the **Bjorgvin folk dance group** performs a one-hour program of traditional dances and music from rural Norway at Bryggens Museum. Tickets are sold at the tourist information center and at the door. *Bryggen, tel. 55/24–89–29. Cost: NKr70. Performances June 8–mid-Aug., Tues. and Thurs. 8:30.*

A more extensive program, **Fana Folklore,** is offered in an evening of folklore, with traditional wedding food, dances, and folk music, plus a concert, at the 800-year-old Fana Church. *A/S Kunst (the Art Association) Torgalmenning 9, tel. 55/91–52–40. Admission: NKr160 (includes dinner). June 5–Aug. 31., Mon., Tues., Thurs., and Fri.*

Concerts are held at **Troldhaugen,** home of composer Edvard Grieg (*see* Tour 3, *above*), all summer. Tickets are sold at the tourist information center or at the door. Performances are given June 26–August 29, Wednesday and Sunday at 7:30; and September 1–October 15, Sunday at 1.

Nightlife Most nightlife centers around the harbor area. **Zachariasbryggen** is a restaurant and entertainment complex right on the water. **Kjøbmandsstuen** is a piano bar with a crowd on weekends. **Engelen** (The Angel) at the SAS Royal Hotel attracts a mixed weekend crowd when it blasts hip-hop, funk, and rock. The **Hotel Norge** piano bar and disco are more low-key, with an older crowd. **Dickens** (8–10 Ole Bulls Plads, tel. 55/90–07–60), across from the Hotel Norge, is a relaxed meeting place for an afternoon or evening drink. **Maxime** (tel. 55/90–07–70) is a packed weekend disco, currently fashionable with the ripped-jean crowd. The complete opposite, **Wessel Stuen**, also on Ole Bull Plads (tel. 55/90–08–20) is a cozy place where you'll find students and the local intelligentsia. **Holbergstuen** (Torgalm. 6, tel. 55/31–80–15) is similar but often attracts a crowd of local sages who hold court.

Bergensers love jazz, and **Bergen Jazz Festival** (Georgernes Verft 3, N–5011 Bergen, tel. 55/32–09–76) is held here during the third week of August. During the winter, **Bergen Jazz Forum** (same address) is *the* place, but it's closed for much of the summer. For rock, **Hulen** (The Cave; Olav Ryesvei 47, tel. 55/32–32–87) has live music on weekends.

Bergen has an active gay community with clubs and planned events. **Homofil Bevegelse** (Gay Movement, Nygårdsgt. 2A, tel. 55/31–21–39) is open Sunday 2–8 PM. **Café Finken** (same address, tel. 55/31–21–39) is open daily until 1 AM.

Mountains and Valleys of the Interior

The central portion of Norway lies in the shadow of the famed fjords but doesn't lack majestic scenery. A land of wide-open vistas and deep forests, it's veined with swift-flowing streams and scattered with peaceful lakes—a natural setting so powerful and silent that a few generations ago, trolls were the only reasonable explanation for what lurked in, or for that matter plodded through, the shadows. These legendary creatures, serious Norwegians explain, boast several heads, a couple of noses (used to stir their porridge of course), and can grow to the size of a village. Fortunately for humans, however, they turn to stone in sunlight.

The tourist board aptly calls the triangle between Oppland and Hedmark counties, south to Lillehammer (and including Peer Gynt country, in Jotunheimen), Troll Park. The otherworldly quality of oblique northern light against wildflower-covered hills has inspired centuries of folk tales, and artists from Wagner to Ibsen, who was awarded a government grant to scour the land for these very stories. Even today, locals claim he applied for the grant just to have the opportunity to hike the hills.

The southern part of the interior, around Hardangervidda, is prime vacation land for wilderness sports lovers, with fishing, canoeing, rafting, hiking, and horseback riding over the plateau in the summer, and skiing, particularly on the slopes of Geilo, in winter. Northward, the land turns to rolling hills and leafy forests, and the principal town, Lillehammer, attracts skiers from around the world to its slopes and trails; in 1994 it hosts the Winter Olympics. At the northern end of the region is the copper-mining town of Røros, which is on UNESCO's World Heritage List—a bucolic little town that's changed little over the past 100 years.

Important Addresses and Numbers

Tourist Information The main tourist offices of the region are in **Geilo** (tel. 62/98–63–00); **Hamar** (Vikingskipet, Olympia Hall, tel. 62/51–02–17 or 62/51–02–25); **Kongsberg** (Storgt. 35, tel. 32/73–50–00); **Lillehammer** (Lilletorget, tel. 61/25–92–99); **Lom** (tel. 61/21–12–86); **Notodden** (tel. 35/01–20–22); **Øyer** (tel. 61/27–79–50); **Rjukan** (Torget 2, tel. 35/09–12–90); **Røros** (Bergmannspl., tel. 72/49–17–22); and **Skien** (Reiselivets Hus, N. Hjellegt. 18, tel. 35/53–49–80).

Arriving and Departing by Car, Train, and Bus

By Car On Route E18 from Oslo, the drive southeast to Kongsberg (84 kilometers/52 miles) takes a little more than an hour. The wide, two-lane Route E6 north from Oslo passes through Hamar and Lillehammer. Route 3 follows Østerdalen (the eastern valley)

from Oslo. Route 30 at Tynset leads to Røros and E6 on to Trondheim, 156 kilometers (97 miles) farther north.

By Train The train from Oslo S to Kongsberg takes 1 hour and 25 minutes. There are good train connections between Oslo and the major interior towns to the north.

By Bus The many bus lines that serve the region are coordinated through Nor-Way Bussekspress in Oslo (Bussterminalen, Galleri Oslo, tel. 22/17–52–90, fax 22/17–59–22).

Getting Around

By Car Roads in the southern part of the interior region are open and flat, while those to the north become increasingly hilly and twisty as the terrain roughens into the central mountains. E18 and Routes 11 and 7 are the chief routes of the south; the northern end of the region is threaded by E16, E6, and Routes 51 and 3. Don't exceed the speed limit: Particularly in the area of Vinstra and Otta, you'll see high-tech markers at the roadside that are actually cameras. Exceed the speed limit and you'll receive a ticket in the mail.

By Train The only train service in the southern part of the region is the Oslo–Stavanger line (via Kristiansand). The midregion is served by the Oslo–Bergen line, which is as much an attraction as a means of transportation. The northern part is served by the Oslo–Trondheim line and two other lines.

By Bus Buses in the region rarely run more than twice a day, so get a comprehensive schedule from the tourist office or Nor-Way Bussekspress and plan ahead. There are good bus connections between Kongsberg and Notodden, Heddal, and Rjukan.

Exploring Mountains and Valleys of the Interior

Numbers in the margin correspond to points of interest on the Mountains and Valleys of the Interior map.

Tour 1: Central Norway

The center of Norway is outdoor country for Norwegians and northern Europeans, who come to ski, hike, dogsled and, in recent years, river raft.

❶ **Geilo,** population 2,700, is dead-center between Bergen and Oslo. The country's most popular winter resort, it often draws more than a million visitors a year to its alpine slopes and cross-country trails; many people ski directly from their hotels and cabins. Recently Geilo has become a popular summer destination, with fishing, boating, hiking, and riding—although, admittedly, it still looks like a winter resort minus the snow. Plan ahead if you plan to visit at Easter, when Norwegians flock there for a final ski weekend.

❷ Geilo is the gateway to **Hardangervidda,** Europe's largest mountain plateau and Norway's biggest national park—10,000 square kilometers of unique scenery, with the largest herd of wild reindeer in Europe, and home to many birds and animals on the endangered list. It also has rich and varied flora, about 450 different species. Touring the plateau, either on horseback or on foot, you can find a trail for any level of proficiency, and

Mountains and Valleys of the Interior

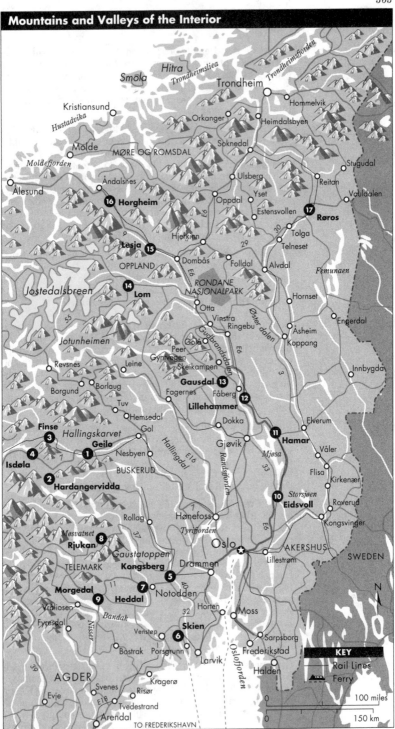

Smola
Hitra
Trondheimslia
Trondheim
Trondheimsfjorden
Kristiansund
Hommelvik
Hustadvika
Orkanger
Heimdalsbyen
Molde
Søknedal
MØRE OG ROMSDAL
Moldefjorden
Ulsberg
Stugudal
Ålesund
Åndalsnes
Oppdal
Yset
Reitan
Vauldalen
16 **Horgheim**
Hjerkinn
Estensvollen
17 **Røros**
Lesja **15**
Dombås
Folldal
Tolga
Telneset
OPPLAND
Rondane
Nasjonalpark
Alvdal
Femunaen
14 **Lom**
Otta
Hornset
Jostedalsbreen
Vinstra
Ringebu
Åsheim
Engerdal
Peer
Gola
Koppang
Jotunheimen
Gyntvegen
Skeikampen
Innbygda
Revsnes
Leine
Gausdal **13**
Fagernes
Fåberg
12
Borlaug
Tuv
Lillehammer
Elverum
Borgund
Hemsedal
Dokka
3 Finse
Hallingskarvet
Gol
Gjøvik
Mjøsa
11 **Hamar**
1 **Geilo**
Nesbyen
Våler
4
BUSKERUD
Flisa
Isdøla
Hallingdal
Kirkenær
2
Rollag
Hønefoss
Roverud
Hardangervidda
10
Storsjøen
Kongsvinger
Randsfjorden
Eidsvoll
Møsvatnet
Tyrifjorden
8
Oslo
AKERSHUS
Rjukan
Gaustatoppen
Lillestrøm
SWEDEN
TELEMARK
Kongsberg
Drammen
5
7 **Heddal**
Notodden
Morgedal
9
Horten
Moss
Bandak
Skien
6 Sarpsborg
Vråliosen
Venstøp
Larvik
Frederikstad
Fyresdal
Nisser
Bøstrak
Porsgrunn
Halden
AGDER
Kragerø
Evje
Svenes
Risør
E18
Tvedestrand
Arendal

TO FREDERIKSHAVN

KEY
Rail Lines
Ferry

100 miles
150 km

N

along the trails, the Norwegian Touring Association (DNT) has built cabins.

❸ The western settlement of **Finse** (on the Bergen railroad) is one of the most frigid places in southern Norway, with snow on the ground as late as August. Here polar explorers Nansen and Scott tested their equipment and the snow scenes in the *Star Wars* movies were filmed. It, too, is a good starting point for tours of Hardangervidda.

At the western end of the vidda, 72 kilometers (44 miles) beyond Geilo, is **Isdøla,** at the junction of the 1-kilometer (0.62 miles, but it seems like 10) road to Fossli and Vøringfossen (Vøring Falls), which has a 141-meter (464-foot) vertical drop. The road down to the valley of Måbødalen was blasted into the mountain early in the century; it has been improved steadily, and now most of the difficult parts are tunneled. Cyclists and hikers can go down the side of the mountain to the base of the falls on the original trail, with 124 swings and 1,300 steps—it takes about 30 minutes—but it's not for amateurs.

At the base is the innermost arm of the **Hardangerfjord.** Although it's not as dramatic as some of the other fjords, it is pastoral, with royal-blue water and lush apple orchards.

Tour 2: Historic Kongsberg and Telemark

Kongsberg, Norway's first industrial town, rose to prominence because of the discovery there of silver in its purest form. The town of Rjukan was the site of the country's entrance into modern technology, with hydroelectric power. Telemark is the birthplace of skiing as we know it today, as well as the birthplace of many ancestors to Norwegian-Americans, for the poor farmers of the region were among the first to emigrate to the United States during the 19th century.

❺ **Kongsberg,** with 20,000 people, was Norway's silver town for more than 300 years. King Christian IV saw the town's natural potential when he discovered that a cow's horn had rubbed moss off a stone—to expose silver. Thereupon, the Danish builder king began construction of the town. The mines are now closed, but the Royal Mint is still going strong.

Norsk Bergverksmuseum (Norwegian Mining Museum), in the old smelting works, documents the development of silver mining and exhibits the pure silver along with gold, emeralds, and rubies from other Norwegian mines. The Royal Mint Museum, in the same building, is a treasure trove for coin collectors, with a nearly complete assemblage of Norwegian coins. Children can pan for silver all summer. *Hyttegt. 3, tel. 32/73–12–75. Admission: NKr25 adults, NKr15 children, NKr20 senior citizens. Open May 18–June 30, Aug. 16–31, daily 10–4; July 1–Aug. 15, weekdays 10–6, weekends 10–4; Sept. 1–30, daily noon–4; Oct. 1–May 17, Sun. noon–4. Guided tours of Underberget, with dinner: NKr220. Only for those 16 and older. Open July–mid-Aug. Tues.–Thurs. at 5.*

Gruvene (the Mines) are 8 kilometers (5 miles) outside town, toward Notodden. Guided mine tours include a 2.3-kilometer (1.4-mile) ride on the mine train into Kongensgruve (the King's mine) and a ride on the first personnel elevator. The temperature in the mine is about 7°C (43°F), so dress accordingly. *Tel. 35/02–02–50. Admission: NKr40 adults, NKr20 children, NKr30*

*senior citizens. Tours June–Aug. 15, daily 11, 12:30, 2 and
3:30; May 18–31 and Aug. 16–31, daily 11, 12:30, 2; Sept.,
Sun. 2.*

Kongsberg Kirke (Kongsberg Church), finished in 1761, was
built during the heyday of the silver mines, with an impressive
gilded Baroque altar, organ, and pulpit all on one wall. It seats
3,000. The royal box and the galleries separated the gentry and
mineowners from the workers. *Admission: NKr10 adults,
NKr5, children. Open May 18–Aug. 31, guided tours lasting 45
min. on the hour, weekdays 10–12, Sat. 10–1. Sun. services at
11 with tours afterward until 1:30. Organ concerts Tues. and
Fri. at 11 during July.*

Time Out | **Peckels Resept** (Peckels gt. 12), in the center of town, is a café
with personality. It serves sandwiches and hot dishes, along
with delicious cakes for lunch.

❻ South of Kongsberg on Routes 40 and 32 is **Skien,** the capital of
the Telemark region. This town of 48,000 is best known as the
birthplace of playwright Henrik Ibsen. **Fylkesmuseet** (the
county museum), a manor house from 1780, has a collection of
Ibsen memorabilia, including his study and bedroom and the
"blue salon" from his Oslo flat (other interiors are at the Norsk
Folkemuseum in Oslo). The museum also has a display of Telemark-style folk art, including rose painting and wood carving.
*Øvregt. 41, tel. 35/52–35–94. Admission: NKr15 adults, NKr10
children. Garden open mid-May–Sept., daily 10–8. Museum
open mid-May–Sept., daily 10–6.*

Venstøp, 5 kilometers (3 miles) northwest of the city, looks just
as it did when the Ibsen family lived there from 1835 to 1843.
The attic was a setting in *The Wild Duck.* The house is part of
Skien's county museum. *Tel. 35/52–35–94. Admission: NKr15
adults, NKr10 children. Open mid-May–Sept., daily 10–6.*

❼ **Heddal,** site of Norway's largest stave church, is 35 kilometers
(20 miles) west of Kongsberg. The church dates from the middle of the 13th century and has exceptional animal-style ornament, along with grotesque human heads, on the portals. *Tel.
33/02–02–50. Admission: NKr15. Open June 21–Aug. 20,
Mon.–Sat. 9–7, Sun. 1–7; May 15–June 20, Aug. 21–Sept. 20,
9–7, Sun. 1–5. Sun. services at 11. July 1–Aug. 10, organ concerts Tues. and Fri. at 11.*

Route 37 northwest from Kongsberg to Rjukan passes the
1,922-meter (6,200-foot) **Gaustatoppen,** a looming, snow-
❽ streaked table of rock popular with hikers. The town of **Rjukan**
may not ring a bell, but mention "heavy water," and anyone
who lived through World War II or saw the film *The Heroes of
Telemark* knows about the sabotage of the "heavy water" factory there, which thwarted German efforts to develop an atomic
bomb. Heavy water was produced as a by-product in the manufacture of fertilizer at **Vemork,** 6 kilometers (4 miles) west of
town, where a museum has been built. Exhibits document both
the development of hydroelectric power and the World War II
events. The first Saturday in July, the work of the saboteurs is
commemorated, but their 8-kilometer (5-mile) path, starting at
Rjukan Fjellstue (mountain lodge) and finishing at the museum, is marked and can be followed at any time. *Industri-
arbeidermuseet Vemork, tel. 35/06–51–53. Admission: NKr35
adults, NKr20 children. Open June 15–Aug. 15, daily 10–6;*

May 1–June 14, daily 10–4; Aug. 15–Sept. 30, weekdays 10–4, weekends 10–6; Oct. 1–31, weekends 11–4.

Rjukan's history actually began in the decade between 1907 and 1916, when the population grew from a few hundred to 10,000 because of a different kind of water, hydroelectric power. Norsk Hydro, one of Norway's largest industries, which uses hydroelectric power to manufacture chemicals and fertilizer, was started here. It is also the site of northern Europe's first cable car, **Krossobanen,** built in 1928 by Hydro to transport people to the top of the mountain, where the sun shone year-round. *Admission: NKr20 adults, one-way, NKr10 children, NKr15 senior citizens. Open June 30–Aug. 25, daily 10–7; May 1–June 30 and Aug. 26–Sept. 30, daily 10–5; Oct. 1–Apr. 1, Fri.–Sun. 10–4.*

❾ Farther into the heart of Telemark is **Morgedal,** the birthplace of modern skiing, thanks to a persistent Sondre Nordheim, who, in the 19th century, attached boards to his boots and practiced jumping from his roof. In 1868, after revamping his skis and bindings, he took off for a 185-kilometer (115-mile) trek to Oslo just to prove it could be done. A hundred years ago, skiers used one long pole, held diagonally, much like high wire artists. Eventually the use of two short poles became widespread, although purists feel that the one-pole version is the "authentic" way to ski. Traditional Telemark skiing is now the rage in Norway, though the trend was begun in the United States.

The **Bjaaland Museum** in Morgedal is named for Olav Bjaaland, who was chosen for Amundsen's expedition to Antarctica because he could ski in an absolutely straight line. The museum collections illustrate the development of Telemark skiing. Also on display are Bjaaland's streamlined polar sled and his photographs of the expedition. *Opposite Morgedal Turisthotell, tel. 036/54–156. Admission: NKr10 adults, NKr5 children. Open June–Aug., daily 10–5.*

Tour 3: Gudbrandsdal

The Gudbrandsdal (Gudbrand's valley) is one of Norway's longest, extending from Lake Mjøsa, north of Oslo, diagonally across the country to Åndalsnes. At the base of the lake is **❿** **Eidsvoll,** where Norway's constitution was signed on May 17, 1814. Most visitors come to the region for the beautiful scenery and the outdoor activities.

⓫ E6 follows the lake halfway to **Hamar.** During the Middle Ages, Hamar was the seat of a bishopric, and part of the cathedral wall, with four Romanesque arches, remains the symbol of the city. Oslo University has sponsored digs around the cathedral precinct just outside town that have turned up thousands of artifacts, which are displayed nearby at **Hedmarkmuseet og Domkirkeodden** (the Hedmark Museum and Cathedral ruins). *Hedmarkmuseet and Domkirkeodden, tel. 62/53–11–63. Admission: NKr30 adults, NKr10 children. Open June 15–Aug. 18, daily 10–6; May 20–June 14, Aug. 19–Sept. 8, daily 10–4. Utvandrermuseum, tel. 62/52–13–04. Open weekdays 8:30–3:30.*

⓬ The winter-sport center of **Lillehammer,** with 23,000 inhabitants, is next. As host for the 1994 Winter Olympics, the small town has built a massive arena blown out of the interior of a

mountain and the world's largest indoor ice rink—designed to look like an upside-down Viking ship—in addition to other venues and accommodations. However, long-term efficiency and planning are keeping expansion surprisingly minimal—ensuring that the town will not be left in Olympic obsolescence. After the games, many of the buildings for the foreign media will be turned over to the local university, and one-third of the athletes' quarters will be transported to Tromsø to be used as housing. Extra beds for 7,000 visitors are located in private accommodations, and transportation to and from Oslo, where many visitors are staying is being increased (cars are not being allowed in Lillehammer). If you plan to attend, make your reservations as early as possible.

The **Lillehammer Olympic Information Center** outlines preparations for the big event through videos and exhibits that also describe Norway's place in international, especially winter, sports. There's a boutique with Olympic clothing and souvenirs, and a cafeteria. *Lillehammer Olympiske Informasjonssenter. Elevgt. 19, tel. 61/27–19–00, fax 61/27–19–50. Admission free. Open Mon.–Sat. 10–8, Sun. 12–8.*

Kulturhuset Banken (the Old Bank), a magnificent, century-old building, is the main venue for cultural events during the Olympics (and later on). It is decorated with both contemporary and turn-of-the-century art. Check out the murals on the ceiling of the ceremonial hall. *Kirkegt. 41, tel. 61/26–68–10. Tours by prior arrangement. Café open weekdays 10–9, Sun. 1–9.*

The new **Olympiaparken** (Olympic Park) includes the Lysgårds-bakkene ski jumping arena, where the Winter Olympics' opening and closing ceremonies are held. From the tower you can see the entire town. Also in the park are **Håkon Hallen,** used for ice hockey, and the **Birkebeineren Stadion** (ski stadium), which holds cross-country and biathlon events.

A highlight of Lillehammer's ski year is the Birkebeiner cross-country ski race, which commemorates the trek of two warriors, whose legs were wrapped in birchbark (hence *birkebeiner*—birch legs), across the mountains from Lillehammer to Østerdalen in 1205 carrying the 18-month-old prince Håkon Håkonsson away from his enemies. The race attracts 6,000 entrants annually. Cartoon figures of Viking children representing Håkon on skis and his aunt Kristin (on ice skates) have been created as official mascots for the games.

Lillehammer claims fame as a cultural center as well. Sigrid Undset, who won the Nobel Prize in literature, lived in the town for 30 years. It is also the site of **Maihaugen,** Norway's oldest (and, according to some, Scandinavia's largest) open-air museum, founded in 1887. The massive collection was begun by Anders Sandvik, an itinerant dentist who accepted folksy odds and ends—and eventually entire buildings—from the people of Gudbrandsdalen in exchange for repairing their teeth. Eventually Sandvik turned the collection over to the city of Lillehammer, which provided land for the museum. In addition to more than 130 structures and 50,000 objects from all over Norway, it has a main building with reconstructed artisans' workshops. *Maihaugvn 1, tel. 61/28–89–00. Admission: NKr50 adults, NKr20 children. Open June–Aug., daily 9–6; May, daily 10–4. Ticket includes guided tour.*

Lillehammer is also home to the **Norsk Vegmuseum** (Norwegian Museum of Transport History), a collection of vehicles ranging from the infancy of the horseless carriage to the present. *Hunder, 2638 Fåberg, tel. 61/27–71–10. Admission: NKr25 adults, NKr12 children. Open June 15–Aug. 31, daily 10–6.*

One of the most important art collections in Norway is housed at the **Lillehammer Bys Malerisamling** (Lillehammer Art Museum). In addition to Munch pieces, the gallery has one of the largest collections of works from the national romantic period. *Kirkegt. 71, Stortorget, tel. 61/26–94–44. Admission: NKr30 adults, NKr15 children. Open Tues.–Fri. 11–7, Sat. 11–3.*

⑬ At **Gausdal,** just north of Lillehammer, you can turn onto the scenic, well-marked **Peer Gynt Vegen** (the Peer Gynt Road), named after the real-life person behind Ibsen's character. A feisty fellow, given to tall tales, he is said to have spun yarns about his communing with trolls and riding reindeer backwards. Traveling along the rolling hills sprinkled with old farmhouses and rich with views of the mountains of Rondane, Dovrefjell, and Jotunheimen, the road is only slightly narrower and just 3 kilometers (2 miles) longer than the main route. It passes two major resorts, **Skeikampen/Gausdal** and **Golå/ Wadahl,** before rejoining E6 at Vinstra. Between Vinstra and Harpefoss, at the Sødorp Church, you can visit Peer Gynt's stone grave and what is said to be his old farm. Although you can walk the grounds, the 15th-century farm is privately owned.

From Vinstra, the road continues along the great valley of the River Mjøsa, birthplace of Gudbrandsdalsost, a sweet, brown goat cheese. The route offers lovely, rolling views of red farmhouses and lush green fields stretching from the valley to the mountainsides are lovely.

⑭ At Otta, Route 15 turns off for the 62-kilometer (38-mile) ride to **Lom,** in the middle of **Jotunheimen** national park. It is a picturesque, rustic town, with log cabin architecture, a stave church from 1170, and plenty of decorative rose painting.

Lom Stavkirke (Lom Stave Church), a mixture of old and new construction, is on the main road. The interior, including the pulpit, a large collection of paintings, pews, windows, and the gallery, is Baroque. *Open May 1–Sept. 30, Mon.–Sat. 10–5, Sun. noon–5.*

⑮ Upper Gudbrandsdal has breathtaking scenery. The area around **Lesja** is trout-fishing country; Lesjaskogvatnet, the lake, has a mouth at either end, so the current changes in the middle. The landscape becomes more dramatic with every mile, as jagged rocks loom up from the river, leaving the tiny settlement of **Marstein** without sun for five months of the year.

⑯ **Horgheim** used to have a gingerbread hotel for elegant early tourists to view **Trollveggen,** the highest overhanging vertical rockface in Europe. Now the tourists have been replaced by expert rock climbers from around the world. Åndalsnes, the end station on the railroad, is the perfect departure point for tours of Central Fjord Country (*see below*).

Tour 4: Røros

At the northern end of the Østerdal, the long valley to the east of Gudbrandsdalen, lies **Røros,** for more than 300 years a company town: Practically everyone who lived there was connected with the copper mines. The last mine in the region closed in 1986 but the town has survived thanks to other industries, including tourism, especially after it was placed on UNESCO's World Heritage List.

The main attraction is the **old town,** with its 250-year-old workers' cottages, slag dumps, and managers' houses, one of which is now City Hall. Descendants of the man who discovered the first copper ore in Røros still live in the oldest of the nearly 100 protected buildings. The tourist office has 75-minute guided tours of this part of town, starting at the information office and ending at the church. *Admission: NKr25 adults, NKr20 senior citizens and students, NKr15 children. Tours: June 1–21 and Aug. 19–Sept. 29, Mon.–Sat. at 11; June 22–Aug. 18, Mon.–Sat. at noon and 3, Sun. at 3. Oct.–May, Sat. at 11.*

The **Røroskirke** (Røros Church), which towers over all the other buildings in the town, is an eight-sided stone structure from 1784, with the mines' symbol on the tower. It can seat 1,600, impressive in a town with a population of only 5,000 today. The pulpit looms above the center of the altar, and seats encircle the top perimeter. Two hundred years ago wealthy locals paid for the privilege of sitting there. *Admission: NKr15 adults, NKr12 senior citizens and students, NKr6 children. Open June 1–21 and Aug. 19–Sept. 29, weekdays 2–4, Sat. 11–1; June 22–Aug. 18, Mon.–Sat. 10–5. Oct.–May, Sat. 11–1.*

Olavsgruva (Olaf's mine), outside town, is now a museum. The guided tour of Olavsgruva takes visitors into the depths of the mine, complete with sound and light effects. Remember to bring warm clothing and good shoes, as the temperature below ground is about 5°C (41°F) year-round. *Rte. 31, tel. 72/41–05–00. Admission: NKr35 adults, NKr25 senior citizens and students, NKr20 children. Guided tours June 1–21 and Aug. 19–Sept. 29, Mon.–Sat. at 1 and 3, Sun. at noon; June 22–Aug. 18, daily at 10:30, noon, 1:30, 3, 4:30, 6. Oct.–May, Sat. at 3.*

Back in town, in the old smelting plant, is **Rørosmuseet** (the Røros Museum), which documents the history of the mines, with working models in one-tenth scale demonstrating the methods used in mining. *Tel. 72/41–05–00. Admission: NKr30 adults, NKr25 senior citizens and students, NKr15 children. Open weekdays 11–3:30, weekends 11–2.*

What to See and Do with Children

Hamar **Jernbanemuseet** (the Railway Museum) documents the development of rail transportation in Norway, with locomotives and rolling stock on both normal and small-gauge track. *Tertittoget,* NSB's last steam locomotive, gives rides from mid-May to mid-August. *Strandvn. 132, tel. 62/51–31–60. Admission: NKr25 adults, NKr10 children. Open June and Aug., daily 10–4; July, daily 10–6.*

Lillehammer **Hunderfossen Park,** 13 kilometers (8 miles) north of Lillehammer, has rides and a petting zoo for small children, plus an energy center, with Epcot-influenced exhibits about oil and

gas and a five-screen theater for everyone. There's also the world's biggest troll. *2638 Fåberg, tel. 61/27–72–22. Admission: NKr60 adults, NKr50 children and senior citizens. Open early June, daily 10–4; mid-June–mid-Aug., daily 10–5.*

Just beyond Hunderfossen is **Lilleputthammer,** a miniature version of Lillehammer as it looked at the turn of the century, complete with animated figures in period dress. There are also rides, a swimming pool, and a water discothèque. *Øyer Gjestegård, 2636 Øyer, tel. 61/27–73–35. Admission to Lilleputthammer and swimming complex: NKr40. Open June 22–Aug. 18, daily 10–7; swimming complex, daily 11–6.*

Off the Beaten Track

Geilo About 35 kilometers (21 miles) northeast of Geilo on Route 7 is **Torpo,** site of a stave church dating from the late 12th century. Its colorful painted ceiling is decorated with scenes from the life of St. Margaret. *Open June–Aug., daily 9:30–5:30.*

Hamar Take a ride on the world's oldest paddleboat, 130-year-old *Skibladner,* also called the "white swan of the Mjøsa," which connects the towns along the lake. The schedule is complicated, with only three stops a week in Eidsvoll and Lillehammer but three stops daily three times a week in Gjøvik. Ask for a schedule from the tourist information or the *Skibladner* office. *Strandgt. 23, 2300 Hamar, tel. 62/52–70–85. June 15–Aug. 10.*

Hell West of Gudbrandsdalen you will find the lush Espedalen valley and some of Europe's biggest stone caldrons. The sight alone is worth a look, and barbecues are held on Sunday throughout the summer, so you can shamelessly "fry in Hell."

Lillehammer The composer of Norway's national anthem and the 1903 Nobel Prize winner in literature, Bjørnstjerne Bjørnson lived at **Aulestad,** in Gausdal, 18 kilometers (11 miles) northwest of Lillehammer, from 1875 until he died in 1910. After his wife, Karoline, died in 1934, their house was opened as a museum. *2620 Follebu, tel. 61/22–03–26. Admission: NKr25 adults; NKr15 children and senior citizens. Open July, daily 10–5:30; June, Aug., daily 10–3:30; Sept., daily 11–2:30.*

Skien From Skien you can take boat tours on the **Telemark waterways,** a combination of canals and natural lakes between Skien and either **Dalen** or **Notodden.** (For trips to Dalen, contact Telemarkreiser, tel. 35/53–03–00; Notodden is served by Telemarksbåtene, 3812 Akkerhaugen, tel. 35/95–82–11, fax 35/95–82–96.) The trip to Dalen takes you through **Ulefoss,** where you can leave the boat and visit neoclassical **Ulefoss Manor,** which dates from 1807. *Ulefoss, tel. 35/94–56–10. Admission: NKr20 adults, NKr10 children. Open June–mid-Aug., Sun–Fri. noon–3.*

Shopping

Geilo **Brusletto & Co.,** in central Geilo (tel. 32/09–02–00), is a purveyor of high-quality hunting knives with silver-inlaid handles made from burnished metal, walnut, and rosewood. Norwegian men wear these knives, used for hunting and hiking, on their belts—something akin to jewelry.

Lillehammer In Lillehammer, most of the stores along Storgate sell souvenirs. Try **Fakkelmannen** (Elvegt. 17, tel. 61/07–13–55) and

Pins'etten (Storgt. 79, tel. 61/25–96–50) for pins; **Ingeborg Svarstad's Vevstugu** (Reichweinsgt. 20, tel. 61/25–12–42), **Marihøna** (Storgt. 79, tel. 61/25–99–80), **Husfliden** (Storgt. 47, tel. 61/25–30–03), and **Reidun's Rosemaling og Brukskunst** (Storgt. 84A, tel. 61/25–84–50) for traditional Norwegian sweaters and handicrafts; and **Toves Brukthandel** (Storgt. 81, tel. 61/25–45–11) and **Loftet Bruktklaer** (Storgt. 81) for good bargains in the secondhand market.

Sports and Outdoor Activities

Although skiing, especially cross-country, is the most popular sport in the area, striking scenery, and fresh air make outdoor possibilities endless—summer or winter. The following is only a sampling of what is available. For additional information on outdoor activities, contact the regional tourist boards or **Telemarkreiser** (tel. 35/53–03–00). Some of the organized activities operate only in summer. If you can't reach them, call the local tourist board.

Bicycling   You can rent a bike and get local maps through any local tourist board. **Askeladdens Eventrreiser** in Oslo (tel. 22/55–55–66, fax 22/44–20–48) organizes a six-day trip that begins in Finse and heads west to the fjords; most of it is on relatively flat or downhill terrain. Students can make the same trip with the more youth-oriented **Terra Nova** in Bergen (tel. 55/32–23–77, fax 55/32–30–15). For details about a five-day mountain-biking trip across Hardangervidda, contact **Ashland's Adventures** (Huk Aveny 17, 1287 Oslo, tel. 22/55–55–66).

Dogsledding   In **Jotunheimen**, Magnar Aasheim and Kari Steinaug (tel. 61/23–87–50, fax 61/23–87–51) have one of the biggest kennels in Norway, with more than 80 dogs. You can travel as a sled-bound observer or control your own team of four to six dogs, most of which are ridiculously friendly Siberian and Alaskan huskies.

Fishing   Fishing throughout the region is excellent, and lakes and rivers are well stocked with trout, grayling, and char. Among the highlights is the Hardanger area, with the Eidefjord, Granvin, and Jondal good choices for salmon and trout. In Kvam, salmon run in the Strandadalselva, Moelven, and Øysteselva (rivers), and trout are plentiful in the mountain lakes. Within the Troll Park, the Gudbrandsdalåen is touted as one of the best-stocked rivers in the country, and the size of Mjøsa trout (locals claim 25 pounds) is legendary. For seasons, permits (you'll need both a national and a local license), and tips, call local tourist boards.

Hiking   You can pick up maps and the information-packed **"Peer Gynt"** pamphlet at the tourism office in Vinstra; then hike anywhere along the 50-kilometer (31-mile) circular route, passing Peer's farm, cottages, and monument. The national parks are also a good hiking choice (*see also* National Parks, *below*).

Elsewhere in the area, hiking possibilities are limitless—particularly around Hardanger and Troll Park. Check with the local tourist board for maps and tips. Overnighting in cabins or hotels is particularly popular on the Peer Gynt trail, where you can walk to each of the **Peer Gynt Hotels** (Box 115, N–2647 Hundorp, tel. 61/29–66–88).

In summer you can hike single-file (for safety purposes, in case of calving or cracks) on the ice and explore ice caves on the

Galdhøpiggen glacier. Call Lom Fjellføring (tel. 61/21–13–88) or the tourist board (tel. 61/21–12–86).

Horseback Riding For day- or week-long trips to the Hardangervidda, on horses or husky Norwegian ponies, contact **Eivindplass Fjellgård** (tel. 32/09–48–45) or **Geilo Hestesenter** (tel. 32/09–01–81). There are several stables in the Peer Gynt area, including **Sulseter Riding School** (tel. 61/29–01–58) and the **Peer Gynt Summer Arena** (tel. 61/29–55–18), both of which offer mountain trips.

Hunting Just south of Lillehammer you can hunt for beaver, and the Østerdalen offers good elk and reindeer hunting. As elsewhere in Norway, you'll need local and national licenses, and in some regions you are permitted to hunt only with a Norwegian. For information, call **Troll Park** (Lillehammer, tel. 61/26–92–00).

Mountaineering and Touring Near **Hardangerjøkulen** (the Hardanger Glacier), about an hour's drive north of Geilo, you can take a guided hike to the archaeological digs of 8,000-year-old Stone Age settlements. Contact **Hallingdal Mountaineering** (tel. 32/08–86–11).

From 1932 to 1953, **musk ox** were transported from Greenland to the Dovrefjell, where about 60 still roam—but it's a good idea to bring binoculars to see them. For information on safaris, call the **Dombaas Tourist Office** (tel. 61/24–14–44). **Elk safaris,** in the Bjødnhovd (not far from Fagernes), and **bear safaris,** in southern Valdres, are also organized. Call the **Valdres Tourist Office** (tel. 61/36–04–00).

National Parks The interior offers several varied national parks. The **Hardangervidda,** Europe's largest plateau and Norway's biggest park, is flat in the east and at its center and more mountainous in the west. Europe's largest herd of reindeer roam the plateau, and trout and char abound in the lakes and streams. About 150 kilometers (94 miles) north is **Ormtjernkampen,** a virgin spruce forest, and **Jotunheimen,** a rougher area spiked with glaciers, as well as Norway's highest peak, the Galdhøpiggen. Farther north is the scrubby, flat, and wide **Rondane** and the **Dovrefjell,** peaked to the west with some of the country's steepest mountains and home to wild musk ox, reindeer, and birds.

Rafting and Canoeing In Geilo they've combined rafting and canoeing with skiing, outfitting rubber rafts with a wood rudder and taking off down the slopes for a bracing, if peculiar, swoosh. Contact the tourist board for details. For rafting in **Dagali** or **Voss, Dagali-Voss Rafting** (Geilo, 32/09–38–20) organizes trips.

The **Sjoa River,** closer to Lillehammer, offers some of the most challenging rapids in the country. Contact **Sjoa Rafting** (tel. 61/23–87–50). **Flaate Opplevelser** (tel. 63/97–29–04) and **Norwegian Wildlife and Rafting** (tel. 61/23–87–27) also have trips in the **Sjoa** and **Dagali** areas.

Skiing **Telemark** is famous as the cradle of skiing, and the region is a center for ski touring. Just to the north, between Bergen and Oslo, is **Geilo** (tel. 32/09–16–95) (24 kilometers/15 miles of Alpine slopes, 130 kilometers/81 miles of cross-country trails; 18 lifts; also a ski-board tunnel). Among the area's other four ski centers, **Vestlia** (tel. 32/09–01–88), west of the Ustedalsfjord, is a good choice for families, as children can play under the guidance of the Troll Klub while parents ski; **Halstensgaard** (no tel.) and **Slaatta** (tel. 32/09–17–10) have a range of alpine and cross-country trails; and **Havsdalsenteret** (tel. 32/09–17–77) attracts a young crowd to its long alpine slopes. One ski pass (NKr140

for adults, NKr90 for children, tel. 32/09–18–09) gives access to all lifts in all five centers. Vestlia is connected to the eastern ski centers by ski taxis (NKr13, tel. 32/09–01–80).

North of Geilo is **Hemsedal** (34 kilometers/21 miles of alpine slopes, 175 kilometers/108 miles of cross-country trails; 17 ski lifts), which together with several nearby areas offers hundreds of miles of alpine and cross-country trails along with comfortable, modern facilities.

North of Oslo, **Lillehammer,** the 1994 Winter Olympics town, is another major skiing center (20 kilometers/12 miles of alpine, 400 kilometers/248 miles of cross-country trails; 7 ski lifts). Within the Lillehammer area, there are five ski centers: **Hafjell** (tel. 61/27–70–78), 10 kilometers (6.3 miles) north, is an Olympic venue with moderately steep alpine slopes; **Kvitfjell** (tel. 61/ 28–07–95), 50 kilometers (31 miles) north, another Olympic site, has some of the most difficult slopes in the world; **Skei** (tel. 61/22–85–55), near Gausdal, 30 kilometers (19 miles) north, has both cross-country and alpine trails; **Galdhøpiggen** (tel. 61/ 21–21–42), 135 kilometers (84 miles) northwest of Lillehammer, sits on a glacier, which makes it great for summer skiing; **Peer Gynt** (tel. 61/29–85–28), 80 kilometers (50 miles) northwest, has respectable downhill but is stronger as a cross-country venue. One ski lift ticket, called a **Troll Pass** (NKr175 for adults, NKr135 for children), is good for admission to all the lifts at all five sites.

To the east of the Gudbrandsdalen is the **Troll-løype** (Troll Trail), 250 kilometers (156 miles) of country trails that vein across a vast plateau that's bumped with mountains, including the Dovrefjells to the north. Ski as much or as little of the tracks as you want, and you can also choose accommodation en route. For information, contact the **Otta Tourist Office** (N-2640 Otta, tel. 61/23–02–44, fax 61/23–09–60).

Beitostølen (9 kilometers/5 miles of downhill slopes, 150 kilometers/93 miles of cross-country trails; 7 ski lifts), on the southern slopes of the Jotunheim range, has everything from torchlit night skiing to paragliding. At the northern end of the region is **Oppdal** (45 kilometers/27 miles of alpine pistes, 186 kilometers/ 115 miles of cross-country trails; 10 ski lifts), another World Cup venue. Like most other areas, it has lighted trails and snow-making equipment.

Dining and Lodging

Highly recommended establishments are indicated by a star★.

Elveseter
Dining and Lodging

Elveseter Hotell. Located 136 kilometers (85 miles) north of Lillehammer in Bøverdalen, this family-owned hotel is like a museum. Imagine a swimming pool in a barn dating from 1579. Every room has a history, and doors and some walls have been painted by local artists. In the public rooms are museum-quality paintings and antiques. There's no place like it. *2687 Bøverdalen, tel. 61/21–20–00, fax 61/21–21–01. 90 rooms with bath or shower. Facilities: 2 restaurants, bar, swimming pool, conference rooms, parking. No credit cards. Closed Sept. 25– May 31. Inexpensive.*

Geilo
Dining and Lodging

Dr. Holms Hotell. Renovated in 1989 to include two new wings and a new kitchen, Dr. Holms is among Norway's top resort hotels. Chef Jim Weiss has made the gourmet restaurant (not to

be confused with the dining room) worth a special trip. His game sausages are full of flavor, and his butterscotch pudding with crunchy topping is sensational. An après-ski stop at Dr. Holms is a must. *3580 Geilo, tel. 32/09–06–22, fax 32/09–16–20. 110 rooms with bath or shower, 14 suites. Facilities: 2 restaurants, 3 bars, fitness room, swimming pool, conference center, garage. AE, DC, MC, V. Expensive.*

Golå
Dining and Lodging
★

Golå Høyfjellshotell og Hytter. Tucked away in Peer Gynt territory, this peaceful hotel is furnished in Norwegian country, with all the extras. The restaurant has a down-to-earth menu of fresh local fish and game, prepared simply and elegantly. *2646 Golå, tel. 61/29–81–08, fax 61/29–85–40. 42 rooms with shower. Facilities: restaurant, ski slopes, outdoor swimming pool, conference rooms, children's Troll Klub, half- and full-board, parking. AE, DC, MC, V. Expensive.*

Kongsberg
Dining and Lodging

Grand. A statue of Kongsberg's favorite son, Olympic ski-jumper Birger Ruud, stands in the park in front of this modern, centrally located hotel. All rooms were refurbished in 1990. *Kristian Augustsgt. 2, 3600, tel. 32/73–20–29, fax 32/73–41–29. 92 rooms with bath or shower, 2 suites. Facilities: 2 restaurants, 2 bars, nightclub, fitness room, swimming pool, conference rooms, parking. AE, DC, MC, V. Inexpensive–Moderate.*

Lillehammer
Dining

Birkebeinerstuene. Centrally located between Storgata and the LOOC Information Center are a ground-floor café and a second-floor restaurant. The café is in traditional Norwegian style, serving cakes, sandwiches, and hot dishes. The restaurant serves lunch specials and à la carte evening meals. The interior is light and airy, the cuisine traditional, and the staff service-minded. *Elvegt. 18, tel. 61/26–44–44. AE, DC, MC, V. Closed Sun. Cafe: Moderate, restaurant: Expensive.*

Lundegården Brasserie & Bar. A piece of the Continent in the middle of Storgata, this restaurant, with its exquisite interior, is a haven where guests can enjoy a light snack in the rattan-furnished bar area or a full meal in the inviting dining room with starched white tablecloths. No detail is overlooked. The varied menu offers such dishes as baked salmon with pepper-cream sauce and seasonal vegetables. *Storgt. 108A, tel. 61/26–90–22. Reservations required. Dress: casual but neat. AE, DC, MC, V. No lunch. Moderate–Expensive.*

Shanghai Chopstick. This is a nice, clean café serving typical Chinese food. *Storgt 83, tel. 61/25–98–68. Inexpensive.*

Zeki Grill og Gatekjøkken. When your purse is empty, everything else is closed, or homesickness overcomes you, a Chicago hot dog costs NKr25. *Storgt 83, tel. 61/25–85–81. Inexpensive.*

Dining and Lodging

Lillehammer Hotel. A five-minute walk from Maihaugen, the hotel has the prime location for the Olympics—next door to Olympic Park, the hub of the games. The rooms are big but anonymous. *Turisthotellvn. 27B, 2600, tel. 61/25–48–00, fax 61/25–73–33. 196 rooms with bath or shower. Facilities: 2 restaurants, bar, nightclub, fitness room, 2 swimming pools, parking. AE, DC, MC, V. Expensive.*

Hammer Hotel. The Home Hotel on Storgatan opened in August 1991. It's named for the old Hammer farm, which first opened its doors to guests in 1665. The rooms are decorated in shades of green with oak furniture, both modern and rustic. Light beer, waffles, and an evening meal are included in the price. *Storgt. 108, 2600, tel. 61/26–35–00, fax 61/26–37–30. 72*

rooms with shower. Facilities: fitness room, conference center, garage. AE, DC, MC, V. Moderate–Expensive.

Mølla Hotell. This converted mill houses one of Lillehammer's new hotels. The intimate reception area on the ground floor gives the feeling of a private home. The bar, Toppen, on the top floor, has a good view of Mjøsa, the town, and the ski jump arena. The restaurant, Kvernhuset, winds down into the basement with old mill equipment kept for atmosphere among seating nooks. Try the Norwegian fillet of lamb with creamed potatoes. *Elvegt. 12, tel. 61/26–92–94, fax 61/26–92–95. 58 rooms with bath. Facilities: wheelchair access, sauna, solarium, exercise equipment. AE, DC, MC, V. Moderate–Expensive.*

Gjestehuset Ersgaard. Dating from the 1500s, originally called "Eiriksgård" (Eirik's Farm), Ersgaard today has all modern facilities. With a homey atmosphere in beautiful surroundings, this white manor house offers views of Lillehammer and Lake Mjøsa. *Nordseterveien 201 (at the Olympic Park), tel. 61/25–06–84, fax 61/25–06–84. 30 rooms, 20 with bath. Facilities: terrace, children's play yard. DC, MC, V. Moderate.*

Dølaheimen Breiseth Hotell. This friendly hotel is located by the railroad station and within walking distance of shops and businesses. The Dølaheimen Kafe serves hearty Norwegian meals. *Jernbanegt. 1–3, tel. 61/25–88–66, fax 61/26–95–00. 89 rooms. Facilities: allergy rooms, sauna, solarium, wheelchair access. AE, DC, MC, V. Inexpensive–Moderate.*

Lodging **Birkebeineren Motell & Apartments.** In these central accommodations breakfasts included except in the apartments. *Olympiaparken, tel. 61/26–47–00, fax 61/26–47–50. 310 beds and 40 chalets. Facilities: sauna, dining room. AE, DC, MC, V. Inexpensive–Moderate.*

Lom **Fossheim Turisthotell.** Arne Brimi's cooking has made this ho-
Dining and Lodging tel famous. He's a self-taught champion of the local cuisine; his dishes are based on nature's kitchen, with liberal use of game, wild mushrooms, and berries. Anything with reindeer is a treat in his hands, and his thin, crisp wafers with cloudberry parfait make a lovely dessert. *2686, tel. 61/21–20–05, fax 61/21–15–10. 54 rooms with bath or shower. Facilities: restaurant, bar, parking. AE, DC, MC, V. Inexpensive–Moderate.*

Oppdal **Oppdal Hotell.** A rather severe, modern, concrete-and-glass,
Dining and Lodging slope-front addition obscures this fine brick building, but inside the mood is lighter. The public rooms are overdecorated, but the bedrooms are understated, small but tastefully furnished, with light wood and pale woven textiles. It's basically a resort, with sports year-round. *O. Skasliens v., 7340, tel. 72/42–11–11, fax 72/42–08–24. 75 rooms with bath or shower. Facilities: 2 restaurants, bar, nightclub, fitness center, conference center, parking. AE, DC, MC, V. Inexpensive–Moderate.*

Øyer **Hafjell Hotell.** The largest hotel between Oslo and Trondheim,
Dining and Lodging near the Olympic alpine facilities, opened in the spring of 1992. It is built in a modern, yet rustic Norwegian style. Stig Søvik, one of Norway's finest chefs, prepares updated versions of Norwegian classics at the restaurant. *2636, tel. 61/27–77–77, fax 61/27–77–80. 138 rooms with bath. Facilities: restaurant, bar, parking. AE, DC, MC, V. Moderate–Expensive.*

Rjukan **Gaustablikk Høyfjellshotell.** Built at the foot of Gaustatoppen
Dining and Lodging near Rjukan, this modern timber hotel is a popular ski resort,

with nine downhill slopes and 80 kilometers (50 miles) of cross-country trails. In summer, these marked trails are perfect for walks and hikes. *N–3660, tel. 35/09–14–22, fax 35/09–19–75. 91 rooms with bath or shower, 14 suites. Facilities: restaurant, bar, nightclub, fitness room, swimming pool, parking. AE, DC, MC, V. Moderate.*

Park Hotell. This newly refurbished hotel is in the center of town. The rooms are tastefully decorated in light colors. *Sam Eydes gt. 67, 3660, tel. 35/09–02–88, fax 35/09–05–05. 39 rooms with bath or shower. Facilities: restaurant, bar, nightclub. AE, DC, MC, V. Moderate.*

Røros
Dining and Lodging

Bergstadens Hotel. The lobby is big, but when there's a fire in the stone fireplace, it is quite cozy. Most of the rooms are decorated in shades of light blue, rose, and gray. The main draw here is the dining room: Chef Kjell Sund sticks to local traditions and products—fish from mountain streams and berries from the nearby forest. *Oslovn. 2, 7460, tel. 72/41–11–11, fax 72/41–01–55. 71 rooms with bath or shower, 2 suites. Facilities: 2 restaurants, bar, nightclub, pool, conference center. AE, DC, MC, V. Moderate.*

Skien
Dining

Boden Spiseri. In the 1970s, Norwegians began their love affair with pepper steak. Boden serves an excellent version, but it also has Norwegian-style food, such as medallions of reindeer. For dessert, the cream-puff swan with ice cream and chocolate sauce is a delight. *Landbrygga 5, tel. 35/52–61–70. Dress: casual. AE, DC, MC, V. No lunch. Moderate.*

Lodging

Høyers Hotell. The old-fashioned exterior, all cornices and pedimented windows, is reflected in the Høyers's lobby, which is an incongruous mixture of old and new. The rooms are modern and light, thanks to the big windows. *Kongensgt. 6, 3700, tel. 35/52–05–40, fax 35/52–26–08. 69 rooms with bath, 1 suite. Facilities: restaurant, bar, nightclub, conference center. AE, DC, MC, V. Inexpensive–Moderate.*

The Arts

Bø i Telemark

During the second week in August, Bø holds its annual **Telemarksfestival** for international folk music and dancing, featuring musicians and dancers from distant lands as well as Norwegian and Sami artists. Nearly every weekend during the summer there's entertainment at **Telemark Sommarland** in Bø—everything from gospel singers to jazz.

Kongsberg

Every June jazz fans descend on Kongsberg for its annual **jazz festival.**

Skien

Henrik Ibsen's home town celebrates its favorite son every August with the **Ibsen-Kultur-festival** (Skien Tourist Office, Box 192, 3701 Skien, tel. 35/53–49–60), which includes concerts as well as drama.

Vinstra

Henrik Ibsen's *Peer Gynt* is performed (in Norwegian) on the first two weekends in August at a small outdoor theater on the shores of Lake Golaa. Contact the Vinstra Tourist Board (Nedregt. 5A, 2640 Vinstra, tel. 61/29–01–66) for additional information.

Central Fjord Country

Drawing from all directions, this fjord-riddled coast, from south of Bergen to Kristiansund, is stippled with islands and grooved with deep barren valleys, with most of the fertile land edging the water. The farther north one travels, the more rugged and wild the landscape. The motionless Sognefjord is the longest inlet, snaking 190 kilometers (110 miles) inland. It is 4,000 feet deep—a depth that often makes it appear black. Some of its sections are so narrow, with rock walls looming on either side, that they look as if they've been sliced from the mountains.

At the top of Sogn og Fjordane county are a succession of fjords referred to as Nordfjord, with Jostedalsbreen, mainland Europe's largest glacier, to the south. Sunnfjord is the coastal area between Nordfjord and Sognefjord, with Florø, the county seat, on an island close to Norway's westernmost point.

The mountains of Møre og Romsdal county are treeless moonscapes of gray rock, stone cliffs that hang out over the water far below. Geirangerfjord is the most spectacular fjord, with a road zigzagging all the way down from the mountaintops to the water beside a famous waterfall.

There is more to the central region than fidgety coasts and peaks. In fact, tourists have been visiting central fjord country ever since the English "discovered" the area some 150 years ago in their search for the ultimate salmon. One of these tourists was Kaiser Wilhelm, who spent every summer except one, from 1890 to 1913, in Molde and helped rebuild Ålesund into one of the most fantastic fits of architectural invention in Scandinavia.

Important Addresses and Numbers

Tourist Information Ålesund (Rådhuset, tel. 70/12–12–02); Åndalsnes (corner Nesgata/Romsdalsvn., tel. 71/22–16–22); Balestrand (dockside, tel. 57/69–12–55); Flåm (railroad station, tel. 57/63–21–06); Geiranger (dockside, tel. 70/26–30–99); Hellesylt (dockside, tel. 70/26–50–52); Loen (tel. 57/87–76–77); Lærdal (tel. 57/66–65–09); Molde (Storgt 1, tel. 71/25–43–30); Olden (tel. 57/87–31–26); Stryn (tel. 57/87–15–26); Ulvik (dockside, tel. 56/52–63–60); Voss (Hestevangen 10, tel. 56/51–17–16).

Emergencies Ålesund Police: tel. 112 or 70/12–13–21. Fire: tel. 111. Ambulance: tel. 113. Hospital Emergency Rooms/Doctors/Dentists: tel. 70–12–33–48. Car Rescue: tel. 70/14–18–33.

Late-Night Pharmacies Ålesund Nordstjernen (Kaiser Wilhelmsgt. 22, Ålesund, tel. 70/12–59–45) is open Wednesday until 6 and Saturday and Sunday from 6 to 8.

Arriving and Departing by Plane

Ålesund's Vigra airport is 15 kilometers (9 miles) from the center of town. Braathens SAFE (tel. 70/12–58–00 Ålesund, 70/18–32–45 Vigra) has nonstop flights from Oslo, Bergen, Trondheim, and Bodø. It's a 25-minute ride from Vigra to town with Flybussen. Tickets cost NKr50. Buses are scheduled according to flights—they leave the airport about 10 minutes after all arrivals and leave town about 60 or 70 minutes before each flight.

Arriving and Departing by Car, Train, and Boat

By Car   From Oslo, it is 570 kilometers (353 miles) on Route E6 to Dombås and then Route 9 through Åndalsnes to Ålesund. The well-maintained two-lane road is inland to Åndalsnes and then follows the coastline out to Ålesund.

The 380-kilometer (235-mile) drive from Bergen to Ålesund covers some of the most breathtaking scenery in the world. Roads are narrow two-lane affairs much of the time; passing is difficult, and in summer traffic can be heavy.

By Train   The **Raumabanen** between Oslo S and **Åndalsnes** runs three times daily in each direction for the 6½-hour ride. At Åndalsnes, buses wait outside the station to pick up passengers for points not served by the train. The 124-kilometer (76-mile) trip to Ålesund takes close to two hours.

By Boat   *Hurtigruten* (the coastal steamer) stops at Skansekaia in **Ålesund,** northbound at noon, departing at 3, and stops southbound at midnight, departing at 1. A catamaran runs between Ålesund and Molde at least twice daily.

Getting Around

By Car   Ferries are a way of life in western Norway, but they are seldom big enough or run often enough during the summer, causing built-in delays. Considerable hassle can be eliminated by reserving ahead, as cars with reservations board first.

By Bus   Bus routes are extensive. The tourist office has information about do-it-yourself tours by bus to the outlying districts. Three local bus companies serve **Ålesund;** all buses depart from the terminal on Kaiser Wilhelms Gate.

By Boat   In addition to regular ferries to nearby islands, boats connect Ålesund with other points along the coast. Excursions by boat are available through the tourist office.

Guided Tours

Orientation   A 1½-hour guided stroll through **Ålesund,** concentrating mostly on the Art Nouveau buildings, departs from the tourist information center (Rådhuset) Saturday and Tuesday at 1 PM from June 15 to August 21.

Special-Interest *Cruises*   The **M/S** *Geirangerfjord* (tel. 70/26–30–07) offers 105-minute guided minicruises (at 10, 1, 3, 5, and 8) on the Geirangerfjord. Tickets are sold at the dock in **Geiranger.**

Flying   Firdafly A/S (tel. 57/86–53–88), based in **Sandane,** offers air tours over Jostedalsbreen. Hotel Alexandra in Loen (*see* Lodging, *below*) arranges group flights. Mørefly A/S (tel. 70/18–35–00) offers 20-minute fjord and mountain-sightseeing trips by helicopter from **Ålesund.**

Hiking   **Aak Fjellsport** (mountain sport) **Center** (tel. 71/22–64–44) in **Åndalsnes** specializes in walking tours of the area, from rambling in the hills for beginners and hikers to full-fledged rockclimbing, along with rafting on the Rauma River. These are the guys who hang out of helicopters to rescue injured climbers, so they know what they're doing.

From Easter through September, **Jostedalen Breførlag** (5828 **Gjerde,** tel. 56/68–32–73) offers glacier tours, from an easy 1½-hour family trip on the Nigard branch (equipment is provided) to advanced glacier courses with rock and ice climbing.

Diving **Ålesund Dykkersenter** (Storgt. 38, tel. 70/12–34–24) has equipment for hire. All certificates are accepted.

Exploring Central Fjord Country

The best way to see fjord country is to make an almost circular tour—from Oslo to Åndalsnes, out to the coastal towns of Åle-sund, Molde, and Kristiansund, then over Trollstigveien to Geiranger, a ferry to Hellesylt, down to Stryn, around Loen and Olden and through the subglacial tunnel to Fjærland, a ferry to Balestrand, connecting with another ferry down to Flåm, where the railroad connects with Myrdal on the Bergen line (*see* Excursions from Bergen, *above*). Then the trip can either continue on to Bergen or back to Oslo.

Numbers in the margin correspond to points of interest on the Central Fjord Country map.

Tour 1: Åndalsnes and the Coast

❶ **Åndalsnes,** an industrial town of 3,000 people, has at least three things going for it: As the last stop on the railroad, it is a gateway to fjord country; **Trollstigveien** (the Trolls' Path), one of Europe's most fantastic zigzag roads, starts here; and **Trollveggen** (the Trolls' Wall), the highest sheer rock wall in Europe (1,000 meters/3,300 feet), which attracts climbers from around the world, is just outside of town.

❷ West 240 kilometers (150 miles), on three islands and between two bright blue fjords, is **Ålesund,** home to 35,000 inhabitants and one of Norway's largest harbors for exporting dried and fresh fish. Nearly 800 buildings in the center of town were destroyed by fire in 1904, which is said to have been started by a tipped oil lamp. In the rush to shelter the 10,000 homeless victims, Kaiser William II led a mercurial rebuilding that married the German Art Nouveau with Viking roots—much of it carried out by an army of young, foreign architects who threw in their own rabid flourishes. Delightfully, nothing has changed. Winding streets are crammed with warehouses topped with turrets, spires, gables, dragonheads, and curlicues, all in a delirious spirit that's best seen while wandering behind the local dock to Kongensgate, the walking street.

You can drive or take a bus (tel. 70/12–65–82) up nearby Aksla Mountain to a vantage point, **Kniven** (the knife), for a splendid view of the city—which absolutely glitters at night.

Time Out **Fjellstua,** a modern lodge at the very top of the mountain, has a terrace with a cafeteria, where the view is especially good.

Near Ålesund is **Runde,** Norway's southernmost major bird rock, one of the largest in Europe, and a breeding ground for some 130 species, including puffins, gannets, and shags. The island is otherwise known for the "Runde Hoard," 1,300 kg of silver and gold coins, which were retrieved from a Dutch ship that sank in 1725. The catamaran leaves from Skateflua quay for the 25-minute trip to Hareid, where it connects with a bus for the

Central Fjord Country

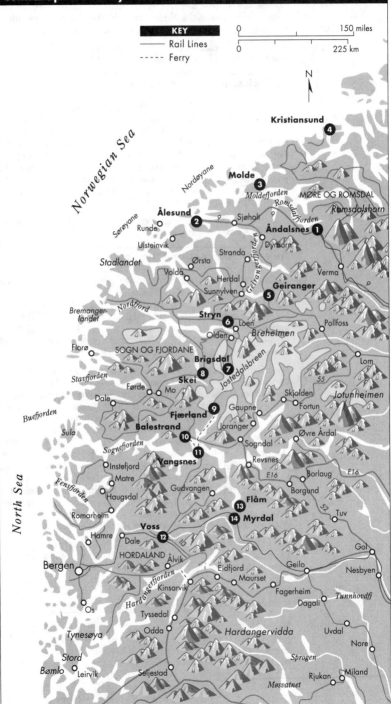

KEY
— Rail Lines
---- Ferry

0 ———————————— 150 miles
0 ———————————— 225 km

N

Norwegian Sea

Kristiansund ④

Molde ③
Moldefjorden
MØRE OG ROMSDAL
Romsdalfjorden
Romsdalshorn

Nordøyane

Ålesund ②
Sjøholt
Åndalsnes ①
Dyrdborn
Verma

Sørøyane
Runde
Ulsteinvik
Stadlandet
Ørsta
Stranda
Herdal
Sunnylven
Geirangerfjorden
Geiranger ⑤

Volda

Nordfjord

Bremanger-landet
Stryn ⑥
Loen
Breheimen
Pollfoss

Olden
Lom

Florø
SOGN OG FJORDANE
Brigsdal ⑦
Jostedalsbreen
55

Stavfjorden
Skei ⑧
Førde
Mo
Skjolden
Jotunheimen

Dale
Fjærland ⑨
Gaupne
Fortun

Buefjorden
Balestrand
Joranger
Øvre Årdal

Sula
⑩
Sogndal
⑪
Sognefjorden
Revsnes

Instefjord
Vangsnes
E16
Borlaug
E16

Fensfjorden
Matre
Gudvangen
Borgund

Haugsdal
Flåm ⑬
52
Tuv

North Sea
Romarheim
Myrdal ⑭

Hamre
Voss ⑫
Gol

Dale
Nesbyen

Bergen
HORDALAND
Ålvik
Eidfjord
Geilo

Hardangerfjorden
Maurset
Fagerheim
Tunnhovdfj

Os
Kinsarvik
Dagali

Tyssedal
Hardangervidda
Uvdal

Tynesøya
Odda
Nore

Stord
Sprogen

Bømlo
Leirvik
Seljestad
Rjukan
Miland

Møsvatnet

50-kilometer (31-mile) trip to Runde. A path leads from the bus stop to the nature reserve. It is also possible to sail around the rock on the yacht *Charming Ruth,* which leaves from Ulsteinvik at 11 on Wednesday and Sunday.

❸ North of Ålesund is **Molde.** During World War II the German air force suspected that King Haakon VII was staying in a red house here and bombed every red house in town. These days the city is known for its yearly jazz festival at the end of July, when big names from around the world gather for a huge jam session. Tickets can be purchased at all post offices in Norway.

Although Molde is a modern town, rebuilt almost entirely after the war, **Kristiansund** was spared the destruction of its historic **❹** harbor, Vågen. Many buildings in the town—which celebrated its 250th birthday in 1992—are well preserved, including **Woldbrygga,** a cooper's (barrelmaker's) workshop from 1875 to 1965, with its original equipment still operational. *Admission: NKr10 adults, NKr5 children. Open weekdays 2–4, Sun. 1–4.*

Tour 2: Geirangerfjord to Sognefjord

Geiranger is the ultimate fjord, Norway at its most dramatic, with the finest sightseeing in the wildest nature compressed into a relatively small area. The mountains lining the Geiranger Fjord tower 2,000 meters (6,600 feet) above sea level. The most scenic route to Geiranger is the two-hour drive along Route 63 over **Trollstigveien** (the Trolls' Path) from Åndalsnes. This road took 100 men 20 summers (from 1916 to 1936) to build, in a constant fight against rock and water. Trollstigveien and Ørneveien (at the Geiranger end) zigzag over the mountains separating two fjords. They're open only during the summer, but there's enough snow for skiing well into July. Trollstigveien has 11 giant hairpin turns, each one blasted from solid rock. Halfway up, the spray from **Stigfoss** (Stig Falls) blows across the bridge.

Time Out **Trollstigen Fjellstue,** near the top of Trollstigveien, is cozy and rustic inside. The *medisterkaker* with *surkål* (mild sausage cakes with caraway-flavored sauerkraut) is a good, hearty meal—be sure to pick up a little tub of *tyttebær* (lingonberry).

❺ Ørneveien (the Eagles' Road), down to **Geiranger,** completed in 1952, with 11 hairpin turns, leads directly to the fjord. The 16-kilometer (10-mile) -long, 960-foot- (-298-meter-) deep Geirangerfjord's best-known attractions are its waterfalls—the Seven Sisters, the Bridal Veil, and the Suitor—and the abandoned farms at **Skageflå** and **Knivsflå,** which are visible (and accessible) only by boat (*see* Guided Tours, *above*). Perhaps the inhabitants left because provisions had to be carried from the boats straight up to Skageflå—a backbreaking 800 feet (248 meters).

If you continue on to Stryn, take the ferry across the Geiranger Fjord to Hellesylt, a 75-minute ride. It's about 50 kilometers (30 miles) from Hellesylt to Stryn on Route 60. Stryn, Loen, and Olden, at the eastern end of Nordfjord, were among the first tourist destinations in the region more than 100 years ago.

❻ **Stryn** is famous for its salmon river and summer ski center, while Loen and Olden are starting points for expeditions to branches of Europe's largest glacier, **Jostedalsbreen.**

● **Brigsdal** is the most accessible arm of the Jostedal glacier. Take a bus (from Stryn, Loen, or Olden) or drive to Brigsdalsbre Fjellstove. The glacier is a 45-minute walk from the end of the road, or you can ride there with pony and trap, as tourists did 100 years ago. Local guides lead tours (*see* Guided Tours, *above*) over the safe parts of the glacier. These perennial ice masses are more treacherous than they look, for there's always the danger of calving (breaking off), and deep crevasses are not always visible.

Time Out **Briksdalsbre Fjellstove** celebrated its 100th anniversary in 1992. Stop at the gift shop or at the cafeteria for delicious homemade cakes, or spend the night at the modern lodge.

It is also possible to visit the **Kjenndal** arm of the glacier on the *M/B Kjendal* (tel. 57/87–76–60), which departs from Sande, near Loen. It sails down the 14-kilometer (9-mile) arm of the lake under mountains covered by protruding glacier arms and past Ramnefjell (Ramne Mountain), scarred by rock slides, to **Kjenndalsbreen Fjellstove.** A bus runs between the lodge (which serves excellent trout) and the glacier.

For many years **Olden** was the home of American landscape artist William H. Singer (d. 1943), scion of a Pittsburgh steel family. A philanthropist, he paid for the road and the regional hospital. His **studio** (open July and August, weekends noon–2) can be visited.

● From Olden it's 62 kilometers (37 miles) of easy though not particularly inspiring terrain to **Skei,** at the base of Lake Jølster, where the road goes under the glacier for more than 6 kilome-
● ters (4 miles) of the journey to **Fjærland,** which, until 1986, was without road connections altogether. In 1991 the **Norsk Bremuseum** (Norwegian Glacier Museum) opened just north of Fjærland. It has a huge screen with a film about glacier trekking and a fiberglass glacial maze, complete with special effects courtesy of the *Star Wars* movies' set designer. *Tel. 57/69–32–88. Admission: NKr60 adults; NKr30 children and senior citizens. Open May–Sept., daily 10–6; Apr., Oct., daily 10–4.*

By 1996 Fjærland should have road connections with Sogndal, but until then, the only way to travel is by ferry, which stops at
● both **Balestrand,** one of the famous destinations of old, and
● **Vangsnes** across from it on the southern bank of **Sognefjord,** one of the longest and deepest fjords in the world, snaking 200 kilometers (136 miles) into the heart of the country. Along its wide banks are some of Norway's best fruit farms, with fertile soil and lush vegetation (the fruit blossoms in May are spectacular). Ferries are the lifeline of the region.

● From Vangsnes it is 80 kilometers (50 miles) south to **Voss,** birthplace of football hero Knut Rockne, and a good place to stay the night, either in the town itself or 36 kilometers (23 miles) away at Stalheim. The road to Stalheim, an old resort, has 13 hairpin turns in one 1½-kilometer (1-mile) stretch of road—and it's 550 meters (1,800 feet) straight down. Voss is connected with Oslo and Bergen by train and by 114 kilometers (71 miles) of roads (some sections are narrow and steep).

● It is also possible to ride a ferry from Balestrand to **Flåm,** from which you can make Norway's most exciting railway journey,
● to **Myrdal.** Only 20 kilometers (12 miles) long, it takes 40 min-

utes to travel 884 meters (2,850 feet) up a steep mountain gorge, and 53 minutes to go down. Don't worry about the brakes. The train has five separate systems, any one of which is able to stop it. A masterpiece of engineering, the line includes 20 tunnels. From Flåm it is also an easy drive back to Oslo on E16 along the Lærdal River, one of Norway's most famous salmon streams and King Harald's favorite.

Off the Beaten Track

Halfway across the southern shore of Lake Jølster (about a 10-minute detour from the road to Fjærland) is **Astruptunet,** the farm of artist Nicolai Astrup (1880–1928). The best of his primitive, mystical paintings sell in the $500,000 range, making him second only to Edvard Munch among Norwegian artists. His home and studio are in a cluster of small turf-roofed buildings on a steep hill overlooking the lake. *Tel. 57/82–77–82. Admission: NKr30 adults, NKr15 children and senior citizens. Open May 19–June 9, Aug. 12–Sept. 1, weekdays, Sun. noon–5, Sat. noon–3; June 10–Aug. 11, weekdays, Sun. 10–6, Sat. 10–4.*

Shopping

Skei in Jølster **Audhild Vikens Vevstove** (Skei, tel. 57/72–81–25, Førde, tel. 57/82–00–84) specializes in the handicrafts, particularly woven textiles, of the Jølster region as well as handicrafts from neighboring areas, including brass, porcelain, and leather goods.

Stryn **Strynefjell Draktverkstad** (6890 Oppstryn, tel. 57/87–72–20) is a women's workshop, started in 1988, that specializes in stylish knickers, trousers, and skirts made of heavy wool fabric. It's a 10-minute drive east of Stryn on Route 15.

Sports and Outdoor Activities

Fishing There are numerous lakes, rivers, and streams around Voss, with trout everywhere; char, salmon, and sea trout reside in these waters. There's also good salmon fishing in the Vosso River (June–mid-August), and the Vangsvatnet and Lønavatnet lakes are good for ice fishing. You can also go sea fishing among the islands south of Bergen near Sunde (call the culture board, at tel. 56/33–75–00), or fish for more trout and salmon in the Etne River in Sunnhordland. As always, a license is required.

Hiking Walks and hikes are especially rewarding in this region, with spectacular mountain and water views everywhere. Be prepared for abrupt weather changes in spring and fall. Voss is a starting point for mountain hikes in Slølsheimen, Vikafjell, and the mountains surrounding Voss. Contact the Voss Tourist Board (Uttraagata 9, tel. 56/51–17–16) for tips. There's also good walking in Sunnhorldland, Osterfjorden, Sotra-Øygarden (among the islands), and the more rugged Nordhorland. The local tourist boards can help you plan hikes.

Skiing **Voss** (40 kilometers/25 miles of alpine slopes; 1 cable car, 8 ski lifts; 8 illuminated and 2 marked cross-country trails) is an important alpine skiing center in Norway, although it doesn't have the attractions or traditions of some of its resort neighbors to the east. The area includes several schools and interconnecting lifts that will get you from run to run. Call the tourist-information office (tel. 56/51–17–16) for details.

Dining and Lodging

Outside of some roadside snack bars and simple cafeterias, restaurants are few in fjord country. Most visitors dine at the hotels, where food is often abundant and simple. Most feature a cold table at either lunch or dinner.

Highly recommended establishments are indicated by a star★.

Ålesund **Gullix.** The decor is a bit much, with stone walls, plants hang-
Dining ing from the ceiling, musical instruments, and even the odd old-
fashioned record player, but you can't fault the food, which
ranges from sautéed monkfish garnished with shrimp, mussels, and crayfish to grilled marinated filet mignon of lamb.
*Rådstugt. 5B, tel. 70/12–05–48. Reservations advised. Dress:
casual but neat. AE, DC, MC, V. Moderate.*

Sjøbua. Within walking distance of the new hotels, this fish restaurant is typical Ålesund. Pick your own fish from the large
tank. The mixed fish and shellfish platter is the most popular
dish on the menu. The lobster soup is excellent, too, but leave
room for the raspberry ice cream with nougat sauce.
*Brunholmgt. 1, tel. 70/12–71–00. Reservations advised. Dress:
casual but neat. AE, DC, MC, V. Closed Sun. Moderate.*

Brosundet Cafe. Hotel Atlantica's coffee shop is one of the most
popular restaurants in town. It has its own bakery, so there's
always homemade bread and rolls. The *sirupsnipper* (spice
cookies) are very popular. You can order anything from
bløtkake (cream cake) and coffee, with free refill, to
peppersteak. *R. Rønnebergsgt. 4, tel. 70/12–91–00. No reservations. Dress: casual. AE, DC, MC, V. Inexpensive.*

Vesle Kari. This tiny maritime-theme café serves typical Norwegian fare—open-face sandwiches and such hot dishes as
kjøttkaker (meat patties), predictable but tasty. *Apoteker-
gaten 2, tel. 70/12–84–04. No reservations. Dress: casual. No
credit cards. Inexpensive.*

Lodging **Bryggen.** Right on Brosundet, Bryggen, formerly a turn-of-
the-century fish warehouse, was restored by the Home hotel
chain in early 1990. The decor in both lobby and guest rooms
illustrates the importance of the fishing industry to Ålesund. A
hot meal is included in the room price, and waffles and coffee
are always available. *Apotekergt. 1–3, N–6021, tel. 70/12–64–
00, fax 70/12–11–80. 76 rooms, 6 suites. Facilities: Fitness
room, conference rooms, fishing, parking. AE, DC, MC, V.
Moderate.*

Hotel Scandinavie. The impressive building with towers and
arches dates from 1905, but the rooms are newly refurbished,
with dark modern Scandinavian furniture, while some textiles
pay a token tribute to Art Nouveau. *Løvenvoldgt. 8, N–6002,
tel. 70/12–31–31, fax 70/12–94–88. 75 rooms with bath, 2
suites. Facilities: 2 restaurants, bar, fitness room, conference
room, garage. AE, DC, MC, V. Moderate.*

Rica Parken. This modern business hotel near Aksla offers panoramic views from most of the small but well-appointed rooms,
which were redecorated in 1990 with rattan furniture and pastel colors. *Storgt. 16, N–6002, tel. 70/12–50–50, fax 70/12–21–
64. 132 rooms with bath, 6 suites. Facilities: restaurant, bar,
nightclub, fitness center, conference rooms, parking. AE, DC,
MC, V. Moderate.*

Scandic. This large postmodernist building complex stands
next to the Exhibition Hall. Its interior design has a maritime

theme. The rooms are both spacious and tastefully decorated. *Molovn. 6, N–6004, tel. 70/12–81–00, fax 70/12–92–10. 120 rooms with bath. Facilities: restaurant, bar, nightclub, swimming pool, fitness center. AE, DC, MC, V. Moderate.*

Åndalsnes
Lodging
Grand Hotel Bellevue. It looks like a white stucco apartment building from the 1950s. The rooms are spare but adequate, all with a view of either the mountains or the fjord. *Åndalsgt. 5, N–6300, tel. 71/22–10–11, fax 71/22–60–38. 46 rooms with bath or shower. Facilities: 2 restaurants, bar, conference room, parking. AE, DC, MC, V. Moderate.*

Balestrand
Lodging
Kvikne's Hotel. This huge wood gingerbread house at the edge of the Sognefjord has been a landmark since 1913. It is fjord country's most elaborate old hotel, with rows of open porches and balustrades. The rooms are comfortable—those in the old section have more personality, but the view's the best part. *N–5850, Balholm, tel. 57/69–11–01, fax 57/69–15–02. 190 rooms with bath or shower. Facilities: restaurant, nightclub, fitness room, fishing, water sports. AE, DC, MC, V. Moderate.*

Fjærland
Lodging
Hotel Mundal. This small, old-fashioned yellow-and-white gingerbread hotel celebrated its 100th anniversary in 1991. All rooms are individually and simply decorated. The dining room is rather dreary, but the food is good. *N–5855, tel. 57/69–31–01, fax 57/69–31–79. 36 rooms with bath. Facilities: 2 restaurants, bar, conference rooms, fishing, parking. No credit cards. Moderate–Expensive.*

Flåm
Lodging
Fretheim Hotell. With the fjord in front and mountains in back, the setting is perfect. The hotel is anonymous, white, and functional. The inside has comfortable lounges, but the rooms won't win any decorating prizes. *N–5743, tel. 57/63–22–00, fax 57/63–23–03. 56 rooms with bath or shower, 28 without. Facilities: 2 restaurants, bar, fishing. AE, MC, V. Moderate.*

Geiranger
Lodging
Union Turisthotel. This family-owned hotel celebrated its 100th anniversary in 1991. The old building was torn down, but the present hotel is a tribute to the old style. It is modern and comfortable, with lots of windows facing the view and light furniture in the relatively large rooms. *N–6216, tel. 70/26–30–00, fax 70/26–31–61. 145 rooms with bath or shower, 10 suites. Facilities: restaurant, bar, nightclub, fitness room, indoor and outdoor swimming pools, parking. AE, DC, MC, V. Expensive.*

Grande Fjord Hotell. Idyllically situated at the edge of the fjord, this small hotel complex has more charm than the big hotels in the area. The rooms are simple but comfortable. *N–6216, tel. 70/26–30–67 (Apr.–Oct.), 70/26–31–77 (Nov.–Mar.). 10 rooms with bath, 5 without, 18 cabins with bath. Facilities: restaurant, parking. No credit cards. Inexpensive.*

Kristiansund N
Lodging
Inter Nor Grand. Practically every Norwegian town has a Grand Hotel. This one's primarily a conference hotel, but the rooms are nicer than most (certainly much nicer than the lobby), with brass beds and light wood furniture. *Bernstorffstredet 1, N–6500, tel. 71/67–30–11, fax 71/67–23–70. 130 rooms with bath/shower. Facilities: 2 restaurants, bar, nightclub, fitness room, conference center, parking. AE, DC, MC, V. Moderate–Expensive.*

Loen
Dining and Lodging
★

Alexandra. It looks like a huge white hospital: More than 100 years ago, English and German tourists stayed here. Even though the original dragon-style building exists only in pictures in the lobby, it is still the most luxurious hotel around. The facilities are first-rate and the dining room was renovated in January 1993, but the food, prepared by Chef Wenche Loen, is the best part. *N–6878, tel. 57/87–76–60, fax 57/87–77–70. 198 rooms with bath. Facilities: 2 restaurants, bar, nightclub, swimming pool, fitness room, gift shop, tennis, boating, conference center. AE, DC, MC, V. Expensive.*

Molde
Dining and Lodging

Inter Nor Alexandra Molde. Spisestuen, the restaurant of Molde's premier hotel, is worth a special trip. Kåre Monsås offers such dishes as pepper-marinated veal fillet. The ice-cream soufflé is an excellent dessert. The rooms, many of which overlook the water, are nondescript but comfortable, with dark-brown wood furniture and textiles in shades of blue. *Storgt. 1–7, N–6400, tel. 71/25–11–33, fax 71/21–66–35. 139 rooms with bath/shower, 11 suites. Facilities: 3 restaurants, 2 bars, swimming pool, fitness room, conference rooms, garage. AE, DC, MC, V. Moderate–Expensive.*

Runde
Lodging

Christineborg Turisthotel. This modern hotel faces the sea and the bird rocks. It's surprisingly comfortable and civilized, a welcome setting for unwinding. *N–6096, tel. 70/08–59–50, fax 70/08–59–72. 31 rooms with shower. Facilities: restaurant, fishing boat. MC, V. Inexpensive.*

Stalheim
Lodging

Stalheim Hotel. A large, rectangular building, much like other Norwegian resort hotels, the Stalheim has been painted dark red and blends into the scenery better than most hotels. It has an extensive collection of Norwegian antiques and even its own open-air museum with 30 houses. *N–5715, tel. 56/52–01–22, fax 56/52–00–56. 127 rooms with bath or shower, 3 suites. Facilities: restaurant, bar, fishing, shop. AE, DC, MC, V. Expensive–Very Expensive.*

Stryn
Lodging

King Oscar's Hall. Mike and Møyfrid Walston have brought back to life a derelict but magnificent hotel from the heyday of the dragon style, 1896, complete with a tower with dragonheads on the eaves. The Great Hall gives new meaning to the word *great* and the number of royal guests, both present and past, is impressive. *N–6880, tel. and fax, 57/87–19–53. 5 suites. Facilities: restaurant, parking. V. Closed Sept.–Apr. Expensive.*

Voss
Lodging

Fleischers Hotel. The modern addition along the front detracts from the turreted and gabled charm of this old hotel. Inside, the old style has been especially well maintained, particularly in the restaurant. The rooms in the old section are comfortable and pleasantly old-fashioned; in the rebuilt section (1993) they are modern and inviting. The motel section offers apartments. *Evangervegen 13, N–5700, tel. 56/51–11–55, fax 56/51–22–89. 86 rooms with bath or shower; 30 apartments. Facilities: restaurant, bar, nightclub, indoor pool, fitness room, tennis, children's playroom, parking. AE, DC, MC, V. Moderate.*

Trondheim and the North

The coast of northern Norway fidgets up from Trondheim, scattering thousands of islands and skerries along the way, until it reaches the northernmost point of Europe. Then it continues even farther, straggling above Sweden and Finland to point a finger of land into Russia.

Long and thin, this area covers an astonishing variety of land- and cityscapes, from bustling Trondheim to elegant Tromsø to colorful Karasjok, capital of the Sami. Some areas, especially when seen from the deck of the mail boats, seem like endless miles of wilderness marked by an occasional dot—a lonely cabin or a herd of reindeer. Views are often exquisite: glaciers, fjords, rocky coasts, and celestial displays of the midnight sun in summer and northern lights (aurora borealis) in winter.

Nordkapp (the North Cape) has a character that changes with the seasons. In summer it teems with visitors and tour buses, and in winter, under several feet of snow, it is bleak, subtle, and astonishingly beautiful. It is accessible then only by squealing snow cat: a bracing and thoroughly Norwegian adventure.

Important Addresses and Numbers

Tourist Information **Trondheim** (Munkegt. 19, tel. 73/92–93–94). Other tourist offices in the region: **Bodø** (Sjøgt. 21, 8000, tel. 75/52–60–00); **Harstad** (Rikard Kaarbøsgt. 20, 9400, tel. 77/06–32–35); **Lofoten** (8300 Svolvær, tel. 76/07–30–00); **Mo i Rana** (8600 Mo, tel. 75/15–04–21); **Narvik** (Kongensgt. 66, 8500, tel. 76/94–33–09); **Tromsø** (Storgt. 61, 9000, tel. 77/61–00–00); **Vesterålen Reiselivslag** (8400 Sortland, tel. 77/02–15–55); and **Nordkapp,** (Nordkapphuset, Honningsvåg, tel. 78/47–28–94).

Emergencies **Trondheim** **Police:** tel. 112. **Fire:** tel. 111. **Ambulance:** tel. 113. **Car rescue:** tel. 73/96–82–00. **Doctors:** tel. 73/99–88–00. **Dentists:** tel. 73/52–25–00.

Other Towns **Bodø:** tel. 112; **Harstad:** tel. 112; **Narvik:** tel. 112; **Tromsø:** tel. 112.

Late-Night Pharmacies **Trondheim** **St. Olav Vaktapotek** (Kjøpmannsgt. 65, tel. 73/52–66–66) is open Monday through Saturday 8:30 AM–midnight and Sunday 10 AM–midnight.

Tromsø **Svaneapoteket** (Fr. Langes Gate 9, tel. 77/68–64–24) is open daily 8:30–4 and 6–9.

Arriving and Departing by Plane

Airports and Airlines Trondheim's **Værnes Airport** is 35 kilometers (22 miles) northeast of the city. **SAS** (tel. 74/82–49–22), **Braathens SAFE** (tel. 74/82–32–00), and **Widerøe** (tel. 74/82–49–22) are the main domestic carriers. SAS also has one flight between Trondheim and Copenhagen daily, except Sunday, and daily flights to Stockholm.

With the exception of Harstad, all cities in northern Norway are served by airports less than 5 kilometers (3 miles) from the center of town. Tromsø is a crossroads for air traffic between northern and southern Norway and is served by Braathens SAFE, SAS, and Widerøe. SAS flies to eight destinations

in northern Norway, including Bodø, Tromsø, Alta, and Kirkenes. Braathens SAFE flies to five destinations, including Bodø and Tromsø. Widerøe specializes in northern Norway and flies to 19 destinations in the region, including Honningsvåg, the airport closest to the North Cape.

Arriving and Departing by Car, Train, Bus, and Boat

By Car **Trondheim** is about 500 kilometers (310 miles) from Oslo: seven to eight hours of driving. Speed limits are 80 kmh (50 mph) much of the way. There are two alternatives, E6 through Gudbrandsdalen or Route 3 through Østerdalen. Roads are decent, for the most part, but can become thick with campers during midsummer, sometimes making the going slow. It's 727 kilometers (450 miles) from Trondheim to Bodø on Route E6, which goes all the way to Kirkenes.

By Train The **Dovrebanen** has five departures daily, four on Saturday, in both directions on the Oslo–Trondheim route. Trains leave from Oslo S Station for the seven- to eight-hour journey. Trondheim is the gateway to the North, and two trains run daily in both directions on the 11-hour Trondheim–Bodø route. For information about trains out of Trondheim, call 73/53–00–10. The **Nordlandsbanen** has two departures daily in each direction on the Bodø–Trondheim route, an 11-hour journey. The **Ofotbanen** has one departure daily in each direction on the Stockholm–Narvik route, a 21-hour journey.

By Bus Buses run only from Oslo to Otta, where they connect with the train to Trondheim. Buses connect Bergen, Molde, Ålesund, and Røros with Trondheim. **Nor-Way Bussekspress** (tel. 22/17–52–90) can help you to put together a bus journey to the North. The Express 2000 travels three times a week between Oslo, Kautokeino, Alta, and Hammerfest. The journey, via Sweden, takes 24, 26, and 29 hours, respectively.

By Boat **Hurtigruten** (the coastal express boat, which calls at 35 ports from Bergen to Kirkenes) stops at Trondheim, southbound at St. Olav's Pier, Quay 16, northbound at Pier 1, Quay 7.

Getting Around

By Plane Northern Norway has excellent air connections through SAS, Braathens SAFE, and Widerøe. (*See* Arriving and Departing by Plane, *above*.)

By Bus Most local buses in **Trondheim** stop at the Munkegata/
Trondheim Dronningens Gate intersection. Some routes end at the bus terminal (Skakkes Gate 40, tel. 73/52–44–74). Tickets cost NKr12 and allow free transfer between buses (tel. 73/54–71–00) and streetcars (**Gråkallbanen,** tel. 72/55–21–63).

The North North of **Bodø** and **Narvik** (a five-hour bus ride from Bodø), beyond the reach of the railroad, buses go virtually everywhere, but they don't go often. Get a comprehensive bus schedule from a tourist office or travel agent before making plans. Local bus companies include **Saltens Bilruter** (Bodø, tel. 75/52–50–25), **Ofotens Bilruter** (Narvik, tel. 76/94–64–80), **Tromsbuss** (Tromsø, tel. 77/67–02–33), **Tromsøexpressen** (Tromsø, tel. 77/67–27–87), and **Finnmark Fylkesrederi og Ruteselskap** (Alta, tel. 78/43–52–11, Hammerfest, tel. 78/41–16–55).

519 M.P.H.

190 M.P.H.

75 M.P.H.

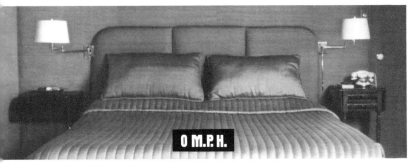

0 M.P.H.

WE LET YOU SEE EUROPE AT YOUR OWN PACE.

Regardless of your personal speed limits, Rail Europe ffers everything to get you over, around and through nywhere you want in Europe. For more infor- nation, call your travel agent or 1-800-4-EURAIL.

We can wire money to every major city in Europe almost as fast as you can say, "Zut alors! J'ai perdu mes valises."

How fast? We can send money in 10 minutes or less, to 13,500 locations in over 68 countries worldwide. That's faster than any other international money transfer service. And when you're *sans* luggage, every minute counts.

MoneyGram from American Express® is available throughout Europe. For more information please contact your local American Express Travel Service Office or call: 44-71-839-7541 in England; 33-1-47777000 in France; or 49-69-21050 in Germany. In the U.S. call 1-800-MONEYGRAM.

MoneyGram

INTERNATIONAL MONEY TRANSFERS.

Ten-minute delivery subject to local agent hours of operation. Local send/receive facilities may also vary. ©1993 First Data Corporation.

By Boat Boat is the ideal transportation in Nordland. The **Hurtigruten** stops twice daily (north and southbound) at 20 ports in northern Norway. It is possible to buy tickets between any harbors right on the boats. **Saltens Dampskibsselskab** (Bodø, tel. 75/52–10–20) has express boats between Bodø and Hamarøy and Svolvær, while **OVDS** (Narvik, tel. 76/94–40–90) ferries and express boats serve many towns in the region. **TFDS, Troms Fylkes Dampskibsselskap** (Tromsø, tel. 77/68–60–88) operates various boat services in the region around Tromsø.

By Car The roads aren't a problem in northern Norway—most are quite good, although there are always narrow and winding stretches, especially along fjords. Distances are formidable. Route 17—*Kystriksvegen* (the Coastal Highway) from Namsos to Bodø—is an excellent alternative to E6. Getting to Tromsø and the North Cape involves additional driving on narrower roads off E6. In the northern winter, near-blizzard conditions and icy roads sometimes make it necessary to drive in a convoy. You'll know it when you see it: Towns are cut off from traffic at access roads, and vehicles wait until their numbers are large enough to make the crossing safely.

You can also fly the extensive distances and then rent a car for sightseeing within the area, but book a rental car as far in advance as possible. There's no better way to see the Lofoten and Vesterålen islands than by car. Nordkapp (take the plane to Honningsvåg) is another excursion best made by car.

By Taxi Taxi ranks are located in strategic places in downtown **Trondheim.** All taxis are connected to the central dispatching office (tel. 73/52–76–00). Taxi numbers in other towns are: **Harstad,** tel. 77/06–20–56; **Narvik,** tel. 76/94–65–00; **Røst,** tel. 77/89–62–90; and **Tromsø,** tel. 77/68–80–20.

Guided Tours

Tromsø The tourist information office sells tickets for **City Sightseeing** (Dampskipskaia) and **M/S *Polstjerna,*** an original Arctic vessel that offers a fishing tour in the waters around Tromsø Island.

Trondheim The Trondheim Tourist Association offers a number of tours. Tickets are sold at the tourist information office or at the start of the tour.

Samiland **Contact Sami Travel A/S** (Kautokeino, tel. 78/48–62–03) for adventure trips to Sami settlements.

Svalbard **Svalbard Polar Travel** (9170 Longyearbyen, tel. 79/02–19–71) arranges combination air-sea visits, from three-day minicruises to 12-day trekking expeditions on the rim of the North Pole. **Spitsbergen Travel** (9170 Longyearbyen, tel. 79/02–24–00) offers specialized "exploring" tours, which focus on the plant and animal life of the region.

Exploring Trondheim and the North

Numbers in the margin correspond to points of interest on the Trondheim and the North map.

Tour 1: Trondheim

❶ Trondheim's original name, Nidaros (still the name of the cathedral), is a composite word referring to the city's location at

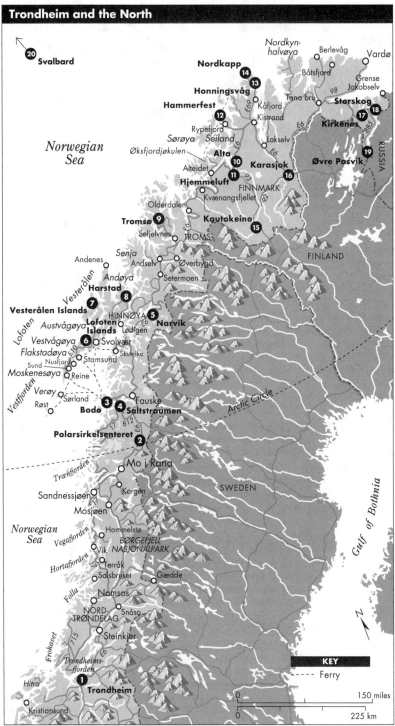

Trondheim and the North

the mouth of the Nid River. After a savage fire in 1681, the wood town was rebuilt according to the plan of General Cicignon, a military man from Luxembourg, who also designed its fort. The wide streets of the city center are still lined with brightly painted wood houses and picturesque warehouses.

Start at Torget, the town square, with the statue of St. Olav in the middle. South on Munkegate is one of the finest collections in Scandinavia, the **Nordenfjeldske Kunstindustrimuseum** (Decorative Arts Museum). It has superb period rooms from the Renaissance to 1950s Scandinavian modern. The Tiffany windows are also magnificent. *Munkegt. 5, tel. 73/52–13–11. Admission: NKr20 adults, NKr10 children. Open June 20–Aug. 20, Mon.–Sat. 10–6, Sun. noon–5; Aug. 21–June 19, Mon.–Sat. 10–3, Thurs. 10–7, Sun. noon–4.*

Continue on Munkegate to **Nidaros domen** (Nidaros Cathedral), built on the grave of St. Olav, who formulated a Christian religions code for Norway in 1024 while he was king. He was killed in battle against the Danes at Stikle Stad. After he was buried water sprang from his grave, and people began to believe that his nails and hair continued to grow beneath the ground. After a series of other miracles, the town became a pilgrimage site for the Christians of northern Europe, and Olav was canonized in 1164.

Although construction was begun in 1070, the oldest existing parts of the cathedral date from around 1150. During the Catholic period, it attracted crowds of pilgrims, but after the Reformation, its importance declined and fires destroyed much of it. The 1814 Constitution decreed that Norway's kings should be crowned at the cathedral. Restoration began around 1870 and the interior was completed in 1930. The facade is still being restored, and the western front, with twin towers and a rose window, has been reinstalled during the past 60 years. The first king of modern Norway, Haakon VII, and Queen Maud, daughter of Edward VII of England, were crowned in the cathedral in 1906. Two years later, the Constitution was altered to eliminate the coronation ceremony, but in 1957, King Olav, and in 1991, King Harald and Queen Sonja, were formally blessed here. *Kongsgårdsgt. 2, tel. 73/50–12–12. Castle admission: NKr10 adults; NKr5 children, senior citizens, students. Ticket also permits entry to Erkebispegården (see below). Open June 1–Aug. 15, weekdays 9:30–12:30, Sun. 1–4; Apr. 1–May 31 and Aug. 16–Oct. 31, Fri. noon–4. Tower Admission: NKr5. Open June 19–Aug. 15, daily every half hour during regular opening hours.*

Next door is Scandinavia's oldest secular building (actually two buildings connected by a gatehouse), from around 1160, **Erkebispegården** (the Archbishop's Palace), the residence of the archbishop until the Reformation. After that, it was a Danish governor's palace, and later a military headquarters. *Tel. 73/50–12–12. Admission: NKr10 adults; NKr5 children, senior citizens, students. Ticket also permits entry to cathedral. Open June 1–Aug. 15, weekdays 9–3, Sat. 9–2, Sun. noon–3.*

Within the Erkebispegården is **Forsvarsmuseet** (the Army Museum), with displays of uniforms, swords, and daggers. **Hjemmefrontmuseet** (the Resistance Museum), also there, documents the occupation of Norway during World War II through objects and photographs. *Tel. 73/51–51–11, ext. 182. Admis-*

*sion: NKr5 adults, NKr2 children. Open June 1–Aug. 31,
weekdays 9–3; year-round, weekends 11–3.*

On Bispegate turn right and follow the river. You'll pass Gamle
Bybro (the Old Bridge) and reach Kjøpmannsgata, where you
can turn left on Kongensgate. Behind **Biblioteket** (the Library,
Kongensgate 2) are the remains of St. Olavskirke (St. Olav's
Church). The crypt of another medieval church can be seen in-
side **Trondhjems og Strindens Sparebank** (a savings bank at
Søndregate 2) during normal banking hours.

Time Out   Two short blocks farther is Nordregate, a pedestrian mall. Pop
into **Erichsens** restaurant/coffee shop (Nordregt. 10) for a
quick lunch, cake and coffee, or a three-course meal.

Continue on Nordregate and turn left on Dronningens Gate. On
the left is **Stiftsgården,** Scandinavia's largest wood building,
built in 1778 as a private home, the result of a competition between two sisters who were trying to outdo each other with the
size of their houses. Today it is the king's official residence in
Trondheim. The interior is sparsely furnished in threadbare
Rococo, Empire, and Biedermeier. *Tel. 73/52–24–73. Admission: NKr20 adults, NKr10 children. Open June 1–Aug. 20,
Mon.–Sat. 10–3, Sun. 10–4.*

The street on the far side of Stiftsgården is Munkegate. To the
right is **Ravnkloa Fiskehall** (fish market), by the water, where
you can see an immense variety of seafood. Past the railroad
station and the quay across the water, you'll come to a former
prison that now houses **Sjøfartsmuseet** (the Maritime Museum). Inside are galleon figureheads, ship models, a harpoon
cannon from a whaling boat, and a large collection of seafaring
pictures. *Fjordgt. 6A, tel. 73/52–89–75. Admission: NKr10
adults, NKr5 children and senior citizens. Open Mon.–Sat.
9–3, Sun. noon–3; closed Sat. in winter.*

Time Out   Down Kjøpmannsgata from the museum is a modern shopping
mall, Olavskvartalet; in its center is **Torgcafeen,** run by the
Grand Hotel Olav, which serves sandwiches, salads, and cakes.

Across the street is the Royal Garden Hotel, built in the same
Hansa style as the buildings that line the wharf. Farther down
are the oldest buildings on the river, dating from the 1700s.

For an unusual museum visit, you can take a half-hour ride to
Fagerheim and the **Ringve Music Museum** at Ringve Gård, the
childhood home of the naval hero Admiral Tordenskiold.
Guides (music students) demonstrate the instruments on display and tell about their role in the history of music. Concerts
are held regularly. *Lade allé 60, tel. 73/92–24–11. Admission:
NKr40 adults, NKr20 senior citizens and students, NKr10
children. Guided tours in English May 20–June 30, daily at
noon, 2; July 1–Aug. 10, daily at 11, 12:30, 2:30; Aug. 11–Aug.
31, daily at 11, 12:30, 2:30; Sept. 1–31, daily at noon; Oct. 1–
May 19, Sun. at 1:30. Tour lasts approximately 75 minutes.*

At the other end of town, **Trøndelag Folkemuseum** has a collection of rustic buildings from the turn of the century, including a dental office and a lace-and-ribbon-maker's workshop.
*Sverresborg, tel. 73/53–14–90. Admission: NKr30 adults,
NKr10 children and senior citizens. Open May 20–Sept. 1, daily 11–6.*

Tour 2: Trondheim to Narvik

Nord Trøndelag, as the land above Trondheim is called, is largely agricultural. Taken on its own, it's beautiful, with farms, mountains, rock formations, and clear blue water, but compared with the rest of Norway, it is subtle, with only an undulating landscape—so many tourists just sleep through it on the night train, or fly over it on their way to the North.

The first town of any size is **Steinkjer,** a military base, boot camp for 3,000 Norwegian army recruits every year. North 350 kilometers (218 miles) is **Mo i Rana** (the poetic name means Mo on the Ranafjord), a center for iron and steel production using ore from nearby mines. Glacier fans can hike on the **Svartisen** (literally Black Ice), an ice cap 30 kilometers (19 miles) north of town.

❷ On a bleak stretch of treeless countryside 80 kilometers (50 miles) north of **Mo i Rana** is the Arctic Circle. **Polarsirkelsenteret** (The Arctic Circle Center), on E6, presents a multiscreen show about Norway. The post office has a special postmark, and you can get your Arctic Circle Certificate stamped. There's also a cafeteria and gift shop. *8242 Polarsirkelen, tel. 75/16–60–60. Admission: NKr30. Open May 1–Sept. 30 (Apr., Oct., cafeteria only).*

❸ **Bodø,** a modern city of about 37,000 just above the Arctic Circle, is best known as the end station of the Nordlandsbanen railroad and the gateway to the Lofoten islands and the North. At Bodø, the Midnight Sun is visible from June 2 to July 10. Like many other coastal towns, it began as a small fishing community, but today it is a commercial and administrative center.

❹ **Saltstraumen,** 33 kilometers (20 miles) southeast of Bodø on Route 80/17, is a 3-kilometer- (2-mile-) long and 500-foot-wide section of water between the outer fjord, which joins with the sea, and the inner fjord basin. During high tide, the volume of water rushing through the strait and into the basin is so great that whirlpools form. This is the legendary mælstrøm—and the strongest one in the world. Sometimes as many as four separate whirlpools can be seen, and the noise made by these "cauldrons" can be both loud and eerie. All that rush of water brings enormous quantities of fish, making the mælstrøm a popular fishing spot.

Time Out | **Saltstraumen Hotel** (tel. 75/58–76–85) is practically on top of the mælstrøm. The restaurant to the left of the entrance serves delicious steamed halibut in butter sauce.

❺ **Narvik,** 336 kilometers (210 miles) north, is more easily reached by rail from Stockholm than from most places in Norway, as it is the end station on the Ofotbanen, the Norwegian railroad that connects with the Swedish railroad's northernmost line. It was originally established as the ice-free port for exporting Swedish iron ore mined around Kiruna.

On May 9, 1940, the German army invaded Norway through Narvik, and German occupying forces stayed for more than five years. After the war, Narvik, which had been leveled by the bombing, was rebuilt. **Krigsminnemuseet** (the War Memorial Museum) documents wartime events with artifacts, models, and pictures. *Torget, tel. 76/94–44–26. Admission: NKr20*

adults, NKr10 children and senior citizens. Open June 15–
Sept. 15, daily 10–10; Sept. 16–June 14, daily 10–2.

Tour 3: The Lofoten Islands

6 Extending out into the ocean north of Bodø are the **Lofoten Is-**
lands, a 190-kilometer (118-mile) chain of jagged peaks, mountaintops rising from the bottom of the sea like open jaws. The
midnight sun is visible here from May 26 to July 17. In the summer, the idyll of farms, fjords, and fishing villages makes it a
major tourist attraction, while in the winter, the coast facing
the Arctic Ocean is one of Europe's stormiest.

Until about 40 years ago, fishing was the only source of income.
Cod and haddock were either dried or salted and sold on the
Continent. Up to 6,000 boats with 30,000 fishermen would mo-
bilize between January and March for the Lofotfiske, the annual cod-fishing event. During the season they fished in open
boats and took shelter during stormy nights in *rorbuer*, simple
cabins built right on the water. Today many rorbuer have been
converted into lodgings, and much of the fishing has been taken
over by year-round factory ships, but many fishing villages,
still with the criss-crossing wood racks set out in the open air
for drying fish, remain, and individual fishermen still go out.

Svolvær, the main town, connected with the other islands by express boat and ferry and by coastal steamer and air to Bodø,
has a thriving summer art colony. A drive on E10, from
Svolvær to the outer tip of the Lofotens (130 kilometers/80
miles)—the town with the enigmatic name of Å—is an opportunity to see how the islanders really live. Scenic stops include
Nusfjord, a 19th-century fishing village on the UNESCO list of
historic monuments; **Sund,** with its smithy; and **Reine.**

Time Out **Gammelbua,** in Reine, serves excellent steamed halibut, homemade fish soufflé, and inspired desserts and cakes.

Off the tip of Moskenesøy, the last island with a bridge, is
Moskenesstraumen, another mælstrøm, not quite as dramatic
as Saltstraumen, but inspiration to both Jules Verne, who
wrote about it in *Journey Beneath the Sea,* and Edgar Allan
Poe, who described it in his short story "A Descent into the
Maelstrom."

7 North of the Lofotens are the **Vesterålen Islands,** with more
fishing villages and rorbuer, and diverse vegetation.

Tour 4: Harstad to the North Cape

East of Vesterålen on Hinnøya, Norway's largest island, is
8 **Harstad,** where the year-round population of 22,000 swells to
42,000 during the annual June cultural festival (the line-up includes concerts, theater, and dance) and its July deep-sea fishing festival.

9 **Tromsø,** the most important city north of the Arctic Circle, and
home to 50,000 people, is 318 kilometers (197 miles) northeast.
At 2,558 square kilometers (987 square miles), it's Norway's
largest city in terms of area, just about the same size as the
country of Luxembourg. The midnight sun shines from May 21
to July 23, and the 13,000 students at the world's northernmost

university are one reason the nightlife here is more lively than in many other northern cities.

Certainly **Ishavskatedralen** (the Arctic Cathedral) is the city's best-known structure. A looming peak of 11 descending triangles of concrete and glass meant it is to evoke the shape of a Sami tent and the iciness of a glacier. Inside, an immense jewel-colored stained-glass window by Norwegian artist Viktor Sparre depicts the Second Coming. At the back of the church is a silver-and-copper organ, a modern adaptation of the omnipresent ships that hang in Scandinavian churches.

The **Tromsø Museum,** part of Tromsø University, offers an extensive survey of local history, lifestyles, and nature, with dioramas on Sami culture, arctic hunting practices, and wildlife. *Universitetet, tel. 77/64–50–00. Admission: NKr10 adults, NKr5 children. Open June–mid-Aug., daily 9–6; mid-Aug.– May, Mon.–Fri. 8:30–3:30, Sat. noon–3, Sun. 11–4. At other times, call for hours.*

Polarmuseet (the Polar Museum), in an 1830s customs warehouse, documents the history of the polar region, with skis and equipment from Roald Amundsen's expedition to the South Pole and a reconstructed Svalbard hunting station from 1910. *Søndre Tollbugt. 11b, tel. 77/68–43–73. Admission: NKr20 adults, NKr5 children. Open May 15–Aug. 31, daily 11–6; Sept. 1–May 14, daily 11–3.*

There are more museums in Tromsø, but to get a real sense of its northerly immensity and peace, take the **Fjellheisen** (cable car) from behind the cathedral up to the mountains, just a few minutes out of the city center. In the late afternoon and on weekends, summer and winter, this is where locals go to ski, picnic, walk their lucky dogs, and admire the view. *Tel. 77/63– 51–21. Admission: NKr40 adults, NKr20 children. Open May– Sept., daily 10–5; June–Aug., daily 10–midnight if it's sunny. At other times, call for hours.*

It's 409 kilometers (253 miles) to Alta on coastal road most of the way. Kautokeino Sami spend the summer in turf huts at **Kvænangsfjellet,** so you might see a few of their reindeer. **Øksfjordjøkelen,** the only glacier in Norway that calves into the sea, is 13 kilometers (8 miles) west of Alteidet.

⑩ Alta is the last marker on the way to the North Cape and a major transportation center into Finnmark, the far north of Norway. Most people come just to spend the night before making **⑪** the final ascent, but it's worth a trek to **Hjemmeluft,** southwest of the city, to see four groupings of 2,500- to 6,000-year-old **prehistoric rock carvings,** the largest in northern Europe. The pictographs, featuring ships, reindeer, and even a man with a bow and arrow, were discovered in 1973. *Tel. 78/43–53–77 (Alta Museum). Admission: NKr10 adults, NKr5 children. Open June 1–June 14 and Aug. 16–Aug. 31, daily 8–8; June 15– Aug. 15, daily 8 AM–11 PM; Sept. 1–May 31, weekdays 9–3, weekends 11–4.*

A detour on the way to the North Cape is to the world's northernmost town, **Hammerfest,** an important fishing center 145 ki-**⑫** lometers (90 miles) from Alta. At these latitudes the "most northerlies" become numerous, but certainly the lifestyles here are a testament to determination, especially in winter, when night lasts for months. In 1891 Hammerfest decided to

brighten the situation and purchased a generator from Thomas Edison. It was the first city in Europe to have electric street lamps.

The journey from Alta to the Cape is 217 kilometers (134 miles) and includes a 45-minute ferry ride from Kåfjord to **⑬ Honningsvåg,** the last village before the Cape. Honningsvåg was completely destroyed at the end of World War II, when the Germans retreated and burned everything they left behind. Only a single wood church, which still survives, was not left in embers. **Nordkappmuseet** (the North Cape Museum), on the third floor of Nordkapphuset (the North Cape House), documents the history of the fishing industry in the region as well as the history of tourism at the North Cape. *9750 Honningsvåg, tel. 78/47-28-33. Admission: NKr15 adults, NKr5 children. Open June 15-Aug. 15, Mon.-Sat. 11-8, Sun. 6-8; Aug. 16-June 14, weekdays 11-3.*

⑭ From Honningsvåg, it's 34 kilometers (21 miles) to **Nordkapp,** on treeless tundra, with crumbling mountains and sparse dwarf plants. The contrast between this near-barren territory and the new **North Cape Hall** is striking. Blasted into the interior of the plateau, it includes a panorama restaurant. A tunnel leads past a small chapel to a grotto with a panoramic view of the Arctic Ocean and to the cliff wall itself, passing exhibits that trace the history of the Cape, from Richard Chancellor, an Englishman who drifted around it and named it in 1533, to Oscar II, king of Norway and Sweden, who climbed to the top of the plateau in 1873, and King Chulalongkorn of Siam (now Thailand), who visited the Cape in 1907. Out on the plateau itself, a hollow sculptured globe is illuminated by the Midnight Sun, which shines from May 11 to August 31. *9764 Nordkapp. Admission: NKr95 adults, NKr35 children.*

Although this area is notoriously crowded in the summer, with endless lines of tour buses, it's completely different from fall through spring, when the snow is yards deep and the sea is frosty gray. Because the roads are closed in winter, the only access is from the tiny fishing village of Skarsvåg via snow cat, a thump-and-bump ride that's as unforgettable as the beautifully bleak view. For winter information, contact the **Skarsvåg Tourist Information Office** (tel. 78/47-52-80). Knivsjellodden, slightly west and less dramatic than the North Cape, is actually a hair farther north.

Tour 5: Samiland

Everyone has heard of Lapland, but few know its real name, Samiland. The Sami recognize no national boundaries, as their territory stretches from the Kola Peninsula in the Soviet Union through Finland, Sweden, and Norway. These indigenous reindeer herders are a distinct ethnic group, with a language related to Finnish. Although still considered nomadic, they no longer live in tents or huts, except for short periods during the summer, when their animals graze along the coast. They have had to conform to today's lifestyles, but their traditions survive through their language, music (called Joikk), art, and handcrafts. Norwegian Samiland is synonymous with the communities of Kautokeino and Karasjok in Finnmark.

⑮ Kautokeino, 129 kilometers (80 miles) southeast of Alta, is the site of the Sami theater and the Nordic Sami Institute, dedi-

cated to the study of Sami culture. It is a center for Sami handicrafts and education, with even a school of reindeer herding.

Guovdageainnu (Kautokeino in the Sami language) **Gilisillju,**
the local museum, documents the way of life of both the nomadic and the resident Sami of that area prior to World War II, with
photographs and artifacts, including costumes, dwellings, and
art. *9520 Kautokeino, tel. 78/45–62–03. Admission: NKr10
adults, children free. Open weekdays 9–3.*

⑯ **Karasjok,** on the other side of the Finnmark plateau, is the seat
of the 39-member Sami Parliament and capital of Samiland. It
has a typical inland climate, with the accompanying temperature extremes. The best time to come is at Easter, when the
communities are celebrating the weddings and baptisms of the
year and taking part in reindeer races and other colorful festivities. In summer, when many of the Sami go to the coast with
their reindeer, the area is not nearly as interesting.

Samid Vuorku-Davvirat (the Sami Collections), is a comprehensive museum of Sami culture, with emphasis on the arts, reindeer herding, and the status of women in the Sami community.
*Museumsgt. 17, tel. 78/46–63–05. Admission: NKr15 adults,
NKr5 children. Open Mon.–Sat. 9–3, Sun. noon–3.*

From late fall to early spring you can go **reindeer sledding.** A
Sami guide will take you out on a wood sled tied to a couple of
unwieldy reindeer, and you'll clop through the barren, snow-
covered scenery of Finnmark. Wide and relatively flat, the col-
orless winter landscape is veined by inky alder branches and
little else. You'll reach a *lavvu*, a traditional Sami tent, and be
invited in to share a meal of boiled reindeer, bread, jam, and
strong coffee next to an open alder fire. It's an extraordinary
experience. *Karasjok Opplevelser, tel. 78/46–73–60.*

Tour 6: The Finnish-Russian Connection

At its very top, Norway hooks over Finland and touches Russia
for 122 kilometers (75 miles). The towns in east Finnmark have
a more heterogeneous population than those in the rest of the
country. A century ago, during hard times in Finland, many in-
dustrious Finns settled in this region, where their descendants
keep the language alive.

⑰ A good way to visit this part of Norway is to fly to **Kirkenes** and
then explore the region by car. Only Malta was bombed more
than Kirkenes during World War II, so virtually everything
has been built within the past 40 years.

From Kirkenes, it's about 60 kilometers (37 miles) to **Grense
Jakobselv,** the Russian border. As a protest against constant
Russian encroachment in the area, King Oscar II built a chapel
⑱ right at the border in 1869. Just east of Kirkenes is **Storskog,**
for many years the only official land crossing of the border between Norway and Russia.

The southernmost part of Finnmark, a narrow tongue of land
⑲ tucked between Finland and Russia, is **Øvre Pasvik** national
park. This subarctic evergreen forest is the western end of
Siberia's *taiga* and supports many varieties of flora found only
here. The area is surprisingly lush, and in good years all the
cloudberries make the swamps shine orange.

Tour 7: Svalbard

㉟ North of the North Cape are the islands of **Svalbard,** the largest of which is Spitsbergen. Officially part of Norway only since 1925, they might have remained wilderness, with only the occasional visitor, if coal had not been discovered late in the 19th century. Today both a Norwegian and a Russian coal company have operations there, and there are two Russian coal miners' communities. The islands offer ample opportunities for ski, dogsled, and skidoo exploring.

The best way to experience Svalbard is by ship, as accommodations on the islands themselves are sparse. The capital, **Longyearbyen,** is 90 minutes by air from Tromsø. It was named for an American, John Monroe Longyear, who established a mining operation there in 1906. Only three species of land mammals— polar bear, reindeer, and Arctic fox—and one species of bird— ptarmigan—have adapted to Svalbard winters, but during the summer months, more than 30 species of birds nest on the steep cliffs of the islands, and white whales, seals, and walruses also come for the season.

Because Svalbard is so far north, it has four months of continual daylight, from April 21 to August 21. Summers can be lush, with hundreds of varieties of wildflowers. The season is so compressed that buds, full-blown flowers, and seed appear simultaneously on the same plant.

What to See and Do with Children

Tromsø Take bus No. 28 to the mainland to ride Fjellheisen (*see* Tour 4, *above*) cable car to **Storsteinen** (the Big Rock), 420 meters (1,386 feet) above sea level, for a great view of the city.

Nordlysplanetariet (the Northern Lights Planetarium), at Breivika, is just outside town. Here, 112 projectors guarantee a 360-degree view of programs, which include a tour through the Northern Lights, the Midnight Sun, and geological history, as well as a film and multimedia show about the city. *Breivika, tel. 77/67–60–00. Admission: NKr50 adults, NKr25 children, NKr40 senior citizens. Open June 1–June 15, weekdays 12:30–7; June 16–Aug. 15, 10–7; Sept.–Apr., weekends 11:30–6.*

At **Tromsø Museum** (*see* Tour 4, *above*) children can listen to animal sounds over earphones, match animal puzzles to their tales, and play with a nearly lifesize dinosaur. An open-air museum is on the same grounds. *Folkeparken, tel. 77/64–50–00. Admission: NKr10 adults, NKr5 children. Open June 1–Aug. 31, daily 9–7; Sept. 1–May 31, weekdays, 8:30–3:30, Wed. also 7–10; Sat. noon–3, Sun. 11–4. Aquarium only: Open June 1– Aug. 31, daily 10–5; Sept. 1–May 31, Sun. only 11–2.*

Off the Beaten Track

In winter this entire region, blanketed by snow and cold, is off the beaten track. As the Norwegians say, there is no bad weather, only bad clothes—so bundle up and explore.

Kirkenes From mid-June to mid-August, the *FFR* (Hammerfest, tel. 78/ 59–25–44) operates visa-free day cruises to Murmansk on a

high-speed catamaran. Booking is required two weeks in advance.

St. Georgs kapell, 45 kilometers (28 miles) west of Kirkenes, is the only Russian-Orthodox chapel in Norway, where the Orthodox Skolt-Sami had their summer encampment. It's a tiny building, and services are held outside, weather permitting.

Mo i Rana **Sætergrotta** and **Grønligrotta** are two of around 200 caves 26 kilometers (16 miles) northwest of Mo i Rana. Sætergrotta, with 2,400 meters (7,920 feet) of charted underground paths, many narrow passages, natural "chimneys," and an underground river, is for serious cave explorers. *Tel. 75/15–04–21. Admission: NKr140 at tourist office. Two-hour guided tours daily at 11 and 2.*

Grønligrotta, Scandinavia's best-known show-cave, even has electric lights. The 20-minute tour goes deep into the limestone cave to the underground river. *Admission: NKr30 adults, NKr15 children. Tours daily on the hour 10–7. Open June 15–Aug. 15.*

Svartisen **Saltens Dampskibsselskap** (tel. 75/72–10–20) offers seven-hour boat tours from Bodø to Svartisen, the second-largest glacier in Norway, near Mo i Rana, on Saturday in summer. The easiest way to get to the glacier is from Mo, 32 kilometers (20 miles) by car to Svartisvatn lake. A boat crosses the lake every hour to within 2½ kilometers (1.5 miles) of the Østerdal arm of the glacier. If you plan to get to the glacier on your own, you should inquire at the tourist office about connecting with a guide. Glacier walking is extremely hazardous and should never be done without a professional guide, because even though a glacier may appear fixed and static, it is always changing; there's always the danger of crevasses.

Shopping

Harstad **Trastadsenteret** (Rik. Kaarbøsgt. 19) sells pottery, weavings, and textile prints by local artists.

Kåfjord **Grenbu** (tel. 77/71–62–73) at Løkvoll in Manndalen on E6 about 15 kilometers (9 miles) west of Alta is a center for Coastal Sami weaving, on vertical looms. Local weavers sell their rugs and wall hangings along with other regional crafts.

Karasjok The specialties of the region are Sami crafts, particularly handmade knives. In **Samelandssenter** (tel. 78/48–73–60) is a large collection of shops featuring northern specialties, including **Knivsmed Strømeng** (tel. 78/48–71–05).

Kautokeino The Frank and Regina **Juhls** silver gallery (tel. 78/48–61–89) sells Sami crafts as well as their own modern jewelry.

Lofoten Lofoten is a mecca for artists and craftspeople; a list of galleries and crafts centers, with all locations marked on a map, is available from tourist offices.

Probably the best-known craftsperson in the region is Hans Gjertsen, better known as **Smeden i Sund** (the blacksmith at Sund; tel. 76/09–36–29). Watch him make wrought iron cormorants in many sizes, as well as candlesticks and other gift items.

Tromsø The city has two major shopping centers: **Veita** (Storgaten 102, tel. 77/65–87–55) and **Pyramiden** (Tromsdalen, tel. 77/63–82–00).

Trondheim Trondheim has an extraordinary number of high-quality art and handicraft stores. In addition to **Husfliden** (Olav Tryggvasonsgt. 18, tel. 73/52–18–74). **Yvonne Verkstedutsalg og Galleri** (Ørjaveita 6, tel. 73/52–73–27) also sells works of local artists. **Olavskvartalet,** across from the Royal Garden Hotel, is a shopping center with many specialty stores.

Sports and Outdoor Activities

Bird-watching From Moskenes, just north of Å (or from Bodø), you can take a ferry to the bird sanctuaries of **Værøy** and **Røst.** Hundreds of thousands of seabirds inhabit the cliffs of the islands, in particular the eider ducks, favorites of the local population, which build small shelters for their nests. Eventually the down collected from these nests ends up in *dyner* (feather comforters).

There are even more birds in Gjesvær on the east coast of the Honningsvåg. Contact Ola Thomassen (tel. 78/47–57–73) for organized outings.

Dogsledding **Canyon Huskies** (tel. 78/43–33–06), in Alta, arranges all kinds of personalized tours, whether you want to stay in a tent or hotel, and whether you want to drive your team or stay in the sled. Like most Norwegian sled dogs, these are very friendly.

Fishing In **Trondheim** the Nidelven (Nid River) is one of Norway's best salmon and trout rivers. You can fish right in the city, but, as usual, you'll need a license. Ask at any sports store. In the waters of **Tromsø,** there are cod, coalfish, haddock, and the occasional catfish. Elsewhere in Finnmark, ice fishing is a passion, often with the entire family involved. (The Sami sometimes ice fish from tiny houses they pull onto the ice with snow cats.) Check with the tourist board to find out if and where any competitions are scheduled. Bring at least your own ice drill.

Hiking In **Tromsø** there's good hiking in the mountains above the city, reachable by funicular. Other regional possibilities begin anywhere outside the cities (usually only a few minutes away). In between the Alta and Karasjok areas, the **Finnmarksvidda** has marked trails with overnight possibilities in lodges. Contact the Norwegian Mountain Touring Association (Stortinsgata 28, N-0161 Oslo) and the Finnmark Travel Association (tel. 78/43–54–44).

Hunting Two licenses are needed to hunt, and for large game, especially moose, lots must be drawn among applicants. Contact the Finnmark Travel Association (tel. 78/43–54–44).

Rafting Deep-sea rafting is a relatively new sport in the area, but one that is as exhilarating as it is beautiful. Several tours are offered, including a three-hour trip to the North Cape. Call **Nordkapp Safari** (tel. 78/47–27–94).

Reindeer Sledding Reindeer sledding is a wonderful Finnmark experience (*see* Tour 5, *above*).

Skiing **Bymarka** and **Estenstadmarka,** the wooded areas on the periphery of Trondheim, are popular among cross-country skiers. At **Skistua** (ski lodge) in Bymarka, and at **Vassfjellet** south of the city, there are downhill runs. In Tromsø, the mountains, only eight minutes away by funicular, are not only a great place to ski, but also to hike (*see* Tour 4, *above*). Elsewhere, you'll have to ask specifics from the tourist board. Listen to the weather reports and pay heed to warnings. Blizzards come in

quickly over the water; the wind alone can knock an ample person clear off his or her feet.

Beaches

In Trondheim, the island of Munkholmen, easily reached by ferry from Ravnkloa, has a popular sandy beach. Elsewhere, most beaches are rocky, and the water is, as the Norwegians say, fresh. However, some of the beaches of Nordland are long and sandy, with temperatures reaching as high as 20°C (68°F).

Dining and Lodging

Dining **Trondheim** is known for several dishes, including *surlaks* (pickled salmon), marinated in a sweet-and-sour brine with onions and spices, and served with sour cream. A sweet specialty is *tekake* (tea cake), which looks like a thick-crust pizza topped with a lattice pattern of cinnamon and sugar.

If you visit northern Norway between May and August, try the specialty of *måsegg* and *Mack-øl*, more for curiosity value than for taste. *Måsegg* (seagulls' eggs), are always served hard-boiled and halved in their shells. They're larger than chicken eggs, and they look exotic, with greenish-gray speckled shells and bright orange yolks, but they taste like standard supermarket eggs. *Mack-øl* (similar to pils), is brewed in Tromsø at the world's northernmost brewery. Otherwise, as in the rest of provincial Norway, most better restaurants are in hotels.

Lodging Most Trondheim hotels have summer rates, but for some, a hotel pass or special booking method is required. Unless otherwise noted, breakfast is included.

At times it seems as though the SAS and Rica hotel chains are the only ones in northern Norway, and often that is true. These are always top-rate, usually the most expensive hotel in town, with the best restaurant and the most extensive facilities. Rustic cabins and campsites are also available everywhere, as well as independent hotels.

In the Lofoten and Vesterålen islands, rorbuer, which have been converted into lodgings or modern versions of these simple dwellings, are the most popular form of accommodation. These rustic quayside cabins, with minikitchens, bunk beds, living rooms, and showers are reasonably priced, and they give an authentic experience of the region. *Sjøhus* (sea houses) are larger, usually two- or three-storied buildings similar to rorbuer.

Highly recommended establishments are indicated by a star★.

Alta **SAS Alta Hotell.** This new glass-and-white hotel does every-
Dining and Lodging thing it can to make you forget that you are in a place where it is dark much of the time. Everything is light, from the reflectors on the ceiling of public rooms to the white furniture in the rooms. *Box 1093, N-9501, tel. 78/43–50–00, fax 78/43–58–25. 155 rooms with bath or shower, 2 suites. Facilities: 3 restaurants, 2 bars, nightclub, conference center, parking. AE, DC, MC, V. Expensive.*

Bodø **Løvolds' Kafeteria.** Freshly caught fish (the Løvolds also sell
Dining fishing gear) and traditional Norwegian dishes are featured at this upstairs cafeteria with a harbor view. It's a good place for

coffee and cake, too, for all pastries are made in-house. *Tollbugt. 9, tel. 75/52–02–61. No reservations. Dress: casual. No credit cards. Moderate.*

Dining and Lodging **Bodø Hotell.** This pale blue-gray modern building has an identity of its own yet fits well into the Bodø street scene. The facade is more interesting than the rooms. *Professor Schyttesgt. 5, N–8000, tel. 75/52–69–00, fax 75/52–57–78. 63 rooms with bath or shower, 3 suites. Facilities: restaurant. AE, DC, MC, V. Moderate.*

Diplomat. This hotel near the harbor is a short walk from the shopping district. The modern rooms are soberly decorated. The restaurant has live entertainment, but the food could be more imaginative. *Sjøgt. 23, N–8000, Bodø, tel. 75/52–70–00, fax 75/52–24–60. 104 rooms with shower (no bathtubs). Facilities: 3 restaurants, bar, nightclub, fitness room, conference center, garage. AE, DC, MC, V. Moderate.*

Hammerfest **Rica Hotel Hammerfest.** The entire hotel was redecorated in
Dining and Lodging 1989. The rooms are functional and small, but the furniture is light and comfortable. *Sørøygt. 15, tel. 78/41–13–33, fax 78/41–13–11. 88 rooms with bath or shower. Facilities: restaurant, bar, nightclub, fitness center, conference center, parking. AE, DC, MC, V. Moderate–Expensive.*

Harstad **Røkenes Gård.** This large, white wood building with an intri-
Dining cately carved portal was built in 1750 as a commercial trading house and inn. Recently it was restored by the ninth generation of descendants, and it is now a cozy restaurant serving regional specialties, such as reindeer and cloudberry parfait. *9400 Harstad, tel. 77/01–74–65. Reservations required at least 24 hours in advance. Dress: casual but neat. AE, DC, MC, V. Closed Sun. Expensive.*

Dining and Lodging **Grand Nordic.** It's a neat, brickred building in the Bauhaus style, with Norwegian 1970s-look leather furniture in the public rooms. Bedrooms, no bigger than necessary, are furnished with dark woods. The restaurant and conference rooms are lighter and more modern. *Strandgt. 9, N–9400, Harstad, tel. 77/06–21–70, fax 77/06–77–30. 85 rooms with bath or shower, 3 suites. Facilities: 2 restaurants, bar, nightclub, parking, conference center. AE, DC, MC, V. Moderate–Expensive.*

Honningsvåg **Hotel Havly.** This simple hotel is cozy and centrally located,
Dining and Lodging with small, spic-and-span rooms, and an ample breakfast buffet. Because this is a seamen's hostel, no alcohol is served. *N–9751 Honningsvåg, tel. 78/47–29–66, fax 78/47–30–10. 35 rooms with shower. Facilities: restaurant, conference rooms. AE, MC, V. Closed Easter, Dec. 24–Jan 2. Inexpensive.*

Karasjok **Karasjok SAS Hotell.** This feels more like a ski chalet than a ho-
Dining and Lodging tel, with bright rooms, done in warm blues and reds, that are
★ cozy rather than industrial. The lobby is more staid, with a seating arrangement up front. The hotel's wonderful Sami restaurant, Goathi, serves traditional fare, including reindeer cooked over open fires. *Box 38, N–9731 Karasjok, tel. 78/46–74–00, fax 78/46–68–02. 56 rooms with shower. Facilities: restaurant, conference rooms, bar, saunas. AE, DC, MC, V. Closed Dec. 24–Jan. 2. Expensive–Very Expensive.*

Kirkenes **Rica Arctic Hotel.** Do not confuse this new hotel with the Rica
Dining and Lodging Hotel Kirkenes, an older establishment, which ends up costing the same during the summer. Rooms here are spacious and

pretty, with white painted furniture and light print textiles. *Kongensgt. 1–3, N–9900, Kirkenes, tel. 78/99–29–29, fax 78/ 99–11–59. 80 rooms with bath. Facilities: restaurant, bar, nightclub, fitness room, swimming pool, conference center, shopping center, parking. AE, DC, MC, V. Moderate–Very Expensive.*

Lofoten Islands
Dining

Fiskekrogen. This quayside restaurant in the fishing village of Henningsvær will prepare your own catch. Chef/owner Otto Asheim's specialties include smoked *gravlaks* (smoking the dill-marinated salmon gives it extra depth of flavor) and sautéed ocean catfish garnished with mussels and shrimp. *8330 Henningsvær, tel. 76/07–46–52. Reservations required. Dress: casual. DC, MC, V. Moderate.*

Dining and Lodging

Nyvåga Rorbu og Aktivitetssenter. Built in 1990, this hotel and recreation complex is a 15-minute drive from the airport. It looks old, but it's brand new. Activities are well organized, with fishing-boat tours, eagle safaris, and deep-sea rafting, plus planned evening entertainment. *8310 Kabelvåg, Storvågan, tel. 76/07–89–00, fax 76/07–89–50. 60 rooms with shower. Facilities: 2 restaurants, conference rooms. AE, DC, MC, V. Moderate–Expensive.*

Henningsvaær Rorbuer. This small group of renovated turn-of-the-century rorbuer, all facing the sea, is just outside the center of Lofoten's most important fishing village. Breakfasts can be ordered from the cafeteria/reception, where there's a fireplace and a TV. Reservations are essential for July. *8330 Henningsvær, tel. 76/07–46–00. 14 1- or 2-bedroom rorbuer with shower. Facilities: cafeteria, sauna, laundry, grill. MC, V. Inexpensive.*

Narvik
Dining and Lodging

Inter Nor Grand Royal. It looks like an office building from the outside, but inside it is a comfortable top-class hotel, with big, rather formal rooms. The main restaurant is also quite formal. *Kongensgt. 64, N–8500 Narvik, tel. 76/94–15–00, fax 76/94–55–31. 112 rooms with bath or shower. Facilities: 2 restaurants, 2 bars, fitness room, conference center. AE, DC, MC, V. Moderate–Expensive.*

Tromsø
Dining

Brankos. Branko and Anne Brit Bartolj serve authentic Yugoslavian food, including *cevapcici* (small, spicy meatballs) and *raznici*, accompanied by their own imported Yugoslavian wines, in their art-filled dining room. *Storgt. 57, tel. 77/68–26–73. Reservations required. Dress: casual but neat. AE, DC, MC, V. No lunch. Moderate–Expensive.*

Compagniet. An old wood trading house from 1837 is now a stylish restaurant serving modern Norwegian food. Chef Morten Lønstad, formerly of Oslo's Feinschmecker, prepares sautéed shrimp with garlic and mussels baked in an herb sauce for starters, while main dishes include grilled monkfish with Dijon-mustard hollandaise sauce. *Sjøgt. 12, tel. 77/65–57–21. Reservations required. Dress: casual but neat. AE, DC, MC, V. No lunch in winter. Moderate–Expensive.*

Dining and Lodging

Hotel With. This recently constructed building on the waterfront in the dock area has spacious rooms decorated in shades of gray with the occasional colorful accent. The sauna/relaxation room on the top floor has the best view in town. As a Home hotel, it offers alcohol-free beer, a hot meal included in the room price, and waffles and coffee at all times. *Sjøgt. 35–37, N–9000, tel. 77/68–70–00, fax 77/68–96–16. 76 rooms with shower. Fa-*

cilities: fitness room, conference rooms, parking. AE, DC, MC, V. Moderate–Expensive.

SAS Royal Hotel. It's a new, modern hotel with splendid views over the Tromsø shoreline, but standard rooms are tiny, and even the costlier "Royal Club" rooms aren't big enough for real desks and tables, so modular ones have been attached to the walls. *Sjøgt. 7, N–9000, tel. 77/65–60–00, fax 77/68–54–74. 193 rooms with bath, 6 suites. Facilities: restaurant, bar, nightclub, business center, parking. AE, DC, MC, V. Moderate–Expensive.*

Polar Hotell. This no-frills hotel gives good value for money in the winter, when none of the bigger hotels have special rates. Rooms are small, and the orange/brown color scheme is a bit dated, but it's a pleasant, unassuming place to stay. *Grønnegaten 45, N–9000, tel. 77/68–64–80, fax 77/68–91–36. 64 rooms with shower (no bathtubs). Facilities: restaurant, bar, conference room. AE, DC, MC, V. Inexpensive–Moderate.*

Trondheim
Dining
★ **Bryggen.** The furnishings are in bleached wood, with dark-blue and red accessories, and the atmosphere is intimate. The menu features a reindeer fillet salad with cranberry vinaigrette and an herb cream soup with both freshwater and ocean crayfish for starters. Meat dishes include breast of chicken with a red-wine sauce and lamb medley. *Øvre Bakkelandet 66, tel. 73/52–02–30. Reservations required. Dress: casual but neat. AE, DC, MC, V. Closed Sun. No lunch. Expensive.*

Havfruen. "The Mermaid" has a maritime dining room with an open kitchen at street level, while in the cellar, 200-year-old stone walls from the original building frame the setting. Fish soup is the most popular starter, while summer main dishes include poached halibut. Desserts are simple—the citrus parfait is especially good. *Kjøpmannsgt. 7, tel. 73/53–26–26. Reservations advised. Dress: casual but neat. AE, DC, MC, V. Closed Sun. No lunch. Moderate–Expensive.*

Hos Magnus. The price/value ratio is excellent at this old-fashioned, cozy restaurant in the new part of Bryggen. The menu ranges from such modern dishes as cognac-marinated moose fillet with mustard dressing to the old local specialty surlaks for appetizers. Grilled, marinated spiral pork chop and fillet of beef with mushrooms and onions are featured on the meat menu. There are ample fish and vegetarian choices, too. *Kjøpmannsgt. 63, tel. 73/52–41–10. Reservations advised. Dress: casual but neat. AE, DC, MC, V. Moderate.*

Lian. In the heights above the city, Lian offers beautiful scenery and Norwegian standards. The oldest part of the restaurant dates from 1700, but the round section, from the 1930s, commands the best view. The food is solid, honest, and hearty, with roast beef, reindeer, smoked pork loin, and the old standby, *kjøttkaker* (Norwegian meat cakes). *Lian, tel. 72/55–90–77. Dress: casual. No credit cards. Closed Mon. Moderate.*

★ **Tavern på Sverresborg.** This big, yellow, wood former ferryman's house at the Trondelag Folkemuseum has been an inn since 1739. The food is authentic Norwegian, including meat and fish prepared with old methods—pickled, salted, and dried. Choices include a plate with four different kinds of herring, roast lamb ribs, trout, meat cakes, and rømmegrøt. Homemade oatmeal bread and rolls accompany all dishes. *Sverresborg allé, tel. 73/52–09–32. Dress: casual but neat. MC, V. No lunch Sept. 2–May 19. Moderate.*

De 3 Stuer. This small bistro chain serves everything home-made, and the daily special features such dishes as fish soufflé, fried fish with sour-cream sauce, split-pea soup with sausage, boiled beef, and lamb stew, all served with dessert and coffee. For lunch, there's smørbrød, crescent rolls, salads, and cakes. *Trondheim Torg, tel. 73/52–92–20; Gågaten Leuthenhaven, tel. 73/52–43–42; Dronningens Gate 11, tel. 73/52–63–20. No reservations. Dress: casual. No credit cards. Dronningens closed Sun. Inexpensive.*

Lodging **Prinsen.** Rooms in this recently remodeled hotel in the center of the city are light, monochromatic to the point of being dull, and decorated with classic furniture. Teatergrillen, named after a nearby theater, serves a good early dinner. *Kongensgt. 30, N–7002, tel. 73/53–06–50, fax 73/53–06–44. 85 rooms with bath or shower, 1 suite. Facilities: 3 restaurants, 3 bars, nightclub. AE, DC, MC, V. Moderate–Very Expensive.*

Royal Garden. The city's showcase hostelry, right on the river, was built in the same style as the old warehouse buildings that line the waterfront, only in glass and concrete. It's a luxury hotel, with big rooms, light wood furniture, and predominantly blue textiles. *Kjøpmannsgata 73, N–7010, tel. 73/52–11–00, fax 73/53–17–66. 297 rooms with bath, 8 suites. Facilities: 3 restaurants, bar, pool, fitness room, shops. AE, DC, MC, V. Moderate–Very Expensive.*

Grand Hotel Olav. Situated in the center of town, this hotel boasts 27 different room models, all impeccably decorated. It is part of a complex that contains shops, conference rooms, and the Olavshallen Concert Hall (home of the Trondheim Philharmonic). *Kjøpmannsgto 48, tel. 73/53–53–10, fax 73/53–57–20. 106 rooms, 5 no-smoking rooms. Facilities: 3 restaurants, bar, pub, nightclub, parking. AE, DC, MC, V. Expensive.*

★ **Bakeriet.** Built as a bakery in 1863, Trondheim's newest hotel opened in March 1991. There's no restaurant, but a hot evening meal is included in the room rate. You can borrow a track suit, and there's free light beer in the lounge by the sauna. Every room has a VCR and a window thermometer. Few rooms look alike, but all are large, with natural wood furniture, beige-and-red-stripe textiles, and stylish in their simplicity. *Brattørgt. 2, N–7011, Trondheim, tel. 73/52–52–00, fax 73/50–23–30. 91 rooms with bath or shower, 1 suite. Facilities: sauna. AE, DC, MC, V. Inexpensive–Moderate.*

Trondheim. If you've always wanted to try mead, the fermented honey drink of the Vikings, you can do it here—it's produced on the premises. The building is old on the outside, with a curved corner and wrought-iron balconies, but inside it's completely remodeled. The rooms are big and light, with what is now considered to be classic Scandinavian bentwood furniture. *Kongensgt. 15, N–7013, tel. 73/50–50–50, fax 73/51–60–58. 140 rooms with shower or bath. Facilities: restaurant, bar, conference room. AE, DC, MC, V. Inexpensive–Moderate.*

Singsaker Sommerhotell. A student dorm that becomes a hotel from June 15 to August 20, it is not much cheaper than many downtown hotels. It's good for the single traveler, though, as the lounge fills up in the evening with other loners. *Rogertsgt. 1, N–7016, tel. 73/52–00–92, fax 73/52–06–35. 104 rooms, 16 with bath. Facilities: bar, fitness room. AE, DC, MC, V. Inexpensive.*

The Arts and Nightlife

The Arts **Olavshallen** (Kjøpmannsgt. 44, tel. 73/53–40–50), a concert and
Trondheim cultural center built in 1989, is the home of Trondheim's
symphony and the nearly 3,000 music students in the city. The
auditorium seats 1,300. The concert and entertainment season
is from September through May.

During the last week in July, the *St. Olav Play* is performed at
the outdoor amphitheater in **Stiklestad,** 98 kilometers (60
miles) from Trondheim. The play, with a cast of 300, commemorates the life of King Olav Haraldsson, who united and brought
Christianity to Norway. Tickets are available from any post office or from Stiklestad Nasjonale Kulturhus (tel. 74/07–12–00).

Tromsø Every year in January the city celebrates **Nordlysfestivalen**
(the Northern Lights Festival) with a series of concerts by distinguished visiting artists at Kulturhuset (the Culture House)
(Grønnegata 87, tel. 77/68–20–64). For concert information and
reservations, contact the festival (tel. 77/68–08–63, fax 77/68–
01–09).

The North Nature takes precedence over the arts in northern Norway,
but Harstad hosts the yearly **Northern Norway Festival** in June.

From June 15 to August 15, **Beaivas Sami Theater** (9250
Kautokeino, tel. 78/48–68–11) offers summer programs of traditional Sami folk songs and modern works.

Nightlife **Olavskvartalet** (*see* Shopping, *above*) is the center of much of
Trondheim the city's nightlife, with a disco, a jazz and blues club, and a bar
and beer hall in the cellar. **Hotell Prinsen** (*see* Lodging, *above*)
has a summer restaurant, **Sommer'n,** open from mid-May to the
end of August, with live music and dancing. **Restauranthuset
Norrein** (Dronningens Gate 12, tel. 73/52–24–23) is an entertainment complex with the **Sunset Club,** a piano bar, and **Bever-
ly,** a postmodern café straight out of California.

Tromsø Tromsø brags that it has 10 nightclubs, not bad for a city of
50,000 at the top of the world. **Compagniet** (*see* Dining, *above*)
has the classiest nightclub; **Charly's** at the SAS Royal Hotel,
and **Papagena** at the Grand Nordic hotel (*see* Lodging, *above*)
are also popular.

6 Sweden

By Chris Mosey

*Updated by
Brian Owens*

Sweden requires the visitor to travel far, in terms of both distance and attitude. Approximately the size of California, Sweden reaches as far north as the Arctic fringes of Europe, where glacier-topped mountains and thousands of acres of pine, spruce, and birch forests are broken here and there by wild rivers, countless pristine lakes, and desolate moorland. In the more populated south, roads meander through mile after mile of softly undulating countryside, skirting lakes and passing small villages with their ubiquitous sharp-pointed church spires. Here, the lush forests, which dominate Sweden's northern landscape, have largely fallen to the plow.

Once the dominant power of the region, Sweden has traditionally looked mostly inward, seeking to find its own, Nordic solutions. During the cold war, it tried with considerable success to steer its famous "Middle Way" between the two superpowers, both economically and politically. Its citizens were in effect benignly subjected to a giant social experiment aimed at creating a perfectly just society, one that adopted the best aspects of both socialism and capitalism.

As it slipped into the worst economic recession since the 1930s, Sweden made adjustments that lessened the role of its all-embracing welfare state in the lives of its citizens. Although fragile, the conservative coalition, which defeated the long-incumbent Social Democrats in the fall of 1991, has been attempting to make further cutbacks in welfare spending as the country faces one of the largest budget deficits in Europe. At the same time, an influx of immigrants is reshaping what was once a homogeneous society. As a result, the mostly blond, blue-eyed Swedes may now be more open to the outside world than at any other time in their history. Indeed, another indication of change is Sweden's formal application to join the European Community (EC), a move that represents a radical break with its traditional go-it-alone policies in defense and many other areas of life.

The country possesses stunning natural assets. In the forests, moose, deer, bear, and lynx roam, coexisting with the whine of power saws and the rumble of automatic logging machines as mankind exploits a natural resource that remains the country's economic backbone. Fish abound in sparkling lakes and tumbling rivers, sea eagles and ospreys soar over myriad pine-clad islands in the archipelagoes off the east and west coasts.

The population is thinly spread, with 8.5 million people inhabiting a country 173,731 square miles in area, Europe's fourth largest. If, like Greta Garbo, one of its most famous exports, you want to be alone, you've come to the right place. A law called *Allemansrätt* guarantees public access to the countryside; you'll seldom encounter signs warning NO TRESPASSING.

Sweden stretches 977 miles from the barren, Arctic north to the fertile plains of the south. Contrasts abound, but they are neatly tied together by a superbly efficient infrastructure, embracing air, road, and rail. You can catch salmon in the far north and, thanks to the excellent domestic air network, have it cooked by the chef of your luxury hotel in Stockholm later the same day.

The seasons contrast savagely: Sweden is usually warm and exceedingly light in the summer, then cold and dark in the winter.

Sweden

Norwegian Sea

Kiruna

Gällivare
Jokkmokk
Luleälven
400

Tärnaby
Arjeplog
Töre
Torneå
E79
Arvidsjaur
Kalix
Sorsele
95
Luleå
Storuman
Piteå
Lycksele
Skellefteå
342
Åsele
Umeälven
92
Umeå
Strömsund
90
E4

Åre
Östersund
E75
Tännäs
Sundsvall
84
Ljungan
Idre
Hudiksvall
70
Bollnäs
Mora
Söderhamn
62
Klarälven
Falun
Gävle
80
Borlänge
Avesta
Fagersta
E4
Karlstad
Uppsala
Västerås
E18
E18
Mälaren
Stockholm
Mellerud
Örebro
E20/E3
Strömstad
Vänern
E20/E3
Uddevalla
Norrköping
Trollhättan
Gotska Sandön
Göteborg
Vättern
Linköping
Baltic Sea
Borås
40
E4
Jönköping
Nässjö
Visby
Falkenberg
E6
Värnamo
E66
Gotland
Oskarshamn
Halmstad
23
Växjö
Öland
Helsingborg
Kalmar
Malmö
Karlskrona
DENMARK
Kristianstad
Trelleborg
Ystad

NORWAY

FINLAND

Gulf of Bothnia

Gulf of Finland

Gotska Sandön

ESTONIA

Gulf of Riga

LATVIA

LITHUANIA

N

0   50 miles
0   75 km

The sea may freeze, and in the north, iron railway lines may snap.

Sweden is also an arresting mixture of ancient and modern. The countryside is dotted with rune stones recalling its Viking past: trade beginning in the 8th century eastward to Kiev and as far south as Constantinople and the Mediterranean, expansion to the British Isles in the 9th through the 11th century, and settlement in Normandy in the 10th century. Small timbered farmhouses and maypoles around which villagers still dance at Midsummer in their traditional costumes evoke both the pagan early history and the more recent agrarian culture.

Many of the country's cities are sci-fi modern, their shop windows filled with the latest in consumer goods and fashions, but Swedes are reluctant urbanites: Their hearts and souls are in the forests and the archipelagoes, and there they faithfully retreat in the summer and on weekends to take their holidays, pick berries, or just listen to the silence. The skills of the woodcarver, the weaver, the leatherworker, and the glassblower are all highly prized. Similarly, Swedish humor is earthy and slapstick. Despite the praise lavished abroad on introspective dramatic artists such as August Strindberg and Ingmar Bergman, it is the simple trouser-dropping farce that will fill Stockholm's theaters, the scatological joke that will get the most laughs.

Again, despite the international musical success of two Swedish rock groups, Roxette and Abba, the domestic penchant is more often for the good old-fashioned dance band. Gray-haired men in pastel-shaded sweaters playing saxophones are more common on TV than heavy-metal rockers. Strangely, in ultramodern concert halls and discos, it is possible to step back in time to the 1950s, if not the 1940s.

Despite the much-publicized sexual liberation of Swedes, the joys of hearth and home are most prized in what remains in many ways an extremely conservative society. Conformity, not liberty, is the real key to the Swedish character: The good of the collective has always come before that of the individual, and this is why socialism had such a strong appeal here.

At the same time, Swedes remain devoted royalists and patriots, avidly following the fortunes of King Carl XVI Gustaf, Queen Silvia, and their children in the media and raising the blue-and-yellow national flag each morning on the flag poles of their country cottages. Few nations, in fact, take as much effort to preserve and defend their natural heritage. It is sometimes difficult in cities such as Stockholm, Göteborg, or Malmö to realize that you are in an urban area. Right in the center of Stockholm, thanks to a cleanup program in the 1970s, you can fish for salmon or go for a swim. In Göteborg's busy harbor, you can sit aboard a ship bound for the archipelago and watch fish jump out of the water; in Malmö hares hop around in the downtown parks. It is this pristine quality to life that can make a visit to Sweden a step out of time, a relaxing break from the modern world.

Before You Go

Government Tourist Offices

In the United States Swedish Travel and Tourism Council (Next Stop Sweden), 655 3rd Ave., 18th floor, New York, NY 10017, tel. 212/949–2333.

In Canada Sweden has no tourist office in Canada. For information write to the U.S. office.

In the United Kingdom Swedish Travel and Tourism Council, 73 Welbeck St., London W1M 8AN, tel. 071/487–3135, fax 071/935–5833.

Tour Groups

General-Interest Cole Travel Service Inc. (310 W. State St., Geneva, IL 60134, tel. 312/232–4450) can arrange bed-and-breakfast holidays at 200 hotels, inns, and guest houses at 130 locations in Sweden. **Scantours Inc.** (1535 6th St., Suite 205, Santa Monica, CA 90401, tel. 213/451–0911) can fix independent packages, escorted tours, and group travel. **Scandinavian American World Tours, Inc.** (795 Franklin Ave., Franklin Lakes, NJ 07417, tel. 201/891–6641) offers deluxe, first-class, and escorted tours. **Bennett Tours** (270 Madison Ave., New York, NY 10016, tel. 800/221–2420) offers tours of Scandinavia. **Watling Sweden** (91–93, Cranbrook Rd., Ilford, Essex, England, tel. 081/553–3883) and **Swedish Chalets** (28 Hillcrest Rd., Orpington, Kent, BR6 9AW, England, tel. 689/24958) offer chalet holidays for the family. **Star Tour of Scandinavia** (209 Edgware Rd., London W2 1ES, tel. 71/706 25–20) and **Scanscape Holidays** (Hillgate House, 13 Hillgate St., London W8 7SP, tel. 071/221–3244) offer low-cost charter flights from the United Kingdom. **Anglers World** (46 Knifesmith Gate, Chesterfield, Derbyshire, England, tel. 246/221717) runs holidays for fishermen in Sweden.

Cruises EuroCruises (Box 30925, New York, NY 10011, tel. 212/691–2099) offers cruises to Sweden from Amsterdam, Helsinki, Leningrad, Newcastle, North Cape, Tallinn, and Turku. **Scandinavian Seaways** (Crown Place, Suite 212, 6499 N.W. 9th Ave., Ft. Lauderdale, FL 33309, tel. 800/533–3755, and Parkeston Quay, Harwich, England, tel. 0255/240–240) offers overnight crossings to Sweden from England and Holland.

When to Go

The best time to visit Sweden is in summer, from mid-May through August, when temperatures are usually high and the days exceptionally long. However, remember to pack some warm and rainproof clothing, just in case. The winters are usually long, dark, and hard, the country covered with snow and ice. January is too dark for skiing, but in February the days start to lengthen and the trails are in prime condition. A word of warning: Temperatures will be far lower than those of central Europe. The following are average daily maximum and minimum temperatures for Stockholm.

Jan.	30F	-1C	May	57F	14C	Sept.	59F	15C
	23	-5		43	6		48	9
Feb.	30F	-1C	June	66F	19C	Oct.	48F	9C
	23	-5		52	11		41	5
Mar.	37F	3C	July	72F	22C	Nov.	41F	5C
	25	-4		57	14		34	1
Apr.	46F	8C	Aug.	68F	20C	Dec.	36F	2C
	34	1		55	13		28	-2

Festivals and Seasonal Events

January 13: Knut signals the end of Christmas festivities and "plundering" of the Christmas tree: Trinkets are removed from the tree, edible ornaments eaten, and the tree itself thrown out.

February (first Thursday, Friday, and Saturday): A **market** held in the small town of Jokkmokk, above the Arctic Circle, features both traditional Lapp artifacts and plenty of reindeer.

Shrove Tuesday: Special buns called *semlor* are eaten; lightly flavored with cardamom, filled with almond paste and whipped cream, they are traditionally placed in a dish of warm milk and topped with cinnamon.

March (first Sunday): The **Vasaloppet 55-mile ski race** from Sälen to Mora in Dalarna attracts entrants from all over the world.

Maundy Thursday: Small girls dress up as witches and hand out "Easter letters" for small change. *Påskris*, twigs tipped with brightly colored chicken feathers, decorate homes.

April 30: For the **Feast of Valborg,** bonfires are lit to celebrate the end of winter. The liveliest celebrations involve the students of the university city of Uppsala, 60 kilometers (37 miles) north of Stockholm.

May 1: Labor Day marches and rallies are held nationwide.

June 6: National Day is celebrated, with parades, speeches, and band concerts nationwide.

June: Midsummer's Day celebrations are held on the Saturday that falls between June 20 and 26. Swedes decorate their homes with flower garlands, raise maypoles, and dance around them to folk music.

August 5–13: Stockholm Water Festival celebrates the city's clean water environment with water-sports performances, a crayfish party, a fireworks competition, and 1,500 other events next to the Royal Palace.

August (second Wednesday): Crayfish are considered a delicacy in Sweden, and on this day, the **Crayfish premiere,** friends gather to eat them at outdoor parties.

November 11: St. Martin's Day is celebrated primarily in the southern province of Skåne. Roast goose is served, accompanied by *svartsoppa*, a bisque made of goose blood and spices.

December: For each of the four weeks of **Advent,** leading up to Christmas, a candle is lit in a four-pronged candelabra.

December 10: Nobel Day sees the presentation of the Nobel prizes by King Carl XVI Gustaf at a glittering banquet held in the Stockholm City Hall.

December 13: On **Santa Lucia Day** young girls (preferably blondes) are selected to be "Lucias," and wear candles (today usually electric substitutes) in their hair and sing hymns along with their handmaidens and "stablelads" at ceremonies around the country.

December 24: Christmas Eve is the principal day of Christmas celebration. Traditional Christmas dishes include ham, rice porridge, and *lutfisk* (ling that is dried and then boiled).

What to Pack

Take a warm sweater and something rainproof with you, even in summer, just in case. In winter, make sure you have lots of warm clothing and a hat or cap with protection for ears. The emphasis should be on sensible clothing. Mosquitoes can be a nuisance in the countryside from June through September, so pack an effective repellent.

Swedish Currency

The unit of currency is the krona (plural kronor), which is divided into 100 öre and is written as SKr. The 10-öre coin was phased out in 1991, leaving only the 50-öre and SKr1 coins. These have recently been joined by an SKr10 coin. Bank notes are at present: SKr20, 50, 100, 500, and 1,000. At press time (summer 1993), the exchange rate was 7.59 to the dollar, 11.76 to the pound, and 5.98 to the Canadian dollar.

Bank Cards

There is an American Express cash and traveler's check dispenser at Arlanda, Stockholm's international airport, and outside the American Express office at Birger Jarlsgatan 1, Stockholm. The 1,000 or so blue Bankomat cash dispensers nationwide have been adapted to take some foreign cards. For more information, contact Bankomat Centralen, tel. 08/7257240.

What It Will Cost

The short answer is a lot! Special tourist rates usually apply in the summer and most of the major hotel chains give discounts. For details, contact any of the Swedish hotel chains or your travel agent. Some sample prices: cup of coffee, SKr16; strong beer, SKr38–SKr55; mineral water, SKr10–SKr17; cheese roll, SKr16; pepper steak, à la carte, SKr120–SKr160; cheeseburger, SKr30; pizza, starting at SKr32.

Passports and Visas

American, British, and Canadian citizens are required to have a valid passport to enter Sweden, but no visa is needed unless you are planning to stay for more than three months.

Customs and Duties

Tourists entering Sweden are allowed to bring with them duty-free one liter of spirits, one liter of wine (includes aperitifs), and two liters of strong beer (exceeding 2.8% alcohol by weight). Travelers from Europe may bring in 200 cigarettes or 250 grams of other tobacco products. Other travelers are allowed to bring in 400 cigarettes or 500 grams of other tobacco products duty-free. More than 13,000 shops are part of a tax-free shopping service for visitors. When you buy goods, you are given a voucher for the value-added tax (VAT) paid on them that

you can cash in when leaving the country. Look for the blue-and-yellow TAX FREE sign. For more information, including a brochure listing shops that are part of the plan, contact: **Sweden Tax-free Shopping,** Information Dept., Box 128, 231 22 Trelleborg, tel. 0410/19560.

Language

Swedish is closely related to Danish and Norwegian and derives primarily from German. After "z," the Swedish alphabet has three extra letters, "å,","ä," and "ö," something to bear in mind when using the phone book. Most Swedes speak English.

Car Rentals

All major companies are represented in Stockholm, many with branches nationwide. For local firms, check the yellow pages under *Biluthyrning.* Many car rentals have special weekend rates off-season.

Rail Passes

A special pass called the **Nordturistkort** (Nordic Tourist Card) allows for unlimited rail travel anywhere in Scandinavia. This pass (second-class only) costs SKr1,980 for adults, SKr1,480 for young people ages 12–25, SKr1,000 for children ages 4–11, and children under 4 travel free (if seats have not been reserved for them).

The **Eurail** and **InterRail** passes are both valid in Sweden. **Statens Järnvägar** (SJ, the Swedish state railway company) also organizes reduced-cost package trips in conjunction with local tourist offices. Details are available at any railway station or from **SJ** (Vasagatan 22, 102 34 Stockholm, tel. 020/757575).

Student and Youth Travel

To and from Stockholm, those under 24 years of age can fly SAS for Skr150 to Skr200 one-way, and farther for Skr350. These tickets cannot be reserved in advance, however, and are offered only if there is room. Airport buses, boat trips, and tourist tickets in Stockholm are free for children under 7 years of age, free on weekends for children ages 7 to 11 when riding with an adult, and half price for ages 7 to 18.

Only Swedish students are given a discount by **SJ.** However, young people up to 26 years old can buy **Transalpino** tickets when traveling between Scandinavian countries that give 20% to 30% discounts on ordinary prices. For further information on student travel, contact the **Swedish National Student Travel Bureau** (Kungsgatan 4, 103 87 Stockholm, tel. 08/234515).

Accommodations In addition to youth hostels, young visitors to Sweden will find low-cost, comfortable accommodations at any bed-and-breakfast establishment displaying the BILTUR-LOGI sign. For further information, contact the **Swedish Travel and Tourism Council** or **Biltur-Logi** (S–79303 Tallberg, Sweden, tel. 0247/50925).

Traveling with Children

On Swedish trains, up to two children under 12 years of age can travel with an adult free, except for a small fee to make a reservation. Each additional child under the age of 12 receives a 50% discount. In summer, families traveling with at least one child under 16 can receive a 50% discount for trips over 140 kilometers (87 miles) in second-class seats. Tickets can be bought only in Sweden. There are special family cars equipped with toys for children on the Stockholm–Malmö and Stockholm–Göteborg lines. Ask for this service when you are making reservations.

Hints for Travelers with Disabilities

Sweden has made great efforts to make life as easy as possible for disabled travelers. There are lifts and ramps for wheelchairs, specially adapted public toilets, and a host of other aids. Special taxi and bus services, help for disabled travelers to board trains, and a list of camp sites, youth hostels, and hotels with special facilities for the disabled are also available. One annual guide, "Hotels in Sweden," lists hotels with rooms adapted for disabled visitors. **Swiss Chalets** (28 Hillcrest Rd., Orpington, Kent BR6 9AW, England) offers holidays in Sweden designed for the disabled.

Getting Around
By Rail **Swedish State Railways (SJ)** offers special "transport chairs" to help physically disabled passengers get into trains and reach their seats. Most InterCity and other long-distance trains have family carriages with large toilets, and a new kind of second-class carriage is offered on the Stockholm–Malmö and Sundsvall–Stockholm–Göteborg routes with carriages that allow passengers to sit in their own wheelchairs.

By Bus With advance notice, most bus companies in Sweden will gladly provide special assistance to disabled travelers. In addition, **Sirius Travel Service** (Stockholm, tel. 08/749–1900) operates taxis and minibuses—with lifts and wheelchair mountings—for disabled passengers. **SHT** (Stockholm, tel. 08/6528100) provides special coaches for group and individual travel.

By Taxi Information on **Fardtjänst,** a Swedish taxi service for the disabled, is available from local tourist offices in Sweden. Short trips are priced on an hourly basis, longer trips by distance.

Hints for Older Travelers

Of special interest to travelers over 50 is the **Reslutskort,** a train pass that costs SKr100 and provides discounts of 25% in second class if trips are taken on Tuesday, Wednesday, Thursday, or Saturday. All passengers can travel first-class for an additional SKr50 on Saturday and long holidays. The Swedish **SARA** hotel chain offers a *SeniorPass* for those 65 and older, with rooms at half price (SeniorPass, SARA Hotels, Svarspost, Kundnr. 31598113, 18201–Danderyd, Sweden).

SAS offers discount tickets to and from Stockholm for those over 65, depending on distance, at a price of up to SKr400. Tickets may be reserved in advance.

Further Reading

One of the easiest and certainly most entertaining ways of finding out about modern Swedish society is to read the Martin Beck detective series of thrillers by Maj Sjöwall and Per Wahlöö, all of which have been translated into English. One of these, *The Terrorists*, was even prophetic, containing a scene in which a Swedish prime minister was shot, a precursor to the murder of Olof Palme in 1986.

Similarly, an entertaining insight into how life was in the bad old days when Sweden was one of the most backward agrarian countries in Europe may be obtained from Vilhelm Moberg's series of novels on poor Swedes who emigrated to America: *The Emigrants*, *Unto a Good Land*, and *The Last Letter Home*.

One Swedish writer of genius was August Strindberg (1849–1912), whose plays greatly influenced modern European and American drama. Perhaps the most enduringly fascinating of these, *Miss Julie*, mixes the explosive elements of sex and class to stunning effect.

Another major talent was the novelist Selma Lagerlöf, the first Swedish writer to win the Nobel Prize in literature, whose works are rooted in local legend and saga. Best for providing insights on things specifically Swedish are the collection *Tales of a Manor* (1899) and the children's book *The Wonderful Adventures of Nils* (1906).

One of the most exhaustive and comprehensive studies in English of the country published in recent years is *Sweden: The Nation's History*, by Franklin D. Scott (University of Minnesota Press). Chris Mosey's *Cruel Awakening, Sweden and the Killing of Olof Palme* (C. Hurst, London 1991) seeks to provide an overview of the country and its recent history seen through the life and assassination of its best-known politician of recent times and the farcical hunt for his killer.

Arriving and Departing

From North America by Plane

Airports and Airlines Stockholm's **Arlanda** airport and Göteborg's **Landvetter** airport are served by **SAS** (tel. 800/251–2350), **British Airways, American, Delta, TWA,** and other major international airlines.

From the United Kingdom by Plane, Car, Ferry, Train, and Bus

By Plane The major airlines flying to Sweden from the United Kingdom include **SAS** (52–53 Condute St. W1R OAU, London, tel. 071/734–4020) and **British Airways (tel. 081/897–4000).**

By Car and Ferry There are excellent links between Harwich and Göteborg and Newcastle and Göteborg aboard **Scandinavian Seaways** ferries (Scandinavian Seaways, DFDS Ltd., Scandinavia House, Parkeston Quay, Harwich, Essex, CO12 4QG, England, tel. 0255/240–240). An alternate approach is through Denmark using ferry crossings to Malmö or Helsingborg.

By Train From London, the **British Rail European Travel Center** (Victoria Station, London, tel. 071/834–2345) can be helpful in

arranging connections through to Sweden's **SJ** (Statens Jarn-vagar).

By Bus   Bus travel is the least expensive alternative, but it is slower and less comfortable.

Staying in Sweden

Getting Around

By Plane   All major cities and towns are linked with regular flights by **Scandinavian Airlines System** (SAS), which recently merged with Linjeflyg to form one airline network under the SAS name. Most Swedish airports are located a long way from city centers but are linked to them by fast and efficient bus services. SAS also operates a limousine service at leading airports. For more information, contact SAS, Inrikes (Flygcity, Klarabergsviaducten 72, 111 64 Stockholm, tel. 020/550550).

By Train   **SJ**, the state railway company, has a highly efficient network of comfortable, electrified trains. On nearly all long-distance routes there are buffet cars, and, on overnight trips, sleeping cars and couchettes in both first and second class. A high-speed train, which takes just less than three hours, runs the Stock-holm–Göteborg route. Look for so-called *röda avgångar* (red departures), which offer 50% reductions. Children under 16 travel at half fare. Up to two children under 12 may travel free if accompanied by an adult. For more information, contact **SJ** (Vasagatan 22, 105 51 Stockholm, tel. 020/757575).

By Bus   There is excellent bus service between all major towns and cities. Consult the yellow pages under *Bussresearrangörer* for telephone numbers of the companies concerned. Recommended are the services offered to different parts of Sweden from Stockholm by **Swebus** (Cityterminalen, Klarabergsviadukten 72, tel. 020/640640).

By Car   There are few expressways, but roads are well maintained and relatively traffic-free. Major car-rental companies such as **Avis, Hertz, Europcar, Bonus, Budget, OK,** and **InterRent** have facilities in all major towns and cities and at airports. It is worth shopping around for special rates. See the yellow pages under *Biluthyrning* for telephone numbers and addresses.

By Boat   An excellent way of seeing Sweden is from its many ferry boats, which ply the archipelagoes and main lakes. In Stockholm, visitors should buy a special *båtluffarkort*. This gives unlimited travel on the white archipelago ferry boats for a 16-day period and is available at the ferry ticket offices. Highly popular four-day cruises are available on the Göta Canal, which makes use of rivers, lakes, and, on its last lap, the Baltic Sea. This lovely waterway, which links Göteborg on the west coast with Stockholm on the east, has a total of 65 locks, and you travel on fine old steamers, some of which date almost from the canal's opening in 1832. The oldest and most desirable is the *Juno*, built in 1874. Prices start at SKr5,400 for a bed in a double cabin. For more information, contact the **Göta Canal Steamship Company** (Box 272, S–401 24 Göteborg, tel. 031/806315).

Telephones

Post offices do not have telephone facilities, but there are plenty of pay phones, and long-distance calls can be made from special telegraph offices called *Telebutik*, or marked "Tele." You can also purchase a **Telefonkort** (Telephone card) from the Telebutik, pressbyrå, or hospitals for SKr45 or SKr80, which works out to be cheaper if you're making numerous domestic calls.

Local Calls The new orange pay phones, which are rapidly replacing the old green models, take 50-öre, SKr1, and SKr5 coins. A local call costs a minimum of SKr2. For calls outside the locality, dial the area code.

International Calls The foreign dialing code is 009 followed by the country code, then the number you require. Sweden's country code is 46. The AT&T USA direct-access code is 020–795–611. The MCI call-USA access code is 020–795–922.

Operators and Information For directory inquiries, dial 07975 for information concerning Sweden, 0013 for the Nordic area, and 0019 for other foreign inquiries. For operator-assisted foreign calls, dial 0018 on green pay phones.

Mail

Postal Rates Letters up to 20 grams and postcards cost SKr3.50 to send inside the Nordic Area, SKr5 to elsewhere in Europe, and SKr6 to the United States and the rest of the world by air. Surface mail costs SKr5.

Tipping

In addition to the 12% value-added tax, most hotels usually include a service charge of 15%; it is not necessary to tip unless you have received extra services. Similarly, a service charge of 13% is usually included in restaurant bills. It is a custom, however, to leave small change when buying drinks. Taxi drivers and hairdressers expect a tip of around 10%.

Opening and Closing Times

Banks **Banks** are open from 9:30 to 3. In the larger cities some stay open until 5:30. All banks are closed on Saturday and Sunday. The bank at Arlanda Airport, Stockholm, is open daily between 7 AM and 10 PM. There is also a bank at Landvetter Airport, Göteborg, which is open daily from 8 to 8. There are "Forex" **currency exchange** offices at Central Station in Stockholm (8 AM–9 PM), Stockholm City Terminal (9 AM–6 PM), Göteborg Central Station (8 AM–9 PM), and at the Malmö tourist office (Hamngatan 1; 8 AM–9 PM).

Museums Most **museums** are open Tuesday through Sunday 10–5, though some have other hours. A free guide called "Stockholm This Week" is available from stores, hotels, and tourist offices.

Stores Shopping hours vary, but most businesses are open 10–6 on weekdays and 9–1 (and sometimes 4) on Saturday. Some grocery shops are open until 9 PM, sometimes even 11 PM, and these are almost exclusively Swedish franchises of 7-Eleven stores.

Shopping

Sweden produces expensive, high-quality handicraft goods that are available at special *Hemslöjd* shops and in leading department stores such as **NK, Åhléns,** and **Pub.** Swedish crystal is a traditional favorite, the leading brands being Orrefors and Kosta Boda. At the glass factories themselves in the south, "seconds" shops provide bargain buys; otherwise expect to pay heavily for the craftsmanship, design, and reputation.

Sports and Outdoor Activities

Bicycling As there are separate bicycle tracks through most cities, and Swedish roads are usually not congested, bicycling is a popular way of getting around. Rental costs average around SKr80 per day. Tourist offices and Sveriges Turist förening (STF; the Swedish Touring Association) in Stockholm (tel. 08/790–3100) have information about cycling package holidays that include bike rentals, overnight accommodations, and meals. The bicycling organization, **Cykelfrämjandet** (tel. 08/321680), publishes an English-language guide to cycling trips.

Boating and Sailing STF, in cooperation with Televerket (Sweden's PTT—Postal, Telephone, and Telegraph authority), publishes an annual guide in Swedish to all the country's marinas with telephone numbers. It is available from STF (tel. 08/790–3250) or in your nearest PTT "Telebutik." The **Swedish Canoeing Association** (Svenksa Kanotförbundet, Skeppsbron 11, 611 35 Nyköping, tel. 0155/69508) publishes a similar booklet for canoers.

Camping There are 760 registered campsites nationwide, many located close to uncrowded bathing places and with fishing, boating, or canoeing; they may also offer bicycle rentals. Prices range from SKr60 to SKr110 per 24-hour period. Many camping places also offer accommodations in log cabins at various prices, depending on the facilities offered, and some have special facilities for the disabled. Most are open between June and September, but about 200 remain open in winter for skiing and skating enthusiasts. An annual catalogue in English is available from tourist bureaus. For additional information, contact **Sveriges Campingvärdarnas Riksförbund** (Kålgårdsbergsgatan 1, Box 255, S–45 117 Uddevalla, tel. 0522/38345).

Golf Sweden has 283 golf clubs; you can even play by the light of the midnight sun at Boden in the far north. The **Swedish Golfing Association** (Svenska Golfförbundet, Box 84, 182 11 Danderyd, tel. 08/622–1500) publishes an annual guide in Swedish with current information; it costs around SKr55, plus postage.

Hiking There are countless trails nationwide, but **Kungsleden** (The King's Trail) through the mountains of Lappland, including Kebnekaise, at 7,000 feet the country's highest peak, is especially rewarding. Information on walking routes and overnight accommodations is available from STF (Box 25, S–101 20 Stockholm, tel. 08/790–3100).

Skiing There are plenty of both downhill and cross-country facilities. The best-known resorts are in the country's western mountains: **Åre** in the north, with 29 lifts; **Idre Fjäll**, to the south of Åre, offering accommodation for 10,000; and **Sälen** in the folklore region of Dalarna. You can ski in summer at **Riksgränsen** in the far north. A new center called the **Discover Sweden Shop**,

now located in the Sweden House (Kungsträdgården, Stockholm, tel. 08/789–2000), has information on skiing and other sport and leisure activities, and will advise on equipment needed.

Tennis Since the time Björn Borg began to win Wimbledon with almost monotonous regularity, Sweden has been a force in world tennis. There are indoor and outdoor courts throughout the country. The **Swedish Tennis Association** (Svenska Tennisförbundet, Lidingövägen 75, Box 27915, S–115 94 Stockholm, tel. 08/667–9770) can supply more information.

Water Sports Windsurfing and waterskiing are extremely popular in Sweden. One can learn the basics and rent equipment at many locations nationwide.

Beaches

There are relatively few sand beaches but thousands of unspoiled *bad*, or "bathing places." These are more likely to be grassy or rocky areas by the lakeside than sandy beaches, though these, too, can be found along both the east and west coasts and on the Baltic resort islands of Gotland and Öland. It is possible to swim in clear, clean waters close to most urban centers.

Dining

In August look for *kräftor* (crayfish), which are boiled with dill, salt, and sugar, then cooled overnight. Swedes eat them with hot buttered toast, caraway seeds, and schnapps or beer. Later comes an exotic assortment of mushrooms and wild berries.

Regional specialties include *spettekaka*, a cake of eggs and sugar made in Skåne, and *Gotlandsflundror*, a smoked flat fish from the island of Gotland. *Husmanskost* (home-cooking) recipes are often served in restaurants as a *dagens rätt* (the daily special). Examples are *pytt i panna* (literally, "put in the pan"—beef and potato hash topped with a fried egg), or pea soup with pancakes, a traditional meal on Thursday.

Sweden is known for its coffee. Jealous Danes theorize that foreigners like their coffee weak and therefore prefer Swedish varieties; Swedes just say it tastes better.

The nation's standard home-cooked meal is basically peasant fare—sausages, potatoes, and other hearty foods to ward off the winter cold. However, it has also produced the *smörgåsbord*, a generous and artfully arranged buffet featuring both hot and cold dishes. You start with the herring, then eat your way through salads, vegetable dishes, meats, cheeses, and breads, winding up with a slice of *tårta* (cake) or some fruit. Fish—fresh, smoked, or pickled—is a Swedish specialty; herring and salmon both come in myriad traditional and new preparations.

The hotel breakfast is often a well-stocked smörgåsbord-style buffet. Lunches are markedly less expensive than dinner. Even in Stockholm, it is still possible to eat the *dagens rätt* (dish of the day) between 11:30 AM and 2 PM for less than SKr60, with bread, salad, and either a light beer or a cup of coffee.

So, you're getting away from it all.

Just make sure you can get back.

Here's a travel tip that will make it easy to call back to the States. Dial the access number for the country you're visiting and connect right to AT&T **USADirect**® Service. It's the quick way to get English-speaking operators and can minimize hotel surcharges.

If all the countries you're visiting aren't listed above, call THE **i** PLAN℠ **1 800 241-5555** before you leave for a free wallet card with all AT&T access numbers. International calling made easy—it's all part of **The i Plan.**℠

AT&T

All The Best Trips Start with **Fodor's**

Dinner is a different matter entirely. An indifferent steak and potatoes can set you back SKr160, and a bottle of mediocre wine with the meal will cost at least that much again. Dinner for two with wine in one of the better Stockholm restaurants could easily cost SKr600 or more.

Category	Cost*
Very Expensive	Over SKr500
Expensive	SKr250–SKr500
Moderate	SKr120–SKr250
Inexpensive	under SKr120

per person, for a two-course meal, including service charge and tax but not wine.

Lodging

Though they are usually extremely clean and efficient, hotels are very expensive all over the country. In mid-1993 the government reduced the tax on hotels and domestic travel services from 21% to 12%, a welcome change for visitors. However, in summer many discounts, special passes, and summer packages are available. Your travel agent or the Swedish Travel and Tourism Council (in New York) will have full details, but some of the better buys are as follows: The **Reso** hotel chain offers the **Piccolo Card,** which costs SKr150 and entitles the holder to a 20% discount on summer rates (June 1–Aug. 31), which are reduced by as much as 50%. The **Scandic Hotel** summer check plan enables you to pay for your accommodation in advance, with a weekend check costing SKr550, and a supplement of SKr150 at city-center hotels. **Sweden Hotels** offer a **Scandinavian Bonus Pass** costing SKr160 that gives between 15% and 50% discounts from May 15 to October 1.

Vandrarhem (youth hostels), also scrupulously clean and well run, are more expensive than elsewhere in Europe. **Sveriges Turistförening** (STF; the Swedish Touring Association, Box 25, S–101 20 Stockholm, tel. 08/790–3100) has 280 nationwide, most with 4- to 6-bed family rooms and 80 with running hot and cold water in the rooms. They are open to anyone irrespective of age. Prices are from SKr60 to SKr90 per night for members of STF or organizations affiliated with the International Youth Hostel Federation. Nonmembers are charged SKr35 extra per night. A hostel handbook is published annually by STF.

Category	Cost*
Very Expensive	over SKr1,500
Expensive	SKr1,200–SKr1,500
Moderate	SKr800–SKr1,200
Inexpensive	under SKr800

All prices are for a standard double room, including tax.

Stockholm

Set at the point where the waters of Mälaren (Lake Mälar) rush into the Baltic, Stockholm is one of Europe's most beautiful capitals. Nearly 1.6 million people now live in the greater Stockholm area, yet it remains a quiet, almost pastoral city.

Built on 14 small islands among open bays and narrow channels, Stockholm is a handsome, civilized city, filled with parks, squares, and airy boulevards, yet it is also a bustling, modern metropolis. Glass-and-steel skyscrapers abound, but you are never more than five minutes' walk from twisting medieval streets and waterside walks.

The first written mention of Stockholm dates from 1252, when a powerful regent named Birger Jarl built a fortified castle and city here. King Gustav Vasa took it over in 1523, and King Gustavus Adolphus made it the heart of an empire a century later.

During the Thirty Years' War (1618–48), Sweden gained importance as a Baltic trading state, and Stockholm grew commensurately. But by the beginning of the 18th century, Swedish influence had begun to wane, and Stockholm's development had slowed. It did not revive until the Industrial Revolution, when the hub of the city moved north from the Old Town area.

Nowadays most Stockholmers live in high-rise suburbs dotted in the pine forests and by lakesides around the capital, linked to it by a highly efficient infrastructure of roads, railways, and one of the safest subway systems in the world. Air pollution is minimal and the city streets are relatively clean and safe.

Important Addresses and Numbers

Tourist Information The main tourist office, **Stockholm Information Service,** in the center of the city at **Sverigehuset** (Sweden House; Kungsträdgården, Box 7542, S–103 93 Stockholm, tel. 08/789–2000) is open every day. Here you will find information on current events, sightseeing, one-day tours, maps, and books. Bookings can be made for tours.

The free publication *Stockholm This Week* is available at most hotels and tourist centers. The Saturday edition of the daily newspapers *Dagens Nyheter* and *Svenska Dagbladet* carry current listings of events, films, restaurants, and museums (in Swedish, of course).

Embassies **U.S. Embassy:** Strandvägen 101, tel. 08/783–5300. **Canadian Embassy:** Tegelbacken 4, tel. 08/237920. **U.K. Embassy,** Skärpögatan 6–8, tel. 08/6670140.

Emergencies Dial 90000 for emergencies. This covers police, fire, ambulance, and medical help, and sea and air rescue services.

Doctors There is a 24-hour national health service emergency number (tel. 08/449200) and private care via City Hälsocentral (tel. 08/206990).

Dentists There is an emergency clinic at St. Erik's Hospital, open 8 AM–7 PM, with provision for acute cases until 9 PM (tel. 08/6541117). The emergency number is 08/6540590.

English-Language Bookstores Nearly all bookshops stock English-language books. The best selections are at **Hedengren's** (Sturegallerian shopping com-

plex, tel. 08/611–5132) and **Akademibokhandeln** (Mäster Samuelsgatan 32, near city center, tel. 08/237990). For English-language newspapers and magazines, try the **Press Center** (Gallerian, Hamngatan, tel. 08/723–0191) or one of the newsstands at Central Station.

Late-Night Pharmacies C. W. Scheele (Klarabergsgatan 64, tel. 08/218934 or 08/218280) is open all night.

Travel Agencies **American Express** is at Birger Jarlsgatan 1 (tel. 08/235330). **SJ,** the state railway company, has its main ticket office at Central Station (Vasagatan 1, tel. 020/757575). For air travel, contact **SAS** (Klarabergsviadukten 72, accessible from Central Station, tel. 020/910150). For other travel agencies, see the yellow pages under *Resor-Resebyråer.*

Arriving and Departing by Plane

Airport Stockholm's **Arlanda** Airport was opened in 1960 at first solely for international flights, but it now also contains the domestic terminal. Arlanda is 41 kilometers (26 miles) from the center of Stockholm and is linked to it by freeway.

Between the Airport and City Center Buses leave both the international and domestic terminals every 10 to 15 minutes from 7:10 AM to 10:30 PM and run to the city terminal at Klarabergsviadukten next to the central railway sta-
By Bus tion. The trip costs SKr50. For more information, call 08/6001000.

By Taxi If you look for a taxi with a large SKr250 sign on the back or side window, or ask for *fast pris* (fixed price), the fare will be SKr250. SAS operates a shared limousine to any point in central Stockholm. This will cost between SKr185 and SKr280, depending upon distance. If two or more people travel to the same address together in a limousine, only one pays the full rate; the others pay half price. For more information and bookings, call 08/797–3700.

Arriving and Departing by Car, Train, and Bus

By Car You will approach the city by either the E3 highway from the west or the E4 from the north or south. The roads are clearly marked and well sanded and plowed during winter.

By Train All trains arrive at Stockholm's Central Station (Vasagatan, tel. 08/762–2000) in downtown Stockholm. From here regular commuter trains serve the suburbs, and an underground walkway leads to the central subway station.

By Bus Buses arrive at various points, all close to the central railway station. There are numerous companies, but the principal one, with services to most parts of the country, is run by **Eurolines,** also known as Continentbus (tel. 08/234810).

Getting Around

The most effective way to get around the city is to purchase a *Stockholmskort* (Key to Stockholm) card. Besides giving unlimited transportation on city subway, bus, and rail services, it offers free admission to 50 museums and several sightseeing trips. The card costs SKr150 for 24 hours, SKr300 for two days, and SKr450 for three days. It is available from the tourist center at Sweden House in Kungsträdgården and from the Hotellcentralen accommodations bureau at Central Station.

Otherwise, tickets may be bought on buses or at the subway barrier. The minimum fare is SKr12. It is cheaper to buy a discount coupon from one of the many Pressbyrån newsstands. The standard discount coupon valid for both subway and buses costs SKr80 and is good for a fixed number of trips (approximately 10) within the greater Stockholm area during an unlimited period of time. If you plan to travel within the greater Stockholm area extensively during a 24-hour period, you can purchase an SKr60 ticket; an SKr150 ticket will allow for 72 hours of travel. People under 18 or over 65 pay a reduced fare. The 24-hour card entitles the holder to admission to Skansen, Gröna Lund, and Kaknäs Tower.

Maps and timetables for all city transportation networks are available from the SL information desks at Sergels Torg. Information is also available by phone (tel. 08/6001000).

By Car Rental cars are readily available in Sweden and relatively inexpensive. Because of the availability and efficiency of public transport, there is little point in using a car within the city limits. However, if you are traveling elsewhere in Sweden, roads are uncongested and well marked, but gasoline is expensive (SKr7 per liter at press time). All major car-rental firms are represented, including **Avis** (Ringvägen 90, tel. 08/6449980) and **Hertz** (Vasagatan 26, tel. 08/240720.)

By Bus and Subway Stockholm has excellent bus and subway service. The subway stations are marked by a blue-on-white T (short for *Tunnelbanan*, or subway). The subway covers more than 60 route miles, and trains run frequently between 5 AM and 2 AM. There are also several night buses.

By Taxi Stockholm's taxi service is efficient but overpriced. To order a cab from one of the three taxi companies, telephone **Taxi Stockholm** (tel. 08/150000), **Taxi 1** (tel. 08/6700000), or **Taxikurir** (tel. 08/300000). **Taxi Stockholm** has an immediate charge of SKr23 whether you hail a cab or order one by telephone. A trip of 10 kilometers (6 miles) costs SKr80 between 6 AM and 7 PM, SKr90 at night, and SKr100 on weekends. If you call a cab, ask the dispatcher to quote you a fast pris, which is usually lower than the meter fare.

Opening and Closing Times

Banks Banks are open weekdays 9:30 AM to 3 PM, but some stay open until 5:30 on most days. The bank at Arlanda Airport is open every day with extended hours, and the Forex currency-exchange offices also have extended hours.

Museums The opening times for **museums** vary widely, but most are open from 10 AM to 4 PM weekdays and over the weekend but closed on Monday. Consult the guide in *På Stan*, the entertainment supplement published in *Dagens Nyheter's* Saturday edition.

Stores Shops are generally open weekdays from 9 AM, 9:30 AM, or 10 AM until 6 PM and Saturday from 9 AM to 1 or 4 PM. Most of the large department stores stay open later in the evenings and some open on Sunday. Several supermarkets open on Sunday, and there is a reasonable number of late-night food shops.

Guided Tours

Orientation A bus tour in English and Swedish covering all the main points of interest leaves each day at 11 AM from the Tourist Center at Sverigehuset and costs SKr135. Other more comprehensive tours, taking in museums, the Old Town, and City Hall, cost SKr200. Tickets are available at the Tourist Center (Kungsträdgården).

City Sightseeing (tel. 08/117023) runs several tours, including the "Domestic Stockholm" tour of the Cathedral and City Hall and the "Royal Stockholm" tour, which features visits to the Royal Palace and the Treasury.

Stockholm Sightseeing (tel. 08/240470) also runs combined boat and bus tours from outside the Grand Hotel and City Hall.

Boat Tours **Strömma Bolaget and Stockholm Sightseeing** (Skeppsbron 22, tel. 08/233375) runs a variety of boat and bus sightseeing tours of Stockholm. Boats leave from the quays outside the Royal Dramatic Theater, the Grand Hotel, and City Hall.

Personal Guides Individual city guides may be hired from Stockholm Information Service's **Guide Centralen** (c/o Hotell centralen, Centralstationen, Nedrebotten, S–111 20 Stockholm, tel. 08/240880), but be sure to book well in advance. Costs average SKr975 for a three-hour tour.

Walking Tours A walking tour of the Old Town leaves every evening at 6:30 from June to mid-September, from the Obelisk, Slottsbacken (Palace Hill).

Highlights for First-Time Visitors

Djurgården (*see* Tour 4)
Drottningholm Palace (*see* Tour 3)
Gamla Stan (Stockholm's Old Town) (*see* Tour 2)
Kungliga Slottet (Royal Palace) (*see* Tour 2)
Stadshuset (City Hall) (*see* Tour 3)
Skansen (*see* Tour 4)
Vasa Museum (*see* Tour 4)

Exploring Stockholm

The center of Stockholm is Sergels Torg, a modern, sunken square. Past the Parliament building on Helgeands Holmen (Holy Ghost Island) and over the tumbling Strömmen (the Current), where Lake Mälar empties into the Baltic, lies the superbly well preserved medieval Gamla Stan (Old Town). Behind the island of Skeppsholmen another stretch of water laps Strandvägen, the waterfront for Östermalm, the upscale residential area. At the end of Strandvägen, a bridge takes you over to Djurgården. Directly south of Gamla Stan is Södermalm (known as Söder), the south island.

Numbers in the margin correspond to points of interest on the Stockholm map.

Tour 1: Modern Stockholm

The heart of the city, **Sergels Torg,** named for Johan Tobias Sergel (1740–1814), one of Sweden's greatest sculptors, is dominated by modern, functional buildings that include

❶ Kulturhuset (the House of Culture), a library, theater, and exhibition center, with an excellent restaurant. Make a slight detour to visit the Åhléns department store, then walk north, along the pedestrian street Sergelgatan in the shadow of five identical concrete-and-glass skyscrapers to **Hötorget** (the Hay **❷** Market), where you'll find **Konserthuset** (the Concert House), a colorful outdoor fruit and vegetable market, and the PUB department store. You might also like to visit **Hötorgshallen,** an underground, old-fashioned food hall, with relatively inexpensive restaurants.

Head east over Sveavägen, where you can make a brief detour to see the spot where Olof Palme was assassinated in 1986 and to visit his grave in Adolf Fredrik's Churchyard nearby.

Next, walk down **Kungsgatan,** Stockholm's main shopping street, to Stureplan. In **Stureplan** you'll find Sturegallerian, a fine modern shopping precinct. South along **Birger Jarlsgatan,** a street named for the nobleman generally credited with founding Stockholm around 1252, there are still more interesting shops and restaurants. When you reach Nybroplan, take a look **❸** at **Kungliga Dramatiska Teatern** (the Royal Dramatic Theater), an imposing building with a gilded roof that faces out over the Baltic harbor. Here occasional productions by Ingmar Bergman, the country's leading director, provoke the imagination.

❹ Heading west up Hamngatan, drop in at **Hallwylska Museet** (the Hallwyl Museum), a private turn-of-the-century palace, with imposing wood-panel rooms, housing a collection of furniture, paintings, and musical instruments in a bewildering mélange of styles assembled by the Countess von Hallwyl, who left it to the state on her death. *Hamngatan 4, tel. 08/666–4499. Admission: SKr40. English guided tour June–July, Sun. and Mon. 1 PM; Sept.–May, Sun. 1 PM.*

Not far along Hamngatan stands **Kungsträdgården,** a park since 1562 but previously the royal kitchen garden. There are usually public concerts and events here in the summer.

❺ On the park you will find **Sverigehuset** (Sweden House), with its excellent tourist center, and on the opposite side of the street the NK department store.

If you have time, head down Kungsträdgårdsgatan to Blasieholmshamnen quay, passing the **Grand Hotel** (where Nobel laureates are accommodated each year) and visit the **❻ National Museum,** with its fine collection of old masters, including some of Rembrandt's major works. *Södra Blasieholmshamnen, tel. 08/666–4250. Admission: SKr40, free Fri. Open Wed., Fri., Sat., Sun. 11–5; Tues., Thurs. 11–9.*

Cross the footbridge to the idyllic island **Skeppsholmen,** where **❼** you'll find two museums. **Östasiatiska Museet** (the Museum of Far Eastern Antiquities), has an arresting collection of Chinese and Japanese Buddhist sculptures and artifacts. *Skeppsholmen, tel. 08/6664391. Admission: SKr30. Open Tues. 11–9, Wed.–Sun. 11–5.*

❽ A little farther along, **Moderna Museet** (the Modern Museum) features a good selection of contemporary art, including works by Picasso, Dali, and Modigliani. The museum has a fine, health-food-oriented canteen and a workshop for children. *Skeppsholmen, tel. 08/666–4250. Admission: SKr40, free Thurs. Open Tues.–Thurs. 11–8; Fri.–Sun. 11–5.*

❾ The adjoining island, **Kastellholmen,** is a pleasant place for a stroll, especially on a summer evening, with fine views of Gamla Stan's seafront, across the Baltic harbor.

Tour 2: Gamla Stan (The Old Town)

Gamla Stan sits on a cluster of small islands between two of Stockholm's main islands and is the site of the medieval city. The narrow twisting cobbled streets are lined with superbly preserved old buildings.

❿ Start at the refurbished stone **Riksdagshuset** (Parliament Building) on **Helgeandsholmen** (Holy Ghost Island). It dates from the end of the 19th century. *Admission free. English guided tours Jan.–June, weekends 1:30; June–Aug., weekdays 12:30, 3.*

⓫ Cross the bridge to **Kungliga Slottet** (the Royal Palace), a magnificent granite edifice designed by Nicodemus Tessin and completed in 1760. There is a fine view here of the Baltic harbor, with the *af Chapman* sailing-ship youth hostel and the Grand Hotel and National Museum in the background. The **State Apartments** feature fine furnishings and Gobelins tapestries. **Livsrustkammaren** (the Royal Armory) boasts an outstanding collection of weaponry and royal regalia, while **Skattkammaren** (the Treasury) houses the crown jewels, which are no longer used, even on ceremonial occasions, in this self-consciously egalitarian country. *Admission: State Apartments SKr25; treasury and royal armory SKr40; treasury and armory open Mon.–Sat. 11–3, Sun. noon–4. State apartments open Tues.–Sat. 10–3, Sun. noon–3.*

It is only a short walk from the palace to Stockholm's 15th-century Gothic cathedral, **Storkyrkan** (the Great Church), where Swedish kings were crowned until 1907. It contains a dramatic wooden statue of St. George slaying the dragon, carved by Bernt Notke of Lübeck in 1489, and the *Parhelion,* a painting of Stockholm dating from 1520, the oldest in existence.

Walk a few yards on Källargränd to the front of Storkyrkan or on Trångsund to the rear until you reach **Stortorget** (the Great Square), which is small but marvelously atmospheric, fronted by magnificent old merchants' houses. Here in 1520 the Danish King Christian II ordered a massacre of Swedish noblemen, paving the way for a national revolt against foreign rule and the founding of Sweden as a sovereign state under King Gustav Vasa, who ruled from 1523 to 1560.

⓭ In **Stockholms Fondbörs** (the Stock Exchange), which also fronts onto the square, the Swedish Academy meets each year to decide the winner of the Nobel Prize for literature. The Stock Exchange itself is computerized and rather quiet. There are no tours in English, but there is a film about the Stock Exchange in Swedish. *Stockholms Fondbörs, Källargränd 2, Stockholm, tel. 08/613–8892.*

⓮ Passing among ancient buildings, you walk down Svartmangatan to **Tyska Kyrkan** (the German Church), with its magnificent oxidized copper spire and airy interior. Then go down Tyska Brinken to Västerlånggatan, where you can walk north, checking out pricey fashion boutiques.

Stockholm

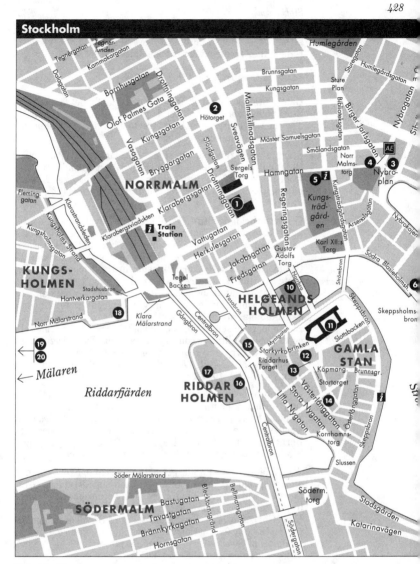

Biologiska Museet, **25**

Drottningholms Slott, **19**

Drottningholms Slottsteater, **20**

Gröna Lund, **23**

Hallwylska Museet, **4**

Historiska Museet, **28**

Kaknästornet, **27**

Kastellholmen, **9**

Konserthuset, **2**

Kulturhuset, **1**

Kungliga Dramatiska Teatern, **3**

Kungliga Slottet, **11**

Moderna Museet, **8**

National Museum, **6**

Nordiska Museet, **22**

Östasiatiska Museet, **7**

Riddarholmskyrkan, **16**

Riddarhuset, **15**

Riksdagshuset, **10**

Skansen, **24**

Stadshuset, **18**

Stockholms Fondbörs, **13**

Storkyrkan, **12**

Svea Hovrätt, **17**

Sverigehuset, **5**

Tyska Kyrkan, **14**

Vasa Museet, **21**

Waldemarsudde, **26**

KOMMENDÖRSGATAN KARLAPLAN

ÖSTERMALM

Narvavägen

Linnégatan

Baněrgatan Karlavägen

Oxenstimsgatan

N. DJURGÅRDEN

Cördegatan

Storpogatan

Skeppargatan

Grevgatan

Styrmangatan

Storgatan

Linnégatan

28

Riddargatan

Strandvägen

27

Strandvägen

Djurgårdsbron

Djurgårdsbrunnsviken

22

Rosendalsvägen

21

7

25

8

KEPPSHOLMEN

Alkärret

Djurgårdsvägen

24

DJURGÅRDEN

Sirishovsvägen

Svensksundsvägen

23

Falkenb G.

Allmänna Gränd

Djurgårds
Slätten

Sollidsbacken

Singelbacken

9

**KASTELL-
HOLMEN**

26

Baltic →

Saltsjön

BECKHOLMEN

KEY

N

AE	American Express Office
𝒊	Tourist Information
—	Rail Lines

0 _____ 500 yards

0 _____ 500 meters

Time Out On Västerlånggatan you can stop for a coffee and a pastry in **Grå Munken** (the Gray Monk) coffee house.

⑮ Cut down Storkyrkobrinken to the 17th-century **Riddarhuset** (the House of Nobles), built in the Dutch Baroque style. Before the abolition of the aristocracy early in the 20th century, it was the gathering place for the First Estate of the realm. Hanging from its walls are 2,325 escutcheons, representing all the former noble families of Sweden. Because of the building's excellent acoustic properties, Riddarhuset is often used for concerts. *Riddarhuset, tel. 08/100857. Admission: SKr20. Open weekdays 11:30–12:30.*

⑯ A short walk takes you over Riddarholmen bridge to **Riddarholmen** (the Island of Knights), on which stands **Riddarholmskyrkan,** a Greyfriar monastery dating from 1270. The second-oldest structure in Stockholm, it has been the burial place for 17 Swedish kings over four centuries. The most famous figures buried here are King Gustavus Adolphus, hero of the Thirty Years' War, and the warrior king Karl XII, renowned for his daring invasion of Russia, who finally fell in Norway in 1718. The latest king to be put to rest here was Gustav V, in 1950. Normally the church is not used for services. The various rulers' sarcophagi, usually embellished with their monograms, are visible in the small chapels given over to the various dynasties. The redbrick structure is distinguished by its delicate iron fretwork spire. *Admission: SKr10. Open May–Aug. 10–3, Sun. 1–3.*

⑰ Riddarholmen is also the site of the white 17th-century palace that houses the **Svea Hovrätt** (Swedish High Court). The quiet and restful quayside here is an excellent place to end an afternoon's sightseeing, sitting by the water's edge, watching the boats on **Riddarfjärden** (Bay of Knights) and beyond it, Lake Mälar. It affords a fine view of the lake, the magnificent arches of **Västerbron** (the West Bridge) in the distance, the southern heights, and above all the imposing profile of Stadshuset (the City Hall), which appears almost to be floating on the water. At the quay you may see one of the Göta Canal ships.

Tour 3: Stadshuset and Drottningholm

Stockholm's City Hall and Drottningholm Palace, outstanding embodiments of Swedish architecture and sensibilities from different centuries, share access from Mälaren.

⑱ Start at the redbrick **Stadshuset,** a powerful symbol of Stockholm, among the most impressive pieces of modern architecture in Europe. Completed in 1923, it was created by Rangnar Östberg, one of the founders of the National Romantic movement. It is both functional (headquarters for the city council) and ornate (its immense Blue Hall is the venue for the Nobel Prize dinner each December, Stockholm's principal social event). A trip to the top of the 348-foot tower, most of which can be achieved by elevator, is rewarded by a breathtaking panorama of the city and Riddarfjärden. *Hantverkargatan 1, tel. 08/ 785–9074. Admission to tower: SKr10. Tour of Stadshuset and tower: SKr25; tours at 10 and noon Sat. Tower open May–Sept., daily 10–4:30.*

Time Out After climbing the tower, relax on Stadshuset's fine grass terraces, which lead down to the bay, or perhaps have lunch in **Stadshuskällaren** (the City Hall Cellar, tel. 08/650-5454), whose kitchen prepares the annual Nobel banquet.

Walk the short distance over Stadshusbron (City Hall Bridge) to the quayside at **Klara Mälarstrand,** from which boats leave ⑲ regularly for **Drottningholms Slott** (Queen's Island Castle), a miniature Versailles dating from the 17th century on an island in Mälaren some 45 minutes from the city center. The royal family once used it as their summer residence, but, tiring of the immensity of the Royal Palace, they moved permanently to one wing of Drottningholm in the 1970s. Drottningholm is one of the most delightful of European palaces, embracing all that was best in the art of living practiced by mid-18th-century royalty. The interiors are from the 17th, 18th, and 19th centuries, and most are open to the public. *Drottningholms Slott, tel. 08/ 759-0310. Admission: SKr30. Open May–Aug., daily 11–4:30; Sept., weekdays 1–3:30.*

The lakeside gardens of Drottningholm are its most beautiful ⑳ asset, containing **Drottningholms Slottsteater** (the Court Theater), the only complete theater to survive from the 18th century anywhere in the world. It was built by Queen Lovisa Ulrika in 1766 as a wedding present for her son Gustav III. It fell into disuse after his assassination at a masked ball in 1792, but in 1922 it was rediscovered. There is now a small theater museum here as well. To obtain tickets for a performance, you must book well in advance. A word of caution: the seats are extremely hard—take a cushion. *Castle tel. 08/759-0310. Admission: SKr30. Open May–Aug., weekdays 11:30–4:30, Sun. 11:30– 4:30; Sept. 12:30–3:30.*

Tour 4: Djurgården and Skansen

Djurgården is Stockholm's pleasure island. On it you will find the outdoor museum Skansen, the Gröna Lund amusement park, and the *Vasa,* a 17th-century warship raised from the bottom of the harbor in 1961, as well as other delights.

You can reach **Djurgården** by sea aboard the small ferries that leave from **Slussen** at the southern end of Gamla Stan or from **Nybrokajen** (the New Bridge Quay) in front of the **Kungliga Dramatiska Teater.** Alternatively, starting at the theater, stroll down the **Strandvägen** quayside, taking in the magnificent old sailing ships permanently anchored here and the fine views over the harbor, and then cross **Djurgårdsbron** (the Djurgården Bridge) to the island. Your first port of call should ㉑ be the **Vasa Museet,** where you can see the *Vasa,* a warship that sank on its maiden voyage in 1628, was forgotten for three centuries, then located in 1956, and raised from the seabed in 1961. Its hull was found to be largely intact, because the Baltic's brackish waters do not support worms that otherwise eat ship's timbers. Now largely restored to her former, if brief, glory, the man-of-war resides in a handsome new museum. *Galärvarvet, Djurgården, tel. 08/666-4800. Guided tours in English every hour. Admission: SKr40 adults, SKr10 children. Open daily 10–5 (Wed. 10–8).*

㉒ Close by is the **Nordiska Museet** (the Nordic Museum), housed in a splendid late-Victorian structure, worth a quick visit for an

insight into Swedish folklore. Its collection includes peasant costumes from every region of the country and exhibits on the Sami (pronounced **sah-mee**; Lapps), formerly seminomadic reindeer herders who inhabit the far north. *Djurgårdsvägen 6– 16, tel. 08/666–4600. Admission SKr50. Open Tues., Wed., Fri. 10–4, Thurs. 10–8, weekends 11–4.*

㉓ Just down the road is **Gröna Lund,** an amusement park that features a range of carnival rides, though on a smaller scale than both Copenhagen's Tivoli and Göteborg's Liseberg. *Djurgårdsvägen, tel. 08/665–7000. Admission: SKr35 adults, children 12 years and under free. Open mid-Apr.–late Aug.*

㉔ Cross Djurgårdsvägen to **Skansen,** a must for any visitor to Stockholm. The world's first open-air museum, it was founded by philologist and ethnographer Artur Hazelius (who is also buried here) in 1891 to preserve traditional Swedish architecture, including farmhouses, windmills, barns, a working glassblower's hut, and churches, brought from all parts of the country. Not only is Skansen a delightful trip out of time in the center of a modern city, it also provides an easily assimilated insight into the life and culture of Sweden's various regions. In addition, the park contains a zoo, a circus, an aquarium, a theater, and cafés. *Djurgårdsslätten 49–51, tel. 08/663–0500. Admission: SKr20 adults (except weekends, SKr30), children under 14 free. Open Sept.–Apr. daily 9–5; May–Aug., daily 9–10.*

Time Out For a snack with a view, try the **Solliden Restaurant** at Skansen. The museum also offers a selection of open-air snack bars and cafés; Gröna Lund has four different restaurants.

㉕ The charmingly archaic **Biologiska Museet** (Biological Museum), in the shadow of Skansen, has a collection of stuffed animals in various simulated environments. *Hazeliusporten, tel. 08/661–1383. Admission: SKr6. Open daily 10–3.*

㉖ Djurgården's treasure is **Waldemarsudde,** the beautiful turn-of-the-century home of Sweden's Prince Eugen, an accomplished painter, who died in 1947. His mansion, bequeathed to the Swedish people, maintains an important collection of Nordic paintings from 1880 to 1940 in addition to the prince's own works. Its grounds are a delight. *Prins Eugens väg 6, tel. 08/ 662–1833. Admission: SKr30. Open Tues.–Sun. 11–5; Tues. and Thurs. 7–9.*

㉗ Finally, eastward on Norra Djurgården is **Kaknästornet,** the radio and television tower, completed in 1967 and, at 511 feet, the highest building in Scandinavia. Here you can eat a meal in a restaurant 426 feet above the ground and enjoy panoramic views of the city and the archipelago. *Mörkakroken, off Kaknäsvägen, tel. 08/667–8517. Admission: SKr20. Open Apr. 15–Sept. 15, daily 9 AM–10:30 PM.*

Cross the Djurgården bridge and proceed up Narvavägen to ㉘ **Historiska Museet** (the Museum of National Antiquities), which houses important collections of Viking gold and silver treasures. **Myntkabinettet** (the Royal Cabinet of Coin), in the same building, boasts the world's largest coin. *Narvavägen 13–17, tel. 08/783–9400. Admission to both: SKr50. Open Tues., Wed., and Fri. noon–5; Thurs. noon–8; weekends 10–5.*

Short Excursions from Stockholm

Numbers in the margin correspond to points of interest on the Excursions from Stockholm map.

Skärgården **Skärgården** (the archipelago) is Stockholm's greatest natural asset: more than 25,000 islands and skerries, many uninhabited, spread across an almost tideless sea of clean, clear water. To sail lazily among these islands aboard an old steamboat on a summer's night is a timeless delight.

Regular ferry services depart from the quayside in front of the Grand Hotel. Cruises on a variety of boats leave from the harbor in front of the Royal Palace or from Nybrokajen, across the road from the Royal Dramatic Theater.

For the tourist with limited time, one of the simplest ways to get a taste of the archipelago's delights is to take a one-hour ❶ ferry trip to **Vaxholm,** an extremely pleasant, though sometimes crowded, mainland seaside town of small, red-painted wooden houses. It is the site of a fortress guarding the approaches to Stockholm. The fortress, **Vaxholms Kastell,** houses a small museum, **Vaxholms Kastell Museum,** showing the defense of Stockholm over the centuries. *Tel. 08/541–30107. Admission: SKr20 or SKr45 including boat fare. Open May 15– Aug. 31, daily noon–3:45; July 3–14, daily 11–6 (when a pontoon bridge temporarily links the island with the mainland). Group admission also at other times by arrangement.*

A more authentic way of getting to know the archipelago is to seek out the *Blidösund.* A coal-fired steamboat built in 1911 that was in regular service for 50 years, it is now run by a small group of enthusiasts, who take parties of around 250 merrymakers on evening cruises. The *Blidösund* leaves from a berth close to the Royal Palace in Stockholm. *SS Blidösund, Skeppsbron 10, tel. 08/117113 or 08/202186. Fare: SKr100. Season: May–Sept.; departs Mon.–Thurs. at 7:30, returns at 11:15.*

The finest of the other steamboats is *Björkfjärden,* which leaves from Nybrokajen, close to the Strand Hotel. *Björkfjärden, Ångfartyget, St. Nygatan 45, tel. 08/233375. Fare: SKr100. Season: June–Aug.*

Mälaren Boats plying the lake leave from a quay close to City Hall. There are regular services and excursions to various points, but the most delightful way to experience the true vastness of ❷ Sweden's third-largest lake is the trip to **Mariefred** aboard the coal-fired steamer of the same name, built in 1903 and still going strong. *Round-trip fare, SKr150; one-way, SKr100. Limited service from May, regular sailings from June. For boat schedules, contact Mariefred Tourist Office, tel. 0159/29790.*

The principal attraction in Mariefred, an idyllic little town of mostly timbered houses, is the 16th-century **Gripsholm Slott** (castle), which contains fine Renaissance chambers, a superbly atmospheric theater dating from the late 1700s, and Sweden's royal portrait collection. *S–64700, tel. 0159/10194. Admission: SKr30. Open May, June, Aug., daily 10–4; July, daily 10–5; Apr. Tues.–Sun. 10–3; Sept., Tues.–Sun. 10–4; Jan.–Mar. and Oct.–Dec., weekends 12–5.*

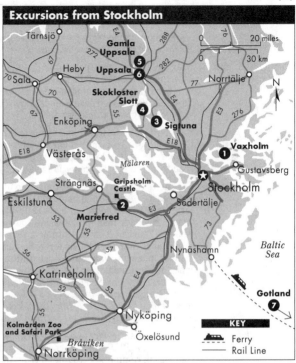

Excursions from Stockholm

You can also travel by narrow-gauge steam railway from Mariefred to a junction on the main line to Stockholm, returning to the capital by ordinary train.

Sigtuna ❸ This extremely picturesque and restful little town of 5,000 is idyllically located some 30 kilometers (20 miles) from Stockholm on a northern arm of Lake Mälar. **Sigtuna** was the principal trading post of the Svea, the tribe that settled Sweden after the last Ice Age. After it was sacked by Estonian pirates, its merchants founded Stockholm sometime in the 13th century. Little remains of Sigtuna's former glory, beyond parts of the principal church. The town hall dates from the 18th century, the main part of town from the early 1800s, and there are two houses said to date from the 15th century. Sigtuna can be reached by taking a commuter train from Stockholm's Central Station to Märsta, where you change to Bus 570 or 575. From June to August it can also be reached by boat from the quay near City Hall. The fare is approximately SKr60.

Skokloster Slott ❹ About 20 kilometers (12 miles) to the northeast of Sigtuna off the E18 highway lies **Skokloster Slott,** a Baroque castle that was the home of a celebrated Swedish soldier, Field Marshal Carl Gustav Wrangel. It is exquisitely furnished with the spoils of his successful campaigns in Europe in the 17th century. *S–14800 Bålsta, tel. 018/386077. Admission: SKr40. Open May–Aug. 31, daily 11–4. Special tours for groups can be arranged in September.*

What to See and Do with Children

In addition to **Skansen** and the **Gröna Lund** amusement park, (*see* Tour 4, *above*) the **Stockholms Leksaksmuseet** (Toy Museum) features a collection of toys and dolls from all over the world and has a playroom for children. *Mariatorget 1, Södermalm, tel. 08/6416100. Admission: SKr25 adults, SKr10 children. Open Tues.–Fri. 10–4, Sat.–Sun. 12–4.*

See also the Saturday *Dagens Nyheter* newspaper for details of children's events at other museums.

Off the Beaten Track

Hidden away over a grocery store, **Strindbergsmuseet Blå Tornet** (Strindberg Museum, Blue Tower) is dedicated to Sweden's most important author and dramatist (1849–1912). This was actually August Strindberg's home from 1908 until his death, and the interior has been lovingly reconstructed with authentic furnishings and other objects (including his pen). It also has a library, a press, and picture archives and arranges literary, musical, and theatrical events. *Drottninggatan 85, tel. 08/113789. Admission: SKr20. Open Tues. 10–4 and 6–8; Thurs.–Sat. 10–4; Sun. 12–4.*

Millesgården is another home that has become a museum dedicated to its former owner, in this case American-Swedish sculptor Carl Milles (1875–1955). His works and his collection of the works of other artists are displayed in the house, and his sculptures top columns on terraces in a magical garden high above the harbor and the city. *Carl Milles väg 2, Lidingö, tel. 08/731–5060. Admission: SKr30. Open: May–Sept., daily 10–5; June–Aug., Wed. 10–9; Oct.–Apr., Tues.–Sun. 11–4.*

Shopping

Shopping Districts The three main department stores are situated in the central city area, as are the **Gallerian** and **Sturegallerian** shopping malls. However, there are interesting boutiques and galleries in **Västerlånggatan,** the main street of the Old Town, and some excellent handicrafts and art shops line the raised sidewalk at the start of **Hornsgatan** in Söder.

Department Stores Sweden's leading department store, **NK** (the initials, pronounced *enn-koh*, stand for *Nordiska Kompaniet*), is located in Hamngatan, just across the street from Kungsträdgården (tel. 08/762–8000). The **Åhléns** department store (tel. 08/246000) is only a short distance up Hamngatan at Klarabergsgatan. **PUB** (the initials of founder Paul U. Bergström) is at Hötorget (tel. 08/791–6000). Greta Garbo worked here before she went into films.

Street Markets There is a **flower and fruit market** every day at **Hötorget** and a **fleamarket** at the suburb of **Skärholmen.** The best streets for **bric-a-brac** and **antiques** are **Odengatan** and **Roslagsgatan** (Odenplan subway station).

Specialty Stores The principal local auction houses are **Lilla Bukowski** **Antiques** (Strandvägen 7, tel. 08/6140800), **Beijers Auktioner** (Birger Jarlsgatan 6, tel. 08/6117870), and **Stockholms Auktionsverk** (Jakobsgatan 10, tel. 08/142440).

Books Both **Hedengrens** (Sturegallerian, tel. 08/611–5132) and **Akademibokhandeln** (Mäster Samuelsgatan 32, tel. 08/214890) have excellent selections of English-language and Swedish books. **Hemlins** (Västerlånggatan 6, in the Old Town, tel. 08/ 106180) carries foreign titles and antique books.

Crystal Swedish crystal is available at a number of stores, among them **Nordiska Kristall** (Kungsgatan 9, tel. 08/104372), **Svenskt Glas,** (Birger Jarlsgatan 8, tel. 08/6797909), **New Scandinavian Design** (Tegelbacken 4, tel. 08/219211), and **NK** (*see* Department Stores, *above*). All feature everything from small bowls to major art works at prices that range from SKr144 to SKr88,000.

Handicrafts Swedish handicrafts from all over the country are available at **Svensk Hemslöjd** (Sveavägen 44, tel. 08/232115). **Stockholms Läns Hemslöjdsförening** (Drottninggatan 14, tel. 08/761–1717) also has an excellent selection. Prices are high, but so is the quality.

Men's Clothing For suits and evening suits for both sale and rental, **Hans Allde** (Birger Jarlsgatan 58, tel. 08/200835) provides good, old-fashioned service. For shirts, there is **La Chemise** (Smålandsgatan 11, tel. 08/6111494).

Women's Clothing There are many boutiques in **Biblioteksgatan** and **Västerlånggatan** in Gamla Stan, in addition to stores such as **Twilfit** (Nybrogatan 11, tel. 08/662–3817; Gallerian, tel. 08/216221; and Gamla Brogatan 36–38, tel. 08/201954). **Hennes & Mauritz** (Hamngatan 14 and 22; Drottninggatan 53 and 56; Hötorget 1–3; Sergelgatan 1, 11, 22; and Sergels Torg 12; all tel. 08/796–5500) is one of the few Swedish-owned clothing stores to have achieved international success.

Sports and Fitness

Participant Sports Stockholm is well supplied with bicycle routes and, except during peak traveling times, bikes may be taken aboard commuter trains for excursions to the suburbs. **Cyckelfrämjandet** (tel. 08/ 321680), a local bicyclists' association, publishes an English-language guide to cycling trips. Bicycles may be rented from **Cykel & Mopeduthyrning** (Strandvägen at Kajplats 24, tel. 660–7959) or from **Skepp & Hoj** (Gälarvärvsvägen 10, tel. 08/ 660–5757). Rental costs average around SKr80 per day.

Golf There are numerous golf courses around Stockholm, among them **Lidingö Golf Club** (Sticklinge on Lidingö, tel. 08/765–7911) and **Nacka Golfbana** (Nacka, tel. 08/773–0431).

Health and Fitness Centers Keeping fit is an obsession with Swedes. **Friskis & Svettis** (Eriksgatan 63, 100 28 Stockholm, tel. 08/6520470) is a legendary local gym specializing in aerobics. Farther along the same road is the **Atalanta Girls Gym** (Eriksgatan 34, tel. 08/6506625). For relatively inexpensive massage, try **Axelsons Friskvård** (Gästrikegatan 12, tel. 08/338988). Otherwise, consult the yellow pages under "Frisk-, hälsovård."

Jogging Numerous parks and footpaths dot the central city area, among them **Haga Park,** which also has canoe rentals, **Djurgården,** and **Liljans Skogen.** An interesting track runs alongside the Karlbergssjö; it can be reached from an alleyway and steps at the side of Eriksbron (the Eric Bridge).

Swimming In the center of town, **Centralbadet** (Drottninggatan 88, tel. 08/ 242402), newly renovated, boasts an extra-large pool and nu-

merous other facilities. **Sturebadet** (Sturegalleriet, tel. 08/ 6796700) also has excellent facilities.

Tennis There are many fine tennis courts in and around Stockholm. **Kungliga Tennishallen** (the Royal Tennis Hall, Lidingövägen 75, tel. 08/667–0350) is where former champion Björn Borg plays. Another good venue is **Tennisstadion** (Fiskartorpsvägen 20, tel. 08/215454).

Spectator Sports There are two main sports stadiums in Stockholm, featuring soccer in summer and ice hockey in winter. The **Globe** (Box 10055, S–12127, tel. 08/725–1000), at 281 feet claimed to be the world's tallest spherical building, has its own subway station just across the water from Söder. The Stockholm Open Tennis Tournament is held here each November. To the north there is **Råsundastadion** (Solnavägen 51, Solna, tel. 08/735–0900).

Beaches

The best bathing places in central Stockholm are on the island of **Långholmen** and at **Rålambshov** at the end of Norr Mälarstrand. Both are grassy or rocky lakeside hideaways. Topless sunbathing is virtually de rigueur.

Dining

Recently restaurant prices have declined and a greater selection of less expensive restaurants has appeared on the scene. Even the higher-priced restaurants in Stockholm have kept their prices down. One factor has been the decrease in the value-added tax on restaurant food from 25% to 21%. Among Swedish dishes, the best bets are fish, particularly salmon, and the smörgåsbord buffet, which is usually a good value. Many restaurants close for either July or August, and most close at Christmas and New Year. It is advisable to telephone first to check that the restaurant is open. Unless otherwise stated, casual dress is acceptable.

Highly recommended restaurants are indicated by a star ★.

Very Expensive **Grands Franska Matsalen.** This classic French restaurant in the Grand Hotel has an inspiring view of the Old Town and the Royal Palace across the inner harbor waters. The food is equally inspiring, and the presence of Sweden's Chef of the Year for 1989, Roland Persson, has only improved matters. The duckling in coriander with honey-and-cinnamon sauce, and the medallions of deer with shiitake mushrooms in wild-berry cream sauce are highly recommended. The thick carpets and elegant decor should be matched by your thick wallet. *Grand Hotel, Blasieholmshamnen 8, tel. 08/221020. Reservations required. Jacket and tie required. AE, DC, MC, V.*

Operakällaren. Stockholm's best-known restaurant has a magnificent location in the Opera House at the end of Kungsträdgården. Operakällaren started business in 1787, so the tone is predictably snobbish but not intrusively so. The decor is lavish Old World style, with deep Oriental carpeting, shiny polished brass, and handsome carved-wood chairs and tables. The crystal chandeliers are said to be Sweden's most magnificent, and the high windows on the south side give fine views of the Royal Palace. Top selections on the grand smörgåsbord table with pickled herring, rollmops (rolled herring), reindeer and elk in season, and ice cream with cloudberry (a yellow blackberry na-

Stockholm Dining and Lodging

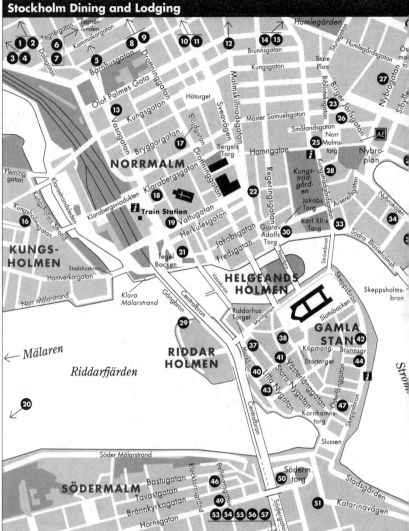

Dining
Aurora, **37**
Bakfickan, **30**
Blå Gåsen, **14**
Butler's, **4**
Cassi, **36**
Clas på Hörnet, **11**
De Fyras Krog, **46**
Den Gyldene
Freden, **47**
Edsbacka Krog, **10**

Glada Enkan, **9**
Grands Franska
Matsalen, **33**
Greitz, **13**
Hannas Krog, **57**
Invito, **15**
Källaren Diana, **44**
KB, **26**
Nils Emil, **56**
Open Gate, **53**
Operakällaren, **30**

Örtagården, **27**
Paul & Norbert, **35**
Prinsen, **23**
Rolfs Kök, **7**
Söders Hjärta, **49**
Stallmästare-
gården, **8**
Tranan, **1**
Ulriksdalsvärdshus, **3**
Wasahof, **2**
Wedholms Fisk, **39**

Lodging
af Chapman, **45**
Alexandra, **55**
Alfa, **54**
Amaranten, **16**
Anno 1647, **51**
Bema, **5**
Berns, **28**
Birger Jarl, **12**
Bosön, **32**
Clas på Hörnet, **11**

Continental, **18**
Diplomat, **31**
Grand, **33**
Gustav af Klint, **52**
Hotel City, **17**
Hotel Gamla Stan, **43**
Lady Hamilton, **38**
Långholmen, **20**
Lord Nelson, **41**
Mälardrottningen, **29**
Mornington, **24**

Reisen, **42**
Royal Viking, **21**
Scandic Crown, **50**
Sergel Plaza, **22**
Skeppsholmen, **48**
Stockholm, **25**
Strand, **34**
Tegnérlunden, **6**
Victory, **40**

tive to Scandinavia) sauce. Resting on its laurels, Opera-källaren tends to be more a Swedish institution than a great gastronomic experience. *Operahuset, Jakobs Torg 2, tel. 08/111125. Reservations required. Jacket and tie required. AE, DC, MC, V.*

★ **Paul & Norbert.** Among the best culinary spots in Stockholm, Paul and Norbert is a quaint, romantic restaurant located on the city's most elegant avenue and overlooking one of its most picturesque bays. It is noted for its French-style preparations of indigenous wild game such as reindeer, elk, partridge, grouse, and fish of various kinds. The decor is rustic but refined. *Strandvägen 9, tel. 08/6638183. Reservations required. AE, DC, MC, V. Closed weekends.*

Ulriksdalsvärdshus. This beautifully situated country inn, built in 1868, offers both Swedish and international cuisine, but is particularly noted for its lunchtime smörgåsbord. It provides a specifically Swedish experience in the park of an 18th-century palace, overlooking orchards and a peaceful lake. The interior is traditional, and guests even stand and sing the Swedish national anthem as the flag is lowered. *Ulriksdals Slottspark, Solna, tel. 08/850815. Reservations advised. Jacket required. AE, DC, MC, V. Closed Christmas. No dinner Sun.*

★ **Wedholms Fisk.** Noted for its fresh seafood dishes, Wedholms appropriately faces a bay in the center of Stockholm. High ceilings, large windows, and tasteful modern paintings from the owner's personal collection create a spacious, sophisticated atmosphere. The traditional Swedish cuisine is simple, straightforward, generous, and delicious, and consists almost exclusively of seafood. Try the poached sole in lobster-and-champagne sauce or the Pilgrim mussels Provençal. *Nybrokajen 17, tel. 08/6117874. Reservations advised. AE, DC, MC, V. Closed Sun.*

Expensive **Aurora.** Extremely elegant, if a little staid, this Old Town cellar restaurant is set in a beautiful 300-year-old house. A largely foreign clientele enjoys top-quality Swedish and international cuisine served in intimate small rooms. The adjacent Old City Club, under the same management, is open for moderate-price lunch Monday through Friday. *Munkbron 11, tel. 08/219359. Reservations required. Jacket and tie required. AE, DC, MC, V. Closed Sun.*

Blå Gåsen. This is a classic Östermalm restaurant: very classy, cozy, and costly. The Swedish/French food is excellent, the service usually impeccable. *Karlavägen 28, tel. 08/6110269. Reservations advised. Jacket and tie required. AE, DC, MC, V.*

★ **Clas på Hörnet.** In the small, intimate ground floor of a restored inn built in 1739, this restaurant is only a little off the beaten track but well worth seeking out for its extremely pleasant, relaxed, and old-fashioned atmosphere. It offers a choice of Swedish or international cuisine, including outstanding *stromming* (Baltic herring). *Surbrunnsgatan 20, tel. 08/165136. Reservations required. Jacket and tie required. AE, DC, MC, V. Closed Christmas.*

Den Gyldene Freden. Sweden's most famous old tavern, "Freden" has recently been restored after being closed for many years. The building dates from 1721 and the restaurant from the following year. The haunt of bards and barristers, artists and ad people, Freden could probably serve sawdust and still be popular, but the staff is worthy of the restaurant's hal-

lowed reputation. The cuisine has a Swedish orientation, but Continental influences are spicing up the menu. Season permitting, try oven-baked fillets of turbot, served with chanterelles and cèpes. The gray hen fried with spruce twigs and dried fruit is another good selection. The menu changes regularly and the friendly staff will gladly make recommendations. *Österlånggatan 51, tel. 08/109046. Reservations advised. AE, DC, MC, V. Closed Sun. No lunch.*

Edsbacka Krog. In 1626, Edsbacka became Stockholm's first licensed inn. This out-of-town Continental/Swedish restaurant boasts reliably superb culinary standards. With its exposed, rough-hewn beams, plaster walls, and open fireplaces, it has the feel of a country inn for the gentry. The owner, Christer Lindström, is an award-winning chef; his tarragon chicken with winter vegetables is worth the occasional long wait. *Sollentunavägen 220, Sollentuna, tel. 08/963300. Reservations advised. AE, DC, MC, V. Closed Sun. No lunch Sat.*

Greitz. Home-style Swedish cuisine is served in this classy and comfortable restaurant. Try the *Sotare* (grilled Baltic herring with parsley and butter). Also good is the *burbot* (local whitefish) stewed in wine with burbot roe and croutons. The decor is revamped cafe style, with the once-stained wood paneling around the room now painted a trendy burgundy red. *50 Vasagatan, tel. 08/234820. Reservations advised. Jacket and tie advised. AE, DC, MC, V. Closed Sun.*

Invito. This elegant and airy Italian restaurant in Östermalm has a pleasant dining room on the ground floor and atmospheric cellar rooms below. *Engelbrektsgatan 37, tel. 08/203934. Reservations required. Jacket and tie required. AE, DC, MC, V.*

Källaren Diana. Something of an institution, this is a great restaurant for authentic Swedish cuisine at the highest level. Located in an atmospheric Gamla Stan cellar, it is noted for such Swedish specialties as cuts of elk and reindeer meat and cloudberry desserts. Nowadays in summer customers may be predominantly foreign or businesspeople from the provinces. *Brunnsgränd 2, tel. 08/107310. Reservations advised. Jacket required. AE, DC, MC, V.*

KB. The most urbane of Stockholm's quality restaurants serves Swedish country fare, painstakingly prepared. The middle-aged waitresses are familiar in the best sense, and the patrons are among the city's most relaxed. There are soft, fitted benches around the smallish dining room, and another, more casual dining room in the bar next door, where you might try the excellent *mejramkorv* (marjoram sausage). Chef Örjan Klein pushes low-cal, low-fat dishes in the best modern tradition (i.e., with visible homage to France). Try the pot-au-feu with chicken and almond potatoes, or the Swedish freshwater crayfish in season. *Smålandsgatan 7, tel. 08/6796032. Reservations advised. AE, DC, MC, V. Closed Sun. No lunch Sat.*

Stallmästaregården. A historic old inn with an attractive courtyard and garden, Stallmästaregården is located in the Haga Park, half an hour from the city center. The fine summer meals are served in the courtyard overlooking the waters of Brunnsviken. *Norrtull, near Haga, tel. 08/6101300. Reservations advised. AE, DC, MC, V.*

Moderate **Bakfickan.** The name means "hip pocket" and is appropriate
★ because this restaurant is tucked round the back of the Opera House complex. It's a budget-price alternative to the nearby Operakällaren and is particularly popular at lunchtime, offer-

ing Swedish home cooking and a range of daily dishes. Counter and table service are available. *Operahuset, Jakobs Torg 2, tel. 08/242700. No reservations. AE, DC, MC, V. Closed Sun.*

Butler's. The menu is short but dependable, specializing in eclectic lamb dishes from southern Europe. Try the saddle of lamb with mixed vegetables Provençal, or the steak tournedos in creamy mustard sauce with garlic and mushrooms. The checkered tablecloths and the French bistro chairs give Butler's an indefinable Continental atmosphere. Butler's is noisy but very trendy for lunch. *Rörstrandsgatan 11, tel. 08/321823. Reservations advised. AE, DC, MC, V. No lunch on weekends.*

De Fyras Krog. The Inn of the Four Estates in Södermalm boasts a good traditional Swedish menu and an intimate, cozy atmosphere. *Tavastgatan 22, tel. 08/6586405. Reservations advised. AE, DC, MC, V.*

Hannas Krog. What started out as an interesting neighborhood spot has become one of Söder's trendiest restaurants. Ranging from Caribbean shrimp specialties to Provençal lamb dishes, the food is good, if a bit pricey. Service is consistent with the restaurant's crowded and relaxed atmosphere. *Skånegatan 80, tel. 08/6438225. Reservations required. AE, DC, MC, V.*

★ **Nils Emil.** This bustling restaurant in Södermalm is known for delicious Swedish cuisine and generous helpings at reasonable prices. It attracts members of the royal family on a regular basis. The paintings of personable owner/chef Nils Emil's island birthplace in the Stockholm Archipelago are by a well-known Swedish artist. *Folkungagatan 122, tel. 08/407209. Reservations required. Jacket and tie advised. AE, DC, MC, V.*

Prinsen. Established in 1897, this lively restaurant has remained an unpretentious, unchanging presence in a fashionable area given to overtrendiness—one reason for Prinsen's popularity with the city's writers, musicians, and artists. The food is primarily robust, if plain, Swedish and French fare, served by attentive waiters negotiating narrow aisles and crowded booths. *Mäster Samuelsgatan 4, tel. 08/6111331. Reservations advised. AE, DC, MC, V.*

Rolfs Kök. Small and modern, this restaurant combines an informal atmosphere with excellent Swedish/French cuisine at reasonable prices. The lamb is usually a good bet. *Tegnérgatan 41, tel. 08/101696. No reservations. AE, DC, MC, V.*

Söders Hjärta. Conveniently located on Söder just across from a floodlit church, this bistro is not far from the Slussen subway station. The cuisine is Stockholm standard, but the adjacent large bar is cheerful and friendly. *Bellmansgatan 22, tel. 08/6401462. Reservations required. AE, DC, MC, V.*

Tranan. A young, Yuppie crowd uses Tranan for its bar, which often features live music, and for its unpretentious restaurant. The stark walls and checkered floor are from Tranan's days as a workingman's beer parlor. Chef Rolf Durr improvises the menu almost daily. Traditional Swedish dishes such as boiled pork sausage and mashed turnip with lashings of sweet mustard are more delicious than they sound. *Karlbergsvägen 14, tel. 08/300765. Reservations advised. AE, DC, MC, V.*

★ **Wasahof.** Popular with newspaper reporters, copywriters, and advertising types, Wasahof is noted for its friendly, bistrolike atmosphere. Often packed and smoky on weekday nights, it offers a tasty menu once you squeeze past the crowded bar. *Dalagatan 46, tel. 08/323440. Reservations advised. AE, DC, MC, V.*

Inexpensive **Cassi.** This centrally located restaurant specializes in French cuisine at reasonable prices. *Narvavägen 30, tel. 08/661–7461. Reservations advised. MC. Closed Sat.*

Glada Enkan. This so-called artists' restaurant, housed in a former widow's home in Vasastan, serves excellent food and wine at (for Sweden) reasonable prices. It's a short walk from the Odenplan subway station. *Norrtullsgatan 45, tel. 08/339575. No reservations. AE, V.*

Open Gate. Located near the Slussen locks, on the south side of Stockholm Harbor, this is a popular, trendy Art Deco Italian-style trattoria that attracts a youngish crowd. Pasta dishes are the house specialty. *Högbergsgatan 40, tel. 08/6439776. No reservations. AE, DC, MC, V.*

★ **Örtagården.** This is a truly delightful vegetarian, no-smoking restaurant above the Östermalmstorg food market. The excellent-value buffet includes soups, salads, and hot dishes and is served in a turn-of-the-century atmosphere. *Nybrogatan 31, tel. 08/662–1728. No reservations. DC, MC, V.*

Lodging

In spite of the prohibitively expensive reputation of Stockholm's hotels, great deals can be found during the summer, when prices are substantially lower and numerous discounts are available. Some 60 hotels offer the **"Stockholm Package,"** providing accommodations for one night, breakfast, and a card giving free admission to museums and travel on public transport. Costs run from SKr305 to SKr655. Details are available from travel agents, tourist bureaus, or **Stockholm Information Service** (Box 7542, S-103 93 Stockholm, tel. 08/789–2000), or from Hotel Centralen (Centralstationen, S-111 20 Stockholm, tel. 08/240880). All rooms in the hotels reviewed are equipped with shower or bath unless otherwise noted.

Highly recommended hotels are indicated by a star ★.

Very Expensive **Amaranten.** A little out of the way, on the island of Kungsholmen, this large, modern Reso hotel is, however, just a few minutes' walk from Stockholm's central train station. Built in 1969, it was refurbished in 1988. A roof garden is featured atop the "executive tower," which contains 52 rooms. The brasserie-style restaurant offers cuisine with a French touch. *Kungsholmsgatan 31, Box 8054, 104 20, tel. 80/654–1060, fax 08/652–6248. 410 rooms. Facilities: restaurants, piano bar, pool, sauna, solarium. AE, DC, MC, V.*

Berns. In a successful attempt to distinguish itself from the rest of the crowd, the 130-year-old Berns opted for a Spartan look in its 1989 renovation. Indirect lighting, modern Italian furniture, and expensive marble, granite, and wood inlays now dominate the decor of the public areas and guest rooms. It was one of August Strindberg's haunts; guests can breakfast in the Red Room, immortalized by his novel of the same name. *Näckströmsgatan 8, S-111 47, tel. 08/614–0700 or 800/448–8355, fax 08/611–5175. 59 rooms, 3 suites. Facilities: restaurant, bar. AE, DC, MC, V.*

Continental. Located in the city center across from the train station, the Continental is a reliable hotel that is especially popular with American guests. First opened in 1966, it was renovated in 1992. It offers four restaurants in different price brackets, all of which have also been renovated. *Klara*

*Vattugränd 4, S-101 21, tel. 08/244020, fax 08/113695. 250
rooms with bath. Facilities: 4 restaurants. AE, DC, MC, V.*

Diplomat. Located within easy walking distance of Djurgården, this elegant hotel is less flashy than most in its price
range. Rooms facing the water have magnificent views over
Stockholm Harbor. Originally a turn-of-the-century house, it
was converted to its present use in 1966. The sometimes slow
and indifferent service is partially compensated for by its calm
and dignified atmosphere. *Strandvägen 7C, S-104 40, tel. 08/
663-5800, fax 08/783-6634. 133 rooms. Facilities: restaurant,
bar, sauna, office, conference room. AE, DC, MC, V. Closed
Christmas and New Year's Day.*

Grand. The city's showpiece hotel is an 1874 landmark on the
quayside at Blasieholmen, just across the harbor from the Royal Palace. Visiting political dignitaries and Nobel Prize winners are accommodated here. The gracious Old World
atmosphere extends to the comfortable and well-furnished
rooms. One of the hotel's best features is a glassed-in veranda
overlooking the harbor, where an excellent smörgåsbord buffet
is served. *Södra Blasieholmshamnen 8, Box 164 24, S-103 27,
tel. 08/221020, fax 08/218-6880. 299 rooms, 20 suites. Facilities: restaurant, piano bar, shop, conference and banquet
rooms. AE, DC, MC, V.*

★ **Lady Hamilton.** This small but charming hotel is in a house dating from 1470 near the Royal Palace in the Old Town. Converted to its present use in 1980, it boasts an extensive
collection of antiques, including one of George Romney's portraits of Lady Hamilton, the English beauty who was the mis-
tress of Lord Nelson at the beginning of the 19th century.
*Storkyrkobrinken 5, S-111 28, tel. 08/234680, fax 08/111148. 34
rooms. Facilities: cafeteria, sauna, minipool. AE, DC, MC, V.
Closed Christmas.*

Reisen. This Reso hotel, dating from 1819, successfully manages to combine elegance with modernity. It has a magnificent
central location on the Old Town waterfront. The rooms have all
been modernized and are well furnished, while the swimming
pool is built under medieval arches. The Quarter Deck restaurant serves high-quality Swedish-French food, and the piano
bar attracts a lively crowd at night. *Skeppsbron 12-14, S-111
30, tel. 08/223260, fax 08/201559. 114 rooms. Facilities: 2 restaurants, 2 bars, indoor pool, sauna, conference rooms. AE,
DC, MC, V. Closed Christmas and New Year's Day.*

Royal Viking. Only yards from Central Station and from the
airport bus terminal, the SAS-owned Royal Viking was built in
1984. The large atrium lobby is spacious, and the split-level
lounge is elegant. Last renovated in early 1990, the guest
rooms lack nothing except space; they have attractive natural
textiles and artwork, sturdy writing desks, minibars, separate
seating areas, and plush robes in the large bathrooms. Triple-
glazed windows and plenty of insulation keep traffic noise to a
minimum, but check whether the current bar pianist is the exu-
berant type before taking a room on the atrium. The staff is
young and inexperienced, and service is at best formal.
*Vasagatan 1, S-101 24, tel. 08/141000 or 800/448-8355, fax 08/
108180. 319 rooms. Facilities: 3 restaurants, 2 bars, nightclub,
indoor pool, sauna, solarium, massage, conference rooms,
SAS ticket counter and check-in, rooms for disabled guests.
AE, MC, V.*

Sergel Plaza. This stainless-steel-paneled high-rise became a
(Reso) hotel in 1984. The lobby is welcoming, with cane chairs

in a pleasantly skylighted seating area. Well-lighted rooms are practical but lack the luxury feel the price tag might lead you to expect; the decor is almost disappointing, with run-of-the-mill furnishings and too many grays. The location is central, right on the main pedestrian mall, but most windows view only office buildings. The best rooms are high up, with a view of the inner-city rooftops and beyond. *Brunkebergstorg 9, S–164 11, tel. 08/226600 or 800/843–6664, fax 08/215070. 406 rooms. Facilities: restaurant, 2 bars, rooms for nonsmokers and the disabled, conference rooms. AE, DC, MC, V.*

Strand. This Old World yellow-brick hotel, built in 1912 for the Stockholm Olympics, was completely and tastefully modernized after its purchase by SAS in 1986. The waterside location is right across from the Royal Dramatic Theater. No two of its rooms are the same; many are furnished with antiques and have rustic touches such as flower painting on woodwork and furniture. *Nybrokajen 9, Box 163 96, S–103 27, tel. 08/678–7800, fax 08/611–2436. 138 rooms. Facilities: restaurant, sauna, kiosk, conference rooms. AE, DC, MC, V.*

Victory. Slightly larger than its brother and sister hotels, the Lord Nelson and Lady Hamilton, this is an extremely atmospheric lodging place in a building that dates from 1640 in the Old Town. It also houses a noted restaurant, Lejontornet, which boasts an extensive wine cellar. *Lilla Nygatan 5, S–111 28, tel. 08/143090, fax 08/202177. 48 rooms. AE, DC, MC, V.*

Expensive **Anno 1647.** The name is the date the building was erected. A
★ small, pleasant, friendly hotel on Söder, the south island, it is three stops on the subway from the city center. *Mariagränd 3, S–116 21, tel. 08/6440480, fax 08/6433700. 42 rooms, 30 with baths. Facilities: restaurant serving light foods only. AE, DC, MC, V.*

Birger Jarl. This is one for nondrinkers: a hotel with no liquor license that is connected to a neighboring church, with weekly services in English. The modern, characteristically Scandinavian hotel opened in 1974. It is a quiet, unpretentious place, only a short walk from Stureplan. *Tulegatan 8, S–104 32, tel. 08/151020, fax 08/317366. 248 rooms. Facilities: cafeteria, fitness center, sauna. AE, DC, MC, V.*

Clas på Hörnet. This may be the most exclusive—and smallest—hotel in town: 10 rooms (eight doubles) in an 18th-century inn converted into a small hotel in 1982. The rooms, comfortably furnished with antiques of the period, go quickly. The restaurant (*see* Dining, *above*) is worth a visit in its own right; a bar opened in 1991 in the adjacent glassed-in pavilion. *Surbrunnsgatan 20, S–113 48, tel. 08/165130, fax 08/612–5315. Facilities: restaurant, bar. AE, DC, MC, V.*

Lord Nelson. A small hotel with nautical atmosphere right in the middle of the Old Town, this is in the same hotel family as the Lady Hamilton and the Victory. Space is at a premium, and the rooms are little more than cabins, though service is excellent. Noise from merrymakers in the pedestrian street outside can be a problem during the summer. *Västerlånggatan 22, S–111 29, tel. 08/232390, fax 08/101089. 31 rooms. Facilities: sauna, conference room. AE, DC, MC, V.*

Mälardrottningen. One of the more unusual places to stay in Stockholm, *Mälardrottningen* (Queen of Lake Mälar), a Sweden Hotels property, was once Barbara Hutton's yacht. Since 1982, it has been a quaint and pleasant hotel, with a crew as service-conscious as any in Stockholm. Tied up on the freshwa-

ter side of Gamla Stan, it is minutes from everything. The small suites are suitably decorated in a navy-blue and maroon nautical theme. Some of the below-deck cabins are a bit stuffy. Its chief assets are novelty and absence of traffic noise. *Riddarholmen 4, S–111 28, tel. 08/243600 or 800/448–8355, fax 08/243676. 59 rooms. Facilities: restaurant, grill, bar, conference rooms. AE, DC, MC, V.*

Mornington. A quiet, modern (Best Western) hotel that prides itself on a friendly atmosphere, the Mornington is within easy walking distance of Stureplan and downtown shopping areas and particularly handy to Östermalmstorg, with its food hall. *Nybrogatan 53, S–102 44, tel. 08/663–1240, fax 08/662–2179. 141 rooms. Facilities: restaurant, bar, rooms for the disabled and nonsmokers, 4 conference rooms, sauna, steam baths. AE, DC, MC, V.*

Scandic Crown. Working with what appears to be a dubious location (perched on a tunnel above a six-lane highway), the Scandic Crown has pulled a rabbit out of a hat. The hotel was built in 1988 on special cushions; you know the highway is there, but it intrudes only minimally, mainly in view. The intriguing labyrinth of levels, separate buildings, and corridors is filled with such details as a rounded stairway lighted from between the steps. The guest rooms are exquisitely designed and decorated in modern style, with plenty of stainless steel and polished wood inlay to accent the maroon color scheme. The hotel is easily accessible from downtown. *Guldgränd 8, S–104 65, tel. 08/702–2500, fax 08/6428358. 264 rooms. Facilities: 2 restaurants, bar, shops. AE, DC, MC, V.*

Moderate   **Alfa.** About 20 minutes from the city center, Alfa is a medium-size, medium-class hotel. Opened in 1972, it has recently been refurbished. *Marknadsvägen 6, S–121 09, tel. 08/810600. 104 rooms with bath. Facilities: restaurant. AE, DC, MC, V.*

Bema. This small hotel has a reasonably central location, on the ground floor of an apartment block near Tegnérlunden. *Upplandsgatan 13, S–111 23, tel. 08/2332675, fax 08/205338. 12 rooms with showers. Facilities: breakfast. AE, DC, MC, V.*

Hotel City. A large, modern-style hotel built in the 1940s but modernized in 1982–83, the City is located near the city center and Hötorget market. Breakfast is served in the atrium Winter Garden. *Slöjdgatan 7, S–111 81, tel. 08/222240, fax 08/208224. 300 rooms with bath. Facilities: restaurant, café, sauna, rooms for the disabled. AE, DC, MC, V.*

Hotel Gamla Stan. A quiet, cozy hotel in the area of town for which it was named, the Gamla Stan has recently been renovated and each of its 51 rooms is uniquely decorated. *Lilla Nygatan 25, tel. 08/24450, fax 08/216483. Facilities: breakfast included. AE, DC, MC.*

Stockholm. Occupying the upper floors of a downtown office building, this Sweden Hotels property has mainly modern decor offset by traditional Swedish furnishings that help create its friendly atmosphere. *Norrmalmstorg 1, S–111 46, tel. 08/6781320, fax 08/611–2103. 92 rooms. Facilities: breakfast. AE, DC, MC, V.*

Tegnérlunden. An extremely good bet for the budget tourist, this moderate-size hotel (owned by Sweden Hotels) is situated only a short walk from the city center opposite a small park, close to the Strindberg Museum. *Tegnérlunden 8, S–113 59, tel. 08/349780, fax 08/327818. 104 rooms. Facilities: rooms for nonsmokers. AE, DC, MC, V.*

Inexpensive **Alexandra.** Although it is in the Södermalm area, to the south of the Old Town, the Alexandra is only five minutes by subway from the city center. It is a small, modern hotel, opened in the early 1970s and renovated in 1988. Only breakfast is served. *Magnus Ladulåsgatan 42, S–118 27, tel. 08/840320. 79 rooms with bath. Facilities: sauna, solarium. AE, DC, MC, V. Closed Christmas and New Year's Day.*

Gustav af Klint. A "hotel ship" moored at Stadsgården quay, near Slussen subway station, the *Gustav af Klint* is divided into two sections—a hotel and a hostel. It was refurbished in 1989. There is a cafeteria and a restaurant, and you can dine on deck in summer. *Stadsgårdskajen 153, S–116 30, tel. 08/404077. 28 cabins, none with bath. AE, DC, MC, V. Closed Christmas and New Year's Day.*

Youth Hostels Don't be put off by the "youth" bit: There's actually no age limit. The standards of cleanliness, comfort, and facilities offered are usually extremely high.

af Chapman. This is a sailing ship built in 1888 that is permanently moored in Stockholm Harbor, just across from the Royal Palace. It is a landmark in its own right. *Västra Brobänken, Skeppsholmen S–111 49, tel. 08/6795015. 136 beds, 2- to 6-bed cabins. Facilities: breakfast.*

Bosön. Out of the way on the island of Lidingö, this hostel is pleasantly situated close to the water. *Bosön, S–181 47 Lidingö, tel. 08/767–9300. 26 beds; 2- to 3-bed rooms. Facilities: breakfast, cafeteria, washing machine, sauna, canoes for rent. V.*

Långholmen. This former prison, built in 1724, was converted into a combined hotel and hostel in 1989. It is located on the island of Långholmen, which has popular bathing beaches. The hotel serves Swedish home cooking. *Långholmen, Box 9116, S–102 72,tel. 08/668–0510. Summer weekends: 254 beds (hotel: 101 2- to 4-bed rooms, all but 10 with showers and WC). Sept.–May, weekdays: 26 beds with shared bath. 32 beds adapted for the disabled. Facilities: cafeteria, restaurant, laundry room, sauna, beach. AE, DC, MC, V.*

Skeppsholmen. A former craftsman's workshop in a pleasant and quiet part of the island, it was converted into a hostel for the overflow from the *af Chapman*, which is an anchor's throw away. *Skeppsholmen, S–111 49, tel. 08/6795017. 152 beds, 2- to 4-bed rooms. Facilities: special rooms for disabled guests, breakfast. No credit cards.*

Camping There are camping sites at Enskede (tel. 08/773–0100), Haninge (tel. 08/745–8259), Slagsta (tel. 0753/77788), Bredäng (tel. 08/977071), and Sollentuna (tel. 08/353475). Camping in the Stockholm area costs SKr50–SKr100 per night.

The Arts and Nightlife

The Arts There are demonstrations of Swedish folk dancing in
Dance **Kungsträdgården** and at **Mosebacken** in Söder during the summer months. Consult the tourist office for details.

Film Foreign movies are not dubbed. The best-quality cinema in town is the **Grand** (Sveavägen, tel.08/112400). The cinema at **Filmhuset** (Borgvägen 1–5, tel. 08/665–1100), headquarters of the Swedish Film Institute, usually has a good program. A curiosity is **Folkets Bio** (The People's Cinema) (Vegagatan 17, tel.

08/736–0035), a leftover from more idealistic times, which shows films that don't get general release.

Music Free concerts are held in **Kungsträdgården** every summer. For details, contact the tourist office. International orchestras often visit **Konserthuset** (Hötorget 8, tel. 08/102110), the main concert hall.

Opera **Operan** (the Royal Opera House) (Jakobs Torg 2, tel. 08/248240), dating from 1898, continues a tradition going back to 1755, when Queen Lovisa Ulrika introduced opera to her subjects. Sweden has continued to produce such names as Jenny Lind, Jussi Björling, and Birgit Nilsson. **Folkoperan** (Hornsgatan 72, tel. 08/6585300), a lively, modern company with its headquarters in Söder, features "opera in the round." It rides roughshod over traditional methods of presentation and interpretation of the classics, generally to scintillating effect.

Theater **Kungliga Dramatiska Teatern** (or Dramaten: the Royal Dramatic Theater) (Nybroplan, tel. 08/667–0680) sometimes stages productions of international interest, even though they are in Swedish. These include works directed by Ingmar Bergman. The **Regina Theater** (Drottninggatan 71a, tel. 08/207000) stages English-language productions.

Nightlife The hub of Stockholm's nightlife is Kungsträdgården, where several popular bars and discothèques line the western edge of the park. On weekends these spots are often packed with tourists and locals.

Bars If you prefer exploring areas not entirely swamped by crowds, you will find a bar-hopping visit to Södermalm rewarding. Start at **Mosebacke Etablissement** (Mosebacke torg 3, tel. 08/641–9020), a combined indoor theater and outdoor café with a spectacular view of the city. Wander along Götagatan with its lively bars and head for the **Pelikan Restaurant** (Blekingegatan 40, tel. 08/743–0695), a former beer hall and now an unpretentious but well-priced restaurant and bar. The trendy **Hannas Krog** (Skånegatan 80, tel. 08/767–5211) features a bar in the cellar with low lights, little furnishing, loud music, and people dressed in black.

Piano bars are also part of the Stockholm scene. Try the **Anglais Bar** at the Hotel Anglais (tel. 08/6141600) or the **Clipper Club** at the Hotel Reisen, Skeppsbron (tel. 08/223260).

Cabaret Stockholm's biggest nightclub, **Börsen** (Jakobsgatan 6, tel. 08/787–8500), offers high-quality international cabaret shows. Another popular spot is the **Cabaret Club,** Barnhusgatan 12 (tel. 08/110608; reservations advised). Drag shows are the main attraction at **Studion** (St. Eriksplan 4, tel. 08/344454).

Casinos These simply do not exist as such. Many hotels and bars have a roulette table and sometimes blackjack, operating according to Swedish rules aimed at restricting the amount you can lose.

Discos **Café Opera** (tel. 08/110026) enjoys a magnificent locale in the Opera Building at the end of Kungsträdgården. A popular meeting place for young and old alike, it features a restaurant, roulette tables, and the longest bar in town, with a disco that starts at midnight, closing at 3 AM. **Daily News** (tel. 08/215655), a glitzy disco located at the other end of Kungsträdgården near the Sweden House, has a restaurant and is open until 3 AM. **King Creole** (Kungsgatan 18, tel. 08/244700) offers big-band

dance music alternating with rock. **Berns** (Berzeli Park, tel. 08/614–0550), an elegant restaurant and bar located in a renovated period building with a large balcony facing the Stockholm Royal Theater, turns into a lively discothèque at night. Other hot spots are **Sture Compagniet** (Sturegatan 4, tel. 08/6117800) and **Sloppy's** (Horngsgatan 136, tel. 08/845610).

Gay Bars   **Pride** (Sveavägen 57, tel. 08/315533) has a restaurant, café, bookshop, and disco, run by homosexuals for homosexuals. It's all totally respectable by local standards and backed by grants from the authorities.

Jazz Clubs   The best venue is **Fasching** (Kungsgatan 63, tel. 08/216267), close to the city center and featuring international and local bands. **Stampen** (Stora Nygatan 5, tel. 08/205793), an overpriced but atmospheric club in the Old Town, features traditional jazz nightly.

Rock Clubs   The best local and international groups can be seen at **Berns** (Berzeli Park, tel. 08/6140720); **Galaxy** (on Strömsburg, an islet in the middle of Strömmen, tel. 08/215400); **Ritz** (Götgatan 51, on Söder, subway: Medborgarplatsen; tel. 08/6424737); **Lido** (on Söder, at Hornsgatan 92, subway: Zinkensdamm; tel. 08/6682333); and **Krogen Tre Backar** (off Sveavägen at Tegnérgatan 12–14, tel. 673–4400).

Excursions from Stockholm

Uppsala

Sweden's principal university town vies for that position with Lund in the south of the country. August Strindberg, the nation's leading dramatist, studied here—and by all accounts hated the place. Ingmar Bergman, his modern heir, was born here. It is a historic site where pagan (and extremely gory) Viking ceremonies persisted into the 11th century. Uppsala University, one of the oldest and most highly respected institutions in Europe, was established here in 1477 by Archbishop Jakob Ulfson. As late as the 16th century, nationwide *tings*, early parliaments, were convened here. Today it is a quiet home for around 170,000 people, built along the banks of Fyris River, a pleasant jumble of old buildings dominated by its cathedral, which dates from the early 13th century.

Tourist Information   The main **tourist office** (tel. 018/117500 or 018/274800) is at Fyris Torg in the center of town. In summer a small tourist information office is also open at Uppsala Castle.

Getting There
By Car   Uppsala is an easy drive 67 kilometers (41 miles) north from Stockholm along the E4 motorway.

By Train   There is regular train service from Central Station. The journey takes 45 minutes.

By Bus   Buses leave the city terminal at Klarabergsviadukten on Friday and Sunday. For information, call 08/237190. There is direct bus service to Uppsala from Arlanda Airport.

Guided Tours   You can explore Uppsala easily by yourself, but guided tours in English for groups can be arranged through the tourist office.

Numbers in the margin correspond to points of interest on the Excursions from Stockholm map.

Exploring Uppsala Ideally you should start your visit with a trip to **Gamla Uppsala**
❺ (Old Uppsala), 5 kilometers (3 miles) north of the town. Here
under three huge **mounds** lie the graves of the first Swedish
kings, Aun, Egil, and Adils, of the 6th-century Ynglinga dynasty. Close by in pagan times was a sacred grove containing a
legendary oak from whose branches animal and human sacri-
fices were hung. By the 10th century, Christianity had eliminated such practices. A small church, which was the seat of
Sweden's first archbishop, was built on the site of a former pagan temple. Today the archbishopric is in Uppsala itself, and
the church, **Gamla Uppsala Kyrka,** is largely for the benefit of
tourists. A small open-air museum nearby, **Disagården,** features old farm buildings, most of them from the 19th century.
Admission free. Open May–Sept., daily 9–5.

Time Out You can drink mead brewed from a 14th-century recipe at the
nearby **Odinsborg Restaurant.**

❻ Back in **Uppsala,** your first visit should be to Uppsala
Domkyrka (Cathedral), whose twin towers (362 feet high) dominate the city. They are the same height as the length of the
nave. Work on the cathedral was begun in the early 13th century; it was consecrated in 1435 and restored between 1885 and
1893. The cathedral remains the seat of Sweden's archbishop.
It is important in the nation's history as the site of the tomb of
Gustav Vasa, the king who established Sweden's independence
in the 16th century. It also houses a silver casket containing the
bones of St. Erik, Sweden's patron saint.

Work on **Uppsala slott** (Uppsala Castle) was started in the 1540s
by Gustav Vasa, who intended it to symbolize the dominance of
the monarchy over the church. It was completed under Queen
Christina nearly a century later. Students gather here every
April 30 to celebrate the Feast of Valborg and optimistically
greet the arrival of spring.

In the excavated castle ruins, **The Vasa Vignettes,** scenes from
the 16th century, are portrayed with effigies, costumes, light,
and sound effects. *Admission: SKr35 adults, SKr15 children
under 15. Open daily, mid-Apr.–late Sept.*

One of Uppsala's most famous sons, Carl von Linné, also known
as Linnaeus, was a professor of botany at the university during
the 1740s and created the Latin nomenclature system for
plants and animals. The **Linné Museum** in his old botanical garden, **Linnéträdgården,** which has been restored to its former
glory, is dedicated to his life and works. The orangery houses a
pleasant cafeteria and is used for concerts and cultural events.
*Svartbäcksgatan 27, tel. 018/136540. Admission to garden
SKr10. Open May–Aug., daily 9–9; Sept.–Apr., daily 9–7.
Admission to museum: SKr10. Open May–Sept., Tues.–Sun.
1–4.*

Uppsala Universitetet (the Uppsala University), founded in
1477, features the **Carolina Rediviva** (the university library),
which contains a copy of every book published in Sweden, in addition to a large collection of foreign literature. One of its most
interesting exhibits is the *Codex Argentus*, a silver Bible written in the 6th century.

Completed in 1625, the **Gustavianum,** which served as the university's main building for two centuries, is easy to spot by its remarkable copper cupola, now green with age. The building houses the ancient anatomical theater where lectures on human anatomy and public dissections took place. The Victoria Museum of Egyptian Antiquities and the Museums for Classical and Nordic Archeology are also in the building. *Akademigatan 3, tel. 018/182500. Admission: SKr20. Open daily noon–3.*

Dining **Domtrappkällaren.** Located in a 14th-century cellar near the cathedral, Domtrappkällaren features excellent French and Swedish cuisine. *Sankt Eriksgränd 15, tel. 018/130955. Reservations required. Dress: casual but neat. AE, DC, MC, V.*

Gotland

Gotland is Sweden's main holiday island, a place of wide, sandy beaches and wild cliff formations called *raukar.* Inland, there is verdant sheep-farming country and glades in which 35 different varieties of wild orchids thrive, attracting botanists from all over the world. Lying in the Baltic just 85 kilometers (53 miles) from the mainland, the island is 125 kilometers (78 miles) in length and 52 kilometers (32 miles) across at its widest point.

Gotland was first inhabited around 5000 BC, and by the time of the Roman Iron Age had become a leading Baltic trading center. Germans arrived later and built most of its churches in the 13th century. They established close trading links with the Hanseatic League in Lübeck. The Danes followed, and it was not until 1645 that Gotland finally became part of Sweden.

Tourist Information The main tourist office is at Bermeisterska huset, Hamngatan 4, Visby (tel. 0498/210982).

Getting There
By Plane Fifteen flights a day arrive in Gotland's airport from Stockholm. For information, call SAS (tel. 08/151000).

By Boat Car ferries sail from Nynäshamn, a small port on the Baltic an hour by car or rail from Stockholm (commuter trains leave regularly from Stockholm's Central Station for Nynäshamn), at 12:40 PM and 11:30 PM during the summer and at 11:30 PM only during the winter. The voyage takes about five hours. Boats also leave from Oskarshamn, farther down the Swedish coast and closer to Gotland. *Kungsgatan 48, Gotland City, tel. 08/236170 or 08/233180; Nynäshamn, tel. 08/5206400.*

Guided Tours Guided tours of the island and Visby, the capital, are available in English by arrangement with the tourist office.

Exploring Gotland
❼ If you have a limited time schedule, you may be content to visit Gotland's capital, **Visby,** a delightful, hilly town of about 20,000 people, in which medieval houses, ruined fortifications, and churches blend with cobbled lanes of fairy-tale cottages, their facades covered with roses reputed to bloom even in November because the climate is so gentle.

In its heyday Visby was protected by a wall, of which 3 kilometers survive today, along with 44 towers and numerous gateways. It is considered the best-preserved medieval city wall in Europe after that of Carcassonne in southern France. The north gate provides the best vantage point for an overall view of the wall.

The cathedral, **St. Maria Kyrka,** is the only one of the town's 13 medieval churches that is still intact and in use.

Near the harbor is **Det Gamla Apoteket** (the Old Apothecary), a late-medieval four-story merchant's house, where a silversmith now works and demonstrates his trade to visitors. *Strandgatan 28, tel. 0498/212889. Admission free. Open daily 9–5.*

In the same street you'll find **Burmeisterska huset,** the home of the Burmeister, or principal German merchant, which today houses the tourist office. *Strandgatan 9, tel. 0498/210982. Admission: free. Open weekdays 8–8, weekends 10–7.*

Fornsalen (the Fornsal Museum) contains examples of medieval artwork, hordes of silver from Viking times, and impressive picture stones that predate the Viking rune stones. *Strandgatan 14, S–62102, tel. 0498/247010. Admission: SKr20 adults, children under 16 free. Open mid-May–Sept., daily 11–6; Sept–mid-May, Tues.–Sun. noon–4.*

Celebrated during early August, **Medieval Week** is a city-wide festival marking the invasion by the Danish King Valdemar of the prosperous island on July 22, 1361. Medieval jousting, a "medieval" open market on Strandgatan, and a variety of street theater performances recreate the period.

The rest of the island is best explored by bicycle. Bicycles, tents, and camping equipment can be rented from **Gotlands Cykeluthyrning** (Skeppsbron 8, tel. 0498/14133). Details of Gotlandsleden, a 200-kilometer (120-mile) route around the island, which avoids military installations (off-limits to foreigners), are available from the tourist office.

The stalactite caves at **Lummelunda,** about 13 kilometers (8 miles) from Visby, are unique in this part of the world and are worth visiting, as is the **Krusmyntagården** (herb garden), 8 kilometers (5 miles) north of Visby, close to the sea.

There are approximately 100 old churches on the island that are still in use today, dating from Gotland's great commercial era. Outstanding among them are **Barlingbro,** dating from the 13th century, with vault paintings, stained-glass windows, and a remarkable 12th-century font; the exquisite **Dalhem,** constructed about 1200; **Gothem,** built during the 13th century, with a notable series of paintings of that period; **Grötlingbo,** a 14th-century church with stone sculpture and stained glass (note the 12th-century reliefs on the facade); **Tingstäde,** a mix of six building periods from 1169 to 1300; **Roma Kloster Kyrka** (Roma Cloister Church), the massive ruins of a Cistercian monastery founded in 1164; and **Öja,** decorated with paintings and housing a famous holy rood from the late 13th century.

Curious rock formations dot the coasts, and two bird refuges, **Stora** and **Lilla Karlsö,** stand off the coast south of Visby. The bird population consists mainly of guillemots, which look like penguins. Visits to these refuges are permitted only in the company of a recognized guide. (Stora Karlsö, tel. 0498/40500; Lilla Karlsö, tel. 0498/41139).

Dining **Gutekällaren.** Despite the name, this is not a cellar restaurant. *Visby* Located aboveground in a building that dates from the 12th century, it features local specialties, many involving lamb.

Stora Torget 3, tel. 0498/210043. Reservations required. AE, DC, MC, V. Expensive.
Lindgården. This atmospheric restaurant specializes in both local dishes and French cuisine. *Strandgatan 26, tel. 0498/ 218700. Reservations required. AE, DC, MC, V. Expensive.*

Göteborg

If you arrive in Göteborg (Gothenberg) by car, don't drive straight through the city in your haste to reach your coastal vacation spot; it is well worth spending a day or two exploring this attractive port. A quayside jungle of cranes and warehouses attests to the city's industrial might, yet within 10 minutes' walk of the waterfront is an elegant, modern city of broad avenues, green parks, and gardens. It is an easy city to explore: Most of the major attractions are within walking distance of one another, and there is an excellent streetcar network. In summer you can take a sightseeing trip on an open-air streetcar.

Sprawling, mostly modern Göteborg, with a population of 500,000, is Sweden's second-largest city. Its heart is Avenyn (the Avenue; actually Kungsportsavenyn, but over the years shortened to simply Avenyn), a 60-foot-wide, tree-lined boulevard that bisects the center of the city in a south–north direction, linking its cultural heart, Götaplatsen, at the southern end, with the main commercial area, now dominated by the huge, modern Nordstan shopping center. Also toward the northern end of Avenyn is the pleasant park of Trädgårds-föreningen (the Horticultural Society—called Trägårn), the best-known of the city's 20 parks.

Beyond Nordstan is the harbor, 22 kilometers (14 miles) of quays with warehouses and sheds covering more than 1.5 million square feet and spread along both banks of the Göta Älv (river), making Göteborg Scandinavia's largest port. It is also the home of Scandinavia's largest corporation, the automobile manufacturer Volvo (which means "I roll" in Latin), as well as of the roller-bearing manufacturer SKF and the world-renowned Hasselblad camera company.

Historically, Göteborg owes its existence to the sea. Tenth-century Vikings sailed from its shores, and a settlement was founded here in the 11th century. Not until 1621, however, did King Gustav II Adolf grant Göteborg a charter in order to establish a free-trade port on the model of others already thriving on the Continent. The west-coast harbor would also allow Swedish shipping to avoid Danish tolls exacted for passing through Öresund, the stretch of water separating the two countries. Foreigners were recruited to make these visions real: The Dutch were its builders—hence the canals that thread the city—and many Scotsmen worked and settled here, though they have left little trace.

Today Göteborg resists its second-city status by being a leader in terms of attractions and civic structures: The Scandinavium was until recently Europe's largest indoor arena; the Ullevi Stadium stages some of the Nordic area's most important concerts and sporting events; Nordstan is one of Europe's largest indoor shopping malls; and Liseberg, Scandinavia's largest amusement park in area, attracts some 2.5 million visitors a year. Over the Göta River is Älvsborgsbron, at 3,000 feet the

longest suspension bridge in Sweden, and under it is the Tingstads Tunnel, at 62 feet the world's widest cut through rock for motor vehicles.

Göteborg is a pleasantly relaxed place from which to explore the west coast of Sweden, where wide, unspoiled beaches and a majestic rocky coastline alternate with timbered fishing villages. From here, too, you can set out on the Göta Canal, Sweden's "blue ribbon," down which barges once sailed laden with exports and imports, but which today provides a picturesque water journey through the Swedish countryside.

Important Addresses and Numbers

Tourist Information The main tourist office is Göteborg's Turistbyrå (Kungsportsplatsen 2, S–411 10 Göteborg, tel. 031/100740). There is also an office at the Nordstan shopping center (Nordstadstorget, 411 05 Göteborg).

Consulates **U.K. Consulate:** Götgatan 15, tel. 031/151327.

Emergencies Dial 90000 (*see* Stockholm, *above*).

Doctors Dial 031/415500 for information on medical services. Emergencies are handled by the **Sahlgrenska Hospital** (tel. 031/601000), **Östrasjukhuset** (tel. 031/374000), and **Mölndalssjukhuset** (tel. 031/861000). There is a private medical service at **City Akuten** (Drottninggatan, tel. 031/101010).

Dentists The national health service emergency number is 031/803140; the private dental service emergency number is 031/117017.

Pharmacy **Vasen** (Götgatan 12, tel. 031/804410), in the Nordstan shopping mall, is open 24 hours.

English-Language Bookstores Nearly all bookshops stock English-language books. The broadest selection is at **Esselte's Eckersteins** store (Södra Larmgatan 11, tel. 031/171100).

Travel Agencies The SJ main ticket office is located at Östra Hamngatan 35 (tel. 031/176860). For other travel agencies see the yellow pages under *Resor-Resebyråer*.

Arriving and Departing by Plane

Airports and Airlines The airport, **Landvetter,** is approximately 26 kilometers (16 miles) from the city center. Among the airlines operating from it are **SAS** (tel. 020/910150), **British Airways** (tel. 020/781144), **Air France** (tel. 031/801110), and **Lufthansa** (tel. 031/805640).

Between the Airport and City Center
By Bus Landvetter is linked to Göteborg by freeway. Buses leave Landvetter every 15 minutes, traveling to Drottningtorget near the central railway station and stopping at the SAS Park Avenue Hotel. The price of the trip is SKr50. For more information, call 031/801235.

By Taxi A taxi to the city center will cost between SKr250 and SKr300. For SAS limousine service, call 031/942424.

Arriving and Departing by Car, Train, and Bus

By Car You arrive on the E20 highway from Stockholm (495 kilometers/307 miles) and the east or on the E6 coastal highway from the south (Malmö is 290 kilometers/180 miles away.) Markings are excellent, and roads are well sanded and plowed in winter.

By Train There is a regular service from Stockholm, taking a little over four hours. All trains arrive at the central railway station in Drottningtorget, downtown Göteborg (tel. 031/175000 or 020/757575). Streetcars and buses leave from here for the suburbs.

By Bus All buses arrive in the downtown area. The principal company is **Continentbus/Swebus** (tel. 031/171500).

Getting Around

By Car **Avis** has offices at the airport (tel. 031/946030) and the central railway station (tel. 031/805780). **Hertz** is at Stampgatan 16A (tel. 031/803730).

By Bus and Tram Göteborg has an excellent transit service. The best bet for the tourist is the **Göteborg Card,** which costs SKr120 for 24 hours and gives free use of public transport, various sightseeing trips, and admission to Liseberg and local museums, among other benefits. It is available at Pressbyrån shops, kiosks, and the tourist office.

By Taxi To order a taxi, telephone 031/650000; for advance bookings, call 031/500504.

Guided Tours

Orientation A 90-minute bus tour of the chief points of interest leaves from outside the main tourist office (Kungsportsplatsen 2) every day from early May to mid-August and on Saturdays in September. Call tourist information, tel. 031/100740, for the schedule.

Highlights for First-Time Visitors

Götaplatsen (*see* Tour 1)
Avenyn (*see* Tour 1)
Elfsborg Fortress (*see* Tour 3)
Harbor (*see* Tour 2)
Liseberg Amusement Park (*see* What to See and Do with Children)

Exploring Göteborg

Numbers in the margin correspond to points of interest on the Göteborg map.

Tour 1: The City Center

Start in **Götaplatsen,** a fine, light, modern square dominated by Carl Milles's statue of **Poseidon,** whose shy, downturned gaze and gentle demeanor lend him a distinctly Swedish aura.
❶ Grouped around the square, you will find **Konserthuset** (the Concert Hall), the art museum and the municipal theater, three quite imposing contemporary buildings in which the city celebrates its important contribution to Swedish cultural life. Konserthuset is the home of the highly acclaimed Göteborg Symphony Orchestra (Konserthuset, Götaplatsen, tel. 031/167000).

❷ **Konstmuseet** (the Art Museum), opened in 1925, contains an impressive collection of the works of leading Scandinavian painters and sculptors; it encapsulates some of the moody introspection of the artistic community in this part of the world.

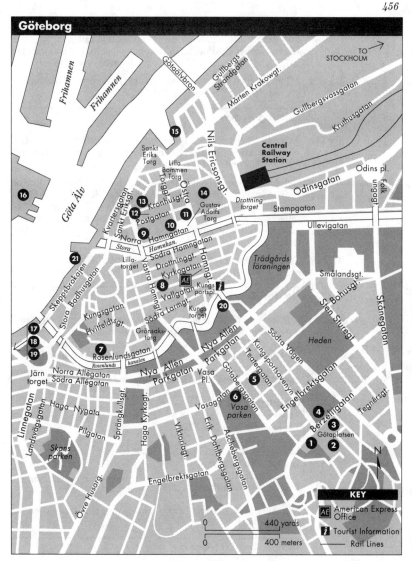

Göteborg

Älvsborgsbron, **18**
Börshuset, **11**
Domkyrkan, **8**
East India Company Building, **9**
Elfsborgs Fästning boat, **21**
Feske Körkan, **7**

Fiskhamnen, **17**
Folkhögskolan, **6**
Götaverkan, **16**
Konserthuset, **1**
Konstmuseet, **2**
Kronhusbodarna, **13**
Kronhuset, **12**
Maritima Centret, **15**

Nordstan, **14**
Paddan boats, **20**
Rådhuset, **10**
Röhsska Konstslöjdsmuseet, **5**
Skarvikshamnen, **19**
Stadsbiblioteket, **4**
Stadsteatern, **3**

Among the artists represented are Swedes such as Carl Milles, Sergel, the Impressionist Anders Zorn, the Victorian idealist Carl Larsson, and Prince Eugen. The small collection of old masters includes Rubens, Rembrandt, and van Dyke. The best collection in Sweden of 19th- and 20th-century French art includes works by Monet, Pissarro, Sisley, Renoir, Cézanne, Gauguin, van Gogh, Rousseau, Matisse, and Picasso. *Götaplatsen, tel. 031/612977. Admission: SKr25. Open weekdays 11–4 (Wed. until 9), weekends 10–5. Closed Mon. Sept.– May.*

❸ **Stadsteatern** (the Municipal Theater) (Götaplatsen, tel. 031/ 819960), while it has a good reputation in Sweden, remains very much a local phenomenon because the vast majority of its pro-
❹ ductions are in Swedish. Also in Götaplatsen, **Stadsbiblioteket** (the Municipal Library) (Götaplatsen, tel. 031/817–7300), boasts a collection of more than 550,000 books, many in English.

From Götaplatsen, stroll northward past the cafés and restaurants along the **Avenyn** to the intersection with Vasagatan. A short way to the left down Vasagatan, at the junction with
❺ Teatergatan, you can visit the **Röhsska Konstslöjdsmuseet** (Museum of Arts and Crafts), with its fine collections of furniture, books and manuscripts, tapestries, and pottery. *Vasagatan, tel. 031/200605. Admission: SKr25. Open Tues. 11–9, Wed.– Fri. 11–4, weekends 10–5.*

❻ Continue left along Vasagatan to **Folkhögskolan,** Göteborg Universitet (Göteborg University), and, if the weather's good, to relax in neighboring **Vasa Park.** Walk northward along Viktoriagatan, crossing the canal and then making an immedi-
❼ ate left to visit one of the city's most peculiar attractions, **Feske Körkan,** an archaic spelling of *Fisk Kyrkan,* the Fish Church. It resembles a place of worship but is actually an indoor fish market.

Following this you may feel inspired to visit the city's principal
❽ place of worship, **Domkyrkan** (Göteborg Cathedral). To get here from Feske Körkan, follow the canal eastward until you come to Västra Hamngatan, then head north to Kyrkogatan. The cathedral, in neoclassic yellow brick, dates from 1802; while it's not particularly attractive from the outside, the interior is impressive. *Kungsgatan 20. Open weekdays 8–5, Sat. 8–3, Sun. 10–3.*

❾ Continue northward on Västra Hamngatan to the **East India Company Building** (formerly the Museum of Cultural History) at the junction with Norra Hamngatan. This palatial structure, once the warehouse and auction rooms of the East India Company, a major Swedish trading firm founded in 1861, now houses Sweden's largest, but still unnamed, museum-in-progress. When completed in 1995, the new museum will blend what was once three separate museums featuring industrial history, archaeology, and general history into one large museum with an emphasis on thematic rather than departmentalized exhibits. The focus will continue to be on Göteborg, its nautical and trading past, and the Swedish west coast, with exhibits on the Iron Age and on crafts and industries of the more recent past. Sections of the museum remain open to the public, particularly exhibits dealing with the East India Company and the company's ship, the *Göteborg,* which sank just outside Göte-

borg on a return voyage from China in 1745 while members of the crew's families watched from shore. *Norra Hamngatan, tel. 031/612770. Admission: SKr25. Open Sept.–Apr., Tues.– Fri. 11–4 (Wed. until 9), weekends 10–5; May–Aug., Mon.– Fri. 11–4, weekends 10–5.*

⑩ Follow Norra Hamngatan eastward to **Gustav Adolfs Torg**, the city's official center, which is dominated by **Rådhuset** (the City Hall) (Gustav Adolfs Torg, tel. 031/611000), built in 1699, with a modern extension by Swedish architect Gunnar Asplund that caused great controversy when it was completed in 1937. Tours must be prearranged.

⑪ On the north side of the square is **Börshuset** (the Stock Exchange) (Gustav Adolfs Torg, tel. 031/835900), built in 1849.

⑫ Head northwest from the square along Östra Hamngatan, turning into Kronhusgatan, to visit **Kronhuset**, the city's oldest secular building, which dates from 1643. It was once the armory, and in 1660 Sweden's Parliament met here to arrange the succession for King Karl X Gustav, who died suddenly while visiting the city. *Postgatan 628, tel. 031/117377. Admission: SKr25. Open Tues.–Fri. 11–4, weekends 10–5.*

⑬ Close by are the **Kronhusbodarna,** carefully restored turn-of-the-century shops and handicrafts boutiques. *Kronhusgatan. Open Mon.–Sat. 10–4, some shops open later in summer.*

⑭ The quaintness of Kronhusbodarna as a shopping experience contrasts sharply with the coldly modern functionalism of **Nordstan,** the vast indoor shopping mall a short distance away off Östra Hamngatan.

Tour 2: The Harbor

Walk across the Götaälvbron (Göta River Bridge) to **Hisingen,** now the mainly industrial area of the city, on the far bank, which was the site of earlier settlements before Göteborg was built. When the city was founded, boats at first anchored in its canals, but larger vessels had to put in farther west, and as a consequence, the harbor developed on both banks of the river.

⑮ A good starting point for a tour of the docks is **Gasverkskajen** (Gas Works Quay), just off Gullbergsstrandgatan. Today this is the headquarters of a local boating association, its brightly colored pleasure craft contrasting with the old-fashioned working barges either anchored or being repaired at Ringön, just across the river. Walk back under the Göta River Bridge and head for **Maritima Centret** (the Maritime Center) at Lilla Bommen. This modern development is aimed at revitalizing the inner harbor. The center contains modern naval vessels, including a destroyer, submarines, a lightship, a cargo vessel, and various tugboats, that can be visited. *Lilla Bommenshamnen, tel. 031/ 101035. Admission: SKr35 adults, SKr20 children 5–12. Open late May–late Aug., daily; Mar.–Nov., weekends only.*

⑯ Continue along the river, down Skeppsbrokajen, for views across the river of the **Götaverkan** and **Cityvarvet** shipyards, which were once the pride of the city but now look distinctly forlorn. Farther along the riverbank, past Masthuggskajen, where boats depart for Denmark, you come to **Stigbergskajen,** where the transatlantic liners once docked. Today most inter-

national visitors arrive by air at Göteborg's Landvetter airport or Arlanda outside Stockholm.

⑰ Just past Stigbergskajen is **Fiskhamnen,** the fishing harbor, where the day's catch is auctioned weekdays at 7. Continue walking and you will see signs of changing times all around. An **⑱** excellent view of **Älvsborgsbron,** (the Älvsborg Bridge), the longest suspension bridge in Sweden, is available from Fiskhamnen. Built in 1967, it stretches 3,000 feet across the river and is built so high that ocean liners can pass beneath. The government is considering plans to turn this part of the harbor into a scenic walkway with parks and cafés. Return to the city side of the river across the mighty bridge and from it look to- **⑲** ward the sea to the large container harbors, **Skarvikshamnen, Skandiahamnen** (where boats depart for England), and **Torshamnen,** which bring most of the cargo and passengers to the city today.

Tour 3: Göteborg from the Water

For a view of the city from the water and an expert commentary in English and German on its sights and history, take one of the **⑳** **Paddan** sightseeing boats. *Paddan* means "toad" in Swedish, an apt commentary on the vessels' squat appearance. The boats pass under 20 bridges and take in both the canals and part of the Göta River. *Kungsportbro, tel. 031/133000. Fare: SKr55. Open early May–mid-June and early Aug.–mid-Sept., daily 10–5; mid-June–early Aug., daily 10–9.*

㉑ There also are regular **boat** trips from the quayside close to the city center to the **Elfsborgs Fästning** (Elfsborg Fortress), built in 1670 on a harbor island to protect the city from attack. *Elfsborg båtar, Stenpiren, tel. 031/7752565. Boats leave 6 times daily, mid-May–mid-Sept. Cost: SKr55 adults, SKr37 children round-trip.*

What to See and Do with Children

Here Göteborg comes into its own with **Lisebergs Nöjes Park,** Scandinavia's largest amusement park and one of the best-run, most efficient parks in the world. It not only features a wide selection of carnival rides but also has numerous restaurants and theaters, all set amid beautifully tended gardens. It's only a short walk from the city center. *Södra Vägen, tel. 031/400100. Admission: SKr35. Open mid-Apr.–mid-May and late Aug.– late Sept., weekends; mid-May–late Aug., daily.*

Shopping

Department Stores The local branch of **NK,** Sweden's leading department store, is at Östra Hamngatan 42 (tel. 031/173300), while that of **Åhléns** is in the Nordstan mall (tel. 031/800200).

Specialty Stores
Antiques **Antikhallarna** (the Antiques Halls) (Västra Hamngatan 6, tel. 031/137799) claim to be the largest of their kind in Scandinavia. You'll find Sweden's leading auction house, **Bukowskis,** on Avenyn (Kungsportsavenyn 43, tel. 031/200360).

Handicrafts The most atmospheric settings for the purchase of Swedish handicrafts and glassware are in the various shops in **Kron-husbodarna** (*see* Tour 1, *above*), but excellent examples of local

handicrafts can also be bought at **Bohusslöjden** (Kungsports-avenyn 25, tel. 031/160072).

Men's Clothing **Gillblads** (Kungsgatan 42–44, tel. 031/108846) and **Ströms** (Kungsgatan 27–29, tel. 031/177100) have good selections.

Women's Clothing For furs, try **Andreassons** (Södra Hamngatan 49, tel. 031/155535), for other fashions, **Gillblads, Ströms** (*see* Men's Clothes, *above*), and **Hennes & Mauritz** (Kungsgatan 55–57, tel. 031/110011) all have standard choices.

Sports and Fitness

Fishing Fishing for mackerel is a popular sport. Among the boats that take expeditions into the archipelago is the M/S *Daisy*, which leaves from Hjuvik on the Hisingen side of the Göta River (tel. 031/963018).

Water Sports Boating, sailing, and windsurfing are all well provided for. Check with the tourist office for details.

Beaches

There are several excellent local beaches. The two most popular (though visitors are unlikely to find them crowded) are **Näset** and **Askim.**

Dining

You can eat well in Göteborg, but you must expect to pay dearly for the privilege. If anything, there is a more casual approach here than in Stockholm, so, unless otherwise indicated, you won't need to dress up. Fish dishes are the best bet here. Check to make sure restaurants are open first, as many close for a month in summer.

Highly recommended restaurants are indicated by a star ★.

Very Expensive **Belle Avenue.** A dramatic tribute to the power of interior decoration, this plush, wood-paneled restaurant entered from the modern lobby of the SAS Park Avenue is another world. The chef at Belle Avenue is expert at utilizing local fishes and creating such gourmet dishes as thin slices of halibut filled with ragout of lobster and artichoke and served with truffles. *Kungsportsavenyn 36–38, tel. 031/176520. Reservations required. Dress: casual but neat. Closed Sat. lunch, Sun., and July. AE, DC, MC, V.*

★ **The Place.** Göteborg's top restaurant, The Place now offers a choice between the restaurant and the less expensive but popular brasserie. Characteristic of both restaurants are the terracotta ceilings, pastel-yellow walls, and white linen tablecloths heightening the warm, intimate atmosphere in which to enjoy the wide selection of contemporary cuisine and quality ingredients. The Place also boasts one of the best wine cellars in Sweden, with Mouton Rothschild wines dating from 1904. *Arkivgatan 7, tel. 031/160333. Reservations advised. Dress: casual but neat. Restaurant closed July. AE, DC, MC, V.*

Expensive **Chablis.** Long popular in Göteborg, this excellent fish restaurant is located at *Aschebergsgatan 22, tel. 031/203545. Reservations advised. AE, DC, MC, V.*

Sjömagasinet. The specialty of this seafood restaurant, with its 18th-century atmosphere and pleasant view of the sea, is fillet

of sole Walewska. *Klippans Kulturreservat, tel. 031/246510. Reservations required. AE, DC, MC, V.*

Stallgården. This is a high-quality fish restaurant, one of whose specialties is curry-stuffed lobster. *Kyrkogården 33, tel. 031/130316. Reservations required. AE, DC, MC, V.*

Moderate **A Hereford Beefstouw.** Probably as close as you come to an American steak house in Sweden, this restaurant has gained popularity in a town dominated by fish restaurants. Diners' beef selections are cooked by chefs at grills in the center of each of the three dining rooms. The rustic atmosphere is heightened by thick wooden tables, pine floors, and landscape paintings. *Linéagatan 5, tel. 031/775–0441. Reservations advised. Dress: casual but neat. AE, DC, MC, V. July dinner only.*

Fiskekrogen. Its name means "Fish Inn," and it has more than 30 fish and seafood dishes to choose from. Lunches are particularly good. *Lilla Torget 1, tel. 031/112184. Reservations advised. AE, DC, MC, V.*

Weise. A centrally located restaurant with a German beer-cellar atmosphere, owned by the same family since 1907, it was once a haunt of local painters and intellectuals and still retains something of that ambience. The tables and chairs date from 1892. It specializes in traditional Swedish home cooking, serving dishes such as pork and brown beans, pea soup, and homemade apple cake. *Drottninggatan 23, tel. 031/131402. Reservations advised. AE, DC, MC, V.*

Inexpensive **Amanda Boman.** This little restaurant is in one corner of the market hall and keeps early opening hours, so unless you eat an afternoon dinner, it is primarily a lunch place. It serves Swedish specialties—fish soup, *gravlax* (marinated salmon), and daily hot dishes. *Saluhallen, tel. 031/137676. AE, DC, MC, V. Closed Sun.*

Gabriel. Fresh shellfish and the fish dish of the day draw crowds to this restaurant on a balcony above the fish hall. You can eat lunch and watch all the trading. *Feskekorka, tel. 031/139051. MC, V. Closed dinner and weekends.*

Minus. This restaurant proves that health food doesn't have to be boring. All food is marked with calorie count, but, fortunately, that doesn't affect the taste. *Andra Långgatan 4B, tel. 031/144199. No credit cards. Closed weekends.*

Lodging

In Göteborg, many hotels offer special summer discounts.

Highly recommended hotels are indicated by a star ★.

Very Expensive **SAS Park Avenue.** The lobby of this modern luxury hotel was renovated in 1991, but it still lacks ambience. The well-equipped rooms are decorated in earth tones. Its excellent location on Avenyn and the bright, airy cocktail bar on the top floor are its chief attractions. *Kungsportsavenyn 36–38, S–400 16, tel. 031/176520, fax 031/169568. 318 rooms. Facilities: restaurant, bar, nightclub, sauna, swimming pool, conference room, SAS airline check-in counter. AE, DC, MC, V.*

Sheraton Hotel and Towers. Opened in 1986, the Sheraton Hotel and Towers is Göteborg's most modern and spectacular international-style hotel. It features an atrium lobby. There are several restaurants with varying prices, including a popular Italian café, open at lunchtime, and a more formal restaurant serving international cuisine. *Södra Hamngatan 59–65, S–401 24, tel.*

031/806000, fax 031/159888. 340 rooms with bath. Facilities: restaurants, nightclub, health club, 16 rooms for the disabled, swimming pool. AE, DC, MC, V. Closed Christmas.

Expensive **Europa.** Large and comfortable, this Reso hotel is situated
★ close to the central railway station and the Nordstan mall. *Köpmansgatan 38, S–401 24, tel. 031/801280, fax 031/154755. 475 rooms, 5 suites. Facilities: restaurant, bar, piano bar, nightclub, gift shop, garage, rooms for the disabled. AE, DC, MC, V.*

Opalen. If you are attending an event at the Scandinavium stadium or if you have children and are heading for the Liseberg amusement park, this Reso hotel is ideally located. Completely renovated in 1990, the rooms are bright and modern. *Engelbrektsgatan 73, S–402 23, tel. 031/810300, fax 031/187622. 241 rooms. Facilities: restaurant, bar, swimming pool, sauna, tennis courts, 2 non-smoking floors. AE, DC, MC, V.*

Panorama. Within reach of all downtown attractions, this Best Western hotel nevertheless manages to provide a quiet, relaxing atmosphere. *Eklandagatan 51–53, S–400 22, tel. 031/810880, fax 031/814237. 340 rooms. Facilities: restaurant, nightclub, swimming pool, sauna, Jacuzzi, garage. AE, DC, MC, V.*

Riverton. Convenient for people arriving in the city by ferry, this hotel is close to the European terminals and overlooks the harbor. Built in 1985 and regularly renovated, it has a glossy marble floor and reflective ceiling in the lobby and rooms decorated with abstract-pattern textiles and whimsical prints. *Stora Badhusgatan 26, S–411 21, tel. 031/101200, fax 031/130866. 190 rooms. Facilities: restaurant, bar, swimming pool, sauna, Jacuzzi, garage, conference rooms. AE, DC, MC, V.*

Moderate **Eggers.** Dating from 1859, Sweden Hotels' Eggers has more
★ Old World character than any other hotel in the city. It is located near the train station and was probably the last port of call in Sweden for many emigrants to the United States. The rooms feature antique furnishings. *Drottningtorget, S–401 25, tel. 031/806070, fax 031/154243. 77 rooms with bath. Facilities: restaurant. AE, DC, MC, V. Closed Christmas.*

Foggs Hotel. A little off the beaten path, but still only five minutes from the city center by car, the Foggs has large, pastel rooms equipped with desks and sofas in addition to the standard amenities. *Gamla Tingstadsgatan 1, S–402 76, tel. 031/222420, fax 031/512100. 121 rooms. Facilities: restaurant, bar, sauna, indoor pool, squash courts, conference rooms. AE, DC, MC, V.*

Hotel Klang. Renovated in 1986, this family-run modern hotel is situated in a 100-year-old former warehouse. The only evidences of its history are the brick walls on the outside and the high ceilings in all the rooms. *Stora Badhusetgatan 28, tel. 031/174050, fax 031/174058. 50 rooms. Facilities: breakfast room, conference room. AE, DC, MC, V.*

Rubinen. Here's an excellent central location on Avenyn, but this Reso hotel can be noisy during the summer. *Kungsportsavenyn 24, S–400 14, tel. 031/810800, fax 031/167586. 190 rooms. Facilities: restaurant, bar, conference rooms, garage. AE, DC, MC, V.*

Inexpensive **Royal.** Located in the city center near the train station,
★ Göteborg's oldest hotel is small, family-owned, and traditional. It was built in 1852 and refurbished in 1991. The rooms are indi-

vidually decorated with reproductions of elegant Swedish traditional furniture. *Drottninggatan 67, S–411 21, tel. 031/80610. 86 rooms with bath. Facilities: breakfast room. AE, DC, MC, V. Closed Christmas and New Year's Day.*

Youth Hostels **Oskupan.** Situated in a modern apartment block, this hotel is 5 kilometers (3 miles) from the railway station. *Merjerigatam 2, S–412 76, tel. 031/401050. 220 beds, 6-bed apartments. Facilities: breakfast. No credit cards. Closed Sept.–May.*
Partille. This hostel is in a pleasant old house 15 kilometers (9 miles) outside the city. *Box 201, Landvettersvägen, S–433 24, tel. 031/446163 or 031/446501. 120 beds, 2- to 4-bed rooms. Facilities: meals to order.*

Camping There are campsites at **Delsjö** (tel. 031/252909), **Kärralund** (tel. 031/252761), and **Askim** (tel. 031/286261).

The Arts and Nightlife

Two free publications in English, available in hotels and at the tourist office, list events, shows, and restaurants: *What's On in Gothenburg* is published monthly, *Gothenburg This Week* weekly. The principal morning newspaper, *Göteborgs Posten*, publishes a weekly listings supplement titled "Aveny," which, while it is in Swedish, is reasonably easy to decipher. "Miss Tourist" (tel. 031/117450), a taped telephone service, lists events in English.

Excursions from Göteborg

Bohuslän

This coastal region north of Göteborg, with its indented, rocky coastline, provides a foretaste of Norway's fjords farther north. It was from these rugged shores that the 9th- and 10th-century Vikings sailed southward on their epic voyages. Today small towns and attractive fishing villages nestle among the distinctively rounded granite rocks and the thousands of skerries and islands that form Sweden's western archipelago, best described by Prince Vilhelm, brother of the late King Gustav V, as "an archipelago formed of gneiss and granite and water which eternally stretches foamy arms after life."

Tourist Information The principal tourist office for the region is **Göteborg Turistbyrå** (Kungsportsplatsen 2, 411 10 Göteborg, tel. 031/100740). There are local offices in **Kungälv** (Fästningsholmen, tel. 030/12035), **Kungshamn** (Hamngatan 6, tel. 0523/37150), **Öckerö** (Stranden 2, tel. 031/965080), **Strömstad** (Torget, Norra Hamnen, tel. 0526/13025), and **Uddevalla** (Kampenhof, tel. 0522/11787).

Getting There *By Car* The best way to explore Bohuslän is by car. The E6 highway runs the length of the coast from Göteborg north to Strömstad, close to the Norwegian border, and for campers there are numerous extremely well-equipped and uncluttered camping places along the coast's entire length.

By Train There is regular service along the coast between all the major towns of Bohuslän. The trip from Göteborg to Strömstad takes about two hours, and there are several trains each day. **SJ** (Göteborg, tel. 031/103000 or 020/757575).

By Bus Buses leave from behind the central railway station in Göteborg (bus lines are: Göteborg bus, tel. 031/801235, and Bohustrafiken, tel. 0522/14030). The trip to Strömstad takes two to three hours.

Exploring *Numbers in the margin correspond to points of interest on the*
Bohuslän *Excursions from Göteborg map.*

Ideally you should drift slowly north, taking full advantage of the uncluttered beaches and small, picturesque fishing villages. Painters and sailors haunt the region in summer.

❶ The first stop north of Göteborg is **Kungälv,** strategically placed at the confluence of the two arms of the Göta River and the site of **Bohus Fästning,** a ruined fortress built by the Norwegians in 1308 where many battles between Swedish, Norwegian, and Danish armies took place. Today Kungälv has become something of a bedroom suburb for Göteborg, but it has a white wooden church dating from 1679, with an unusual Baroque interior. (*See also* Exploring the Göta Canal, *below*).

There is excellent deep-sea mackerel fishing from **Skärhamn** on the island of Tjörn, which can be reached by road bridge from Stenungsund.

❷ **Uddevalla,** a former shipbuilding town at the head of a picturesque fjord, is best known for a battle in which heavy rains doused musketeers' matches, effectively ending hostilities.

Lysekil, off the E6 highway on a promontory at the head of the Gullmarn Fjord, has been one of Sweden's most popular summer resorts since the 19th century. It specializes in boat excursions to neighboring islands and deep-sea fishing trips. The best bathing is at Pinnevik Cove.

❸ A little to the north lies the **Sotenäs** peninsula and the attractive island of **Smögen,** which can be reached by road bridge. It is locally renowned for its shrimp.

Stop at **Tanumshede** to see Europe's largest single collection of Bronze Age rock carvings at **Vitlycke.** They cover 673 square feet of rock and depict battles, hunting, and fishing. The carvings are close to the main road and well marked.

❹ **Strömstad,** a popular Swedish resort, boasts that it has more summer sunshine than any other town north of the Alps. Formerly Norwegian, it has been the site of many battles among warring Danes, Norwegians, and Swedes. A short trip over the Norwegian border takes you to Halden, where Sweden's warrior king, Karl XII, died in 1718.

There are regular ferry boats from Strömstad to the **Koster Islands,** another favorite holiday spot, with uncluttered beaches and trips to catch prawn and lobster.

The Swedish Riviera

The coastal region south of Göteborg is the closest that mainland Sweden comes to having a resort area (locally dubbed the "Swedish Riviera"). Fine beaches abound, and there are plenty of opportunities for many sporting activities. The region stretches down to Båstad in the country's southernmost province, Skåne.

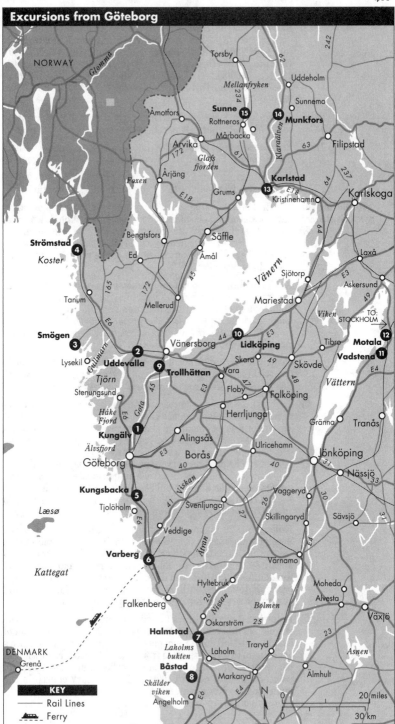

Excursions from Göteborg

Tourist The regional tourist office is VästSvenska Turistråd (West
Information Swedish Tourist Board) (Kungsportsplatsen 2, 411 10 Göteborg, tel. 031/818200). Local offices are in **Båstad** (Stortorget 1,
tel. 0431/75045), **Falkenberg** (Stortorget, tel. 0346/17410),
Halmstad (Lilla Torg, tel. 035/109345), **Kungsbacka** (Storgatan
41, tel. 0300/34284), **Laholm** (Rådhuset, tel. 0430/15216 or
0430/15450), and **Varberg** (Brunnsparken, tel. 0340/88780 and
0340/88770).

Getting There To reach the Swedish Riviera, simply follow the E6 highway
By Car south from Göteborg. It parallels the coast.

By Train Regular service connects the Göteborg central station with all
major towns. Contact **SJ** (Göteborg, tel. 031/103000 or 020/
757575).

By Bus Buses leave from behind Göteborg's central railway station.

Exploring the The first stop heading south from Göteborg is **Kungsbacka,** to-
Swedish Riviera day fast becoming one of its bedroom suburbs; it holds a market
5 on the first Thursday of every month. From the top of an Ice
Age sand ridge at the nearby village of Fjärås, there is a fine
view of the coast, and on the slopes of the ridge are Iron Age
and Viking graves.

At **Tjolöholm,** 12 kilometers (7 miles) down the road, you encounter Tjolöholms Slott (Tjolöholm Castle), a manor house
built by a Scotsman at the beginning of this century in mock
English Tudor style. *S–43033 Fjärås, tel. 0300/44200. Admission: SKr35 adults, SKr10 children 4–14. Open June–Aug.,
daily; Apr.–May, Sept., weekends.*

Nearby is the tiny 18th-century village of **Äskhult,** the site of an
open-air museum. *Tel. 0300/42159 or 0300/34619. Admission:
SKr10 adults, SKr2 children. Open June–Aug.*

6 The next town along the coast is **Varberg,** a busy port with connections to Grenå in Denmark and some good beaches. It is best
known for a suit of medieval clothing preserved in the museum
in the 13th-century **Varbergs Fästning** (Varberg Fortress). The
suit belonged to a man who was murdered and thrown into a
peat bog. The peat preserved his body, and his clothes are the
only suit of ordinary medieval clothing in existence. The museum also contains a silver bullet said to be the one that killed
Karl XII. *Tel. 0340/18520. Admission: SKr10. Open daily
10–7. Guided tours June–Aug., daily; May and Sept., Sun.*

Falkenberg, 29 kilometers (18 miles) farther south, is one of
Sweden's most attractive resorts, with fine beaches and salmon
fishing in the Ätran River. Falkenberg's Gamla Stan (Old
Town) features narrow, cobblestone streets and quaint old
wooden houses. Here you'll find Törngren's, a pottery shop,
probably the oldest still operating in Scandinavia, owned and
run by the seventh generation of the founding family.

7 **Halmstad,** 148 kilometers (92 miles) south of Göteborg, is the
largest seaside resort on the west coast, with a population of
50,000. The **Norreport** town gate, all that remains of the town's
original fortifications, dates from 1605. The modern Town Hall
has interior decorations by the so-called Halmstad Group of
painters, formed here in 1929. A 14th-century church in the
main square contains fragments of medieval murals and a 17th-
century pulpit.

❽ By the time you reach **Båstad,** 188 kilometers (117 miles) from Göteborg, you are in Skåne, Sweden's southernmost province. Båstad is the most fashionable resort in Sweden, where ambassadors and local captains of industry have their summer houses. Aside from this, it is best known for its tennis. In addition to the **Båstad Open,** a Grand Prix tournament in late summer, there is the annual **Donald Duck Cup** in July for children ages 11 to 15; it was the very first trophy won by Björn Borg, who later took the Wimbledon men's singles title an unprecedented five times in a row. Spurred on by Borg and other Swedish champions, such as Stefan Edberg and Mats Wilander, thousands of youngsters take part in the Donald Duck Cup each year. For details, contact **Svenska Tennisförbundet** (the Swedish Tennis Association), Lidingövägen 75, Stockholm, tel. 08/6679770).

Time Out   **Norrviken Gardens** (tel. 0431/71070), 3 kilometers (2 miles) northwest of Båstad, are beautifully laid out in different styles, with a restaurant, a shop, and a pottery studio.

The Göta Canal

The **Göta Canal** is actually 614 kilometers (380 miles) of interconnected canals, rivers, lakes, and even a stretch of sea. It links Stockholm with Göteborg and had been a Swedish dream ever since it was first suggested by Bishop Hans Brask of Linköping in the 16th century. In 1718 King Karl XII ordered the canal to be built, but work was abandoned when he was killed in battle the same year. Not until 1810 was the idea again taken up in earnest. The driving force was a Swedish nobleman, Count Baltzar Bogislaus von Platen (1766–1829), and his motive was commercial. Von Platen saw in the canal a way of beating Danish tolls on shipping passing through the Öresund and of enhancing the importance of Göteborg by linking the port with Stockholm on the east coast. At a time when Swedish fortunes were at a low ebb, the canal was also envisaged as a means of reestablishing faith in the future and boosting national morale.

The building of the canal took 22 years and involved a total of 58,000 men. The linking of the various stretches of water required 87 kilometers (54 miles) of man-made cuts through soil and rock, the building of 58 locks, 47 bridges, 27 culverts, and 3 dry docks. Unfortunately, the canal never achieved the financial success hoped for by von Platen. By 1857 the Danes had removed shipping tolls, and in the following decade the linking of Göteborg with Stockholm by rail effectively ended the canal's commercial potential. The canal did come into its own as a 20th-century tourist attraction, however.

Tourist   Regional tourist offices are **Bohusturist** (Uddevalla, tel. 0522/
Information   14055), **Västergötlands Turistråd** (Skövde, tel. 0500/18050), and **Turistbolaget AB** (Linköping, tel. 013/125055). Local tourist offices along the route include **Karlsborg** (N. Kanalgatan 2, 0505/12120), **Linköping** (Agatan 39, tel. 013/206835), and **Vadstena** (Rådhustorget, tel. 0143/15125).

Exploring the   Drifting lazily down this lovely series of waterways, across the
Göta Canal   enormous lakes, Vänern and Vättern, through a microcosm of all that is best about Sweden—abundant fresh air, clear, clean

water, pristine nature, well-tended farmland—it is difficult to conceive of the canal's industrial origins.

Traveling the entire length of the canal by passenger boat to Stockholm takes four or six days. For details, contact the **Göta Canal Steamship Company** (Box 272, S–401 24, Göteborg, tel. 031/806315). A bicycle path runs parallel to the canal, offering another way to tour the country. For information on sailing your own boat, contact AB Göta Kanalbolaget (tel. 0141/53510).

The trip from Göteborg takes you first along the Göta Älv (river), a wide waterway that 10,000 years ago, when the ice cap melted, was a great fjord. Some 30 minutes into the voyage the boat passes below a rocky escarpment, topped by the remains of **Bohus Fästning** (Bohus Castle), distinguished by two round towers known as Father's Hat and Mother's Bonnet. It dates from the 14th century and was once the mightiest fortress in western Scandinavia, commanding the confluence of the Göta and Nordre rivers. It was strengthened and enlarged in the 16th century and successfully survived 14 sieges. From 1678 onward, the castle began to lose its strategic and military importance and fell into decay, until 1838, when King Karl XIV passed by on a river journey, admired the old fortress, and ordered its preservation.

The boat passes **Kungälv** (*see also* Exploring Bohuslän, *above*), a pleasant riverside town, then **Lödöse,** once a major trading settlement and a predecessor of Göteborg that is today a quiet village. The countryside becomes wilder, with pines and oaks clustered thickly on either bank between cliffs of lichen-clad granite.

Some five hours after leaving Göteborg the boat arrives in **Trollhättan,** 89 kilometers (55 miles) upriver. This is a pleasant industrial town of around 50,000 inhabitants, where a spectacular waterfall was in 1906 rechanneled to become Sweden's first hydroelectric plant. Most years, on specific days the waters are allowed to follow their natural course, a fall of 106 feet in six torrents. This is a sight that is well worth seeing. The other main point of interest is the area between what were the falls and the series of locks that allowed the canal to bypass them. Here are disused locks from 1800 and 1844 and a strange Ice Age grotto where members of the Swedish royal family have carved their names since the 18th century. Trollhättan also has a fine, wide marketplace and pleasant waterside parks.

Soon after leaving Trollhättan, the boat passes **Hunneberg** and **Halleberg,** two strange, flat-top hills, both more than 500 feet high. The woods surrounding them are extraordinarily rich in elk, legend, and Viking burial mounds. The boat proceeds through **Karls Grav,** the oldest part of the canal. This was begun early in the 17th century, its purpose to bypass the Ronnum Falls on the Göta River, which have been harnessed to a hydroelectric project. Finally the boat reaches **Vänern,** Sweden's largest and Europe's third-largest lake: 3,424 square kilometers (2,123 square miles) of water, 145 kilometers (90 miles) long and 81 kilometers (50 miles) wide at one point. The canal enters the lake at **Vänersborg,** a town of around 30,000 inhabitants that was founded in the mid-17th century. The church and the governor's residence date from the 18th century, but the rest of the town was destroyed by fire in 1834.

Vänersborg is distinguished by its fine lakeside park, the trees of which act as a windbreak for the gusts that sweep in from Vänern.

It takes about eight hours to cross Vänern. On an inlet at the southernmost point of its eastern arm lies the town of **Lidköping,** which received its charter in 1446 and is said to have the largest town square in Sweden. Lying 24 kilometers (15 miles) to the north of it, on an island off the point dividing the eastern arm of Vänern from the western, is **Läckö Slott** (Läckö Castle), one of Sweden's finest 17th-century Renaissance palaces. Its 250 rooms were once the home of Magnus Gabriel de la Gardie, a great favorite of Queen Christina. Only the Royal Palace in Stockholm is larger. In 1681 Karl XI, to curtail the power of the nobility, confiscated it, and in 1830 all its furnishings were auctioned. Many of them have since been restored to the palace.

On a peninsula to the east, the landscape is dominated by the great hill of **Kinnekulle,** towering 900 feet above the lake. The hill is rich in colorful vegetation and wildlife and was a favorite hike for the botanist Linnaeus.

Then, at the lakeside port of **Sjötorp,** the **Göta Canal** proper begins: a cut through earth and granite with a series of locks raising the steamer to Lanthöjden, at 304 feet above sea level the highest point on the canal. The boat next enters the narrow, twisting lakes Viken and Bottensjön and continues to Forsvik though the canal's oldest lock, built in 1813. It then sails out into **Vättern,** Sweden's second-largest lake, nearly 129 kilometers (80 miles) from north to south and 31 kilometers (19 miles) across at its widest point. Its waters are so clear that in some parts the bottom is visible at a depth of 50 feet. The lake is subject to sudden storms that can whip its normally placid waters into a choppy maelstrom.

Some 259 kilometers (161 miles) from Göteborg, the boat finally anchors at **Vadstena,** a little-known historic gem of a town. Vadstena grew up around the monastery founded by St. Birgitta, or Bridget (1303–1373), who wrote in her *Revelationes* that she had a vision of Christ in which he revealed the rules of the religious order she went on to establish. These rules seem to have been a precursor for the Swedish ideal of sexual equality, with both nuns and monks sharing a common church. Her order spread rapidly after her death, and at one time there were 80 Bridgetine monasteries in Europe. Little remains of the Vadstena monastery, however; in 1545 King Gustav Vasa ordered its demolition, and its stones were used to build **Vadstena Slott** (Vadstena Castle), the huge fortress dominating the lake. Swedish royalty held court here until 1715. It then fell into decay and was used as a granary. Today it houses part of the National Archives and is also the site of an annual summer opera festival. *Tel. 0143/15123. Admission: SKr30. Open mid-May–mid-Aug., daily noon–5.*

Vadstena Kyrka is also worth visiting. The triptych altarpiece on the south wall features St. Birgitta presenting her book of revelations to a group of kneeling cardinals. There is also a fine wood carving of the Madonna and Child from 1500.

If you continue down the canal to Stockholm, you sail through **Motala,** where Baltzar von Platen is buried close to the canal. He had envisaged the establishment of four new towns along

the waterway, but only Motala fulfilled his dream. He designed the town himself, and his statue is in the main square.

At Borenshult a series of locks takes the boat down to Boren, a lake in the province of Östergötland. On the southern shore of the next lake, Roxen, lies the city of **Linköping,** capital of the province and home of Saab, the aircraft and automotive company. Once out of the lake, you follow a new stretch of canal past the sleepy town of **Söderköping.** A few miles east, at the hamlet of Mem, the canal's last lock lowers the boat into Slätbaken, a Baltic fjord presided over by the ruins of the ancient **Stegeborg** fortress. The boat then steams north along the coastline until it enters Mälaren through the Södertälje Canal and finally anchors in the capital at Riddarholmen.

Lodging   **Kungs-Starby Wärdshus.** This recently renovated manor house
Vadstena   on the outskirts of town, reached on Route 50, is surrounded by a park. The bedrooms are small and functional. *S–59200, tel. 0143/11420. 45 rooms with shower. Facilities: restaurant, sauna, swimming pool, solarium. AE, DC, MC, V. Inexpensive.*
Vadstena Klosterhotel. This hotel is housed in what is Sweden's oldest secular building, parts of which date from the 13th century. *Klosterområdet, off Lasarettsgatan, S–59230, tel. 0143/ 11530, fax 0143/13648. 29 rooms with bath. Facilities: restaurant, satellite TV, rooms for allergy sufferers. AE, DC, MC, V. Inexpensive.*

Värmland

This province, close to the Norwegian border on the north shores of Vänern, is rich in folklore. It was also the home of Alfred Nobel and the birthplace of other famous Swedes, among them the Nobel Prize–winning novelist Selma Lagerlöf, the poet Gustaf Fröding, former Prime Minister Tage Erlander, and present-day opera star Håkan Hagegård. It is a part of the country favored by artists, with a timeless quality to it, a place where Swedes often take their own holidays. Värmland's forested, lake-dotted landscape, along with that of Dalarna, farther north, embodies Sweden as a whole.

Tourist   The regional tourist office is **Värmlands Turistråd** (Södra
Information   Kyrkogatan 10, Karlstad, tel. 054/102160). There are local tourist offices in **Karlstad** (Bibliotek, Västratorggatan 26, tel. 054/195901) and **Sunne** (Sunne Turistcentrum, tel. 0565/ 13530).

Getting There   Follow E3 and then E18 west from Stockholm or Route 45 north
By Car   to E18 from Göteborg.

By Train   There is regular service to Karlstad from Stockholm and Göteborg on SJ.

Exploring   Värmland's principal city, **Karlstad** (population 74,000), 255 ki-
Värmland   lometers (158 miles) from Göteborg, is situated on Klaraälven
13   (the Klara River) at the point where it empties into Vänern. Karlstad was founded in 1684, when it was known as Tingvalla. It later changed its name to honor King Karl IX, Karlstad meaning "Karl's Town." It was totally rebuilt after a fire in 1865. In **Stortorget,** the main square, there is a statue of Karl IX by the local sculptor Christian Eriksson. The **Värmlands Museum** has rooms dedicated to both Eriksson and the poet Fröding. *Sandgrun, Box 335, S–65108, tel. 054/111419. Admission: SKr15. Open daily noon–4 (Wed. noon–8).*

The **Marieberg Skogspark** (Marieberg Forest Park) is also worth visiting. A delight for the whole family, the park has restaurants and an outdoor theater. Karlstad is also the site of an **Emigrant Registret** (Emigrant Center, Norra Strandgatan 4, tel. 054/15926) that maintains detailed records of the Swedes' emigration to America. Visitors of Swedish extraction can trace their ancestors at the center's research facility.

Värmland is, above all, a rural experience. You can drive along the Klaräalven, through the beautiful Fryken Valley, to Ransater, where author Erik Gustaf Geijer was born in 1783 and where Erlander, the former prime minister, also grew up.

⑭ The rural idyll ends in **Munkfors,** where some of the best-quality steel in Europe is manufactured, but just past it, you'll find the little village of **Sunnemo,** with its beautiful wooden church. A little farther north, the town of **Uddeholm** on Lake Råda is home of the Uddeholm Corporation, which produces iron and steel, forestry products and chemicals. Continuing north around the lake, you can return to Munkfors and then make a

⑮ diversion west to **Sunne,** from which it is only 55 kilometers (34 miles) to **Mårbacka,** the estate where Nobel Prize winner Selma Lagerlöf was born in 1858. It is preserved as it was when she died in 1940. *Östra Ämtervik, S–68600 Sunne, tel. 0565/ 31027. Admission: SKr35. Open May–Aug., daily 9–6.*

Turning south and heading back toward Karlstad, you can stop off at **Rottneros Herrgårds Park** (Rottneros Manor), the Ekeby of Lagerlöf's *Gösta Berlings Saga* (The Tale of Gösta Berling). The house is privately owned, but its park can be visited and features a fine collection of Scandinavian sculpture, including works by Carl Milles, Norwegian artist Gustav Vigeland, and Wäinö Aaltonen of Finland. *S–68602 Rottneros, tel. 0565/ 60295. Admission: SKr45 adults, SKr20 children under 15. Open mid-May–early Sept., daily 9–6.*

Dining **Inn Alstern.** Overlooking Lake Alstern, this restaurant serves
Karlstad Swedish and Continental cuisine in an elegant atmosphere. *Morgonvägen 4, tel. 054/834900. Reservations advised. Dress: casual but neat. AE, MC, V. Expensive.*

Dining and **Stadshotellet.** On the banks of Klarälven (the Klara River), this
Lodging hotel built in 1870 is steeped in tradition. Completely
Karlstad renovoted in 1991, all the rooms are decorated differently: some in modern Swedish style, others evoking their original look. *Kungsgatan 22, S–651 04, tel. 054/115220, fax 054/ 188211. 143 rooms. Facilities: 2 restaurants, bar, nightclub, sauna. AE, DC, MC, V. Expensive.*

Gösta Berling. Located in the center of town, this small hotel, named for the hero of the Selma Lagerlöf novel, surrounds guests in genuine Värmland ambience. *Drottninggatan 1, S–652 24, tel. 054/150190, fax 054/154826. 66 rooms. Facilities: restaurant, bar, sauna. AE, DC, MC, V. Moderate.*

The South and the Kingdom of Crystal

The southernmost provinces of Sweden—Halland, Skåne, and Blekinge—are different in character from the rest of the country, both in appearance and in the temperament of their inhabitants. This is an extension of the fertile plain of northern Europe, rich farming country, and the people generally are more easygoing than their compatriots farther north. The south is a place of windswept, flat meadows and gently rolling hills, of timber-framed farmhouses in whose yards strut geese being fattened to supply local restaurants with the region's specialty dish. Danish for hundreds of years before being incorporated into Sweden in 1658, the region even today seeks its inspiration from mainland Europe, viewing the rest of Sweden—especially Stockholm—with some disdain. Skåne even has its own independence movement, and the dialect here is so akin to Danish that many Swedes from other parts of the country have trouble understanding it.

While not strictly part of the south, the so-called Kingdom of Crystal, in Småland, is easily reached from here. This is an area of small glassblowing firms, such as Kosta Boda and Orrefors, that are world-renowned for the quality of their products. In addition to visiting these works (and perhaps finding some bargains), the traveler forms an insight into a poorer, harsher way of life that led thousands of peasants to emigrate from Småland to the United States in search of a better life. Those who stayed behind developed a reputation for their inventiveness in setting up small industries to circumvent the region's traditional poverty and are also notorious for being extremely careful—if not downright mean—with money.

Important Addresses and Numbers

Tourist Information

Skånes Turistråd, the Skåne Tourist Council, is at Skiffervägen 38, Lund (tel. 046/124350). There are tourist offices in the following towns: **Helsingborg** (Knutpunkten, tel. 042/120310), **Kalmar** (Larmgatan 6, tel. 0480/15350), **Karlskrona** (Stadsbiblioteket, tel. 0455/83490), **Lund** (Kyrkogatan 11, tel. 046/355040), **Malmö** (Skeppsbron 2, tel. 040/300150), **Ronneby** (Kallingevägen 3, tel. 0457/17650), and **Ystad** (S:t Knuts Torg, tel. 0411/77681). For visitors to the Kingdom of Crystal, the **Småland Tourist Office** is at Jönköping (tel. 036/199570) and Växjö (tel. 0470/47575).

Arriving and Departing by Plane

Airport and Airlines

Malmö's airport, **Sturup,** was opened in 1972. Sturup is approximately 30 kilometers (19 miles) from Malmö and 25 kilometers (16 miles) from Lund. It has two international destinations, Amsterdam, served by KLM, and Oslo, served by Braathens SAFE. Domestic Swedish airlines—SAS, Transwede Airways AB, and Malmö Aviation—serve the Stockholm airports and use them as hubs for connections with other domestic destinations, especially SAS, which also makes international connections via Stockholm's Arlanda. The airlines represented include: **SAS** (tel. 040/357150 or 020/727000), **KLM** (tel. 040/

500530), **Braathens SAFE** (tel. 040/501850), and Malmö Aviation (tel. 040/500330), and **Transwede Airways AB** (tel. 040/501820).

SAS offers discounts on trips to Malmö. You can buy a round-trip ticket, Stockholm–Malmö, for the price of a one-way ticket under the current "Jackpot" discount package (SKr849). The cost for an additional member of the family is SKr424 and children between 2 and 18 get 50% off the going fare. Hertz car rentals are available for SKr850 for the weekend if you book an SAS flight. For more information, contact SAS (161 87 Stockholm, tel. 020/910150 or 020/727000).

Between the Airport and City Center By Bus Buses leave hourly for Malmö and Lund from the Sturup airport. The price of the trip is SKr60 to either destination. For further information on bus schedules, routes, and fares, call 040/501100.

By Taxi A taxi from the airport to Malmö costs about SKr250, and to Lund approximately SKr200. For SAS limousine service, call 040/501834 or 040/357140.

Arriving and Departing by Car, Train, and Boat

By Car Malmö is 620 kilometers (384 miles) from Stockholm. You take the E4 freeway to Helsingborg, then the E6 to Malmö and Lund. From Göteborg, take the E6.

By Train There is regular service from Stockholm to Helsingborg, Lund, and Malmö. The journey takes around 6½ hours. All three railway stations are centrally situated.

By Boat The most common form of arrival in southern Sweden is by boat. Several regular services run from Copenhagen to Malmö, including Hovercrafts that make the trip in less than an hour, and a bus/ferry service from Copenhagen Station, which also goes to Lund. There are also regular ferry connections to Denmark, Germany, and Poland from such ports as Malmö, Helsingborg, Landskrona, Trelleborg, and Ystad. **Stena Line** (Kungsgatan 12–14, Stockholm, tel. 08/141475, and Danmarksterminalen, Göteborg, tel. 031/858000) is one of the major Swedish carriers.

Day-trippers can pick up tickets at Malmö Harbor and catch one of the hourly Copenhagen-bound Hovercrafts operated by the following ferry lines: **Flybåtarna** (tel. 040/103930), **Pile** (tel. 040/234411), and **Hopping Linje** (040/110099). **Skandlines** (tel. 040/362000) runs the only car-ferry service between Dragör, Denmark, and Limhamn, a town that adjoins Malmö's southern edge. For travelers from Denmark who want to rent a car as soon as they arrive, **Avis** (tel. 040/77830), **Hertz** (tel. 040/74955), and **InterRent** and **Europcar** (tel. 040/380240), which share an office, all have locations at Malmö Harbor.

Getting Around

By Car Roads are uncluttered and extremely well marked and maintained. Traveling around the coast counterclockwise from Helsingborg, you take the E6 to Landskrona and then on to Malmö, then the E66 to Lund, Kristianstad, Solvesborg, Karlshamn, Ronneby, Karlskrona, and up the coast to Kalmar.

By Train The major towns of the south are all connected by rail. A special *Öresund Runt* (Around Öresund) ticket for trains and ferries to Denmark is available from the Malmö Tourist Office (Skeppsbron 2, tel. 040/3001507; price: SKr125).

Exploring the South and the Kingdom of Crystal

Numbers in the margin correspond to points of interest on the South and the Kingdom of Crystal map.

Southern Sweden is a world of its own, clearly distinguished from the rest of the country by its geography, culture, and history. Skåne (pronounced *Skoh*-neh), the southernmost province, is known as the granary of Sweden. It is a comparatively small province of beautifully fertile plains, sand beaches, scores of castles and châteaus, thriving farms, medieval churches, and summer resorts. The two other southern provinces, Blekinge and Halland, are also fertile and rolling and edged by seashores. Historically, these three provinces are distinct from the rest of Sweden: they were the last to be incorporated into the country, having been ruled by Denmark until 1658. They retain the influences of the Continental culture in their architecture, language, and cuisine. Småland, to the north, is larger than the other provinces, with a harsh countryside of stone and woods. It is noted for its glass industries, as well as furniture and other wooden products, and for the historic region around Kalmar.

Tour 1: The South

❶ The first town of any importance is **Helsingborg** (still sometimes spelled the old way, Hälsingborg). With a population of 108,000, the town seems to the first-time visitor arriving by boat little more than a nondescript ferry terminal (it has connections to Denmark, Norway, and Germany). Actually, it has a rich history, having first been mentioned in 10th-century sagas and since been the site of many battles between the Danes and the Swedes. Together with its twin town, Helsingör, across the Öresund (Elsinore in William Shakespeare's *Hamlet)*, it controlled shipping traffic in and out of the Baltic for centuries. Helsingborg was officially incorporated into Sweden in 1658 and totally destroyed in a battle with the Danes in 1710. It was then rebuilt, and Jean-Baptiste Bernadotte, founder of the present Swedish royal dynasty, landed here in 1810. The **Stadshuset** (Town Hall) has a small museum featuring exhibits on the city and the region. *Södra Storgatan 31, tel. 042/105963. Admission: SKr10 adults, SKr5 children 7–16. Open May–Aug., Tues.–Sun. noon–5; Sept.–Apr., Tues.–Sun. noon–4.*

All that remains of Helsingborg's castle is **Kärnan** (the Keep). The surviving center tower, built to provide living quarters and defend the medieval castle, is the most remarkable relic of its kind in the north. The interior is divided into several floors, where there are a chapel, a kitchen, and other medieval fittings. It stands in a park and offers fine views over the Öresund from the top. *Kärngränden, tel. 042/105991. Admission: SKr10. Open June–Aug., daily 9–8.*

Sofiero Slott (Sofiero Palace), 5 kilometers (3 miles) outside the town, was once a royal summer residence. Built in 1865 in the

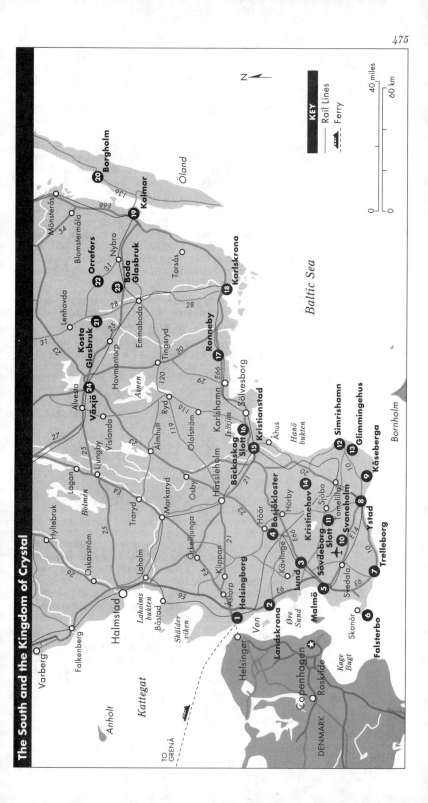

The South and the Kingdom of Crystal

KEY
- Rail Lines
- Ferry

40 miles
60 km

N

Kattegat

Anholt

Varberg

Falkenberg

Halmstad

Laholms bukten
Skälder viken
Båstad

Laholm

Oskarström

Hyltebruk

Lagan

Bolmen

Ljungby

Alvesta

Växjö **24**

Kosta Glasbruk **21**

Lenhovda

Åseda

Blomstermåla

Mönsterås

Borgholm **20**

Orrefors **22**

Kalmar **19**

Boda Glasbruk **23**

Nybro

Öland

Torsås

Karlskrona

Ronneby **17**

18

Sölvesborg

Karlshamn

Baltic Sea

Bornholm

Hanö bukten

Åhus

Kristianstad

Bäckaskog Slott **16**

15

Hässleholm

Osby

Markaryd

Traryd

Tranemö

Emmaboda

Tingsryd

Ryd

Älmhult

Olofström

Hoor

Höör

Hörby

Sjöbo

Bosjökloster **4**

Kristinehov **14**

Simrishamn **12**

Glimmingehus **13**

Kåseberga **9**

Ystad **8**

Svaneholm Slott **10**

Sövdeborg Slott **5**

11 Tomelilla

Trelleborg **7**

Skanör

Falsterbo

Malmö

Lund **3**

Helsingborg **1**

Landskrona

2

Ven

Øre Sund

Helsingør

Copenhagen

Roskilde

Køge Bugt

DENMARK

TO GRENÅ

Dutch Renaissance style, it has a fine park designed by Crown Princess Margareta. *Solfierovägen (on road to Laröd), tel. 042/145259. Admission: SKr20 adults, Skr12 children. Open May–Sept., daily 10–6.*

② The 17th-century Dutch-style fortifications of **Landskrona,** 40 kilometers (25 miles) down the coast, are among the best-preserved of their type in Europe. Though it appears to be just another modern town, Landskrona actually dates from 1413, when it received its charter. Author Selma Lagerlöf worked here at the town's elementary school in 1888 and began her novel *Gösta Berlings Saga.*

Landskrona's **Citadellet** (castle) was built under orders of the Danish King Christian III in 1549 and is all that remains of the original town, which was razed in 1747 on orders of the Swedish Parliament to make way for extended fortifications. The new town was then built on land reclaimed from the sea. Local handicrafts workshops in the castle grounds sell their products during the summer. *Slottsgatan, tel. 0418/16980. Admission: SKr10. Open June–Aug., daily 11–4.*

Three kilometers (2 miles) north of the town lies the **Borstahusen** recreation area, with long stretches of beach, a marina, and a holiday village with 74 summer chalets.

From Landskrona harbor there are regular 25-minute boat trips to the island of **Ven,** where the Danish astronomer Tycho Brahe lived from 1576 to 1597 and conducted his pioneering research. The foundations of his Renaissance castle, **Uranienborg,** can be visited, as can **Stjärneborg,** his reconstructed observatory. The small **Tycho Brahe Museet** is dedicated to Brahe and his work. *Landsvägen, Ven, tel. 0418/72058. Admission: SKr5. Open May–Sept., daily 11–5.*

Ven is also ideal for camping (check with the local tourist office in Landsvägen, tel. 0418/79493), and there are special paths across the island for bicycles (rentals are available at Bäckviken, the small harbor).

③ Head inland now to **Lund,** one of the oldest towns in Europe, founded in 1020 by the legendary King Knud (Canute), monarch of Scandinavia and Britain. In 1103 Lund became the religious capital of Scandinavia and at one time had 27 churches and eight monasteries, before King Christian III of Denmark ordered most of them razed to use their stones for the construction of Malmöhus Castle in Malmö. Lund lost its importance until 1666, when its **university** was established. It is now one of Sweden's two chief university towns and one of the nicest of Swedish towns, having managed to preserve its historic character.

Its monumental gray stone Romanesque **cathedral** is the oldest in Scandinavia, consecrated in 1145. Its crypt features 23 finely carved pillars, but its main attraction is an astrological clock, *Horologum Mirabile Lundense* (the miraculous Lund clock), dating from 1380, which was restored in 1923. It features an amazing pageant of knights jousting on horseback, trumpets blowing a medieval fanfare, and the Magi walking in procession past Virgin and Child as the organ plays *In Dulci Jubilo.* It plays at noon and 3 PM on weekdays and at 1 and 3 PM on Sunday.

Esaias Tegnér, the Swedish poet, lived from 1813 to 1826 in a little house immediately behind the cathedral. Today it is the **Tegnér**

Museet in his honor. *Gråbrödersgatan, tel. 046/691319. Admission: SKr10. Open first Sun. each month noon–3.*

On the southern side of the main square is **Drottens Kyrkoruin** (the Church Ruins of Drotten), an "underground" museum of Lund's middle ages located in the cellar of a modern five-story building. The foundations of three Catholic churches are here: the first and oldest was built of wood in approximately AD 1000. It was torn down to make room for one of stone built in about 1100; this was replaced by a second stone church built around 1300. *Kattensund 6, tel. 046/355291. Admission: SKr10. Open weekends 10–2.*

Kulturen (the Museum of Cultural History), is both outdoor and indoor museum, featuring 20 old cottages, farms, and manor houses from southern Sweden plus an excellent collection of ceramics, textiles, weapons, and furniture. *Adelgatan, tel. 046/ 150480. Admission: SKr30 adults, children under 15 free. Open May–Sept., daily 11–5; Oct.–Apr., daily 12–4.*

One street over and east of the cathedral is the **Botaniska Trädgården** (the Botanical Gardens), which contain 7,500 specimen plants from all over the world—very pleasant on a summer's day. *Ostravalsgatan 20, tel. 046/107320. Admission free. Open daily 6 AM–8 PM; greenhouses open noon–3.*

Time Out Drop by **Storkällaren** (Stortorget 5, tel. 046/115173) in the center of town, a great place to watch and meet locals after a stroll around.

About 30 miles (38 kilometers) farther inland off Route 23, ❹ north of E66, is **Bosjökloster,** an 11th-century white-painted Gothic castle with lovely grounds on Ringsjö, the second-largest lake in southern Skåne. The castle's original owner donated the estate to the church, which turned it over to the Benedictine order of nuns. They founded a convent school for the daughters of Scanian nobility, no longer in existence, and built the convent church with its tower made of sandstone. The 300-acre castle grounds, with a 1,000-year-old oak tree, a network of pathways, a children's park, a rose garden, and an indoor-outdoor restaurant, are ideal for picnics. *Höör, tel. 0413/250 48. Admission: SKr25 adults, SKr12 children 16 and under. Open May–Oct. Castle grounds open 8–8. Restaurant and exhibition halls open 10–6.*

❺ **Malmö,** just 31 kilometers (19 miles) to the southwest, is very different from Lund. Capital of the province of Skåne, with a population of about 250,000, this is Sweden's third-largest city.

Visitors can purchase **Malmökortet** (the Malmö Card), which entitles the holder to, among other benefits, free admission or discounts to most museums, concert halls, nightclubs, and theaters, and many shops and restaurants. A one-day card costs SKr110 for adults and SKr55 for children; a two-day card costs SKr200 and SKr100, respectively; and one for three days costs SKr280 and SKr140. The cards are available at most hotels, newspaper kiosks, and tourist offices in Malmö, Lund, and Trelleborg.

The city's castle, **Malmöhus,** completed in 1542, was for many years used as a prison (James Bothwell, husband of Mary, Queen of Scots, was one of its notable inmates). Today it houses four museums, including an art museum with a collection of

Nordic art, a toy museum, a marine museum, and a puppet theater. *Malmöhusvägen, tel. 040/341000. Admission: SKr30. Open Tues.–Sun. noon–4.*

Farther down Malmöhusvägen there's a clutch of tiny red-painted shacks called **Fiskehodderna** (the Fish Shacks) adjoining a dock where the fishing boats come in every morning and unload their catch. The piers, dock, and huts were restored in 1991 and are now a government-protected district.

Nearby is the old town, where the **St. Petri Church,** from the 14th century, is an impressive example of the Baltic Gothic style, with its distinctive stepped gables. Inside there is a fine Renaissance altar.

Rådhuset (the City Hall), dating from 1546, dominates Stortorget, a huge, cobbled market square, and makes an impressive spectacle when illuminated at night. In the center of the square stands an equestrian statue of Karl X, the king who united this part of the country with Sweden in 1658. Off the southeast corner of Stortorget is Lilla Torg, an attractive small cobblestone square surrounded by restored buildings from the 17th and 18th centuries. A sports museum occupies **Baltiska Hallen.** *John Ericssons Väg, tel. 040/342688. Admission free. Open Mon.–Fri. 8–4.*

Also downtown, the **Rooseum,** located in a turn-of-the-century brick building that was once a power plant, is one of Sweden's most outstanding art museums, with exhibitions of contemporary art and a quality selection of Nordic art. *Gasverksgatan 22, tel. 040/121716. Admission: SKr20 adults, children under 16 free. Open Tues.–Fri., noon–7, weekends noon–5. Guided tours weekends at 2.*

On a tiny peninsula 32 kilometers (20 miles) from Mälmö, at the country's southwesternmost corner, are the idyllic towns of ❻ **Falsterbo** and **Skanör,** both popular summer resorts. Ornithologists gather at Falsterbo every fall to watch the spectacular migration of hundreds of raptors.

Continuing on from Malmö, you can make your way through ❼ ❽ **Trelleborg,** Sweden's southernmost town, to **Ystad,** a medieval city on the coast, and a smuggling center during the Napoleonic Wars. If you are driving, go by way of **Torup Slott** (Castle), a good example of the square fortified stronghold, built about 1550. Ystad has preserved its medieval character with winding, narrow streets and hundreds of half-timbered houses from four or five different centuries. The principal ancient monument is **St. Maria Kyrka,** begun shortly after 1220 as a basilica in the Romanesque style but with later additions.

Some 24 kilometers (15 miles) east of Ystad, on the coastal road leading to the harbor town of Simrishhamn, is the charming ❾ fishing village of **Kåseberga.** On the hill behind it stand the impressive **Ales stenar** (Ale's stones), an intriguing 76-meter (251-foot) arrangement of 58 Viking rune stones in the shape of a ship. The stones are still something of a puzzle to anthropologists.

Inland, the gentle rolling hills and fields of Skåne are broken every few miles by lovely castles, chronologically and architecturally diverse, which have given this part of Sweden the name Château Country. Often they are surrounded by beautiful grounds and moats. A significant number of the estates have

remained in the hands of the original families and are still inhabited. If you drive back toward Malmö on E14, you'll come to **⑩ Svaneholm,** one of Skåne's outstanding Renaissance strongholds. First built in 1530 and rebuilt in 1694, the castle today features a museum occupying four floors with sections on the nobility and the peasants. On the grounds are a noted restaurant, walking paths, and a lake for fishing and rowing. *Skuderup, tel. 0411-40012. Admission: SKr10 adults, SKr2 children. Open May–Sept., Tues.–Sun. 11–5; Sept.–Christmas and Mar.–May, Wed.–Sun. 11–5. Closed Christmas–Mar. 1.*

On your return trip to Ystad on E14, you might want to turn left at Skårby and drive about 56 kilometers (35 miles) north to **⑪ Sövdeborg Slott** (Sövdeborg Castle). Built in the 16th century and restored in the mid-1840s, the castle consists of three two-story brick buildings and a four-story-high crenellated corner tower. The Stensal (Stone Hall), with its impressive stuccowork ceiling is the main attraction. *Sjöbo, tel. 0416-16012. Admission: SKr45. Groups by prior arrangement only.*

Time Out   If your next stop is Simrishamn, have lunch at **Trydegården** (Tryde 13, Route 19, tel. 0417/137 29), a restaurant in an elegantly renovated farmhouse just west of Tomelilla that combines the best in Skåne haute cuisine with Mediterranean flair; try the wild-boar pâté with elderberry sauce.

⑫ Follow Route 12 until you reach **Simrishamn** on the coast, a bustling fishing village of 25,000 that swells to many times that number during the summer. Built in the mid-1100s, this picturesque town of cobblestoned streets is lined with tiny brick houses covered with white stucco. The medieval St. Nicolai's Church, which dominates the town's skyline, was once a landmark for local sailors. Inside are models of sailing ships.

⑬ Glimmingehus (Glimminge House), located about 10 kilometers (6 miles) southwest of Simrishhamn off Route 410, is Scandinavia's best-preserved medieval stronghold. Built between 1499 and 1505 to defend the region against invaders, this late-Gothic castle was lived in only briefly. The walls are 2½ meters (8 feet) thick at the base, tapering to 2 meters (6½ feet) at the top of the 26-meter (85-foot)-high building. On the grounds are a small museum and a theater. There are concerts and lectures throughout the summer and a medieval festival at the end of August. *Hammenhög, tel. 0414/30289. Admission: SKr20 adults, SKr5 children under 12. Open Apr., May, Sept. 9–5; June–Aug. 10–6.*

On your way to Kristianstad you might want to stop off at **⑭ Kristinehov,** a castle located about 2 kilometers (1 mile) north of Andrarum. Known as the pink castle, Kristinehov was built in 1740 by Countess Christina Piper in the late Caroline style. Open to the public during the summer, the castle has a hunting museum, exhibits, extensive paths, a children's playground, and safari tours in a protected wildlife area with boars and stags. Check the schedule for outdoor summer concerts. *Andrarum, tel. 0417/26110. Admission: SKr15 adults, SKr8 children ages 7–15. Open May 1–June 30 and Aug. 19–Sept. 30, weekends 11–5 and by arrangement; July 1–Aug. 18, Tues.–Sun. 11–5.*

⑮ **Kristianstad** was founded by Danish King Christian IV in 1614 as a fortified town to keep the Swedes at bay. Its former ramparts and moats are today wide, tree-lined boulevards. **Holy Trinity Church,** consecrated in 1628, is an excellent example of so-called Christian IV–style architecture.

⑯ About 10 kilometers (6 miles) northeast of Kristianstad is **Bäckaskog Slott** (Bäckaskog Castle), located on a strip of land between two lakes. Originally founded as a monastery by a French religious order in the 13th century, it was turned into a fortified castle by Danish noblemen during the 16th century and later appropriated by the Swedish government and used as a residence for the cavalry. The castle was a favorite of the Swedish royalty until 1900. *Fjälkinge, tel. 044/53250. Admission: SKr20 adults, SKr8 children under 12. Open May 15– Aug. 15, daily 10–5; open to groups off-season by prior arrangement.*

⑰ **Ronneby,** a spa town 85 kilometers (53 miles) east of Kristianstad on Route 66, has a picturesque waterfall and rapids called **Djupadal,** where a river runs through a cleft in the rock just 5 feet wide but 50 feet deep. There are boat trips on the river each summer.

⑱ A little farther along the coast is **Karlskrona,** a small city built on the mainland and five nearby islands. It achieved great notoriety in 1981, when a Soviet submarine ran aground a short distance from its naval base. The town was laid out in the Baroque style on the orders of Karl XI in 1679. In 1790 it was severely damaged by fire. Its **Admiralitetskyrkan** (Admiralty Church) is Sweden's oldest wooden church, and two other churches, **Holy Trinity** and **Frederiks,** were designed by the 17th-century architect Nicodemus Tessin. **Arsenal Museet** (the Arsenal Museum), dating from 1732, is the oldest museum in Sweden, detailing the history of the country's navy. *Admiralitetsslatten, tel. 0455/83490. Admission: SKr10. Open daily 9–8.*

⑲ If you follow E66 north for 82 kilometers (51 miles), you'll reach the attractive coastal town of **Kalmar.** Opposite the Baltic island of Öland, the town is dominated by the imposing **Kalmar Slott,** Sweden's best-preserved Rennaissance castle, part of which dates from the 12th century. Here in 1397 Sweden, Norway, and Denmark signed the Kalmar Union, which lasted until 1521, when King Gustav Wasa rebuilt the castle. The living rooms, chapel, and dungeon can be visited. The castle now houses **Kalmar Läns Museum** (Kalmar District Museum), which has good archaeological and ethnographic collections. *Skeppsbrogatan, tel. 0480/15350. Admission: SKr25. Open daily 10–4.*

The **Kronan Museet** in the harbor area features the remains of the royal ship *Kronan,* which sank in 1676. Consisting primarily of cannon, wood sculptures, and old coins, they were raised from the seabed in 1980. *Skeppsbrogatan, tel. 0480/15350. Admission: SKr25. Open daily 10–4.*

The limestone plateau of **Öland,** 139 kilometers (86 miles) long and 37 kilometers (23 miles) at its widest point, was first settled some 4,000 years ago. It is linked to the mainland by one of the longest bridges in Europe (6 kilometers/4 miles). Öland is fringed with fine sandy beaches and is dotted with old windmills and such archaeological remains as the massive stone walls of the 6th-century Gråborg Fortress, the 5th-century for-

tified village of Eketorp, and the medieval Borgholm Castle.
The royal family has a summer home at Solliden, on the out-
20 skirts of **Borgholm,** the principal town. In spring and fall,
Öland is a way station for hundreds of species of migrating
birds.

Tour 2: The Kingdom of Crystal

An hour or so west of Kalmar off Route 25, scattered among the
rocky woodlands of Småland province, are isolated villages
whose names are bywords for quality when it comes to fine
crystal glassware. In the streets of Kosta, Orrefors, Boda, and
Strombergshyttan, red-painted cottages surround the actual
factories, which resemble large barns. The region is the home
of 16 major glassworks, and visitors may see glass being blown
and crystal being etched by skilled craftspeople. *Hyttsil* evenings are also arranged, a revival of an old tradition in which
Baltic herring (*sil*) is cooked in the glass furnaces of the *hytt*
(literally "cabin" but meaning the works). Most glassworks also
have shops selling seconds at a discount.

Fifteen kilometers (9 miles) north of Route 25 on Route 28 is
21 **Kosta Glasbruk,** the oldest works, dating from 1742 and named
for its founders, Anders *K*oskull and Georg Bogislaus *Sta*el von
Holstein, two former generals. Faced with a dearth of talent
locally, they initially imported glassblowers from Bohemia.
The Kosta works pioneered the production of crystal (to qualify
for that label, glass must contain at least 24% lead oxide). *Tel.
0478/50300. Open mid-June–early Aug. Shops and museum,
open weekdays 9–6, Sat. 9–3, Sun. 9–4. Demonstrations weekdays 9–3:30.*

On Route 31, 17 kilometers (11 miles) north of Route 25 is
22 **Orrefors,** one of the best known of the glass companies. It came
on the scene late—in 1898—but set particularly high artistic
standards. The skilled workers in Orrefors dance a slow, delicate minuet as they carry the pieces of red-hot glass back and
forth, passing them from hand to hand, blowing and shaping
them. The basic procedures and tools are ancient, and the finished product is the result of unusual teamwork, from designer
to craftsman to finisher. One of Orrefors's special attractions is
a magnificent display of pieces made during the past century.
Tel. 0481/34000. Open 8–3.

23 **Boda Glasbruk,** part of the Kosta Boda company, is just off
Route 25, 42 kilometers (26 miles) west of Kalmar. *Tel. 0481/
24030. Open 8–3.*

24 Farther west on Route 25 is **Växjö,** where the **Småland Museum**
has the largest glass collection in northern Europe. *Södra
Jarnvägsgatan 2, S–35104, tel. 0470/45145. Admission:
SKr10. Open weekdays 9–4, Sat. 11–3, Sun. 1–5. Closed holidays.*

Växjö is also an important sightseeing destination for some
10,000 American visitors each year, for it was from this area
that their Swedish ancestors set sail in the 19th century. The
Emigrants' House, located in the town center, tells the story of
the migration, during which close to a million Swedes—one
quarter of the population—departed for the promised land.
The museum exhibits provide a vivid sense of the rigorous jour-

ney, and an archive room and research center allow American visitors to trace their ancestry.

What to See and Do with Children

Kulturen (the Museum of Cultural History), is both outdoor and indoor museum, featuring 20 old cottages, farms, and manor houses from southern Sweden plus an excellent collection of ceramics, textiles, weapons, and furniture. *Adelgatan, tel. 046/ 150480. Admission: SKr30 adults, children under 15 free. Open May–Sept., daily 11–5; Oct.–Apr. 12–4.*

Located on the other side of the park from Malmöhus, **Aq-va-kul** is a swimming-pool complex that offers a wide variety of bathing experiences for children and their parents, from water slides to bubble baths. *Regementsgatan 24, tel. 040/300540. Admission: SKr55 adults, SKr35 children ages 7–15, SKr20 children under 7. Open Mon., Wed. 9–9, Tues., Thurs., Fri. 9–8, weekends 9–5.*

Frasses Music Museum contains an eclectic collection of music oddities, such as self-playing barrel organs, antique accordions, children's gramophones, and the world's most complete collection of Edison phonographs. *Padar Mörksvagen 5, tel. 0414/14520. Admission: SKr10 adults, SKr3.50 children under 12. Open June–Aug., Sun. 2–6.*

About 4 miles (6 kilometers) north of Växjo, a castle ruin called **Kronobergs Slott,** built during the 1300s, lies on the edge of the Helgasjön (Holy Lake). The Småland guerilla fighter, Nils Dacke, used the castle as a base in his attacks against the Danish occupiers during the mid-1500s. You can eat waffles under the shade of birch trees or tour the lake on the toylike *Thor,* Sweden's oldest steamboat. *Tel. 0470/45145. Two boat tours offered: canal trip to Årby (SKr100 adults, SKr50 children) or round-the-lake trip (SKr75 adults, SKr35 children). Boat runs June 25–Aug. 30.*

Off the Beaten Track

On the mainland coast opposite Öland, off E66, numerous picturesque seaside towns dot the coastline, such as Pataholm, with its cobblestoned main square; Timmernabben, which is famous for its caramel factory; and Mönsterås, from which the Borgholm-bound car ferries depart. Miles of clean, attractive, and easily accessible, if windy, beaches line this strip of the coast.

Dining and Lodging

Highly recommended establishments are indicated by a star ★.

Helsingborg
Dining and Lodging
★

Grand Hotel. In one of Sweden's oldest hotels, the dining room has a long reputation for excellence, with a good selection of wines at reasonable prices. There are special rose-colored rooms for women guests. The hotel is near the railway station and ferry terminals. *Stortorget 8–12, S-251 11, tel. 042/120170, fax 042/118833. 130 rooms. Facilities: restaurant, piano bar. AE, DC, MC, V. Expensive.*
Villa Thalassa. This youth hostel has fine views over Öresund. *Dag Hammarskjölds väg, tel. 042/110384. 145 beds, 4- to 6-bed*

rooms (in winter 2-bed rooms are also available). Facilities: conference rooms. No credit cards. Inexpensive.

Kalmar **Romantik Hotel Slottshotellet.** Situated in a gracious old town
Lodging house on a quiet street, Slottshotellet bears no resemblance to a hotel from the outside. But inside, it offers a host of modern facilities. Only breakfast is served. *Slottsvägen 7, tel. 0480/ 88260, fax 0480/11993. 36 rooms with shower. AE, DC, MC, V. Expensive.*

Stadshotellet. Located in the city center, Best Western's Stadshotellet is a fairly large, Old World hotel. The main building dates from the 19th century. It features a fine restaurant. *Storgatan 14, tel. 0480/15180, fax 0480/15847. 140 rooms with bath or shower. Facilities: restaurant, Jacuzzi, disco. AE, DC, MC, V. Closed Christmas. Expensive.*

Continental. Located about 93 meters (100 yards) from the train station, the Continental is a fairly basic but comfortable family hotel. Only breakfast is served. *Larmgatan 10, tel. 0480/ 15140. 40 rooms, most with bath or shower. AE, DC, MC, V. Closed Christmas. Inexpensive.*

Lund **Fiskaregatan.** Chefs Rikart Nilsson and Lars Fogelkous believe
Dining in getting to know their guests and in taking an unconventional approach to do so. One example is their "gourmet evening" with nine courses—interrupted by a stroll around the town at the halfway stage in April and October (no fixed date). A specialty is stuffed breast of pheasant. *Lilla Fiskaregatan 14, tel. 046/151620. Reservations advised. Dress: casual. AE, DC, MC, V. Moderate.*

Lodging **Grand.** This elegant red-stone Best Western hotel is located close to the railway station in a pleasant square. *Bantorget 1, S–221 04, tel. 046/117010, fax 046/147301. 87 rooms. Facilities: restaurant with vegetarian menu by arrangement, conference rooms, sauna. AE, DC, MC, V. Very Expensive.*

Concordia. Located in a 100-year-old building in the city center, this Sweden Hotels property was completely renovated recently. *Stålbrogatan 1, S–222 24, tel. 046/135050, fax 046/ 137422. 50 rooms. Facilities: rooms for nonsmokers and the disabled. AE, DC, MC, V. Moderate.*

Djingis Khan. This English-style hotel has a pleasing aspect and is situated in a quiet part of town. *Margarethevägen 7, S– 222 40, tel. 046/140060, fax 046/143626. 55 rooms. Facilities: rooms for allergy sufferers and the disabled, conference rooms, sauna, solarium, gymnasium, bicycles for rent (SKr25). AE, DC, MC, V. Moderate.*

Hotel Lundia. Only 100 meters (330 feet) from the train station, Best Western's Hotel Lundia is ideally located for families who want to be within walking distance of the city center. Built in 1968, the modern four-story square building has transparent glass walls on the ground floor. *Knut den stores gata 2, Box 1136, S–221 04, tel. 046/124140, fax 046/141995. 97 rooms. Facilities: restaurant, nightclub, garage. AE, DC, MC, V. Moderate.*

STF Vandrahem Tåget. So named because of its proximity to the train station (*tåget* means "train"), this youth hostel faces a park in central Lund. *Bjerredsparken, Vävareg. 14, S–22 37 Lund, tel. 046/142820. 108 beds. No credit cards. Inexpensive.*

Malmö **Årstiderna.** Marie and Wilhelm Pieplow's restaurant (the name
Dining means "The Seasons" in Swedish) has a pleasant, intimate at-
★ mosphere. It is known for large portions and a good medium-

priced wine list. *Grynbodsgatan 9, tel. 040/230910. Reservations advised. Jacket and tie required. AE, DC, MC, V. Expensive.*

Johan P. This extremely popular restaurant specializes in seafood and shellfish prepared in Swedish and Continental styles. White walls and white tablecloths give it the air of an elegant French restaurant, which contrasts with the generally casual dress of the customers. An outdoor section opens during the summer. *Saluhallen, Lilla Torg, tel. 040/971818. Dress: casual. Reservations advised. AE, DC, MC, V. Expensive.*

Kockska Krogen. Located in the cellar of a 16th-century house, one of the few in Malmö, this popular restaurant serves internationally influenced Swedish food. Glassware, cutlery, and decor are calculated to re-create a 16th-century atmosphere. *Stortorget, tel. 040/70320. Reservations advised. Dress: casual. AE, DC, MC, V. Expensive.*

La Mélisse. This friendly little restaurant usually gives extremely good value. The special menu, *Kvartersmenyn*, is an excellent bet, with four courses for SKr200. *Foreningsgatan 37, tel. 040/116816. Reservations advised. Dress: casual. AE, DC, MC, V. Expensive.*

Valvet. Centrally located in the St. Jörgen hotel, this restaurant was expanded in late 1992 from the cellar so that it now also occupies the balcony overlooking the lobby. Although the wine list has been deemphasized, the restaurant still offers Swedish cuisine with a French accent and excels at grilled meats and fish. *Stora Nygatan 35, tel. 040/77300. Reservations advised. Dress: casual. AE, DC, MC, V. Expensive.*

Anno 1900. Here is a curiosity: a charming little restaurant located in a former working-class area of Malmö. It is a popular local luncheon place with a cheerful outdoor garden terrace for summer eating. Try the *dagens rätt* (daily special), which may be meat or fish. *Norra Bulltoftavägen 7, tel. 040/184747. Reservations required. Dress: casual. AE, MC, V. Moderate.*

B & B. It stands for *Butik och Bar* (Bar Shop) because of its location in the market hall in central Malmö. There's always good home cooking, and sometimes even entertainment at the piano. The restaurant is extremely popular with a young crowd on weekday nights. *Saluhallen, Lilla Torg, tel. 040/127120. Reservations advised. Dress: casual. AE, DC, MC, V. Moderate.*

Dining and Lodging
★ **Mäster Johan Hotel.** The unpretentious exterior of this new Best Western hotel disguises a plush and meticulously crafted interior. The 1990 top-to-bottom redesign of a 19th-century building, with the focal point an Italianate atrium breakfast room, is unusually personal in tone for a chain hotel. The rooms are impressive, with exposed Dutch brick walls, recessed lighting, oak floors, Oriental carpets, and French cherry-wood furnishings. *Mäster Johansgatan 13, tel. 040–71560, fax 040/127242. 70 rooms. Facilities: 24-hour room service, breakfast room, sauna. AE, DC, MC, V. Expensive.*

SAS Royal. This modern luxury hotel has rooms in four styles: Scandinavian, Oriental, Italian, and Grand. *Östergatan 10, S–211 25, tel. 040/239200, fax 040/112840. 221 rooms. Facilities: restaurant. AE, DC, MC, V. Expensive.*

Sheraton. Ultramodern, in steel and glass, the Sheraton opened in 1989. *Triangeln 2, S–200 10, tel. 040/74000, fax 040/232020. 214 rooms. Facilities: restaurant, bar, fitness center, sauna. AE, DC, MC, V. Expensive.*

★ **Baltzar.** A turn-of-the-century house in central Malmö has been converted into a small, comfortable hotel. *Södergatan 20, tel. 040/72005. 41 rooms. AE, DC, MC, V. Inexpensive.*

Prize Hotel. Centrally located in the newly renovated Malmö Harbor area, this spanking-new hotel features a large front entrance and lobby atrium inventively created out of a narrow strip of empty space between two buildings. The rooms, though small, are comfortable and equipped with cable TV, telephone, and radio. This low-overhead, minimal-service hotel doesn't add a surcharge to the telephone bill. You get exactly what you pay for. *Carlsgatan 10C, tel. 046/40112511. 109 rooms. Facilities: breakfast room. AE, DC, MC, V. Inexpensive.*

Öland
Dining and Lodging

Halltorps Gästgiveri. This manor house from the 17th century has modernized duplex rooms decorated in Swedish landscape tones and an excellent restaurant. *S–38792 Borgholm, tel. 0485/85000, fax 0485/85001. 35 rooms. Facilities: restaurant, sauna, tennis court. AE, DC, MC, V. Moderate.*

Växjö
Lodging

SARA Statt. A conveniently located, traditional hotel, SARA Statt is popular with tour groups. The building dates from the early 19th century, but the rooms themselves are modern, and the hotel has a resident piano bar and an à la carte restaurant. *Kungsgatan 6, tel. 0470/13400, fax 0470/44837. 130 rooms with bath or shower. AE, DC, MC, V. Closed Christmas Eve. Expensive.*

Esplanad. Centrally located, the Esplanad is a small, family hotel offering basic amenities; it has recently been renovated. Only breakfast is served. *Norra Esplanaden 21A, tel. 0470/22580, fax 0470/26226. 27 rooms, most with shower. MC, V. Closed Christmas and New Year's Day. Inexpensive.*

Dalarna: The Folklore District

Dalarna is considered to be the most typically Swedish of all the country's 24 provinces, a place of forests, mountains, and red-painted wooden farmhouses and cottages by the shores of pristine, sun-dappled lakes. It is the favorite site for Midsummer celebrations, in which Swedes don folk costumes and dance to fiddle and accordion music around maypoles garlanded with wildflowers.

Dalarna played a key role in the history of the nation. It was from here that Gustav Vasa recruited the army that freed the country from Danish domination in the 16th century.

The region is also important artistically, both for its tradition of naïve religious decoration and for producing two of the nation's best-loved painters, Anders Zorn (1860–1920) and Carl Larsson (1853–1915), and one of its favorite poets, the melancholy, mystical Dan Andersson, who sought inspiration in the remote camps of the old charcoal burners deep in the forest.

Important Addresses and Numbers

Tourist Information
There are tourist offices in the following towns and villages: Falun (Stora Torget, tel. 023/83637), **Leksand** (Norsgatan, tel. 0247/80300), **Ludvika** (Sporthallen, tel. 0240/86050), **Mora e**

(Ångbåtskajn, tel. 0250/26550), **Rättvik** (Torget, tel. 0248/10910), and **Sälen** (Sälen Centrum, tel. 0280/20250).

Emergencies For **emergencies,** dial 90000, **Falun Hospital** (tel. 023/82900) or **Mora Hospital** (tel. 0250/25000).

Pharmacies There are no late-night pharmacies in the area, but doctors called to emergencies can supply medicines. **Vasen** pharmacy in Falun (Åsagatan, tel. 023/20000) is open until 7 PM.

Arriving and Departing by Plane

Airports and Airlines Dalarna is served by two airports: **Dala** at **Borlänge** and **Mora** Airport. There are regular daily **Linjeflyg** (tel. 0243/39090) flights from Stockholm to Dala Airport (seven each weekday, two on Saturday, five on Sunday). Mora Airport is served by the problem-plagued private company **Salair** (tel. 0250/30175), with four flights daily from Stockholm.

Between the Airport and Town Dala Airport is 8 kilometers (5 miles) from Borlänge, where there are half-hourly bus connections to Falun, 26 kilometers (17 miles) away. Mora Airport is 10 kilometers (6 miles) from town.

By Bus There are buses every half hour from Dala Airport to Borlänge. The price of the trip is SKr12. From Mora Airport there are buses three times daily into town. The fare is also SKr12.

By Taxi A taxi from Dala Airport to Borlänge costs around SKr90, to Falun approximately SKr200. A taxi to town from Mora Airport costs SKr89. Taxis are best ordered in advance through your travel agent or when you make an airline booking.

Arriving and Departing by Car, Train, and Bus

By Car From Stockholm it is 275 kilometers (170 miles) on Highway 70 leads to Borlänge. From Göteborg the drive is 438 kilometers (272 miles): E3 to Örebro and Route 60 north from there to Borlänge.

By Train There is regular daily train service from Stockholm to both Mora (tel. 0250/11619) and Falun (tel. 023/15830).

By Bus Buses run only on weekends. For information, call **Eurolines** (also known as Continentbus, tel. 08/234810).

Getting Around

By Car **Avis** has offices in **Borlänge** (tel. 0243/87080) and Mora (tel. 0250/16711). **Hertz** has an office at **Dala** Airport (tel. 0243/39807) and agents in **Falun** (tel. 023/18440) and **Mora** (tel. 0250/11760). **InterRent** and **Europcar** have offices in **Borlänge** (tel. 0243/19050) and **Falun** (tel. 023/18850).

Guided Tours

The tourist office in **Falun** can arrange one-day guided coach tours in English of Falun and the region around Lake Siljan. The guide costs around SKr850, the coach, with driver, SKr4,200 (coaches can seat around 50 persons). Other tourist offices can arrange tours or advise on public transport.

Exploring Dalarna

Numbers in the margin correspond to points of interest on the Dalarna map.

❶ **Falun** is the traditional capital of Dalarna, though in recent years the nondescript railway town of Borlänge has been growing in importance. Falun's history has always been very much bound to its copper mine. This has been worked since 1230 by Stora Kopparbergs Bergslags AB (today just *Stora*), which claims to be the oldest limited company in the world. Its greatest period of prosperity was the 17th century, when it financed Sweden's "Age of Greatness," and the country became the dominant Baltic power. In 1650, Stora produced a record 3,067 tons of copper; probably as a result of such rapid extraction, 37 years later its mine shafts caved in. Fortunately, the accident was on Midsummer's Day when most of the miners were off duty, and as a result no one was killed. Today the major part of the mine is an enormous hole in the ground that has become Falun's principal tourist attraction, with its own museum, **Stora Museum.** *Tel. 023/114750. Admission: SKr50, including entry to mining museum; admission to museum alone, SKr5. Open May–Aug., daily 10–4:30. Sept.–Apr., daily 12:30–4:30.*

❷ At **Sundborn,** a small village east of Falun off Route 80, you can visit **Carl Larsson Gården,** the lakeside home of the Swedish artist Carl Larsson, its turn-of-the-century fittings and furnishings carefully preserved. Larsson was an excellent draftsman who painted idyllic scenes from his own family's apparently unceasingly happy and well-adjusted life. His grandchildren and great-grandchildren are on hand to show you the house and a selection of his paintings, which owe much to local folk-art traditions. *Tel. in summer, 023/60053; in winter, 023/60069. Admission: SKr45. Open May 1–Sept. 30, Mon.–Sat. 10–5, Sun. 1–5. Call ahead to arrange for off-season visits.*

The real center of Darlana folklore is the area around **Lake Siljan,** the largest of the 6,000 lakes in the province. From
❸ Falun take Route 80 north to **Rättvik,** a pleasant town of timbered houses on the eastern tip of Lake Siljan surrounded by wooded slopes. Rättvik is a center for local folklore, and several shops sell handmade articles and produce from the surrounding region.

Every year hundreds of people wearing traditional costumes arrive in longboats to attend Midsummer services at the town's 14th-century church, **Rättvik Kyrka,** which stands on a promontory stretching into the lake. Its interior contains some fine examples of local naïve religious artwork.

Only a short distance away, the open-air museum **Rättvik Gammalgård** gives the visitor an idea of the peasant lifestyles of bygone days. *Admission free; guided tour: SKr10. Open mid-June–mid-Aug., Mon.–Sat. 11–6, Sun. 12–6.*

❹ South of Rättvik on Route 70 is **Leksand,** on which thousands of tourists converge each year for the Midsummer celebrations and, in July, for *Himlaspelet* (The Play of the Way that Leads to Heaven), a traditional musical with an all-local cast, staged in the open near the town's church. It is easy to get seats for this; the local tourist office will have details.

Dalarna

Leksand is also an excellent vantage point from which to watch the "church boat" races on Siljan. These vessels are claimed to be successors to the Viking longboats and were traditionally used to take peasants from outlying regions to church on Sunday. On Midsummer Eve, the longboats, crewed by people in folk costumes, skim the lake. Consult the local tourist office for dates and times.

In the hills around Leksand and elsewhere near Siljan you will find the *fäbodar*, small settlements in the forest where cattle were taken to graze during the summer. Less idyllic memories of bygone days are conjured up by **Käringberget,** a 720-foot-high mountain north of town where alleged witches were burned to death in the 17th century.

After Leksand, take the small road toward Mora along the southern shores of Siljan, passing through the small communities of Siljansnäs and Björka, before stopping at **Gesunda,** a pleasant little village at the foot of a mountain (with a chair lift) from which there are unbeatable views over the lake.

It is also worth paying a quick visit to **Sollerön,** a large island connected to the mainland by bridge, from which there are fine views of the mountains surrounding Siljan and several excellent bathing places. The church here dates from 1775.

⑤ Mora, a pleasant, relaxed lakeside town of 20,000, was the home of Anders Zorn (1860–1920), Sweden's leading Impressionist painter, who lived in Stockholm and Paris before returning to his roots here, painting the local scenes for which he is now famous. His former private residence, a large, sumptuous

home designed with great originality and taste by the painter himself, has retained the same exquisite furnishings, paintings, and decor as it had when he lived there with his wife. The garden, also a Zorn creation, is open to the public. Next door, the **Zorn Museet** (Zorn Museum), built 19 years after the painter's death, contains many of his best works. *Vasagatan, tel. 0250/16560. Zorn Home: Admission: SKr20. Open Mon.–Sat. 12:30–5; Sun. 1–5. Museet: Admission: SKr15. Open Mon.–Sat. 10–5, Sun. 1–5.*

South of town, near the lake, you'll find **Zorns Gammalgård,** a fine collection of old wooden houses from local farms, brought here and donated to the town by the artist.

Mora is also the finishing point for the 90-kilometer (53-mile) *Vasalopp,* the world's longest ski race, running from Sälen, a ski resort close to the Norwegian border. The race commemorates a fundamental piece of Swedish history: the successful attempt by Gustav Vasa in 1521 to rally local peasants to the cause of ridding Sweden of Danish occupation. Vasa, only 21 years old, arrived in Mora and described to the locals in graphic detail a bloodbath of Swedish noblemen ordered by the Danish King Christian in Stortorget in Stockholm. Unfortunately, no one believed him and the dispirited Vasa was forced to abandon his attempts at insurrection and take off on either skis or snow shoes for Norway, where he hoped to evade Christian and go into exile. After he left, confirmation reached Mora of the Stockholm bloodbath, and the peasants, already discontented with Danish rule, relented, sending two skiers after Vasa to tell him they would join his cause. The two men caught up with the young nobleman at Sälen. They returned with him to Mora, where an army was recruited. Vasa marched south, defeating the Danes to become king and the founder of modern Sweden. The race, held on the first Sunday in March, attracts thousands of competitors from all over the world. There is a spectacular mass start at Sälen before the field thins out. The finish is eagerly awaited in Mora, though in recent years the number of spectators has fallen, thanks to the often frigid temperatures and the fact that the race is now usually televised live.

From Mora, take Route 70 back along the eastern shore of Siljan to Rättvik and Falun, leaving it at Färnäs to make an excursion to **Nusnäs,** the lakeside village where the small, brightly red-painted wooden Dala horses are made. These were originally carved by the peasants of Dalarna as toys for their children, but their popularity rapidly spread with the advent of tourism in the 20th century. Mass production of the little horses started at Nusnäs in 1928. In 1939 they achieved international popularity after being shown at the New York World's Fair. Since then they have become a Swedish symbol. Today some of the smaller versions available in Stockholm's tourist shops are even made in East Asia. However, at Nusnäs you can watch the genuine article being made, now with the aid of modern machinery but still painted by hand. Naturally you'll be able to buy some to take home.

Directly east of Falun, on the coast of the Gulf of Bothnia, is the port town of **Gävle,** which achieved dubious renown at the time of the Chernobyl nuclear accident in 1986 by briefly becoming the most radioactive place in Europe. A freak storm dumped extra-large amounts of fallout from the Soviet Union on the town. For a while farmers had to burn newly harvested hay and

keep their cattle inside. However, the scare soon passed and today one can visit the town in perfect safety. Gävle is worth visiting for two relatively new museums.

Joe Hill Museet (the Joe Hill Museum), dedicated to the Swedish emigrant who went on to become America's first well-known protest singer and union organizer, is located in Hill's former home in the oldest section of Gävle. Once a poor, working-class district, ironically this is now the most picturesque and highly sought-after residential part of town, and nearby are some art studios and handicrafts workshops. The museum is furnished in the same style as when Hill lived here. Though it contains very few of his possessions, it does display Hill's prison letters. The house itself bears witness to the poor conditions that forced so many Swedes to emigrate to the United States (an estimated 850,000 between 1840 and 1900). When his mother died in 1902, Joe and his brother sold the house and used the money to emigrate to the United States. Hill, whose original Swedish name was Joel Hägglund, became a founder of the International Workers of the World and was executed for the murder of a Salt Lake City grocer in 1914, but he protested his innocence right up to the end. *Nedre Bergsgatan 28, tel. 026/613425. Admission: SKr10. Open 10–5.*

Also in Gävle you will find the **Skogsmuseet Silvanum** (Silvanum Forestry Museum). Its name means "The Forest" in Latin, and when it was inaugurated in 1961, it was the first such museum in the world; it remains the largest. The museum provides an in-depth picture of the forestry industry in Sweden, still the backbone of Sweden's industrial wealth. Trees cover more than 50% of the country's surface area. Forest products account for 20% of Swedish exports. Silvanum includes a forest botanical park and an arboretum that contain examples of every tree and bush growing in Sweden. *Kungsbäcksvägen 32, tel. 026/614100 or 026/615570. Admission free. Open Tues.–Sun. 10–4.*

What to See and Do with Children

Near Gesunda, **Tomteland** (Santaland) somewhat unconvincingly claims to be the home of Santa Claus, or Father Christmas. It features Santa's workshop and kiosks, where you can buy toys. There are rides in horse-drawn carriages in summer and sleighs in winter. *Gesundaberget Sollerön, S–79200 Sollerön-Gesunda, tel. 0250/29000. Admission: SKr60. Open mid-June–mid-Aug. and Dec.*

Shopping

Apart from its little red wooden horses (*see* Nusnäs, *above*), Dalarna offers knitwear and handicrafts, available in *hemslöjd* (handicrafts) shops throughout the region.

Sports

All the region's tourist offices can supply details of **skiing** vacations. The principal ski resort is Sälen, starting point for the Vasalopp. **Canoes** and **kayaks** can also be rented at most of the lakeside campgrounds.

Dining and Lodging

Do not expect too much in Dalarna. Traditionally, visitors to the area—many from elsewhere in Scandinavia or from Germany—make use either of the region's many well-equipped campsites or of *stugbyar* (small villages of log cabins, with cooking facilities), usually set idyllically by lakesides or in forest clearings.

Highly recommended establishments are indicated by a star★.

Falun
Dining and Lodging

Grand. Now part of the Reso chain, this conventional, modern hotel has fine light rooms and is close to the town center. *Trotzgatan 9–11, S–791 71, tel. 023/18700, fax 023/14143. 183 rooms. Facilities: restaurant, bar, rooms for allergy sufferers and the disabled, conference center, gymnasium, sauna, pool, solarium. AE, DC, MC, V. Expensive.*

Birgittagården. This small hotel, 8 kilometers (5 miles) out of town, run by the religious order Stiftelsen Dalarnas Birgitta Systrar (the Dalarna Sisters of Birgitta), is alcohol-free and set in a fine park. It is open year-round. *Uddnäs Hosjös S–79146, tel. 023/32147 fax 023/32471. 25 rooms. Facilities: restaurant, rooms for the disabled, conference rooms. No credit cards. Inexpensive.*

Lodging
★

Bergmästaren. This is one of Dalarna's best hotels. Situated in the middle of town, it is decorated according to local custom and was completely refurbished in 1985. It is open year-round. *Bergskolegrand 7, S–791 26, tel. 023/63600, fax 023/22524. 90 rooms. Facilities: breakfast, gymnasium, sauna, solarium, conference center, parking with engine warmers. AE, DC, MC, V. Expensive.*

Scandic. This ultramodern, spanking-new Legolike high-rise hotel is located in the expanded Lugnet sports and recreation center outside Falun, where the 1993 World Skiing Championships took place. The comfortable, modern rooms have good views. *Svärdsjögatan 51, 791 31 Falun, tel. 023/221 60, fax 023/12845. Facilities: restaurant, snack bar, pub, pool, sauna, exercise room, conference rooms. AE, DC, MC, V. Moderate.*

Falun. Ulf Henriksson and Bernt Brick run this small, friendly but bland-looking hotel just 1,300 feet from the railway station. *Centrumhuset, Trotzgatan 16 S–791 71, tel. 023/29180. 25 rooms, 15 with bath/shower. Facilities: breakfast. AE, DC, MC, V. Inexpensive.*

Mora
Dining and Lodging

Mora. A pleasant little hotel, situated in the center of town, 5 kilometers (3 miles) from the airport, the Mora is part of the Best Western chain. *Strandgatan 12, S–792 01, tel. 0250/11750, fax 0250/18981. 138 rooms. Facilities: restaurant, bar, rooms for nonsmokers, conference rooms, sauna, pool, game room. AE, DC, MC, V. Expensive.*

King's Inn. This modern, reasonably sized hotel is 2 kilometers (1 mile) from the center of town and only 100 meters (330 feet) from the Mora train station. *Kristeneberg, S–792 01, tel. 0250/15070, fax 0250/17078. 47 rooms. Facilities: restaurant, rooms for the disabled, conference rooms, gymnasium, sauna, pool, solarium. AE, DC, MC, V. Moderate.*

Moraparken. This modern hotel sits in a park by the banks of the Dala River, not far from the center of town. *Parkgarten 1, S–79201, tel. 0250/17800. 75 rooms. Facilities: restaurant; rooms for the disabled, nonsmokers, and allergy sufferers;*

conference rooms; sauna; indoor pool; tennis courts; jogging tracks; beach; fishing. AE, DC, MC, V. Inexpensive.

Siljan. Part of the Sweden Hotel group, this small, modern hotel affords views over the lake. *Moragatan 6, S–79200, tel. 0250/13000, fax 0250/13098. 46 rooms. Facilities: restaurant, rooms for nonsmokers and the disabled, sauna, conference rooms. AE, DC, MC, V. Inexpensive.*

Norrland

The north of Sweden, Norrland, is a place of wide-open spaces where you can "listen to the silence." Golden eagles soar above snowcapped crags, huge salmon fight their way up wild, tumbling rivers, rare orchids bloom in Arctic heathland, and wild rhododendrons splash the land with color.

In the summer the sun shines at midnight above the Artic Circle. In the winter it hardly shines at all. The weather changes with bewildering rapidity. A June day can dawn sunny and bright; then the skies may darken and the temperature drop to around zero as a snow squall blows in. Just as suddenly, the sun comes out again and the temperature starts to rise.

Here live the once-nomadic Lapps, or Same, as they prefer to be known, generally smaller and darker than Swedes, with high cheekbones and slightly slanting eyes. They carefully guard what remains of their identity, while doing their best to inform the public about their culture. Many of them still earn their living herding reindeer, but as open space shrinks, the younger generation is turning in greater numbers toward the attractions of the cities. There are 17,000 Same in Sweden. Often the Same exhibit a sad resignation to the gradual disappearance of their way of life as the modern world makes incursions. This is best expressed in one of their folk poems: "Our memory, the memory of us vanishes/We forget and we are forgotten."

Yet there is a growing struggle, especially among younger Same, to maintain their identity and, thanks to their traditional closeness to nature, they are now finding allies in Sweden's Green movement. They refer to the north of Scandinavia as *Sapmi*, their spiritual and physical home, making no allowance for the different countries that now rule it.

Nearly all Swedish Same now live in ordinary houses, having abandoned the *kåta* (Lapp wigwam), and some even herd their reindeer with helicopters. Efforts are now being made to protect and preserve their language, which is totally unlike Swedish and bears much more resemblance to Finnish. The language reflects their closeness to nature. The word *goadnil*, for example, means "a quiet part of the river, free of current, near the bank or beside a rock."

Nowadays many Same depend on the tourist industry for their living, selling their artifacts, such as expertly carved bone-handled knives, wooden cups and bowls, bark bags, silver jewelry, and leather straps embroidered with pewter thread.

The trouble with Norrland, from the traveler's point of view, is its size. It stretches 1,000 kilometers (620 miles) from south to north, makes up more than half of Sweden, and is about the size of Britain. On the west there are mountain ranges, to the east a

wild and rocky coastline, and in between boundless forests and moorland. Its towns are often little more than a group of houses along a street, built around a local industry such as mining, forestry, or hydropower utilities. However, thanks to Sweden's excellent transportation infrastructure, Norrland is no longer so inaccessible and even a traveler with a limited time schedule should be able to get at least a taste of it. Its wild spaces are ideal for open-air holidays. Hiking, climbing, canoeing, river rafting, and fishing are all popular in summer; skiing, skating, and dogsledding in winter.

A word of warning: In summer mosquitoes are a constant nuisance, worse even than in other parts of Sweden, so be sure to bring plenty of repellent. Fall is perhaps the best season to visit Norrland. Roads are well maintained, but you should watch out for *guppar* (holes) following thaws. Highways are generally traffic-free, but keep an eye out for the occasional reindeer or two.

Important Addresses and Numbers

Tourist Information Norrbottens Turistråd covers the whole area (Sandviksgatan 53, Luleå, tel. 0920/94070). There are tourist offices at **Kiruna** (Hjalmar Lundbohmsvägen 42, tel. 0980/18880), **Luleå** (Rådstugatan 9, tel. 0920/93746), and **Jokkmokk** (Stortoget 4, tel. 0971/12140).

Emergencies For **emergencies** dial 90,000. You can also call **Kiruna Health Center** (Thulegatan 29, tel. 0980/173000), **Luleå district nurse** (emergency tel. 0920/71400), and **Jokkmokk Health Center** (Lappstavägen 9, tel. 0971/11350).

Pharmacies There are no late-night pharmacies in the area, but doctors called to emergencies can supply medicines. The pharmacy at Kiruna Hospital (Thulegatan 29, tel. 0980/12220) is open until 5 PM.

Arriving and Departing by Plane

There are two non-stop SAS flights a day from Stockholm to **Kiruna Airport** (tel. 0980/12410) and three additional flights via Luleå. Check SAS (tel. 0980/83100) for specific times.

Between the Airport and Town It is 9 kilometers (6 miles) from the airport to the center of Kiruna. **Buses** connect with the flights from Stockholm. The fare is SKr25. A **taxi** from the airport to the center of Kiruna costs SKr90.

Arriving and Departing by Train

The best and cheapest way to get to Kiruna is to take the 5:40 PM sleeper from Stockholm on a Tuesday or Wednesday, when the fare is reduced to SKr554 single. The regular one-way price is SKr876, double for return. You arrive at 11:26 AM the next day.

Getting Around

By Car In Kiruna **Avis** has a branch at Industrivägen 10 (tel. 0980/16060). **Hertz** is at Industrivägen 5 (tel. 0980/19000), and **InterRent** and **Europcar** are at Växlaregatan 20 (tel. 0980/14365).

Guided Tours

Numerous guided tours are available through the various tourist offices. For example, a two-hour tour of a local iron mine costs SKr75. A 45-minute flight in a seaplane taking off from a nearby lake costs SKr520. Tours of Same villages and holy places are available. Contact the **Swedish Same Association** (Brogatan 5, S–902 48, Umeå, tel. 090/141180) or **Sameturism AB** (tel. 0980/83388) for up-to-date information.

Exploring Norrland

Norrland is best discovered from a base in Kiruna, located in the center of the alpine region that has been described as Europe's last wilderness. You can tour south and west to the mountains and national parks, east and south to Sami villages, and farther south still to Baltic coastal settlements.

Tour 1: Kiruna

Numbers in the margin correspond to points of interest on the Norrland map.

❶ **Kiruna** is the most northerly city in Sweden, spread over a wide area between two mountains largely composed of iron ore, which are its raison d'être. They are called Luossavaara and Kirunavaara. The city, named for the latter, was established in 1890 as a mining town, but true prosperity came only with the building of the railway to the Baltic port of Luleå and the northern Norwegian port of Narvik in 1902. Kiruna has the world's largest underground iron mine, with reserves estimated at 500 million tons. Automated mining technology has largely replaced the traditional miner in the Kirunavaara underground mines, which are some 500 kilometers (310 miles) long.

Kiruna lies at the eastern end of Lake Luossajärvi and with 26,000 inhabitants is one of Norrland's largest cities. It is, at 1,670 feet above sea level, the highest city in Sweden, with an estimated fifth of its population Finnish immigrants who came to work in the mine.

Because the municipality is spread over such a large area, Kiruna is often called "the world's biggest city" (it covers the equivalent of half the area of Switzerland). It is also a city of remarkable contrasts, from the seemingly pitch-black, months-long winter to the summer, when the sun never sets and it is actually possible to play round-the-clock golf for 50 days at a stretch. Here, too, the ancient Same culture exists side by side with the high-tech culture of cutting-edge satellite research. In recent years the city has diversified its economy and now houses the Esrange Space Range, which sends rockets and balloons to probe the upper reaches of the earth's atmosphere, and the Swedish Institute of Space Physics, which has pioneered the investigation of the phenomenon of the northern lights. The city received a boost in 1984 with the opening of *Nordkalottvägen*, a 170-kilometer (105-mile) -long road to Narvik.

One of Kiruna's few buildings of interest is **Kiruna Kyrka** (Kiruna Church), on Gruvvägen, near the center of the city. It was built in 1921, its inspiration a blending of a Sami kåta with a

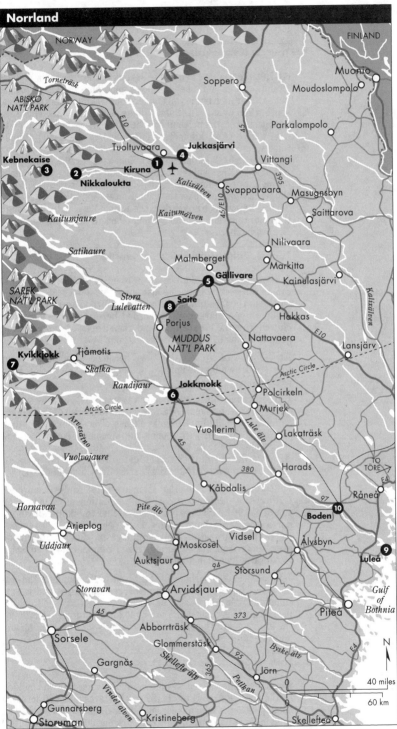

Norrland

Swedish stave church. The altarpiece is by Prince Eugen (1863–1947), Sweden's painter prince.

Tour 2: Kebnekaise

At 7,000 feet above sea level, **Kebnekaise** is Sweden's highest mountain, but you'll need to be in good physical shape just to get to it. From Kiruna you travel about 60 kilometers (37 miles) south, then west to the Same village of **Nikkaloukta.** There are two buses a day from Kiruna in the summer. From Nikkaloukta it is a hike of 21 kilometers (13 miles) to the Fjällstationen (mountain station) at the foot of **Kebnekaise,** though you can take a boat for 7 kilometers (4 miles) across **Lake Ladtjojokk.** Kebnekaise itself is easy to climb in good weather, with no need for mountaineering equipment. If you feel up to more walking, the track continues past the mountain station to become part of what is known as **Kungsleden** (the King's Way), a trail through the mountains and Abisko National Park to Riksgränsen on the Norwegian border.

Tour 3: Jukkasjärvi and Jokkmokk

Jukkasjärvi is just 16 kilometers (10 miles) east of Kiruna and can be reached by bus. The history of this Same village by the shores of the fast-flowing **Torneälven** (Torne River) dates from 1543, when a market was recorded here. There is a wooden **church** from the 17th century and a small **open-air museum** that gives a feeling of Same life in times gone by.

At the peak of winter, this town becomes a popular spot for tourists drawn by the annual construction of the world's largest igloo.

Here, if you are gastronomically adventurous, you may sample one of the most unusual of Same delicacies: a cup of thick black coffee and small lumps of goat cheese. These you marinate in the coffee, fish out with spoons, and consume. Then you drink the coffee. The taste sensation is intriguing, to say the least. Afterward, try riding the rapids of the Torne River in an inflatable boat. In winter Jukkasjärvi also offers dogsled rides.

Follow Route 45/E10 104 kilometers (65 miles) south to **Gällivare,** a mining town with a population of 22,000, then Route 45 106 kilometers (66 miles) farther to **Jokkmokk,** an important center of Same culture. Each February it is the scene of the region's largest market, nowadays an odd event featuring everything from stalls selling frozen reindeer meat to Same handcrafted wooden utensils.

Jokkmokk makes perhaps the best base in Norrland for the outdoor vacationer. The village has three campsites and is surrounded by wilderness. The local tourist office sells fishing permits, which cost SKr25 to SKr40 for 24 hours to SKr200 for the entire year. The office can also supply lists of camping and housekeeping cabins.

Tour 4: Sarek National Park

Sarek is Sweden's largest high mountain area and was molded by the last Ice Age. It totals 197,000 hectares (487,000 acres), a small portion of which is forest, bogland, and waterways. The remainder is bare mountain. The park has 90 peaks some 6,000

feet above sea level. The mountains have been sculpted by glaciers, of which there are around 100 in the park. The Rapaätno River, which drains the park, runs through the lovely, desolate **Rapadalen** (Rapa Valley). There is a surprising variety of landscape, luxuriant green meadows contrasting with the snowy peaks of the mountains. Animals to be found here include elk, bear, wolverine, lynx, ermine, hare, Arctic fox, red fox, and mountain lemmings. Birdlife includes ptarmigan, willow grouse, teal, wigeon, tufted duck, bluethroat, and warbler. Golden eagles, rough-legged buzzards and merlins also have been spotted here.

Visiting Sarek demands a good knowledge of mountains and a familiarity with the outdoors. Sarek can be dangerous in winter because of avalanches and snowstorms. However, in summer, despite its unpredictable, often inhospitable climate, it attracts large numbers of experienced hikers. The best entry point is at **Kvikkjokk**, a village reached by a small road to the east of Jokkmokk (*see* Tour 3, *above*). Hikers can then choose between a trail through the Tarradalen (Tarra Valley), which divides the Sarek from the Padjelanta National Park, located on the northwest side of Sarek, or part of the Kungsleden trail (*see* Tour 2, Kebnekaise, *above*), which crosses the southern end for a distance of about 16 kilometers (10 miles).

Tour 5: Muddus National Park

Established in 1942, this park is less mountainous and spectacular than Sarek, its 49,300 hectares (121,770 acres) comprising mainly virgin coniferous forest, some of whose trees may be up to 600 years old. The park's 1,490 hectares (3,680 acres) of water is composed primarily of two huge lakes at the center of the park and the Muddusjokk River, which tumbles spectacularly through a gorge with 330-foot-high sheer rock walls and includes a 140-foot-high waterfall. Muddus is reached by taking the road southwest of Gällivare to **Saite** en route to the Porjus power station and is well signposted. The highest point of Muddus is **Södra Stuobba** Mountain, 629 meters (2,076 feet) above sea level. Well-marked trails lead through the park, where you can pick cloudberries in the autumn. There are four well-equipped overnight communal rest huts and two tourist cabins. The park contains bears, elk, lynx, wolverines, moose, ermines, weasels, otters, and many bird species.

Tour 6: Luleå and the East Coast

Driving south from Kiruna, continuing along E10 at Gällivare, you pass several small former mining villages before coming into the **Kalixälv** (Kalix River) valley, where the countryside becomes more settled, with small farms and fertile meadows replacing the wilder northern landscape. Follow E4 west from Töre, and some 347 kilometers (215 miles) from Kiruna, you reach **Luleå**, a port at the top of the Gulf of Bothnia, at the mouth of the Luleälv (Lule River). The most northerly major town in Sweden, Luleå was situated some 10 kilometers (6 miles) farther inland when it was first granted its charter in 1621, but by 1649 trade had grown so much that the town was moved closer to the sea. The development of Kiruna and the iron trade is linked, by means of a railway, with the fortunes of Luleå, where a steelworks was set up in the 1940s. Luleå, along

with Piteå, Skellefteå, Umeå, and Sundsvall, farther south down the coast road, remains an important northern port. It also boasts a beautiful archipelago of hundreds of islands. Luleå, like most of its fellow ports on the east coast, is a very modern and nondescript city, but it has some reasonable hotels. There is also, at **Norrbottens Museet** (the Norbotten Museum), one of the best collections of Same ethnography in the world. *Hermelinsparken, tel. 0920/93829. Admission: SKr10. Open daily 10–5.*

➓ From Luleå you can take Route 97 north to **Boden,** the nation's largest garrison town, dating from 1809, when Sweden lost Finland to Russia and feared an invasion of its own territory. **Garnisonsmuseet** (the Garrison Museum), contains exhibits from Swedish military history, with an extensive collection of weapons and uniforms. *Garnisonsmuseet, Boden, tel. 0921/ 62000. Admission: SKr20. Open daily 10–5.*

You can then return through ever wilder and more desolate countryside to Jokkmokk and Kiruna.

Sports and Outdoor Activities

All the regional tourist offices can supply details of skiing holidays, but never forget the extreme temperatures and weather conditions. For the really adventurous, the Kebnekaise mountain station (*see* Tour 2, *above*) offers combined skiing and climbing weeks at SKr3,475. It also offers week-long combined dogsledding, skiing, and climbing holidays on the mountains, which vary in price from SKr3,995 to SKr4,995. Because of the extreme cold and the danger involved, be sure to have proper equipment. Consult the mountain station well in advance for advice (tel. 0980/55042).

Dining and Lodging

The two are often synonymous at these latitudes. Standards of cuisine and service are, unlike prices, not high, but hotels are usually exceptionally clean and staffs scrupulously honest.

Highly recommended establishments are indicated by a star ★.

Dining Norrland specialties include *surströmming* (fermented herring), *palt* (a stuffed dumpling), *mandelpotatis* (almond-shaped potatoes), and *tunnbröd* (thin bread made from barley flour) eaten with butter, potatoes, and elk meat, or fermented herring. Trout and salmon are common, as are various cuts of elk and reindeer. But to the foreign palate, the most acceptable of Norrland's culinary specialties is undoubtedly *löjröm*, pinkish caviar from a species of Baltic herring, which is eaten with chopped onions and sour cream, and the various desserts made from the cloudberries that thrive here.

Lodging This is limited, but the various local tourist offices can supply details of bed-and-breakfasts and holiday villages equipped with housekeeping cabins. The area is also rich in campsites, though, with the highly unpredictable climate, this may appeal only to the very hardy.

Jokkmokk **Hotel Jokkmokk.** Although located in the center of town, a
Dining and Lodging modern hotel of this level of luxury seems incongruous in this
★ remote region, but welcome nevertheless. The hotel can ar-

range helicopter trips to the Sarek and Muddus national parks, and there is excellent fishing nearby. *Solgatan 45, S–96 231, tel. 0971/11320, fax 0971/11625. 75 rooms. Facilities: restaurant, pool, solarium, sauna, gymnasium, conference rooms. AE, DC, MC, V. Expensive.*

Gästis. This small hotel in central Jokkmokk was opened in 1915. *Herrevägen 1, S–96 231, tel. 0971/10012, fax 0971/10012. 30 rooms. Facilities: restaurant, dancing, sauna. AE, DC, MC, V. Moderate.*

Jokkmokks Turistcenter. This complex is prettily situated in a forest area, near a lake, 3 kilometers (2 miles) from the railway station. *Box 75, S–96 222, tel. 0971/12370, fax 0971/12476. 26 rooms, 84 cabins. Facilities: conference rooms, sauna, solarium, 4 outdoor swimming pools, canoe and bicycle rentals. MC, V. Inexpensive.*

Jukkasjärvi
Dining and Lodging
★

Jukkasjärvi Wärdshus och Hembygdsgård. The restaurant specializes in Norrland cuisine and is the lifework of its manager, Yngve Bergqvist. The hotel has four rooms, and there are 45 cabins around it. *Box 24, S–98021, tel. 0980/21190, fax 0980/21406. 4 rooms, 45 cabins, 30 with bath and kitchen. Facilities: restaurant, rooms for the disabled, conference rooms. AE, DC, MC, V. Inexpensive.*

Kebnekaise
Lodging

Kebnekaise Fjällstation. Recently renovated, this rustic, wooden mountain station consists of seven separate buildings. The rooms accommodate 2 to 4 or groups of up to 15, but none has shower or bath. It is 19 kilometers (12 miles) from Nikkaloukta by footpath or by a combination of boat and hiking, or by helicopter. *S–98 129 Kiruna, tel. 0980/55042, fax 0980/55048. (Contact Abisko tourist office off-season, S–98024, Abisko, tel. 0980/4000). 200 beds. Facilities: restaurant, bar, commissary, sauna, guided mountain tours. AE, V. Closed mid-Aug.–mid-Mar. Inexpensive.*

Kiruna
Dining and Lodging

Ferrum. Part of the Reso Hotels chain, this late-1960s-vintage hotel, renovated in 1991, is situated near the railway station. *Lars Janssonsgatan, S–981 31, tel. 0980/18600, fax 0980/14505. 170 rooms with shower. Facilities: 2 restaurants, bar, sauna, solarium. AE, DC, MC, V. Expensive.*

Kebne och Kaisa. These twin modern hotels are close to the railway station and the airport bus stop. *Konduktörsgatan 7, S–98134, tel. 0980/12380, fax 0980/82111. 54 rooms with shower, 2 rooms with kitchenette. Facilities: breakfast, sauna, solarium. AE, DC, MC, V. Moderate.*

Fyra Vindar. This small hotel, dating from 1903, also has the advantage of being close to the railway station. *Bangårdsvägen 9, S–98134, tel. 0980/12050. 18 rooms, not all with bath. Facilities: breakfast. DC, MC, V. Inexpensive.*

STF Vandrarhem. Formerly a hospital for the aged, this modernized, 1926 building now serves as a youth hostel. It faces a large park near the railway station. *Skytegatan 16A, S–127 84, tel. 0980/17195. 35 2-bed–5-bed rooms. Closed mid-Aug.–mid-June. No credit cards. Inexpensive.*

Luleå
Dining and Lodging

Luleå Stads Hotell. This large, centrally located Best Western hotel has nightly, sometimes rowdy dancing. *Storgatan 15, S–972 32, tel. 0920/67000, fax 0920/67092. 135 rooms, 3 suites. Facilities: restaurant, café, discothèque, rooms for the disabled and allergy sufferers, conference rooms, sauna, solarium. AE, DC, MC, V. Expensive.*

SAS Luleå. As you might expect of an SAS hotel, this one is

large, modern, and centrally situated. *Storgatan 17, S–972 32, tel. 0920/94000, fax 0920/88222. 212 rooms. Facilities: restaurant, rooms for the disabled and allergy sufferers, conference rooms, nightclub, sauna, swimming pool, solarium. AE, DC, MC, V. Expensive.*

Amber. A particularly fine old building houses this hotel close to the railway station. *Stationsgatan 67, S–972 34, tel. 0920/ 10200. 16 rooms. Facilities: restaurant, rooms for allergy sufferers and nonsmokers. AE, DC, MC, V. Moderate.*

Arctic. Right in the center of town, the Arctic is renowned locally for its restaurant. *Sandviksgatan 80, S–972 34, tel. 0920/ 10980. 95 rooms. Facilities: restaurant, rooms for the disabled, conference rooms, sauna. AE, DC, MC, V. Moderate.*

Aveny. This small hotel is close to the railway station. *Hermelinsgatan 10, tel. 0920/221820. 24 rooms. Facilities: rooms for nonsmokers and allergy sufferers, solarium. AE, DC, MC, V. Moderate.*

Scandic. This hotel, located on Lake Sjö, has an extremely pleasant location but is 2 kilometers (1 mile) from the railway station. *Banvägen 3, S–973 46, tel. 0920/28360, fax 0920/69472. 158 rooms. Facilities: restaurant, rooms for the disabled and allergy sufferers, conference rooms, gymnasium, sauna, indoor pool, solarium. AE, DC, MC, V. Moderate.*

Conversion Tables

Distance

Kilometers/Miles   To change kilometers to miles, multiply kilometers by .621.
To change miles to kilometers, multiply miles by 1.61.

Km to Mi	Mi to Km
1 = .62	1 = 1.6
2 = 1.2	2 = 3.2
3 = 1.9	3 = 4.8
4 = 2.5	4 = 6.4
5 = 3.1	5 = 8.1
6 = 3.7	6 = 9.7
7 = 4.3	7 = 11.3
8 = 5.0	8 = 12.9
9 = 5.6	9 = 14.5

Meters/Feet   To change meters to feet, multiply meters by 3.28.
To change feet to meters, multiply feet by .305.

Meters to Feet	Feet to Meters
1 = 3.3	1 = .31
2 = 6.6	2 = .61
3 = 9.8	3 = .92
4 = 13.1	4 = 1.2
5 = 16.4	5 = 1.5
6 = 19.7	6 = 1.8
7 = 23.0	7 = 2.1
8 = 26.2	8 = 2.4
9 = 29.5	9 = 2.7

Weight

Kilograms/Pounds   To change kilograms to pounds, multiply by 2.20.
To change pounds to kilograms, multiply by .453.

Kilo to Pound	Pound to Kilo
1 = 2.2	1 = .45
2 = 4.4	2 = .91
3 = 6.6	3 = 1.4
4 = 8.8	4 = 1.8
5 = 11.0	5 = 2.3

6 = 13.2	6 = 2.7
7 = 15.4	7 = 3.2
8 = 17.6	8 = 3.6
9 = 19.8	9 = 4.1

Grams/Ounces To change grams to ounces, multiply grams by .035.
To change ounces to grams, multiply ounces by 28.4.

Grams to Ounces	Ounces to Grams
1 = .04	1 = 28
2 = .07	2 = 57
3 = .11	3 = 85
4 = .14	4 = 114
5 = .18	5 = 142
6 = .21	6 = 170
7 = .25	7 = 199
8 = .28	8 = 227
9 = .32	9 = 256

Liquid Volume

Liters/U.S. Gallons To change liters to U.S. gallons, multiply liters by .264.
To change U.S. gallons to liters, multiply gallons by 3.79.

Liters to U.S. Gallons	U.S. Gallons to Liters
1 = .26	1 = 3.8
2 = .53	2 = 7.6
3 = .79	3 = 11.4
4 = 1.1	4 = 15.2
5 = 1.3	5 = 19.0
6 = 1.6	6 = 22.7
7 = 1.8	7 = 26.5
8 = 2.1	8 = 30.3
9 = 2.4	9 = 34.1

Vocabulary

Danish Vocabulary

	English	Danish	Pronunciation
Basics	Yes/no	Ja/nej	yah/nie
	Please	Vær så god	**ver** soh god
	Thank you very much	Tak	tak
	You're welcome	Velbekomme	**vel**-be-ko-me
	Excuse me (to apologize)	Undskyld	**unsk**-ul
	Hello	Goodag	gu-**day**
	Goodbye	Farvel	fa-**vel**
	Today	I dag	ee **day**
	Tomorrow	I morgen	ee **morn**
	Yesterday	I går	ee **gore**
	Morning	Morgen	**more**-n
	Afternoon	Eftermiddag	**ef-tah**-mid-day
	Night	Nat	nat
Numbers	One	een/eet	**een**/eet
	Two	to	toe
	Three	tre	tre
	Four	fire	fear
	Five	fem	fem
	Six	seks	sex
	Seven	syv	syoo
	Eight	otte	**oh**-te
	Nine	ni	nee
	Ten	ti	tee
Days of the Week	Monday	mandag	**man**-day
	Tuesday	tirsdag	**tears**-day
	Wednesday	onsdag	**ons**-day
	Thursday	torsdag	**trs**-day
	Friday	fredag	**free**-day
	Saturday	lørdag	**lore**-day
	Sunday	søndag	**soo**(n)-day

Useful Phrases	Do you speak English?	Taler du engelsk	te-ler **doo** in-galsk
	I don't speak . . .	Jeg taler ikke Dansk	yi tal-ler **ick** Dansk
	I don't understand.	Jeg forstår ikke	yi fahr-store **ick**
	I don't know.	Det ved jeg ikke	deh **ved** yi ick
	I am American/ British.	Jeg er amerikansk/ britisk	yi ehr a-mehr-i-**kansk**/ bri-**tisk**
	I am sick.	Jeg er syg	yi ehr **syoo**
	Please call a doctor.	Kan du ringe til en læge?	can **doo** rin-geh til en lay-eh
	Do you have a vacant room?	Har du et værelse?	har **doo** eet va(l)r-sa
	How much does it cost?	Hvad koster det?	va cos-ta **deh**
	It's too expensive.	Det er fahr duurt	deh ehr **fohr** dyrt
	Beautiful	Smukt	smukt
	Help!	Hjælp	yelp
	Stop!	Stop	stop
	How do I get to . . .	Hvordan kommer jeg til?	vore-**dan** kom-mer yi til
	. . . the train station?	banegarden	**ban** eh-gore-en
	. . . the post office?	postkonoret	**post**-kon-toh-raht
	. . . the tourist office?	turistkonoret	too-**reest**-kon-tor-et
	. . . the hospital?	hospitalet	hos-peet-**tal**-et
	Does this bus go to . . . ?	Går denne bus til?	**goh** den-na boos til
	Where is the W.C.?	Hvor er toilettet	vor **ehr** toi-le(tt)-et
	On the left	Til venstre	til **ven**-strah
	On the right	Till højre	til **hoy**-ah
	Straight ahead	Lige ud	**lee** u(l)
Dining Out	Please bring me . . .	Mø jeg få	mo yi **foh**
	menu	menu	me-**nu**
	fork	gaffel	gaf-**fel**
	knife	kniv	kan-**ew**

spoon	ske	skee
napkin	serviet	serv-**eet**
bread	brød	brood
butter	smør	smoor
milk	mælk	malk
pepper	peber	**pee**-wer
salt	salt	selt
sugar	sukker	**su**-kar
water/bottled water	vand	van
The check, please.	Regning	**ri**-ning

Finnish Vocabulary

	English	*Finnish*	*Pronunciation*
Basics	Yes/no	Kyllä/Ei	kue-la/**ee**
	Please	Olkaa hyvä	ol-kah **hue**-va
	Thank you very much.	Kiitoksia paljon	**kee**-tohk-syah **pahl**-yon
	You're welcome.	Olkaa hyvä	ol-kah **hue**-va
	Excuse me. (to get by someone)	Anteeksi	**ahn**-teek-see
	(to apologize)	Suokaa anteeksi	**soo**-oh-kah **ahn**-teek-see
	Hello	Hyvää päivää terve	**hue**-va **paee**-va **tehr**-veh
	Goodbye	Näkemiin	**na**-keh-meen
	Today	Tänään	**ta**-naan
	Tomorrow	Huomenna	**hoo**-oh-men-nah
	Yesterday	Eilen	**ee**-len
	Morning	Aamu	**ah**-moo
	Afternoon	Iltapäivä	**eel**-tah-**pay**-va
	Night	Yö	**eu**-euh
Numbers	One	Yksi	**uek**-see
	Two	Kaksi	**kahk**-see
	Three	Kolme	**kohl**-meh
	Four	Nelja	**nel**-ya
	Five	Viisi	**vee**-see
	Six	Kuusi	**koo**-see
	Seven	Seitseman	**sate**-seh-man

Eight	Kahdeksan	**kah**-dek-sahn
Nine	Yhdaksän	**uef**-dek-san
Ten	Kymmenen	**kue**-meh-nen

Days of the Week

Monday	maanantai	**mah**-nahn-tie
Tuesday	tiistai	**tees**-tie
Wednesday	keskiviikko	**kes**-kee-veek-koh
Thursday	torstai	**tohrs**-tie
Friday	perjantai	**pehr**-yahn-tie
Saturday	lauantai	**loo**-ahn-tie
Sunday	sunnuntai	**soon**-noon-tie

Useful Phrases

Do you speak English?	Puhutteko englantia?	**poo**-hoot-teh-koh **ehng**-lahn-tee-ah
I don't speak . . .	En puhu suomea . . .	ehn **poo**-hoo **soo**-oh-mee-ah
I don't understand.	En ymmärrä.	ehn **eum**-mar-ra
I don't know.	En tiedä.	ehn **tee**-eh-da
I am American/ British.	Mina olen amerikkalainen/ englantilainen.	**mee**-na **oh**-len ah-**mehr**-ee-kah-lie-nehn/**ehn-**glahn-tee-lie-nehn
I am sick.	Olen sairas.	**oh**-len **sigh**-rahs
Please call a doctor.	Haluan kutsua lääkärin.	**hah**-loo-ahn **koot**-soo-ah **lay**-ka-reen
Do you have a vacant room?	Onko teillä vapaata huonetta?	**ohn**-koh **teel**-la **vah**-pah-tah **hoo**-oh-neht-tah?
How much does it cost?	Paljonko tämä maksaa?	**pahl**-yohn-koh ta-ma **mahk**-sah
It's too expensive.	Se on liian kallis.	**say** ohn **lee**-ahn **kah**-lees
Beautiful	Kuanis	**kow**-nees
Help!	Auttakaa!	**ow**-tah-kah
Stop!	Seis!/ Pysähtykka!	say(s) **peu**-sa-teu-kay
How do I get to . . .	Voitteko sanoa miten pääsen-n . . .	**voy**-tay-koh **sah**-noh-ah **mee**-ten **pay**-sen
. . . the train station	asema (. . . pääsen asemalle?)	**ah**-say-mah (**pay**-sen **ah**-say-mah-lay)
. . . the post office?	posti (. . . paasen postiin?)	**pohs**-tee (**pay**-sen **pohs**-teen)

. . . the tourist office?	matkatoimisto (. . . pääsen matkatoimistoon?)	**maht**-kah-**toy**-mees-toh (**pay**-sen **maht**-kah-**toy**-mees-tohn)
. . . the hospital?	sairaala (. . . pääsen sairaalaan?)	**sigh**-rah-lah (**pay**-sen **sigh**-rah-lahn)
Does this bus go to . . . ?	Kulkeeko kämä bussi-n	**kool**-kay-koh ta-ma **boo**-see-n?
Where is the W.C.?	Missä on W.C.?	**mee**-sa ohn **ves**-sah
On the left	Vasemmalle	**vah**-say-mahl-lay
On the right	Oikealle	**ohy**-kay-ah-lay
Straight ahead	Souraan eteenpäin	**swoh**-rahn **eh**-tayn-pa-een
Dining Out Please bring me . . .	Tuokaa minulle . . .	**too**-oh-kah **mee**-new
menu	ruokalista	**roo**-oh-kah-lees-tah
fork	haarukka	**hahr**-oo-kah
knife	veitsi	**vayt**-see
spoon	lusikka	**loo**-see-kah
napkin	lautasliina	**low**-tahs-lee-nah
bread	leipä	**lay**-pa
butter	voi	**voh**(ee)
milk	maito	**my**-toh
pepper	pippuri	**pee**-poor-ee
salt	suola	**soo**-oh-lah
sugar	sokeri	**soh**-ker-ee
water/bottled water	vesi/ kivennäisvesi	**veh**-see/**kee**-ven-eyes-veh-see
The check, please.	Lasku, olkaa hyvä/Saanko maksaa	**lahs**-kew, **ohl**-kah **heu**-va/ **sahn**-koh **mahk**-sah

Icelandic Vocabulary

	English	*Icelandic*	*Pronunciation*
Basics	Yes/no	já/nei	yow/nay
	Thank you very much.	kærar þakkir takk	**kie**-rahr **thah**-kihr **tah**kk
	You're welcome.	Ekkert að-þakka	**ehk**-kehrt ath **thah**-ka
	Excuse me. (to get by someone)	Afsakið	**ahf**-sah-kith(e)

(to apologize)	Fyrirgefið	**feer**-ee-geh-vith(e)
Hello	Góðan dag	goh-than **dahgh**
Goodbye	bless	bless
Today	í dag	**ee dahgh**
Tomorrow	á morgun	ow **mohr**-gun
Yesterday	í gær	ee **gah-eer**
Morning	morgun	**mohr**-gun
Afternoon	eftirmiðdagur	**ehf**-teer-mihth-dahg-ur
Night	nótt	noht

Numbers	One	einn	**ehnn**
	Two	tveir	**tveh**-eer
	Three	Þrír	threer
	Four	fjórir	**fyohr**-eer
	Five	fimm	fehm
	Six	sex	sex
	Seven	sjö	sy-uh
	Eight	átta	**owt**-tah
	Nine	níu	**nee**-uh
	Ten	tíu	**tee**-uh

Days of the Week	Monday	mánudagur	**mown**-ah-dah-gur
	Tuesday	Þriðjudagur	**thrithe**-yoo-dah-gur
	Wednesday	miðvikudagur	**meethe**-veek-uh-dah-gur
	Thursday	fimmtudagur	**feem**-too-dah-gur
	Friday	föstudagur	**fuhs**-too-dah-gur
	Saturday	laugardagur	**loy**-gahr-dah-gur
	Sunday	sunnudagur	**soon**-noo-dah-gur

Useful Phrases	Do you speak English?	Talar Þú ensku?	**tah**-lahr thoo **ehn**-skoo
	I don't speak Icelandic	Ég tala ekki islensku . . .	**yeh** tah-lah **ehk**-keh **ees**-lehn-skoo
	I don't understand.	Ég skil ekki	yeh **skeel ehk**-keh
	I don't know.	Ég veit ekki	yeh **vayt ehk**-keh
	I am American/ British.	Ég er ameriskur/ breskur	yeh ehr **ah**-mehr eeskur/brehs-koor
	I am sick.	Ég er veik(ur)	yeh ehr vehk(oor)

Please call a doctor.	Viltu hringja í lækni, takk	veel-too **hreeng**-yah ee **lahk**-nee **tah**-kk
Do you have a vacant room?	Átt þú laust herbergi	owt thoo laysht **hehr**-behr-ghee
How much does it cost?	Hvað kostar Það	kvathe kohs-tahr thathe
It's too expensive.	Þuð er of dýrt	thahthe ehr ohf deert
Beautiful	Falleglur/t	**fahl**-lehg-loor
Help!	Hjálp	hyalp
Stop!	Stopp	stohp
How do I get to . . .	Hvernig kemst ég	**kvehr**-neeg kehmst **yehg**
. . . the post office?	á pósthúsið	ow pohst-hoos-ihthe
. . . the tourist office?	á ferðamálaráð	ow **fehr**-tha-mow-lahr-owthe
. . . the hospital?	á spitalan	ow **spee**-tah-lahn
Does this bus go to . . . ?	Fer Þessi vagn	fehr **thehs**-see **vakn**
Where is the W.C.?	hvar er salernið	kvahr ehr sahl-ehr-nihthe
On the left	til vinstri	teel **veen**-stree
On the right	til hægri	teel **hie**-ree
Straight ahead	beint áfram	baynt **ow**-frahm
Dining Out Please bring me . . .	get ég fengið	geht yehg **fehn**-gihthe
menu	matseðil	**maht**-seh-theel
fork	gaffal	**gah**-fahl(t)
knife	hnif	hneef
spoon	skeið	skaythe
napkin	servetta	sehr-**veht**-tah
bread	brauð	braythe
butter	smjör	smyoor
milk	mjólk	myoolk
pepper	pipar	**pay**-pahr
salt	salt	sahlt
sugar	sykur	**say**-koor
water/bottled water	vatn	vahtn
The check, please.	reikninginn	takk **rehk**-nihn-ghihn

Norwegian Vocabulary

	English	*Norwegian*	*Pronunciation*
Basics	Yes/no	Ja/nei	yah/nay
	Please	Vær så snill	**vehr** soh snihl
	Thank you very much.	Tusen takk	**tews**-sehn tahk
	You're welcome.	Vær så god	**vehr** soh goo
	Excuse me.	Unnskyld	**ewn**-shewl
	Hello	God dag	goo **dahg**
	Goodbye	Adjø	ah-**dyur**
	Today	i dag	ee **dahg**
	Tomorrow	i morgen	ee **moh**-ern
	Yesterday	i går	ee **gohr**
	Morning	morgen	**moh**-ern
	Afternoon	ettermiddag	**eh-terr**-mid-dahg
	Night	natt	naht
Numbers	One	en	ehn
	Two	to	too
	Three	tre	tray
	Four	fire	**feer**-eh
	Five	fem	fehm
	Six	seks	sehks
	Seven	syv, sju	shew
	Eight	åtte	**oh**-teh
	Nine	ni	nee
	Ten	ti	tee
Days of the Week	Monday	måndag	**mahn**-dahg
	Tuesday	tirsdag	**teesh**-dahg
	Wednesday	onsdag	**oonss**-dahg
	Thursday	torsdag	**tohsh**-dahg
	Friday	fredag	**fray**-dahg
	Saturday	lørdag	**loor**-dahg
	Sunday	Søndag	**suhn**-dahg
Useful Phrases	Do you speak English?	Snakker De engelsk?	**snahk**-kerr dee **ehng**-ehlsk
	I don't speak Norwegian.	Jeg snakker ikke norsk.	yay **snahk**-kerr **ik**-keh nohrshk
	I don't understand.	Jeg forstår ikke.	yay fosh-**tawr** **ik**-keh
	I don't know.	Jeg vet ikke.	yay veht **ik**-keh

I am American/ British.	Jeg er amerikansk/ engelsk.	yay ehr ah-mehr-ee-kahnsk/ehng-ehlsk
I am sick.	Jeg er dårlig	yay ehr **dohr**-lee
Please call a doctor.	Vær så snill og ring etter en lege.	vehr soh snihl oh ring **eht**-ehr ehn **lay**-geh
Do you have vacant room?	Jeg vil gjerne ha et rom?	yay vil **yehr**-neh hah eht room
How much does it cost?	Hva koster det?	vah **koss**-terr deh
It's too expensive.	Det er for dyrt.	deh ehr for **deert**
Beautiful	vakker	**vah**-kehr
Help!	Hjelp!	yehlp
Stop!	Stopp!	stop
How do I get to . . .	Hvor er	voor **ehr**
. . . the train station?	jernbanestasjonen	yehrn-bahn-eh sta-**shoon**-ern
. . . the post office?	posthuset	**pohsst**-hewss
. . . the tourist office?	turistkontoret	tew-**reest**-koon-toor-er
. . . the hospital?	sykehuset	**see**-keh-hoo-seh
Does this bus go to . . . ?	Går denne bussen til . . . ?	gohr **den**-nah boos teel
Where is the W.C.?	Hvor er toalettene?	voor ehr too-ah-**leht**-ter-ner
On the left	Til venstre	teel **vehn**-streh
On the right	Til høyre	teel **hooy**-reh
Straight ahead	Rett fram	reht **frahm**
Dining Out menu	meny	meh-**new**
fork	gaffel	**gahff**-erl
knife	kniv	kneev
spoon	skje	shay
napkin	serviett	ssehr-**vyeht**
bread	brød	brur
butter	smør	smurr
milk	melk	mehlk
pepper	pepper	**pehp**-per
salt	salt	sahlt
sugar	sukker	**sook**-kerr

water/bottled water	vann	vahn
The check, please.	Jeg vil gjerne betale.	yay vil **yehr**-neh beh-**tah**-leh

Swedish Vocabulary

	English	*Swedish*	*Pronunciation*
Basics	Yes/no	Ja/nej	yah/nay
	Please	Var snäll; Var vänlig	vahn snehll vahr **vehn**-leeg
	Thank you very much.	Tack så mycket.	tahk soh **mee**-keh
	You're welcome.	Var så god.	vahr shoh **goo**
	Excuse me. (to get by someone)	Ursäkta.	oor-**shehk**-tah
	(to apologize)	Førlåt.	fur-**loht**
	Hello	God dag	goo **dahg**
	Goodbye	Adjø	ah-**yoo**
	Today	I dag	ee **dahg**
	Tomorrow	I Morgon	ee **mor**-ron
	Yesterday	I går	ee **gohr**
	Morning	Morgon	**mohr**-on
	Afternoon	Eftermiddag	**ehf**-ter-meed-dahg
	Night	natt	naht
Numbers	One	en	ehn
	Two	tva	tvoh
	Three	tre	tree
	Four	fyra	**fee**-rah
	Five	fem	fem
	Six	sex	sex
	Seven	sju	shoo
	Eight	åtta	**oht**-tah
	Nine	nio	nee
	Ten	tio	tee
Days of the Week	Monday	Måndag	**mohn**-dahg
	Tuesday	Tisdag	**tees**-dahg
	Wednesday	Onsdag	**ohns**-dahg
	Thursday	Torsdag	**tohrs**-dahg
	Friday	Fredag	**freh**-dahg
	Saturday	Lørdag	**luhr**-dahg
	Sunday	Sondag	**sohn**-dahg

Useful Phrases	Do you speak English?	Talar ni engelska?	**tah**-lahr nee **ehng**-ehl-skah
	I don't speak . . .	Jag talar inte svenska . . .	yah **tah**-lahr **een**-teh **sven**-skah
	I don't understand.	Jag förstår inte.	yah fuhr-**stohr** **een**-teh
	I don't know.	Jag vet inte.	yah **veht** **een**-teh
	I am American/ British.	Jag är amerikan/ engelsman.	yah ay ah-mehr-ee-**kahn**/ **ehng**-ehls-mahn
	I am sick.	Jag är sjuk.	yah ay **shyook**
	Please call a doctor.	Jag vill skicka efter en läkare.	yah veel **shee**-kah **ehf**-tehr ehn **lay**-kah-reh
	Do you have a vacant room?	Har Ni något rum ledigt?	hahr nee noh-goht **room** **leh**-deekt
	How much does it cost?	Vad kostar det?/ Hur mycket kostar det?	vah **kohs**-tahr deh/hor **mee**-keh **kohs**-tahr deh
	It's too expensive.	Den är for dyr.	dehn ay foor **deer**
	Beautiful	Vacker	**vah**-kehr
	Help!	Hjälp	yehlp
	Stop!	Stopp, stanna	stop, **stahn**-nah
	How do I get to . . .	Kan Ni visa mig vägen till	kahn nee **vee**-sah may **vay**-gehn teel
	. . . the train station?	stationen	stah-**shoh**-nehn
	. . . the post office?	posten	**pohs**-tehn
	. . . the tourist office?	en resebyrå	ehn-**reh**-seh-**bee**-roh
	. . . the hospital?	sjukhuset	**shyook**-hoo-seht
	Does this bus go to . . . ?	Går den här bussen till ?	gohr dehn hehr **boo**-sehn teel
	Where is the W.C.?	Var är toilett/ toaletten	vahr ay twah-**leht**
	On the left	Till vänster	teel **vehn**-stur
	On the right	Till höger	teel **huh**-gur
	Straight ahead	Rakt fram	rahkt **frahm**
Dining Out	Please bring me . . .	Var snäll och hamta at mig	vahr snehl oh **hehm**-tah oht may

menu	matsedeln	**maht**-seh-dehln
fork	en gaffel	ehn **gahf**-fehl
knife	en kniv	ehn **kneev**
spoon	en sked	ehn **shehd**
napkin	en servett	ehn sehr-**veht**
bread	brød	bruh(d)
butter	smør	smuhr
milk	mjølk	myoolk
pepper	peppar	**pehp**-pahr
salt	salt	sahlt
sugar	socker	**soh**-kehr
water	vatten	**vaht**-n
The check, please.	Far jag be om notan?	fohr yah beh ohm **noh**-tahn

515

Index

In this index the Scandinavian letters å, æ, ä, ø, ö and þ have been alphabetized as though they were the English letters a, o, and p. In Scandinavia these letters are found at the *end* of the alphabet in telephone directories and other alphabetized lists.

Aalborg, Den., *116, 117, 123, 126, 128–129*
Aalborg Jazz Festival, *49*
Admiralitetskyrkan, *478*
Ærø Island, *111*
Ærøkøbing, Den., *111, 112–113*
Afangar, *253–254*
Ahtari wildlife park, *220*
Akershus Slott, *311*
Åkirke, *134*
Åkirkeby, Den., *134*
Akureyri, Ice., *269–270, 273*
Akvariet, *356*
Åland Islands, *199, 203–204, 205–206*
Ales stenar, *498*
Ålesund, Nor., *384–385*
Álftafjöroður, *275*
Ålholm Slot, *99–100*
Allinge, Den., *133, 137*
Almannagjá gorge, *261*
Almindingen, *134*
Alþingishús, *250*
Alta, Nor., *395, 401*
Amalienborg, *71*
American Express, *8*
Ammassalik, Gre., *146*
Amuri Museum of Workers' Housing, *219*
Amusement parks
Bornholm, *134*
Copenhagen, *74, 76*
Denmark, *124, 135*
Finland, *204, 219–220*
Göteborg, *462*
Helsinki, *185*
Iceland, *263*
Jylland, *120, 123*
Norway, *344*

Oslo, *317*
Stockholm, *432*
Åndalsnes, Nor., *379, 385*
Andersen, Hans Christian, *72, 98, 104, 106, 107–108*
Anne Hvides Gård, *110*
Apartment and Villa Rentals, *33*
April Jazz/Espoo, *159*
Aquariums, *76, 356*
Arbæjarsafn, *250–251*
Arbejdermuseet, *77*
Architecture itinerary, *36–38*
Arctic Open Golf Tournament, *231*
Arctic Rally, *159*
Arendal, Nor., *339*
Århus, Den., *116, 117, 121–122, 126–127, 128*
Århus Festival, *49*
Århus Jazz Festival, *49, 121*
Århus Rådhus, *122*
Arktikum, *210*
Armfelt-Museo, *182*
Arnarstapi, Ice., *266*
Árni Magnússon Institute, *252*
Around Fyn Regatta, *48*
Arsenal Museet, *478*
Art galleries and museums
Bergen, *354–355*
Denmark, *95, 98, 106–107, 108, 109, 124*
Copenhagen, *68, 72, 73–74, 75, 76*
Finland, *217, 218, 221*
Göteborg, *456, 457*
Helsinki, *175, 178, 179, 181, 182, 184*
Iceland, *270*
Norway, *332, 333–334, 338, 343,*

365, 367, 368, 391
Oslo, *307, 310, 311–312, 313, 314, 315, 317, 318*
Reykjavík, *251–252*
Stockholm, *427, 435*
Sweden, *452, 470, 484*
Ásbyrgi national park, *272*
Åsgårdstrand, Nor., *334*
Ásgrímur Jónsson Museum, *251*
Åskhuet, Swe., *466*
Ásmundur Sveinsson Gallery, *251*
Assens, Den., *109*
Astruptunet, *383*
ATMs (automated teller machines), *7–8*
Aulestad, *370*
Auning, Den., *122*

Baby-sitting services, *21*
Bakkafjörður, Ice., *277*
Bakkagerði, Ice., *275*
Bakken amusement park, *76*
Balestrand, Nor., *382, 385*
Baltic Herring Festival, *160*
Baltiska Hallen, *476*
Bank Holiday Weekend, *231*
Barnafossar, *265–266*
Barnekunst Museum, *317*
Båstad, Swe., *464*
Beaches, *30–31. See also under cities and countries*
Bed-and-breakfasts, *169*
Beds, sizes of, *32*
Benneweis Circus, *76*
Bergen, Nor.,

348–361
the arts, *360*
beaches, *357*
business hours, *351*
children, attractions for, *356*
currency exchanges, *349*
emergencies, *349*
guided tours, *351–352*
hotels, *359–360*
nightlife, *360–361*
restaurants, *357–359*
shopping, *356*
sightseeing, *352, 354–356*
sports, *356–357*
tourist information, *349*
transportation, *349–351*
Bergenhus Festning, *352*
Bergen Jazz Festival, *360*
Bergen Music Festival, *287*
Bergman, Ingmar, *448*
Bergþórshvoll, Ice., *279*
Bicycling, *30*
Copenhagen, *63, 79*
Denmark, *56–57, 100, 106, 112, 125, 130–131*
Finland, *165, 167, 203, 212*
Helsinki, *187*
Iceland, *272*
Norway, *297, 344, 371*
Oslo, *320*
Stockholm, *437*
Sweden, *420, 452*
tours, *4*
Bilfröst, Ice., *267*
Billund, Den., *116, 120*
Bindslev Ørne Reservat, *124*

Biologiska Museet,
433
Bird-watching, *297,*
342, 344, 400
Birkebeiner Race,
287
Bjaaland Museum,
366
Blaafarveværket, *316*
Blidösund
(steamboat), *433*
Blönduós, Ice., *269*
Boating and sailing,
30
Bergen, *357*
Denmark, *57*
Finland, *167, 205,*
220, 222
Göteborg, *459*
Iceland, *265*
Norway, *299, 306, 345*
Sweden, *420, 425, 485*
Boat travel. *See*
Ferry service
Boda Glasbruk, *479*
Boden, Swe., *493*
Bodø, Nor., *393,*
401–402
Bogø Island, *99*
Bog people,
preserved, *120, 121,*
122
Bohus Festning, *464,*
468
Bohuslän, *463, 467*
Bø i Telemark, Nor.,
376
Bomarsund, Fin., *204*
Borgafjörður, Ice.,
265–266, 268
Borgarbókasafn,
251–252
Borgarnes, Ice.,
265–266, 267
Borgholm, Swe., *476*
Bornholm, *129–139*
the arts, *139*
beaches, *136–137*
children, attractions
for, *135*
emergencies, *130*
guided tours, *131*
hotels, *137–138*
nightlife, *139*
restaurants, *133,*
137–138
shopping, *135–136*
sightseeing, *131–135*
sports, *136*
tourist information,

129–130
transportation,
130–131
Bornholm Museum,
131
Bornholms Dyre og
Naturpark, *135*
Borøoy Island, *153,*
154
Borrehaugene, *334*
Børsen, *69*
Borstahusen, *476*
Bøsdalafossur
(waterfall), *153*
Botaniska
Trädgården, *476*
Botanisk Have
(Copenhagen), *73*
Brændesgårdshaven,
135
Brahe, Tycho, *73, 476*
Brandt's
Klædefabrik, *108*
Brattahlið, Gre., *144*
Breakfasts, *32*
Breidablikk, *342*
Breioðamerkur
sands, *276*
Breioðsdalsvík, Ice.,
276
Brú, Ice., *269, 273*
Bryggen buildings,
352
Bryggen Museum,
354
Bryne, Nor., *346*
Búðahraun lavafield,
266
Búðir, Ice., *266, 267*
Budolfi Kirke, *123*
Buekorpsmuseet, *356*
Burmeisterska huset,
451
Bus travel, *28*
Bergen, *350–351*
Copenhagen, *62, 63*
Denmark, *53, 54, 93,*
105–106, 117, 130
Faroe Islands, *150*
Finland, *164, 172,*
173, 200, 209, 216
Göteborg, *454*
Helsinki, *173*
Iceland, *236–237, 264,*
269, 274, 278
Norway, *293, 332,*
337, 362, 378,
388–389
Oslo, *304, 305*
Reykjavík, *246, 247*

Sweden, *416,*
417–418, 463,
466, 479
By Museum, *95*

Cameras,
Camcorders and
Laptops, traveling
with, *11–12*
Camping
Denmark, *60, 136*
Finland, *169*
Iceland, *243–244, 280*
Norway, *297–298*
Stockholm, *448*
Sweden, *420, 453, 461*
Canoeing
Denmark, *100, 125*
Finland, *167, 212,*
216, 222
Norway, *298, 372*
Sweden, *486*
Carl Larsson Gorden,
482
Carl Nielsen
Museum, *108*
Carmelite Kloster, *95*
Car museum, *99–100*
Carolina Rediviva,
451
Car rentals, *16–17*
Car travel, *28*
Bergen, *350, 351*
Copenhagen, *62*
Denmark, *52, 54–55,*
92, 93, 105, 117, 130
Faroe Islands, *150*
Finland, *164,*
172–173, 208–209,
216
Göteborg, *455*
Helsinki, *171*
Iceland, *260, 264,*
268, 274, 277
Norway, *294–295,*
332, 333, 336, 337,
361–362, 378, 388,
389
Oslo, *304, 305*
Reykjavík, *247*
Sweden, *415–416,*
424, 464, 490
Cash machines, *7–8*
Casinos
Copenhagen, *90*
Denmark, *104, 116,*
129
Helsinki, *180, 198*
Stockholm, *449*
Castles

Bergen, *356*
Copenhagen, *68,*
70–71, 73
Denmark, *95, 96,*
99–100, 104, 106,
110–111, 115
Finland, *174, 202,*
204, 217, 221
Helsinki, *181–182*
Norway, *334, 370, 391*
Oslo, *307, 311, 314*
Stockholm, *446, 448,*
451, 454
Sweden, *450, 468,*
469–470, 478
Caverns
Norway, *394*
Sweden, *453*
Cemeteries
Denmark, *123–124*
Oslo, *312*
Charlottenborg,
70–71
Children, traveling
with, *19–21. See*
also under cities and
countries
Children's Festival,
160
Christiania
commune, *77*
Christiansborg Slot,
68
Christiansholm
festning, *340*
Christianskirkjan,
153
Christiansø, Den.,
135
Christmas events
Norway, *288*
Sweden, *408*
Chronology of
Scandinavia, *38–43*
Churches
Bergen, *354, 355*
Copenhagen, *69, 70,*
71–73
Denmark, *95, 96, 97,*
98, 99, 108, 120, 123,
124, 132, 133–134
Faroe Islands, *152,*
153
Finland, *202, 218,*
220, 221
Göteborg, *457*
Greenland, *144*
Helsinki, *178, 180,*
181, 182–183
Iceland, *262, 269,*

271, 278

Norway, *338, 340, 342, 365, 366, 368, 369, 370, 391, 392, 395*

Oslo, *310, 312, 314, 317–318*

Reykjavík, *250, 251*

Stockholm, *430*

Sweden, *460, 452, 470, 479, 491*

Citadellet, *473, 475*

Citizen's Emergency Center, *2*

City Cards, *18*

Climate, *4–5. See also under cities and countries*

Clothing for the trip, *5. See also under cities and countries*

Cobalt mines, *316*

Colleges and universities

Copenhagen, *73*

Göteborg, *458*

Helsinki, *180*

Lund, *476*

Oslo, *307*

Reykjavík, *252*

Uppsala, *450*

Convents

Denmark, *95*

Finland, *203, 219*

Conversion tables, *501–502*

Copenhagen, Den., *60–66, 68–81, 84–91*

the arts, *89*

beaches, *80–81*

business hours, *63–64*

casinos, *90*

children, attractions for, *76*

Christianshavn, *69–70*

climate, *48*

currency exchanges, *61–62*

embassies, *61*

emergencies, *61*

English-language bookstores, *62*

excursions, *75–76*

festivals, *48–49*

free attractions, *76*

guided tours, *64*

hotels, *86–89*

Istedgade district, *74–75*

Kongens Nytorv, *70*

nightlife, *89–91*

Nyboder district, *72*

Nyhavn, *71*

pharmacies, *61*

Rådhus Pladsen, *65*

restaurants, *70, 71, 72, 81, 84–86*

shopping, *77–79*

sightseeing, *65, 68–75*

sports, *79–80*

Strøget, district, *72–75*

taxis, *63*

tourist information, *61*

transportation, *62–63*

travel agencies, *62*

Copenhagen Carnival, *48*

Copenhagen Jazz Festival, *49*

Costs of the trip, *9*

Covered wagons, *111*

Credit cards, *7–8, 33*

Crystal works, *466*

Currencies, *7*

Customs, *10–11*

Cygnaeuksen Galleria, *179*

Czarina's Stone, *174*

Dalarna folklore district, *480–492*

Dalen, Nor., *370*

Dance

Copenhagen, *89*

Stockholm, *450*

Danmarks Akvarium, *76*

Dansk Presse museum, *108*

Davíðshús, *270*

Davids Samling museum, *76*

De Kongelige Stald, *69*

Den Fynske Landsby, *108*

Den Gamle By, *122*

Den Gamle Gård, *109*

Den Geografiske Have, *120*

Den Hirschsprungske Samling, *73–74*

Den Lille Havefrue (statue), *72*

Denmark, *44–60. See also Bornholm; Copenhagen; Faroe Islands; Fyn and the central islands; Greenland; Jylland;*

Sjælland and its islands.

beaches, *57*

books on, *52*

business hours, *56*

car rentals, *50*

climate, *48*

costs of the trip, *49*

currency, *49*

customs and duties, *50*

disabled travelers, *51*

festivals and seasonal events, *48–49, 128*

government tourist offices, *2, 48*

hotels, *59–60*

language, *50*

mail, *56*

older travelers, *51*

passports and visas, *49–50*

rail passes, *50–51*

restaurants, *58*

shopping, *56*

sports, *56–57*

student and youth travel, *51*

taxes, *49*

telephones, *55*

timing the visit, *48*

tipping, *56*

transportation in, *54–55*

transportation to, *52–53*

Det Gamla Apoteket, *452*

Det Kongelige Bibliotek, *68–69*

Det Norske Utvandrersenteret, *343*

Dettifoss waterfall, *272*

Dimmuborgir lava field, *271*

Dinesen, Isak, *93, 95*

Disabled travelers. *See also under cities and countries*

hints for, *21–22*

sports participation, *299*

Disagården, *449*

Discount Cards, *19*

Djupadal waterfall, *477*

Djúpivogur, Ice., *276*

Djurgården Island, *452–453*

Dogsledding, *147, 306, 371, 400*

Doll and Toy Museum, *185*

Dominican monastery clock, *119*

Domkirke (Bergen), *354*

Domkirke (Viborg), *123*

Dómkirkjan (Reykjavík), *250*

Domkyrka (Uppsala), *450–451*

Domkyrkan (Göteborg), *458*

Donald Duck Cup, *457*

Døndalen forest, *133*

Dormitory accommodations, *169*

Dragør, Den., *75*

Drammen, Nor., *333*

Drammens Museum, *333*

Drekkingarhylur pool, *261*

Drottningholms Slott, *430–431*

Dueodde Fyr, *135, 137*

Dueodde Strand, *134*

Duties, *10–11*

Dyrhólaey promontory, *278*

Easter events

Iceland, *231*

Norway, *287*

Sweden, *410*

Ebeltoft, Den., *122*

Eckerö, Fin., *204*

Educational tours, *4*

Egeskov Slot, *110*

Egilsstaðir, Ice., *275, 276–277*

Ehrensvärd Museo, *181*

Eidsvoll, Nor., *366*

Einar Jónsson Museum and Sculpture Garden, *251*

Eiði, *153, 154*

Eiran Sairaala, *178*

Ekkodalen, *134*

Eksperimentarium, *75*

Elderhostel program, 23

Eldgjá volcano, *278*

Electricity, *6*

Elfsborgs Fästning, *460*

Elmelunde, *99*

Elveseter, Nor., *373*

Emanuel Vigeland Museum, *318*

Emergencies, *2*
Denmark, *61, 92, 105, 117, 130, 141, 149*
Finland, *171, 199, 208, 215*
Iceland, *245–246, 264, 277*
Norway, *303, 336, 349, 377, 387*
Sweden, *422, 456, 483*

Erichsens Gård, *131*

Erkebispegården, *391*

Esbjerg, Den., *120*

Esja mountain, *249*

Eskifjörður, Ice., *275*

Espoo, *186*

EurailPass, *17–18*

Evje Mineralsti, *341*

Eysturoy Island, Faroe Islands, *153, 154*

Fåberg, Nor., *368*

Fåborg, Den., *109, 113*

Fåborg Museum for Fynsk Malerkunst, *109*

Falkenberg, Swe., *466*

Falster, Den., *99*

Falsterbo, Swe., *478*

Falun, Swe., *477–479, 491*

Fanefjord, *99*

Fanø Island, *127*

Fantoft Stavkirke, *355*

Fårevejle, Den., *97*

Farm vacations,
Denmark, *59*
Finland, *162*
Iceland, *243*

Farm Zoo, *253*

Faroe Islands, *148–150, 152–155*
emergencies, *149*
guided tours, *150*
hotels, *154–155*

restaurants, *154–155*
sightseeing, *150, 152–154*
tourist information, *149*
transportation, *149–150*

Fårup Sommerland, *124*

Fennefoss Museum, *341*

Ferjukot wild salmon farm, *265*

Ferry service, *28–29*
Bergen, *350*
Copenhagen, *63*
Denmark, *53, 121, 130, 141–142*
Faroe Islands, *149–150*
Finland, *163, 164, 174, 200*
Greenland, *144*
Helsinki, *176*
Iceland, *235–236, 237–238, 265, 274, 278*
Norway, *292, 293–294, 333, 337, 378, 388, 389*
Oslo, *305*
Sweden, *417, 418, 472*

Feske Körkan, *460*

Festivals and seasonal events. *See under cities and countries*

Film
Copenhagen, *89*
Helsinki, *198*
Oslo, *330*
Reykavík, *259*
Stockholm, *450*

Fimmvörðuháls mountain pass, *279*

Finland, *157–225.*
See also Helsinki; Lapland
the arts, *207, 225*
beaches, *166, 205*
business hours, *166*
car rentals, *161*
children, attractions for, *204, 221*
children, traveling with, *162*
climate, *159*
costs of, *160*
currency, *160*
customs and duties,

161
disabled travelers, *162*
emergencies, *199, 215*
farmhouse holidays, *162*
festivals and seasonal events, *159–160*
government tourist offices, *157, 159*
guided tours, *200, 216–217*
hotels, *169–170, 205–207, 222–225*
Lakelands, *215–225*
language, *161*
mail, *166*
nightlife, *225*
older travelers, *162*
passports and visas, *161*
rail passes, *161–162*
restaurants, *166–167, 203, 204, 205–207, 222–225*
shopping, *166, 205, 221–222*
sightseeing, *200, 202–204, 217–221*
south coast, *199–201, 202–207*
sports, *166, 205, 222*
taxes, *160, 166*
taxis, *165*
telephones, *165*
timing the visit, *159*
tipping, *166*
tourist information, *199, 215*
transportation in, *163–165*
transportation to, *163, 200, 216*

Finlandiatalo, *182, 197*

Finnish Aviation Museum, *185*

Finnish Glass Museum, *221*

Finnish-Russian connection, *397*

Finse, Nor., *364*

Fishing, *30*
Bergen, *357*
Denmark, *100, 112, 125, 136*
Finland, *167, 212*
Göteborg, *459*
Greenland, *147*
Iceland, *240, 263, 267, 272, 276*

Norway, *298, 344–345, 371, 383, 400*
Oslo, *320*

Fjærland, Nor., *382, 385*

Fjords
Bergen, *351*
Faroe Islands, *153*
Greenland, *145*
Iceland, *264–267, 275*
Norway, *351–352, 364, 382*

Flagstad, Kirsten, *370*

Flåm, Nor., *382–383, 385*

Flaskeskibs-samlingen, *111*

Flatey, Ice., *266*

Fljótshilíð, Ice., *281*

Fløybanen cable car, *354*

Fnjóskadalur Valley, *270–271*

Folkhögskolan, *460*

Folklore performances
Bergen, *360*
Reykavík, *259*

Fornsalen, *456*

Forsvarsmuseet (Oslo), *314*

Forsvarsmuseet (Trondheim), *391–392*

Forts
Bergen, *352*
Copenhagen, *72*
Denmark, *118, 132, 135*
Faroe Islands, *152*
Finland, *204*
Göteborg, *459*
Norway, *332, 340*
Sweden, *433, 465, 467, 470*

Fourth of July festivals, *49*

Fountains, *72, 175*

Fram-museet, *315*

Fredensborg, Den., *96, 101*

Fredensborg Slot, *96*

Frederiksborg, Den., *101*

Frederiksborg Slot, *96*

Fredrikstad, Nor., *332*

Fredriksten festning, *495*
332
Fredriksvern, *338*
Frelsers Kirke, *70*
Friends Overseas, *20*
Frihedsmuseet, *72*
Fríkirkjan, *252*
Frilandsmuseet, *76*
Fróði, Sæmundur,
statue of, *252*
Fylkesmuseet, *365*
Fyn and the central
islands, *104–116*
the arts, *115*
beaches, *112*
casinos, *116*
children, attractions
for, *111*
emergencies, *105*
guided tours, *106*
hotels, *112–115*
nightlife, *115–116*
pharmacy, *105*
restaurants, *109,*
112–115
shopping, *111–112*
sightseeing, *106–111*
sports, *112*
tourist information,
105
transportation,
105–106
Fyn rundt (regatta),
109–110

Gallen-Kellela estate,
183–184
Galleri F15, *332*
Gällivare, Swe., *445*
Gamla Uppsala
Kyrka, *452*
Gamle Aker Kirke,
312
Gamle Rådhus
(Oslo), *311*
Gamle Rådhuset
(Bergen), *354*
Gammel Estrup Slot,
122
Gardens
Copenhagen, *71, 73*
Denmark, *107–108,*
109, 120, 124, 125
Finland, *204*
Helsinki, *185, 186*
Iceland, *270*
Reykjavík, *253*
Sweden, *451, 454,*
468, 479
Garnisonsmuseet,

Gausdal, Nor., *368*
Gaustatoppen
mountain, *365*
Gävle, Swe., *487*
Gay bars
Copenhagen, *91*
Helsinki, *196*
Oslo, *331*
Stockholm, *449*
Gefion Springvandet,
72
Geilo, Nor., *362, 370,*
373–374
Geiranger, Nor., *381,*
385
Genealogy resources
Norway, *343*
Sweden, *470*
Gesunda, Swe., *486*
Geysers, *258*
Geysir geyser, *280*
Gilleleje, Den., *97*
Gimle Gård, *340*
Glaciers
Iceland, *275–276*
Norway, *381, 393,*
395, 399
Glass works
Finland, *220–221*
Norway, *316–317*
Sweden, *478–479*
Glaumbær Folk
Museum, *269*
Goðafoss waterfalls,
271
Gola, Nor., *374*
Gold panning,
211–212
Golf
Bergen, *357*
Copenhagen, *79–80*
Denmark, *57, 101,*
112, 125, 136
Finland, *213, 222*
Helsinki, *187*
Iceland, *231, 240,*
267, 272, 280
Norway, *298, 345*
Oslo, *320*
Reykjavík, *254*
Stockholm, *438*
Sweden, *421*
Gol stave Church,
314
Göta Canal, *466–469*
Göteborg, Swe.,
453–460
the arts, *460*
beaches, *455*

children, attractions
for, *455*
consulates, *453*
emergencies, *453*
English-language
bookstores, *454*
excursions, *459–460*
guided tours, *456*
hotels, *457–458*
nightlife, *458–459*
restaurants, *458*
shopping, *457*
sightseeing, *456, 457*
sports, *458*
tourist information,
453
transportation, *453*
travel agencies, *454*
Gotland Island, *459*
Government tourist
offices, *2*
Grábrók volcanic
cone, *266*
Græsholmen Island,
135
Grasagarður, *253*
Greenland, *142,*
144–148
clothing for the trip,
140
emergencies, *141*
guided tours, *142*
hotels, *147–148*
language, *140*
nightlife, *148*
restaurants, *147–148*
shopping, *146–147*
sightseeing, *142,*
144–146
sports, *147*
timing the visit, *140*
tourist information,
141
transportation,
141–142
Grense Jakobselv, *397*
Grete Waitz Race,
287
Grieg, Edvard, *355*
Grieghallen, *355*
Grimstad, Nor.,
339–340
Gripsholm Slott, *437*
Gröna Lund
amusement park, *431*
Gröngvistin Talo, *175*
Grovane i Vennesla,
Nor., *341*
Grund, Ice., *270*
Gruvene mines,

364–365
Gudbrandsdal, Nor.,
366–368
Gudhjem, Den., *133,*
137
Guest houses, *243*
Gullfoss waterfall,
262
Guovdageainu
Gilisillju, *397*
Gustavianum, *451*

Hadeland, Nor.,
316–317
Hå gravesite and
parsonage, *341*
Haihara Doll and
Costume Museum,
220
Håkonshallen, *352*
Halden, Nor., *332*
Hallgrímskirkja, *251*
Hallormsstaður
Forest Reserve, *275,*
277
Hallwylska Museet,
427
Halmstad, Swe., *467*
Hamar, Nor., *366,*
369, 370
Hamarsfjörður, *275*
Häme Castle, *221*
Hämeenlinna, Fin.,
219, 220–221,
222–223
Hammeren, Den., *132*
Hammerfest, Nor.,
395–396, 402
Hammershus
fortress, *132*
Hammer Sø, *132*
Handball, *255*
Handicraft
itineraries, *36–38*
Hanko, Fin., *199,*
200, 202, 206
Hans Christian
Andersen Festival,
49
Hans Christian
Andersen Hus,
107–108
Hans Christian
Andersens
Barndomshjem, *108*
Hanseatisk Museum,
352
Hardangerfjord, *364*
Hardangervidda, *362,*
364, 372

Harstad, Nor., *394–396, 399, 402*
Hattula Church, *221*
Haugesund, Nor., *284*
Haugfossen, *316*
Haukadalur, Ice., *263*
Havis Amandan Patsas, *175*
Havnar Kirkja, *152*
Health clubs
Copenhagen, *80*
Health concerns, *13–14*
Health insurance, *14*
Heavy water production, *365*
Heddal, Nor., *365*
Hedmarkmuseet og Domkirkeodden, *366*
Heimaey Island, *280*
Hekla volcano, *279*
Helicopter travel
Faroe Islands, *150*
Greenland, *141*
Hell, Nor., *370*
Hella, Ice., *279*
Hellerup, Den., *79*
Helligånds Kirken, *70*
Helligandsklosteret, *123*
Helligdomsklipperne rock formation, *133*
Hellnar, Ice., *266*
Helsingborg, Swe., *474, 481*
Helsingin Pitajan Kirkko, *185*
Helsingin Yliopisto, *180*
Helsingør, Den., *95–96, 101–102*
Helsinki, Fin., *170–175, 178–189, 192–199*
the arts, *197–198*
business hours, *166*
children, attractions for, *185*
climate, *159*
currency exchanges, *171*
embassies, *171*
emergencies, *171*
English-language bookstores, *171*
excursions, *183–185*
festivals, *159–160*
free attractions, *185*
guided tours, *173–174*

Hietalahden Tori, *178*
hotels, *193–197*
Kaivopuisto, *179*
Kauppatori, *174*
metro system, *173*
nightlife, *198–199*
restaurants, *175, 179, 180, 182, 183, 187–189, 192–193*
Senaatintori, *180*
shopping, *186–187*
sightseeing, *174–175, 178–183*
sports, *187*
taxis, *172*
tourist information, *171, 175*
transportation, *163–165*
travel agencies, *172*
Helsinki Festival, *160*
Hemsedal, Nor., *370*
Henie, Sonja, *315*
Henie-Onstad Center, *315*
Herregården, *338*
Heureka Suomalainen Tiedekeskus, *184*
Heyerdahl, Thor, *312*
Hiking, *30*
Bergen, *357*
Denmark, *57, 136*
Finland, *167, 213*
Greenland, *147*
Iceland, *240–241, 272, 280*
Norway, *298, 345, 371–372, 378–379, 383, 400*
Oslo, *321*
Sweden, *420*
Hill, Joe, *488*
Hillerød, Den., *96*
Historisk Museum (Oslo), *307*
History of Scandinavia, *38–43*
Hjemmefrontmuseet, *391–392*
Hjemmeluft, Nor., *395*
Hlíðarendi, Ice., *279*
Höfn, Ice., *275–276, 277*
Højerup Kirke, *98–99*
Hólar, *269*
Hollufgård, *109*
Holmenkollbakken, (ski museum), *313*

Holmenkollen Ski Festival, *287*
Holmens Kirke, *69*
Holy Trinity Church, *4*
Home exchanges, *32–33*
Honningsvåg, Nor., *396, 402*
Horgheim, Nor., *368*
Horseback riding
Copenhagen, *80*
Denmark, *57*
Finland, *213*
Iceland, *241, 263, 267, 272, 276, 280*
Norway, *298, 371–372*
Reykavík, *254–255*
Horse racing, *159*
Horten, Nor., *333–334*
Hospitalsdalen, *144*
Hotel Continental (Oslo), *307, 310*
Hotels, *31–33. See also under cities and countries*
children, accommodations for, *21*
disabled travelers, accommodations for, *22*
reservations, *32*
Hot springs, *272*
Houses, historic
Denmark, *93, 95, 106, 108, 109, 110, 118, 122, 123, 133*
Finland, *219, 221*
Greenland, *145*
Helsinki, *175, 178, 179, 182, 183–184*
Iceland, *252, 254, 269, 270, 276*
Norway, *334, 338, 340, 342, 343, 352, 354, 355, 392*
Stockholm, *435*
Sweden, *472, 478*
Hraunfossar, *265–266*
Humlebæk, Den., *95*
Hunderfossen park, *369–370*
Hunting, *147, 345, 372, 400*
Húsafell park, *266*
Húsavik, Ice., *272, 273*
Húsey, Ice., *277*

Hvalsey Kirke, *144*
Hvannadalshnúkur glacier, *276*
Hveragerði, Ice., *262, 263*
Hverfjall ash cone, *271*
Hvolsvöllur, Ice., *280*
Ibsen, Henrik, *339–340, 365, 368*
Ibsenhus, *339–340*
Icebergs, *144*
Iceland, *227–281. See also Reykavík*
alcoholic beverages, *242–243*
books on, *234*
business hours, *238–239*
car rentals, *233*
children, attractions for, *263*
climate, *230*
clothing for, *231*
costs of, *232*
currency, *231–232*
customs, *232*
disabled travelers, *233*
eastern region, *274–277*
electricity, *231*
emergencies, *260, 264, 268, 277, 260*
festivals and seasonal events, *230–231*
Golden Circle excursion, *260–264*
government tourist offices, *2, 229–230*
guided tours, *260, 265, 269, 274, 278, 260*
health concerns, *233*
hotels, *243–244, 263–264, 267–268, 273–274, 276–277, 280–281*
language, *233*
mail, *238*
money brought to, *231*
northern region, *268–274*
passports and visas, *232*
restaurants, *241–242, 261, 263–264, 267–268, 271, 273, 276–277, 280–281*
shopping, *239, 272*

sightseeing, *261–262,*
265–267, 269–272,
275–276, 278–280
southern region,
277–281
sports, *240–241, 263,*
267, 272, 276, 280
taxes, *232*
telephones, *238*
timing the visit, *230*
tipping, *238*
transportation in,
236–238, 260
transportation to,
234–236, 260,
264–265, 268–269,
274, 277–278
the west and western
fjords, *264–268*
Iceland National
Day, *231*
Iittala Glassworks,
220–221
Ilola
Mäkitupalaiskylä,
184
Ilulissat/Jacobshavn,
Gre., *145, 147*
Inari, Fin., *211, 213*
Inarijärvi, *211*
Inarin Porofarmi,
211
Independence Day
(parade), *160*
Ingólfsgarður pier,
253
Insurance, *14–16*
Interhostel, *23*
International Jean
Sibelius Violin
Competition, *160*
International
Women's Theater
and Cultural
Festival, *121*
Isafjörður, Ice.,
266–267
Isdøla, Nor., *364*
Ishavskatedralen, *395*
Itinerary
recommendations,
33–38
Ivalo, Fin., *211, 213*

Jan-Karls Gardenin
Ulkorlmamuseo, *204*
Jelling, Den., *121*
Jeløy, Nor., *330*
Jens Bangs Stenhus,
123

Jernbanemuseet, *369*
Joe Hill Museet, *488*
Jogging. *See* Running
Jökulsárgljúfur
National Park, *272*
Jökulsárlón lagoon,
275–276
Jons Kapel, *132*
Jostedalsbreen, *381*
Jotunheimen
national park, *368,*
372
Joulupukin Pajakylä,
210
Juhannus (festivals),
159
Jukkasjärvi, Swe.,
494, 496
Julianehåb Museum,
144
Jutland Pass, *118*
Jylland, *116–119,*
120–129
the arts, *128*
beaches, *125*
casinos, *129*
children, attractions
for, *124*
emergencies, *117*
festivals, *42*
guided tours, *118*
hotels, *125–128*
nightlife, *128–129*
restaurants, *121,*
125–128
shopping, *125*
sightseeing, *118,*
120–124
sports, *125*
tourist information,
116–117
transportation,
117–118

Kaamos Jazz
(festival), *160*
Kafhellir sea cave,
271
Kåfjord, Nor., *399*
Kainuu Jazz
(festival), *159*
Kaknästornet, *435*
Kaleva Church, *220*
Kalmar, Swe., *477,*
479
Kangerlussuaq/-
Søndre Strømfjord,
145
Karasjok, Nor., *397,*
399, 402

Kardemomme By,
341
Käringberget, *483*
Karlstad, Swe., *473*
Kärnan, *475*
Kåseberga, Swe., *477*
Kastellet, *72*
Kastellholmen
Island, *425*
Kaupingintalo, *174*
Kaustinen Folk
Music Festival, *160*
Kautokeino, Nor.,
396–397, 399
Keldby, *99*
Kemijärvi, *210*
Kerling mountain,
270
Kerteminde, Den.,
106–107, 113
Kierkegaard, Søren,
75
Kiilopää, *213*
Kingdom of Crystal,
478
Kinnekulle, *470*
Kirkenes, Nor., *397,*
398–399, 402–403
Kirkja, *271*
Kirkjubøur, Faroe
Islands, *152*
Kirkjubæjarklaustur,
Ice., *278, 280*
Kittelsen, Theodor,
338
Kittilä, *211*
Kjarvalsstaoðir, *251*
Kjerringøy, Nor., *387*
Klaksvík, Faroe
Islands, *153, 154*
Klampenborg, Den.,
102
Kleppjárnsreykir
horticultural center,
265
Klokketårnet, *109*
Knud Rasmussens
Fødehjem, *145*
Knuthenborg Safari
Park, *100*
Københavns
Bymuseum, *75*
Københavns
Synagoge, *73*
Københavns
Universitet, *73*
Køge, Den., *98*
Køge Kunst Museet
Skitsesamling, *98*
Køge Museum, *98*

Kolding, Den., *118,*
120, 127
Koldinghus, *118*
Kommandør
Christensens
Hvalfangstmuseum,
334
Kongaminnid, *144*
Kongaminniö, *152*
Kongelige Teater, *70*
Kongens Haven
(Copenhagen), *73*
Kongeparken
Amusement Park,
344
Kong Haakon VIIs
kilde, *338*
Kongsberg, Nor.,
364–365, 374, 376
Kongsberg Kirke, *365*
Kongsgård, *342*
Kongsten festning,
332
Kon-Tiki Museum, *315*
Korkeasaari
Elaintarha, *185*
Korskirken, *317–318*
Kosta Glasbruk, *480*
Koster Islands, *469*
Kragerø, Nor., *338*
Krigøminnemuseet,
393–394
Kristiansand, Nor.,
336–338, 340–341,
343–345, 346–347,
348
Kristianstad, Swe.,
479
Kristiansund, Nor.,
381, 385
Kristnes, Ice., *270*
Kronan Museet, *472*
Kronborg Slot, *95,*
104
Kronhuset, *459*
Krossobanen, *366*
Kuhmo Chamber
Music Festival, *160*
Kultamuseo, *210–211*
Kultaranta, *203*
Kulturen, *478*
Kulturhistoriska
Museet (Göteborg),
490
Kulturhistoriske
Museum (Silkeborg),
121
Kulturhuset, *428*
Kulturhuset Banken,
367

Kulusak, Gre., *146*
Kungälv, Swe., *470*
Kungliga Dramatiska Teatern, *429–430*
Kungsbacka, Swe., *468*
Kunsthallen, *108*
Kunstindustrimuseet (Oslo), *311–312*
Kuopio, Fin., *217–218, 223*
Kuopio Music and Dance Festival, *159*
Kværndrup, Den., *110*
Kverkfjöll hot springs, *272*
Kvikkjokk, Swe., *493*
Kvinesdal, Nor., *337*

Läckö Slött, *469*
Ladby, Den., *107*
Lagerlöf, Selma, *477*
Lake Siljan, *487*
Laki Volcano, *278*
Landmannalaugar, *279*
Landsbókasafnið, *248, 250*
Landsbrugs Museum, *133*
Landskrona, Swe., *479*
Landsmuseet, *144*
Landsstýri, *152*
Langeland Island, *111*
Language, *13*. See also under countries
Lapland. See also Samiland
children, attractions for, *211–212*
emergencies, *208*
Finland, *207–215*
guided tours, *209*
hotels, *213–215*
restaurants, *210, 213–215*
shopping, *212*
sightseeing, *210–211*
sports, *212–213*
tourist information, *208*
transportation, *208–209*
Larsen, Johannes, *106–107*

Larsson, Carl, *488*
Larvik, Nor., *338*
Laugardalur, *253*
Laugarvatn, *261–262, 263–264*
Laxfoss waterfall, *265*
Ledaal stately house, *342*
Legoland, *48, 120*
Lejre, Den., *97*
Lejre Forsøgscenter, *97*
Leksand, Swe., *487*
Lenin Museum, *220*
Lepramuseet-St. Jørgens Hospital, *352*
Lesja, Nor., *368*
Libraries
Copenhagen, *68–69*
Göteborg, *458*
Kuopio, *224*
Reykjavík, *248, 250, 251–252*
Stockholm, *428*
Trondheim, *392*
Uppsala, *454*
Lighthouses, *135, 341*
Lilla Holmen, *204*
Lilla Karlsö bird refuge, *461*
Lillehammer, Nor., *366–368, 369, 370–371, 374–375*
Lillehammer Bys Malerisamling, *368*
Lilleputthammer, *370*
Lindesnes Fyr, *341*
Lindholm Højo, *123–124*
Linnaeusgården, *454*
Linnanmäki, *185*
Linné Museum, *454*
Lintula convent, *219*
Lisebergs Nöjes Park, *454*
Liselund Slot, *99*
Listasafn Islands, *252*
Ljósavatn church, *271*
Lödöse, Swe., *470*
Loen, Nor., *386*
Lofoten Islands, *394, 399, 403*
Lögurinn lake, *275*
Lolland Island, *99–100, 102*
Lom, Nor., *368, 375*

Lom Stavkirke, *368*
Longyearbyen, Nor., *398*
Lónkot, Ice., *273*
Louisiana museum, *75, 95*
Luggage
airline rules on, *6–7*
insurance for, *15*
Luleå, Swe., *498*
Lummelunda, *454*
Lund, Swe., *478, 482*
Luostotunturi, Fin., *210*
Lurblæserne, *65*
Lyngby, Den., *76*
Lyngør, Nor., *338–339*
Lysekil, Swe., *466*
Lysøen, *356*
Lystiland, *204*
Lýsuhóll, Ice., *266*

Madsebakke, *133*
Mælstrøms, *394*
Magnus Cathedral, *152*
Maihaugen, *367*
Malmö, Swe., *478–479, 483*
Mandal, Nor., *341*
Mannerheim Museo, *179*
Mårbacka, *472*
Mariakirken (Bergen), *354*
Maria Kyrka (Gotland), *452*
Mariefred, Swe., *436–437*
Mariehamn, Fin., *203–204*
Marienlyst Slot, *95*
Marinemuseet, *333*
Markarfljót River, *279*
Marstein, Nor., *368*
Matthíasarhús, *270*
Medicinsk Historisk Museum, *77*
Medieval Week, *464*
Menntaskólinn í Reykjavík, *250*
Merdøgaard, *339*
Merdøy Island, *339*
Merenkulkijoiden Muistomerkki statue, *178*
Middelfart, Den., *109, 118*

Midnight Sun, *386*
Midsummer's Night festivals, *49, 287*
Miðvágur, Faroe Islands, *153*
Mikael Agricolan Kirkko, *178*
Mikkeli, Fin., *221*
Mineral springs, *341*
Mining sites
Norway, *364–365, 369*
Sweden, *487–488*
Minjasafnið, *270*
Moderna Museet, *427*
Mööruvellir farm, *270*
Moesgård Forhistorisk Museum, *122*
Mo i Rana, Nor., *393, 399*
Molde, Nor., *381, 386*
Monasteries
Denmark, *123*
Finland, *218*
Stockholm, *433–434*
Monastery of Valamo, *218*
Money, *7–9*
Møn Island, *99, 102*
Møns Klint, *99*
Mønsted Kalkgruber, *124–125*
Møntergården, *108*
Mora, Swe., *488, 491*
Morgedal, Nor., *366*
Moskenesstraumen, *394*
Mountaineering, *298, 372*
Mountain huts, *244*
Mountains itinerary, *34–35*
Mount Baula, *266*
Muddus National Park, *496*
Munch, Edvard
Munchmuseet, *313*
Munchs lille hus, *334*
Museet for Fotokunst, *108*
Museet for Samtidskunst, *310*
Museums. See also Art galleries and museums
Bergen, *352, 354, 356*
Copenhagen, *68, 69, 72, 75, 76, 77*
Denmark, *93, 95, 97,*

98, 99–100, 106, 108, 109, 110, 118, 120, 121, 122, 131, 134
Finland, 202, 203–204, 210–211, 219, 220
Greenland, 144, 145–146
Helsinki, 175, 178, 179, 181, 182, 183–184, 185
Iceland, 269, 270
Norway, 332, 333–334, 339, 340, 341, 343, 364, 366, 367, 368, 369, 381, 382, 391–392, 393–394, 395, 396, 397
Oslo, 307, 311, 313, 314, 315, 317
Reykjavík, 248, 251–252
Stockholm, 434–435
Sweden, 450, 451, 455, 459, 468, 478, 479, 490–491, 493, 495

Music, classical
Bergen, 360
Helsinki, 197
Reykavík, 259
Stockholm, 448
Tromsø, 103

Music, popular
Bergen, 364
Copenhagen, 91
Norway, 286, 376
Stockholm, 448

Mykines atoll, 153–154
Mykineshólmur, 154
Myntkabinette, 434
Myrdal, Nor., 382–383
Mýrdalur, Ice., 281
Mývatn lake, 271, 273
Myyrmäki Kirkko, 184–185

Naantali, Fin., 199, 203, 206
Naantali Music Festival, 159, 207
Naantalin Luostarikirkko, 203
Námaskarð mountain ridge, 272
Nanortalik, Gre., 142
Narsaq, Gre., 144

Narsarsuaq, Gre., 144, 147–148
Narvik, Nor., 393–394
Nasinnuela Observation Tower, 219–220
Nasjonalgalleriet (Oslo), 307
National Museet (Copenhagen), 68
National Museum (Stockholm), 427
Nationaltheatret (Oslo), 307, 320
Náttúrufræðistofnun, 248
Náttúrugripasafnið, 270
Narvik, Nor., 403
Neksø Museum, 134
Neskaupsstaður, Ice., 275
New Year's events, 160
Nidaros domen, 391
Nielsen, Carl, 109
Nikkaluotka, Swe., 493
Nikolaj Kirke, 70
Nonnahús, 270
Nordenfjeldske Kunstindus- trimuseum, 391
Nordiska Museet, 426
Nordkapp, Nor., 396
Nordkappmuseet, 396
Nordlysplanetariet, 398
Nordturist Card, 28
Norðurlandahúsið, 152
Norges Hjemme- frontmuseum, 311
Norræna Húsið, 252
Norrbottens Museet, 495
Nørresundby, Den., 123–124
Norrviken Gardens, 468
Norsk Bergverksmuseum, 364
Norsk Bremuseum, 382
Norsk Folkemuseum, 314, 317
Norsk Hermetikkmuseum,

343
Norsk Vegmuseum, 368
North Cape Hall, 396
Northern Light Festival, 287
Norway, 283–406. See also Bergen; Oslo; Sørlandet region; Trondheim
the arts, 376
beaches, 299–300
business hours, 296
car rentals, 274
central fjord country, 377–386
children, attractions for, 369–370
children, traveling with, 290
climate, 287
clothing for, 288
costs of, 289
currency, 289
customs and duties, 289–290
disabled travelers, 290
emergencies, 377
festivals and seasonal events, 287–288
Finnish-Russian connection, 397
government tourist offices, 2, 286
guided tours, 378–379
health concerns, 290
holidays, 287
hotels, 301–302, 332, 335, 373–376, 384–386
language, 290
mail, 295
money from abroad, 289
mountains and valleys of the interior, 361–376
nightlife, 401
northern region, 387–388, 391–406
older travelers, 290–291
passports and visas, 289
restaurants, 300–301, 332, 334, 335, 365, 373–376, 381, 382, 384–386
shopping, 296–297, 370–371, 383

sightseeing, 332, 333–335, 362, 364–369, 379, 381–383
sports, 297–299, 371–373, 383
taxes, 297
telephones, 295
timing the visit, 286–287
tipping, 295–296
tourist information, 332, 333, 361, 377
transportation, 291–295, 332, 333, 361–362, 377–378
Notodden, Nor., 370
Núpsstaður, 278
Nusfjord, Nor., 394
Nusnäs, Swe., 487
Nuuk/Godthåb, Gre., 144, 148
Nyborg, Den., 106, 113
Nyborg Museum, 106
Nyborg Slot, 106
Ny Carlsberg Glyptotek, 74
Nykøbing Falster, Den., 102–103
Nylars, Den., 134
Nylars Kirke, 134
Nyord Island, 99

Obrestad, Nor., 341
Oddernes Church, 340
Odense, Den., 107–109, 113–114
Odsherred, 97
Ólafsvik, Ice., 266, 267–268
Öland plateau, 480, 484
Olavinlinna Castle, 217
Olavsgruva, 369
Olavs kloster, 317–318
Olden, Nor., 382
Older travelers, hints for, 22–23. See also under cities and countries
Olympiaparken, 367
Opera, 89, 159, 197–198, 259
Oppdal, Nor., 375
Örfirisey peninsula, 253

Orienteering, *167*, *298*

Orre, Nor., *342*

Orrefors, *480*

Orthodox Church Museum, *218*

Oscarshall Slott, *314*

Oslo, Nor., *302–307*, *310–321*, *324–332*
the arts, *330*
Bygdøy Peninsula, *314–315*
children, attractions for, *317*
climate, *287*
currency exchanges, *303*
embassies, *303*
emergencies, *303*
English-language bookstores, *303*
excursions, *332–335*
festivals and seasonal events, *287–288*
Frogner Park, *312–313*
guided tours, *305–306*
hotels, *326–329*
nightlife, *330–331*
panoramic views, *311*
restaurants, *310*, *313*, *315*, *321*, *324–326*
shopping, *318–320*
sightseeing, *306–307*, *310–315*
sports, *320–321*
subway system, *305*
taxis, *305*
tourist information, *302–303*
transportation in, *304–305*
transportation to, *303–304*
travel agencies, *303*

Oslo Domkirke, *310*

Östasiatiska Museet, *429*

Østerlars, Den., *133–134*

Osterlars Kirke, *133–134*

Outokumpu, Fin., *221*

Øvre Pasvik national park, *397*

Öxaráfoss, *261*

Øyer, Nor., *375*

Package deals for

independent travelers, *3–4*

Paddleboats, *370*

Palaces. *See* Castles

Parks, national
Finland, *212*
Greenland, *147*
Iceland, *272*, *276*
Norway, *341*, *362*, *364*, *368*, *372*, *397*
Sweden, *494–495*

Passports, *9–10*

Pedersker, Den., *135*, *137*

Peer Gynt Vegen, *368*

Pelle the Conqueror Tour, *131*

Photographers, tips for, *11–12*

Þingvellir, Ice., *261*, *264*

Þjóðhátíð 1874 festival, *231*

Þjóðleikhús, *248*, *250*

Þjóðminjasafn, *252*

Planetariums and observatories
Breivika, *394*
Copenhagen, *74*
Helsinki, *184*
Trondheim, *398*

Plane travel
airlines, *24*, *26*
Bergen, *349*
with children, *20*
Copenhagen, *62*
Denmark, *52–53*, *54*, *92*, *105*, *117*, *130*, *141*
discount flights, *24–26*
Faroe Islands, *149*
Finland, *163*, *172*, *200*, *208*, *209*, *216*
flying times, *26–27*
Göteborg, *455*
Greenland, *140*
Helsinki, *170*
Iceland, *234–235*, *236*, *264*, *268*, *274*, *277*
insurance for, *14*
luggage, rules on, *6–7*
Norway, *291*, *292*, *336*, *377–378*, *387–388*
Oslo, *303–304*
Reykjavík, *246*
in Scandinavia, *27*
smoking rules, *26*
Stockholm, *425*
Sweden, *418*, *453*,

473–474, *484–485*, *494*
tips on, *26*

Poet's Way tour, *220*

Pohjoismainen Taidekeskus, *181*

Polarmuseet, *395*

Polarsirkelsenteret, *393*

Pommern Museefartyget, *203–204*

Pori Jazz (festival), *159–160*

Poro Kuninkuusajot Reindeer Races, *159*

Þorri Banquets, *231*

Þórsmörk nature reserve, *279*

Porvoo, Fin., *184*

Porvoo and Edelfelt-Vallgren Museo, *184*

Prekestolen, *343*

Prescription drugs, *1–5*

Presedentinlinna, *174*

Preus Fotomuseum, *334*

Puijo Tower, *219*

Punkaharju ridge, *217*

Pyhätunturi, *210*

Pyynikki, Fin., *219*

Pyynikki Open Air Theater, *220*

Qagssiarssuk, Gre., *144*

Qaqortoq/Julianehåb, Gre., *142*, *144*, *148*

Qasigiannguit/Christianhåb, Gre., *148*

Qeqertarsuaq/Disko, Gre., *145*

Qeqertarsuaq/Godhavn, Gre., *145*

Queen's Birthday (Denmark), *48*

Råbjerg Mile, *124*

Rådhus (Copenhagen), *59*

Rådhus (Oslo), *310*

Rådhuset (Göteborg), *460*

Rådhuset (Malmö), *477*

Rafting, *263*, *298*,

372, *400*

Railroads
Denmark, *121*
Norway, *341*, *364*
Randers, Den., *116*, *122*

Rannikkoty-kistö-museo, *182*

Rasaseporin Linna, *202*

Rasmus Meyers Samlinger, *355*

Rasmussen, Knud, *145*

Rättvik Gammalgård, *487*

Rauma, Fin., *204–205*

Ravnendalen, *340–341*

Redningsselskapets Museum, *333–334*

Reindeer farms, *211*, *212*

Reindeer races, *159*

Reindeer sledding, *397*, *400*

Reine, Nor., *394*

Restaurants, *31*. *See also under cities and countries*

Retretti, *217*

Retretti Taidekeskus, *221*

Reykholt, Ice., *265*, *268*

Reykjavík, Ice., *244–248*, *250–260*
the arts, *259*
business hours, *247*
children, attractions for, *253*
climate, *230*
currency exchanges, *246*
embassies, *245*
emergencies, *245–246*
English-language bookstores, *246*
festivals, *230–231*
guided tours, *248*
hotels, *258–259*
nightlife, *260*
restaurants, *248*, *250*, *252*, *255–257*
shopping, *254*
sightseeing, *248*, *250–252*
sports, *254–255*
tourist information,

245
transportation,
246–247
travel agencies, 246
Reykjavík Arts
Festival, 231
Reykjavík Marathon,
231
Ribe, Den., 116, 120,
127
Ribe Domkirke, 120
Riddarholmskyrkan,
430–431
Riddarhuset, 430
Riihimäki, Fin., 221
Riksdagshuset, 428
Ringve Music
Museum, 392
Risør, Nor., 338
Rjukan, Nor., 365,
375–376
Rock carvings
Denmark, 133
Norway, 395
Sweden, 463
Rockne, Knut, 379
Rød Herregård, 331
Rødvig, 98–99
Roma Kloster Kyrka,
454
Rønne, Den., 131,
137–138, 139
Ronneby, Swe., 479
Rø Plantage, 133
Røros, Nor., 369, 376
Rosenborg Slot, 73
Rosenkrantztårnet,
354
Roskilde, Den., 96,
103–104
Roskilde Domkirke,
96
Roskilde Festival, 49,
96
Rottneros Herrgårds
Park, 473
Round Zealand
Regatta, 48
Rovaniemi, Fin., 210,
213–214
Royal Copenhagen
Museum, 76
Roykstovan
farmhouse, 152
Runde bird rock, 379,
381, 386
Rundetårn, 73
Runestener, 121
Rungstedlund, 93, 95
Running and jogging

Copenhagen, 80
Helsinki, 183
Norway, 298–299
Oslo, 321
Reykjavík, 255
Stockholm, 437
Ruskis Luonnon-
suojelualue, 184
Russiske Ortodoks
Kirke, 71–72

Saamelaismuseo, 211
Saariselkä, Fin., 212,
213, 214
Sailing. See Boating
St. Halvards Kirke,
317–318
St. Knuds Kirke, 108
St. Olav's Church,
152
Saite, Swe., 495
Sakskøbing, Den.,
99–100
Saksûn, Faroe
Islands, 152–153
Sälen, Swe., 480
Salmon farms, 265
Saltstraumen, 393
Samid
Vuorku-Davvirat,
397
Samiland, see
Lapland
Finland, 207–215
Norway, 389, 396–397
Sandefjord, Nor., 334
Sandoy, Faroe
Islands, 154
Sandur, Faroe
Islands, 154
Sandvig, Den., 133
Santa Claus home,
486
Santa Claus Village,
210, 212
Sarek National Park,
495
Särkäniemi
Amusement Center,
219–220
Saubær, Ice., 270
Sauðárkrókur, Ice.,
269, 273
Savonlinna, Fin.,
217, 223–224
Savonlinna Opera
Festival, 159
Scandinavian Guitar
Festival, 207
Scandinavian Rail

Pass, 19
Science centers, 79,
186
Scuba diving, 57,
345–346, 379
Seacoast itinerary,
33–34
Seaside cabins, 160
Sel, 276
Senior Rail Card, 28
Setesdalsbanen
railway, 341
Seurasaaren
Ulkomuseo, 183
Seurasaari, 185
Seven Gardens, 109
Seyðisfjörður, Ice.,
277
Ship Museum, 480
Ships, historic, 182,
203–204, 480
Ship travel. See also
Ferry service
from North America,
27
from United Kingdom,
27
Shopping, 29–30. See
also under cities and
countries
Shrove Tuesday, 159,
410
Sibelius, Jean, 221
Sigtuna, Swe., 438
Silkeborg, Den., 116,
121, 128
Silver mines, 351
Sima power station,
350
Sinebrychoffin
Taidemuseo, 175,
178
Singer, William, 382
Sisimiut/-
Holsteinsborg, Gre.,
145
Sjælland, 91–94,
95–104
the arts, 104
beaches, 101
casinos, 104
children, attractions
for, 100
emergencies, 92
guided tours, 93
hotels, 101–104
nightlife, 104
pharmacies, 92
restaurants, 97,
101–104

shopping, 100
sightseeing, 93,
95–100
sports, 100–101
tourist information, 92
transportation, 92–93
Sjøfartsmuseet
(Stavanger), 343
Sjøfartsmuseet
(Trondheim), 392
Sjømannadagur, 231
Skaftafell National
Park, 276, 277
Skägården, 437–438
Skagen, Den., 124,
128
Skagen Museum, 124
Skálafjörður, 153
Skálholt Cathedral,
262
Skálholt Music
Festival, 231, 262
Skanör, Swe., 480
Skansen museum,
437–438
Skansin, 152
Skating, 255, 299
Skei, Nor., 382, 383
Skien, Nor., 370, 376
Skiing, 30
Bergen, 357
Finland, 167, 213
Helsinki, 187
Iceland, 241
museum on, 313
Norway, 299, 366,
367, 372–373, 383,
400–401
Oslo, 321
Reykjavík, 255
Sweden, 421, 491
Skógafoss, 279
Skógar, Ice.,
278–279, 281
Skogbrand Insurance
building, 311
Skogsmuseet
Silvanum, 490
Skokloster Slott, 438
Skt. Nicolai Kirke
(Vejle), 120
Skt. Nikolai Kirke
(Køge), 98
Skt. Olai's Kirke, 95
Skútustaðir, Ice., 271
Slættaratindur
mountain, 153
Slagen, Nor., 334
Sleigh rides, 306
Slottet, 307

Slottsfjellet, *334*
Småland Museum, *472*
Smögen Island, *457*
Snæfellsjökull, *266*
Snæfellsnes Peninsula, *266, 268*
Snappertuna, Fin., *200, 202*
Snogebæk, Den., *138*
Snowmobiling, *241, 280*
Soccer, *80, 255*
Sodankylä, Fin., *210*
Söderköping, Swe., *472*
Sofiero Slott, *476*
Sognefjord, *382*
Solfiero Slott, *473*
Sollerön Island, *488*
Sømods Bolcher, *76*
Sønderho, Den., *120*
Sørlandet region, Nor., *335–348*
the arts, *348*
beaches, *345–346*
children, attractions for, *343–344*
emergencies, *336*
guided tours, *337–338*
hotels, *346–348*
nightlife, *348*
restaurants, *339, 346–348*
shopping, *344*
sightseeing, *338–343*
sports, *344–346*
tourist information, *335–336*
transportation, *336–337*
Sörvágur, Faroe Islands, *154*
Spiralen tunnel, *333*
Sports, *30. See also* specific sports; under cities and countries
Sporveismuseet, *317*
Stadshuset, *433–434*
Stadsteatern, *458*
Stalheim, Nor., *386*
Statens Museum for Kunst, *73*
Stavanger, Nor., *337–338, 342–343, 344, 345, 347–348*
Stavanger Domkirke, *342*
Stavern, Nor., *338*

Stege, Den., *99*
Stegeborg fortress, *469*
Steinkjer, Nor., *393*
Stenersen Collection, *354–355*
Stevns Klint, *98*
Stifsgården, *392*
Stigfoss, *381*
Stjärneborg, *478*
Stjórnarráð, *250*
Stock exchanges
Copenhagen, *79*
Göteborg, *460*
Helsinki, *430*
Stockholm, *430*
Stockholm, Swe., *422–449*
the arts, *447–448*
beaches, *437*
business hours, *424*
children, attractions for, *435*
climate, *412*
embassies, *422*
emergencies, *422*
English-language bookstores, *422–423*
excursions, *433–434, 449–453*
festivals, *412–413*
guided tours, *425*
hotels, *443–447*
nightlife, *448–449*
panoramic views, *432*
restaurants, *430, 431, 432, 437, 440–443*
shopping, *435–436*
sightseeing, *425–427, 430–434*
sports, *436–437*
subway system, *424*
taxis, *424*
tourist information, *422–424*
transportation, *423*
travel agencies, *423*
Stockholms Fondbörs, *429*
Stockholms Leksaksmuseet, *435*
Stokkatovan farmhouse, *152*
Stora bird refuge, *455*
Stora Museum, *456*
Storebælt Udstillings Center, *98*
Storskog, Nor., *397*
Stortinget, *310*
Stortorvet, *310*

Streymoy, Faroe Islands, *154–155*
Strömstad, Swe., *458, 460*
Stryn, Nor., *381, 383, 386*
Student and youth travel, *18–19*
Denmark, *51*
Sweden, *409*
Studenterluden Park, *307*
Stykkishólmur, Ice., *266, 268*
Submarine Vesikko, *182*
Sulfur pits, *265*
Sund, Fin., *204*
Sund, Nor., *394*
Sundborn, Swe., *495*
Sunnemo, Swe., *453*
Suomen Kansallismuseo, *182*
Suomenlinna, *181–182, 185*
Suomen Rakennustaiteen Museo, *179*
Suðuroy, Faroe Islands, *154, 155*
Surfing, *57*
Surtsey Island, *280*
Svalbard Islands, *389, 398*
Svaneke, Den., *134, 138*
Svartifoss, *276*
Svartisen glacier, *399*
Svea Hovrätt, *433*
Svendborg, Den., *109–110, 114–115*
Svendborgs Omegns Museum, *110*
Svenska Teatern, *175*
Sverigehuset, *412*
Svolvær, Nor., *394*
Svörtuloft Cliffs, *266*
Sweden, *408–500. See also* Göteborg; Stockholm
ATM's, *413*
beaches, *420*
Bohuslän region, *464–465, 468*
books on, *416*
business hours, *418*
car rentals, *414*
Chateau Country, *478*
children, attractions for, *487*

children, traveling with, *415*
climate, *412*
clothing for, *413*
costs of, *413*
credit cards, *408*
currency, *413*
customs and duties, *413–414*
disabled travelers, *415*
emergencies, *454, 486*
festivals and seasonal events, *412–413*
Göta Canal, *461–464*
government tourist offices, *2, 411*
guided tours, *486, 490*
hotels, *421*
Kingdom of Crystal *472–474, 476–485*
language, *414*
mail, *418*
Norrland, *496–497*
older travelers, *415*
passports and visas, *413*
rail passes, *414*
restaurants, *421*
shopping, *421, 490*
sightseeing, *425–434, 449–451, 455–459, 464–471, 474–482, 487–490, 494–498*
southern provinces, *484–488*
sports, *419–420*
student travel, *414*
Swedish Riviera, *475–477*
telephones, *418*
timing the visit, *411–412*
tipping, *418*
tour groups, *411*
tourist information, *475, 482, 489*
transportation, *415, 416–417, 475–476, 482, 490*
Värmland, *469–472*
Swimming
Copenhagen, *80*
Helsinki, *187*
Iceland, *241, 263, 267, 272, 276, 280*
Lapland, *213*
Norway, *299*
Oslo, *321*
Reykavík, *255*
Stockholm, *438*

Synagogues, 73

Tähtitorninvuori observatory, 179

Taideteol- lisuusmuseo, 179

Tamminiemi, 183

Tammisaaren Museo, 202

Tammisaari, Fin., 199, 202, 206–207

Tampere, Fin., 159, 219–220, 224–225

Tampere International Short Film Festival, 159

Tampere International Theater Festival, 160

Tampere Jazz (festival), 160

Tankavaara, Fin., 210–211, 214–215

Tapiola, 186

Tar Skiing Race, 159

Tarvaspää, Fin., 183–184

Tåsinge Island, 110

Tatania's Palace, 120

Teaterhistorisk Museet, 69

Teatermuseet, 311

Tegnér Museet, 477

Teknisk Museum, 317

Temppeliaukion Kirkko, 182–183, 198

Tennis
Copenhagen, 80
Denmark, 57
Finland, 205
Helsinki, 187
Norway, 299
Stockholm, 438
Sweden, 421, 470
tournaments, 280, 461

Terrarium, 111

Theater
Copenhagen, 89
Helsinki, 175, 198
Norway, 363, 409
Oslo, 319–321
Reykavík, 248, 250, 259
Stockholm, 428–429

Thorvaldsens Museum, 68

Thurø Island, 110

Tilsandede Kirke, 124

Timing the visit, 4–5. See also under countries

Tinganes, 150

Tivoli amusement park, 74, 124, 263

Tivoli Gardens, 48

Tivoliland, 124

Tjodhilde Kirke, 144

Tjolöholm, Swe., 465

Tøjhusmuseet, 69

Tollstöðin, 253

Tomteland, 486

Tønsberg, Nor., 334

Torpo, Nor., 370

Tórshavn, Faroe Islands, 150, 152, 154–155

Torup Slott, 477

Tour groups, 2–4

Toy Museum, 76

Trælleborg, Den., 98

Train travel, 28. See also Railroads
Bergen, 350
Copenhagen, 63
Denmark, 50–51, 53, 54, 92, 93, 105–106, 117, 121
Finland, 163–164, 200, 207, 209, 216
Göteborg, 456
Norway, 291, 292–293, 332, 333, 337, 362, 378, 388
Oslo, 304
rail passes, 17–18, 28, 50–51, 161–162, 409
Stockholm, 425
Sweden, 413, 415, 416, 418, 457, 466, 472

Traveler's checks, 7

Trelleborg, Swe., 477

Troense, Den., 110–111

Troldeskoven, 100

Troldhaugen, 355

Trolleskoe, 133

Trollhättan, Swe., 468

Trøllkonufingur, 153

Trollveggen, 368

Tromsø, Nor., 389, 394–395, 398, 399, 403–404, 406

Tromsø Museum, 395, 398

Trøndelag Folkemuseum, 392

Trondheim, Nor., 387–389, 391–406
the arts, 406
beaches, 401
children, attractions for, 398
emergencies, 387
guided tours, 389
hotels, 401–405
nightlife, 406
restaurants, 392, 393, 394, 401–405
shopping, 399–400
sightseeing, 389, 391–398
sports, 400–401
tourist information, 387
transportation, 387–389

Tryvannstårnet TV tower, 313

Tuen, Den., 124

Tunnel-bridges, 98

Tuomiokirkko, 172

Turku, Fin., 199, 200, 202, 207

Turku Music Festival, 160

Turun Linna, 202

Turun Tuomiokirkko, 180, 202

Tusenfryd amusement park, 317

Tvøroyri, Faroe Islands, 154

Tycho Brahe Planetarium, 74

Tyska Kyrkan, 430

Uddeholm, Swe., 473

Uddevalla, Swe., 464

Ulefoss, Nor., 370

Ullandhaug, 343

Undset, Sigrid, 360

University Art Museum, 252

University of Iceland, 252

Uppsala, Swe., 453–454

Uranienborg, 476

Urho Kekkonen National Park, 212

U.S. embassy (Oslo), 312

U.S. Government Travel Briefings, 2

Uspenskin Kirkko, 180

Uummannaq Island, 145–146

Vaglaskógur, 270–271

Vágur, Faroe Islands, 153, 154, 155

Valbergtårnet, 343

Valdemar's Slot, 110–111

Valtionneuvosto, 180

Valtion Taidemuseo, 181

Vänern lake, 469

Vänersborg, Swe., 469

Vang, Den., 132

Vangsnes, Nor., 382

Vantaa, Fin., 184–185

Vappu celebrations, 159

Vapunaatto celebrations, 159

Varberg, Swe., 466

Vår Frelsers Gravlund, 312

Värmland, Swe., 470

Värmlands Museum, 472

Vasa Museet, 431

Vatnajökull glacier, 275–276

Vättern lake, 470

Vaxholm, Swe., 435

Växjö, Swe., 480, 482

Vejle, Den., 120, 128

Vemork, Nor., 365–366

Ven Island, 478

Venstøp, 365 '

Verdenskort, 125

Vermo Cup Horse Event, 159

Vesitorni, 204

Vest-Agder Fylkesmuseum, 340

Vesterålen Islands, 394

Vestfirðir, Ice., 266–267

Vestfold Fylkesmuseum, 334

Vestlandske Kunstindus- trimuseum, 354

Vestmannaeyjar Islands, 279–280, 281

Viborg, Den., *116,*
122–123
Viðimýri, Ice., *269*
Viðoy, Faroe Islands,
153, 155
Viebæltegård, *110*
Vigelands anlegget
(sculpture), *312*
Vigelandsmuseet, *313*
Viherpaja Icelandic
Japanese and Cactus
Gardens, *185*
Vík, Ice., *278*
Viking artifacts
Denmark, *93, 95, 97,
107, 121, 123–124,
134*
Faroe Islands, *150,
152*
Finland, *202*
Greenland, *143*
itinerary for, *35–36*
Norway, *334*
Oslo, *314, 315*
Reykjavík, *252*
Sweden, *477*
Vikingeskibshallen,
97
Viking Festival, *49*

Vikings, books on, *25*
Vikingskiphuset, *314*
Villa Ensi, *178*
Village
reconstructions, *96*
Villa Johanna, *178*
Vindmølleparken,
122
Vinstra, Nor., *376*
Viðey Island,
253–254
Visas, *9–10*
Visulahti Tourist
Center, *221*
Vitlycke, Swe., *466*
Vitöycke, Swe., *457*
Volcanoes, *266, 278,
279, 280*
Vor Frue Kirke,
72–73
Voss, Nor., *382, 386*
Vuoren Peikon
Leikkipuisto, *221*

Walter Runebergin
Kulttuuri,
Kokoelma, *184*
Waterfalls
Faroe Islands, *153*

Iceland, *261, 262,
265–266, 271, 272,
276, 279*
Norway, *381*
Oslo, *316*
Sweden, *480*
Waterskiing, *167, 345*
Weather information,
5
Western Union, *8*
Whaling industry,
334
Wildlife preserves
Denmark, *124, 135*
Finland, *220*
Iceland, *273*
Norway, *397*
Sweden, *455*
Windmill parks, *122*
Windsurfing, *30*
Denmark, *57, 112,
136*
Finland, *222*
Norway, *299, 345*
Sweden, *423, 462*
Winter Olympics,
287
Woldbrygga
Workshop, *381*

W. Ø. Larsens
Tobaksmuseet, *77*

Yachting, *see* Boating
Ymerbrønden
sculpture, *109*
Youth hostels, *19, 21*
Denmark, *59–60, 109*
Göteborg, *464*
Helsinki, *194*
Iceland, *244, 264,
268, 273–274, 277,
281*
Norway, *302*
Stockholm, *448*
Sweden, *417*

Zoological Gardens,
76
Zoological Museum,
76
Zoos
Copenhagen, *76*
Helsinki, *185*
Norway, *344*
Reykjavík, *253*
Zorn Museet, *487*
Zorns Gammalgård,
487

Personal Itinerary

Departure *Date*

Time

Transportation

Arrival *Date*   *Time*

Departure *Date*   *Time*

Transportation

Accommodations

Arrival *Date*   *Time*

Departure *Date*   *Time*

Transportation

Accommodations

Arrival *Date*   *Time*

Departure *Date*   *Time*

Transportation

Accommodations

Fodor's Travel Guides

Available at bookstores everywhere, or call 1–800–533–6478, 24 hours a day.

U.S. Guides

Alaska

Arizona

Boston

California

Cape Cod, Martha's Vineyard, Nantucket

The Carolinas & the Georgia Coast

Chicago

Colorado

Florida

Hawaii

Las Vegas, Reno, Tahoe

Los Angeles

Maine, Vermont, New Hampshire

Maui

Miami & the Keys

New England

New Orleans

New York City

Pacific North Coast

Philadelphia & the Pennsylvania Dutch Country

The Rockies

San Diego

San Francisco

Santa Fe, Taos, Albuquerque

Seattle & Vancouver

The South

The U.S. & British Virgin Islands

The Upper Great Lakes Region

USA

Vacations in New York State

Vacations on the Jersey Shore

Virginia & Maryland

Waikiki

Walt Disney World and the Orlando Area

Washington, D.C.

Foreign Guides

Acapulco, Ixtapa, Zihuatanejo

Australia & New Zealand

Austria

The Bahamas

Baja & Mexico's Pacific Coast Resorts

Barbados

Berlin

Bermuda

Brazil

Brittany & Normandy

Budapest

Canada

Cancun, Cozumel, Yucatan Peninsula

Caribbean

China

Costa Rica, Belize, Guatemala

The Czech Republic & Slovakia

Eastern Europe

Egypt

Euro Disney

Europe

Europe's Great Cities

Florence & Tuscany

France

Germany

Great Britain

Greece

The Himalayan Countries

Hong Kong

India

Ireland

Israel

Italy

Japan

Kenya & Tanzania

Korea

London

Madrid & Barcelona

Mexico

Montreal & Quebec City

Morocco

Moscow & St. Petersburg

The Netherlands, Belgium & Luxembourg

New Zealand

Norway

Nova Scotia, Prince Edward Island & New Brunswick

Paris

Portugal

Provence & the Riviera

Rome

Russia & the Baltic Countries

Scandinavia

Scotland

Singapore

South America

Southeast Asia

Spain

Sweden

Switzerland

Thailand

Tokyo

Toronto

Turkey

Vienna & the Danube Valley

Yugoslavia

Special Series

Fodor's Affordables

Caribbean

Europe

Florida

France

Germany

Great Britain

London

Italy

Paris

Fodor's Bed & Breakfast and Country Inns Guides

Canada's Great Country Inns

California

Cottages, B&Bs and Country Inns of England and Wales

Mid-Atlantic Region

New England

The Pacific Northwest

The South

The Southwest

The Upper Great Lakes Region

The West Coast

The Berkeley Guides

California

Central America

Eastern Europe

France

Germany

Great Britain & Ireland

Mexico

Pacific Northwest & Alaska

San Francisco

Fodor's Exploring Guides

Australia

Britain

California

The Caribbean

Florida

France

Germany

Ireland

Italy

London

New York City

Paris

Rome

Singapore & Malaysia

Spain

Thailand

Fodor's Flashmaps

New York

Washington, D.C.

Fodor's Pocket Guides

Bahamas

Barbados

Jamaica

London

New York City

Paris

Puerto Rico

San Francisco

Washington, D.C.

Fodor's Sports

Cycling

Hiking

Running

Sailing

The Insider's Guide to the Best Canadian Skiing

Skiing in the USA & Canada

Fodor's Three-In-Ones (guidebook, language cassette, and phrase book)

France

Germany

Italy

Mexico

Spain

Fodor's Special-Interest Guides

Accessible USA

Cruises and Ports of Call

Euro Disney

Halliday's New England Food Explorer

Healthy Escapes

London Companion

Shadow Traffic's New York Shortcuts and Traffic Tips

Sunday in New York

Walt Disney World and the Orlando Area

Walt Disney World for Adults

Fodor's Touring Guides

Touring Europe

Touring USA: Eastern Edition

Fodor's Vacation Planners

Great American Vacations

National Parks of the East

National Parks of the West

The Wall Street Journal Guides to Business Travel

Europe

International Cities

Pacific Rim

USA & Canada

WHEREVER YOU TRAVEL, *H*ELP IS NEVER FAR AWAY.

From planning your trip to providing travel assistance along the way, American Express® Travel Service Offices* are always there to help.

Scandinavia

DENMARK
American Express Travel Service
Amagertorv 18
(Stroget)
Copenhagen
45-331-22301

ICELAND
Urval Utsyn Travel
13 Posthusstraeti
Reykjavik
354-1 26900

FINLAND
Area Travel Agency Ltd.
Pohjoisesplanadi 2
Helsinki
358-0-628788

NORWAY
American Express Travel Service
Karl Johansgatan 33/35
Oslo
47-2-286-1300

SWEDEN
American Express Travel Service
Birger Jarlsgatan 1
Stockholm
46-8-679-5200

Please look for other American Express Travel Service Offices in central locations throughout Scandinavia.

Before You Go

Government Information Offices

Tourist Information In the United States
Scandinavian Tourist Board, 655 3rd Ave., New York, NY 10017, tel. 212/949–2333, fax 212/983–5260. This is the umbrella organization that includes the **Danish Tourist Board,** the **Finnish Tourist Board,** the **Iceland Tourist Board,** the **Norwegian Tourist Board,** and the **Swedish Travel and Tourism Council.**

In Canada **Danish Tourist Board,** Box 115, Station N, Toronto, Ontario M8V 3S4, tel. 416/823–9620, fax 416/823–8860. **Finnish Tourist Board,** 1200 Bay St., Suite 604, Ontario M5R 2A5, tel. 416/964–9159, fax 416/964–1524. For information on other Scandinavian countries, contact the Scandinavian Tourist Board (*see above*).

In the United Kingdom **Danish Tourist Board,** Sceptre House, 169 Regent St., London W1R 7FB, 071/734–2637, fax 071/494–2170. **Finnish Tourist Board,** 66 Haymarket, London SW1Y 4RF, tel. 071/839–4048, fax 071/321–0696. The Icelandic Tourist Board does not have an address in London, but **Icelandair** (172 Tottenham Court Rd., London WP1 9LG, tel. 081/388–5599) can supply tourist information. **Norwegian Tourist Board,** 5 Lower Regent St., London SW1Y 4LX, tel. 071/839–2650, fax 071/839–6114. **Swedish Travel and Tourism Council,** 73 Welbeck St., London W1M 8AN, tel. 071/487–3135, fax 071/935–5833.

U.S. Government Travel Briefings
The U.S. Department of State's **Citizens Emergency Center** issues Consular Information Sheets, which cover crime, security, and health risks as well as embassy locations, entry requirements, currency regulations, and other routine matters. For the latest information, stop in at any U.S. passport office, consulate, or embassy; call the interactive hotline (tel. 202/647–5225); or, with your PC's modem, tap into the Bureau of Consular Affairs' computer bulletin board (tel. 202/647–9225).

Tours and Packages

Should you buy your travel arrangements to Scandinavia packaged or do it yourself? There are advantages either way. Buying packaged arrangements saves you money, particularly if you can find a program that includes exactly the features you want. You also get a pretty good idea of what your trip will cost from the outset. Generally, you have two options: fully escorted tours and independent packages. Escorted tours are most often via motorcoach, with a tour director in charge. They're ideal if you don't mind having limited free time and traveling with strangers. Your baggage is handled, your time rigorously scheduled, and most meals planned. Such tours are therefore the most hassle-free way to see a destination, as well as generally the least expensive. Independent packages allow plenty of flexibility. They generally include airline travel and hotels, with certain options available, such as sightseeing, car rental, and excursions. Such packages are usually more expensive than escorted tours, but your time is your own.

While you can book directly through tour operators, you will pay no more to go through a travel agent, who will be able to tell you about tours and packages from a number of operators.

1 Essential Information